SERVICES MARKETING

SERVICES MARKETING

SECOND EDITION

K. Rama Mohana Rao

Andhra University

Pearson

Original edition, entitled *SERVICES MARKETING,* 2nd Edition by K. Rama Mohana Rao published by Pearson Education Ltd., Copyright © 2009.

Indian Subcontinent Reprint

ISBN 978-81-317-3225-0

First Impression, 2011
Thirteenth Impression, 2024
Fourteenth Impression 2025

Published by Pearson India Education Services Pvt. Ltd, CIN: U72200TN2005PTC057128.

Head Office: 1st Floor, Berger Tower, Plot No. C-001A/2, Sector 16B, Noida - 201 301, Uttar Pradesh, India.
Registered Office: Featherlite, 'The Address' 5th Floor, Survey No 203/10B, 200 Ft MMRD Road, Zamin Pallavaram, Chennai – 600 044.
Website: in.pearson.com; Email: companysecretary.india@pearson.com

Printed in India at Repro India Ltd., Rewari

Dedicated to

Lord Sri Venkateswara

About the Author

K. Rama Mohana Rao is a professor in the Department of Commerce and Management Studies, Andhra University where he has been teaching marketing management and services marketing to MBA students for over 25 years. In addition to teaching and overseeing research students, Professor Rao has completed 14 research projects funded by public and private organizations. He has published research papers in national and international journals of repute and authored five books.

Professor Rao is a member of many expert committees, academic and professional bodies. He has organized national seminars, workshops and training programs for academicians and business executives.

Professor Rao holds two postgraduate degrees—one in commerce and the other in business administration—and a doctorate degree from Andhra University.

Brief Contents

Preface xxix

1. Introduction to Services Marketing 1
2. Marketing Management: Core Concepts 22
3. The Marketing Environment 42
4. The Services Sector in the Indian Economy 59
5. Consumer Behaviour in Services 91
6. Marketing Information System and Research 117
7. Services Strategy 149
8. Market Segmentation 169
9. Competition Analysis and Strategies 184
10. Service Demand Management 199
11. The Service Product 219
12. Service Branding and Positioning 242
13. Physical Evidence 259
14. Pricing 275
15. Distribution 291
16. Internal Marketing 308
17. External Marketing 327
18. Interactive Marketing 347
19. Service Quality Management 373
20. Service Failures and Recovery 396
21. Customer Relationship Management 414
22. International Marketing of Services 440
23. Consumer Protection in Services 459
24. Services Marketing in India 487

Case 1 Beauty Care by Marico: Kaya Skin Clinics 521
Case 2 Life Insurance Corporation: Restructuring for Growth 524
Case 3 McDonald's in India 527
Case 4 Subway's Marketing Strategy in India 530
Case 5 Cox and Kings: Service with a Difference 533
Index 537

Contents

Preface *xxix*

1. Introduction to Services Marketing **1**

Introduction 2
Services Defined 3
India and China—The World's Two Fastest Growing Telecom Service Markets **4**
Differentiating Goods from Services 6
Why Services Marketing? 7
Characteristics of Services 9
Intangibility *9*
Inseparability *9*
Variability *10*
Perishability *10*
Customer Participation *11*
Lack of Ownership *11*
The Growth of the Services Sector 13
The Department for Professional Employees, AFL-CIO: Fact Sheet 2002–05 on Services Sector **14**
Reasons for Growth in the Services Sector 14
Intermediate Demand from Firms *15*
Final Demand from Customers *15*
Career Opportunities in the Services Sector 17
Insurance *18*
Call Centres *18*
Non-government Organizations *18*
Knowledge Process Outsourcing (KPO) *18*
Human Resources *19*
IT-enabled Services *19*
Hospitality *19*
Entertainment *19*
Aviation *19*
Summary *20*
Key Terms *20*
Brief Questions *20*
Essay Questions *20*
Assignments *20*
References *21*

2. Marketing Management: Core Concepts **22**

Introduction 23
The Marketing Offer 23
Core Concepts 24
Needs, Wants and Expectations 24
Markets 24
Exchange 25
Customer Value 25
Demand Management 26
Segmentation, Targeting and Positioning 26
***The Powerful Consumer* 27**
Creating Value 28
Communicating Value 28
Delivering Value 28
Goods Marketing Versus Services Marketing 29
Marketing Philosophies 30
The Production Concept 31
The Product Concept 31
The Selling Concept 31
The Marketing Concept 32
The Holistic Marketing Concept 33
Marketing Challenges 35
Customers 35
Business Trends 36
Technology 36
Marketing Planning 37
***Database Marketing* 38**
Marketing Tasks 39
Summary 39
Key Terms 40
Brief Questions 40
Essay Questions 40
Assignments 40
References 40

3. The Marketing Environment **42**

Introduction 43
The Micro-environment 44
***Organized Retailing: The New Growth Frontier* 44**
Other Divisions of the Company 45
Suppliers 45
Intermediaries 46
Competitors 46

Customer Markets 46
Other Publics 46
The Macro-environment 47
The Demographic Environment 48
The Economic Environment 49
The Natural Environment 50
The Technological Environment 50
***Industrial Policy 1991: The Focus on Market Economy* 51**
The Political and Legal Environment 52
The Social and Cultural Environment 52
The Company's Response to the Marketing Environment 56
Summary 57
Key Terms 57
Brief Questions 57
Essay Questions 57
Assignments 57
References 58

4. The Services Sector in the Indian Economy 59

Introduction 60
Contribution to the Gross Domestic Product 60
Shares of Sub-sectors 61
Contribution to Employment 61
Reasons for the Growth of Services in India 62
***Operational Characteristics of Services Sector Enterprises in India* 64**
Economic Affluence 64
The Changing Role of Women 64
Cultural Changes 65
The IT Revolution 65
The Conservation of Natural Resources 66
The Development of Markets 66
The Unbundling of Corporations 66
The Increased Consciousness of Healthcare 67
Economic Liberalization 67
Migration 67
Export Potential 67
Key Service Businesses in India 68
Insurance 68
***Service Tax* 69**
Transport 70
Telecommunications 72

IT and ITeS 74
Electricity 75
Postal Services 76
Tourism 77
Banking 79
Healthcare 81
Education 83
Entertainment and Media Services 85
Retailing 88
Summary 88
Key Terms 88
Brief Questions 89
Essay Questions 89
Assignments 89
References 89

5. Consumer Behaviour in Services **91**

Introduction 92
Buyers, Consumers and Customers 92
Factors Influencing Consumer Behaviour 92
Cultural and Social Factors 93
Consumers in India 96
***Middle-class Consumers: The Potential Market for a Host of Services* 99**
Personal and Physical Factors 99
Psychological Factors 101
How Do Consumers Develop Expectations? 104
The Zone of Tolerance 105
Determinants of the Maximum Service Level 105
Determinants of the Minimum Service Level 107
Determinants of the Maximum and Minimum Service Levels 107
Service Perception 108
Consumer Purchase Decision Process 109
Problem Identification and Definition 109
Information Search 111
Evaluation of Service Alternatives 112
Service Purchase and Consumption 112
Post-purchase Evaluation 113
Summary 114
Key Terms 114
Brief Questions 115
Essay Questions 115

Assignments *115*
References *115*

6. Marketing Information System and Research **117**

Introduction 118
Marketing Information System: A Definition 118
Sources of Marketing Information 119
Internal Information Sources *119*
External Information Sources *120*
MIS Begins and Ends with the Information User 121
Identifying and Assessing Information Needs *121*
Collecting Information *122*
Marketing Research 123
Information Technology and Marketing Information System ***124***
Marketing Research Application and Importance *124*
Marketing Research Organizations *127*
The Marketing Research Process 128
Defining the Problem *129*
Selecting the Sources of Information and Data-collection Methods *131*
Online Marketing Research ***136***
Designing the Questionnaire *138*
Selecting the Sample *142*
Collecting the Data *145*
Analysing and Interpreting the Data *145*
Preparing and Presenting the Research Report *145*
Information Analysis and Distribution 146
Summary *146*
Key Terms *147*
Brief Questions *147*
Essay Questions *147*
Assignments *147*
References *148*

7. Services Strategy **149**

Introduction 150
The Process of Strategic Planning 150
The Steps in Strategic Planning *151*
Selecting the Right Strategy Is the Success Key ***156***
A Market-oriented Service Strategy 156
The Strategic Management Trap *157*
The Service-oriented Approach *158*

A Service-oriented Organization Structure 159
The Service Triangle 160
The Services Marketing Mix 162
Strategy Implementation 164
Corporate Strategy and Social Responsibility 165
Strategy Evaluation and Control 166
Summary 166
Key Terms 167
Brief Questions 167
Essay Questions 167
Assignments 167
References 168

8. Market Segmentation 169

Introduction 170
Undifferentiated Marketing 170
Differentiated Marketing (Market Segmentation) 170
Bases for Market Segmentation 172
Consumer Characteristics 172
Consumer Responses (Behavioural Segmentation) 174
Technographic Segmentation 177
Market Segmentation System 178
Criteria for Market Segmentation 178
Substantiality 178
Measurability 178
Accessibility 179
Differentiability 179
Customization 179
Customizing the Service Around a Standardized Core 180
Creating Customizable Services 180
Offering Point-of-delivery Customization 180
Offering Standard Modules that Can Be Combined in Unique Ways 180
Stages in Market Segmentation 181
Search 181
Selection 181
Strategy 181
Summary 182
Key Terms 182
Brief Questions 182
Essay Questions 182

Assignments *183*
References *183*

9. Competition Analysis and Strategies **184**

Introduction 185
Competitive Threats 185
Competition from the Industry Perspective 187
Monopoly *187*
Oligopoly *187*
Monopolistic Competition *188*
Pure Competition *188*
Competition from the Market Perspective 188
Competition Leads Life Insurance Market Development in India *189*
Competition Analysis 190
Future Objectives *190*
Current Strategy *190*
Assumption *191*
Capabilities *191*
Competition Strategies 192
Market Leaders *192*
Market Challengers *193*
Market Followers *194*
Market Nichers *194*
Achieving Competitive Advantage 194
Regulated Competition in the Indian Telecom Sector *195*
Summary *197*
Key Terms *197*
Brief Questions *197*
Essay Questions *198*
Assignments *198*
References *198*

10. Service Demand Management **199**

Introduction 200
Demand Situations 200
Negative Demand *200*
No Demand *200*
Latent Demand *201*
Seasonal Demand *201*
Demand Patterns 202
Irregular Demand *202*
Falling Demand *202*

Demand to the Level of Optimum Capacity *203*
Demand Exceeds Optimum Capacity *203*
Demand Below the Optimum Capacity *204*
Excess Demand *204*
Demand Variations 205
Demand Forecasting Methods 207
Demand Management 208
Shifting Demand to Match Service Capacity *208*
Increasing Demand to the Level of Optimum Capacity *210*
Capacity Management 211
High Demand *212*
Low Demand *212*
Waiting-line Management 213
Developing Operational Logic *213*
Top 10 Predictions for the IT/ITeS Sector in India 214
Establishing a Reservation Process *215*
Differentiating Waiting Customers *216*
Making Waiting Fun *216*
Summary *216*
Key Terms *217*
Brief Questions *217*
Essay Questions *217*
Assignments *217*
References *218*

11. The Service Product **219**

Introduction 220
The Basic Service Package 220
Service Product Classification: The Consumer's Perspective 222
The Customer Value Hierarchy 223
The Flower of Service 224
Information *225*
Consultation *225*
Order Taking *225*
Hospitality *226*
Safekeeping *226*
Exceptions *226*
Billing *226*
Payment *226*
The Development of a New Service 227
What Is a New Service Product? *227*
Steps in the Development of a New Service *228*

Success Factors for a New Product **234**

The Service Product Mix 234

Service-line Decisions 234

Service Differentiation 236

Service Life-cycle Management 238

Summary 239

Key Terms 240

Brief Questions 240

Essay Questions 240

Assignments 240

References 241

12. Service Branding and Positioning 242

Introduction 243

Service Branding 243

Goods Branding Versus Services Branding 244

Choosing Brand Elements 245

Benefits of Branding 247

The Brand Value Chain **247**

Corporate Branding for Services 248

Indian Consumers' Brand Loyalty and Performance Rating of Select Service Brands **249**

Brand Equity 251

Service Positioning 253

Frame of Reference 253

Positioning Strategies 254

Summary 257

Key Terms 257

Brief Questions 257

Essay Questions 257

Assignments 258

References 258

13. Physical Evidence 259

Introduction 260

The Concept of Physical Evidence 260

Elements of Physical Evidence 261

The Concept of a Servicescape 261

Types of Servicescapes 262

Servicescape Dimensions 263

The Impact of Colour on Consumer Behaviour **266**

Servicescape Effects on Behaviour 267

Using Visual Merchandising to Influence Consumer Perceptions at Retail Service Outlets **269**
Other Tangibles 269
Role of Evidence in Services Marketing 270
Guidelines for Developing a Physical Evidence Strategy 272
Summary 273
Key Terms 273
Brief Questions 273
Essay Questions 273
Assignments 273
References 274

14. Pricing **275**

Introduction 276
The Pricing of Services 276
Service Attributes that Influence Pricing Decisions **277**
Influence of Non-monetary Costs 278
Price–Quality Relations 278
The Objectives of Pricing 279
Approaches to Pricing 280
Cost-based Pricing 280
Competition-based Pricing 281
Demand-based Pricing 282
Pricing Strategies Linked to Value Perceptions 285
Low or Reduced Price Is Value 285
Price Discrimination in Services **286**
Value Is Everything Expected in a Service 287
Value Is Price Versus Quality Relationship 287
Value Is Special Packages Offered by the Company 287
Summary 288
Key Terms 289
Brief Questions 289
Essay Questions 289
Assignments 289
References 290

15. Distribution **291**

Introduction 292
Service Transactions 292
Service Locations and Service Providers 293
Service Locations 293
Service Providers 294

Distribution Flows of Services 294
Distribution by Company-owned Channels 295
Channels for Service Distribution 296
Franchising 296
Franchisee Satisfaction Is the Key 297
Agents and Brokers 299
Electronic Channels 300
Services e-Retailing 301
The Design of a Service Distribution System 303
The Strategies for Channel Management 304
Control Strategies 304
Empowerment Strategies 305
Partnering Strategies 305
Summary 305
Key Terms 305
Brief Questions 306
Essay Questions 306
Assignments 306
References 306

16. Internal Marketing 308

Introduction 309
Employees Caught in Between 310
Employee Satisfaction 310
Emotional Labour 311
Objectives of Internal Marketing 311
Roles of a Service Employee 312
The Internal Marketing Product 313
Strategies for Internal Marketing 314
Employee Development—Facilitating Practices 314
Staffing 315
Internal Marketing Challenges 316
Training 318
Organizing 319
Supporting 320
Motivating 321
Evaluating 322
Rewarding 323
Retaining 323
Summary 324
Key Terms 324

Brief Questions 325
Essay Questions 325
Assignments 325
References 325

17. External Marketing **327**

Introduction 328
The Need for External Marketing 328
Integrated Marketing Communications 329
Designing a Communication Campaign 331
Selecting the Target Audience 331
Determining the Objectives of Communication 331
Generating the Message 332
Selecting the Media 333
Budgeting for Marketing Communications 333
Integrating Communications Mix Elements 334
The New Age Specialist Ad Agencies ***335***
The Objectives of Integrated Marketing Communications 335
Word-of-mouth Communication 336
Themes of External Marketing Campaigns 337
Information 338
Education 338
Persuasion 339
Reinforcement 339
Training 339
Efficiency 339
Leadership 340
Relationship 340
Image Building 340
Price Versus Quality 340
Demand Management 340
Recovery 340
Successful Communication Campaigns 341
Success in External Marketing 342
The Five Rules of Effective Campaigns ***343***
Matching Service Promises with Delivery 344
Managing Horizontal Communication 344
Summary 344
Key Terms 345
Brief Questions 345
Essay Questions 345

Assignments 345
References 345

18. Interactive Marketing **347**

Introduction 348
Customer Interaction 348
Quality-generating Resources 349
A Service Encounter 350
Employee Participation 350
Customer Participation 352
***Customer Roles in Service Delivery* 353**
Moments of Truth 355
Managing Moments of Truth 356
***Service Cycles* 360**
The Service Interaction Process 361
The Joining Phase 362
The Intensive Consumption Phase 362
The Detachment Phase 363
Integrating the Phases 364
Enhancing Employee Participation 364
Verbal Communication Skills 364
Non-verbal Communication Skills 364
Transactional Analysis 366
Enhancing Customer Participation 368
Defining the Processes Where Customers Have to Perform 369
Providing an Appropriate Customer Mix 369
Managing Customer Expectations 369
Summary 370
Key Terms 370
Brief Questions 370
Essay Questions 370
Assignments 371
References 371

19. Service Quality Management **373**

Introduction 374
How is Service Quality Perceived? 374
Image 375
Expected Versus Experienced Quality 375
Total Perceived Quality 376
Determinants of Service Quality 377

The Process for Service Quality Management 378
Service Quality Audit 380
The GAP Model of Service Quality 381
Quality Management in Sterilization Services 384
SERVQUAL 385
Total Quality Services Marketing 386
Five Myths and Truths of Service Quality 387
Zero Defects Versus Zero Defections 390
Service Excellence 391
Research on Service Quality 392
Summary 393
Key Terms 394
Brief Questions 394
Essay Questions 394
Assignments 395
References 395

20. Service Failures and Recovery 396

Introduction 397
Reasons for Customer Grievances 397
Customer Response to Service Failures 398
Classification of Complainers on Service Failures 400
Complaint Management 401
The Customer Complaint Management System 401
Service Recovery 403
Benefits of Service Recovery 404
Consumer Grievance Recovery Strategies 405
Recovery Strategies 405
Measuring Satisfaction with Transaction—Specific Service Recovery 406
Effective Service Recovery 409
Summary 411
Key Terms 412
Brief Questions 412
Essay Questions 412
Assignments 412
References 412

21. Customer Relationship Management 414

Introduction 415
Benefits of CRM 416

Benefits to the Company 416
Benefits to Consumers 416
Three Drivers of Successful CRM 417
Customer Value 417
Customer Satisfaction 417
Customer Retention 418
A CRM Framework 420
Selection of Customers 420
Customer-related Inputs 421
Organization-related Inputs 423
Selection of Customers 425
Customer Classification Based on Acquisition Costs and Retention Costs 425
The Goals of CRM 426
The Organizational System for CRM 426
Operationalization 427
CRM Budget 428
Employee Orientation 428
Efficiency Measurement and Reward 429
The Interaction Process 430
Roles of Employees 430
Roles of Customers 431
Moments of Truth 431
The Customer Response 431
The Customer Experience 432
Value Analysis 432
Future Benefits 432
e-CRM 432
Applications of e-CRM 433
Benefits of e-CRM 433
Market for e-CRM 434
Types of e-CRM 435
Operational CRM 435
Analytical CRM 435
Collaborative CRM 436
Criteria for the Selection of e-CRM Software 436
Summary 437
Key Terms 437
Brief Questions 437
Essay Questions 438
Assignments 438
References 438

22. International Marketing of Services **440**

Introduction 441
What is International Marketing? 441
Companies' Orientation to International Marketing 442
The International Marketing Environment 444
Asian Versus Western Cultures: The Impact on Travel and Tourism Services 445
Trade Barriers 446
The World Trade Organization (WTO) 447
Measures for Promoting Indian Services Exports 448
The Marketing Programme 449
Market-entry Strategies 450
Selecting a Country for Entry 451
Country-of-origin Effect 452
Value Creation 452
Value Communication 454
Value Delivery 455
Summary 456
Key Terms 457
Brief Questions 457
Essay Questions 457
Assignments 457
References 458

23. Consumer Protection in Services **459**

Introduction 460
Consumer Expectations from Industries and Businesses 461
Product Design and Development 461
Product Quality and Performance 462
Product Representation 462
Optimum Use of Resources 462
Fairness in Transactions 463
Consumers' Concerns 463
The Consumer Movement in India 464
Legal and Administrative Mechanisms for Consumer Protection in India 467
The Consumer Protection Act (1986) 467
National Consumer Disputes Redressal Commission 471
Provisions of the Act for Professional Services, Education Services and PSUs 474
Disruption of Services by Illegal Strikes 478
The Right to Information Act (2005) 480
The Administrative Mechanism 481
Business Response to the Consumer Movement 482

Summary 484
Key Terms 485
Brief Questions 485
Essay Questions 485
Assignments 485
References 486

24. Services Marketing in India **487**

Introduction 487
The Marketing of Banking Services: A Case Study on the State Bank of India 487
Product Policies and Strategies 488
New Product Planning and Development 488
Product Additions and Deletions 489
Pricing Policies and Strategies 489
The Distribution Network 491
External Marketing 495
Internal Marketing 496
Marketing of Transport Services: A Case Study on APSRTC 498
The Service Product Mix 499
Pricing 500
The Distribution Network 500
External Marketing 501
Internal Marketing 502
Marketing of Hospital Services 503
The Basic Service Package (Product) 504
The Physical Environment 504
Pricing 505
The Distribution Network 506
Internal and Interactive Marketing 506
External Marketing 507
Marketing of Educational Services 508
The Product 509
Pricing 509
The Distribution Network 510
People 511
Promotion 512
Interactive Marketing 513
Marketing of Tourism Services 513
Marketing Approach for Tourism Services 514
The Product 514
Physical Evidence 514
Pricing 515
The Distribution Network 515

People *516*
Promotions *517*
The Process *517*
Key Terms *518*
Brief Questions *518*
Essay Questions *518*

Case 1. Beauty Care by Marico: Kaya Skin Clinics **521**

Case 2. Life Insurance Corporation: Restructuring for Growth **524**

Case 3. McDonald's in India **527**

Case 4. Subway's Marketing Strategy in India **530**

Case 5. Cox and Kings: Service with a Difference **533**

Index *537*

Preface

The services sector continues to play a pivotal role in shaping the growth map of the economies of both developing and developed countries the world over. This sector has achieved phenomenal growth during the last 25 years, creating employment opportunities in large numbers. Its contribution to the development of the manufacturing as well as the agricultural sectors cannot be overemphasized. Services marketing has become increasingly challenging due to the dynamic nature of the business environment. The second edition of *Services Marketing* has been thoroughly revised and new chapters and features added to make it easier to learn and study from.

Organization

As markets become increasingly complex, a rising number of researchers believe that marketing is a management function and organizations should focus on establishing, strengthening and developing customer relations. Thus, modern services organizations and managers need to look beyond the tried-and-tested 4Ps approach. They have to appreciate the utility of establishing and maintaining customer relationships in marketing. This textbook introduces the key concepts of both the approaches so readers can develop a comprehensive understanding of various strategic dimensions of services marketing in a systematic manner

The second edition of *Services Marketing* comprises 24 chapters in all. Chapter 1 defines and explains the concept of services marketing. Chapters 2 and 3 review the basic concepts in marketing management. Chapter 4 examines the major services in India and their developmental perspectives along with specific reasons for the growth of the services sector in India. Chapters 5 and 6 explain the concepts of consumer behaviour, marketing research and marketing information systems.

Chapter 7 explains strategic planning and identifies the seven Ps of a services marketing mix. Chapters 8–18 explore the strategic issues related to segmentation, competition, demand and capacity management and the seven Ps. Chapters 19–21 discuss concepts that are important to services strategy but are oriented towards building, sustaining and enhancing customer relationships.

Chapter 22 talks of international services marketing which is a necessity in the current era of economic liberalization and globalization. Chapter 23 highlights legal issues on consumer protection, a relatively grey area for most managers. Chapter 24 integrates these seemingly diverse concepts through five detailed illustrative cases from various sectors, exemplifying how real-world service organizations have successfully blended these concepts to their advantage.

Chapter 24 is followed by five short case studies, handpicked to highlight various service-related issues and scenarios that managers face on a regular basis.

New in the Second Edition

The thoroughly revised and updated *Services Marketing* reflects the major trends and forces impacting marketing in this era of customer value and relationships. Here are just some of the major changes you'll find in this edition:

- In addition to revising and updating the existing chapters, *seven new chapters* have been added to strengthen the conceptual foundation of the book and expand its horizon: Marketing Management: Core Concepts; Marketing Environment; Marketing Information System and Research; Competition Analysis and Strategies; Services Branding and Positioning; Service Failures and Recovery; and International Services Marketing.
- The *pedagogy* of the book has been vastly improved to make the book more reader friendly and valuable to students. A chapter-opening vignette, services marketing insight boxes, margin notes and short caselets have been added to each chapter to give readers an insight into real-world scenarios, problems, solutions and applications. Further, assignments have been included to the end-of-chapter exercises as well.
- *Five case studies* have been appended at the end of the book to describe the issues services organizations face in the real world. These are analysis-oriented case studies that will enable students explore the problems that real-world companies face under the guidance of an instructor.
- The *teaching and learning package* has been enhanced to meet the requirements of students and instructors.

Features

The book includes several features designed to help students comprehend the concepts presented in the chapter:

The Marketing Environment

3

Learning Objective

Each chapter includes learning objectives that outline the chapter goals.

LEARNING OBJECTIVES

After studying this chapter, you will be able to:

- Understand the influence of the marketing environment on business
- Describe micro-environmental forces
- Describe macro-environmental forces

The retail boom began in India in the early years of the 21st century. Many established companies in other businesses and new companies entered the business in a big way. Organized retailing, which was limited to only a few cities in India, spread to almost all cities. Attracted by the business opportunity, Chandan Enterprises Ltd, a goods transport services company, decided to venture into retailing. The plan was to construct four malls in metros initially and then spread the network to all cities over a period of 10 years. The company had worked out the investment and required resources and identified financiers. Since the company was in the transport business, the management thought that it could leverage its competencies in transport for the retailing business.

The company constituted a panel of experts to conduct environmental analysis and suggest strategic measures. The committee analysed both micro- and macro-environmental forces and submitted its report to the management. The report highlighted the following issues:

- Competition with existing retail companies would be intense.
- Efficient supply chain management would be critical.
- Customer markets were well informed and clear in their expectations.
- Economic conditions were likely to affect the business in future.
- Policy changes by the government were likely to impact the business.
- Though core cultural values of consumers were intact, some changes in the culture might affect the business.
- Grocery retailing had more opportunities than other formats.

The management of the company scrutinized the report in detail and decided to focus mainly on grocery items and to offer general items as support products. The company, however, looked for some more information on the forces affecting the business so that it could improve its marketing strategy.

Questions:

1. Do you think the issues highlighted by the expert committee are relevant? Why?
2. What is the information needed on the marketing environment for this business?
3. What mechanism do you suggest to monitor the marketing environment?
4. Is it the right decision to focus on grocery retailing based on the report?

Opening Vignette

The opening vignette presents a real-world situation within the scope of the chapter content. Each vignette ends with a set of discussion questions, the answers to which may be found within the chapter. These vignettes have been included to illustrate the application of concepts to solve real-world problems.

Education: There is a marked difference in the behaviour of an educated person and an uneducated person regarding the purchase of goods and services.

VLCC

VLCC, with the tagline "Shaping your confidence", entered the business of body management services in 1989. The company attracted customers in large numbers by focusing on aspirational references. The models portrayed in the advertisements and the real case examples communicated through various media served as a powerful reference to the prospects to get influenced and buy the services of the company.

Today, VLCC is the single largest player in the organized sector with a pan-India presence of nearly 225 outlets across 75 cities in India and a few outlets outside India. The company has acquired the status of India's largest health and beauty brand by way of offering highly customized services based on multi-disciplinary, integrated scientific approach to study body compositions and offering solutions to consumer problems.

Caselets >>>>>>>>>>

Each chapter includes two short caselets illustrating the real-life application and implementation of concepts discussed within the chapter.

Customer Relationship Management 425

SELECTION OF CUSTOMERS

The customer- and organization-related input forms the basis for finalization of customers. The concept of establishing relationships with selective customers is based on the assumption that the larger customer base is costlier to build relationships. Therefore, companies choose the policy of meritocracy. Meritocracy is the selection of the customers on some merits. It demands a shift in the customer care philosophy from providing the highest level of care for every customer to tailored care to each customer needs based on the value of interactions. Meritocracy identifies long-term valuable customers based on historical and future potential value in terms of profits, sales and life style changes. Profitability is one of the serious considerations in the selection of customers for CRM. Customer profitability depends on the factors such as acquisition costs, retention costs, number of face-to-face telephone contacts, sales revenue from the customer, referral value, synergic value and duration of relationship (see "Service Marketing Insight: Customer Classification Based on Acquisition Costs and Retention Costs").

When the value of customers to the enterprise vary widely, the top customers account for the vast majority of the business; it is called steep skew.

"The selection of customers for relationships is based on the customer- and organization-related input. There should be a right alignment between the two to find out right customers in right size to serve and to maximize benefits of relationships."

<<<< Margin Notes

Key concepts and definitions from each page are presented as margin notes to help the student grasp and retain the concept and its context.

21.1 Services Marketing Insight | **Customer Classification Based on Acquisition Costs and Retention Costs**

The classification of customers—based on acquisition costs and retention costs—made by Jacquelyn S. Thomas, Werner Reinartz and V. Kumar is useful for CRM policy makers. The researchers have classified customers into four groups: casual, low maintenance, high maintenance and loyal. *Casual customers* are easy to acquire and easy to retain. Since acquisition costs and the retention costs are low, the sales staff and relationship management section forget this group to build relations. The second category is *low-maintenance customers*. The cost of acquisition of these customers is high, but the cost of retention is low. These customers are judicious in their approach in the selection of the company; once they establish relationships they prefer to continue loyalty with the company, until the company's CRM personnel commit too many mistakes. The third category is *high-maintenance customers*. The acquisition cost of these customers is low, but their maintenance proves costly to the concerns. These customers are triers and put efforts in evaluating the value of the offering of the existing company with competitive offers. They don't mind cutting off relations, when the company is lagging behind in offering services. The fourth category is *loyal customers*. These customers are difficult both to acquire and to maintain and are highly sensitive of the quality of services. This is the premium group and to tackle them with specialized efforts is necessary. They provide ample opportunities to the company, to maintain and enhance relationships, and require only one thing: the company should treat them as special and offer faultless high-end services.

Source: Jacquelyn S. Thomas, Werner Reinartz and V. Kumar, "Getting the Most out of All Your Customers," Harvard Business Review *(July–August 2004).*

<<<< Services Marketing Insight

Two services marketing insight boxes have been included in each chapter. These boxes provide additional input to readers on the practical developments in the subject being discussed in the chapter.

Competition Analysis and Strategies 197

SUMMARY

- Service companies face competition from different angles and in different ways.
- Competitive threats may arise from existing companies in the same business, new entrants, substitutes, and the bargaining power of both suppliers and buyers.
- Service buyers can also be potential competitors in case of services offered to the household sector and the organized sectors.
- The industry concept of competition is to identify competition in terms of the number of sellers and the degree of differentiation.
- From the industry perspective, competition is identified in four structures: monopoly, oligopoly, monopolistic and pure competition.
- Monopoly results when a single seller offers services to the buyers in a region. The presence of few sellers offering services to large number of buyers is called oligopoly. In monopolistic competition, sellers and buyers are present in large number. Service differentiation is the key characteristic. In pure competition, almost all characteristics of perfect competition exist with marginal variation.
- The market concept of competition refers to the companies serving the same need of consumers.
- For the design of a competitive strategy, marketers need to analyse competitors.
- The competition analysis covers future objectives, current strategy, assumptions and capabilities of competitors.
- The strengths and weaknesses of the competitors should be analysed carefully to arrive at a competitive strategy.
- An effective market intelligence system and the flow of right information from both internal and external sources are necessary for competition analysis.
- Competition strategies depend on the roles the company plays in the market. The four roles are market leader, market challenger, market follower and market nicher.
- A market leader focuses on market expansion, defending market share and expanding its market share.
- A market challenger chooses to attack the leader and other competitors.
- A market follower tries to imitate the best of competitors to gain advantages.
- A market nicher selects an area to specialize and carve a niche for itself.
- Service firms should carry out internal analysis to know their competencies and to identify the resources that can help it gain a competitive advantage.

KEY TERMS

benchmarking *196*
competitive advantage *190*
competitive threats *185*
core competencies *196*
market challenger *193*
market follower *194*
market leader *192*
market nicher *195*
monopolistic competition *188*
monopoly *187*
oligopoly *187*
pure competition *187*
strategic group *190*
value chain analysis *196*

BRIEF QUESTIONS

1. What are competitive threats?
2. What is competitive advantage?
3. What is benchmarking?
4. Explain niche marketing.
5. What are market follower strategies?

Summary

A detailed summary recapitulating the salient points discussed in the chapter is included for a quick review.

Key Terms

A complete list of key terms is provided at the end of the chapter for easy reference.

Brief Questions

Each chapter includes a few short-answer questions at the end for students to test their understanding of the key concepts discussed in the chapter.

Essay Questions

Each chapter includes essay questions designed to test the student's ability to analyse concepts and apply them to real-life situations.

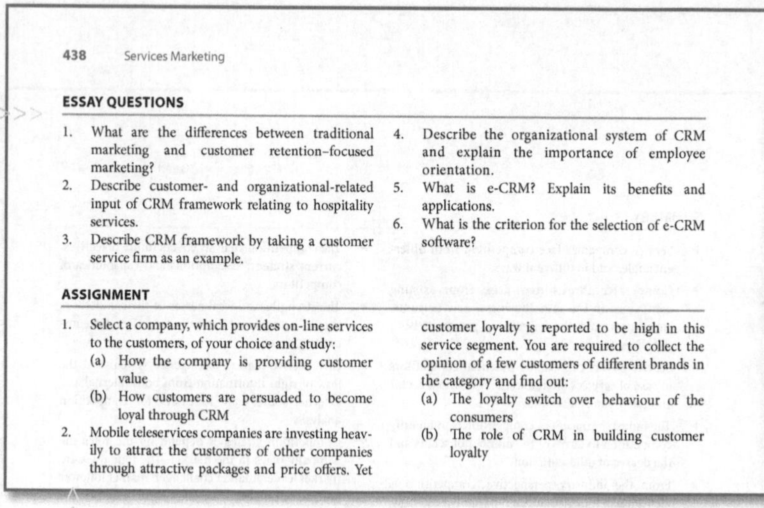
438 Services Marketing

ESSAY QUESTIONS

1. What are the differences between traditional marketing and customer retention-focused marketing?
2. Describe customer- and organizational-related input of CRM framework relating to hospitality services.
3. Describe CRM framework by taking a customer service firm as an example.
4. Describe the organizational system of CRM and explain the importance of employee orientation.
5. What is e-CRM? Explain its benefits and applications.
6. What is the criterion for the selection of e-CRM software?

ASSIGNMENT

1. Select a company, which provides on-line services to the customers, of your choice and study:
   (a) How the company is providing customer value
   (b) How customers are persuaded to become loyal through CRM
2. Mobile teleservices companies are investing heavily to attract the customers of other companies through attractive packages and price offers. Yet customer loyalty is reported to be high in this service segment. You are required to collect the opinion of a few customers of different brands in the category and find out:
   (a) The loyalty switch over behaviour of the consumers
   (b) The role of CRM in building customer loyalty

Assignments

Two assignments have been included at the end of each chapter to help readers apply the concepts to practical, real-world problems and data sets to foster experiential learning.

The Teaching and Learning Package

For the instructors the following aids are provided in addition to the text.

- PowerPoint slides
- Instructors' manual

Acknowledgements

I express my deep gratitude to all my teachers and colleagues in the university, friends in the industry and other academic and research institutions, whose encouragement and support helped me to complete this work. I sincerely thank my research students, S. G. Rama Rao, Y. Srinivasulu, P. V. V. Satyanarayana Murthy, D. Appala Raju, D. Srinivasa Prasad and K. Ratna Manikyam for their help and support in the revision process.

I sincerely acknowledge the support and encouragement from my wife, K. Soujanya, and my daughters, K. Lakshmi Manasa and K. Sindhura.

Finally, I thank the editorial team of Pearson Education, particularly Soma Banerjee, for their efforts in bringing out the book.

The Development of this Book

The feedback and suggestions from several instructors who used the first edition of this book has been immensely useful to the development of this edition of *Services Marketing*. Although we could not incorporate all their suggestions, we do acknowledge that their feedback was invaluable to our attempt at making this book more valuable to students.

Consultant Board

The consultant board provided us a critical and detailed analysis of each chapter and worked with us in developing the book. We wish to thank the following individuals for their timeless dedication and commitment.

Rajesh Panda
Symbiosis Institute of Business Management, Pune

Usha Kiran Rai
Banaras Hindu University, Varanasi

A. Vidyadhar Reddy
Osmania University, Hyderabad

Sukhendu Samajdar
International School of Business, Kolkata

Soumya Singh
Indian School of Mines, Dhanbad

Introduction to Services Marketing

1

LEARNING OBJECTIVES

After studying this chapter, you will be able to:

- Understand the concept of services marketing
- Describe the emergence of marketing thought in the services sector
- Appreciate the reasons for a distinctive marketing approach for services
- Understand the specific characteristics of services
- Describe the reasons for growth in the services sector
- Identify career opportunities in the services sector

After successfully completing his business engagements at Kozhikode, G. S. Rao headed to the airport to catch the 8:00 a.m. flight to Chennai from where he was to catch the connecting flight to Visakhapatnam to reach his office for a board meeting.

Suddenly his phone rang. He was informed that the flight to Visakhapatnam had been cancelled. Panic quickly gave way to anger when he was informed that no alternatives were available. Following the call, Rao received an SMS confirming the same. The message provided a contact number for queries and alternative arrangements. A quick call to the number proved futile. Extremely annoyed with the airline employees' total lack of concern, courtesy and empathy towards the stranded passengers, Rao stalked off to look for alternatives himself. Within minutes, he received another call from the airlines confirming that they had put him on a Chennai–Hyderabad flight. From Hyderabad, he could take a connecting flight to Visakhapatnam. However, he was asked to report at the Chennai airport at 8:00 a.m., which was impossible for him since his flight from Kozhikode was scheduled to land in Chennai at 9:45 a.m. He was asked to contact the duty manager at the Chennai airport for further information.

On landing at Chennai, Rao promptly contacted the duty manager only to be rudely told that there was no possible solution to his problem. All his attempts to find another flight proved futile. As a last recourse, he went back to the duty manager. Just as he was about to present his case again, another airline employee rushed into the cabin, looked at Rao and asked, "Are you to Visakhapatnam? Let me see if I can accommodate you in another flight." He arranged a ticket to Visakhapatnam for Rao on another airline for an additional payment of INR 3,100. A visibly relieved Rao accepted the offer immediately and resolved never to fly the same airlines again in the future.

Questions:

1. Do you think the airlines handled the issue in the best possible manner?
2. If you were the manager responsible for handling these problems, how would you resolve the problem?
3. Do you think marketing of services need a specialized approach?
4. What are the key factors to be managed to retain customer confidence?
5. How to manage customer confidence when substitute arrangements are not in your control?

> *Affluence in a society and growth in services are correlated. The affluent sections of the society consume services provided at a high price. Thus, services become business propositions.*

INTRODUCTION

The concept of "service" is as old as humankind and began when man started serving himself (self-servicing). When a part of the society became affluent, it started utilizing the services of others at a price. Then, services became a business proposition. However, until the beginning of the twentieth century, the focus of economies was to produce more and more tangible goods and sell agricultural and manufactured products. Services such as accounting, banking, insurance and transportation were considered to be support to manufacturing units. But nowadays, services influence our lifestyle and the quality of life significantly. All human beings have become service producers as well as consumers. We cannot imagine our lives in the absence of services. Transportation, education, communication, healthcare, hospitality, entertainment, banking, information technology, electricity and a host of other such services have become a part of our lives.

> *An economy is called a* ***service economy*** *when the contribution of the services sector to the GDP of the nation is more than 50 per cent.*

Over the years, services have increasingly assumed an important role in the economic development of many countries, including India. All developed countries and many developing countries either have emerged or are emerging as service economies or service societies. An economy is called a *service economy* when the contribution of the services sector to the GDP of the nation is more than 50 per cent. In 1948, the economy of the United States was the first to be declared as a service economy with about 53 per cent contribution of the services sector to the GDP of the nation. There is an argument that the statistics of the services sector's contribution in many countries is a gross underestimation of the truth, since the value of the services produced by the manufacturers of goods in the industrial sector is not included in the service output value. There is a large "hidden services sector" that is not classified under the services sector. The term *hidden services sector* refers to the service output generated in the manufacturing sector as a support to the tangible product output and included in the overall value of the tangible output of the manufacturing sector. In other words, though the service output is generated, its value is included in the goods output for the purpose of the calculation of GDP. In almost all economies, the beginning of most services was in the public sector. Most organizations enjoyed the status of monopoly. The situation of excessive demand over supply and the absence of competition or negligible competition led many service organizations to be insensitive to the concept of marketing. The management and the marketing literature, which developed until the 1970s, depicted manufacturing organizations and suggested that the same philosophies and technology be applied to service organizations also.

During the early 1980s, the deregulation of services in many parts of the world, particularly in the areas of banking and insurance, telecommunications, transportation and healthcare services, led to intensified competition among various organizations. The growth in size and volume of business and the growing demand made organizations identify the gap between the available technical support and the support required to face the distinctive marketing challenges. The American Marketing Association took up the task of developing marketing technology and organized a series of marketing conferences on themes related to services marketing. In 1977, Lynn Shostack, the then Vice President at Citibank, wrote an article "Breaking Free from Product Marketing" in the *Journal of Marketing*. This article influenced the course of thought related to services marketing. She asserted, "New concepts are necessary if services marketing is to succeed ... merely adopting product marketing's labels does not resolve the question of whether product marketing can be overlaid on service businesses. Could marketing itself be 'myopic' in having failed to create relevant paradigms for the services sector?"[1] Since then, efforts have been on to develop new concepts, strategies and techniques for handling marketing problems of service organizations.

> *The **hidden services sector** refers to the service output generated in the manufacturing sector as a support to the tangible product output and included in the overall value of the tangible output of the manufacturing sector for the purpose of the calculation of GDP.*

Since the 1980s, there has been a huge growth in the number of publications and empirical research reports. Several key issues and concepts have been brought forth, including service quality, customer relationship marketing, internal marketing, designing of service packages, interactive marketing, moments of truth, service encounter management, customer evaluation process, customer-perceived service quality, service failures and recovery strategies, losses of customer defections and so on.

Now, services have become a critical source of wealth to economies in many ways. Economies experience an increase in employment with the growth in the services sector. While employment in the manufacturing sector is receding every year, employment in the services sector is rising. Services provide the required infrastructure and support for the growth and development of the manufacturing and agricultural sectors. Services contribute to the enhancement of productivity, optimal use of resources, qualitative managerial decision-making and so on, which impact economic development and the standard of living in a society. Services not only boost consumption but also induce investment. The services sector does not squeeze out the manufacturer, but rather serves as an important supplement to the growing power. For instance, the development of the telecom sector in many countries has significantly increased the productivity in the industry as well as business sectors. The technological revolution in this sector has opened up many opportunities for the growth and development of almost all sectors. The growth of the telecom sector in India and China—the world's two fastest growing telecom service markets—is discussed in "Services Marketing Insight: India and China—The World's Two Fastest Growing Telecom Service Markets."

> *Services contribute to the enhancement of productivity, optimal use of resources, qualitative managerial decision making and so on, which impact economic development and the standard of living in a society.*

SERVICES DEFINED

The term *service* has been defined by several marketing analysts and associations. The study of such definitions provides an understanding of the direction of evolution of the concept of services. It also provides the changing perception of service by the society in general and business concerns in particular.

1.1 Services Marketing Insight | **India and China—The World's Two Fastest Growing Telecom Service Markets**

The telecommunication sector, a prime support service for rapid economic growth, has undergone transformation throughout the world. Technological advances have revolutionized the range and quality of services offered by this sector. The rapid growth of the telecom sector has brought about a qualitative change not only in the way businesses and organizations function, but also in the lifestyle of people. It is no surprise that India and China, which together account for over 40 per cent of the world's population, are the fastest growing telecom markets globally. The two countries together were estimated to have a subscriber base of about 1.2 billion by the end of the year 2010, with India claiming 438 million and China 750 million.

India achieved a growth rate of 95.6 per cent from August 2006 to August 2007 in the mobile subscriber base. The country recorded a hefty 8 million plus monthly mobile subscriber addition in 2007 as a result of new schemes and increased penetration in rural and semi-urban areas by telecom companies. This growth put India on the third place globally in terms of the total subscriber base. China undoubtedly was the world's largest telecom market with a total mobile subscriber base of 515.67 million as of August 2007. The subscriber base grew steadily at 8 per cent from August 2006 to August 2007.

The telecom sector in India has 12 players—eight in the GSM segment and four in the CDMA segment—whereas there are only two players in China—China Mobile and China Union (GSM and CDMA). China Mobile was the market leader with 69 per cent market share as of August 2007. In India, none of the telecom companies had managed to capture such a high market share. Bharti Airtel was the dominant player with a market share of 24.15 per cent. GSM was the dominant technology in both the countries, accounting for about 92 per cent of the market share in China and over 70 per cent of the market share in India. In China, the telecom market is largely state owned because of which the benefits of a truly competitive market cannot be exploited. On the other hand, India, with 74 per cent foreign direct investment, offers a relatively open telecom market wherein all competitive forces have enough freedom to operate. Industry experts predict that the trend of increasing subscribers in India will continue; China will see an increase in the number of wireless subscribers, but slowly.

Source: Adapted from "Closing the Gap: A Comparison of the Telecom Sectors in India and China," tele.net, *8, no.12 (December 2007): 16–18.*

The following definitions present the thoughts of various personalities and associations that have contributed significantly, over the last four decades—from 1960 onwards—to services management and marketing.

The American Marketing Association was the first to define services as "activities, benefits or satisfactions which are offered for sale or provided in connection with the sale of goods."[2] This definition provides a limited view of services in that it does not provide for valuing services involved in the production of tangible goods. However, this was the first major attempt to identify services differently in valuing the output of a society. W. J. Regan, in his definition, classified services into two categories. According to him, "services represent either tangibles, yielding satisfaction directly (transport, housing) or intangibles, yielding satisfaction jointly when purchased either with commodities or other services (credit, delivery)."[3] This definition tried to focus on services that are offered directly to consumers as products.

According to R. Judd, service is "a market transaction by an enterprise or entrepreneur where the object of the market transaction is other than the transfer of ownership of a tangible commodity."[4] In this definition, the following three broad areas of services are recognized:

1. Right to possess and use a product (rented goods business)
2. The custom creation, repair or improvement of a product (owned product services)
3. No product element, but an experience (non-goods services)

Through this definition an attempt was made to give an independent status to more and more services and to focus the attention of researchers on further development.

W. J. Stanton provided a comprehensive view of services.. According to him, services are "separately identifiable, intangible activities which provide want-satisfaction when marketed to consumers and/or industrial users and which are not necessarily tied to the sale of a product or another service."[5] This definition focuses on the following issues for recognition:

1. Services are those activities that are identifiable separately.
2. Services are intangibles that provide want satisfaction to consumers.
3. Services are marketed directly to consumers and also to the industrial users.
4. Services may or may not be tied with the sale of goods.
5. Services may or may not be tied with the sale of other services.

According to J. Lehtinen, a service product is "an activity or a series of activities which take place in interaction with a contact person or a physical machine and which provides consumer satisfaction."[6] This definition recognizes the services provided by machines such as vending machines and ATMs, besides the services provided by contact persons.

> "***Services*** *may be defined as intangible activities performed by persons, machines, or both for creating value perceptions among consumers. The quality of services results in perception and value assessment by the consumer.*"

P. Kotler and P. N. Bloom defined a service as "any activity or benefit that one party can offer to another that is essentially intangible and does not result in the ownership of anything. Its production may or may not be tied to a physical product."[7] This definition more or less follows the earlier ones. The focus was on the absence of ownership as a special feature of services, which has significant business implications.

According to C. Grönroos, "a service is an activity or series of activities of more or less intangible nature that normally, not necessarily take place in interactions between the customer and service employees and/or physical resources or goods and/or systems of the service provider, which are provided as solutions to customer problems."[8] This definition attempted to include all important issues relating to services management.

V. A. Zeithaml and M. J. Bitner said, "Services are deeds, processes and performances."[9] Although it seems that the definition is more precise, it provides a marketing orientation to the concept of services. This definition implies that the consumer is interested in deeds, processes and performances in perceiving the value of the service.

Services may be defined as intangible activities performed by persons or machines or both for the purpose of creating value perceptions among consumers. Since services are intangible activity(ies) or benefit(s) produced by the service provider, in association with the consumer, its quality results in perception and value assessment by the consumer. Services are interaction-based performances whose quality is perceived by consumers.

DIFFERENTIATING GOODS FROM SERVICES

It is very difficult to draw a clear, demarcating line between goods and services in a marketing offer. According to T. Levitt, a renowned marketing specialist, "In almost every tangible pure physical product, an intangible service component is associated. Therefore, everybody is in service." He classified products into two categories: search goods and experience goods.[10] *Search goods* are those that are packaged and customers can see, evaluate and go for a trial before making a purchase. For example, scooters, fans, locks and so on. *Experience goods* are those that can be evaluated only after purchase and consumption. For example, a holiday, travel and so on.

> *Marketable products are classified into five categories: pure tangible goods, tangible goods with accompanying service, hybrid, service with accompanying tangible goods and pure services.*

P. Kotler, one of the world's leading authorities on marketing, classified products into the following five categories for establishing the goods–services relationship:[11]

1. *Pure Tangible Goods:* These are like commodities that are identical or homogeneous. Differentiating these goods with supplier identity is difficult. Consumers do not attach any specific value to a little-associated service. Agricultural and unbranded goods (mostly from tiny and small-scale sectors) fall under this category.
2. *Tangible Goods with Accompanying Services:* In this case, consumers give greater importance to the tangible part of the marketing offer. However, the services accompanying tangible goods are also part of the value assessment done by buyers. Buyers get the title of tangible goods transferred and get ownership of the goods. The accompanying services, though, accounting for a minor share in the total offer, provide a competitive advantage to the seller. In the light of significant developments that took place in technology development, most producers are unable to find technical advantage of tangible factors and find enormous sources of differentiation in accompanying services. A vast majority of manufacturing goods fall under this category. The role of services under this category is to support the tangible product. Services are identified and valued only in association with tangible goods.

3. *Hybrid:* This is a typical marketing offer where tangible goods and services may be given equal importance by consumers. For example, people patronize restaurants for both food and service. However, the contribution of goods and services may not be equal in all restaurants despite being important to consumers. In a five-star hotel, services take a prominent place when compared to food items, whereas in ordinary restaurants the proportion may be more or less equal. In fast food outlets, food may dominate as compared to services. Therefore, there is a possibility of having a hybrid category of products, but it is uncommon to have a significant portion of such products in any economy.
4. *Services with Accompanying Tangible Goods:* This is a marketing offer in which the intangible part is dominant. People buy services but not tangible goods involved in the production of services. Accompanying goods play a major role in the value assessment of services by the consumer. For example, people buy mobility services from a transport organization. To provide these services, transport organizations need tangibles such as buses, trucks, trains, helicopters, aeroplanes and the like. Although consumers do not buy tangibles, the condition of vehicles—both on the interior and the exterior—facilities, comfort, speed and so on play a major role in assessing the value of the service. A vast majority of service products fall under this category.
5. *Pure Service:* Pure service is a marketing offer where consumers confine themselves to valuing only the service they receive and nothing else. Services without any support of goods can serve the purpose of users and are capable of giving satisfaction to consumers. Services such as teaching, consultancy, idea selling and the like fall in this category.

Figure 1.1 presents the tangibility spectrum, illustrating goods and services with varied proportions of tangibility and intangibility.

WHY SERVICES MARKETING?

The basic questions that confront everyone are: Why should there be a separate learning on services marketing? Are the marketing concepts and techniques developed for the manufacturing sector not applicable to services? Do services require distinctive strategies in marketing? The answers to these questions provide the basic platform for an understanding of services marketing.

A different marketing approach is necessary for services marketing because services differ from goods in many respects. The following are the differences between physical goods and services.

> *The six characteristics of services, intangibility, inseparability, variability, perishability, customer participation and lack of ownership, greatly affect marketing programmes.*

- Services are intangible. Goods are tangible.
- Services are heterogeneous whereas goods are homogeneous.
- Services are produced in buyer–seller interactions. Goods are produced in a factory.

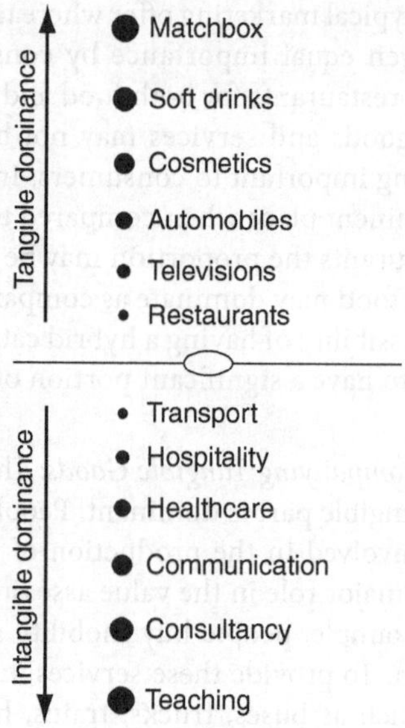

Fig. 1.1 The tangibility spectrum

- Production, distribution and consumption take place simultaneously in the case of services. In the case of goods, the three are separate and independent functions.
- Consumers are co-producers in services. Consumers do not generally participate in the production of goods.
- Services cannot be stored. Goods can be stored.
- In the sale of services, the transfer of ownership does not take place, whereas in the case of goods, it does take place.

Considering the core differences between goods and services, six characteristics of services can be identified

Bharti Airtel

Sunil Bharti Mittal founded Bharti in 1976—a time when the telecom industry was a purely public sector enterprise requiring huge capital investment to set up the requisite infrastructure. Since its inception, Bharti Airtel Limited, the first private telecom service provider, has consistently been the market leader in mobile services, with 24.15 per cent market share in 2007. As of 31 March 2008, Bharti had an aggregate of 62.26 million customers, of which 61.98 million were mobile customers. The success of the company may be attributed to the services marketing model adopted by them, which yielded rich dividends. The model integrates customized product packages and price offerings, accessibility through widely connected network, extensive as well as exclusive distribution systems, skilled and motivated human resources, qualitative interaction experiences, image building through effective communication campaign in credible media and minimization of service deficiencies through professional management practices. The strategy of extensive roll out ahead of competition, especially in new villages, was unique and successful. The brand Airtel became very popular in India. The company developed strategic partnerships with various companies in the world.

CHARACTERISTICS OF SERVICES

Services have basically six characteristics that greatly affect the design of marketing programmes. They are: (1) intangibility, (2) inseparability, (3) variability, (4) perishability, (5) customer participation and (6) lack of ownership.

Intangibility

Services are intangible. Unlike physical products, they cannot be seen, tasted, felt, heard or smelt before they are bought. Intangibility creates a feeling of uncertainty about the outcome of a service. For example, a tourist does not know about the exact outcome of experience before consuming the service; a woman who purchases the services of a beauty parlour for getting a facial cannot foresee the exact result. This characteristic of the service makes buyers look for evidence of quality in the service offer. Buyers try to draw quality inferences from the components of service environment such as the place, people, equipment, communication material, symbols and the technical design of the service package. To handle the given marketing problem, service providers need to manage evidence. They should try to make the intangible tangible to the best possible extent. The service design should be able to transform intangible services into concrete benefits. Let us take an example of an insurance company that wants to position itself as a modern insurance company.

> ***Intangibility** is the key characteristic that distinguishes services from goods. In the absence of physical form for identification, verification or trail, service consumers are often uncertain about the outcome of a service. The critical challenge to the service company, therefore, is to facilitate the transformation of intangible services into concrete benefits.*

The process of a company to make a service tangible should include:

- *Location and Physical Setting:* The location at which service outlets are established should be accessible to target consumers. The physical setting must be convenient for both employees and customers. The layout and the traffic flow should be planned in such a way that waiting lines should not be long. The exterior design must be attractive and indicative of the service level and the interior should be designed meaningfully.
- *Employees and Agents:* Employees and agents should be sufficient in number and busy in interactions. They should possess a pleasant and neat appearance, sharpness and knowledge of the service and the customers.
- *Hardware, Tools and Techniques:* The company should be equipped with the latest hardware that can support the service process and help the employees in providing speedy and quality services to customers. The company should create an impression that it uses the state-of-the-art technology in serving customers.
- *Communication:* The material used for communicating with customers should suggest efficiency and speed.

Inseparability

> *Production, delivery and consumption are inseparable and simultaneous processes in the case of services. Inseparability creates problems in market expansion, particularly in offering standard services and establishing service production units.*

Services cannot be separated from the service provider. In fact, the production, delivery and consumption of a service take place simultaneously in the buyer–seller interactions. This characteristic of a service creates problems to the marketer, particularly in the case of market expansion. No matter where service providers intend to offer services, they should have service production units that offer the same service quality standards. However, some service organizations have reduced direct interactions by introducing new technologies. For example, banking organizations have introduced cheque, credit card, telebanking and ATM facilities to minimize direct buyer–seller interactions. Thus, the customers of State Bank of India can interact through interest (online banking), telephone, ATM, besides other conventional means. The Indian Railways can be accessed through telephone, authorized agencies, Internet and so on.

Variability

> *__Variability__ creates problems in standardization and communication of services to customers. Service firms struggle to build customer confidence and manage consistency in service offerings because of this characteristic.*

> *Service companies often try to capitalize on the variability characteristic of services. They introduce many changes in the service offer quite often to deliver more value to the customer without disturbing the basic structure of the service offer, thus promoting innovation as a core strength.*

Services are highly variable. It is almost impossible to have the same service from the same seller the second time. No two customers can receive identical service, even though they experience it simultaneously. For example, the experiences of bus travellers vary with the seats they occupy. The experiences of passengers sitting on the window side, inner side, front end and rear end of the bus will not be similar, though they avail the service simultaneously. A receptionist of a hotel cannot extend the same kind of smile to customers during all her working hours. Further, experiences vary with the knowledge, co-customers, the ability to participate, mood, and other behavioural variables of service consumers. Service organizations face major problems in standardizing and communicating service standards because of this variability. While customers expect from a company the communication relating to service standards to arrive at a purchase decision, service providers often struggle to develop service standards.

However, the variability of services can be used as an opportunity by service organizations. Since innovation is the key to success, this characteristic offers enormous opportunities to introduce several changes in the service offer without disturbing the basic structure of the offer. The service provider can offer better experiences and delight customers by introducing surprise changes in the service package.

Perishability

> *__Perishability__ is a serious problem in the face of fluctuating demand. This characteristic necessitates careful planning for optimal capacity utilization and demand management.*

Services perish; they cannot be stored. A half-full train that leaves the railway station means that the service of the empty half remains unused. An unutilized service capacity cannot be used further. When the demand is stable, perishability cannot be a problem to the service organization. However, service firms face many problems when demand fluctuates. The major challenge to these firms is to balance the supply–demand positions. Thus, demand management is one of the major tasks for service firms. To cite an example: Andhra Pradesh State Road Transport Corporation (APSRTC),[11] established in 1932, found a place in the *Guinness Book of World Records* in 1999 for operating the largest number of buses. The corporation has a fleet of about 20,000 buses which cover 6.63 million km and carry 127.87 million people to their destinations every year. The corporation has received several awards for its performance on various counts. APSRTC faced a serious problem of falling occupancy ratio from 1997–98 to 2006–07. Local transporters like autos, rickshaws and other tiny private transporters took away the demand from the corporation. The corporation's future was in jeopardy due to accumulated losses. It primarily worked on changing the attitude of the front-line employees from public sector ego state to passenger-friendly behaviour besides other measures. In 2007–08, the corporation made a profit after 10 years of successive losses. The occupancy ratio increased from 65 per cent in 2004–05 to 70 per cent in 2007–08. Demand management thus became vital for the corporation's success.[12]

Customer Participation

Service production is not a one-sided activity. Customers are co-producers of a service. The production quality of the service greatly depends on the ability, skill and performance of the employee as well as the ability and performance of the customer. In the service interaction, although the employee and the customer are not the equal part of production, the role of the customer cannot be overemphasized. Service firms should make customers aware of the service package and the production process through proper communication media. For example, tourists can perceive the architecture, appearance and environmental beauty of Taj Mahal at Agra in many ways. But if informed about the legendary love story of Shah Jahan and Mumtaz Mahal, and the significance of the Taj Mahal as a symbol of their love, the tourist involvement, experience and perceived quality change significantly. Tourists perceive greater value of their visit to the Taj Mahal. Service companies, therefore, should take necessary steps to ensure customer participation, leading to a quality experience of the service. Customer participation is greatly influenced by the content, media and the mode of communication with the customer. It may be necessary to "train" customers for effective participation in the service process and also to learn the methodology of quality perception and assessment. Perfection from the organization's side in service production cannot ensure positive results unless consumers too are effectively involved in the process. Therefore, specific and special orientation to different groups of customers is necessary.

> *Customers are co-producers of services; the service quality depends equally on the performance of the service provider and on the ability and performance of the customer. Therefore, customer participation, which alters the "perception" of the service quality, is the responsibility of the service provider.*

Customization is one of the key strategies the service firms adopt to ensure efficient and effective participation of customers. Customer participation is active in services such as medical treatment, hairdressing, health clubs, colleges and beauty care centres.

Lack of Ownership

Service consumers acquire experience, not ownership, since services are intangible and perishable. However, this characteristic adds to the problems of the service marketer. Convincing the customer with tangible goods on which they will have ownership through transfer of title is much easier than selling an experience where nothing remains after consumption, except the memory of it. Customer dissonance would be higher in the case of services than of goods.

> *Convincing the customer by the ownership of tangible goods through the transfer of the title is much easier than selling an experience where nothing remains after consumption, except its memory. Customer dissonance is higher in the case of services than of goods.*

Due to these characteristics of services, service providers face varied problems and challenges in marketing, as compared to the producers of goods. The marketing challenges and strategic options due to service characteristics are presented in Table 1.1.

Table 1.1 Marketing Challenges and Strategic Options in Services Marketing

Service Characteristics	Marketing Problems/Challenges	Strategic Options
Intangibility	• Cannot be communicated easily • Consumer suspects due to absence of concrete evidences • Design of total service package is not possible • Comparative presentation is not possible	• Making the service process tangible to the maximum possible extent • Managing and promoting word-of-mouth communication • Strengthening internal and external marketing • Using relationship marketing
Inseparability	• Problems of market expansion • Maintenance of service quality • Compulsory presence of consumer • Limited production capacity • Operation at limited capacity	• Minimizing customer interactions • Innovating techniques of indirect interaction • Standardization to the maximum possible extent • Developing distribution network with quality control mechanisms
Variability	• Limited scope for standardization • Not possible to communicate exactly what the consumer is going to receive • Quality can be determined only after the service is consumed	• More focus on standardization • Internal marketing and employee retention • Positioning variation as a strength of innovation • Promoting research and innovations
Perishability	• Storage of service is not possible • Sales volume should match the capacity • Time pressure in sales	• Demand management • Capacity management • Tactical approaches • Continuous study on demand patterns and competitive parameters
Customer participation	• Customers are not controllable • Production quality also depends on the customer's knowledge and ability to participate • Customers are evaluated at every stage of service production	• Effective external marketing • Customer education and training • Effective interactive marketing • Management of movements of truth • Effective internal marketing
Lack of ownership	• Nothing remains after consumption • Very less time for the consumer to evaluate the product • High consumer dissonance	• Making communication tangible • Customer relationship marketing • Managing high level of company image

Pantaloon Retail

Pantaloon Retail (India) Limited, the flagship enterprise of Future Group, is the leading retailer operating multiple retail formats in both the value and lifestyle segment of the Indian market.

Kishore Biyani led the company's foray into organized retailing with the pantaloons family store that opened in 1977. The company launched Big Bazaar in 2001 as a unique Indian hypermarket format integrating the look, touch and feel of Indian bazaars, with the aspects of modern retail-like choices, convenience and quality. The opening of the100th Big Bazaar store in just 7 years stands as a testimony of its successful growth. With a vision of delivering everything, everywhere, every time for every Indian consumer in the most profitable manner, Big Bazaar adopted "Indianness" in every sphere of its activity. This retail format exploited successfully the latent demand that existed in urban India for a new buying and shopping experience. Big Bazaar effectively addressed the typical service characteristics such as tangiblization of services, variation in offerings and involving customers in service processes. The 30,000 strong skilled employees, who are driven by the corporate doctrine "Rewrite rules, Retain values," contribute in generating quality experiences for customers. The well-crafted service business strategy led the company to grow in terms of size as well as profits.

The characteristics described in Table 1.1 necessitate a distinctly different approach for services marketing. This does not mean that the traditional marketing philosophies, methods and techniques are totally irrelevant to the services sector. In fact, the fundamentals of marketing are the same for both the sectors. What is required is the development of an adaptable mechanism to a different environment, keeping in view the service characteristics.

Thus, services marketing is nothing but the application of suitably modified and customized traditional marketing philosophies to the services sector.

> *Services marketing challenges are typical due to the distinctive characteristics of services. Conventional marketing strategies are less likely to generate optimum results. The different strategic approaches based on the foundations of traditional marketing are necessary to address services marketing challenges effectively.*

THE GROWTH OF THE SERVICES SECTOR

The growth of the services sector is a global trend. As mentioned already, many economies have already become service economies and others are following in their footsteps. In 2007, services accounted for 66.4 per cent of the GDP in the United States. More than 80 per cent of the workforce in the United States is employed in the services sector. The growth of services is directly linked to the development of the economy. The majority of the workforce in all developed countries in the world, including the UK, France, Germany, Japan, and Canada, is engaged in service organizations. The Fact sheet 2002–05 shown in "Services Marketing Insight: The Department for Professional Employees, AFL-CIO: Fact sheet 2002–05 on Services Sector" testifies the growth of services in the United States. J. B. Quinn and C. E. Gagnon[13] identified the contributions of the services sector to any economy in the following respects:

> *The growth of services is directly linked to the development of an economy. The majority of the workforce in all developed countries in the world, including the UK, France, Germany, Japan, and Canada, are engaged in service organizations.*

- People value services as highly as manufactured goods. Services are not something one looks at after goods needs have been met.
- The value addition by service firms is very well comparable to, and even higher than, the value addition by the manufacturers of goods.

1.2 Services Marketing Insight

The Department for Professional Employees, AFL-CIO: Fact Sheet 2002–05 on Services Sector

- Over the last 50 years, the rising share of employment in the services sector and the declining share in the goods-producing sector have transformed the U.S. labour market. In 1950, 45 per cent of the non-agricultural labour force was employed in the services sector while 65 per cent was employed in the goods-producing sector. In 2001, the services sector accounted for more than 80 per cent of the non-agricultural labour force, while the goods-producing sector employed less than 20 per cent.
- The services sector will be the main source of employment growth and output between 2000 and 2010. Employment in the services sector will increase by almost 20 per cent between 2000 and 2010, while employment in the goods-producing sector will increase by less than 6 per cent.
- The variety of industries that comprise the service industry will collectively account for three out of every five new jobs created in the U.S. economy between 2000 and 2010.
- Expected to generate almost 13 million jobs, the service industry overshadows the 3.1 million jobs expected to be created by retail trade, the next largest source of employment growth. Together, these two industry divisions make up about 73 per cent of the total non-farm wage and salary employment growth between 2000 and 2010.
- The largest source of employment growth in the economy is projected in the personnel supply services industry. Professional employment in the industry will increase by 66 per cent between 2000 and 2010.
- The economy's fastest growing industry, and the second largest in terms of employment, is computer and data processing services. This industry is expected to nearly double between 2000 and 2010, adding another 1.8 million jobs. Computer specialists account for almost half of all employees in this industry.
- Educational services were one of the largest employers in 2001, providing 11.3 million jobs. The industry is expected to add 1.9 million new jobs between 2000 and 2010. The number of job openings for teachers is expected to increase substantially by 2010 due to the projected increases in enrolments and retirements.
- Social services rank among the fastest growing industries. The number of non-governmental wage and salary jobs is expected to increase to 42 per cent, compared with only 15 per cent for all industries combined.

Sources: DPE Research Department, "The Service Sector Vital Statistics" Fact sheet 2002–05, www.dpeaflcio.org, Washington, DC, 2005.

- The services sector is at least as capital intensive as the goods sector, and many service industries have a high technology impact.
- Service industries tend to be just as concentrated as manufacturing, and service firms tend to be sufficiently big in scale to be important and sophisticated buyers.
- Service industries develop productivity increases that are big enough to support continuing real growth in per capita income.

> *"The two major reasons identified as responsible for the growth of services sector are: growth in the intermediate demand from firms and growth in the final demand from customers."*

REASONS FOR GROWTH IN THE SERVICES SECTOR

The services sector has registered substantial growth in many economies. The changing economic, social and technological scenarios have contributed to the growth of services in many respects. The growth in trade within and across countries, the potential capacity of services in exploiting the optimum value of productive resources, the intensified competition across the sectors and the realization of the value of services by a major part of the society created and enhanced the demand for services.

The reasons for the growth of the services sector can be attributed to the growth in the intermediate demand from firms and the final demands from customers.

Intermediate Demand from Firms

Manufacturing firms realized the importance of the staff function when line managers' sub-optimal performance in decision-making relating to operational activities and the growth of the business was identified. Manufacturing firms started bundling a number of services functions such as selling, marketing research, advertising, labour welfare, HRD, financial advisors, strategic advisors and so on. The growth of competition and the pace of change in consumer exposure and expectations forced organizations to look for specialized services.

Manufacturing companies started unbundling themselves by way of closing support service departments to benefit from the highly specialized support services of outside organizations. The concept of self-reliance by way of minimizing or avoiding dependence on others was used by firms to reduce uncertainties, maintain confidentiality and grow big. The professional service companies offering quality services at a relatively low price compared to the production cost of service departments inside the manufacturing companies. Further, they could concentrate more on their core competencies to retain a sustained competitive edge. The wave of specialist services during the last three decades changed management philosophies and encouraged them to outsource many services. Service companies also require specialized service from micro-level professional support service companies. Hence, the demand for special services has gone up.

> *"The unbundling of corporations is one of the major changes to have taken place in recent years. The traditional philosophy of self-reliance was given up to develop networking with dependable supply and support service companies. The availability of micro-level professional and specialized services at a relatively low price has helped companies become focused on their competencies."*

Final Demand from Customers

The direct demand from customers for a variety of services has gone up. The marginal utility from goods has diminished, at least in a relative sense, and services have grown in importance. People spend more and more on services. The demand for health services, polybion laser services, travel, entertainment, sports and the like have registered a significant growth in recent years. The following are the reasons identified for the growth in demand for services directly from customers.

> *"The reasons for the growth in demand for services from final consumers are: increased affluence, more leisure time, rising number of working women, growth in DINKs, greater life expectancy, greater complexity of products, greater complexity in life, greater concern for resource scarcity and ecology and increased number of new products and the young generation."*

- *Increased Affluence*: The majority of the population in developed economies and significant groups in developing economies has become more affluent. The 250-million strong middle-income households of India with their desire for a variety of products and services attract many multinational companies to the country. The demand for personal services, travel, tourism, entertainment, clubs and the like greatly depends on the affluence of the society. If travellers have little money, they carry their luggage themselves. If they are affluent, they engage a porter for the same job. Affluence reduces the scope of self-service and creates opportunities for many service people and organizations.

- *More Leisure Time:* People across the world want increasingly more leisure time to engage in personal and family activities. There is a significant change in defining the holidays or leisure period even in the semi-urban and rural pockets of India. Apart from travelling, entertainment, personal care and so on, people now spend more time on education, training and skill development for themselves as well as their children.
- *Increased Percentage of Working Women:* The steady rise in the percentage of employed women in many economies has spurred the growth of services that can reduce their burden. More affluent than their non-working counterparts, these women have led to an increased demand for services such as crèches, babysitting, household domestic help, health services, fitness services, special education services and so on.
- *Growth in the Population of DINKs:* The term DINK—dual income, no kids—refers to couples too busy with their respective careers to have children. More often than not, such people postpone starting a family till it is too late to do so. In some societies, where the divorce rate is high, marriage is perceived as a short-term relationship. In such societies, neither partner prefers to have children whose future is uncertain if the marriage fails. In many developed societies, DINK is on the rise. DINK couples spend liberally on services.
- *Greater Life Expectancy:* Economic prosperity and improved standard of living have resulted in greater life expectancy. As a result, there has been a significant growth in the population of senior citizens accompanied by a greater demand for nursing homes and healthcare services with the increasing population of the elderly. For example, in India, the population above the age of 60 years had increased from 14.13 million in 1981 to 76.62 million in 2001.
- *Greater Complexity of Products:* The rapid pace of change in technology offers greater choice, allowing people to regularly use increasingly complex products such as computers, automobiles, television, kitchen appliances and so on that need specialists for maintenance and repair. Therefore, the demand for such services is growing day by day.
- *Greater Complexity in Life:* In today's society, people are required to play a number of roles. There is a demand for such services that can reduce or share their burden. As such, there is an increased demand for income tax consultants, legal consultants, counselling, employment services, labour supply services, baby care centers and so on.
- *Greater Concern for Resource Scarcity:* A majority of the population, despite limited or scarce financial resources, want to avail and utilize a number of services. Owning a tangible product for various services requires financial strength. On the other hand, many such goods may

not be used to the optimum capacity by individuals. Hence, there is a demand for leisure services such as car rentals, computer hardware rentals, accommodation and door-to-door service.

- *Greater Concern for Ecology:* In recent years, many economies have become concerned about the environment and ecological balance. The governments of various countries have taken the responsibility to promote various public organizations to protect the environment from pollution and other hazards and to maintain the ecology through the conservation of forests, protection of animals, birds, insects and other important species. They have been using various media for campaigning and taking up several programmes to make people participate in the process. Schemes like Vana Mahotsav and water conservation are examples of this.
- *Increasing Number of New Products:* Consumers have been exposed to a wide variety of choice in recent years. The life of products and services is shrinking owing to the rapid introduction of new or improved products. Consumers being very busy, are unable to understand a product completely before taking a decision to purchase the product or service. As such, consultancy services are enjoying increased demand. For example, if a person wants to invest in shares, the complex information inputs of the share market certainly drive him/her to confusion and uncertainty. Brokers or consultancy services facilitate a smooth process.
- *The Young:* The younger generation tends to use more and more services than the older generation, who depends on themselves for a number of activities. The younger generation would be able to cope up with the pace of change only through consumption of a number of services. For example, a graduate in computers can learn new languages during the course but it takes a lot of time. By the time he/she has expertise in a language, there is a danger that the programme may get outdated. Therefore, they prefer to take training through other institutions to be competitive.

CAREER OPPORTUNITIES IN THE SERVICES SECTOR

The growth of the services sector in many economies resulted in the growth of employment opportunities. The services sector provides enormous business opportunities to creative entrepreneurs. Value creation, communication and delivery through cost-effective means with reasonable profits further develop many unexploited and under-exploited areas of the services sector. The services sector in India stands as an example of the growing employment opportunities. The details of major industries in the services sector are presented in Exhibit 1.1.

Market trends indicate that finance professionals are in great demand in banking, trading, real estate and the like. Another new economy sector is the retail sector. Bharti Enterprises, in a tie-up with Wal-Mart, forecast a billion-

Exhibit 1.1	Major Industries Classified under the Services Sector
1. Transportation and public utilities	10. Entertainment services
2. Communication	11. Healthcare services
3. Electric, gas and sanitary services	12. Legal services
4. Wholesale and retail trade	13. Educational services
5. Finance, insurance and real estate	14. Social organizations offering services
6. Hospitality services	15. Government services—civilian-cum-military
7. Personal services	16. State and local government services
8. Business services	17. Tourism services
9. Accounting services	

dollar market for the organized retail sector by the end of the year 2010, creating 2 million new jobs. The spurt in the advertising industry during the postreform period has thrown open a vista of opportunities in areas such as client servicing, creative department, media department, production, television, photography, market research, exhibition, event management and direct marketing. The top ten career options for the youth of India in the services sector are shown in Exhibit 1.2. The following are the services sectors offering good career opportunities.[14]

Insurance

In India, this sector was opened to private companies as a part of the economic reforms. A variety of services from life and health to travel and house insurance are offered by different companies. More and more individuals are being employed as agents, development officers and administrative officers.

Call Centres

The call centre is the first customer interface with a company. Call centre executives are often fresh graduates, and sometimes undergraduates, who have knowledge of computers and are trained to respond to customer queries promptly and politely, using state-of-the-art telephony and computing technology to give correct information. The sector is likely to employ 2.3 million people by the end of the year 2010.

Non-government Organizations

Characteristics such as genuine interest in helping people, patience, the ability to be empathetic and to be able to provide hope and relief make one eligible for entry-level jobs in NGOs and social welfare organizations.

Knowledge Process Outsourcing (KPO)

Knowledge Process Outsourcing is emerging as a lucrative job destination for the youth. KPO may create 0.25 million jobs spanning different backgrounds

Exhibit 1.2	Top 10 Emerging Career Options for the Youth of India in the Services Sector
1. Software Engineering	6. Tourism Management
2. Call Centre	7. Radio Jockeying
3. Animation/Graphics	8. TV Presentation/Journalism
4. Hotel Management	9. Investment Banking
5. Advertising	10. Fashion Photography

as science, engineering, law, accounting, pharmaceuticals and technological stream and the legal field is expected to boom, netting around 80,000 jobs by the end of the year 2010.

Human Resources

The hugely growing HR and recruitment companies are themselves hunting for good human resources. Placement agencies often require the services of graduates or postgraduates in their headhunting or recruitment campaigns for job openings in organizations.

IT-enabled Services

The huge demand for manpower by companies abroad wanting to provide information and support services to their customers using technology has led to ITeS becoming a booming sector in India.

Hospitality

With business travel on the rise, the hotel industry would require a workforce of around 95,000 by the end of the year 2010. Graduates in home science, commerce, physics and engineering can look forward to suitable openings at different levels of work.

Entertainment

This sector offers great job opportunities. It is estimated that about 300,000 professionals will be employed by the end of the year 2010. The animation industry is growing at the rate of 30 per cent per year.

Aviation

This sector is growing at a whopping 25 per cent per year, creating new job opportunities. Alteon Training, a subsidiary of Boeing Company, forecasts that the number of pilots required in India will increase from 3,000 to 15,000 in coming years. Cabin crew, airline managers and ground staff constitute the rest.

SUMMARY

- Services are interaction-based performances whose quality is perceived by consumers.
- The services sector is growing rapidly in almost all parts of the world.
- The hidden services sector refers to services output within the manufacturing sector. It is not counted in calculating the contribution of services sector to the GDP of a country.
- Services are becoming a critical source of wealth in many ways to economies.
- The services sector will not squeeze out the manufacturer, but rather serve as an important supplement.
- Services differ from goods in many respects, and as such the marketing of services is altogether a different proposition.
- Service characteristics such as intangibility, inseparability, variability, perishability, customer participation and lack of ownership offer new challenges to service marketers.
- Innovation is the key to the success of services marketing.
- The two reasons attributed to the growth of services sector are: growth in the intermediate demand from firms and growth in the final demand from customers.
- The career opportunities in services sector are growing in various business segments.

KEY TERMS

affluence *15*
customer participation *11*
DINK *16*
hidden services sector *2*
intangibility *9*
inseparability *9*
intermediate demand *15*
perishability *10*
service economy *2*
variability *10*

BRIEF QUESTIONS

1. Define services.
2. Explain the emergence of the marketing thought for services.
3. What are the career opportunities in the services sector?
4. List 10 major service industries.
5. What are the marketing challenges due to the intangible character of services?
6. Explain customer participation in services.
7. Discuss the challenges and opportunities arising from the variability character of services.

ESSAY QUESTIONS

1. "Many economies in the world are becoming service economies." Is this a positive direction? Give reasons.
2. Explain the reasons for the growth of the services sector.
3. Differentiate between goods and services.
4. Why should there be a different marketing approach to services?
5. What are the characteristics of services? What challenges do the characteristics offer to services marketing?
6. "Traditional marketing is also applicable to services. The only difference is that it has to be applied to the services sector." Comment.

ASSIGNMENTS

1. India and China are the emerging economic powers of the new millennium. The services sector has registered a substantial growth in India since the implementation of liberalization policies. The contribution of the services sector to the GDP of India was 54.2 per cent in 2004. The success in this sector is regarded as "India's services revolution." In China, however, the services sector has lagged well

behind the manufacturing sector (or the secondary sector, according to Chinese terminology), though its role in the economy improved slightly in the last 15 years. From 1990 to 2004, the services sector, as a proportion of China's GDP, increased modestly from 34.3 per cent in 1990 to 40.7 per cent in 2004.

(a) Why have the two countries taken very different trajectories in developing their service economies?

(b) What are the implications for future development in the two economies?

2. The unexpected growth of telecommunications, particularly in mobile services in India, has contributed significantly to the changing lifestyle and human interaction processes. Teledensity, the major indicator of telecom growth in a country, is on the increase. It has shown a sharp rise from 1.90 in 1997–98 to 18.23 in 2006–07. Though the National Telecom Policies of 1994 and 1999 gave high priority to providing telecom services to rural areas, the teledensity has increased from 0.4 to 2.00 in these areas, as compared to the urban areas where it shot up from 5.80 to 45.00. This disparity in the teledensity between the urban and rural areas became a cause of concern to the Indian government. The Department of Telecommunication (DoT) and the Telecom Regulatory Authority of India (TRAI) took several measures to increase teledensity in rural areas. The Indian government's Bharat Nirman plan for rural infrastructure 2005–09 includes telephone connectivity to every village as one of its prime tasks. The kind of measures being implemented in rural areas will certainly increase teledensity in rural India in the near future.

(a) What will be the impact of the growth of telecommunication services on the lifestyle of rural people?

(b) How do you correlate teledensity with rural development?

REFERENCES

1 G. L. Shostack, "Breaking Free from Products Marketing," *Journal of Marketing: Theory and Practice*, 41, no. 2 (1977): 73–80.

2 American Marketing Association, quoted in Harsh V. Verma, *Services Marketing.* (Delhi: Pearson Education, 2008), p. 26.

3 W. J. Regan, "The Service Revolution," *Journal of Marketing*, 27, no. 3 (1963): 57–62.

4 R. C. Judd, "The Case for Redefining Services," *Journal of Marketing*, 28, no. 1 (1964): 58–59.

5 W. J. Stanton, *Fundamentals of Marketing*, 4th ed. (New York: McGraw-Hill Inc., 1975), p. 545.

6 J. Lehtinen, *Customer Oriented Service Firm* (Finland: Espoo, 1983), p. 21.

7 P. Kotler and P. N. Bloom, *Marketing Professional Services* (Upper Saddle River, NJ: Prentice Hall, 1984), p. 174.

8 C. Grönroos, *Service Management and Marketing; Managing the Moments of Truth in Service Competition*. (Lexington, D. C.: Heath/Lexington books, 1990), p. 27.

9 V. A. Zeithaml and M. J. Bitner, *Services Marketing.* (New York: McGraw-Hill Inc., 1996), p. 3.

10 T. Levitt, "Marketing Intangible Products and Product Intangibles," *Harvard Business Review*, 59, no. 3 (1981): 94–102.

11 P. Kotler and K. L. Keller, *Marketing Management*, 12th ed. (Delhi: Pearson Education, 2006), pp. 373–74.

12 www.apsrtc.gov.in, APSRTC, Performance Trends from 1998-99 to 2008-09, Central MIS, Hyderabad, 2009,1

13 B. Quinn and C. E. Gagnon (1986), pp. 95–96 quoted in Christian Grönroos, *Service Management and Marketing; Managing the Moments of Truth in Service Competition*. (Massachusetts: Maxwell Macmillan; Lexington: D.C. Heath/ Lexington Books, 1990), p. 7.

14 P. K. Dutta (2009). "Fascinating Career Oppor tunities." *Employment News*, xxx III, no. 39 (December 30, 2008–January 5, 2009), http://www.employmentnews.gov.in/career_details-fascinating-career-opportunities-for-freshers-210-209.html.

Marketing Management: Core Concepts

2

LEARNING OBJECTIVES

After studying this chapter, you will be able to:

- Understand the core concepts of marketing
- Describe the philosophies of marketing
- Understand the marketing challenges
- Understand the process of marketing planning

Mr Mukherjee, a retired service man, decided to spend his time in social service. He remembered reading reports of various organizations regarding the health hazards of rural and tribal people in India. These reports suggested that polluted drinking water was the root cause for many diseases afflicting these people. The problem of clean drinking water—a known problem for many decades—was unfortunately not resolved either by successive governments or by non-government organizations. It was a Herculean task in view of the magnitude of the problem and resource limitations, compounded further by the poor commitment of various organizations. As a responsible citizen, Mr. Mukherjee wanted to find a solution to this problem—albeit on a small scale.

Mr Mukherjee decided to invest the money from his retirement benefits. He also convinced a few friends to invest in the project. He identified 10 villages as the first target. These villages did not get pure drinking water and depended on water from tanks and ponds for all their needs. Mr Mukherjee established a water purifying plant at a central location to be able to supply water to all the 10 villages. He planned to offer drinking water in reusable plastic cans with a capacity of 10 litres at INR 5. The expected revenue was expected to be sufficient for distribution services.

Mr Mukherjee contacted village heads and opinion leaders and explained his service motto and the need for such a service. However, their response was far from encouraging. Villagers were not convinced that drinking water was responsible for their ill health and said they could not afford to pay for it. If it were supplied free of cost, it would have been easy for him to convince people to use safe drinking water. Mr Mukherjee was unable to satisfy their demand as logistics involved regular expenditure. For plant maintenance, he was confident of getting support from others as it involved a relatively nominal amount. He realized that marketing skills were necessary to sell his services to the target group.

Questions:

1. What are the critical marketing issues involved in the service?
2. What is the marketing philosophy of Mr Mukherjee?
3. How do you develop a marketing plan for the service?
4. How do you apply segmentation, targeting and positioning for this service?

INTRODUCTION

Marketing is the service function of an organization that connects the company with the targeted part of the society. Marketing is the process of identifying needs, wants and expectations of people and providing utility value to the satisfaction of consumers through an exchange process. The American Marketing Association defines marketing as "an organizational function and a set of processes for creating, communicating, and delivering value to customers and for managing customer relationships in ways that benefit the organization and its stake holders."[1] This definition identifies three critical processes of marketing: creating value, communicating value and delivering value. Another important focus is on managing customer relationships. Therefore, marketing aims to build customer relationships through the exchange of value beneficial to both the company and customers. Marketing is the science of serving markets. It involves systematic processes and formulations towards the achievement of customer satisfaction and retention. Marketing is an art. Every process and formulation needs to be carried out creatively. Consumers prefer the companies that can successfully blend the professionalism of formulated marketing and creative marketing performances.

> *"**Marketing** is the science of serving markets. It involves systematic processes and formulations towards achievement of customer satisfaction and retention. Marketing is an art. Every process and formulation needs to be carried out creatively."*

Marketing can be understood from two perspectives—the management perspective and the social perspective. From the management point of view, marketing is the art and science of creating, delivering and communicating superior customer value[2] to the chosen target markets. It includes building, maintaining and enhancing relationships with customers to satisfy them better than the competitors. From the society point of view, marketing can be understood as a societal process by which individuals and groups obtain what they need through creating, offering and freely exchanging products and services of value with others.[3]

The importance of marketing in the socio-economic system of a country can be noticed through the utilities generated by marketing. Utilities are the values which society derives from marketing. At least four utilities are created by marketing: time, place, possession and image utility. Marketing plays a supporting role in creating form utility.[4] When services or goods are made accessible to customers, the place utility is created. When they are offered at the time customers want them, the time utility is created. When ownership or a legally protectable assurance is given to consumers, the possession utility is created. When a psychological value is created for the perception of consumers, the image utility is created. Marketers play a critical role in creating an identifiable form of a marketing offer in terms of either designing the service package or developing a tangible good such as a tour package or a toothpaste.

THE MARKETING OFFER

Companies decide marketing offers based on the assessment of market needs and company's vision and mission. Researchers have identified 10 broad entities that are marketed widely over the globe: goods, services, events, experiences, persons, places, properties, ideas, organizations and information. These are all demanded by various people belonging to different geographic regions. A variety of products are offered under each category to satisfy the ever-changing, divergent needs of people. A company may concentrate on a single/a few items in an entity or a few entities.

CORE CONCEPTS

Marketing is a dynamic field. To understand the marketing function properly, it is necessary to have a clear understanding of the fundamental concepts of marketing. The following are the core concepts of marketing.

Needs, Wants and Expectations

> *Service companies should focus on consumer needs, wants and expectations and find ways to satisfy these. Need orientation is critical as consumers find different ways to satisfy a need. Wants change from time to time. Consumer expectations are influenced by many factors which change with time. Only those companies that are capable of adapting to such changes can survive.*

The purpose of marketing is to satisfy the needs of people selectively. *Needs* are human requirements. Needs are either physiological or psychological. Every human being needs food, clothing and shelter. They also need entertainment, identity, education, relationships, and so on to lead life on desired lines. People may not be consciously aware of all their needs. The job of the marketer is to serve the known needs, make customers aware of subconscious needs and then serve those needs. *Wants* are the means people find to satisfy their needs. In other words, wants are the specific objects that people believe to be capable of satisfying their needs. Marketers create wants. They offer a wide range of choices to consumers to find the right objects to satisfy their needs.

Consumers develop *expectations* of the objects selected for the satisfaction of a need. The expectations may be based on past experiences, the promises made by marketers, word of mouth, the knowledge base on related products or experiences, and so on. Marketers need to understand the expectations of people while designing marketing offers and make sure that the product delivered to the customer ultimately matches the expectations. Consumers are satisfied with a marketing offer only when their expectations are fully met.

The study of consumer needs, wants and expectations is critical for service marketers. A consumer may satisfy a need through many ways. For example, a consumer may watch television, go to movie theatres and clubs, attend parties, or browse through desired programmes/play games on Internet to satisfy their entertainment needs. The desired objects for satisfying the need may change from time to time. Similarly, the expectations of the quality, accessibility, and cost of such services also may change over time. Therefore, it is necessary to focus on the needs, the wants and the expectations of the target consumers to design and develop service offers and also to modify the offers from time to time.

Markets

In conventional terms, a market is a place where buyers and sellers interact and transactions take place. In marketing, the term *market* is used contextually. A common understanding is that a market consists of current and potential buyers who share a common need and belief that a specific good or service satisfies the need. Marketers classify markets using different criteria such as product, demographic feature, geography, period and types of buyers.

> **Market** *contextually refers to a group of present and potential buyers of a company or product. Market identification is the basic foundation for marketing management.*

The following four types of markets are important to the companies: consumer markets, business markets, global markets and government markets. The consumer market consists of household consumers while the business market consists of business organizations. *Global markets* refer to the markets outside a country. Government markets consist of government organizations buying goods and services for the public use. The market of non-profit organizations is another type of market which consists of non-profit NGOs serving the society.

Exchange

The central theme of marketing is exchange. An *exchange* occurs when one party obtains something from the other party by transferring something of value to the other. Thus, for an exchange to take place two parties are required. Each party has something valued by the other party. Both the parties have an understanding and willingness to sacrifice the products on hand for want of the products held by the others.

Customer Value

It is very difficult to conceptualize value from the point view of customers. The value of a product or service is reflected in the consumers' assessment of perceived tangible and intangible benefits against sacrifices. Customer-perceived value is the key concept of services marketing. Customer-value perception is influenced by internal factors, service processes and performances, service environment, situational factors and so on. Thus, a patient's value perception of a healthcare service depends on the patient's knowledge of the disease, their motivation level, the seriousness of the problem, the treatment process (right from reception to billing and payment), the care and concern of doctors and paramedical staff, the availability of support services such as medical shops, diagnostic services, canteen and drinking water, movement space and sitting arrangement, ventilation, hygiene, co-patients' and accompaniers' composition and behaviour, speed of delivery, price, and the assurances of the service unit. The available number of potential value generating sources may be many for a service provider. Many service providers identify a few sources and concentrate only on them. Service marketers should explore the possibilities of value generation to create value as desired by consumers. Continuous search for value-generating resources helps service companies find new ways of satisfying consumers and develop competitive advantage. The created value needs to be communicated to the target consumers effectively by the marketer to develop proper understanding and right kind of consumer expectations. The delivered value should match the communicated value. Value creation has to be a continuous process requiring investment

> *The central theme of marketing for an organization is to provide better value to customers than its competitors. To achieve the goal of marketing it is necessary to understand value perceptions of consumers and communicate and deliver effectively the value created by the company to them.*

in research and development, involvement of people, customer focus, development of core competencies, and establishment of collaborative networks that strengthen the value-generation tasks. Every company needs to identify the value chain[5] by identifying various facilitating and supporting processes required for the value delivery process.

Demand Management

The critical task of marketing managers is to find enough customers for the optimum utilization of capacity. Demand for a product exists only when three conditions are satisfied in the market—desire, ability and willingness of people to buy services. People should have the desire to use or consume products and services. This desire generates action tendencies in individuals towards satisfying the desire. When people do not have ability in terms of financial strength they fail to satisfy their desires. Therefore, they cannot buy the desired products or services. Thus, the desire must have the support of ability to generate demand for a service. Desire and ability are not enough for demand generation. People should be willing to spend on the product or service. Some people may not like to spend more despite having the desire and the ability to have the product or service due to several reasons. Thus, demand is generated only when these three conditions are positive in a market in relation to a product or service. In an open market, demand is not controllable. Marketers face different demand situations in different regions, in different segments, and in different periods. When the demand is less than the desired level, marketers should work out strategies to raise the demand to the optimum level. When the demand is more than the desired level, marketers should work on strategies to bring down the demand to the level of capacity, without any negative effects on the company in the long run. The company's efforts to bring down excess demand are termed as *demarketing*. (The demand management strategies for service companies are discussed in detail in Chapter 10.)

Consumers have gained power from the positive developments in the business environment in recent years. The more the consumer is empowered, the more the demand for quality services (see "Services Marketing Insight: The Powerful Consumer"). The patterns of demand for various services are influenced significantly due to the growing size of powerful consumers.

Segmentation, Targeting and Positioning

The era of market generalizations is gone. Specializations and super specializations are the order of the day. *Market segmentation* helps companies reach specific groups of customers with specialized offers. Market segmentation is nothing but dividing a market into segments, taking into consideration the homogeneity in satisfying a specific need or a set of needs. A company may choose to serve one segment, a group of segments or all segments with differentiated marketing offers. Market segmentation is widely used by service companies to reach markets effectively. The hospitality industry, for example,

2.1 Services Marketing Insight | **The Powerful Consumer**

The rapidly changing business environment has empowered consumers like never before. Many service markets have been transformed from being a sellers market to a buyers market. About two decades back, getting a telephone connection was akin to winning a lottery. Today, companies are knocking at the doors of prospective consumers. Instant connections, bundled with additional free gifts, backed by a service at the doorstep of the customer through mobile vans have become the order of the day. The entry of private players to the banking sector has brought about a similar paradigm shift in the banking industry. In the past banks commanded customers, today customers command banks. The state-owned transport companies learned the power of consumers the hard way. What factors have enabled such drastic changes in the producer–consumer relationship? The key inputs to consumer power are:

- ***Increased Purchasing Power*:** Consumer affluence is on the increase. The growing middle-income and rural-rich segments now demand services of their choice.
- ***Increased Choice*:** Intense market competition has created more choices for consumers. Companies are becoming highly innovative; consumers can now select the best among a wide variety of choices.
- ***Increased Information Input*:** Thanks to the digital revolution, consumers have an easy access to reliable information on all offerings. They follow opinions and feedback references through a variety of media.
- ***Increased Access*:** Markets have become increasingly accessible to consumers. Online marketing has erased geographical boundaries. The enhanced investments on infrastructure and logistics by various countries have reduced access costs to the consumer. Time costs, energy costs and transportation costs of consumers have reduced significantly with the development of the communication network, Internet facilities, and so on. Consumers today are willing to purchase quality services even from distant companies.
- ***Increased Empowerment*:** Consumers today are more empowered. They are able to take decisions on their own. The increased literacy rate, the mass communication revolution and so on have made consumers knowledgeable and able to make right purchasing decisions.

The powerful consumer is a check to service companies in planning and executing their marketing operations. Companies should be truthful to their consumers. A small deviation in this respect may lead to a major setback to the company.

may segment the market based on income, purpose of the visit, expected comforts and so on. Healthcare service companies may segment the market based on disease type, income of consumers, and so on. The segment chosen to serve is called the target market. *Target marketing* is a strategic decision that determines the market to be served and also the tactics to be used to reach the market. Thus, the target market for a premier hotel may be higher-income group tourist segment or business people segment or both. A healthcare institution may target patients with heart ailments. Once the target market is finalized, the marketer should find an appropriate market positioning strategy. *Positioning* is projecting the desired image of the product to consumers to help them identify the critical values of the marketing offer to perceive. The differentiated value of the service needs to be communicated to the consumer. (Positioning strategies are discussed in Chapter 12.) Thus, segmentation, targeting and positioning, popularly called STP, are critical to the strategic designs of marketing.

> *Companies may choose to serve the total market with an undifferentiated product or serve a part or more of the market with differentiated offers. When differentiation is the option, markets need to be segmented. The segment that a company selects to serve is called the **target market**. The differentiated offer should be positioned in the minds of consumers to create right perceptions of the marketing offer.*

Creating Value

The critical theme of marketing is value creation. Companies need to understand the value perceptions of consumers and create value offering. Marketing requires networking of various value-generating resources such as suppliers, employees and support services to develop a service package that offers better value to customers than competitors. Customer-perceived value is the basis for creating value packages. It is necessary to identify the factors influencing customer perceptions through marketing information system and research continually to work on generating value perceptions. Companies develop an organization mechanism to create value as per the needs and expectations of the target market.

> ***Value creation** is the critical task of marketing, which requires the knowledge of the factors influencing the customer-perceived quality relating to a product or service to develop a value offer to the customer better than competitors. Service companies need to develop a network of various value-generating resources and utilize them optimally.*

Communicating Value

The value created needs to be communicated effectively to the target audience. The communication campaign should inform consumers about the marketing offer; it should encourage them to develop expectations and to find areas to perceive value. Companies need to select and use the right communication channels to reach consumers effectively and to achieve set communication objectives. Integrated marketing communications helps companies communicate value effectively. This approach integrates the operations of different communication channels, both personal and non-personal, and helps in optimizing the results of the campaign by eliminating waste and variations. Each market segment requires a different communication channel mix. The requirements of B2B market and B2C market vary significantly. Service companies should be able to customize the communication campaign to the extent possible, considering the needs and expectations of the market segment.

> *Value created should be communicated effectively. Companies use the integrated marketing communications approach to plan and execute the communication campaign.*

Delivering Value

Delivering value is the ultimate marketing activity. The service delivery system should be developed to provide accessibility to customers and to offer quality services as per the basic specifications of the value created. Service companies generally prefer to have their own service outlets to deliver value to the customer. This measure provides absolute control over the operations and helps provide reliable, responsive and credible services to the customer. Companies also use private channels such as franchisees and agents/brokers as intermediaries to deliver value, if they find it appropriate under different conditions. It is a challenging task to maintain the quality standards of private channels. Customer-perceived quality is greatly influenced by interactive processes, employees' behaviour at the service outlet, the physical environment, systems and procedures and the composition of customer groups at the service delivery point. Value delivery, therefore, requires effective functional performance at service outlets.

> ***Value delivery*** *is an important process in services marketing. Service companies should provide accessibility, reliability and credibility in delivering value to consumers. The service delivery process is influenced by the physical environment, employees' behaviour, systems and processes, and so on.*

GOODS MARKETING VERSUS SERVICES MARKETING

The basic principles of marketing are common for both goods and services. However, due to the distinctive characteristics of services a differentiated marketing programme is essential for services to optimize the results. The key points of difference between goods and services marketing are:

1. Goods marketing is relatively easy as tangible goods stand as evidence to persuade customers. The intangibility of services makes services marketing rather difficult to handle. Creating tangible evidence in support of services is the critical challenge here.
2. In the case of goods, the consumer is involved only with the final product and the sales process. In contrast, the consumer is involved both with the production and sales of services. In fact, customer participation is critical to the perceived value and the utility of the service.
3. Consumers interact with only the marketing team when purchasing goods. Consumers who purchase services interact with many departments, not just the marketing team.
4. Internal marketing is not a prominent feature of goods marketing. Since consumers interact with only the marketing team, other employees of the organization play a supportive role. Internal marketing is prominently applied to services marketing as employees play a vital role in the entire process.
5. Standardization of services is not possible. Since the consumer is an equal contributor to the final service, each customer perceives and evaluates the utility of the service differently. On the other hand, precise standards can be formulated and communicated to customers in goods marketing.
6. In goods marketing, the marketing mix deals with the four Ps—product, price, place and promotion. These four parameters cannot be used to characterize services completely. Additional parameters including physical evidence, people and process need to be considered.
7. There are multiple channel options in goods marketing as compared to limited options in services marketing.
8. Problems in product quality can be identified before the product is sold to customers. Here, quality refers to the technical specifications and the features of the product. The quality of services, on the other hand, includes not only technical features but also the functional performance. Quality problems in services can be identified only in the presence of customers.

Table 2.1 highlights the points of distinction in an easy-to-remember manner.

Table 2.1 The Differences Between Goods and Services Marketing

Goods Marketing	Services Marketing
1. Tangible goods stand as an evidence to convince customers. The task of the marketer is relatively easy to persuade customers.	1. Intangibility of services creates evidence problems. Creating tangible evidences in support of services is the critical challenge.
2. Limited consumer connectivity. Consumers connect only with output and sale processes.	2. Greater consumer connectivity. Consumers connect with production as well as sale processes.
3. Only marketing department deals with consumers directly	3. Many departments of the organization deal with consumers directly in different processes.
4. Precise standards can be formulated and communicated to consumers.	4. Total standardization is not possible in services.
5. The marketing mix consists of four Ps—product, price, place and promotion.	5. Service characteristics demand the inclusion of a few more elements in the mix. The marketing mix of services consists of seven Ps—product, price, physical evidence, place promotion, people and process.
6. Multiple channel options.	6. Limited channel options.
7. Quality problems can be detected before goods are offered to customers.	7. Quality problems occur mostly in the presence of customers.
8. Quality primarily measured on the technical features of the product.	8. Quality primarily measured on the technical features as well as functional performance of the service.
9. Consumers can compare choices by examining them keeping side by side.	9. Services cannot be compared by experiencing simultaneously.
10. Employees of the organization (other than marketing) play an indirect and supportive role. Therefore, internal marketing is not prominently practised in goods marketing.	10. Employees (of all departments) play a vital role in services marketing. Internal marketing is, therefore, prominently applied to services marketing.

MARKETING PHILOSOPHIES

The marketing philosophy of a company guides its marketing activities. As shown in Fig. 2.1, there are five competing philosophies under which companies conduct their marketing activities:

1. The production concept
2. The product concept
3. The selling concept
4. The marketing concept
5. The holistic marketing concept

Each of these concepts is discussed in detail in the following sections.

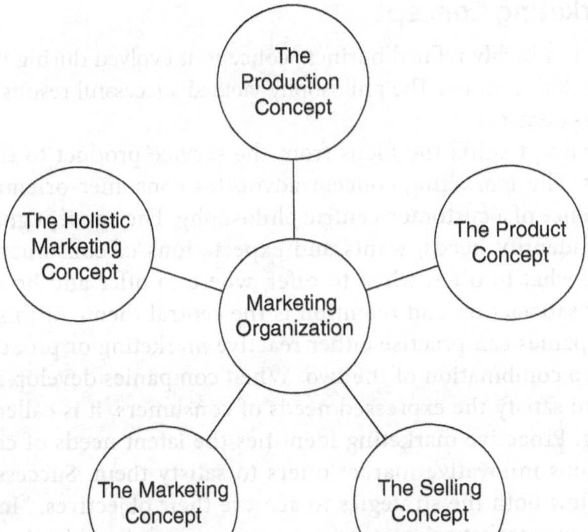

Fig. 2.1
Marketing philosophies

The Production Concept

The companies adopting the production philosophy believe that they can satisfy consumers by making services accessible to consumers at a low cost. The focus is on increasing productivity and reducing cost. Companies work on volume economies, supported by scientific methods applied to processes, to achieve desired results. This philosophy works when demand is more than capacity and when there are entry barriers. Services including electricity, transport, education and healthcare rely on this philosophy to achieve their business objectives in India.

The Product Concept

The companies following this philosophy offer a variety of innovative features in the belief that consumers favour quality. Thus, the focus of these companies is on improving product features continually to create additional product value. Companies such as beauty care, advertising, interior designing, fabric designing, and entertainment work with this philosophy to achieve their goals.

The Selling Concept

Some companies believe that consumers do not buy enough when they are not persuaded. Companies such as insurance, fitness and security systems, following this philosophy undertake aggressive sales campaigns to convince customers.

The Marketing Concept

Regarded as a highly refined business concept, it evolved during the second half of the 20th century. The philosophy yielded successful results in almost all business domains.

> *"The marketing concept recognizes the theme of customer orientation. It makes organizations believe that the beginning and end of marketing is the customer only. All the resources of the company should be directed towards customer satisfaction and retention."*

This concept shifts the focus from the service product to the service consumer. The marketing concept advocates consumer orientation and the pursuance of a customer-centric philosophy. The concept guides companies to identify needs, wants and expectations of consumers to conceptualize what to offer, when to offer, where to offer and how to offer. Customer satisfaction and retention is the central theme of this philosophy. Companies can practise either reactive marketing or proactive marketing, or a combination of the two. When companies develop a marketing offer to satisfy the expressed needs of consumers, it is called reactive marketing. Proactive marketing identifies the latent needs of consumers and develops innovative market offers to satisfy them. Successful companies follow both the strategies to achieve their objectives. "In order to achieve a true market orientation, a company needs to make the customer the epicenter of its business perspective. At the same time, those within the organization must also become involved, and become supportive, with these marketing efforts."[6]

For example, NIIT, the leading IT education and training service company has adopted the marketing concept successfully. The marketing-oriented

NIIT

NIIT, established in 1981, adopted the marketing concept successfully by creating a niche in the education and training services for information and communication technology and promoted it as the most powerful business domain. Driven by its vision of developing global talent, the company is building a pool of employable, industry-ready professionals globally.

NIIT identified and defined the needs and expectations of the target market and developed a variety of programmes for the specific target groups. NIIT's programmes touch 5 million learners every year. NIIT's expertise in learning content development, training delivery and education process management has made the company the most preferred training partner, worldwide. Research-based innovation has enabled the company to develop programmes and curricula that use cutting-edge instructional design methodologies and training delivery. These initiatives indicate the company's core competencies in creation and delivery of market-oriented services.

The company is also leveraging the high-quality infrastructure, technology tools and faculty of the best universities in the world. The networking with world-class companies facilitates an unmatched delivery and unique educational experience that meets the existing needs and prepares for the future. NIIT could capitalize the early entrant advantage through its successful marketing programmes. The competition from conventional academic institutions and many private companies failed to affect the company's prospects. NIIT focussed on the market needs and responded very effectively by creating new programmes and modifying the programmes offered. The market expansion with franchisee networking and alliances with competent partners led the company towards the accomplishment of its marketing objectives.

approach adopted by the company supported its growth and development over the years.

> *Reactive marketing* is to respond to the identified needs and wants of consumers in the form of a marketing offer that satisfies them. Proactive marketing is to innovate new marketing offers to cater to the new needs of consumers. Consumers are influenced to recognize the new needs that benefit them more.

The Holistic Marketing Concept

The rapidly changing business scenario has increasingly forced companies to adopt an integrated, unified approach that goes beyond traditional applications of the marketing concept. P. Kotler aptly termed this approach as *holistic marketing*. According to him: "The holistic marketing concept is based on the development, design and implementation of marketing programmes, processes and activities that recognizes their breadth and interdependencies. Holistic marketing recognises that 'everything matters' with marketing."[7] Holistic marketing comprises four components—integrated marketing, relationship marketing, internal marketing and socially responsible marketing (see Fig. 2.2). The focus and scope of each of these components are examined in the following sections.

Integrated Marketing

It refers to the integration of marketing programmes, designed to provide value to consumers. Service companies develop a marketing mix consisting of seven Ps: product, price, place, promotion, physical evidence, people and process (see Chapter 7). The quality of the service offer depends on how effectively these elements of the marketing mix are designed, integrated and executed. "A market-driven strategy needs a company to understand its market truly and the customers that comprise this market. This effort allows for a more effective integration of all activities that may impact customer value, which in turn affects both return-on-investment and profitability."[8]

Relationship Marketing

Marketers have realized the limitations in transactional marketing and found a remedy in relationship marketing as it lays a strong foundation for the future. Establishing linkages with other firms has become one of the biggest emerging

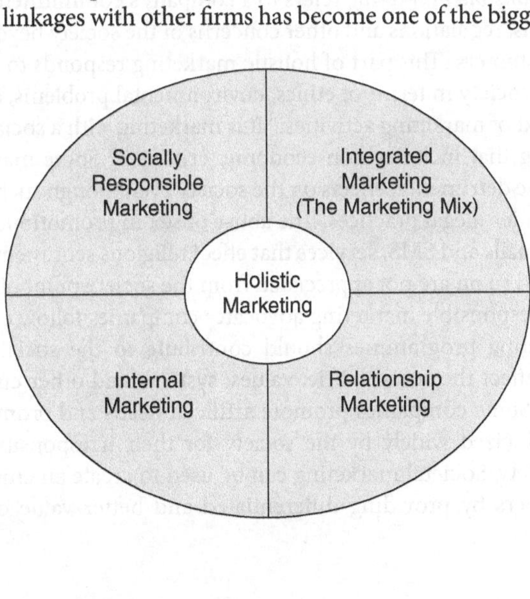

Fig. 2.2
Holistic marketing

> *Relationships with various parties connected to the business are considered vital to the long-term success of the company. Relationship marketing aims at building, maintaining and enhancing relationships with individuals, groups and organizations and sharing value with them.*

challenges. It is necessary to interact with other companies including associates, partners, buyers and sellers to provide beneficial outcomes to each other and customers.[9] Relationship marketing embraces the human approach to develop bonds with varied parties connected to the company and those who are capable of adding value at different levels. Companies need the support of internal departments, suppliers, financial institutions, regulatory bodies, intermediaries, support services and, most importantly, customers. This focus on relationship not only requires building relationships but also needs maintenance and enhancement of relationships. Companies derive many values from relationships and can be successful in relationship marketing only when they are prepared to share the value with customers. Relationships must be a win-win proposition and companies should evolve the formula of sharing benefits with parties connected to the business. A well-managed customer relationship programme generates life-time customer value to the company.

Internal Marketing

Treating employees as internal customers is the central theme of internal marketing. Employee satisfaction is considered the foundation for achieving satisfaction of final customers. *Internal marketing* focuses on building skilled, motivated and service-oriented workforce and assumes vital significance in high customer contact businesses. Companies need to study the needs, wants and expectations of internal customers and devise right programmes to satisfy them. Internal customers expect better value compared to the competitive value offerings from the employer. It is necessary, therefore, to conduct employee satisfaction surveys periodically to identify internal problems and to initiate measures for rectification. Satisfied employees become the core competency of the organization.

> ***Societal marketing** directs companies to focus on social well being along with satisfying the target consumers. It promotes the organizational commitment towards ethics, values, consumerism and social responsibilities of the business.*

Socially Responsible Marketing

Socially responsible marketing refers to a company's commitment towards the values, norms, regulations and other concerns of the society beyond the target group of customers. This part of holistic marketing responds to broader concerns of the society in terms of ethics, environmental problems, and legal and social context of marketing activities. "It is marketing with a social dimension, or marketing that includes non-economic criteria."[10] Some marketing practices will have detrimental effects on the society even though such practices do not come under illegal practices. The abuse of sex in promotional campaigns, unwanted emails and SMS, services that effect religious sentiments and trigger emotions and so on are not appreciated from the society point of view.

Socially responsible marketing advocates companies follow ethics in business. Marketing programmes should contribute to the social good. They should not affect the social fabric, values, systems and other cultural beliefs and norms. Some companies promote artificial needs and promise miracles. They are criticized widely by the society for their irresponsible behaviour towards society. Societal marketing can be used to create an emotional bond with customers by providing differentiated and better value consistently.[11]

Societal marketing programme basically consists of three major components: symbolism, management, and employees' behaviour and communication.[12] Symbolism refers to the visual identity given to the marketing offer often using tangibles. The behaviour of management and employees refer to service offerings, service quality, service inclination and empathetic interactive behaviour. Communications refer to all forms of communication media used to reach the target audience including word-of-mouth communication.

The application of holistic marketing can be found in the functioning of DTDC Courier & Cargo Ltd. All the components of the holistic marketing are part of the company's marketing strategy.

> ***Holistic marketing*** *is the combination of integrated marketing, relationship marketing, internal marketing and socially responsible marketing and covers every aspect of business. Therefore, holistic marketing becomes a business philosophy rather than a marketing philosophy.*

MARKETING CHALLENGES

Marketers today face far more serious challenges than their counterparts of yesteryears. The challenges basically are from three important areas—customers, business trends and technology.

Customers

Customers are empowered today due to the revolution in information and technology. The digital revolution has provided information access to consumers and empowered them to take qualitative purchase decisions. Customers became knowledgeable, information seekers and rational in many purchase decisions. They are demanding customized offerings and exhibiting their interests to interact with the company and participate in the design of

DTDC

DTDC Courier & Cargo Ltd. has become the nation's largest domestic delivery network by focusing on the four components of holistic marketing. The company offers a wide range of services—from domestic express, domestic air cargo and domestic ground express to international air express to international economy express. It created service accessibility through a network of 4,000 franchised outlets supported by 176 company offices located in various parts of the country. The IT infrastructure enabled the company to deliver 10.5 million parcels per month to customers across the world. DTDC Shopping Net provides additional value to customers. Their "Right-First-Time" approach intends to prevent service failures in every area of business. Customer value addition is DTDC's core solution.

DTDC's 13,000 employees deliver 10 million consignments every month. Internal marketing ensures employee commitment to use it as the key strength of the company. One of the company's key objectives is to encourage employees to adopt new technologies, processes and systems for improved, reliable and speedy services.

Relationships with customers, partners and franchisees are the strength of the company. Besides international associates and franchisees, the company is associated with Reliance ADAG Group for the IT support. DTDC is also a socially committed organization. The company regularly participates and conducts activities such as organize blood donation camps and encourage skills of under-privileged and visually impaired children. It contributes towards development of sports, protection of environment by minimizing pollution and reducing national wastage.

products and services. They are fairly in a good position to assess value and compare values of competing offers. Marketers should learn changes in consumers and accordingly modify their orientation towards consumers. Many companies are using technology to establish person-to-person interactions with consumers. Successful companies make use of the positive developments in consumers to better their marketing performances. In other words, they have realized consumers to be the core competency of the organization. They do not leave any opportunity to interact with customers to gain the advantage of creativity, feedback and relationships.

Business Trends

Business is undergoing tremendous changes worldwide. *Globalization* is one trend that has made many companies reorient themselves to reach the markets available in other countries and also prepare to face competition from multinational giants. The advancements in support services such as transportation and communication have facilitated many companies to reach easily the markets outside the country.

The emergence of the World Trade Organization (WTO) has been wiping out business boundaries in a phased manner with a vision of making the world a business village. The demands of today's market place transcend localization of global knowledge and skills. Many of today's global customers demand consistent products and services on a worldwide basis.[13]

Deregulation of business is another trend that has affected the business. Many countries have deregulated industries to promote competition. Services such as airlines, insurance, and telecom, which are deregulated in India, have brought a visible change in the business system in a very short period of time. *Privatization* is another trend that has an impact on the business. Private ownership and management of the erstwhile public sector monopoly businesses in India has impacted the business environment significantly. The growth of organized retailing in India and in many developing countries during the last decade has influenced the business significantly. Mergers and acquisitions in various business domains and, more particularly, the industry convergence to explore new opportunities by leveraging the competencies of two or more different industries, have been building a new order of business. The changes in the system are vibrant. Therefore, one has to learn to adapt one's business to these fast-emerging changes to achieve success.

> *"Companies face many marketing challenges due to the fast-changing business environment. Today consumers are more empowered and demanding quality performance. The economic and business policy changes by governments and ever-changing technologies create new challenges to companies."*

Technology

The digital revolution and rapidly changing technologies have led to many changes in the business. Most businesses are now technology driven. The pace of change in technology is unimaginable; it has resulted in shorter product life and increased the risk of failures. Disintermediation is one change that could be made possibly due to technology. The online dotcom companies have come up in a big way to create a new business order that provides customer convenience at very low cost. "High-tech markets are characterized by a continuous shortening of product and market cycles. On the other hand, ever-increasing technological uncertainty and the importance of systems technology (office data bank, communication networks and interface-related technology, etc.) breaks down the product development cycles associated with traditional technology."[14] Technological innovations create many new opportunities. Companies need to orient themselves to adapt to changing technologies quickly to exploit business opportunities. (See "Services Marketing Insight: Database Marketing".)

MARKETING PLANNING

The management process of marketing basically consists of planning a marketing programme, implementing and evaluating the programme to find out its performance level. *Marketing planning* has been defined as all rational, incremental and intuitive processes that guide a firm's marketing to its future.[15] Planning includes goal setting and developing strategies to achieve goals. "As market opportunities change, firms will need to adapt their plans in order to pursue these developing opportunities. Adaptation is achieved through the process of flexibility in marketing planning, decision making, which is the extent to which managers are willing to explore alternative and new decision-making options, with respect to objectives, strategies, tactics, implementation and control."[16] To achieve flexibility in marketing planning, six key management processes are proposed: proactive management, competitive aggression, innovative management, organizational learning, market orientation and deploying slack resources.[17]

Implementation refers to the design of marketing operations to carry out the strategy. *Performance evaluation* is to compare the set targets with the actual performance. Companies aspiring to meet the challenges of today's rapidly changing markets and increasing global competition require management decisions to be based on well-conceived strategies. Clearly defined strategies and plans are vital if the firm has to achieve its objectives while optimizing the use of its limited resources.[18] As market opportunities change, firms will need to adapt their plans in order to pursue these developing opportunities. The following are the steps followed in the strategic marketing planning process.[19]

> *"Marketing activities need to be planned, executed and controlled effectively. **Marketing planning** is the critical stage in marketing management. It involves setting objectives based on situation analysis, selection of the target market and developing a marketing mix suitable to satisfy the target market."*

1. *Situation Analysis:* It involves reviewing the existing marketing programme, the external environmental forces, the internal environment, analysing the competition, company resources and competencies and the current strategy of the company. The situation analysis provides a right understanding on where the company stands in the setting of the business environment.

2.2 Services Marketing Insight | **Database Marketing**

Marketing management has become information intensive in the highly networked environment. Data-related marketing techniques are gaining unprecedented popularity. The digital revolution has transformed the process of collecting, storing, accessing and sharing information for managerial decision making.

What Is Database Marketing?

Database marketing refers to the use of information and communication technology to collect, classify, store, access and share marketing information for providing information support at the right time and in the right form to marketing managers. The rise of database technologies and electronically mediated communications has led to the emergence of new forms of marketing power.

Common Perceptions

The opinion of marketing experts on the potential ability of database technologies to change the course of marketing is divided.

- One group believes that the new medium revolutionizes marketing by rendering Kotler's conception of marketing mix obsolete. It is capable of creating new wealth for companies and generating processes that delight customers.
- Another group does not believe that these new technologies will change the time-honoured marketing rules. However, they agree that there will be increased use of computer networks and database technologies in marketing exchanges.
- The third group is sceptical of the impact of these technologies on marketing. This group is concerned over the threatening effects of new information technologies on the consumer privacy and corporate domination.

Advantages

Digitalization involves transformation of physical matter into electronically generated bits and bytes. The consumer who visits the service outlet becomes a set of data points. In other words, the customer becomes a digital representation of their movements and behaviour. The digital matter can be stored and transferred. It becomes free flowing and free floating in technical and symbolic terms. Through digitization, companies can have a vast network of consumer and product databases. Marketers are analysing consumer behaviour in detail with the support of this digitized database. The store of massive database can be accessed and analysed with the lightening speed. Software packages are capable of producing a digital facsimile of the real-time consumer. The digital database provides customer's identity to the marketer. Thus, database marketing helps in understanding consumer behaviour and strengthen customer relationship management initiatives.

Source: *Detlev Zwick and Nikhilesh Dholakia, "Whose Identity is it Any Way? Consumer Representation in the Age of Database Marketing,"* Journal of Macro Marketing, *24, no. 1 (June 2004): 31–43.*

2. *Setting Marketing Objectives:* Based on the situation analysis, companies set realistic and measurable objectives. Marketing objectives should fit in the broader perspective of company's overall business strategy.
3. *Selecting the Target Markets:* The company identifies target markets to serve and estimate the market demand.
4. *Developing the Marketing Mix:* The elements of the marketing mix are aligned appropriately to maximize the value to the customers.

5. *Preparing the Annual Marketing Planning:* The annual marketing plan serves as a guide to a business unit to carry out marketing activities. The plan clearly states what and how is to be achieved.

MARKETING TASKS

Marketing organizations need to carry out a variety of tasks as per the demands of the situation. These organizations deal with mostly uncontrollable elements such as consumers and other micro-environmental forces to execute their operations. Therefore, tasks vary with time, segment, product and region. However, the following 12 tasks are commonly considered to be the vital tasks of marketing:

1. Identifying business opportunities
2. Developing strategies and plans
3. Identifying right markets to serve
4. Creating value
5. Communicating value
6. Delivering value
7. Building customer relations
8. Developing value networks
9. Building brand equity
10. Promoting long-term growth
11. Exploiting technology for building competencies
12. Promoting social interests

All these tasks are parts of holistic marketing. It is critical to manage these marketing tasks effectively to achieve organizational objectives. Only an efficiently designed organizational mechanism can handle these tasks effectively.

SUMMARY

- Marketing has evolved over the years as a critical function of business organizations.
- The basic focus of marketing is to create, communicate and deliver value to customers.
- Marketing is both a science and an art. It is a combination of formulations and creativity.
- Marketing can be understood from the management and social perspectives. The management perspective describes the companies' response to the needs of consumers. The societal perspective describes the process of exchange between individuals or groups with companies and the utilities generated by the processes of marketing to the society at large.
- In a society, goods, services, persons, places, events, ideas, experiences, properties, organizations and information are marketed.
- The understanding of the needs, wants and expectations of consumers is critical to marketers.
- Exchange is at the heart of marketing.
- Customer value analysis and demand management are important concepts of marketing.

- Market segmentation, targeting and positioning are critical to the strategic designs of marketing.
- Business concerns adopt a marketing philosophy oriented towards achieving business goals.
- The production concept, product concept, selling concept, marketing concept and holistic marketing concept are the five different philosophies of marketing.
- Holistic marketing is comprehensive and covers every aspect of marketing. It involves integrated marketing, relationship marketing, internal marketing and socially responsible marketing.
- Marketing is a dynamic field and challenges are an integral part of it.
- The changes in consumer behaviour, business trends and technology are the critical challenges to marketers.
- Marketing management involves the planning, execution and control of various marketing operations.

KEY TERMS

Customer value *25*	Proactive marketing *33*	Societal marketing *34*
Holistic marketing *33*	Relationship marketing *33*	Situation analysis *38*
Needs, wants and expectations *24*	Reactive marketing *33*	Target marketing *27*
Positioning *27*		

BRIEF QUESTIONS

1. Define marketing from the point of view of management and society.
2. What is integrated marketing?
3. What are the social issues in marketing?
4. What are marketing tasks?
5. Differentiate between needs, wants and expectations.

ESSAY QUESTIONS

1. Explain the importance of marketing in the changing business scenario.
2. What are the core concepts of marketing? How are they influence the marketing management programme?
3. What are the various marketing philosophies that a company can adopt?
4. Explain holistic marketing.
5. What are the marketing challenges faced by marketers?
6. Explain the marketing planning process.

ASSIGNMENTS

1. Select two branches of life insurance companies in your locality—one from the public sector and another from the private sector. Interact with the branch managers and other employees of both the companies to find:
   (a) The marketing tasks and their approaches towards the performance of the tasks.
   (b) The marketing planning process.
2. Cellular services in India have successfully reached the common man. People from the lower-income group also are utilizing these services liberally. Interview selected users of these services from lower- and middle-income groups to find out:
   (a) Their value perceptions of the service.
   (b) The marketing strategies that influenced them the most.

REFERENCES

1 American Marketing Association, 2004.

2 Philip Kotler et al., *Marketing Management: Defining Marketing for the 21st Century.* (Singapore: Pearson Prentice Hall, 2007), p. 6.

3 Ibid.

4 William J. Stanton and Charles Futrell, *Fundamentals of Marketing.* (New York: McGraw Hill International Edn., 1989), p. 8.

5 Michael E. Porter, *Competitive Advantage: Creating and Sustaining Superior Performance.* (New York: Free Press, 1985).
6 Richard C. Leventhal, "The Importance of Marketing," *Journal of Consumer Marketing,* 21, no. 6 (2005): 3–4.
7 Philip Kotler et al., *Marketing Management: Defining Marketing for the 21st Century.* (Singapore: Pearson Prentice Hall, 2007), p. 17.
8 Richard C. Leventhal, "The Importance of Marketing," *Journal of Consumer Marketing,* 21, no. 6 (2005): 3–4.
9 Dennis A. Pitta, Frank F. Franzak and Michael W. Little, "Maintaining Positive Returns in the Value and Supply Chain: Applying Tomorrow's Marketing Skills," *Journal of Consumer Marketing,* 21, no. 7 (2004): 510–519.
10 J. Handerman and S. Arnold, "The Role of Marketing Actions with a Social Dimension: Appeals to the Institutional Environment," *Journal of Marketing,* 63 (July, 1999): 33–48.
11 H. Meyer, "When the Cause is Just," *Journal of Business Strategy,* 20 (1999): 27–31.
12 C. B. M. Van Riel and J. M. T. Balmer, "Corporate Identity: The Concept, Its Measurement and Management," *European Journal of Marketing,* 31, no. 5 (1997): 341.
13 Andrew Inkpen and Kannan Ramaswamy, "End of the Multinational: Emerging Markets Redraw the Picture," *Journal of Business Strategy,* 28, no. 5 (2007): 4–12.
14 Martin Benkenstein and Brian Bloch, "Strategic Management in High-tech Industries," *Marketing Intelligence & Planning,* 12, no. 1 (1994): 15–21.
15 J. Saunders, J. Saker and G. Smith, "Afterword: An Agenda for Research into Strategic Marketing Planning", *Journal of Marketing Management,* 12, no. 1–3 (1996): 215–30.
16 Gordon Greenley, Graham Hooley and John Saunders, "Management Processes in Marketing Planning," *European Journal of Marketing,* 38, no. 8 (2004): 933.
17 Ibid, p. 934.
18 Steven Ward and Aleksandra Lewandowska, "Is the Marketing Concept Always Necessary?," *European Journal of Marketing,* 42, no. 1/2 (2008): 222–223.
19 William J. Stanton and Charles Futrell, *Fundamentals of Marketing,* (New York: McGraw Hill International Edn., 1989), p. 53, 57.

The Marketing Environment

3

LEARNING OBJECTIVES

After studying this chapter, you will be able to:

- Understand the influence of the marketing environment on business
- Describe micro-environmental forces
- Describe macro-environmental forces

The retail boom began in India in the early years of the 21st century. Many established companies in other businesses and new companies entered the business in a big way. Organized retailing, which was limited to only a few cities in India, spread to almost all cities. Attracted by the business opportunity, Chandan Enterprises Ltd, a goods transport services company, decided to venture into retailing. The plan was to construct four malls in metros initially and then spread the network to all cities over a period of 10 years. The company had worked out the investment and required resources and identified financiers. Since the company was in the transport business, the management thought that it could leverage its competencies in transport for the retailing business.

The company constituted a panel of experts to conduct environmental analysis and suggest strategic measures. The committee analysed both micro- and macro-environmental forces and submitted its report to the management. The report highlighted the following issues:

- Competition with existing retail companies would be intense.
- Efficient supply chain management would be critical.
- Customer markets were well informed and clear in their expectations.
- Economic conditions were likely to affect the business in future.
- Policy changes by the government were likely to impact the business.
- Though core cultural values of consumers were intact, some changes in the culture might affect the business.
- Grocery retailing had more opportunities than other formats.

The management of the company scrutinized the report in detail and decided to focus mainly on grocery items and to offer general items as support products. The company, however, looked for some more information on the forces affecting the business so that it could improve its marketing strategy.

Questions:

1. Do you think the issues highlighted by the expert committee are relevant? Why?
2. What is the information needed on the marketing environment for this business?
3. What mechanism do you suggest to monitor the marketing environment?
4. Is it the right decision to focus on grocery retailing based on the report?

INTRODUCTION

Business organizations operate in a social system to provide value to target groups in the society. They take resources from the society and create a new form that is beneficial to customers. Society–business interaction is natural and inseparable. It is obvious that the changes in the environment of the business affect the business either positively or negatively. While some changes create opportunities, others pose threats. Companies should learn to identify and exploit opportunities, defend themselves against threats. They require an organizational mechanism to monitor trends in the business environment and feed the management with relevant information to enable it to take the right decisions at the right time.

The 21st century began on an optimistic note. The growing economies, revolution in digital technologies, emergence of knowledge societies, global accessibility, scientific innovations to optimize resource utility, greater understanding among many countries on trade regulations and procedures and so on opened up many business opportunities. Companies got access to global technologies and resources. Consumers, on the other hand, also got access to the best available goods and services in the world. Companies are now competing to come up to global standards even if they operate in local markets. To accomplish this and develop competitive advantages, companies need to understand the wide disparities in environmental forces across the globe.

The economic meltdown, which began in the United States in 2008, affected many economies of the world. Top-rated business companies went through a turbulent phase because of the changing business environment. Some companies could defend themselves successfully, while many more failed to protect themselves. Yet, some innovative companies could find business opportunities even during this turbulence in the marketing environment. Therefore, it is necessary to know what is happening to develop the ability to predict future trends in environmental forces.

It is necessary at this point to clarify as to what really constitutes the marketing environment of a company. According to P. Kotler and G. Armstrong,[1] a company's marketing environment consists of the actors and forces outside marketing that affect marketing managements' ability to develop and maintain successful relationships with its target customers. The marketing environment is the combination of several forces influencing the company's business prospects directly or indirectly, closely or distantly, strongly or weakly, or positively or negatively. It can be categorized into two parts: the micro-environment and the macro-environment. The micro-environment consists of forces that are close to the company that can directly or indirectly affect the company's ability to serve customers. The micro-environment of a company includes other divisions of the company—suppliers, intermediaries, markets, competitors and other publics. The macro-environment consists of forces that affect the company prospects directly or indirectly.

> *"The marketing environment consists of actors and forces outside the marketing organization which influence the functioning of the organization directly or indirectly. Service companies need to learn the changes and develop mechanisms to respond effectively to the changes in the marketing environment."*

They include demographic, economic, natural, technological, political, legal, social and cultural forces.

One of the major changes in the Indian marketing environment in recent years is the retail revolution. The growth of organized retailing in India influenced consumer behaviour and lifestyles significantly, and expanded business opportunities for many manufacturing and service companies. The emerging growth perspectives of this sector are discussed in "Services Marketing Insight: Organized Retailing: The New Growth Frontier".

THE MICRO-ENVIRONMENT

Companies need to monitor micro-environmental forces continuously as their impact on the company's ability is direct and rapid. Figure 3.1 presents the micro-environmental forces that are capable of influencing a company.

3.1 Services Marketing Insight — Organized Retailing: The New Growth Frontier

The beginning of the 21st century was marked by the retail revolution in India. India has the highest retail density in the world. There are about 15 million retailers in the country; most of them are the owners of mom-and-pop stores. Organized retailing is now set to change the retail business environment. Indian consumers are evolving rapidly and accepting the modern retail formats.

Organized retailing in India is highly underdeveloped as compared to the emerging markets in Asia and other developed countries. The share of organized retailing in India is only 4.6 per cent, as compared to 85 per cent in the United States and 17 per cent in China. It indicates the potential for growth of this sector in India. In India, organized retailing has been growing at over 35 per cent per annum since 2004. It focused primarily on the 300-million urban middle class and another 200-million rural rich. Large corporate groups such as ITC, Reliance, Tata, Raheja, Jubilient and the Future Group infused staggering amounts of capital into the organized retail sector. Industry studies indicate that there will be 1200 hyper markets and 3000 super markets in India by 2011.

The TATA Strategic Management Group projects that the overall retail market will grow at 5.5 per cent compound annual growth rate (CAGR) to touch INR 16,770 billion by 2015. The total retail value was INR 12,000 billion in 2006 and the organized retail was expected to grow much faster at a CAGR of 21.8 per cent. Thus, the total value of organized retailing was expected to grow from INR 280 billion in 2004 to INR 2464.31 billion in 2015. The Foreign Direct Investment (FDI) was not allowed in multi-brand retailing. However, 100 per cent equity was allowed for cash-and-carry wholesale trading but there was no dividing line between this activity and retail trading. Inroads into the activity in the domestic economy were also made by foreign enterprises through franchising. Later the government moved to introduce FDI in multi-brand speciality forms like consumer electronics, sports goods, building and construction equipment and stationary. This move attracted more capital investment into the sector and greater choices to consumers.

Source: India Retail Report 2007, Tata Strategic Management Group Report, available at *www.tata.com.*

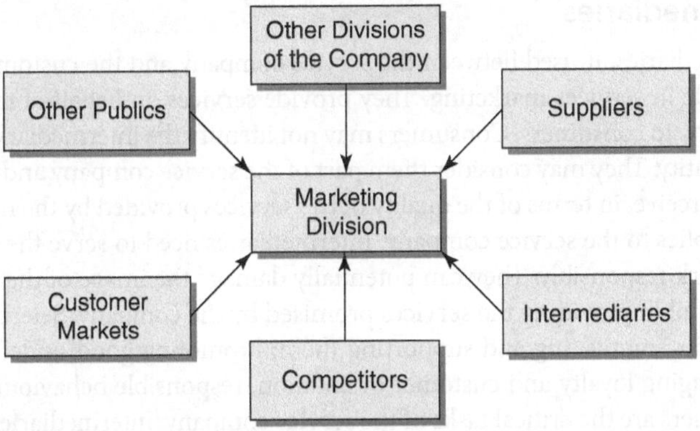

Fig. 3.1 Micro-environmental forces

Other Divisions of the Company

The marketing division of an organization cannot formulate its plans in isolation. It needs to work with the other departments to achieve the common goal, i.e., company objectives. The marketing division works with finance, human resources, research and development, purchases, accounting and top management to develop and execute its plans and programmes. Requisite and timely support from the other departments of the company is a critical factor in the success of the marketing team. For example, the plans of the marketing division to open new service outlets in some strategic locations need the support of finance, human resources, research and development and, of course, the top management. The role of these divisions is pivotal in executing such plans. An obligatory performance of these divisions based on rules and regulations may not adequately support the marketing division. Motivated and involved support is expected from other divisions of the company. The marketing department should build relationships based on mutual understanding and trust with the other departments of the company to achieve its objectives.

> *The influence of micro-environmental forces on business is more direct and rapid than macro-environmental forces. The micro-environment consists of other departments within the company—suppliers, intermediaries, competitors, markets and other publics. Service companies should build, maintain and enhance relationships with individuals, groups or organizations that are part of the micro-environment.*

Suppliers

Suppliers form an important link in providing quality services to customers. Suppliers are firms and individuals that provide the resources needed by the company to produce its goods and services. In addition to resources, they also provide support services to the organization. Trends and developments affecting suppliers can, in turn, seriously affect a company's marketing plan.[2] The service quality of the company is largely influenced by the quality of resources and support services provided by its suppliers. Thus, the quality of services of a beauty shop depends on the quality of creams, lotions, powders and the tools and instruments used. The beauty shop depends on suppliers for all these resources. Similarly, the maintenance of air conditioners, the power supply, the sanitary services and so on from suppliers also influence the final service quality. Service companies need to have good relations with suppliers to prevent any disruptions in the supply of products and services and to improve the quality of supplies and services.

Intermediaries

Intermediaries, if used between the service company and the customer, play a vital role in services marketing. They provide services on behalf of the service company to consumers. Consumers may not identify the intermediary as a separate entity. They may consider them part of the service company and whatever they perceive, in terms of the quality of the services provided by the intermediary, applies to the service company. Intermediaries need to serve the company and work responsibly. They can potentially damage the image of the company if they fail in providing the services promised by the company. Selecting intermediaries; motivating and supporting them; promoting good understanding, encouraging loyalty and customer orientation, responsible behaviour towards consumers are the critical tasks of the service company. Intermediaries can add value to the company if the relationship is managed effectively.

Competitors

In their attempts to reach out to customers, service companies face competition on many fronts—competitors encourage switchovers, try to influence and entice customers and so on. The *competitive environment* affects the number and types of competitors the marketing manager must face. It also affects the behaviour of these competitors. Although marketing managers usually can't control these factors, they can choose strategies that avoid head-on competition. And where competition is inevitable, they can plan for it.[3]

Service companies should recognize competitors and understand their strengths and weaknesses. Based on this understanding, service companies should draw up an appropriate strategy to either attack their competitors or defend their market share. Companies are becoming increasingly aware that competition is a reality that has to be dealt with continuously. Companies now understand that consumers prefer those service providers who provide better value than competitors. Competitors' strategies should be monitored, and counter-strategies should be deployed to protect the interests of the company in the market.

Customer Markets

Service companies may serve the needs of individual customers, industrial markets, government markets or international markets. The needs, choices, preferences of these markets change frequently, which impact the business prospects of the company. Companies capable of adapting to these changes quicker than others stand to benefit from the change. It is necessary to study the composition of each market, the potential changes in needs and preferences, the emerging opportunities and threats, and to develop strategies to face them effectively.

Other Publics

Service companies should also recognize the public who take interest in it as part of their business or activity. Publics such as financial institutions,

AIR

All India Radio (AIR) is a national broadcasting service, planned, developed and operated by Prasar Bharati (Broadcasting Corporation of India). AIR began as a government organization to inform, educate and entertain the masses. Before independence, the network was limited to six stations covering 2.5 per cent of the area and 11 per cent of the population. After independence, the organization grew and established a network of 232 broadcasting centres, with 149 medium-frequency, 54 high-frequency and 171 FM stations. The coverage was 91.79 per cent of the area serving 99.14 per cent of the people in the country.

Though marketing was not a problem till the entry of the television, Radio Ceylon did pose a serious threat to AIR in the 1950s. It was then that the *Vividh Bharti* service was introduced which made AIR a household name. Following the introduction of television, AIR focused on rural India. However, the growth of new private channels in the early 2000s adversely affected the growth of AIR. Though the market for sound broadcasting was being revived in the urban areas by the private players, AIR did not benefit from it. The private FM radio channels had correctly identified the changes in consumer expectations—something that AIR had failed to do thus far. In a somewhat delayed response to competition, AIR launched two FM channels.

Till date, though not an established player in the urban market, AIR continues to be the market leader with its huge network within and outside India. This public sector organization is required to balance social responsibilities and commercial objectives, unlike private players. Yet, market orientation is a much-needed focus for AIR to serve people better than competitors.

media, government, citizen action groups and social organizations often impact a business. Financial institutions lend the required financial support to the company. Since their finance is in the company, they try to watch the company progress and interfere in the company affairs when the situation warrants it. The media plays a critical role in shaping public opinion either in favour of or against the company by communicating interpreted facts to people. The government can influence any business or company at any point of time, if the situation demands. Citizen action groups including consumer associations and environment groups act as watchdogs to bring any misconduct of the company towards the society to light and to agitate for social justice. Social organizations are opinion leaders and are capable of influencing the business prospects of a company. Service companies need to develop positive relationships with all these publics. Many companies have established public relations departments to manage their relationships with all these groups.

THE MACRO-ENVIRONMENT

The macro-environment of a service company comprises those forces that impact the business in the form of opportunities and threats. The changes in the macro-environment should be monitored carefully. It requires marketing intelligence and information inflows to the company and a skilled team to analyse and interpret changes, taking into consideration the core competencies and weaknesses of the company. Six macro-environmental forces are identified and presented in Fig. 3.2. These include:

1. The demographic environment
2. The economic environment
3. The natural environment
4. The technological environment
5. The political and legal environment
6. The social and cultural environment

We now examine and analyse each of these environmental forces to understand the impact they might have on the marketing of services.

The Demographic Environment

The term *demographic environment* refers to the composition of society in terms of population size, density, location, age, sex, occupation and so on. Demographic characteristics and corresponding changes impact the service business significantly. Therefore, service marketers are interested in the demographic factors of the market. India ranks second in terms of population in the world, next only to China. As per the 2001 census, the population of India stands at 1,027 million.[4] The size of the population, the economic growth rate and the prospects of the country with its natural

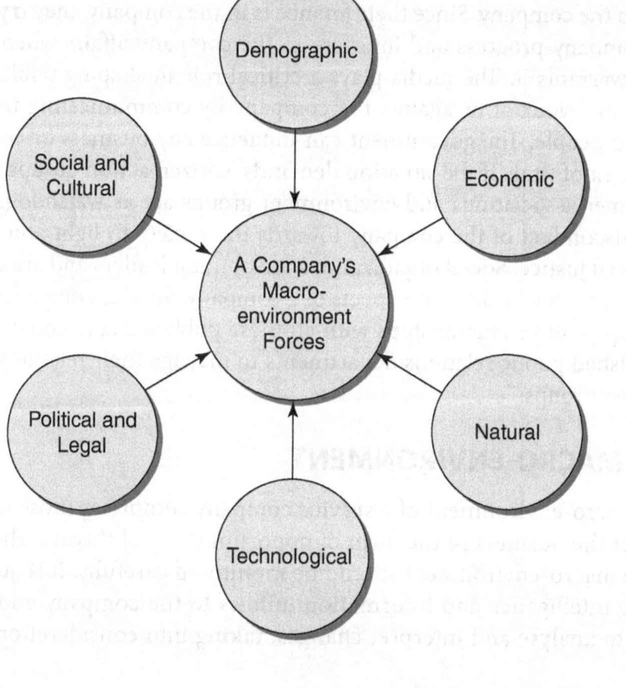

Fig. 3.2
Macro-environmental forces

resources and human resources transformed the country into a destiny for many multinational companies to market their products and services. The Indian consumer is amongst the youngest in the world as compared to the ageing population of the United States, China, Japan, the United Kingdom and so on. Over 65 per cent of the population is below 35 years old; 54 per cent of the population is below 25 years of age. In contrast, the population in Europe and Japan is declining. Immigration is largely responsible for keeping a positive growth rate in the United States. Even China, which is currently young, would witness rapid ageing in the next 20 years. The sex ratio in India is 933 per 1,000 males. Kerala has the highest female sex ratio of 1,058 while Haryana has the lowest female sex ratio of 861. The falling sex ratio in various parts of the country is a serious concern that has many marketing implications for services.

> *The* ***demographic environment*** *is the key macro-environmental force influencing the service business. The composition of societies in terms of age, sex, occupation, location and so on is changing fast and such changes are impacting the businesses significantly.*

The density of population is another demographic factor influencing the service business decisions. The average density of population in India is 325 persons per square kilometre. West Bengal has the highest population density of 903 persons while Arunachal Pradesh has the lowest population density of 13 persons per square kilometre. The density of population influences the choice of service location, the distribution system, the service package, the cost–output ratio and other marketing decisions.

The Economic Environment

The economic environment refers to the factors affecting consumer purchasing power and consumption patterns. Assessing the economic environment means evaluating factors that influence consumer and business buying patterns, such as the amount of confidence people have in the health of the economy.[5] According to a study conducted by the Centre for Monitoring Indian Economy (CMIE) in 2004, the expenditure on services increased from INR 1,400,420 million to INR 5,270,240 million during 1993–1994 to 2003–2004, a net growth of 276.3 per cent. The share of services in total consumer expenditure varied between 23.67 per cent and 29.85 per cent. The data indicates that consumer spending on non-durable goods is the highest followed by services. The monthly per capita expenditure on all items in rural India increased from INR 579 in 2004–2005 to INR 695 in 2006–2007.[6] The increase is much higher in urban areas, where the monthly per capita expenditures increased from INR 1,105 to INR 1,312 during the same period. The data indicates that there is higher per capita spending in urban areas as compared to rural areas. This is the reason why many companies focus on urban markets. However, taking the size of the rural population into consideration, even the small indulgences of rural consumers translate into big business volumes to the companies, if managed properly. Although many advertisers would prefer to show their services as part of an affluent lifestyle, working-class or blue-collar people represent a vast group of consumers that marketers cannot ignore. Lower-income, or downscale consumers may actually be more brand loyal

> *The **economic environment** refers to consumers' purchasing power and consumption patterns. The changes in these two areas are visible worldwide and particularly in the fast-growing economies like India and China. The increases in the consumer expenditure result in greater demand for goods and services.*

than wealthier consumers, because they cannot afford to make mistakes by switching to unfamiliar brands.

The changing lifestyles, due to television and telecommunications, migration to urban areas, migration to other countries, financial support by banks and other financial institutions through liberal lending, emergence of women entrepreneurs and so on create opportunities for business to exploit the emerging potential.

The industrial policy of 1991 brought about many changes in the Indian economy, impacting industry and business. The policy changes touched the roots of the economic system and changed the complexion of the business environment. Many service businesses could prosper by the exploitation of the emergent opportunities in domestic and international markets. The major changes initiated in the policy are discussed in "Services Marketing Insight: Industrial Policy 1991: The Focus on Market Economy".

The Natural Environment

> *All business organizations depend on natural resources. The **natural environment**, therefore, is critical for their business planning. The shortage of some natural resources, increased pollution and so on are serious concerns of the society and business.*

It refers to availability of natural resources for the production of services. The production of goods as well as services is dependent on natural resources directly or indirectly. The abundance or shortage of some resources impacts management and marketing decisions of the service companies significantly. For example, the scarcity of oil resources in India affects the business of transport services and retailing services directly and all other services indirectly. The oil crisis of 1990s and its impact on the Indian business is well recorded. The scarcity of the resources influenced changes in the economic system of the country in a big way. The shortage of electric power is another example of the negative effects of scarce natural resource on service business. All service organizations need electric power to carry out their operations. A breakdown in power supply breaks the service process in many businesses. In India, for decades the supply–demand gap in electricity has been existing. Energy conservation, oil conservation, controlled use of gas and so on have become the priority areas of the government due to the scarcity of natural resources. Marketers should study the trends in the natural environment. The availability of resources for present and future needs and the shortage of resources need to be analysed. One of the serious concerns of the natural environment is the increased pollution. The operations of the service companies should not contribute to the increase in pollution. On the other hand, it is good if companies consider the control of the environmental pollution a social responsibility and work towards it. Such activities of the company promote its positive image in the society and help in promoting its services.

The Technological Environment

The most influencing environment in recent years is the technological environment. Technological advancements kept the word status quo at a distance. Technology has a tremendous impact on our lives—our life-styles, our consumption

3.2 Services Marketing Insight

Industrial Policy 1991: The Focus on Market Economy

A major shift in the economic environment in India took place with the industrial policy statement of the Government of India in 1991. The policy provided a new direction to the Indian business. The policy stated that "the government will continue to pursue a sound policy framework encompassing encouragement of entrepreneurship, development of indigenous technology through investing in research and development, bringing in new technology, dismantling the regulatory system, developing the capital markets and increasing competitiveness for the benefit of the common man."

The objective of the policy statement was to maintain a sustained growth in productivity and gainful employment and attain international competitiveness. The policy basically focused on five important areas.

1. ***Industrial Licensing:*** Industrial licensing was abolished for all industries, except those specified, irrespective of the levels of investment. This change helped many small and medium entrepreneurs, who had been unnecessarily hampered by the erstwhile licensing system. The economy was opened for competition in all sections. Efficient and innovative companies could find their rightful place in the market.
2. ***Foreign Investment:*** Foreign investment facilitated technology transfer, marketing expertise, modern management techniques and promotion of exports. Visualizing the benefits, the policy allowed foreign investment in the interests of the country's industrial development.
3. ***Foreign Technology Agreement:*** As per the policy "the government will provide automatic approval for technology agreement related to high-priority industries within specified parameters.... Indian companies will be free to negotiate the terms of technology transfer with their foreign counterparts...." This measure was to induce the Indian industry to develop indigenous competence for the efficient absorption of the foreign technology.
4. ***Public Sector Policy:*** The priority areas for the growth of the public sector were identified. An essential infrastructure service was among them. According to the policy, "Competition will also be induced in these areas by inviting private sector participation. In the case of selected enterprises, part of Government holdings in the equity share capital of these enterprises will be disinvested in order to provide further market discipline to the performance of public enterprises."
5. ***Monopolies and Restrictive Trade Practices (MRTP) Act:*** The MRTP Act was restructured by eliminating the legal requirement for the prior governmental approval for the expansion of present undertakings and the establishment of new undertakings. The MRTP Commission was given more powers to execute the provisions of the Act.

Source: Statement on Industrial Policy, Ministry of Industry, Government of India, 1991. Available online at www.siadipp.nic.in/publicat/nip079.htm.

patterns and our economic well-being.[7] The digital revolution has impacted the business in many ways. The Internet changed the lifestyles of people and fortunes of many businesses. Many things that were considered not possible two decades ago are made possible through technological innovations. In the individual

> Technology has led to many changes in the business management. New technological innovations have created new business opportunities to service companies. The digital revolution transformed the business and introduced changes in consumer lifestyles throughout the world, creating many opportunities to service companies.

sphere, entertainment, music, education, healthcare and communication have been greatly impacted by technology. In addition to this, many new technologies are emerging and a fusion and convergence of different technologies is also taking place.[8] Technology facilitates speed, accuracy, reach, interactions with masses, inexpensive processes and operations, control of operations and so on. New technologies create new market opportunities. Marketers should study the trends in the technological environment. If they fail to notice changes, they may soon find their services outdated, lose market opportunities and leave chance to competitors.

The Political and Legal Environment

In a democratic setup, the political party that gets the majority in the parliament forms the government in the country. The philosophies and priorities of the party naturally reflect in the functioning of the government. Thus, the government initiates policy changes, in all required areas from time to time. These policy changes may create business opportunities or threats. The 1991 industrial policy of the government of India is a major change in the Indian business system. Some companies could exploit the opportunities and some companies faced severe threats due to the policy changes. Service companies are not an exception to this. The opening up of insurance, telecom and banking sectors to private players, introduction of service tax, facilitation of FDI inflow, export promotion schemes, establishment of regulatory bodies such as IRDA and TRAI, privatization policy, changes in various laws governing business, introduction of FEMA and Competition Act and so on are the major changes in the policy and legal system that impacted service business companies significantly. Legislation at all levels exercises more influence on the marketing activities of an organization than on any other phase of its operations.[9]

> Companies carry out their business operations under political and legal systems of a country. The policies of the government and the existing laws governing the business are important influencers. The increased legislation and government initiated policy changes in recent years impact service companies significantly.

Increasing legislation is one of the major trends in the legal environment. A number of legislations covering issues of fair trade practices, safety, pricing, trade, pollution, consumer protection and other areas have enacted for economic, social and political purposes. Marketers should understand the implications of legislations and public policy on marketing activities. They should workout their marketing plans within the legal framework of the land in which services are operated. The government policy often creates opportunities to private companies. The privatization policy, special economic zones, public–private participation policy and so on have created many business opportunities particularly for service companies. Therefore, it is necessary to keep a watch on the changing trends in the political and legal environment.

The Social and Cultural Environment

Culture exists to satisfy the needs of the people within a society. It offers order, direction and guidance in all phases of human problem solving by providing "tried-and-true" methods of satisfying physiological, personal and social needs. Culture is also associated with what a society's members consider to be a necessity and what they view as a luxury.

India is a multi-lingual, multi-cultural and multi-religious society. However, the predominance of the Hindu religion throughout the length and breadth of the country makes people believe that the Indian culture is the reflection of the Hindu culture. Since the Hindu culture itself has diversity as a core value, it is very difficult to study the cultural values of India. The core cultural values of Indians are described here.

Governed by Customs and Traditions

Indians prefer the customary way of life and believe that such lifestyle is honourable. Their consumption habits are influenced by customs. Though every Indian is not clearly exposed to descriptive customs, they learned from the elders and follow them to the best possible extent. Celebratory occasions and rituals and the way in which those occasions have to be organized are learnt from customs and traditions. Festivals such as Dussehra, Diwali and Pongal require distinctive arrangements and organizational processes. Many goods and services such as ornaments, clothes, gift items, movies, tourist places, hotels and restaurants, transport services find peak demand during festival seasons as Indians give top priority to the celebration of festivals. They even take loans, even at a higher rate of interest, but do not compromise on the level of celebration. Indians find an opportunity to display their social status and affection towards relatives and friends by following customs and traditions without significant deviations.

Social Relationships Are Dominant Influencers

Indians prefer to see themselves as members of the society and accord the highest respect to social relationships. They feel comfortable in following the norms and values of the society; prefer to sacrifice their individualism for the sake of social relationships; want the society to recognize them as good, intelligent, special and highly esteemed. It is the dream of the majority of Indians that other members of the society should feel envious of them. However, they also take care to ensure that their behaviour does not harm others.

Conservative and Contented

Conservativism is one of the important values of Indians. They don't like to waste any resource. Most of their activities relating to consumption of goods and services are planned. This does not mean their purchasing behaviour is highly balanced and rational. They do have emotions but they keep an upper limit for deviations from the conservative plan developed in advance. Indians are content with normal living conditions because the loyalty levels of Indians are very high towards products and sellers as long as products do not deviate significantly the traditional pattern.

Part of the Family

Indians are collectivists as far as orientation towards families is concerned. Family members play an important role in influencing the purchase behaviour of an individual. Family relationships are given great importance, and the love and affection of the family members evokes emotions in individuals. Individuals prefer and like to sacrifice something for their family members. Indian buyers read the satisfaction of their family members on their choice and performance of goods and services. With the emergence of the nuclear family system, every member of the family has started influencing the purchase behaviour of other members of family. This is why the promotional campaigns of almost all companies in India are targeted at families not individuals.

Health and Fitness Conscious

Health and fitness is an important element of Indian customs. Indians believe that health is wealth of the highest value. According to the Indian philosophy, the healthy being is equipoised both in pleasure and in pain, in success and in failure. The use of traditionally identified natural health items in products and services receives an instant appreciation from the Indian community if communicated properly.

Humanitarianism

One of the moral standards adapted by the Indian society is humanitarianism. Indians believe that service to humanity is service to God. By every possible means Indians try to extend a helping hand to others even when it requires some amount of sacrifice from them. If any business proposition is linked with service to the deprived or service to humankind, Indians encourage such business concerns.

Women Carry Special Respect

In ancient India, women were by and large treated "equal to men". They were treated and honoured and considered to be the "embodiment of all divine virtues on earth". They were considered not only as pivots of domestic life but also of the entire social organization.[10] In the medieval periods, the status of women was lowered and several restrictions were imposed on them. After independence, governments encouraged women in all areas, and now women enjoy full freedom and equal rights. Irrespective of the changes in the role and status of women in the Indian society, women have received special respect throughout. The housewife plays almost all roles in purchase decisions such as initiator, influencer, user, decider, approver, buyer and also serves as a reference and sometimes an opinion leader.

Predominance of Religious Faith

Indians prefer to follow the religious code and accept those products and services that conform to the standards of their religion. Anything that appears deviant or against religious faith is rejected by people. It may sometimes invite agitation from religious groups. For example, the exploitation of sex for business purposes in advertising and other media is not acceptable in the Indian society beyond a particular proposition. If any company attempts to introduce any service that affects the religious sentiment of people, the service is rejected.

Change is the Last Option

Indians are resistance to change. They accept changes slowly and to the level sustainable. They prefer to continue with time-tested practices, and only after visualizing greater value with the change will they make a passive initiation to adapt to the change. In the rating of alternatives, the new option finds the lowest position. Companies seeking the acceptance by Indians of newly introduced products need to be patient. Innovators and early adopters constitute a small in proportion in India as compared to the West.

Tolerance

Tolerance is one of the great virtues of Indians. Several cultural groups, each of which migrated into the country with their own customs, cultures and lifestyles, live amicably with the ethnic population. The cultural coexistence in India is a symbol of tolerance. This cultural value significantly influences the complaining behaviour of individuals. Indians react only when the mistakes of businessmen exceed the threshold level of tolerance. They provide ample opportunity to businessmen to rectify their mistakes.

Defined Lifestyle at Different Stages of the Life Cycle

According to Hinduism, each individual must divide his life into four stages (*ashramas*) to lead an ideal life. The four *ashramas* (stages) are:[11] *Brahmacharya* (student life), *Grihastha* (family life), *Vanaprastha* (retired life) and *Sanyasa* (life of renunciation). During the first stage of life, students were taught the discipline of life by the family, society and teachers. In the second stage (family life), a man was expected to lead a married life and perform the duties of a householder—bringing up children and offering reverence to ancestors. The third stage was the retired-life stage during which parents were expected to take social welfare work and were relieved of the responsibilities of children. At this stage, they were relieved from all attachments with family members and relatives so that they could develop new interests and activities oriented towards social development. In the fourth phase of life (*Sanyasa)*, people were free from all burdens. Individuals focused on developing universal consciousness. People at this stage were expected to rise above fears, passions and hatred. This stage was not a life of inaction, but a life of action with high level of motivation and interest.

The description of the four stages of life and the suggested behavioural tendencies are of great help to marketers to design products and services and to relate them to any of these four stages of life.

> *Despite many changes in the cultural and social environment in India the core cultural values of Indians are intact. The changes in family systems and the changing role of women impact service businesses greatly.*

The core values are not common to every citizen of India, as individuals differ in their likes, dislikes, attitudes, perceptions, interests, opinions and all other behavioural dimensions. Homogeneity is far from reality in any group in a society. The cultural values, however, are great influencers of behaviour and, therefore, a proper understanding of the values is immensely helpful to companies offering goods and services to the consuming public.

Balaji Telefilms

The market for entertainment services is huge in India. India is the fastest growing entertainment market, producing the largest number of films in many languages in the world. The entry of television opened new vistas in this area. Balaji Telefilms, established in 1994, could capitalize the latent demand for household entertainment needs. The launch of highly successful teleserials including *Kyunki Saas Bhi Kabhi Bahu Thi, Kahani Ghar Ghar Ki,* and *Karam Apnaa Apnaa* helped the company make a mark for itself.

The company entered the market as a content provider for television. It identified marketing opportunities in the environment and became a leading entertainment content provider in India. Creativity, insight and discipline were the philosophies of the company. The management focused on careful planning, disciplined action and specialization to reflect in all stages. The key factors of their success included conceptualization, content focus, talent pool management, constant improvization and management with innovation drive.

The company's careful adherence to processes and systems right from the level of ideation and conceptualization has helped it in providing quality services. Idea banks are created with relevant and inspiring thoughts for future applications.

The exploration of new genres is the key strategy of the company. It has understood the market environment to identify the future entertainment needs and created a niche for non-fiction, animation, reality shows and events on the small screen market. Balaji Telefilims is poised as a media powerhouse and has developed the solid infrastructure of about 32 state-of-the-art studios in the country. To expand its business content beyond Hindi, the company had strategic alliances with other companies to access Telugu, Tamil, Kannada, Bengali language audiences.

Balaji Telefilms Ltd. stands as an example for its ability to analyse the marketing environment from the management perspective and to exploit opportunities successfully.

THE COMPANY'S RESPONSE TO THE MARKETING ENVIRONMENT

> *"Service companies should develop an environment management system to study, respond and influence micro- and macro-environmental forces. Though environmental forces are not within the control of any organization, successful companies follow proactive methods to exploit emerging opportunities or to defend from threats due to the changes in the environment."*

Service companies need to conceptualize the micro- and macro-environments specific to their business and develop an organizational mechanism to study the changing trends. They should equip themselves with the ability to respond effectively to the changes in the marketing environment. The companies which make things happen, by keenly assessing the trends and projecting them accurately for the future, are considered excellent companies. Companies which watch the changes and respond timely and efficiently are rated as good companies. Some companies are blind and do not know what is happening around them. Such companies are likely to fail in a short period. The marketing environment should not be viewed as uncontrollable. Successful companies try to influence the environment to respond in their favour. They take the marketing environment from the management perspective. They influence the actors in the micro-environment and also work on influencing the forces of the macro-environment. Thus, service companies should play a proactive role in managing the marketing environment.

SUMMARY

- Service companies are part of the society and work to satisfy the needs of society. The changes in the environment in which a business is operated are likely to affect the company's prospects.
- The marketing environment of a company can be divided into the micro-environment and the macro-environment.
- The micro-environment consists of other divisions of the company—suppliers, intermediaries, competitors, customer markets and other publics.
- Macro-environmental forces include demographic, economic, natural, technological, social and cultural, and political and legal environments.
- The forces in the marketing environment influence the company's ability to face the situations.
- Services companies should identify the actors in the micro-environment and promote good relationships with them for mutual gain.
- The trends in the macro-environment should be studied periodically to identify business opportunities or threats from the changes in the environment.
- Service companies should develop competencies to exploit opportunities quickly and in a better way than competitors.
- Companies should analyse the marketing environment from the management perspectives and try to influence the environment to create a favourable setting for the company.
- Excellent companies make things happen, good companies respond effectively to the changes in the environment while poor companies fail to respond properly.
- An organizational mechanism to study the micro- and macro-marketing environment and the impact of changes on them is necessary for service companies.

KEY TERMS

customer markets *46*
core cultural values *55*
demographic environment *48*
economic environment *49*
micro-environment *44*
macro-environment *47*
natural environment *54*
suppliers *45*
technological environment *54*

BRIEF QUESTIONS

1. What is the micro-environment?
2. How do other publics influence the service business?
3. Explain the term *technological environment*.
4. What is the impact of the natural environment on the services sector?
5. How do you manage the micro-environment?

ESSAY QUESTIONS

1. Explain the importance of the micro-marketing environment and the direct and indirect influence of the actors of the micro-environment on a service organization.
2. What are the macro-environmental forces that affect the service business? How?
3. Explain the socio-cultural environment prevalent in India.
4. "Technology creates opportunities as well as threats." Discuss.
5. How should a service company respond to its marketing environment?

ASSIGNMENTS

1. Divide the class into five member groups to study and prepare a report on:
   (a) Demographic changes in India.
   (b) The emerging business opportunities in the services sector due to demographic changes.
2. Identify the core cultural values of the Indian society and find out:
   (a) The changing requirements of the society due to cultural changes.
   (b) The impact of cultural changes on service industry.

REFERENCES

1 Philip Kotler and Gary Armstrong, *Principles of Marketing* (New Delhi: Prentice Hall of India, 2002), p. 87.

2 Philip Kotler, John Bowen and James Makens, *Marketing for Hospitality and Tourism*. (Delhi: Pearson Education, 2005), p. 131.

3 William D. Perreault, Jr., and E. Jerome McCarthy, *Basic Marketing—A Global Managerial Approach*. (New Delhi: Tata McGraw-Hill, 2002), p. 99.

4 Census of India, 2001, www. censusindia.gov.in.

5 Michael R. Solomon and Elnora W. Stuart, *Marketing—Real People, Real Choices*. (Delhi: Pearson Education, 2005), p. 109.

6 NSS report.527; Household Consumer Expenditure in India, 2006-07, 15

7 William J. Stanton and Charles Futrell, *Fundamentals of Marketing*. (New York: McGraw-Hill, 1989), p. 30

8 V. S. Ramaswamy and S. Namakumari, *Marketing Management*. (New Delhi: Macmillan, 2009), p. 53

9 William J. Stanton and Charles Futrell, *Fundamentals of Marketing*. (New York: McGraw-Hill, 1989), p. 28

10 Ram Ahuja, *Society in India*. (New Delhi: Rawat Publications, 2002), p. 127.

11 Ibid, pp. 10–11.

The Services Sector in the Indian Economy

4

LEARNING OBJECTIVES

After studying this chapter, you will be able to:

- Describe the status of the services sector in India
- Understand the reasons for the growth of services
- Identify the key services in India

In 1770, India was the second largest economy in the world, contributing more than 20 per cent of the world output.[1] Two centuries later, in 1970, India's contribution had plummeted to three per cent, thanks to the economic stagnation during the imperialist British regime and the inward-looking, state interventionist policies followed since independence. The 1991 reforms removed the obstacles to economic freedom and helped India catch up and find its place in the global economy.

Currently, India is recognized as one of the fastest growing economies in the world. The economy has shown positive signs and a consistent growth rate. Before the global economic meltdown of 2008, it was estimated that India's GDP would surpass that of the United States before 2050[2] and India would once again become the world's second largest economy.

The two major sectors of the Indian economy that will help India achieve this growth are the services sector and industry—the growth drivers of the economy. The growth of the services sector has been consistent, and its contribution to the development of industry is vital. A quarter of the total services is directly linked to industry in sectors such as trade, transport, electricity, software and construction. This sector is opening up business opportunities for young, innovative and enthusiastic entrepreneurs.

Questions:

1. Do you think the growth of the services sector in India will continue?
2. What are the real reasons for the growth of this sector?
3. Do you think government policy alone is responsible for the development of this sector?
4. How can this sector be further strengthened?

INTRODUCTION

India has been pursuing a planned approach to achieve economic growth and development. Since its independence in 1947, the economic activities to be developed were categorized into three sectors in the order of priority: primary, secondary and tertiary. The primary sector includes agriculture, animal husbandry, fishing and forestry. These areas are considered fundamental to the further development of the economy. The secondary sector includes manufacturing industry and construction. The tertiary sector covers services, including distribution. The development of each of these sectors has been carried out in a phased manner. The first three Five Year Plans focused on the primary sector the next two on the secondary sector. From the sixth Five Year Plan onwards, the focus has been on the tertiary sector. As a result, the services sector has been growing rapidly since the 1980s.

Contribution to the Gross Domestic Product

One of the key indicators of the growth of the services sector is its contribution to the gross domestic product (GDP) of the country. While considering services for this purpose, there are two important dimensions that need special attention: hidden services and the services in the unorganized sector. As defined in Chapter 1, *hidden services* are the services that are used internally by manufacturing organizations. The output value of such services becomes part of the value of tangible goods, thus remaining hidden. There are a large number of services that are not accounted for output assessment for the purpose of GDP calculation. Examples include personal services, maid services and a host of professional services such as the services offered by barbers, carpenters, washermen, goldsmiths, priests, and nurses. These services are predominant in almost all semi-urban and rural parts of the country, but a proper accounting system to assess the value of the output is conspicuously absent. Barring these two important dimensions, the service output is valued for the purpose of the GDP. Figure 4.1 shows the contribution of agriculture, industry and services to the GDP in India. The share of the agricultural sector in the GDP of the country was 57.1 per cent in 1950–1951, that is, in the beginning of the planned era, services occupied the second position with 28.6 per cent and the contribution of industry to the GDP was 14.3 per cent. There was a significant change in the proportions of these three sectors by the end of 2000–2001. The share of agriculture had gone down to 24.7 per cent; the services sector became the major contributor with 48.8 per cent share in the GDP, and the contribution of industry to the GDP was 26.4 per cent. In the early 2000s, change continued with greater pace. The contribution of the services sector to the GDP reached 57 per cent by the end of 2008–2009. The contribution of industry was 26 per cent while the share of agriculture was the lowest (17 per cent). Between 2005–2006 and 2008–2009, the growth rate of the services sector varied between 9.6 per cent and 11.2 per cent (see Table 4.1).

> *“The place of the services sector in the Indian economy is pivotal. The sector contributed 29 per cent to the GDP of the country in 1950–1951 and registered consistently high growth rates over the years to become the largest contributor to the GDP with a 57 per cent contribution in 2008–2009.”*

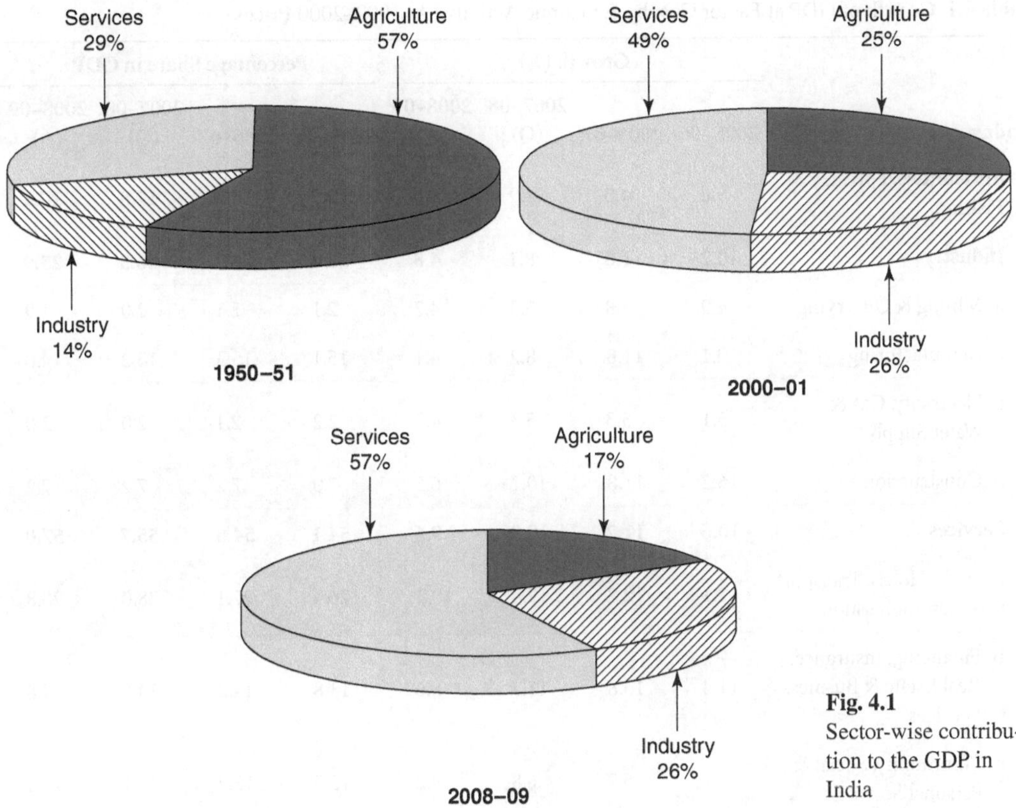

Fig. 4.1
Sector-wise contribution to the GDP in India

Shares of Sub-sectors

Among the major sub-sectors of services, the share of trade was consistently dominant and varied between 25.1 per cent and 28.3 per cent during 1981–1982 to 2006–2007, as shown in Table 4.2. The other major contributors were real estate, banking, insurance and public administration. Public administration was the second major contributor until 1986–1987 but real estate services occupied the second place from 1991–1992 to 2006–2007. The share of railways declined from 4.4 per cent to 2.2 per cent. Hotels and restaurants registered marginal improvement. The share of other transport was consistent with minor variations. The banking and insurance sector registered consistently impressive upward performance by improving its share from 6.5 per cent to 11.3 per cent. Communications was the other major performer. The share of communications increased from a mere 1.8 per cent to 7.5 per cent by the end of 2006–2007.

> *"The share of the services sector in total employment is significant. The sector employs 107.02 million people in the country and contributes 23.4 per cent to the total employment."*

Contribution to Employment

Agriculture has continued to be the major contributor to employment in India. The services sector ranked a distant second in 2004–05. As can be seen

Table 4.1 Growth of GDP at Factor Cost by Economic Activity (At 1999–2000 Prices)

Industry	Growth (%)				Percentage Share in GDP			
	2005–06	2006–07	2007–08 (Q)	2008–09 (A)	2005–06	2006–07	2007–08 (Q)	2008–09 (A)
1 **Agriculture, Forestry & Fishing**	**5.8**	**4.0**	**4.9**	**2.6**	**19.5**	**18.5**	**17.8**	**17.1**
2 **Industry**	**10.2**	**11.0**	**8.1**	**4.8**	**26.4**	**26.7**	**26.5**	**25.9**
a Mining & Quarrying	4.9	8.8	3.3	4.7	2.1	2.1	2.0	1.9
b Manufacturing	9.1	11.8	8.2	4.1	15.1	15.3	15.2	14.8
c Electricity, Gas & Water Supply	5.1	5.3	5.3	4.3	2.2	2.1	2.0	2.0
d Construction	16.2	11.8	10.1	6.5	7.0	7.2	7.2	7.2
3 **Services**	**10.6**	**11.2**	**10.9**	**9.6**	**54.1**	**54.8**	**55.7**	**57.0**
a Trade, Hotels, Transport & Communication	12.1	12.8	12.4	10.3	26.4	27.1	28.0	28.8
b Financing, Insurance, Real Estate & Business Services	11.4	13.8	11.7	8.6	13.8	14.3	14.6	14.8
c Community, Social & Personal Services	7.1	5.7	6.8	9.2	13.9	13.4	13.1	13.4
4 **GDP at Factor cost**	**9.5**	**9.7**	**9.0**	**7.1**	**100.00**	**100.00**	**100.00**	**100.00**

Source: *Department of Economic Affairs, Ministry of Finance, Monthly Economic Report, March 2009, p. 2.*
Q = Quick estimates; A = Advanced estimates

"The shares of various sub-sectors of services in India reveal that trade is the major contributor followed by real estate, banking and insurance and public administration. Communications achieved remarkable progress from a mere 1.8 per cent in 1981–82 to 7.5 per cent in 2006–2007."

in Table 4.3, this sector provided 22.8 per cent employment in 1999–2000. The share of the services sector in the total employment increased to 23.4 per cent in 2004–2005. Among the sub-sectors of services, trade, hotels and restaurants provided employment to a large number of persons (37.32 million in 1999–2000 and 47.11 million in 2004–2005) followed by community, social and personal services (33.20 million in 1999–2000 and 35.67 in 2004–2005).[3]

REASONS FOR THE GROWTH OF SERVICES IN INDIA

The services sector in India is growing impressively and contributing significantly to the development of industry and agriculture in the country besides promoting economic growth. The operational characteristics of the services sector are shown in "Services Marketing Insight: Operational Characteristics of Services Sector Enterprises in India". The following are the major reasons for the growth of services in India.

Table 4.2 Share of Different Sub-sectors Within Services (At 1999–2000 Prices)

	1981–82	1986–87	1991–92	1996–97	2001–02	2006–07
Trade	28.3	27.0	25.1	27.3	26.6	26.7
Hotels & Restaurants	2.0	2.0	2.0	2.4	2.6	2.5
Railways	4.4	4.0	3.5	2.7	2.3	2.2
Other Transport	9.5	9.4	9.5	10.0	9.2	10.1
Storage	0.4	0.3	0.3	0.2	0.2	0.1
Communications	1.8	1.7	1.7	2.3	4.3	7.5
Banking & Insurance	6.5	8.1	10.2	10.7	11.2	11.3
Real Estate	13.8	14.8	16.0	15.1	14.7	14.1
Public Administration	14.7	15.3	14.5	12.4	12.8	10.6
Other Services	18.8	17.5	17.1	16.8	16.2	14.9
Total	100	100	100	100	100	100

Source: National Accounts Statistics.

Table 4.3 Employment Statistics (Disaggregated)

	Sectoral Share (million) 1999–2000	Sectoral Share (%) 1999–2000	Sectoral Share (million) 2004–05	Sectoral Share (%) 2004–05	Elasticity
Agriculture Forestry & Fishing	237.56	59.8	267.57	58.4	1.52
Mining & Quarrying	2.27	0.6	2.74	0.6	0.82
Manufacturing	48.01	12.1	53.51	11.7	0.34
Electricity, Gas & Water Supply	1.28	0.3	1.37	0.3	0.33
Construction	17.62	4.4	25.61	5.6	0.88
Trade, Hotels & Restaurants	37.32	9.4	47.11	10.3	0.59
Transport, Storage & Communication	14.69	3.7	17.38	3.8	0.27
Financing, Insurance, Real Estate & Business Services	5.05	1.3	6.86	1.5	0.94
Community, Social and Personal Services	33.20	8.4	35.67	7.8	0.28
All Services Excl. Construction	90.26	22.8	107.02	23.4	
Total	397.0	100	457.87	100	0.48

Source: C Rangarajan et al., "Revisiting Employment and Growth," ICRA Bulletin—Money & Finance, 2007, 3(2); data sourced from NSSO 2004-05, based on 61st Round Survey.

4.1 Services Marketing Insight | **Operational Characteristics of Services Sector Enterprises in India**

The National Sample Survey Organization of the Government of India conducted a study in 2006–2007 to find out the operational characteristics of services sector enterprises in the country. The findings of the study help understand the big picture vis-à-vis the services sector in India. According to the study:

- There were about 16.5 million* functional services sector enterprises India during 2006–2007.
- 60 per cent of the enterprises were in rural India and 40 per cent in urban India.
- Own-account enterprises constituted 85 per cent of the total.
- Uttar Pradesh had the highest share in the total number of enterprises (14 per cent) followed by West Bengal (13 per cent), Andhra Pradesh (10 per cent), Maharashtra (9 per cent) and Tamil Nadu (7 per cent). These five states together accounted for 53 per cent of enterprises in India.
- About 35 million persons were estimated to be working in the services sector.
- About 59 per cent of service enterprises were not registered with any agency.
- About 74 per cent of enterprises had fixed premises of operation. Out of them, 32 per cent were located in household premises and 41 per cent were located outside household premises.
- 81 per cent of owners/managing partners were literates.
- About 86 per cent of enterprises did not receive any financial support from government or non-government agencies.

*Excluding transport via railways, air, pipelines, real estate of self-owned buildings, monetary intermediation, trade unions, religious organizations, political organizations, all-government and public sector organizations, government-aided institutions, service companies registered under the Factories Act 1948, wholesale and retail trade, repair and maintenance services, public administration and defence, and extra territorial organizations and bodies.

Source: NSS Report No. 528, Service Sector in India, 2006-07, NSS 63rd Round.

Economic Affluence

Affluence is one of the key factors that fuelled the demand for services. The economic liberalization process initiated in the country during the last decade of the 20th century has had a positive impact on Indian households. Their income as well as expenditure has been pushed up, creating a demand for many goods and services. The growth of middle-income households and rural rich in India has resulted in increased demand for many services.

The Changing Role of Women

Women constitute nearly 50 per cent of the population. In the past, Indian women confined themselves to household activities. There were many restrictions on their movements, education, occupations and role in the society. Earlier, educating women was considered a sin. Entertainment was beyond their reach. They neither had a choice in selecting their life partners nor in living their lives as they liked; they even had no right to live after the demise of their husbands. Over a period of time, there has been a change in the traditional way of thinking. Now, women receive education; there are special schools and colleges for the purpose. Indian women have proved to be competent in work and, in some areas, more efficient than their male counterparts. Women work in the defence services, the police services, the postal services, transport services, software services, health services, hospitality services and so on. In fact, it is very difficult to name an area where women do not excel. The percentage of working women has been growing. Women employment in the organized sector increased from 3.89 million in 1992 to 4.93 million in 2004. The percentage share of women's employment rose from 14.4 per cent in 1992 to 18.7 per cent in 2004. The share of employed women increased from 12.8 per cent to 15.9 per cent in the public sector and from 19.4 per cent to 24.8 per cent in the private sector during the period.[4] The changing role of women in society has created a market for a number of products, particularly a number of services. Earning women prefer to hire services to reduce the load of the innumerable roles that they are required to perform. They are well informed and have the ability to choose the right service and also influence the family members in purchase decisions. The demand by women is forcing service organizations to be more innovative in their approach.

> *"The changing role of women in the society has created a market for a number of services. The earning women prefer to hire services to minimize the innumerable roles they are required to play. The demand generated by women is forcing the service companies to be more innovative in their approach."*

Cultural Changes

Culture is an embodiment of values, knowledge, traditions, taboos, habits and behaviour, which passes from generation to generation. The influence of culture on the lifestyles of people is significant. Culture is not static; in fact, it is a process of development. Change is the underlying philosophy of culture. Some societies change faster, some at a medium pace and the others at a slower pace. The pace of change of the Indian culture is not uniform. However, during the last century the factors of change were prominent. The changed role of women is one example and the change in the family systems is another. The emergence of the nuclear family system in place of the traditional joint family system created a demand for a host of services—entertainment, education, healthcare, hospitality, telecommunications, posts, transport and tourism, to mention a few. There has been a marked change in the thought process relating to expenditure, investment, leisure time, children's education, time management and so on, which has created a market for services.

The IT Revolution

India has occupied a vital position in the area of information technology for the last two decades. IT has become one of the key service businesses of the country. India has the largest *software-skilled population* in the world. The domestic market and the international market have grown substantially. Many state governments, realizing the potential for this area, have put IT as their top priority. States such as Karnataka, Andhra Pradesh, Madhya Pradesh, Tamil Nadu, Maharashtra and Delhi have already achieved substantial progress in information technology. It is expected that IT-enabled services will have a bright future in the years to come.

The Conservation of Natural Resources

Population growth, greater industrialization and indiscriminate consumption have affected the environment, ecological balance and natural resources. The government and social organizations, realizing the negative effects of such changes, have promoted several service organizations to take up social marketing. A lot of money is being spent on forestation, safeguarding rare animals and birds, controlling water pollution, and conserving oil and energy. Research is on to develop new technologies that can promote optimal use of natural resources and prevent further damage to the environment.

The Development of Markets

The growth of the wholesaler–retailer population during the last few decades in the country is sine qua non for the development of markets in India. Urban India has become a cluster of wholesaling and retailing businesses. Retailing has spread to every nook and corner of urban India. In rural India too, retailing enjoys a significant presence. A new breed of organizations, offering marketing services for a number of products produced by small-scale and tiny-sector units, has come up. Marketing services are also offered by the government to small agricultural farmers, artisans (handlooms and handicrafts) and other traditional business sectors such as promotion of regulated markets, marketing cooperatives, export promotion councils and developmental boards.

The Unbundling of Corporations

Manufacturing organizations have identified the need for future orientation. To facilitate this requirement, they have promoted support services handled by "staff" in the organization. The *staff* is a group of persons not engaged in manufacturing but in serving line managers to help them function effectively and suggesting developments for a better future. The changing competitive situation and demand–supply positions have forced manufacturing organizations to shift their philosophy from production orientation to market orientation. Marketing is a service function that has been added to the organization. Pressures in the market have further forced manufacturing organizations to have specialized divisions for marketing research, advertising, accounting, auditing, human resource management, financial management, strategy development and human resource development, all of which are service functions. The concept of self-reliance has made manufacturing organizations become a huge bundle of activities. However, intense competition, rapid technological development and the emerging new-world business order, particularly during the last two decades of the 20th century, have forced organizations to unbundle a majority of service functions and concentrate on the core business. Industry support services have attained independent status and achieved

> *Intense competition forced companies to use highly specialized services to gain competitive advantage. Consequently, companies started unbundling themselves and began to purchase services from various specialist organizations, creating opportunities for many service providers.*

tremendous growth by offering creative and quality services. The growth of advertising agencies, marketing research organizations, distribution agencies, financial consultancy firms, management consultancy firms, human resource consultancy firms, accounting service organizations, human resource training centres and so on can be credited to the unbundling process of manufacturing organizations.

The Increased Consciousness of Healthcare

The healthcare market has grown substantially in India. The growing consciousness of people regarding health issues has led to increased life expectancy. The growth of health centres, fitness clubs, diagnostic centres, medical counselling, psychological counselling, health-related information sites reflect the growing demand for healthcare services. The government as well as social organizations have taken up mass campaigns through different media to create awareness among illiterate persons and rural population on healthcare. Immunization campaigns, child care campaigns, campaigns on preventive medicine and family planning are some of the programmes intended to promote healthcare in rural India.

Economic Liberalization

The economic liberalization process, which started in 1991, brought about many changes in the Indian business scenario. Multinationals were permitted to enter the Indian market. Disinvestments and privatization policies put an end to the state-owned monopolies in many service areas. Delicensing policies encouraged many entrepreneurs to establish businesses wherever they wanted. Liberal lending policies and lower interest rates motivated many people to become self-employed. These changes led to a major shift in the competitive scenario. Banking, insurance, telecommunications, power projects, advertising , marketing research, hospitality , courier services and air transport witnessed intense competition due to the entry of multinational companies. The influx of time-tested service technologies from various parts of the world changed the attitude of the Indian consumer towards service.

Migration

Rural to semi-urban and urban migration has been one of the reasons for the growth of services in India. Migration to urban areas in search of jobs and a better livelihood resulted in the expansion of cities and townships, causing real estate, rentals, transportation and infrastructure services to expand rapidly. The demand for urban placement services and personal services has also increased.

> *India is one of the potential sources of services to many countries in the world. Tourism and software services are among the major foreign exchange earners of the country and their growth rate is also very high.*

Export Potential

The export market for services has been on the rise throughout the world. India is considered to be a potential source for services. There are a number of services that India offers to various parts of the world. Services that are commonly offered to international consumers are banking, insurance, transportation, communication, data, accounting, construction labour, design engineering, entertainment, maintenance, education, healthcare, tourism, software and commercial. Tourism and software services are among the major foreign exchange earners of the country and their growth rate is also very high compared to other sectors. The exports of commercial services from India increased from USD 16 billion in 2000 to USD 72.8 billion in 2006. The share of services exports from India in world exports increased from 1.1 per cent in 2000 to 2.7 per cent in 2006.

KEY SERVICE BUSINESSES IN INDIA

The services sector plays an important role in the progress and development of the Indian economy. The contribution of this sector to the exchequer is substantial (see "Services Marketing Insight: Service Tax"). In order to provide a better understanding of the development of services in India and its significance in the economic prosperity of the country, a brief description of a few key services—insurance, postal services, transport, tourism, telecommunications, banking, IT & ITeS, healthcare, electricity, entertainment and media services, education and retailing—is presented in the following sections.

Insurance

In India, the insurance business started in the early years of the 20th century. Marine insurance was the earliest form of insurance transacted in India and was followed by fire insurance. Many foreign companies established their branches in India for business prospects. In 1907, the Indian Mercantile Insurance Company was established as the first company of the Indian origin. The nationalization of the insurance business was a major milestone in the development of the insurance business in India. The life insurance business was nationalized in 1956 by taking over 245 private insurers' business. The General Insurance Corporation (GIC) was established in 1972 by taking over the business of 107 insurers. The GIC has four subsidiaries: National Insurance, Oriental Insurance, New India Assurance and United India Insurance. Apart from the Life Insurance Corporation (LIC) and GIC, there are three more organizations in the insurance business in the public sector: Employees State Insurance, Deposit Insurance Corporation and Export Risk Insurance Corporation. LIC and GIC are the most popular insurance companies in the life and non-life insurance business, respectively. These two companies, with a well-defined market system and a distinguished portfolio, occupy the mega market share in the total insurance business in India.

In the absence of competition from the private sector, the insurance business in India has not grown to its potential. India's life insurance premium as a percentage of the GDP is 1.8 per cent as against 5.2 per cent in the United States, 6.5 per cent in UK and 8 per cent in South Korea.

4.2 Services Marketing Insight | **Service Tax**

Service tax is a tax on services. This tax is levied on the transaction of certain services specified by the central government under the Finance Act, 1994. A person who provides taxable service on the receipt of service charges is required to pay service tax to the government. Every person who has provided a taxable service of value exceeding INR 900,00 in the preceding financial year is required to register with the central excise or service tax office. The word "person" includes any company or association or body of individuals, whether incorporated or not. Thus, this expression includes any individual, Hindu undivided family (HUF), proprietary firm or partnership firm, company, trust, institution and society.

The growth in the services sector attracted the attention of the government as a tax-generating resource. The Government of India introduced service tax for the first time in 1994. There were at least four reasons for the introduction of services into the ambit of the tax structure.

- The continuous increase in the share of services in the GDP and the decrease in the share of industry led to a situation of declined excise tax revenue and reduced tax base.
- The absence of tax on services distorted consumer choices by encouraging spending on services at the expense of goods.
- The traders unable to claim VAT on their service inputs due to non-coverage of services under the tax purview.
- The improvement in equity arising out of subjecting affluent sections of society to taxation, as most services correlated positively with the affluence of people.

For the reasons mentioned above, a 5 per cent tax was introduced in 1994 on three specified services: telephone, general insurance and stock brokerage. Over the years, the number of services brought under service tax increased, and by 2006–2007 there were 106 specified services under tax net. Service tax is required to be paid at the rate of 12.36 per cent (2008–2009) on the value of taxable services. The contribution of the services sector to the exchequer is increasing phenomenally each year. The service tax revenue was only INR 4.07 billion in 1994–1995. The service tax revenue increased to INR 375.96 billion in 2006–2007 and further to INR 506.03 million in 2007–2008. In 2008–2009, the revenue from service tax was INR 644.60 billion. These figures indicate that the contribution of the services sector to the exchequer is substantial and increasing at a very high proportion year by year.

Source: Annual Financial Statements of the Central Government, Ministry of Finance, Government of India.

With the Insurance Regulatory and Development Authority Act, 2000 (IRDA), the insurance market in India was opened to the private sector. As a result, many private insurance companies entered the market, in collaboration with foreign companies. The market has now become highly competitive and challenging. There are 22 life insurance companies and 21 non-life insurance companies competing in India.[5]

LIC is the biggest personal insurance company in India. It has seven zonal offices, 100 divisional offices and 2,048 fully computerized branch offices spread all over the country. The agency network of the corporation is considered the biggest and strongest. The wide area network of LIC covers divisional offices and branch offices. The corporation has tie ups with some banks and other service providers to offer on-line premium collection facilities to consumers.[6]

> "*Insurance recorded a substantial growth after it was opened to private companies. Though public sector companies dominated both the life and the non-life segments, the growth rate of private companies is far ahead of public sector companies. The low penetration of this service in the country, particularly in rural India, offers a great potential for its growth.*"

According to ASSOCHAM,[7] the insurance sector in India grew by a CAGR of approximately 175 per cent during 2006–2008. Private insurance companies adopted intensive marketing strategies causing the market share of public sector companies such as LIC and GIC to come down to 70 per cent in 2008–2009 from over 97 per cent in 2002–2003. ASSOCHAM estimated that insurance businesses in India would grow by over 200 per cent by 2010–2011. The private insurance business would grow by 140 per cent and the state-owned companies would achieve around 35–40 per cent growth. The general insurance business grew at a healthy rate of 16 per cent annually during 2004–2005 to 2008–2009. The growth was led by motor insurance and health insurance, which grew by 16 per cent and 37 per cent, respectively, annually. However, its market penetration level was just 0.60 per cent against the world average of 2.14 per cent. India ranks 136th on penetration levels and lags behind China (106), Thailand (87), Russia (86), Brazil (85), Japan (61) and the United States (9).[8] The reasons identified for its low penetration are low consumer preference, untapped rural markets and limited distribution channels. Thus, there is a great potential for the general insurance business in India.

Transport

The movement of people and goods from one place to another place is called *transportation*. This service is as old as humanity. Transportation is a key service in the development of any nation as it contributes to economic, industrial, social and cultural development. There are four popular means of transport: roadways, railways, waterways and airways. Rail and road are the two dominant means of transport, carrying more than 95 per cent of the total traffic generated in the country.

India has an extensive road network of more than 3.3 million kilometres, connecting the entire country. It is one of the largest networks in the world. It comprises national highways, state highways, district roads, rural roads and special purpose roads, especially for ports and military services. The length of national highways is about 65,590 kilometres, which caters to about 40 per cent of the total road transport demand. The Government of India has recognized the importance of roads and has given a lot of importance to it during the last three decades in spite of the high capital requirement in construction as well as the maintenance of roads. In addition to personalized transport, passenger road transport services are offered by public and private operators. There were about 73 million registered automobiles in India in 2003–2004, which included two wheelers (71.6 per cent), cars (13 per cent), buses (1 per cent), trucks (5 per cent) and other vehicles (9.4 per cent). Out of the 53 State Road Transport Undertakings operating in the country, 15 are operated by local operators and 38 are operated by state governments. Almost all states have facilitated the entry of private operators in passenger transport services.[9]

India has a long coastline on the east as well as the west. Therefore, transport through waterways has assumed significance. Ports became an important infrastructure in the country. India has 12 major ports and 200 minor and intermediate ports. The major ports are located at Chennai, Cochin,

Ennore, Kandla, Kolkata, Marmagao, Mumbai, New Mangalore, Paradip, Tuticorin and Visakhapatnam. These major ports handle nearly 75 per cent of India's port traffic. The major products being transported through these means are POL (petroleum and oil lubricants), coal, iron ore, fertilizers and raw materials, foodgrains, oils and other liquids. Traditionally, most ports in the world are owned by the public sector. But privatization of port facilities and services has now gathered momentum. An enabling policy framework has been put in place by the Government of India. Depending on the nature of the facility/service, private operators can enter into a service contract, a management contract, a concession agreement or a divestiture to operate port services. Areas opened up to the private sector on a Build, Operate and Transfer (BOT) basis include construction of cargo-handling berths and dry docks, container terminals and housing facilities and ship-repair facilities.[10]

The Indian Railways is one of the largest railway networks in the world. It has a network of 63,140 kilometres, connecting various parts of the country. Railways carried about 7,000 million passengers during 2008–2009. The passenger kilometres travelled during the year was 778 billion kilometres. In other words, the number of passengers travelled has grown more than four times, while the number of passenger kilometres has increased about eight times during the last fifty years. Goods transport is the major operation of the Indian Railways. Items such as coal, raw materials for steel plants, iron ore for exports, cement, foodgrains, fertilizers, mineral oils and so on are transported to various destinations from the originating points in the country. The earnings from the transport of goods carried constitute 70 per cent of the total revenues.

Railways is facing competition from other modes of transport. To face this competition, it has rationalized freight structure. Heavy investments are being made towards electrification, track modification, introduction of state-of-the-art technology for safety and security, modernization of railway coaches and so on. Improvement in passenger amenities has been given priority in recent years. Station amenities have been improved in many stations. Real-time train running information is provided to the passenger through Satellite Imaging for Rail Navigation (SIRMAN). The computerized passenger reservation system is the largest network in the world. As many as 32 million passengers avail this facility each month. Freight operations information is provided to all customers. Some steps have been taken to ensure safety in rail transport.

Civil aviation is another growing sector in Indian transport. This sector provides three categories of services: operational, infrastructural and regulatory-cum-developmental services. Operational services include domestic air services and international air services. Domestic air services are provided by Indian Airlines Limited and private airlines, operating both scheduled and non-scheduled services. International air services are provided by Air India Limited, Indian Airlines Limited and other international airlines, operating to and fro from India. Infrastructural facilities are taken care of by the Airports Authority of India. Private participation is significant in civil aviation

> *The transportation sector is showing great signs of development. Roadways and railways carry 95 per cent of the traffic in this country. Railways, a public sector monopoly,is the most profitable public sector company. Air transport has achieved an impressive growth; ports have also recorded a good progress.*

in India. There are 11 scheduled passenger operators and one cargo operator in the country. The combined fleet size was 407 aircraft according to the economic survey of 2008–09. There are also 99 non-scheduled operators with 241 aircrafts. The demand for air transport services increased sharply since the beginning of the 21st century until 2008. During 2008 the number of passengers declined by 5 per cent.[11] Due to the economic slowdown and steep rise in the cost of ATF (air turbine fuel), many operators have been facing trouble in recent times. Air India, the major public sector player, is the major sufferer of the crisis. The company is in deep crisis and a re-engineering programme is on the anvil as the Government of India has restructured the top management of the company by inducting private directors in the management board.

Telecommunications

Telecommunications is one of the fastest growing service industries in the world. The present era is described as the "information age." The need for the growth and development of telecommunications in any part of the world cannot be overemphasized. The industry has achieved tremendous progress in the developed world. In India, it is only during the last decade that progressive developments have taken place in this sector. India's telephone network is one of the largest in the world with a wide range of services such as fixed lines, cellular, Internet, paging and VSAT. The telecom service network expanded from about 84,000 connections (fixed line) at the time of independence to about 414 million working connections in February 2009. About 113.36 million telephones at the rate of more than 14 million were added every month during 2008–2009 (11months). There were 37.73 million fixed telephone lines and 376.12 mobile connections by February 2009.[12] The share of wireless phones increased from 24.3 per cent in March 2003 to 90.88 per cent in February 2009. The market share of the public sector in the fixed line segment was 86.71 per cent in 2008–09 while the wireless telephone segment was dominated by the private sector with 85.5 per cent market share during this period.[13]

In spite of the significant growth in the telecom sector in the recent past, the teledensity in India was abysmally low compared to other countries. Countries such as the United States, UK, Australia, Korea and Japan have a teledensity of more than 100 whereas India's teledensity stands at 35.65, far lower than the world average of 49.45.[14] Teledensity increased substantially during 1997–1998 to 2008–2009 from 1.90 to about 35.65. However, there is a wide gap between the urban and the rural sectors in terms of teledensity. The urban teledenstity in India increased from 5.80 per cent to 83.66 per cent whereas the rural teledensty increased from 0.4 per cent to 13.81 per cent during the period.[15]

The Government of India recognized the telecom sector as one of the prime movers of the economy. It has taken up many regulatory and policy initiatives towards establishing a world-class telecommunications infrastructure in India. All telecom operations in the country are under the control of the Ministry of Communications. The ministry is responsible for all major policy changes, planning, supervision and spectrum of control. The Department of Telecommunications (DoT) was formed in 1985, after its separation from the Department of Posts and Telecommunications. The department plays the role of a policy maker, planner, developer and an implementation body as far as telecommunications is concerned.

In order to reduce the burden of DoT as a service provider as well as a regulator, the Government of India formed the Telecom Regulatory Authority of India (TRAI), through an act in the Parliament, as an independent regulatory body for supervising telecom development in India. Bharat Sanchar Nigam Limited (BSNL) and Mahanagar Telephone Nigam Limited (MTNL) are the two public sector undertakings operating a wide range of telecom services.

Considering the pace of change in this sector, the Government of India has initiated some key policy changes.

Major Policy Initiatives After 2000

- National long distance (NLD) service was opened to operators with effect from 13 August 2002.
- National Frequency Allocation Policy 2002 was evolved.
- The monopoly of Videsh Sanchar Nigam Limited (VSNL) in international long distance (ILD) was terminated on 31 March 2002.
- A national Internet backbone (NIB) covering all states has been commissioned.
- The Indian Telegraph Act was amended for the establishment of USOF. Non-lapsable USOF was created on April 2002.
- The interconnection usage charge regime was introduced.
- Internet Service Providers (ISPs) allowed setting up submarine cable landing stations for international gateways for the Internet.
- The broadband policy was announced on 14 October 2004.
- ISPs have been permitted to use underground copper cables for establishing last mile linkages.
- FDI ceiling has been raised to 74 per cent for various telecom services.
- The operation of automated spectrum management was commenced in January 2005.
- The access service provider can provide Internet telephony, Internet services and broadband services. They can use the network of the NLD/ILD service.
- Internet Protocol based Virtual Private Network service is permitted to ISPs.
- Delicensing has been done of 2.40–2.4835 GHz frequency band for the indoor and outdoor use and 5.15–5.13 GHZ frequency band for the indoor use.

Targets for The Future

- To reach a telecom subscriber base of 600 million by 2012.
- To provide 200 million rural telephone connections by 2012, that is, to reach a rural teledensity of 25 per cent.
- To provide telephone connections on demand across the country at an affordable price.
- To reach a target of 20 million broadband connections and 40 million Internet connections by the end of 2010 as envisaged in the Broadband Policy 2004.
- To provide broadband connections on demand across the country by 2012.
- To provide Third Generation (3G) services in all cities/towns with more than 0.1 million population.
- To facilitate introduction of mobile TV.
- To provide broadband connectivity to every secondary school health centre, GP on demand.
- To make India a hub for telecom equipment manufacturing by facilitating establishment of telecom-specific SEZs.

Telecommunications has tremendous growth potential. The rapid growth in cellular, radio paging, value-added services, Internet and global mobile communication by satellite services, besides basic telephone services, is an indicator of the bright future of this sector.

> *"Telecom revolution is the major landmark in the development of the economy. Particularly cellular services recorded a substantial growth. The teledensity increased impressively in urban India, and in the rural segment it leaves much to be desired.*

IT and ITeS

The rapidly growing software industry has achieved a turnover of $ 8.3 billion during the last decade of the 20th century with an average growth rate of more than 50 per cent. The main reason for this consistent growth is the cost advantage that India offers compared to other developed and developing countries. Indian software companies provide high-quality, low-cost software solutions using state-of-the-art technologies. Indians have proved their expertise in software technology and services and are known throughout the world as excellent software professionals.

Trade in IT and IT-enabled (BPO) services has been the major driver of growth in exports in recent years. The turnover of this sector is estimated to have increased 10-fold between 1998–1999 and 2007–2008,[16] from USD 6 billion to nearly USD 64 billion. The growth of exports is phenomenal; the value of the exports rose from USD 2.7 billion to over USD 40 billion. The contribution of this sector to the GDP has been on the increase. It was 1 per cent in 1999–2000 and became 4 per cent in 2007–2008.

In spite of the slowdown in the software industry in the United States, Indian companies could defend their business by expanding into newer markets and retaining their earlier customers. Indian software companies have constantly strived to stay abreast of global technology trends by embracing new technologies that are gaining pre-eminence. Indian companies strengthened off-shore services to continue their dominance in the software export sector. In 2007, India was the leader in both the IT and BPO offshore segments accounting for an estimated 64 per cent of offshore IT spends and 41 per cent of offshore BPO spends.

Computer software is the thrust area in the growth plan of the Indian economy. The focus is to develop the industry for export as well as for domestic needs. On the domestic front also, software industry registered a healthy growth rate. It is estimated that IT and BPO industries have a large growth potential as only about 20 per cent of the potentially addressable market had been captured in 2007. The addressable market in the global offshore IT industry is estimated to be of the order of USD 220–250 billion and in the BPO segment to be of the order of USD 160–190 billion.

The IT sector has contributed significantly to the progress of the country. The technological breakthroughs and innovations in applications benefited various other sectors in manufacturing and service. The role of the sector in the increased productivity is well registered. The domestic IT market in India was valued at approximately INR 54 billion in 2006. This segment has grown at a CAGR of 19.7 per cent since 2002.[17] The major strength of this sector is the availability of large pool of English-speaking engineering graduates in the country. The employment in this sector grew from about 200,000 in 1997–1998 to over 1.6 million in 2006–2007. Taking into consideration the bright prospects of this sector, the central and the state governments have provided support through many positive initiatives: Export Oriented Units (EOUs), Software Technology Parks (STPs), Special Economic Zones (SEZs) and Electronic Hardware Technology Parks (EHTPs). The Export Promotion Capital Goods (EPCG) scheme, the Star Export House Scheme & Target Plus Scheme, services tax exemptions and certain specific customs and excise duty exemptions for inputs and specified capital goods for IT hardware and software are the major fiscal incentives to this sector.[18]

> *"IT and BPO services have been the major drivers of growth in export in recent years. The turnover recorded a 10-fold increase during 1998–1999 to 2007–2008. India is the leader in both IT and BPO offshore segments in the world."*

Electricity

We cannot live without energy. Electricity is the most convenient and relatively cheaper source of energy. It plays a crucial role both in the industrial and agricultural sectors. The development of electricity is concomitant with the nation's economic and industrial development. Recognizing its importance the Government of India has taken several measures during the planned era for its development.

Electricity is generated in India using hydro, thermal and nuclear sources. By the end of 2008–2009, the total power generated by the three sources was 723.80 billion kWh. Out of the total capacity, hydroelectricity accounts for 113.08 billion kWh, thermal electricity accounts for 590.10 billion kWh and nuclear electricity, a relatively new source, accounts for 14.71 billion kWh. Though hydel power generation is cheaper as compared to other sources, its dependence on water resources compelled the country to go for thermal power. This is the reason why thermal power occupies the lion's share of the total power generated.

The consumers of electricity can be broadly categorized into six groups: domestic consumers, commercial consumers, industrial consumers, traction, agricultural consumers and others. Industry is the major consumer of electricity, followed by agriculture and domestic consumers.

Electricity in India is generated and managed by the State Electricity Boards (SEBs), the central sector and the private sector. The State Electricity Boards, which shoulder the major responsibility of the sector, are financially sick and suffer from managerial inefficiencies. The large amount of dues owed by SEBs to the central power sector undertakings was a major impediment to the development of the power sector. The private sector is a recent entry to this sector. It could not, so far, make inroads into the sector due to many procedural and social factors involved.

The end user of electricity experiences many problems in the country. Scheduled power cuts, unscheduled outages and incorrect voltage are common in most states, leading to enormous disruptions in the economic life. People are dissatisfied with the performance of the sector. The demand–supply gap is increasing day by day. Transmission and distribution (T&D) losses is one of the serious problems being faced by the sector. The following are some reasons for such losses: energy sold at low voltage, sparsely distributed loads over large rural areas, inadequate investment in the distribution system, improper billing and theft, besides indiscriminate grid extension despite low load densities. According to the Eleventh Five Year Plan, T&D losses for the country as a whole are estimated to be in the range of 35 to 45 per cent as against the acceptable loss of 18 per cent.

The government has taken up an energy conservation campaign in order to direct the use of electricity for right purposes. It is estimated that one unit of energy saved at consumption saves 3 units of fresh capacity addition. The Energy Conservation Act 2001, was enacted to provide an institutional mechanism and to develop the delivery mechanism for large-scale penetration of energy efficiency in the country.

The Government of India has taken up Mission 2012 with the aim to provide power to all. A comprehensive plan has been developed to address all the problems confronting the sector. With these initiatives, we can hope for more power generation.

Postal Services

The Indian postal system is one of the most extensive networks in the world. The system provides communication, transportation and other services. Except for courier services, postal operations in India are still a government monopoly. The Indian postal system is the largest postal system in the world. The Indian postal system has 155,000 post offices and outlets established in various parts of the country. It is, in particular, the best linking system in rural India as 90 per cent of postal outlets are in rural areas. In a country with more than a billion people, postal service outlets are offered for every 7,160 inhabitants, covering an area of 21.2 square kilometres on an average. In addition,

5,405 *panchayat sanchar sewa kendras* are also providing basic postal facilities in rural areas. Compared to China, Indonesia and even the United States, the Indian postal system has a greater penetration of the market. The mail profile has changed in recent years significantly, with increased volume of mails to B2C and B2B segments.

In order to improve the speed and volume of money-order transmission, the Department of Posts introduced Very Small Aperture Terminal (VSAT) centres. Many post offices have been computerized. The department has joined hands with the private sector as well for providing quality services. The post office savings bank has introduced a number of new financial services in collaboration with IDBI principal, Prudential ICICI, Western Union Financial Services Limited and so on. Nearly 210 million people used India post to save INR 3,540 billion during 2008–2009.[19] It partnered with Invest India Company to train and educate the employees of post offices as well as its customers on various issues relating to financial markets. The department is modernizing mail offices to provide a proper work environment for improving ergonomics and ambience of post offices. India post presently is served by as many as 0.54 million employees to run its operations throughout the country.

A major problem of the postal department is its deteriorating financial position. Most postal services are heavily subsidized, taking the social and welfare issues into consideration. The total expenditure in percentage of receipts for posts was 123 per cent in India as compared to 101 per cent in UK and 102 per cent in the US. The financial position of the postal department is not going to improve unless the prices of services are determined on a commercial basis. With the emergence of the private sector as a player in the areas of courier service and express service and with the development of information technology applications in every field, the Department of Posts stands to face competition.[20]

The Department of Posts is adapting itself to the changing market dimensions in spite of financial impediments. Competition from courier services and other service companies is becoming more intense day by day. However, the department has no parallel challenge in terms of its huge network connecting every part of India. The objective of the eleventh Five Year Plan is to work towards making India Post a major player in logistics and supply chain management by providing distribution channels, inventory management, packaging services, warehousing, transportation and time-definite distribution programmes. It is proposed to establish logistics centres in metro cities and major business towns and a logistics centre for international operations. India Post also needs to enter the international parcel and logistics business and function as the logistics partner for providing event-specific services for trade fairs, commonwealth games and state-sponsored events.[21]

Tourism

India has all the features to be a preferred destination for tourists. It is the second most populous country with a land frontier of 15,200 kilometres and a coastline of about 6,000 kilometres. The country has a rich cultural heritage. There are a number of places in the country of scenic beauty—forests, landscapes, waterfalls, mountain ranges, lakes, rivers, seashores, temples, holy places, historical monuments, which make India an exciting and fascinating destination.

> *India is considered to have a great potential for tourism services. Tourism in India has two dimensions: domestic tourism and international tourism. Domestic tourism occupies mighty share and there are a few million foreign tourists visiting the country every year.*

Tourism in India has two dimensions: domestic tourism and international tourism. Domestic tourism occupies a mighty share of the total tourism of India. India attracts a few million foreign tourists every year (see Table 4.4). The foreign tourist arrivals increased from 2.726 million in 2003 to 4.977 million in 2007. The country is earning foreign exchange resources from this sector. The sector's contribution increased from USD 4,463 million in 2003 to USD 11,956 million in 2007. Tourism in India has a variety of tourism products: heritage and culture tourism (with 26 and 14 potential world heritage sites at the core); ecotourism (wildlife in national parks); adventure tourism (mountain climbing, mountain trekking, river-based sports including rafting, and skiing); wellness (Ayurveda and yoga institutes in Kerala and Rishikesh) and medical tourism (being developed by private sector hospital chains); beach tourism (centred around Goa); religious tourism (e.g., Varanasi, Haridwar, Tirupati, Bodh Gaya and Ajmer); MICE (meetings, incentives, conferences and exhibitions) tourism; desert tourism and rural tourism.

Tourism is an export-oriented services sector. This sector has the potential to create substantial employment opportunities not only for sattled personnel but also for unskilled and semi-skilled workers. The National Council for Applied Economic Research (NCAER) estimated that this sector provides employment to 51.1 million people in the country. Recognizing the potential for the growth of this sector the Government of India has been taking several measures to develop tourism. Several state governments are also actively involved and are investing a lot of money on various tourism projects. The

Table 4.4 Foreign Tourist Arrivals and Estimated Foreign Exchange Earnings

Years	Arrivals	% Change over the Previous Year	Foreign Exchange Earning in INR million	% Change over the Previous Year	Foreign Exchange Earning in Million USD	% Change over the Previous Year
2003	2,726,214	14.3	207,290	37.6	4,463	43.8
2004	3.457,477	26.8	279,440	34.8	6,170	38.2
2005	3,918,610	13.3	331,230[a]	18.5	7,493	21.4
2006	4,447,167	13.5	4037,580	21.9	8,934	19.2
2007[b]	4,977,193	12.4	494,130[a]	22.4	11,956	33.8

[a]Revised estimates [b]Estimates

Source: *Ministry of Tourism, Government of India, Tourism Statistics, 2007 at a Glance.*

department of tourism, the ministerial wing of the Government of India, is working to make tourism the most prominent services sector in the country. It has divided the country into six regions—north, north-east, east, south, west and central region. In order to promote and facilitate the flow of foreign tourists into the country, overseas offices were established in six countries: the United States, UK, Germany, Australia, Japan and UAE. The tourism sector is open to the private sector. Private participation is encouraged by the union as well as the state governments in almost all tourism projects taken up in recent years.

Tourism is the world's largest export-oriented service, accounting for about 8 per cent of the total world exports or more than 30 per cent of international trade in services. Though India's share is very less compared to even a small country such as Singapore, tourism is the third largest foreign exchange earner for the country. Tourism is a dynamic field and is subject to constant changes caused by consumer as well as societal trends. One of the reasons identified for the slow growth of the sector in India is the lack of professionalism in marketing tourism services. Hence, a strategic approach in the marketing of tourism services is necessary to achieve good results.

Banking

Banks are established to identify the needs in the society for financial help, to device and deliver products and to earn profits for their efforts. The banking sector in India comprises commercial banks and cooperative banks. Commercial banks have been in existence for many decades. They mobilize savings and make them available to various sections of the society, including individuals, associations, large and small industries and trading units. To promote saving among farmers and to meet their credit needs for cultivation, primary cooperative credit societies or banks have been set up in villages. To support these institutions, Central Cooperative Banks and State Cooperative Banks have also been established. The funds of the Reserve Bank of India meant for the agricultural sector actually pass through these institutions. The cooperative credit movement has spread to urban areas also and there are many Urban Cooperative Banks established under State Cooperative Banks.

The Indian banking system has a very long history. Though money lending and indigenous banking in one form or the other was in operation in ancient India, modern banking is a product of the British rule. The Bank of Hindustan, the first joint-sector bank of India, was established in Calcutta in 1770 by one of the agency houses. The Bank of Bengal and two other presidency banks—the Bank of Bombay and the Bank of Madras—received their charters in 1809, 1840 and 1843, respectively. The year 1921 witnessed the taking over of the business of the three presidency banks by the Imperial Bank of India. The Reserve Bank of India was constituted and became operational in April 1935. The World War II period saw a proliferation of banking institutions in the country, and by 1947, 558 commercial banks were operating in India. As a sequel to the failure of the Palai Central Bank in 1960, the Reserve Bank tightened its control over the commercial banks by making several amendments to the banking laws and carried out tidying operations. The 1960s also witnessed a process of voluntary and forced amalgamations, along with voluntary liquidation of banking institutions in the country. The most momentous event relating to the banking industry was the nationalization of 14 major banks in July 1969. Subsequently, widespread branch expansion, functional diversity, introduction of an array of schemes and programmes based on the recommendation of various committees and study groups took place. The spirit of experimentation and the degree of transformation recorded by the Indian banking system in the aftermath of nationalization received wide appreciation. The main objectives were to extend the banking network in rural areas and to provide assistance to the agriculture and small-scale sectors.

By the end of June 1969, there were 89 commercial banks operating with 8,262 offices, with the scheduled commercial banks accounting for deposits of INR 46,460 million and advances of INR 35,990 million. Subsequent years saw Indian banks respond to specific targets and sub-targets relating to the priority sector credit and credit deposit ration in rural and semi-urban branches. Banks started associating themselves with poverty alleviation programmes. In 1980, six more large private sector banks were nationalized, bringing the number of nationalized banks to 20. Public sector banks acquired a share of 80 to 90 per cent of the total business. Indian banks have emerged as a prominent instrument of socio-economic development in the country, ensuring effective distribution among different sectors. The banks elicit interest particularly from the third world countries.

Public sector banks play an important role in the economic development of the country. In the post-liberalization era, that is, after 1991, revolutionary changes took place in the banking sector. Banks started concentrating on exploring new business opportunities rather than generating revenues from conventional streams. The real motivating force behind the new economy drive was the information technology explosion. The new entrants, being adequately equipped technologically, were able to lure the metropolitan markets with their innovative products. Public sector banks faced grim and fierce competition that forced them to make the transition from the "brick-and-mortar" network to the "bricks-and-clicks" scenario.

> *"The banking sector in India consists of the public sector, private sector, cooperative and foreign banks. The nationalization of major banks helped the economy achieve the balanced growth. The changes in technology and the ever-increasing competition are forcing the banks to provide high-quality services."*

Recognizing that nationalized banks need to augment their capital base to cope with the changing operational environment, the government has permitted banks to access the capital market, both at home and abroad. However, the amount of capital which can be raised by nationalized banks from the capital market has been constrained by the minimum shareholding of 51 per cent by the Central Government. The last decade of the 20th century witnessed an explosion in information technology throughout the world. As a result the Internet and e-commerce have arrived in a big way in the banking sector. Most banks have adapted themselves to the changing environment and are attempting to move their customers from traditional banking branches to electronic channels such as ATMs, PCs and mobile phones. Indian banks have a gigantic task of striking an appropriate balance between banking operations of international standards and commitment to social welfare. There is

UTI

Unit Trust of India is a public-sector organization that was created by the UTI Act, 1963 to facilitate the flow of investment from the public to capital market. For almost two decades, UTI remained the sole vehicle for investment in the capital market by the citizens of India. In the mid-1980s, when public-sector banks were allowed to offer mutual fund services, UTI successfully sold the concept of investment in the capital market and achieved commendable progress during 1990s. The flagship scheme UTI-64, UTI-Master Share and Master Plus were the most successful fund schemes. A few bad decisions affected the image of UTI and the business results in 2001. The Government of India came to its rescue. The UTI Act was repealed and UTI was bifurcated into UTI Mutual Fund and Specific Understanding of UTI (SUUTI). However, UTI lost its market dominance rapidly.

UTI Mutual Fund, under a new management, quickly responded to market requirements by initiating turnaround measures. It focused on regaining investor confidence, which was vital for success. It built a large distribution network of 103 branches, 439 chief representatives and over 28,000 certified agents to promote and develop the business. In addition, it tied up with various banks and institutions to help increase the volume of business. India Post was also used as one of the distributors. The company had over 70 schemes in the domestic market and had the largest investor base of over 9 million by June 2008. The company regained its revenue earning capacity and financial strength. The success in the domestic front led the company to extend its operations to foreign countries. Currently, UTI MF has its operations in Japan, Singapore, London, Dubai, and Bahrain.

a need to reset socio-economic objectives in the larger interest of the nation by taking into consideration factors such as severe competition, customer sophistication, business diversification, product/service innovation, asset and liability mismatch, increased business risks (Internet risk, market risk, credit risk, payment risk and so on), NPA menace, capital restructuring, cyber/e-banking, e-commerce and universal banking.

Indian banks have performed well in terms of growth, asset quality and profitability since 2001. The banking index has grown at a compounded annual rate of over 51 per cent compared to 21 per cent growth in the market index over the last ten years. Policy makers such as RBI, Ministry of Finance and other regulatory entities have helped strengthen this sector.

Healthcare

Healthcare is one of the top priorities of individuals as well as the government. India has two streams of medical care—indigenous or traditional medicine and modern medicine. The indigenous/traditional medical system has two wings—Ayurveda and Homeopathy. There are about 350,000 Ayurvedic practitioners in the country. India is believed to have the largest number of homeopathic practitioners in the world.

European doctors, who were employed by the erstwhile East India company, introduced modern medicine in India during the 17th century. However, modern medicine became popular only in the 19th century. Allopathic medicine became dominant and a number of hospitals were established during the period.

India has built up a vast healthcare infrastructure and manpower at primary, secondary and tertiary levels. The vast network of public health institutions in the country includes three types of service units in rural areas. As per the report of the high-level group on the services sector of 2008, there were 3,910 community health centres, 22,669 primary health centres and 144,988 sub-centres in rural areas. In urban areas, 7,663 government hospitals rendered healthcare services.[22]

Improvement in the health status of the population is a major thrust area for the government under the social development programmes. The expenditure on healthcare constitutes 5.2 per cent of the GDP. The department of health formulated the National Health Policy 2002 with an objective of achieving an acceptable standard of good health in the country.

Private sector corporate hospitals offer quality services with the state-of-the-art technology. The entry of the corporate sector has brought in a dynamic shift in healthcare services. Having an assured growth in demand due to the increasing population, rise in pollution levels, emergence of communicable diseases, epidemics and falling living conditions, the healthcare sector has prospects of high level growth. There has been considerable corporate investment already in hospitals in the country with the help of FIIs and foreign equity, and this is likely to continue. Some of the big names are Apollo Hospitals, Fortis Healthcare, Max Healthcare and Wockhardt. Apollo is the world's third largest and India's largest health provider, followed by Fortis. Wockhardt, an established name in cardiac care, has an international alliance with Harvard Medical International. Max Healthcare is another large player.[23]

> *Healthcare services have grown in many dimensions. The entry of corporate hospitals in the private sector has provided quality services with the support of state-of-the art technology. Health tourism is on the rise and India has become an attractive destination for medical value travel. Telemedicine is another phenomenon, and health insurance is picking up as a support service.*

Another business dimension of the Indian healthcare services is health tourism. India has become an attractive destination for the medical value travel. People from SAARC countries are visiting the country in large numbers for the purpose. The NRIs settled in the United States and UK are availing the healthcare services in India. The alternative system of medicine, Ayurveda in particular, enhanced the attractiveness of this services sector. Tourists, domestic as well as foreign, undergo treatment for fitness as well as for many types of chronic diseases. Kerala is the most attractive destination for ayurvedic medical services.

A recent phenomenon in this sector is telemedicine. Telemedicine can be real time (synchronous) or at a later point in time (asynchronous). Synchronous telemedicine requires the presence of two sets of medical professionals, one at either end, present at the same time with a "tele" link between them, which allows a real-time interaction to take place. There are devices, such as tele-opthalmoscope or tele-stethoscope, which can be attached to computers, or the videoconferencing equipment, which aid in interactive examination. Asynchronous telemedicine does not require the simultaneous presence of medical professionals at both ends. It involves acquiring and storing medical data such as X-rays, pathology slides or ECG, which can be viewed by the specialists at the other end offline, at a time convenient to the latter.[24] Telemedicine offers high market potential for expert healthcare service. The remotest rural parts of the country can access the services of expert medical professionals through telemedicine.

Health insurance is picking up slowly as a support to the development of market for healthcare services in India. Several health insurance schemes are available to the people from many service companies.

Education

Education is a critical input for the development of human resources. India, with a population of over a billion, cannot afford to ignore this area. The Government of India has been striving hard to promote education in the country after independence. Due to continuous efforts, the literacy rate, which was only 18.33 per cent in 1951, rose to 65.4 per cent in 2001. Among males, the literacy rate was 75.85 per cent and among females the literacy rate was 54.16 per cent at the end of 2001. In the 11th plan period, an amount of INR 2,700 billion was allotted to this sector. Out of this about 50 percent was allocated to elementary education and literacy, 20 percent to secondary education and 30 percent to higher education including technical education.

In India, the offerings of educational services have been classified into different levels such as primary level, secondary level, high school and junior college level, degree college for general education and professional education and universities, deemed universities and institutes of national importance. There are 18,064 colleges and 367 universities/deemed universities and institutions of national importance in the country. The primary schools, secondary schools, high schools and junior colleges have been established through out the country.

As per the 2001 census, 193 million were in the age group of 6 to 14 years and out of them nearly 81 per cent attended schools at the primary, middle and upper primary level. The number of registered teachers at the elementary level was 3.2 million, of which female teachers accounted for 37 per cent (2000–2001). The pupil teacher ratio was 1:43 at the primary education level, and at the upper primary level the ratio was 1:38. The student enrolment at the secondary level was about 28.8 million. Technical and professional education plays a vital role in developing quality manpower in the country. In 2008, there were 2,388 approved engineering colleges at the degree level established in the country. Besides this, more than 1,100 institutes imparted masters' courses on computer applications. The number of medical colleges and dental colleges was 320 and 301, respectively. There were 1,231 approved management institutes imparting management courses at the post-graduate level by the end of 2008.[25]

The Government of India has taken up a number of programmes to achieve full literacy in the country. The Constitution was amended in 2002 to achieve the goal of education by making free and compulsory education a fundamental right for all the children in the age group of 6 to 14 years. Towards the fulfillment of the goal, *Sarva Shiksha Abhiyan* was launched in association with the states. In order to impart education to adults, adult education programmes were taken up throughout the country. Though the number of out-of-school children in the age group of 6 to 14 brought down from 32 million in 2001–2002 to 7.1 million in July 2006, the data was far from the set objectives. The general enrolment ratio in secondary education is just more than 50 per cent. This speaks of high potential in this area of business. The higher education scenario leaves much to be desired. The university and college enrolments in the country account for only 11 per cent (18–23 age group). When compared with developed countries, with an enrolment of 54.65 per cent and the world average of 23.2 per cent, the position of India is not convincing. The quality of higher education in the country is another area of concern. Though there are regulating bodies such as University Grants Commission (UGC), All India Council for Teacher Education (AICTE) and National Council for Teacher Education (NCTE) at national level and state level to regulate the services, the quality of the education attracts criticisms from many quarters. To promote quality standards in higher education institutions' the UGC established the National Assessment and Accreditation Council (NAAC) to undertake accreditation of institutions. Although the impact of the NAAC on educational institutions is impressive, much has to be done in this direction.

> *"Education is the key driver of an economy. Education services in India are offered mostly by the government. The private sector participation is increasing but not to the level of the requirement. Only 11 per cent of the youth are having access to higher education. The National Knowledge Commission suggested useful measures to promote these services at all levels."*

The National Knowledge Commission constituted by the Government of India in 2005 recommended measures for the improvement of this sector. The following are the main recommendations:

- Passing a central legislation affirming the right to education
- Teaching English as a language along with the first language
- Setting up a National Translation Mission
- Setting up an Independent National commission on libraries
- Creating of national web-based portals on key sectors to serve as a single window for information
- Developing web-based network connecting all healthcare establishments
- Bringing about general changes in the school system to encourage decentralization, local autonomy in the management of schools, and flexibility of disbursal of funds
- Creating of 1,500 universities by 2015, partly by restructuring the existing ones
- Launching a massive science outreach programme, upgrading available infrastructure, revitalizing the teaching profession and revamping teacher training at all levels
- Replacing regulation in all professional education streams including medical, legal, management and engineering education, by subgroups on different streams under the proposed independent regulator
- Changing the focus of distance to a national ICT infrastructure, improving regulatory structures, developing web-based common open resources, establishing a credit bank and providing a national testing service.

The central government envisaged a massive expansion of the institutions of higher learning and technical education in the XIth plan. The major initiatives were:

- Central assistance for setting up 370 new colleges and 30 new central universities
- Expansion of intake capacity in the existing institutions with UGC additional funding for 166 universities and 5,625 colleges and support to the hitherto uncovered universities (150) and colleges (8,775) in partnership with states
- Expansion and upgradation of 200 technical institutions in the states
- Expansion of intake capacity of centrally funded institutions of excellence (IITs, IIMs, NITs, IIITs and NITTRs)
- Upgrading of seven technical universities
- Setting up of new technical institutions (8 IITs, 7 IIMs, 5 IISERs, 2 SPAs, 10 NITs, 20 IITs, and 50 centres for training and research in frontier areas).

Though the major responsibility of providing educational services is on the shoulders of the government, the role of the private sector can't be overemphasized. The private sector has entered at all levels and focuses on imparting quality education. The growth in population and the changing dynamics of environment at macro- and micro-levels promises a high level of growth prospects for the educational services in the country. Not only the higher and middle-income groups, but a significant portion of the lower income groups in urban as well as rural areas has recognized the importance of education and particularly quality education. They are prepared to invest to their maximum possible capacity on the children's education. The liberal financing by banks and other financial institutions further facilitates the growth of this sector. In spite of several impediments such as school dropouts, infrastructural constraints, quality variations, lack of proper vision and financial problems for public institutions and universities, this sector is set to reach new heights each year.

Entertainment and Media Services

Entertainment and media services, one of the oldest in the country, comprise films, radio, music, live entertainment, advertising and television. The performance of this sector is highly impressive during the last two decades and it is expected to grow at a CAGR of 18 per cent until the end of 2010 and beyond. The growth of this sector during 2004–2006 and the estimated growth up to 2011 are shown in Table 4.5.

The revenue share of various sub-sectors[26] of entertainment and media services are shown in Table 4.6.

The Indian film industry produces more than 1,000 films every year. The broadcasting sector which includes radio and television is marching ahead.

> *Entertainment and media services have a great influence on the people of the country. This sector has recorded an impressive growth, and projections are highly favourable to this sector. The Indian film industry has achieved greater penetration in the country and is finding markets outside also.*

Table 4.5 Growth of the Indian Entertainment and Media Industry (INR million)

Annual Growth	2004 Revenue	2005 Revenue	2006 Revenue (E)	2011 Revenue (F)	CAGR
Television	128,700	158,000	191,200	519,000	
Annual Growth (%)		23	21	20	22
Filmed Entertainment	59,900	68,100	84,500	175,000	
Annual Growth (%)		14	24	20	16
Radio	2,400	3,200	5,000	17,000	
Annual Growth (%)		33	56	21	28
Music	6,700	7,000	7,200	8,700	
Annual Growth (%)		4	3	9	4
Live Entertainment	7,000	8,000	9,000	19,000	
Annual Growth (%)		14	13	6	16
Entertainment Industry#	204,700	244,300	296,900	738,700	
Annual Growth (%)		19	22	20	
Print media	87,800	109,500	127,900	232,000	
Annual Growth (%)		25	17	13	13
OOH advertisement	8,500	9,000	10,000	21,500	
Annual Growth (%)		6	11	13	17
Internet Advertisement	600	1,000	1,600	9,500	
Annual Growth (%)		67	60	16	43
Total Entertainment and Media Industry[a]	301,600	363,800	436,400	1,001,700	
Annual Growth Rate (%)		21	20	18	18

Source: *Industry estimates and PwC analysis/Federation of Indian Chambers of Commerce and Industry (FICCI): Indian Entertainment and Media Industry, March 2007.*

Note: E = Estimates; F = Forecasted

[a]The figures taken above include only the legitimate revenues in each segment. Revenues from the animation and gaming segments have not been included in the industry size as these are traditionally included in the Indian IT and software revenues

Table 4.6 Revenue Shares of the Entertainment Market in India

Sub-sectors	2006 (%)	2011(%)
Television	45	51
Flamed Entertainment	19	18
Print Media	29	23
Radio	1	2
Music	2	1
Live Entertainment	2	2
Out-of-Home Advertising	2	2
Internet Advertising	0	1

Source: *Industry estimates and PwC analysis/FICCI: Indian Entertainment and Media Industry, March 2007.*

Television has reached 108 million homes (with 68 million cable and satellite homes). Direct-to-home (DTH) subscription is around 5.6 million (Doordarshan share 4.0 million and private DTH 1.6 million). The number of radio sets was 132 million. There are 229 AIR channels and 42 FM stations.[27]

This sector is emerging as a vibrant business domain. The opening up of international markets and corporatization of the film and the television sectors attract huge investments and highly talented creative personnel into this

The Times Group

The Times Group is the largest media services conglomerate in India. The 170-year old group is known as the market driver in all media platforms. Started in 1838 with the launch of *The Bombay Times* and *Journal of Commerce*, the group passed through many milestones by adapting itself to the changes in the business environment of media services within and outside the country. The success of its brands is the testimony for the competence of the management in this highly creative and challenging business arena. The group brands include: The Times of India—world's largest broadsheet English daily; The Economic Times—India's largest and world's second largest financial daily; Navbharat Times—popular hindi daily newspaper; Maharashtra Times—popular marathi daily newspaper; Mumbai Mirror—leading morning newspaper in Mumbai; Radio Mirchi—India's largest FM radio network; Planet M—India's largest chain of music stores; Zoom—lifestyle television channel; Times Now—television news channel (in association with Reuters); Femina—India's largest women's magazine (published in association with BBC); Filmfare—India's largest English film magazine (published in association with BBC); Times Jobs—India's leading job portal; Simply Marry—India's leading matrimonial portal; Magic Bricks—India's premier real estate portal and Remit2Home—caters to the global remittance market. The group offers services to varied segments of the market with differentiated products. The group launched its Web portal as early as in 1999 to create world-class media services. With continuous innovation as its driving philosophy, the group has developed benchmark standards in media services in India.

sector. The advancements in filming and broadcasting technologies and the growing use of the Internet in the country have put this sector on the road to development.

Retailing

Retailing is recognized as the sunrise sector of India in the 21st century. Though retailing is a very old service and widely spread in India, the sector has caught the attention of big corporations in recent years. Though India has a high density of retailing, it stands poor with less than 5 per cent in organized retailing. When compared to developed and many developing countries, this share of organized retailing is very poor. The companies into this business should address the changing needs of Indian consumers by providing a good buying and shopping experience, adding up to a satisfying experience for their customers. The high growth rates registered in this business during the last five years signalled a high growth potential to these services. The trends of retailing are discussed in "Services Marketing Insight: Organized Retailing-The New Growth Frontier" in Chapter 3.

SUMMARY

- The planners of the Indian economy developed a growth model by identifying three sectors: primary sector which represents agriculture, secondary sector which represents manufacturing sector and tertiary sector which represents services.
- The services sector was given greater emphasis from the sixth Five Year Plan onwards.
- The contribution of services sector to the GDP of the country was 29 per cent at the beginning of the planned era. The share increased to 57 per cent by the end of 2008–2009.
- Trade, communications, real estate, public administration and transport are the major contributors in the services sector.
- In 2004, the services sector contributed a 23.4 per cent of the total employment and was next only to agriculture in this respect.
- There are many reasons for the growth of services. The major reasons include economic affluence, changing role of women, cultural changes, IT revolution, conservation of natural resources, development of markets, unbundling corporations, increased consciousness of healthcare, economic liberalization, migration and export potential for Indian services.
- The key service businesses in India are insurance, transport, telecommunications, software, electricity, education, postal services, tourism, banking, healthcare, entertainment and media services and retailing.
- India is marching ahead with the consistent growth of services in many domains.
- The services sector is contributing substantially to the government exchequer besides earning foreign exchange resources.
- The policy measures of the government, particularly liberalization, privatization and globalization gave required boost to the services sector in India.

KEY TERMS

Economic growth *62*
Economic affluence *64*
Economic liberalization *67*
Export potential *67*
Gross domestic product *60*
Hidden services *60*
Primary sector *60*
Secondary sector *60*
Service tax *69*
Tertiary sector *60*
Unbundling corporations *66*

BRIEF QUESTIONS

1. Write a brief note on the insurance business in India.
2. Explain the growth and development of transport services in India.
3. What are the recent changes in telecom services?
4. "Indian software services are booming." Comment.
5. What are the problems of electricity services in India?
6. Briefly explain the status of postal services in India.
7. What are the challenges faced by the Indian banking sector?
8. How can healthcare services be developed in India?

ESSAY QUESTIONS

1. State the reasons for the growth of the services sector in India.
2. What are the key service businesses in India? What is their contribution to the growth of the sector?
3. What is the contribution of services sector to the growth and development of the Indian economy?
4. What are the prospects for educational services in India?

ASSIGNMENTS

1. Entertainment and media services have grown rapidly in recent years. Now the markets outside the country are accessible to this sector. Corporatization and collaborations with foreign companies have expanded the scope of the business. You are required to search the secondary sources of information to find out:
   (a) The changing trends in the business.
   (b) The critical factors to be addressed for the balanced growth of this sector.
2. The gap between demand and supply of electricity services is ever expanding in the country. The central as well as state governments are trying to fill the gap by taking various measures. You are required to find out through secondary sources of information:
   (a) The status of these services in various states of the country.
   (b) What are the alternative sources of energy available and their ability to solve the problem?

REFERENCES

1 ENS Economic Bureau, "Higher Investments Can Boost Growth to 10%: Goldman Sachs," *Indian Express*, January 25, 2007.

2 Dinesh Narayanan, "India to Overtake United States by 2050: Report," *The Times of India*, January 24, 2007.

3 C. Rangarajan et al. , "Revisiting Employment and Growth," *ICRA Bulletin—Money & Finance* 3(2); data sourced from NSSO 2004–05, based on 61st Round Survey, 2007.

4 Directorate of General Employment and Training, *Quarterly Employment Review*, Ministry of Labour, Government of India, Central Statistical Organization, *Women And Men In India*, 2007.

5 www.irdaindia.org.

6 www.licindia.com.

7 www.assocham.org.

8 *Economic Times*,"India's General Insurance Penetration Level at 0.60 Per Cent of Its GDP: Report," *The Economic Times*, 21 July 2009.

9 Eleventh Five Year Plan, Planning Commission, Government of India, www.planningcommission.nic.in.

10 Economic Survey 2008–09, Government of India, www.indiabudget.nic.in.

11 Ibid.

12 Department of Telecommunications (2007), www.dot.gov.in.

13 TRAI Annual Report 2006–07, www.trai.gov.in.

14 International Telecommunication Union, referred in Eleventh Five Year Plan, Planning Commission, Government of India.
15 TRAI Annual Report 2006–07, www.trai.gov.in.
16 Report of the High Level Group on Service Sector, Planning Commission, Government of India, (March 2008), p. 51.
17 Eleventh Five Year Plan, Planning Commission, Government of India, www.planningcommission.nic.in.
18 Report of the High Level Group on Service Sector, Planning Commission, Government of India (March 2008), p. 60.
19 www.indiapost.gov.in.
20 Ibid.
21 Eleventh Five Year Plan, Planning Commission, Government of India, www.planningcommission.nic.in.
22 Report of the High Level Group on Service Sector, Planning Commission, Government of India (March 2008), p. 96.
23 Ibid, p. 98.
24 Ibid, p. 102.
25 www.pib.nic.in.
26 Industry Estimates and PWC Analysis/FICCI: Indian Entertainment and Media Industry, March 2007.
27 Eleventh Five Year Plan, Planning Commission, Government of India, www.planningcommission.nic.in.

Consumer Behaviour in Services

5

LEARNING OBJECTIVES

After studying this chapter, you will be able to:

- Understand the importance of consumer behaviour and the factors influencing it
- Describe the factors influencing consumer expectations and perceptions
- Understand the consumer purchase decision process
- Identify the distinctive behaviour patterns of consumers in services

Reach is a successful retail chain in Delhi with a number of outlets that attract shoppers from the middle-income group. Started in a moderately busy locality a few years ago, Reach's claim to fame was the large variety of economy-range, ready-made fabrics and other household items offered at relatively low prices. The consistency in product assortment and the pricing policy helped establish a loyal customer base in the locality. Encouraged by the success of this outlet, the management set up more outlets in Delhi, and other northern states with the same business formula. Eventually, new Reach outlets, based on the same business model, were launched in several southern states such as Karnataka, Tamil Nadu and Andhra Pradesh to make the most of the retail boom. Experienced and trained employees were relocated from the northern states to the newly launched outlets to ensure smooth implementation of the system. Despite an enthusiastic initial response, the management noticed a decline in the footfall within two months of the launch. Diminishing sales and regular complaints from customers forced the management to review the business format. During the review process, the management discovered that the customers were dissatisfied with the behaviour of the staff and the overall shopping experience. The plan to successfully ride the retail wave and establish a national presence seemed to flounder in the face of such dismal customer response. The management realized that the decision to extend the business model to the southern states without the prerequisite research was a mistake. Now, with the poor performance of these outlets, the need to modify service design and execution is necessary. The question remains: Will that be enough?

Questions:

1. Why do you think that the concept of Reach malls was not so successful in the southern states?
2. What kind of information would be helpful to Reach? How to obtain such information?
3. Do you agree that there are differences in the consumer behaviour of South Indian and North Indian people?
4. What are the changes do you suggest for Reach to be successful in South India?

INTRODUCTION

The study of consumer behaviour lays the foundation for the marketing of services. It is necessary to know well the needs, wants and expectations of consumers to serve them better. Consumer behaviour is inconsistent and unpredictable, making it difficult to categorize and forecast.

Consumer behaviour, as a field of study, is rooted in the marketing strategy that evolved in the late 1950s when some marketers began to realize that they could sell products more easily if they produced only those products that they had already determined that consumers would buy.[1] Organizations realized that they could survive and succeed only when they responded to the market needs and expectations, rather than persuading customers to buy what the firm had designed already. This marketing concept advocates consumer-oriented marketing. The basic foundation of marketing, therefore, lies in the firm's information and perception of consumers' needs, wants and expectations, which contribute to the decision on how to expend the available resources. In other words, a marketing organization should have up-to-date information on what consumers buy; when they buy; where they buy; why they buy; how frequently they buy and how often they use consumer goods and services. The information on these issues helps a firm design its entire organization policy, particularly its business strategy, product designing and scheduling, promotional strategy, pricing and distribution strategies.

BUYERS, CONSUMERS AND CUSTOMERS

The scope of the term consumer is wider than buyer. All buyers are human beings but consumers include human beings and others who consume goods and services. The study of consumer behaviour includes all those who influence the purchase and consumption behaviour of buyers and customers directly or indirectly.

__Customers__ are those buyers who exhibit a fixed consumption pattern over a period of time. Companies try to convert buyers into customers. The larger the customer base, the more valuable the company. __Consumers__ are identified from the perspective of a company, shop, brand, product class and so on.

There are three important terms in marketing that are commonly used as interchangeable terms—buyer, consumer and customer. There exists a marked difference in the meaning of these terms, the understanding of which is of strategic significance for marketer. A consumer is one who consumes goods and/or services. The term *consumer* includes human beings, animals, birds, trees and all those who have the capacity to consume. *Buyers* are those who buy goods and/or services. All buyers are human beings; they also represent those consumers who can't become buyers on their own. Therefore, all consumers are not buyers and all buyers need not be consumers. The term *customer* finds meaning from the point of view of the seller. We can find a customer for a company, shop, brand, product class and so on. If buyers repeatedly buy the products of one company, they are called customers of the company. If buyers repeatedly purchase from a single sales outlet, they are called customers of that shop. A buyer's behaviour is influenced significantly by the behaviour of those consumers who the buyer represents.

The study of buyer behaviour alone limits the information base of the firm while the study of consumer behaviour expands the understanding of organizations. The expectations of buyers are different from that of customers, and the study of these two groups of people helps in designing strategies for influencing a buyer to become a customer.

FACTORS INFLUENCING CONSUMER BEHAVIOUR

Behaviour is conveyed to others via both verbal and nonverbal communication. Even when no words are exchanged, personality can still communicate loud and clear.[2] Identifying the factors that influence consumer behaviour helps marketers study them in detail from the point of view of the service being marketed. Research indicates that the behaviour of consumers is influenced broadly by three important factors, as illustrated in Fig. 5.1. These are:

1. Cultural and social factors
2. Personal and physical factors
3. Psychological factors

The factors influencing consumer behaviour can broadly be categorized into cultural and social factors, personal and physical factors, and psychological factors. Service providers need to clearly understand these factors to effectively reach out to the consumer with their marketing offers.

Cultural and Social Factors

The behavioural determinants of consumers are summarised in Fig. 5.2. Service marketers need to study all these factors at micro level in order to develop better understanding on consumer behaviour. This kind of study helps basically in assessing consumer expectations and consumer perceptions. The knowledge of key issues of consumer expectations and the process of service consumer perception provides a solid base in marketing strategy development.

Cultural factors have the deepest influence on the behaviour of human beings. Culture is transmitted through language and the modelling of behaviour, when conditions permit humans to communicate through shared language, by living in the same historic period and when they are sufficiently proximal to influence each other.[3] Thus, culture is acquired. There are three sources of cultural learning. Parents, grandparents, elders and other members of a family teach and train children how to behave. This is called *formal learning*. Children observe and imitate the behaviour of others in society with whom they interact. This is called *informal learning*. Children learn many things from educational institutions and the environment, developing analytical abilities. This is called *technical learning*. Thus, cultural learning forms the basis of the consumption habits of individuals.

__Culture__ is shared values, systems and norms of a society. Culture influences the development of personalities. The dimensions of culture include complexity, rigidity, collectivism and individualism.

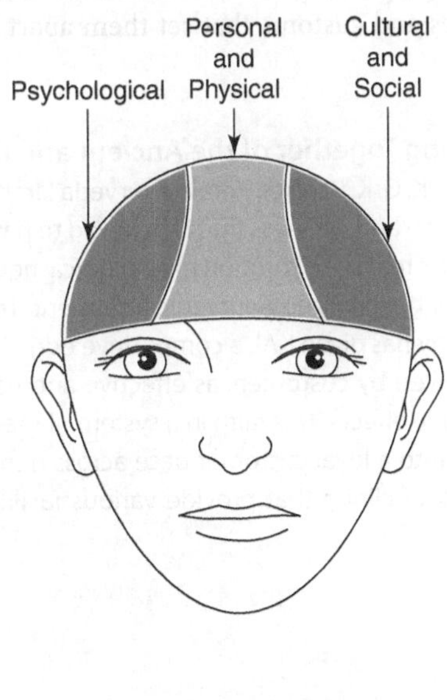

Fig. 5.1
Factors influencing consumer behaviour

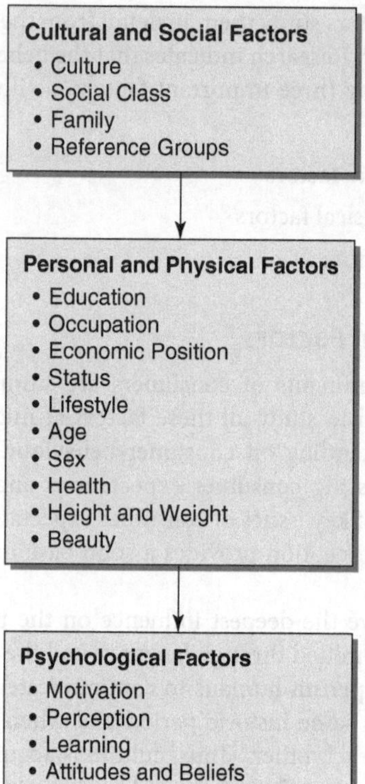

Fig. 5.2 Determinants of consumer behaviour

The presence of different ethnic groups within a geographic region adds to the cultural diversity of the region. The migration of groups and individuals from one place to another is accompanied by the simultaneous migration of core cultural systems, leading to the existence of multiple subculture groups within geographic regions. The members of a specific subculture possess beliefs, values and customs that set them apart from other members of

Kerala Ayurveda Limited—The Coming Together of the Ancient and the Modern

Established as early as 1945 by late Vaidyan K. G. K. Paniker, Kerala Ayurveda Limited (KAL) systematized Ayurveda, the ancient Vedic science of health and wellness that is believed to have been handed down from Brahma, the Hindu God of creation, to great seers through mythological figures. Paniker was a pioneer in the fact that he created a system of hospitalized Ayurvedic treatment. The successful marriage of ancient wisdom with modern technology has given KAL a competitive edge in the current market.

The services offered by KAL are perceived by customers as effective and natural, with a touch of the traditional and no impending risk of side effects. This faith in a system of medicine that is rooted in the ancient Indian culture has translated into a loyal customer base across geographical and cultural borders. Today, KAL has a global network of clinics that provide various facilities and treatments in accordance with the tenets of Ayurveda.

Table 5.1 Subcultural Categories

Categories	Examples of Classification
Nationality (i.e., Birthplace of Ancestors)	Indian, Burmese, Bangladeshis, Nepalese
Religion	Hindu, Muslim, Christian, Jain
Geographic Region	North, South
Age	Senior citizen, Teenager, Middle-aged
Gender	Female, Male
Occupation	Bus Driver, Mechanic, Engineer
Social Class	Lower, Middle, Upper

the same society. In addition, they adhere to most of the dominant cultural beliefs, values and behavioural patterns of the larger society. When we look at the Indian culture, each Indian is a product of the Indian way of life and at the same time a member of various subcultures. For example, an 11-year-old boy may simultaneously be a South Indian, Hindu, Tamilian and preteen. We would expect that the membership of each different subculture would provide its own set of specific beliefs, values, attitudes and customs. Table 5.1 lists typical subcultural categories and corresponding examples of specific subcultural groups. This list is by no means exhaustive; elementary school teachers, politicians, girl scouts and millionaires—in fact, any group that shares common beliefs and customs—may be classified as a subculture.

Subcultural analysis enables the marketing manager to focus on sizeable and natural market segments. When carrying out such an analysis, the marketer must determine whether the beliefs, values and customs shared by the members of a specific subgroup make them desirable candidates for special marketing attention. Subcultures, therefore, are relevant units of analysis for market research.

> *Subcultural groups exist in various geographic regions because the core cultural system travels from place to place when people migrate. Subcultural groups have relatively greater homogeneity in cultural beliefs, values and behavioural patterns.*

Another important dimension of culture is social class. Social classes are relatively homogeneous and follow a hierarchical order. The most popular variable that decides the hierarchy of social class is income. However, other variables such as occupation, education and place of residence can also be used, either separately or in combination, to decide social hierarchy. Based on income, a society can be divided into nine groups—upper-upper class, upper-middle class, upper-lower class, middle-upper class, middle-middle class, middle-lower class, lower-upper class, lower-middle class and lower-lower class. The changes in consumer income and expenditure are discussed in "Services Marketing Insight: Consumers in India."

Product and brand preferences among various social classes differ considerably. The major social groups that influence consumer behaviour are family and reference groups.

5.1 Services Marketing Insight | **Consumers in India**

India became the second fastest growing economy in the world. The Center for Monitoring Indian Economy (CMIE) studied consumer expenditure on different product categories during 1993–1994 to 2003–2004. The study reveals that the expenditure on services increased from INR 1400.42 billion to INR 5270.24 billion and services achieved a growth of 276.3 per cent during this period. The share of services in total consumer expenditure varied between 23.67 and 29.85 per cent.

According to the study, about 80 per cent of urban consumers were literate as against 56 per cent of rural consumers. The average monthly consumer expenditure varied between INR 386 and 652 among different household types in rural areas and between INR 541 and 1031 in urban areas. The data indicates that there is higher per capita spending in urban areas as compared to rural areas, which is why many companies focus on urban markets. However, taking the size of the rural population into consideration, even the small indulgences of rural consumers could translate into big business volumes to the companies, if managed properly.

The Affluent Consumer: Affluent households constitute an especially attractive target segment because its members have incomes that provide them with a disproportionately larger share of all discretionary income—the extras that allow the purchase of luxury cruises, time-sharing ski-resort condos, surfing on the Internet and so on. The National Council for Applied Economic Research (NCAER) report on the Indian consumer market indicated that the number of high-income households increased substantially in India during this period.

The very rich households (with annual income of over INR 215,000) increased to 6.2 million in 2006. The consuming class (with annual income of INR 45,000 to INR 215,000) grew to 90.9 million households. The number of households in the aspirants (with annual income of INR.16,000 to INR.22,000) and the destitute groups (with annual income of less than INR.16,000) decreased significantly.

The affluent consumer group in India is not substantial in size when compared to its population. The study estimated that the annual income of about 1 million households in India was more than INR 1 million each, putting the total number of affluent consumers at 5.6 million. The demand for premium products has been rising continuously in India, indicating the growth of the affluent consumers segment. The growth in market size for telecommunications, education, healthcare, tourism and other services in India during the last one-and-a-half decades has been substantial.

Source: NCAER. Ten Year White Book—The Indian Consumer Market 1997–2007.

Family

A *family* is a very close social group within which individuals interact regularly. The members of a family share values, habits, lifestyles and so on. Relationships within a family are mutually inspiring, influencing the life pattern of each and every individual. The influence of the family on the purchase behaviour of an individual, therefore, cannot be overemphasized.

One of the significant cultural identities of India is its well-structured family system. Indians prefer to be recognized as members of a family rather than as individuals. A family reflects togetherness with love and affection; concern for the overall development and growth of its members;

a managerial system with different positions, roles, responsibilities and control mechanisms. It adapts to changes in its environment together as a unit, to either face different threats or exploit emerging opportunities. The joint family system was deep rooted in India. A joint family is a group of people who generally live under one roof, eat together, cook at one hearth, hold property in common, participate in common family worship and are related to each other as some particular type of kindred.[4] The family system in India, however, is not rigid but flexible in inviting changes in accordance with the changes in the economic environment. Without losing the spirit of the joint family system, modified family structures started emerging due to industrialization, migration and other factors. Several research studies confirmed the fact that the Indian family system has undergone some structural changes during the second half of the 20th century. Ram Ahuja[5] carried out a critical study of the empirical works of many researchers and concluded that there are five major changes in the Indian family. These include:

1. The number of fissioned families is increasing, but they fulfil their traditional obligations towards their parental families despite living separately.
2. There is more jointness in traditional (rural) communities and more nuclearity in communities exposed to the forces of industrialization, urbanization and westernization.
3. The size of the (traditional) joint family has become smaller.
4. As long as the old cultural values persist among people; the functional joint family will be sustained in the Indian society.
5. The changes from a traditional to a contemporary family system is accompanied by several features including trends new local residence, functional jointness, equality of individuals, equal status for women, increasing opportunity to individual members to achieve their aspirations and the weakening of family norms.

A notable change in the Indian family is reflected in the evolving husband-wife and parent-child relationships. Housewives, under the traditional family system, had no or limited voice in the decision-making process. In the contemporary family system, the role of housewives has increased significantly as they play a dominant or equal role in areas such as disciplining the children, purchasing household goods and services, planning the family expenditure, selecting items for the husband and children, and acquiring permanent assets, particularly in the middle- and higher-income households. While the husband continues to play an instrumental role, the wife is expressive and participates actively in the decision-making process. The emergence of nuclear families within the broad framework of the joint family system has increased the importance of children in the family. In the past, parents exercised power over their children in deciding their education, occupation, marriage and careers. In the changing scenario parents have started consulting with children and also respecting their opinion on various issues including changes in consumption patterns. Workers has identified dominant trends in the Indian family system. These are:

> One of the significant cultural identities of India is its well-structured family system. The influence of the family on consumer behaviour is quite significant. Though there has been a shift from the joint family system to the nuclear family system in India during the last two decades, the core values remain intact.

1. Increasing importance of nuclear family
2. Transference of some functions (educational, recreational, protective, etc.) to some other institutions
3. Fundamental change in the family age structure, that is, proportionately fewer children to care for and proportionately more elderly persons surviving. This has necessitated the transfer of the support function from the family to the State and private insurance companies. This has affected the family power structure too.
4. Freedom to women due to their education and increasing economic independence
5. Declining reliance of children upon family controls
6. Changing values of youth. Though they respect and fear their parents, yet they want parental "support" to achieve their individual interests.
7. Liberalization of attitudes and practices towards sex
8. Change from pre-puberty to post-puberty marriages
9. Decreasing family size

These characteristics of the present-day Indian family are indicative of the change in the structure and family ties.

> **Reference groups** serve as guides to consumers either directly or indirectly to respond to various stimulations. Reference groups such as family, friends, relatives, co-workers, opinion leaders and aspirational personalities support the consumer psychologically in marketing purchase decisions.

Reference Groups

A *reference group* is any person or group that serves as a point of comparison (or reference) for an individual while forming either general or specific values, attitudes or a specific guide for behaviour.[7] Consumers are generally influenced by primary groups, secondary groups, aspiration groups, associative groups and disassociate groups. The *primary group* consists of family, relatives, friends, neighbours and co-workers with whom a person has regular and informal interaction. The *secondary group* consists of the people connected with religion, region and profession, wherein the interactions are more formal and occasional. The *aspiration group* consists of those persons with whom an individual develops an interest to join. Individuals try to associate themselves formally with some groups, with whom opinions and attitudes can be shared. Such groups are called *associative groups*. The *disassociate group* consists of those persons whose behaviour is against the value system and lifestyle of an individual. Reference groups influence the attitudes of people and help in forming opinions on various stimulations. Marketers, while designing marketing communications, try to identify the opinion leaders of the target market. The study of reference groups is of immense help in this direction.

5.2 Services Marketing Insight | **Middle-class Consumers: The Potential Market for a Host of Services**

The middle class in India is the most attractive group for companies. The strength of the Indian market lies with middle-income consumers. According to a study by the NCAER, in 1998 India had a middle class of 53.4 million households with an annual income of INR 45,000 to 215,000. Out of them, 27.5 million households lived in urban areas, and 25.9 million households lived in rural areas. The total number of middle-income consumers was around 297 million. The middle class constituted 30 per cent of the population in 1998–1999, and the proportion was expected to touch 40 per cent by 2006–2007. As a result of the growth and development of agriculture, industry and services, particularly software services, expansion of markets and so on, there has been a virtual explosion in the middle class in India. The size of the Indian middle class exceeds the total US population. The middle-income households are well educated with high aspirations. Exposed to global lifestyles, they spend more than they earn. Their high confidence levels, combined with an aggressive business outlook and high risk-taking abilities, have resulted in a significantly higher demand for many goods and services. Goods and services such as cellular services, courier services, transport, computers, economy-segment cars and other automobiles, electrical and electronics, beauty products and services, and health care services are finding great potential in India. The fast-changing lifestyles of this segment continue to be of a subject of significant importance to marketers.

Source: NCAER. Ten Year White Book—The Indian Consumer Market 1997–2007.

Personal and Physical Factors

Personal factors—including education, occupation, economic position, status, personality and self-concept and lifestyle—influence the behaviour of an individual. Physical factors such as age, sex, health, height, weight and beauty also influence an individual's behaviour. Personal and physical factors influence decisions on the type of service, the choice of the service provider, quality requirements, customer's participative role and so on.

Education: There is a marked difference in the behaviour of an educated person and an uneducated person regarding the purchase of goods and services.

VLCC

VLCC, with the tagline "Shaping your confidence", entered the business of body management services in 1989. The company attracted customers in large numbers by focusing on aspirational references. The models portrayed in the advertisements and the real case examples communicated through various media served as a powerful reference to the prospects to get influenced and buy the services of the company.

Today, VLCC is the single largest player in the organized sector with a pan-India presence of nearly 225 outlets across 75 cities in India and a few outlets outside India. The company has acquired the status of India's largest health and beauty brand by way of offering highly customized services based on multi-disciplinary, integrated scientific approach to study body compositions and offering solutions to consumer problems.

Educated persons have knowledge and exposure and analytical abilities. In addition to the fact that they are, to a great extent, rational in approach, educated persons can obtain adequate product information and assess the value of the offering. In contrast, uneducated persons are mostly emotional and dependent on others in their purchase decisions.

Occupation: Occupation influences the behaviour of individuals. The behaviour of a teacher compared to that of a police officer, a doctor to that of a lawyer, a politician to that of a social worker is conspicously different due to different lifestyles and choices on account of to occupational influences.

Economic Position: The financial background, regularity of income, future flow of income, financial obligations and discretionary money—all have direct or indirect influence on the behaviour of an individual. After all, the ability to buy is a key factor for the demand generation of any product, be it services or goods. The growing economic power of the Indian middle class is presented in "Services Marketing Insight: Middle-Class Consumers—The Potential Market for a Host of Services."

Status: People are basically status conscious—whether it is ascribed status or achieved status. Ascribed status is the status people get due to their family position. The status of their parents, grandparents and family members becomes the minimum position for the individuals of the family. *Achieved status* is the position acquired by individuals through their own efforts. People try to display their status prominently through their purchasing decisions.

Personality and Self-concept: Personality refers to an individual's response tendencies across situations and over time.[8] Personality factors influence an individual's buying behaviour. Personality—generally displayed in terms of self-confidence, dominance, sociability, economy, defensiveness, adaptability and aggressiveness—is shaped by both generic and environmental influences.[9] *Self-concept*, also called self-image, influences product selection and usage. Researchers have identified four different kinds of self-image: (1) actual self-image (how individuals see themselves); (2) ideal self-image (how individuals would like to see themselves); (3) social self-image (how individuals feel others see them) and (4) ideal social self-image (how individuals would like others to see them).

> *"Personal factors such as the level and type of education, occupation, economic position, status, personality, self-concept and lifestyle influence purchase behaviour in vital ways. The choice of several services such as hospitality, transport, tourism, healthcare, insurance and banking are influenced greatly by these factors."*

Lifestyle: People belonging to the same culture and social class may lead different lifestyles because lifestyle is influenced by the individual's activities, interactions and opinions. The lifestyle of an individual can be visualized by identifying his/her interactions with the environment. The study of psychographics (the science of using psychology and demographics) is useful in understanding the lifestyles of people and in designing suitable marketing strategies. Marketers exploit the lifestyle concept to position their services effectively. For example, the Tivoli Group offers hospitality services through garden resorts, the daffodils hotels and holiday villages with luxury lifestyle positioning. With a campaign theme "Let's celebrate life in style," Tivoli focuses on setting new benchmarks on the way people share their happy moments.

Age: The needs and consumption patterns of people vary with ages; they are not the same for children, youth, middle-aged and old people. The type of services required at old-age homes are different from that of baby crutches. Similarly, the entertainment services required for different age groups differ significantly.

Sex: The difference between men and women is also reflected in their consumption behaviour. Marketers have identified gender as a powerful segmentation strategy, and many products are offered exclusively to either women or men. Further, many services such as, hostel services, beauty care services and fitness services are offered differently to these two groups.

Health: The physical fitness of individuals—whether male or female—has an impact on their consumption behaviour. Services such as dietary, health care, and fitness find demand based on the health and physical fitness of people.

Height and Weight: These important physical characteristics greatly influence the consumption behaviour of people.

Beauty: Though beauty is a perceptual factor, the consciousness of beauty is overwhelmingly present in the world. The level of consciousness varies between men and women. Though it is debatable whether beauty is physical or mental, it has led to the mushrooming of beauty parlours and clinics all over the world, indicating the rising demand in this segment.

> *Physical factors such as age, sex, health, height, weight and beauty have a bearing on the choice of services*

Psychological Factors

Psychological factors greatly influence the behaviour of individuals. The most important among them are motivation, perception, learning, attitudes and beliefs.

Motivation

A motive is a strong feeling, urge or desire that a goal-oriented individual seeks to satisfy. Motivation starts with an internal stimulation triggered by either physiological or psychological needs. *Motivation* refers to the process that causes people to behave as they do. It occurs when a need is aroused that the individual wishes to satisfy. Once a need has been activated, a state of tension exists that drives the consumer to attempt to reduce or eliminate the need.[10] The pressure of internal stimulation creates tension in the individual and activates them to satisfy an unfulfilled need. Abraham Maslow[11] studied consumer motivation and developed the hierarchy of needs. According to him, there are five levels of needs—physiological, security, social, esteem and self-actualization needs. Maslow states that generally human beings first satisfy their lower-order needs, that is, physiological needs and later security needs and social needs and then move upwards. The need-satisfaction process of a society has a tremendous impact on the marketability of various goods and services.

> *Abraham Maslow's widely accepted theory of motivation identifies five levels of human needs, starting from biogenic needs to psychogenic needs. Some psychologists have identified power, affiliation and achievement needs as the three needs that influence consumer motivation.*

Perception

Perception is the way we look at the world around us. The five senses of the human body—touch, smell, taste, sound and vision—provide basic input to the human brain to develop an understanding of something. This is called perception. Consumers are bombarded with information on products through advertisements, in-store displays, special offers, and so on. The perception process has implications for marketers because consumers absorb and make secure of the vast quantities of information competing for their attention.[12] It is not possible for an individual to respond to every stimulation that is attempted by a host of sellers. Therefore, consumers tend to develop a selection system which generally has three dimensions:

1. *Selective Attention:* Paying attention to only a few selected stimulations.
2. *Selective Retention:* Retaining only those stimulations which consumers can relate to or those that consumers believe will be useful in the future.
3. *Selective Distortion:* The process of erasing the retained information when individuals feel that the information is useless, either for present or future needs.

By understanding this process of selectivity, marketers compete to get the customer's attention first and, then, to find a place in the consumer's memory. Product positioning is one strategy that is used by marketers to reduce the perceptual strain of consumers. Marketers take a risk when they identify either one or a few features of the product and offering it for consumer perception. Consumers consider only these factors to develop perceptions about the product. Airtel, for example, positioned its mobile services with the tagline "Express yourself." It portrays the specific benefits of using mobile service in general and Airtel in particular. It touches the sensitive part of human communication as a majority of Indians find it difficult to effectively communicate with others, besides facing problems in finding right means. The "Dil ki baat" campaign of Airtel aimed to touch the inner most core of a viewer's heart. The advertisement did not mention any of the product features. Everything was cute there: a little girl playing with a poorer girl; an old couple watching a young couple; a teacher interacting flawlessly with her deaf student and finally a girl practicing gymnastics. Each clip by itself was satisfying; that satisfaction has been carried several notches higher in this particular advertisement. The ad simply plays on emotions. Finally, it conveys to the consumer the kind of satisfaction one gets by using Airtel services to express self so naturally, completely and heartfully.

> *“ **Perception** is the process of selecting, mapping and interpreting the stimulations to derive meanings. Consumers' decision making is influenced by the way marketing stimulations are perceived.*

Learning

Learning is one of the important dimensions of consumer behaviour. *Learning* is the process by which people acquire knowledge and experience.[13] Human beings learn through trial and error, past experience, experiences of others and by relating to different experiences. Learning is a continuous process. Often, the new knowledge is the basis for future consumption behaviour. Learning is a natural instinct for human beings; therefore, they intentionally learn many things that they consider useful for their future. Sometimes learning is incidental; it does not take much effort. People seeking to satisfy an unfulfilled need start learning many things related to their needs. For example, a person may want to undergo some diagnostic tests. The person then seeks information on available diagnostic services, their accessibility, price, reliability, service packages, preparatory requirements for some tests and so on. The person also tries to identify the best diagnostic centre. To this end, they seek for information available in newspapers and local media. He/she may obtain information through reading articles on health checkups in magazines, following TV programmes, conversations of friends, neighbours and colleagues on health matters. All consumers may not seek information relating to an object equally. The extent of search depends mostly upon the involvement of the person in satisfying the need. Marketers should work on uncovering the learning motives of consumers and provide right stimulations capable of meeting consumer expectations. Learning may be based on observation and/or on the individual's mental activity. Observational learning is based on the observation of others' behaviour in a similar situation and the consequences due to their behaviour. When satisfied with the outcome of others' behaviour, the individual tries to imitate the behaviour. The learning based on mental activity refers to the complex processing of information in the human mind. Consumers use their knowledge inventory in the memory to understand and learn their experiences. The receptive capacity of the sensory inputs, the organization of knowledge inventory and the retrievable capacity of the individual influence the processing of information in the consumer mind greatly. The response to a stimulation and reinforcement is greatly influenced by the learning of an individual. Marketers need to study the learning process of prospective consumers in order to reach them with the right information effectively.

Attitudes and Beliefs

People develop beliefs and attitudes through activities, interactions, learning and results. *Belief* is the descriptive thought that a person holds about something. An *attitude* is a person's point of view towards something.[14] People tend to develop attitudes towards an object or idea. It is nothing but developing a favourable or unfavourable opinion through evaluations, feelings and tendencies. Attitudes influence beliefs and beliefs influence attitudes. Attitudes once formed are relatively consistent and are difficult to change.

Attitudes, however, are not permanent but change when better stimulations influence the person. The factors responsible for attitude formation are also responsible for attitude change.

> *Marketers try to understand the way consumers form and change their attitudes. Attitudes are influenced by past experience, word-of-mouth communication, personality and marketing stimulations.*

Attitudes may be formed as a result of direct consumption experience of a product or service, evaluation of marketing communications through various media, the influence of family members and friends and/or word-of-mouth communication. Insurance companies, for example, use advisors/agents mostly to influence attitude formation of prospective buyers. The advisors/agents help prospective buyers in identifying the needs, understanding and evaluating various information inputs, addressing their concerns and finally developing a positive attitude towards the policy and the company. Many service companies use mass communication media to influence the attitudes (e.g., cellular services, retailing and entertainment services). Word-of-mouth communication often impact powerfully in forming attitude towards services such as tourism, education, hospitality and health care.

If marketing offers fit into the attitudes and beliefs of people, they are more likely to get accepted. A strategic approach is necessary to influence consumers to develop positive attitude towards company services.

HOW DO CONSUMERS DEVELOP EXPECTATIONS?

Consumers have different types of expectations from a service. Service marketers should know the expectations of customers. The knowledge of customer expectations helps marketers design comprehensive service packages capable of delivering satisfaction. In the past, it was believed that companies succeed by selling value. However, a new question plagues marketers these days: How do customers define value? Customers' expanded concept of value includes the convenience of purchase, after-sales service, and dependability. Companies should meet all these customer expectations to survive in the competitive environment.[15] There are two levels of expectations of service customers: maximum service level and minimum service level.

The *maximum service level* is a blend of what the customer believes "can be" and "should be." For example, if you take the services of your college placement cell, your expectations in all likelihood would be a right job in a right location at the right salary. However, you are also aware of constraints in obtaining jobs—the vacancy positions in various companies, the competition and the changing expectations of the market. Due to this reason you may have low expectations from the acceptance of the service. This low level of expectations is called the minimum service level.

The *minimum service level* is the lowest acceptable expectation—the lowest level of performance acceptable to the customer. As shown in Fig. 5.3, there is a zone of tolerance between the maximum service level and the minimum service level.

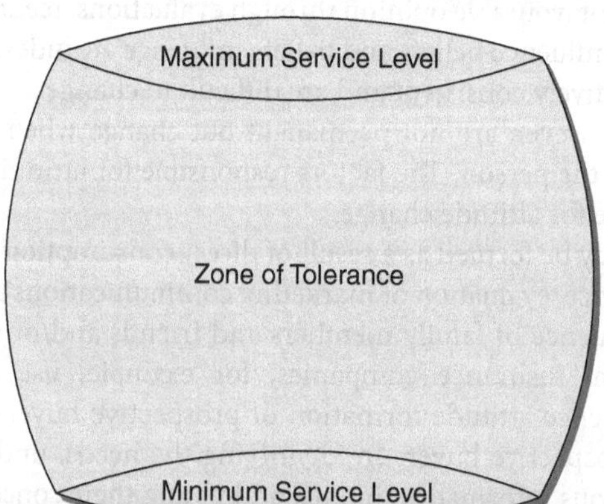

Fig. 5.3
Zone of tolerance

In the process of service production and consumption, five levels of service performance vis-à-vis customer response might result (see Table 5.2).

The Zone of Tolerance

The *zone of tolerance* is the extent to which customers identify or are willing to accept the variation between the two levels of expectations—the maximum service level and the minimum service level. If the performance of the service is below the minimum service level, customers are frustrated and highly dissatisfied, whereas if the performance of the service is above the maximum service level, customers are delighted. When the performance of the service falls in the tolerance zone, customers do not particularly notice the service performance. The service gets the customer's attention in a positive or negative way only when the service performance is outside the tolerance zone. For example, if a customer goes to a bank to withdraw money, his/her maximum level of expectations may be that the bank should provide the service within 10 minutes, as per the time specification of the bank. If the bank takes 15 minutes, the customer may not notice the delay because he/she considers 15 minutes as tolerable. If the bank takes more than 15 minutes, the customer is displeased. On the other hand, if the bank takes only 5 minutes, the customer is highly pleased.

"Consumers' expectations from services depend on many factors. The two levels of the expectations of service customers are the minimum service level and the maximum service level. The minimum service level indicates the bottom-line expectations of consumers, whereas the maximum service level indicates the higher level of expectations of consumers. If the consumer's experience exceeds the maximum service level, the customer is likely to get delighted."

The tolerance zone is low in the case of important factors, while the tolerance zone is high in the case of not very important factors. For example, your zone of tolerance will be very low if the tailor delays the delivery of clothes that you want to wear for your birthday party; it will be significantly higher if the clothes are just meant to be casual wear. Further, the tolerance zone differs from customer to customer, for the first time service and the recovery service. The zone of tolerance of an individual or a group depends on the position of minimum level and maximum level expectations, so it is important to know the factors influencing these levels to estimate the zone of tolerance. Figure 5.4 illustrates the determinants of customer expectations.

Determinants of the Maximum Service Level

The three important factors that influence the maximum level of service expectations in an individual are needs and wants, derived expectations

Table 5.2 The Five Levels of Service Performance

Levels of Service Performance	Customer Response
1. Exceeding maximum expected level	Highly satisfied or delighted
2. Maximum service level	Satisfied
3. Adequate service level	Indifferent
4. Minimum service level	Dissatisfied
5. Below minimum level	Highly dissatisfied

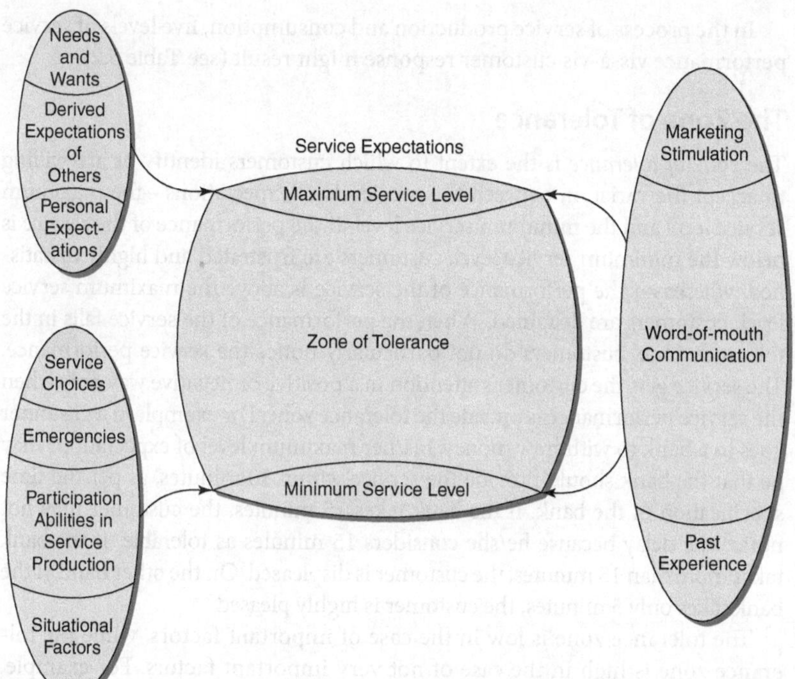

Fig. 5.4 Determinants of customer expectations

> *It is important to marketers to identify the zone of tolerance. This zone is indicative of some deficiencies in a service. Marketers need to work to keep the service performance either at par or above the maximum service level.*

of others and personal expectations. The physical, psychological, social or functional needs of a person are vital factors in shaping the maximum level of service expectations. The entertainment needs of a housewife differ significantly from that of a businessman. The level of expectations of a businessman and a house wife differ in terms of the preference of programmes on a TV channel. The service needs of a retired person from an insurance agent are less than that of an in-service employee. The retired person has more time at his disposal and prefers to attend to some services personally, while an in-service employee, due to paucity of time, requires greater services from an agent. Wants are the means to satisfy the needs. The maximum level of expectations of consumers is influenced by the selection of the means to a great extent. If you want to have lunch and the choice is between a restaurant of a five-star hotel and a roadside ordinary restaurant, service level expectations differ significantly.

The maximum level of service expectations is influenced when customer expectations are driven by others. Thus, a grandson who wants to celebrate the 50th marriage anniversary of his grandparents represents the entire family in selecting the various items required for organizing the celebrations successfully. Therefore, his needs are mostly driven by the derived expectations from other family members. The personal expectations of a consumer reflect the generic attitude towards the service, marketing communication and the "proper" conduct of the service provider. In a five-star hotel a consumer may expect a steward to be dressed in a uniform, to be active in attending to customer calls and to serve food at the proper time.

> *The determinants of the maximum level of service expectations include needs and wants, personal expectations of consumers and derived expectations of others.*

Determinants of the Minimum Service Level

The four important factors that influence a consumer's minimum level of service expectations are service choices, emergencies, participative abilities in service production and situational factors. If consumers have multiple service providers of different levels of quality offerings, the minimum level of expectations depends on the selection of the provider. For a passenger of a bus in a rural area, the tolerance zone of the waiting time is very high as he/she has very few alternatives for mobility. The tolerance zone is narrow for an urbanite who has a greater choice of mobility service providers. In emergency situations such as ambulance service of a hospital and electricity services during peak hours of business, people expect fast service, in which case the minimum level of expectations is high.

The participative abilities of a customer also influence the minimum level of expectations. If consumers perceive that they do not possess the required skills in the participation of the service production process or if they feel that their role in taking the service from others is not adequate, they tend to develop low level of expectations. Thus, a patient who did not follow the directions of a physician may not develop a negative impression of the physician. The tolerance zone of consumers expands when they feel that they are not performing their roles perfectly. There are some factors beyond the control of service providers; these factors are called situational factors. When consumers understand situational factors, their tolerance zone is generally high. For example, in the case of emergency services during major accidents, natural calamities or war periods that affect a large number of people, service expectations generally are lower.

> *The minimum level of service expectations is specifically influenced by alternatives available, emergencies, participation abilities in the service process and situational factors.*

Determinants of the Maximum and Minimum Service Levels

Marketing communication, word-of-mouth communication and the past experience of consumers influence both the maximum and minimum level of expectations. Service organizations communicate with the target market to inform them about the features of the service and service promises. Consumers develop expectations on the basis of direct information from the company. Ambiguous and unclear service promises through external marketing programmes may leave ground for consumers to make implied assumptions. At times consumers perceive some service-related cues and develop expectations. For example, by looking at the exterior of a hotel, a consumer may develop some expectations about the quality of its service.

Word-of-mouth communication in services is one of the most powerful methods of influencing a consumer's mind. People seek information from

> The factors such as stimulations of marketers, word-of-mouth communication and past experience of consumers influence both maximum and minimum level of service expectations

earlier users or co-customers about the service performance. Based on the information, they develop expectations. Highly involved consumers may go for an expert advice also. Past experience is another force in shaping customers' expectations. While availing a service, customers are likely to share their previous experience with the same service provider or service outlet, service organizations or comparable services.

SERVICE PERCEPTION

Service marketers must find out whether customers are satisfied with the quality of the service. The evaluation of services differs from person to person, culture to culture and situation to situation. There are four important factors that usually influence the service perception of customers: (1) service encounters, (2) evidence of service, (3) image and (4) price.

A *service encounter* is a situation where a customer interacts with a service provider. In some services, there may be many service encounters and in some services there may be a few encounters. The most vivid impression of a service occurs to the customer in a service encounter. Service encounters include the behaviour of service contact employees, service processes, competency of service personnel, quality of service, service environment, timeliness of support services, systems and procedures, customer care and concern, responsiveness to customers' specific problems, and the service motive of the company and its personnel. Customers experience many moments and use these experiences to develop overall perception on the service. Most consumers try to identify gaps between their service expectations and their actual experiences. When actual experiences are better than expected, the perceptions of consumers tend to be positive. When negative gaps (the actual experience does not match the level of expectations) are identified customers get dissatisfied. All service moments may not either influence or equally influence consumers in quality perceptions because of the differences in their perceptual process, perceptual ability and other behavioural patterns. Service marketers should focus on identifying the key factors influencing the perceptions of service consumers and the differences in their perceptions. The moments of interaction are most important to service providers; they should look for opportunities to excel and create delightful experiences for consumers.

The evidence of a service is another major factor that influences consumers' perceptions. The intangible nature of a service creates doubts in the minds of consumers, so they search for evidence of their interactions with organizations. For example, when a customer deposits money in a bank, they find the evidence of the transaction in the form of either receipt or passbook entry or access to online verification of the deposit. Evidence ensures that the service process has been completed successfully. Evidences at every stage of a service process develop positive perceptions in consumers.

The image of an organization influences the perceptions of consumers; it communicates expectations. A positive image makes people more open to favourable word-of-mouth communication. A neutral image may not cause any harm but a negative image certainly affects the business of the organization.

Consumers frequently rely on price as a surrogate indicator to develop expectations and perceptions of a service because services are intangible. Generally, a high price indicates high-quality expectations, and a low price indicates low-quality offerings. Thus, the service quality expectations of economy class passengers of air transport services differ significantly from that of executive/business class passengers. The higher income group consumers generally associate high price with status/esteem value.

> *Service perceptions basically are influenced by four important factors—service encounter, evidence of service, image and price—and depend on how consumers relate these factors to their belief system and memory.*

CONSUMER PURCHASE DECISION PROCESS

The objective of any organization in any sector is to develop and provide market offerings that satisfy consumers' needs and wants, thereby ensuring its own economic survival. Towards this end, organizations need to fill the gap between customer expectations and customer perceptions. Marketers should have complete understanding of the behavioural characteristics of consumers, their expectations, evaluation processes and purchase decision processes. There is an argument that the consumer's behaviour is the same for both goods and services. But services specialists do not agree with this argument. Though the basic determinants of behaviour may be common for both goods and services, as far as expectations, evaluation and selection of services are concerned, the behaviour of consumers is definitely different. The characteristics of the service such as intangibility, inseparability, variability and customer participation lead to differences in the consumer evaluation process in all the stages of the buying process.

> *The study of the purchase decision process of consumers provides vital clues to service providers to understand their consumers better. The four stages in the process—problem identification and definition, information search, alternatives evaluation, and purchase and consumption—are not followed uniformly by all consumers. The distinctiveness in their behaviour for various services or service features needs to be analyzed carefully.*

Consumers generally follow a four-stage process in making purchase decisions related to services: (1) problem identification and definition; (2) information search; (3) alternatives evaluation and (4) purchase and consumption. Figure 5.5 outlines the consumer purchase decision process.

Problem Identification and Definition

Problem identification is the first step in the consumer decision-making process. An understanding of the process that consumers follow to recognize and define a problem provides some clues about the information why a buyer buys what they intend to. This information helps marketers identify the ways by which they can influence buyers to recognize their needs. Problem identification represents a perceived gap between the existing level and the desired level of consumer living. Every gap identified by the consumer is not a need. The perceived gap must cross a level, called a threshold level, to become a felt need. A threshold level refers to the minimum amount of tension or intensity necessary for a feeling to occur. Only a felt need can ignite the buying process. The two factors that help an individual recognize the problem are external stimulations and internal stimulations. Marketing communication, word of mouth, personal observations, expiry of service contracts and future expectations are the external factors that

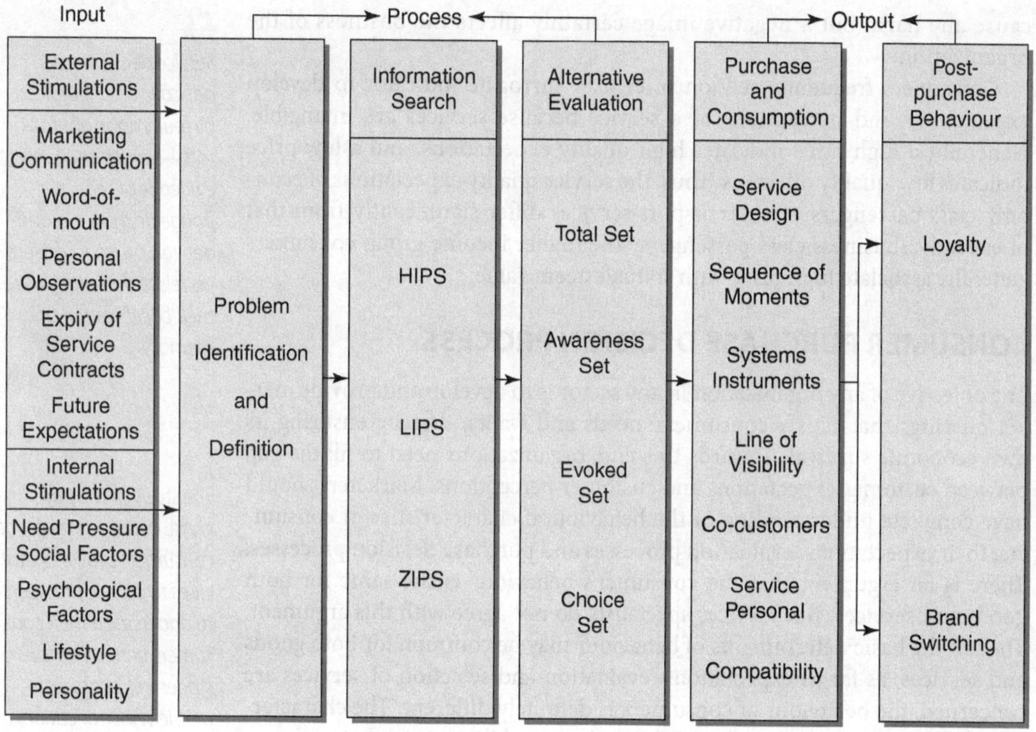

Fig. 5.5
The consumer purchase decision process

make an individual identify his/her needs. The pressure of needs, social factors, psychological factors, lifestyle and personality are the internal factors that help problem identification and definition. A number of organizations constantly communicate a variety of services, their benefits and applicability to consumers through various media. These communications persuade, provoke and instigate consumers and build an inside need pressure. Word-of-mouth communication is the most powerful tool to influence individuals; they perceive that they get reliable information through word-of-mouth communication.

Apart from the efforts of marketers and word-of-mouth communication, individuals observe trends in the society, leading to identification of the gaps in living patterns. Individuals might have entered into service maintenance contracts with various organizations for a time frame. On the expiry of the contract, an individual takes these gaps into consideration for taking a decision on whether to renew the service, discontinue or change the service provider, or minimize or enhance the service level. Consumers are future oriented; insurance, share consultancy, banking and healthcare are the most prominent services with which they link up their future expectations.

Unfulfilled needs motivate individuals to satisfy them. The pressure generated due to the unfulfilment of a need makes an individual recognize the problem in its entirety. Social factors such as the relationship between an individual and the society make him/her identify the need for certain services. Membership in social organizations and status-related services are examples in this respect. Psychological factors such as motivation, perception, attitudes and beliefs, lifestyle patterns and personality traits also generate internal stimulations and contribute to the recognition of problems.

> *The input sources for the identification of consumer problems can be broadly categorized into external stimulations and internal stimulations. External stimulations are the communications from service providers, word of mouth, personal observations, expiry of service contracts and future expectations. Internal stimulations are the pressure of needs, social factors, psychological factors, personality and lifestyle.*

Information Search

Information search depends on certain properties of market offers. Economists have identified the following two categories of properties of consumer products:

- *Search Qualities:* The attributes of the offer can be determined by the consumer before purchasing a product, for example, tangibles, style, price, feel and smell.
- *Experience Qualities:* The attributes of the offer can be known either during the consumption or after the purchase, for example, taste and wearability.

  Later, a third category was identified as credence qualities.
- *Credence Qualities:* The attributes of the offer that the consumer may find impossible to evaluate even after the purchase and consumption. For example, very few consumers have the knowledge and expertise to evaluate medical services or mechanical services as to whether these services are necessary or are performed properly even after the consumption of the services.

In services, experience and credence qualities dominate. Consumers employ different evaluation processes. They generally obtain information from two different sources—personal sources such as friends, relatives and/or experts, and non-personal sources such as mass media or selective media. Consumers depend to a greater extent on personal sources because of the following reasons. First, mass and selective media cannot communicate information about experience qualities effectively. Consumers can obtain quality information from friends, relatives and experts. Second, if the product is in the high involvement category, personal influence becomes pivotal in the evaluation of a service offer. Also, consumers may feel there is a greater risk in selecting a little-known alternative. Hence, consumers seek and rely more on information from personal sources than from non-personal sources when evaluating services before purchase.

Consumers do not react similarly to every felt need. The reaction of buyers depends on the level of involvement in problem solving. The following three types of search behaviours are identified in this respect:

- *HIPS*—High involvement problem solving
- *LIPS*—Low involvement problem solving
- *ZIPS*—Zero involvement problem solving or routinized response

> *Information search is influenced by the level of involvement of a consumer in problem solving. The high involvement indicates more efforts on information search, the low involvement indicates moderate search and the zero involvement triggers routinized response and no further information search.*

Thus, in the case of premium services, special services and personal services, people exhibit high involvement in problem recognition and definition. Services such as beauty care, healthcare, hospitality, consultancy and advertising often attract high-involvement consumers. In high-involvement problems people spend time, energy and, if necessary, money to look for information to find the right service and service provider. The zone of tolerance is very low in this category. Low involvement, generally, is with low-price services and those with less influence on life styles. Thus, services such as courier and local transport mostly attract people with low involvement. Once a consumer begins patronizing a particular service, the involvement in decision making gets reduced slowly to the zero level. Supplier services, personal services and so on have a very loyal clientele.

Perceived risk is another important property that influences the information search. Some degree of perceived risk accompanies all transactions, but there is more risk in the purchase of services because services are intangible and non-standardized.

Evaluation of Service Alternatives

Generally, the evoked set of alternatives is smaller in the case of services, when compared to goods. The evoked set of alternatives means a group of products in a given service category that a consumer considers an acceptable option. Unlike manufactured goods that are offered in numerous retail outlets, services are offered by very few business houses in a given geographic area because they are produced locally. Consumers cannot have multiple brands of services at one unit. It is also very difficult to compare the services offered by competitors in the absence of proper standardization. Alternative services cannot be experienced simultaneously as such critical weights cannot be established accurately and compared. For most non-professional services, the choice often would be between the self-service and hiring someone to perform them. Housewives may choose between cleaning their own homes and hiring servant maids or between taking care of their children and putting the children in day-care centers. For many services, consumers often consider themselves as sources. Thus, for many non-professional services the consumers' evoked set frequently includes self-service.

Service Purchase and Consumption

People often describe service production and delivery as "drama," where service personnel are actors, customers constitute the audience, the physical environment is the setting and the service process is the performance. The service design, the roles given to the service personnel, the environment design for the role performances of sellers and buyers in service encounters have a significant impact on the decision-making process of buyers. The sequence of moments, systems, instruments and the total line of visibility (the total area of the service outlet, people and their activities and other infrastructural facilities visible to the consumers) have a serious impact on purchase decisions. Many consumers try to have a look beyond the visible line to arrive at a final decision relating to purchase, wherever it is possible.

Another important attribute is customer compatibility. The number of other customers present at the service outlet, their status in the society, gender and composition of the group are the factors that generally influence the preference of customers. In general, the presence, behaviour and similarity of other customers receiving services have a strong impact on the satisfaction and dissatisfaction of any given customer.

Customer compatibility has been identified as an important factor in services, especially in situations where:

- Customers are in close physical proximity to each other such as in crowded trains.
- Verbal interaction among customers is likely such as in restaurants, clubs and bars.
- Customers are engaged in numerous and varied activities such as in a library or swimming pool.
- The service environment attracts a heterogeneous customer mix such as public parks.
- Customers need to wait occasionally for the service such as in hospitals.
- Customers are expected to share time, space or service utensils with one another, such as in health clubs.

> *Customer compatibility influences the customer's preference of a service. The co-customer's expected behaviour, status, gender and other features at the service outlet play an important role in the decision making of service consumers.*

Customers may be incompatible for many reasons—differences in beliefs, values, experiences, ability to pay, appearance, age, and health, to name a few. The service marketer must anticipate and deal with heterogeneous consumers who have the potential to be incompatible. The service marketer can also bring homogeneous customers together and solidify relationships between them.

Post-purchase Evaluation

> *Service production and consumption process is not the end of the story. Service providers should understand and try to collect the information on the post-purchase evaluation of service consumers to improve further the service process.*

Since consumers participate to a greater extent in service production and consumption, they may feel more responsible for their satisfaction or dissatisfaction when purchasing services. When a female consumer goes for a hair cut, the result depends on her specifications to the hair stylist. After the hair cut, if she is disappointed, she may blame herself for not communicating her own needs clearly or the stylist for lack of skill or both. Consumers complain less frequently about services than goods due to their belief that they themselves are partly responsible for their dissatisfaction. Therefore, once customers are convinced with a particular service provider, it is more likely that they become loyal to the brand. Brand switching is less frequent with services than with goods. Continuing with a service provider reduces at least half the problem in the service encounter.

SUMMARY

- Consumer orientation is the key for the success of any service organization. Therefore, the study of consumer behaviour is of vital importance to marketing managers.
- Consumer behaviour is influenced by cultural and social factors, personal and physical factors and psychological factors.
- Formal learning, informal learning and technical learning are the three sources of cultural learning.
- Sub-cultural groups exist in various geographical areas due to migration of persons and groups from one place to another.
- Social class is relatively a homogeneous group and follows a hierarchal order. Income is the major variable to decide the social hierarchy followed by occupation, education and other such variables.
- Reference group serves as a frame of reference for an individual while making purchase decisions.
- Personal factors such as education, occupation, income, status, personality and self-concept have impact on service consumer behaviour.
- Physical factors such as age, sex, health, height, weight and beauty also have remarkable influence on the behaviour of service consumers.
- Motivation, perception, learning, attitudes and beliefs are the psychological factors that influence the behaviour of service consumers.
- Motivation starts with an internal stimulation triggered by either physiological or psychological needs.
- People perceive through their five senses—touch, smell, taste, sound and vision.
- People learn through trial and error, past experience, experiences of others and by relating themselves to different experiences.
- The study of consumer expectations is important to know the level of service desired by consumers.
- The variation between minimum service level and maximum service level expectations is called the zone of tolerance.
- When the service performance is outside the zone of tolerance, the service gets the consumer's attention either in a positive or negative way.
- The maximum level of service expectations is influenced by needs and wants, derived expectations of others and personal expectations.
- The minimum level of service expectations is influenced by service choices, emergencies, participation abilities in service production and situational factors.
- Marketing stimulation, word-of-mouth communication and past experience influence both maximum and minimum level of service expectations.
- Consumers generally follow a four-stage process in marketing purchase decisions: (1) problem identification and definition, (2) information search, (3) alternative evaluation, and (4) purchase and consumption.
- The study of consumers' post-purchase evaluation is important to know the satisfaction levels of the consumers.
- If the result of the post-purchase evaluation is positive, the likely behavioural response is brand loyalty. If it is negative, brand switching may result.

KEY TERMS

Attitudes *102*
Beliefs *102*
Buyer *92*
Credence qualities *111*
Culture *93*
Customer *92*
Customer compatibility *113*
Evoked set *112*
Experience qualities *111*
External stimulations *111*
HIPS *111*
Internal stimulations *111*
Learning *102*
LIPS *111*
Maximum level service *103*
Minimum level service *104*
Motivation *100*
Perception *101*
Reference group *97*
Search qualities *111*
Service encounter *108*
Social class *94*
Threshold level *109*
ZIPS *111*
Zone of tolerance *105*

BRIEF QUESTIONS

1. Explain the impact of cultural and social factors on the behaviour of service consumers.
2. How do personal and physical factors influence the behaviour of service consumers?
3. Explain the role of psychological factors in influencing the behaviour of service consumers.
4. What are the determinants of the maximum level of service expectations?
5. Explain the determinants of the minimum level of service expectations.
6. Explain service perception.
7. Discuss post-purchase behaviour in services.

ESSAY QUESTIONS

1. Explain the determinants of consumer behaviour and state how they differ in the case of services.
2. Discuss the consumer decision process in relation to a service of your choice.
3. What is the zone of tolerance? What is its significance in services marketing?
4. How do consumers develop perception? Discuss the relation between consumer expectations and perceptions.
5. "Consumers often exhibit distinctive behavioural patterns in relation to purchase of services." Discuss.
6. Discuss the importance of the study of consumer behaviour in services marketing.
7. How can the behaviour of service consumers be influenced? Illustrate with suitable examples.
8. How would you carry out a study on consumer behaviour in relation to cellular services?

ASSIGNMENTS

1. Indian Airlines was established in 1953 as a public sector company and enjoyed monopoly in the air transport in India until 1994. The competition from the private sector intensified after this sector was liberated. The growth in air passengers due to increased affluence after the implementation of the new economic policy in the country encouraged the companies to enhance the service package to customers and also to focus on the service quality. Indian Airlines faced some bitter experience in providing customer services as consumers started pointing out the differences comparing private company services or shifting loyalties to the competitors. Indian Airlines wanted to know the influencing factors for these kinds of change in consumer behaviour.
   You are required to interview a group of air passengers to:
   (a) Identify the changing expectations of air passengers.
   (b) Find out the influencing factors for the change in consumer behaviour.
2. Television is one of the popular entertainers in India. Many TV channels in many languages are accessible to people. Some channels are general and some are specialized in sports, music, movies, animals, diction, news and so on. Some channels could get high viewership and some could not. Some programmes in a channel get higher viewership and some programmes in the same channel do not.
   You are required to interact with different segments of T.V. viewers such as housewives, children and employees and find out:
   (a) What are the criteria for selecting a channel for viewing?
   (b) How many channels do they select generally? How do they evaluate a channel?

REFERENCES

1 Leon G. Shiffman and Leslie Lazar Kanuk, *Consumer Behaviour*, 7th ed. (Delhi: Pearson Education, 2002), p. 5.
2 Paul R. Timm, *Customer Service: Career Success Through Customer Loyalty*, 4th ed. (Delhi: Pearson Education, 2008), p. 42.
3 Harry C. Triandis and Eunkook M. Suh, "Cultural Influences on Personality," *Annual Review Psychology*, 53 (2002): 135.
4 Karve I. "Kinship Organisation in India," *Deccan College Monograph*, Pune, 1953, p. 21.
5 Ram Ahuja, *Society in India*. (New Delhi: Rawat Publications, 2002), p. 103.
6 Ibid.

7 Leon G. Shiffman and Leslie Lazar Kanuk, *Consumer Behaviour,* 7th ed. (Delhi: Pearson Education, 2002), p. 264.

8 Joy D. Lind Quist and M. Joseph Sirgy, *Shopper, Buyer and Consumer Behaviour: Theory and Marketing Application*, 2nd ed. (New Delhi: Biztantra, 2003), p. 148.

9 Harry C. Triandis and Eunkook M. Suh, "Cultural Influences on Personality", *Annual Review Psychol,* 53 (2002): 135.

10 Michael R. Solomon, *Consumer Behaviour,* 4th ed. (New Delhi: Prentice Hall, 2002), p. 102.

11 Abraham. H. Maslow, *Motivation and Personality,* 2nd ed. (New York: Harper & Row, 1971).

12 Michael R. Solomon and Elnora W. Stuart, *Marketing: Real People, Real Choice*, 3rd ed. (Delhi: Pearson Education, 2005), p. 201.

13 Srivastava K. K. and Sujata Khandri, *Consumer Behaviour: In Indian Context*, (New Delhi: Galgotia Publishing, 2003), p. 341.

14 William D. Perreault, Jr., and E. Jernu MC Carthy, *Basic Marketing: A Global Management Approach,* 14th ed. (New Delhi: Tata McGraw Hill, 2002), p. 162.

15 Michael Treacy and Fred Wiersema, "Customer Intimacy and Other Value Disciplines", *Harvard Business Review,* (Jan–Feb,1993): 84.

Marketing Information System and Research

6

LEARNING OBJECTIVES

After studying this chapter, you will be able to:

- Understand the importance of the marketing information system
- Describe the process of marketing research
- Understand the applications of marketing research
- Describe the research methods for service research

A management graduate from a premier business school, Venkat started his career with a multinational company engaged in the production and marketing of tangible consumer goods.

Five years into the job, he managed to break free from the monotony of a deadline-driven workday. He began to scout for feasible options with the idea of setting up his own outfit with low capital investment. He realized that the services sector offered all he had ever sought from his job—creativity, flexibility and satisfaction.

Venkat wanted to do something that would benefit the educated, unemployed section of society. After much thought, he decided to set up a consultancy service that would market business ideas to these people. These ideas, put into action, would give employment to the youth, making them self-reliant and enabling them to settle down. Thus came into existence, Life Settle.

Venkat proceeded to put together a formal business proposal. He was very clear that creativity and innovation would be the core competencies of the organization. The primary market would be the educated, unemployed youth willing to start something on their own with some professional help from Life Settle. The educated housewives from the middle-income group could also be targeted by Life Settle.

He knows that the single critical factor in the success of Life Settle would be customer confidence. Focusing on the other aspects of the business would be possible only after this hurdle has successfully been cleared. Even then, he is aware, this one hurdle will never be overcome completely—he will have to be at it consistently. Customer confidence is fragile and short-lived. However, sustaining customer confidence, according to Venkat, would be easier than building it.

Venkat plans to undertake an extensive market research to ensure that he is able to reach out to his target audience effectively, establish customer confidence and formalize the services that Life Settle will eventually offer to customers. To this end, he has put together a team of market researchers and asked them to suggest a research plan suitable for Life Settle.

Questions:

1. Do you think Venkat's decision to undertake the marketing research exercise is justified?
2. Do you think a specialized marketing strategy is needed for Life Settle? What purpose do you think the market research will serve?
3. If you were Venkat, would you adopt the same path as him? Why or why not?
4. In your opinion, what points should Venkat keep in mind while designing the market research programme?

> The quality of managerial decision making is influenced greatly by the availability, relevance, accuracy and timeliness of information. Marketing organizations should ensure the continuous flow of desired information across managerial positions.

INTRODUCTION

Information is the basic input for decision making. Access to correct information in the right form and at the right time ensures quality in managerial decision making. In this highly competitive business environment, the effective use of marketing information is a critical managerial skill. Marketing managers need information from a variety of sources, both internal and external, to take appropriate decisions at an appropriate time. The data available from various sources generally vary in quality, quantity, form and degree of credibility. This feature makes it necessary to manage marketing information.

Developments in the last century have enabled organizations to gather information from numerous sources. Simultaneous developments in IT and analytical sciences such as statistics and mathematics ensured that the available data is more credible and presented in a usable form. In present times, the problem of marketing managers in developed countries is discarding unnecessary information, not gathering information. In spite of the easy inflow of the information, managers often feel that they are not supplied with full information or right information to take decisions qualitatively. M. Harper Jr. aptly stated that: "To manage a business is to manage its future and to manage the future is to manage information."[1] A well-defined system, therefore, is necessary to provide reasonably accurate information of the right kind and order. It should also ensure timely and continuous flow of information to the right person. Therefore, every marketing organization should develop an information system for collecting, analysing and disseminating information to support managerial decision making.

MARKETING INFORMATION SYSTEM: A DEFINITION

> **The marketing information system** is a future-oriented, interactive and interrelated structure of people, equipment and procedures to ensure a continuous flow of right information to aid marketing managers in the design, development, execution and control of the marketing programme.

The marketing information system (MIS) is a future-oriented, interactive and interrelated structure of people, equipment and procedures to arrange a continuous flow of the right information to aid the marketing manager in the design, development, execution and control of the marketing programme. The following are the features of the marketing information system:

1. It is an interactive and interrelated structure of people, equipment and procedures.
2. It is a continuous process.
3. It is future oriented.
4. It supports decision making.
5. It identifies problems.
6. It generates, sorts, analyses and distributes information to right persons.
7. It distributes accurate information at the right time.
8. It aids business executives in the management of their marketing programmes.

9. It is a part of the total organizational information system.
10. It helps in the improvement of the overall effectiveness of the organization.

Service companies need to have an MIS that is as effective and functional as the MIS of manufacturing companies. The information needs and processing methodologies are similar in both types of organizations. However, the research in service companies is focused on consumer behaviour as a clear understanding of consumers' motives, perceptions, attitudes, beliefs, learning, cultural, social and personal factors is essential for developing effective marketing programmes.

SOURCES OF MARKETING INFORMATION

The sources of marketing information can broadly be divided into two categories—internal information sources and external information sources. Figure 6.1 presents the details of marketing information sources.

Internal Information Sources

Internal information can be obtained from different departments within the organization. The records and reports of these departments provide information to managers. Internal information—relating to production, facilities, capacity, equipment, human resources, accounting system, financial position, marketing operations and research and development activities—is supplied to managers routinely, after assessing the information needs of each managerial position. Such information is not expensive and helps to control various activities. It is credible, timely and accurate, and can be easily generated and controlled.

> ***Internal information sources*** *constitute an important part of the marketing information system. The data- and information-recording system in various functional departments of a service company helps managers critically analyse and understand the happenings and trends in various dimensions.*

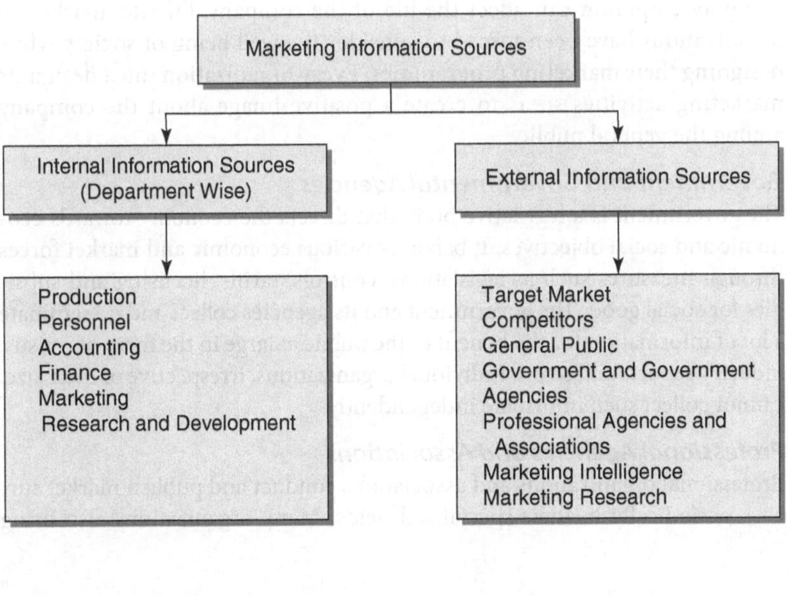

Figure 6.1
Marketing information sources

"Companies should identify and use credible sources of external information for accurate, sufficient and timely information. The sources are used to get data and information for exploring new markets, needs and applications of the existing products and identifying opportunities and threats.

External Information Sources

External information sources provide data and information that help in exploring new markets, needs and applications of the existing products and identifying threats from various sources and opportunities in the changing environment. It also helps in the development of the organization and provides useful data to correct the activities.

The sources of external information include the target market, competitors, the general public, governments, governmental agencies and market research. We looked at each of these in detail in this section.

Target Market

The target market consists of present and potential buyers that the company has chosen to serve. It constitutes an important source of information. The complaints and suggestions offered by buyers on services often become precious information to the marketing department.

Competitors

A close observation of competitors' movements is an important source of information. Competitors' actions, reactions, strategies, and so on are important inputs in building up organizational strengths to successfully face them. For example, Air India changed its market orientation after the introduction of private airline services; their aggressive market promotion strategies started attracting new customers and building customer loyalty. The business orientation of the State Bank of India, Andhra Bank and other public sector banks changed when private-sector and foreign banks introduced innovative approaches to position their services.

General Public

The public opinion of the services offered by an organization is critical information, which leads to its success or failure in the market. A negative public opinion can affect the life of the company. Of late, marketing organizations have been forced to consider the well being of society while designing their marketing programmes. Every organization must design its marketing activities so as to create a positive image about the company among the general public.

Government and Governmental Agencies

The government is a legislative body that directs the economy towards economic and social objectives. It balances various economic and market forces through measures such as legislations, controls, tariffs, licensing and subsidies for social good. The government and its agencies collect and disseminate a lot of information for the benefit of the public at large in the form of census, industry reports and so on. Individual organizations, irrespective of their size, cannot collect such informate independently.

Professional Agencies and Associations

Professional organizations and associations conduct and publish market surveys periodically in their specialized fields. Many organizations also bring out books and periodicals, which often provide very useful information to marketing organizations. Some organizations collect and sell data for profit.

Universities and Other Institutions

Universities organize research activities as part of their academic activity. A research represents factual information since the researchers' interest is academic. In addition to universities, other academic institutions and voluntary organizations also provide very useful information. Universities, for example, undertake research projects with the support of some funding agencies besides the regular doctoral research projects. These reports are of great help to the industry.

Marketing Intelligence

Marketing intelligence deals with information pertaining to happenings in the marketing environment. Everyday changes in the external environment necessitate alterations in an organization's strategic and marketing plans. Marketing intelligence mostly comes from the personnel of the organization. The personnel in marketing, service outlets, finance, engineering, research and development are capable of providing marketing intelligence. The marketing intelligence system trains and motivates the company personnel to observe and study the changes in the environment and report the same to the management. Marketing intelligence may be used either for defensive or offensive purposes. *Defensive intelligence* is to avoid threats to the company's position. *Offensive intelligence* is to find new opportunities to expand marketing activities. Apart from company personnel, intermediaries, suppliers, customers and other allies also provide marketing intelligence. The marketing intelligence system has to design suitable programmes to obtain intelligence from these sources.

Marketing Research

The functions of marketing research are to gather, sort, analyse and interpret information to aid managers in solving a marketing problem. The later part of the chapter presents a detailed discussion of this aspect.

MIS BEGINS AND ENDS WITH THE INFORMATION USER

The concept of MIS is that it begins and ends with the person who uses the information (see Fig. 6.2). It starts with the identification and assessment of the information needs of marketing managers; collection of the information from internal records, marketing intelligence, marketing research and other external sources and analysis of the collected information in view of organizational requirements and ends with the distribution of this information to managers for better planning, execution and control.

> *"The marketing information system begins with the assessment of information needs for effective planning, execution and control of marketing operations. The information collected from the internal and external marketing environment through the three sources—internal records, marketing intelligence and marketing research—are processed and distributed to the right persons as a support to decision making."*

Identifying and Assessing Information Needs

Identifying and assessing information needs is the first major step in deciding the flow of information. Understanding the current situation helps identify

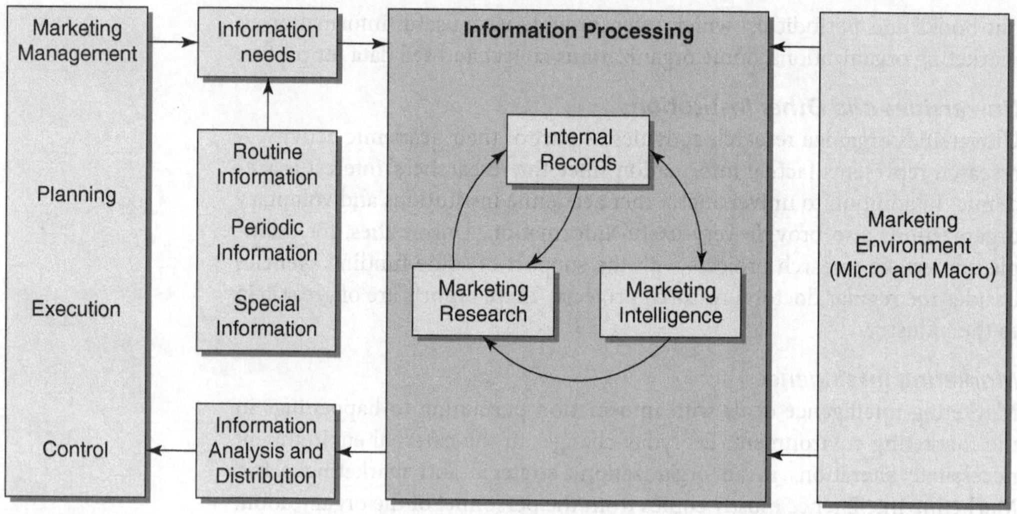

Figure 6.2
The marketing information system

> *Information needs are generally assessed by circulating a set of questions to managers or through interviewing them personally. However, in finalizing the needs, managerial judgement plays a vital role as there may be attitude and behavioural problems of managers in their information needs assessment.*

the gap between the information needs of managers and the supplied information. This assessment is easily done by circulating a questionnaire and/or through personal interviews. The real problem is with the assessment of information needs as there may be many points of view regarding this. There may be some managers who, on account of their poor judgement, want total information on all subjects to be supplied to them irrespective of its application. There may be other managers who do not have complete knowledge of information needs for better decision making. They may struggle with the current problems and lack a comprehensive future outlook. There may be yet other managers who are too ambitious and feel every bit of information may be useful in an unexpected situation. The marketing organization should carefully identify the needs and assess them in the light of organizational objectives. It should also evaluate the cost of information against the value of information as information does not have any value of its own. Rather, its value depends on the purpose and effectiveness of its use. Therefore, in the absence of an acceptable measure, this evaluation is a difficult job. However, organizations apply their own measures to assess the benefit versus the expected cost of such information. When the cost of the additional information exceeds the benefit, the company may not prefer to share such information with its managers.

Collecting Information

Once the organization decides what information to share with its managers on a regular basis, it has to chalk out a plan to collate the necessary information. There are three major sources for processing information: (1) internal records, (2) marketing intelligence and (3) marketing research. Apart from these three sources, the organization also gets information directly from the external environment through complaints and suggestions from customers as reactions to the decisions of the marketing organization.

Internal Records

Internal sources provide regular and periodic information to the marketing information system.

Marketing Intelligence

Marketing intelligence alerts the marketing organization either to safeguard its market position or to exploit the new opportunities in the ever-changing marketing environment.

Marketing Research

Marketing research is a very important component of the marketing information system. The term *research* signifies two important aspects: (1) a methodical, unbiased and complete investigation of a subject matter to establish principles and (2) an investigation of a problem to discover pertinent information to help solve it. Marketing research has a wider application in the science of marketing, both in the formulation of new principles and in assisting managers to solve specific problems. The other two components of the marketing information system—internal records and marketing intelligence—often fail to provide adequate and satisfactory information to marketing managers. Internal records are designed basically for efficient departmental functioning. The form and contents of these records may not be capable of furnishing the total information required by marketing mangers. Marketing intelligence often gathers information in bits and pieces that may not help in assessing the situation and taking decisions. Therefore, marketing managers require formal studies capable of presenting detailed, reliable and accurate information. Thus, marketing research is of great importance to marketing managers. Companies rely heavily on information technology to strengthen the marketing information system. The most commonly used technologies for the purpose are discussed in "Services Marketing Insight: Information Technology and Marketing Information System".

MARKETING RESEARCH

Marketing research is a problem-oriented systematic design, collection, analysis and distribution of adequate and factual information to marketing managers to assist them in decision making. The following are the features of marketing research:

> **Marketing research** *is a problem-oriented systematic design, collection, analysis and distribution of adequate and factual information to marketing managers to assist them in decision making.*

1. Marketing research is problem oriented. It starts with a problem and ends with suggesting a solution.
2. The purpose of marketing research is to help mangers solve specific problems.
3. It is a formalized means of collecting information.
4. It analyses problems related to the marketing of goods and services.
5. It can be used to obtain facts related to a host of marketing problems.

Marketing research became prominent only after the industry recognized the concept of marketing. As consumer satisfaction was identified as a key

> **6.1 Services Marketing Insight — Information Technology and Marketing Information System**
>
> The rapid pace of change in information technology has had a positive impact on marketing management. The market place is moving to the market space and the workplace is moving to the workspace. A wide variety of computer-based tools and approaches is available to process information and services as a support to decision making. The four most commonly used technologies in marketing information systems are:
>
> 1. ***Decision Support Systems (DSS):*** These are computer-based systems that support marketing managers through direct interaction with data and analytical models in decision making. The DSS has three components—dialog, data and model. The dialog component links the user to the system. The data component allows the user to access relevant data directly or use the data as an input to the model component. The model component uses mathematical models to analyse the data.
> 2. ***Data Warehouses and Data Mining:*** Service organizations collect data from various sources within and outside the organization, which is organized, stored and updated under different heads such as customers, market segments and competitors. This sorted and organized data comprises a database. This process of assembling and retrieving data is called database management. Some companies move beyond the database to create large and complex data repositories, called data warehouses. *Data warehouses* enable marketing managers to understand market behaviour better and address consumer needs more efficiently. *Data mining* is an advanced use of data warehouses. It applies advanced statistical and artificial intelligence techniques to identify patterns and meaningful relationships within masses of data.
> 3. ***Executive Information System (EIS):*** An EIS provides access to summarized performance data in an easy-to-use fashion to executives. It uses graphics to display and visualize data. It identifies critical information required by executives and, hence, saves their time.
> 4. ***Expert System (ES):*** An ES is a real-world use of artificial intelligence (AI). The technology that attempts to mimic our senses and emulate certain facets of human behaviour such as reasoning and communicating is called *artificial intelligence*. An ES provides an automated analysis or problem-solving model to executives. Like an expert, it consults the base of knowledge and reasons out a solution based on the characteristics of the problem.

element for the success of any business activity, firms were forced to direct their attention to the development of new products, markets and marketing strategies. Marketing research helps managers address these challenges on the marketing front. Organizations engage in marketing research for two basic reasons—to identify and to solve marketing problems.[2]

Marketing Research Application and Importance

Marketing research has been used widely by all business concerns—both in the manufacturing and in the service sectors. The growing complexity of the business environment, intensified competition and changing behaviour of consumers due to the changes in social, cultural, economic, technological and political systems generate scores of problems for marketing managers.

Marketing research is used in many areas. The important areas where marketing research is used prominently by service companies, shown in Fig. 6.3, are discussed here.

> *Marketing research has been used prominently to study the market potential, market share, market characteristics, sales trends, business trends, market forecasting, competitors, existing as well as new products and company image in the market.*

1. *Sales Analysis:* Sales analysis is an important research activity which helps managers identify many problems and take corrective actions. Data relating to region-wise sales performance, item-wise sales performance, reasons for positive performance, reasons for negative performance, region-wise and service-wise sales growth rate, etc. help managers integrate their efforts to improve the overall efficiency and to maximize the profitability of the concern.
2. *Testing the Existing Products:* Marketers cannot rest with the successful performance of the existing service mix. They have to strive hard to maintain it as competitors always strive hard to offer better services. Testing the performance of existing services, time and again, is of great help in this direction. For the purpose, companies conduct service product research, price research, advertising research, dealer's research and so on.
3. *Testing the New Service Products:* Marketing research undertakes test marketing of new services. It tests the market acceptance, suitability from various angles and helps managers in developing a service very close to the expectations of consumers.

Fig. 6.3
Marketing research applications to services

4. *Testing Service Design and Blueprinting:* Service design includes technical features of the service product. The design is blueprinted with clarity of processes. The expected roles of employees and customers in service production and consumption play a vital role in the success or failure of the service. Before commercializing the service, the service provider needs to test the design and blueprint to ensure everything conceptualized is translated well into the service form. It also helps identify variations or defects and correct them before the product is offered to the target market.
5. *Study of Services Gaps:* One of the prominent quality assessment models used by service providers is *gap analysis*. There are five possible gaps between the actual and desired service quality (see Chapter 19 for details):
   i. *Management Perception Gap:* The difference between the expected service by customers and the management's perceptions of consumer expectations
   ii. *Quality Specification Gap:* The difference between the company's perception of customer expectations and customer-driven service designs and standards
   iii. *Service Delivery Gap:* The difference between customer-driven service designs and standards and the service delivery
   iv. *Market Communication Gap:* The difference between the service delivery and external communications to customers
   v. *Perceived Service Quality Gap:* The gap between the perceived service and the expected service

   Marketing research can be used to identify the existing gaps and the root cause for these gaps so as to take appropriate measures to eliminate these gaps.
6. *Services Recovery:* When service failures occur, service firms initiate the service recovery process by taking some corrective measures or by compensating consumers for service deficiencies. This process is to protect the image of the company and to heal the wounds of consumers (physical or psychological) due to service failures. Marketing research is useful to evaluate the effectiveness of service recovery strategies and to find out the recovery expectations of consumers when services failures occur.
7. *Market Potential:* The term *market potential* refers to the total expected demand for an industry's product at a given period of time. It is an aggregate expected demand of all the competitive products put together for the same purpose. Sales potential means the expected sales of a particular brand at a given period of time. It is necessary to any marketing organization to measure both the aspects. Marketing research can be used to get the required information.
8. *Market Share:* An organization's objective is to increase its market share while maintaining the existing share. It is not an easy task to achieve

this objective. The organization has to take a score of timely decisions for the purpose. The analysis of its own strengths and weaknesses in the market, competitor's strengths and weaknesses, competitor's strategies and expected movements, changes in the consumer needs and wants and so on are the areas in which a thorough understanding is necessary.

9. *Market Characteristics:* As marketing is consumer oriented, learning the market characteristics forms the basis for a marketing strategy. Information about buyers such as their socio-cultural background, economic background, demography, psychological patterns, and attitudes and habits are to be studied in detail.
10. *Business Trends:* Marketing organizations should be watchful of the trends in business. The stage of the business cycle, its direction, its impact on the economy, general marketing implications on company's services are important areas of information.
11. *Market Forecasting:* This includes short-term forecasting and long-term forecasting. This forecast helps in the development of long-term marketing planning and annual marketing plans.
12. *Competitive Offers:* Marketers should study not only their company's services mix but also the competitors' service offerings. A comprehensive knowledge of competitive offers serves as very useful information input to marketing managers.
13. *Company Image:* Company image is a broad term basically refers to the goodwill of the company. Marketing research is used to identify the contributing factors for building and maintaining the image of a company.

The list of applications mentioned here is far from exhaustive, and there are numerous other areas of applications. The scope of marketing research is wider and changes along with the changes in the marketing field.

Marketing Research Organizations

A marketing research department generally is headed by a vice president. The marketing research manager reports to him. The department may have researchers, including problem analysers, survey designers, behavioural scientists and statisticians. Whether having a marketing research department is a strategic decision or not mostly depends on the company's size, financial resources, human resources, markets, competition and so on. A company can undertake marketing research by its own personnel or may leave a part or the entire programme to outsiders. Small firms generally purchase the services of outside organizations whereas big companies prefer to have their own marketing research department. The research organizations outside the company can be grouped into three categories:

> **Marketing research** *can be carried out by the company itself or by using the services of professional organizations. There are firms specialized in offering three categories of services: syndicated research services, custom marketing research and specialty line marketing research.*

Syndicated Service Research Firms

These organizations undertake periodic research, collect consumer and trade information and sell this information to service companies.

Custom Marketing Research Firms

Companies may hire these firms to undertake marketing research. These firms participate in the total marketing research process, and the final report is the property of the client.

Specialty-line Marketing Research Firms

These firms render some specialized services to the company's marketing research department. Survey design, field service, statistical assistance and so on are the examples of specialized services. Nielsen India, for example, provides customized research services to many companies.

THE MARKETING RESEARCH PROCESS

Good research generates dependable data derived from practices conducted professionally; these data can be relied on for managerial decision making.[3] According to D. R. Cooper and P. S. Schindler, there are nine defining characteristics for the scientific method of research: (1) Clearly defined purpose (2) Detailed research process, (3) Thoroughly planned research design, (4) High ethical standards, (5) limitations frankly revealed, (6) adequate analysis for the decision maker's needs, (7) findings presented unambiguously, (8) conclusions justified and (9) researcher's experience reflected.[4]

There are seven major steps in the process of marketing research, as shown in Fig. 6.4. In the following sections, we discuss each of these seven steps in detail.

Nielsen India

Nielsen India, a leading market research agency, offers specialized services to various companies in marketing information and research. It offers key services in the areas of market performance measurement, analytical tools and market information analysis, diagnostic services and market opportunity identification and analysis. The business consultancy services of the company combine qualitative and fact-based recommendations to its clients on where to play, how to win, micro-economic impact systems, shopper management, etc. The agency created a unique retail-measurement technique that gave clients the first reliable objective information about competitive performance and the impact of their marketing and sales programmes on revenues and profits. The company is a pioneer in providing space management solutions to retailers. The company introduced the space and planogram management software solution my.spaceman in 2009, which enables easier integration with client data and planning systems. New analytical reporting capabilities of the software increase the effectiveness and efficiency of the space management process. It quickens the process of implementing customer-centric assortment and space management initiatives at the cluster and store-specific level. Nielsen's research services package includes syndicated services, customized services and speciality-line market research services. The agency developed a reliable and updated database on various trends in business sectors and captured sizable market share in this segment. Customized service offerings are the core competency of the agency.

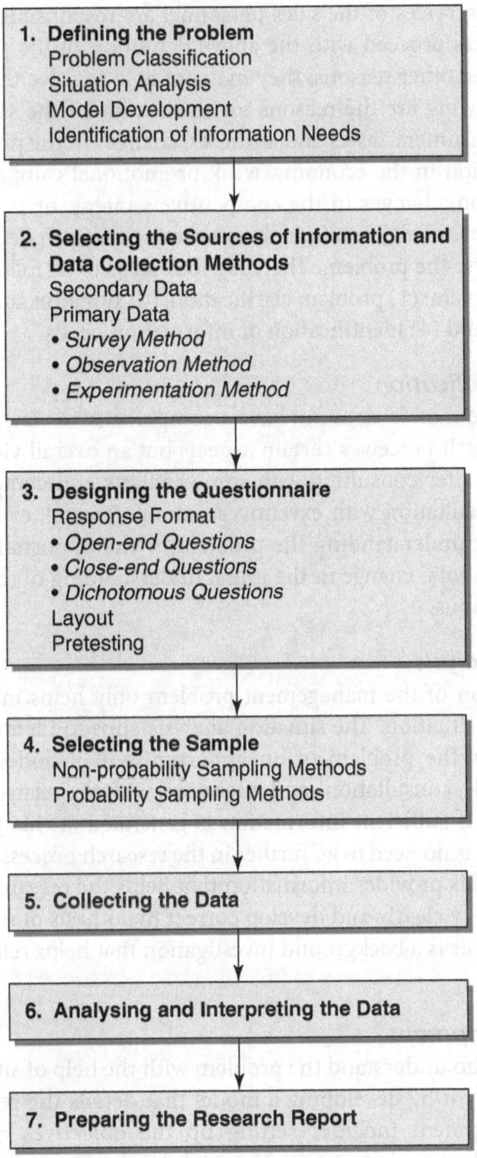

Fig.6.4
The marketing research process

Defining the Problem

This is the first and most critical step in the marketing research process. Various decisions in the subsequent steps of the research process depend on the definition of the problem. If the problem definition is not correct, the entire research process becomes a waste. The marketing research organization should carefully define its problem. For example, marketers may notice a decline in the sales of a service in a particular segment. They may understand

> *The output of the marketing research depends on the clarity of the researcher's understanding of the problem. The researcher consults many functionaries of the organization to understand the problem fully.*

that the poor services of the sales personnel are responsible for the decline. If the marketers proceed with the above definition of the problem without considering the other reasons, they may not able to solve the original problem. The following are the reasons for the decline of the sales of a service: changes in consumers' tastes and attitudes, changes in the purchasing power, general recession in the economy, weak promotional campaign, increase in the competition, changes in the competitive strategy, or poor performance of the sales personnel. Therefore, the marketing research department should carefully analyse the problem. There are four steps to be followed in defining a research problem: (1) problem clarification, (2) situation analysis, (3) model development and (4) identification of information needs.

Problem Clarification

The management often does not have a comprehensive view of a problem or an opportunity. It perceives certain aspects but an overall view point can be achieved only after consulting with some analysts and company personnel. Therefore, consultation with executives, sales personnel, experts and others help in clearly understanding the problem or the opportunity. Sometimes, there may be a total change in the initial understanding of the problem after such consultations.

Situation Analysis

The clarification of the management problem only helps in identifying the context of the situation. The situation analysis aims to identify the variables responsible for the problem or an opportunity. It includes verification of internal records, consultations and interviews with the related personnel and other experts. If sufficient information is generated at this point to solve a problem, there is no need to go further in the research process. Otherwise, the situation analysis provides information that helps the researcher understand the problem very clearly and develop correct hypothesis of the problem. The situation analysis is a background investigation that helps refine the research problem.[5]

> *A **model** is a simplified presentation of a reality. The model of the research problem depicts the relevant variables and their connectivity, research objectives and expected outcome. It determines the scope of the study and eliminates unnecessary information flow.*

Model Development

Researchers who understand the problem with the help of situation analysis should simplify it by developing a model that details the research process. Model development includes setting up the objectives of the research project, identifying relevant variables and developing ways to relate these variables to the objectives. The researcher should keep the following aspects in mind:

1. What will be the outcome with the objectives defined?
2. How will they be useful in problem solving?
3. Will the objectives produce enough information?
4. What is the possibility of generating unnecessary information?
5. Are the variables measurable? If so, to what extent?

6. What is the accuracy level required and will be?
7. What will be the cost and benefit of the total research project?

Keeping these aspects in mind, researchers develop the best possible model of the problem.

Identification of Information Needs

The last step in the problem definition is to develop a statement of the needed information under different heads. The statement is prepared based on the preceding three steps in the definition process.

Selecting the Sources of Information and Data-collection Methods

Information can be broadly obtained from two sources: secondary sources and primary sources. The data generated for solving the problem at hand are called *primary data;* the data developed for the purpose of some other problem are called *secondary data*.

Secondary Data

The role of secondary data in marketing research has, of late, been pivotal due to the availability of large number of databases commercially and the development of information technology. Secondary data has some advantages over primary data. It can be gathered quickly and, relatively, inexpensively. This factor helps the manager take quick decisions either to control the situation or to solve the problem. But, the secondary data suffer from many limitations in application. Secondary data may not be available to all marketing problems; in some cases the available secondary data may not be sufficient. The second limitation is relevance. Since secondary data is developed for some other purpose, the data may not fit the requirements of the problem at hand. Differences in the units of measurement, data classification, time to which the data belongs and so on reduce the relevance of the data to apply to the present situation. The third limitation is accuracy. It is very difficult to determine the accuracy of secondary data. In spite of these limitations, secondary data is used in many marketing research projects. The Central Statistical Organization (CSO) is the major source of data relating to trends in various fields of activity. The activities of the CSO include National Income Accounting, conduct of Annual Survey of Industries, Economic Census and its follow-up surveys, compilation of Index of Industrial Production, as well as Consumer Price Indices for Urban Non-manual Employees, human development statistics, gender statistics and so on. The periodic reports developed by the organization are known for methodical accuracy and consistency. The data provided by the CSO is useful to service companies to understand the geographic and demographic trends in the country, which is helpful in designing marketing strategies.[6] The National Council for Applied Economic Research (NCAER) is another organization which provides credible secondary information to business organizations.

> "***Secondary data*** *can be obtained quickly and at less cost. However, availability, accuracy, sufficiency, relevance, methodology and credibility are to be studied carefully before selecting secondary sources.*"

NCAER

The National Council of Applied Economic Research (NCAER), an independent, non-profit research institution, was established in 1956 with the objective of conducting research on applied economics and providing data and information to policy makers and other clients. It is the premier research institute of India in applied economics. The NCAER has done pioneering research work during the last 50 years on the policy analysis and application of modern quantitative techniques to development issues, regional development and planning, household income, consumption, savings, investments and energy. The NCAER is a syndicated research organization. It conducts periodic research on various social and economic issues of the country and provides very useful database to the industry and business. The NCAER achieved unique status in the country for designing and executing large-scale sample surveys on regional and human development and many consumer products. The reports of the organization carry high level of credibility because of the quality standards adopted in the research process and the use of state-of-the-art computation methodology. The clientele of the council includes planning commission, state governments, public and private sector companies, and international agencies. It has built up a rich database on economic and commercial data for the referral use of its clientele.

Sources of Secondary Data The sources of secondary data can be divided into internal sources and external sources.

- *Internal Sources:* Internal sources include accounting records relating to various departments in the organization, sales force reports and other miscellaneous reports such as special audit reports and earlier marketing research.
- *External Sources:* External sources include the government and its agencies, professional organizations and institutions, trade associations, private business firms, advertising media, universities and other educational institutions, syndicated services, computerized databases and other published sources.

Primary Data

Marketing researchers try to get useful information as much as possible from secondary data. If they find information is inadequate after the sources are exhausted, they proceed to the collection of primary data. Primary data collection is time consuming and expensive as compared to secondary data collection. But the data will be precious in its use and application. There are three methods of collecting primary data: (1) the survey method, (2) the observation method and (3) the experimentation method. All these methods can be used in a research project but normally are not used due to many limitations. The selection of a method is influenced by the availability of time, finance, human resources and other facilities.

> *Though **primary data** is costly and time consuming, it provides useful and comprehensive data and information that is totally relevant and accurate.*

The Survey Method The survey method of obtaining information is based on the questioning of respondents.[7] It is the most common method of collecting primary data. This method can be used to obtain information relating to consumer attitudes, beliefs, opinions, knowledge, personality factors, ownership, past behaviour, intended behaviour and other descriptive aspects. A typical characteristic of the survey method is that it can be used to produce original data. It may be the only logical method, perhaps, to study consumers' behaviour.

In the survey method, information is collected from respondents systematically. For the purpose, the researcher should select the sample, design a questionnaire, administer it among the sample respondents and analyse the data collected in the light of research objectives.

Based upon the method of communication used, surveys can be divided into three types: personal interview, mail survey and telephone survey.

> *The three methods of* ***primary data collection****—survey, observation and experimentation—are complementary to each other. The choice depends on the availability of time, finance, human resources, and other factors.*

Personal Interviews: A personal interview offers greater flexibility than the other two options. It may take place in two forms: individual interview and group interview. In individual interviews, each individual respondent is interviewed separately whereas in group interviews, a trained interviewer interviews a group of 6 to 10 persons at a time by introducing the problem to the group and inviting responses from the group.

An individual interview offers a great opportunity to the researcher to observe the feelings through body movements and facial expressions. It offers greater scope to extract as much information as possible depending on the situation. Researchers can read the respondents and accordingly they can adjust or amend the questions (additions, deletion, sequence, modification and so on). Apart from obtaining answers to the questions, individual interviews help in understanding the realities about the respondents. The researchers can easily estimate the respondents' socio-economic conditions, standard of living and so on, and such information is of great value for marketing. Respondents may be contacted at their residences, offices, shopping and other locations. The familiar surroundings help the respondents feel free in expressing their opinions. The results of the individual interview greatly depend on the interviewers. The interviewers should have good conversational abilities, good communication skills, good knowledge and understanding of the problem and objectives of the research programme, common sense, expertise in time management and a pleasing personality. They should have an ability to get an acceptance from the respondents, to create interest about the problem and to make the respondents understood the problem in a short span of time.

> *Person-to-person interviews and group interviews are widely used in survey research. The skills of the interviewer can be exploited well to generate qualitative information. Respondents also find comfortable as the interviewer clarifies all their doubts on the questions and supports in giving right answers.*

A group interview provides an opportunity to read the group behaviour on a particular problem. It is less costly and time consuming as compared to the individual interview. The interviewers should have the knowledge of consumer behaviour and group dynamics, apart from the problem and company information. The result depends on their ability in obtaining the required information from the group.

In this method, a group of respondents is selected from a specific area and invited on a particular date to a specified place. The interviewers introduce the problem, start with some broad questions and move slowly to specific issues. They encourage participation of respondents and direct the discussion to the specific problem. The entire discussion is recorded through videos and tapes and later analysed to understand the group behaviour. Though, this method helps in understanding consumer thought and feelings, the quality mostly depends on the interviewers. The major problem of this method is to select members of the group. This method suffers from the sampling error to a greater extent since it is not possible to cover a large sample.

Mail Surveys: Under this contact method, the researcher sends questionnaires to respondents by mail. This method can be executed in several ways. Questionnaires may be sent directly by post. They may be distributed by means of magazine and newspaper inserts or through company boys to the residence of respondents and have them collected after some time. They may be distributed at shopping stores, offices and other places with a request to respondents to mail the filled in questionnaires back to the researcher. Questionnaires may also be sent to the respondents via e-mail provided they have Internet access. The advantages of this method are:

1. The questionnaires can be used to collect the large volume of information.
2. The cost per respondent is much lower as compared to the personal interview.
3. The respondents can take up the questionnaire at their convenient time to answer.
4. In the absence of the interviewer, the respondent can feel free in filling the questionnaire.
5. The respondent is not under the influence of the interviewer, which ensures the quality of information.
6. Personal information and some information which the respondent may not be willing to disclose in the presence of an outsider may be obtained through this method.

However, mail interviews have the following drawbacks.

1. Mail questionnaires are not very flexible. The indirect way of questioning does not help the researcher to probe and change the questions depending on the responses to the earlier questions.
2. It is very difficult to develop a standard pattern of questions that suits exactly to each and every respondent.
3. The method is helpless in case respondents need some clarification or some more information to answer some questions.
4. It is time consuming. Busy respondents in their day-to-day activities may not complete it within the time schedule though they do not have the unwillingness to do it.

5. A low response rate is the major factor limiting the application of this method.
6. Obtaining correct addresses is a difficult proposition.

In spite of these limitations, mail surveys are popularly used by many organizations. Many of the drawbacks are subjective and can be overcome by applying sufficient care in the questionnaire development. The low response rate is the major factor; to reduce it, the company may offer some benefits such as free gifts, coupons, or prizes to respondents.

Telephonic Interviews: In this contact method, the interviewer contacts the respondent by phone with a set of questions on hand. If a company needs quick information, a telephone interview is by far the best method to contact respondents. The researchers can interview directly without making their formal presence to the respondents. The respondents feel free to answer various questions in the absence of the formal presence of the interviewer. The researchers can probe, alter or modify their questions depending on the responses to the earlier questions, can obtain information relating to some personal facts of respondents and can clarify doubts and provide additional information, if required, to respondents. This method is less costly, less time consuming and more effective. However, this method has many limitations in application. It is very difficult to obtain the respondent's consent by telephone for an interview. The interview should be very short so that large quantities of information cannot be obtained. It is very difficult to draw full attention of the respondent by phone. The questions must be short, simple and easily understandable to respondents. It is not possible to observe the respondent personally. The total sample should possess telephones.

The three types of surveys have advantages as well as limitations. The selection of one of the three depends on many factors. The information needs, types of respondents, nature of respondents, time, finance, facilities and other factors influence the decision.

Of late, online marketing research has been used by many companies to gain the advantage of time and cost. The details of online marketing research are presented in "Services Marketing Insight: Online Marketing Research".

The Observation Method Observation is the process of noting and recording information about people and their behaviour without asking specific questions.[8] Useful information can be collected through observational research. Under this approach, the consumers' actions and situations are observed keenly and carefully to derive some inferences. The observation method is not a substitute to the survey and experimentation method but it is complementary to these two methods. At least three conditions are to be met for the application of this method: (1) the data for observation must be accessible, (2) the behaviour of the object must be repetitive, frequent and otherwise predictable and (3) an event must cover a reasonably short span of time.

> **Observational research** *is possible when the event is observable and covers a reasonably short span of time, and the behaviour of the object is frequent, repetitive or predictable.*

If anybody requires the accuracy of the data and the cost involved in obtaining it, the observation method is certainly preferred in some situations.

6.2 Services Marketing Insight

Online Marketing Research

The Web-based online marketing research enabling researchers to offer clients a fast and cost-effective method for many marketing research projects such as brand research, customer satisfaction, concept testing, new product research, positioning studies, advertising research, and pricing research. Many companies realized the potential of this research tool in exploring the new areas of marketing research applications.

The specific advantages of the online research are:

- Large number of respondents can be researched at one time.
- Less expensive and fastest research results.
- Global access at the click of the button.
- It can be interactive to ensure accuracy and quality.

Guidelines for commissioning online research

It is necessary to follow some guidelines to commission an online research effectively. The key considerations are:

- Provide the detailed brief about the company expectations to the researcher.
- Communicate the important issues to be focussed in research.
- Make sure that the researcher has necessary resources to interview a representative sample. Pre-screened access panels, if available, reduce the risk of deception.
- The respondents should be of average or above average the literacy level, otherwise they are hard to reach.
- Use scaling techniques in framing questions.
- Include visual display materials such as advertising copy, concept statement, and photos.
- Make sure that the respondent finds benefit by way of participation.

Limitations of online marketing research in India

- Internet users are limited in number. Therefore, the sample cannot be truly representative.
- All Internet users may not be willing to respond to the survey. Only some percentage of users is accessible.
- The methodologies of online research are still evolving. The accuracy and credibility of the results are questionable in many studies.

The limitations do not denigrate the valuable role of online research in today's fast-paced business environment. This tool yields very good results when the same degree of responsibility is shown as in the case of the traditional method of market research; the respondent interface is designed with social expertise and sensitivity to technology users and the case is taken to target the right audience.

There is a strong need of creativity in online research. Crafting old ways into new technologies may not help in exploiting the potential of this powerful tool. Companies must ensure that they are pushing for the highest professional standards and challenging the norms consistently if they opt for this method.

Sources: www.rbg.org.uk, November 2007, and www.powerdecisions.com.

For example, voters' turn out to political meetings, traffic counts and cine goer's turn out to new movies can be studied through observation method more qualitatively and at a less expense. In some cases, observational research is the only way to collect information; for example, children, animals and birds food preferences can be known only through observation.

Observation may be made on a natural situation. The observers does not disturb the natural situation and does not reveal their formal presence.

They observe closely the natural happenings and draw inferences. For example, a researcher may select the entrance of a shopping mall to observe the composition of customers such as males, females, families and groups and changes in composition of customers during peak periods, slack periods, and so on.

A researcher may create a situation to observe the behaviour. For example, a researcher may introduce himself as a consumer and observe the behaviour of salesmen.

Generally, the observation is made in an indirect way. The person being observed is not informed about it. One-way mirrors, hidden cameras and so on are used mostly to prevent respondents from becoming aware of their being observed.

Observation may be structured or unstructured. In structured observation, the researcher decides in advance what are to be observed and ignores all the other behavioural acts. Structured observation reduces the consumption of time and energy and increases the quality of observation. In unstructured observation the researcher is free to observe the objects. It is more useful in exploratory research.

Observation may be direct or indirect. In direct observation, the researcher observes the current behaviour of the object. However, it is not possible to observe the results or effects of actions through direct observation. Indirect observation is necessary for the purpose. The examination of secondary sources of information and physical traces (for example, verification of a waste basket may reveal the various items and their number consumed by a family) are some of the methods used for indirect observation.

Apart from human observation, many mechanical devices are also being used for observational research. A television meter can be used to observe a family's television viewing habits. There are physiological measures to identify human reactions to a particular stimulation: A brain wave analysis method is used to measure the degrees of rational and emotional responses to stimulations; eye tracking is used to record movements of the eye in relation to a stimulus; a psychogalvanometer identifies the emotional reactions to various stimulations by way of measuring the rate of perspiration; a voice pitch analysis technique is used to examine relative changes in the vibration frequency of the voice. These methods/mechanical devices help in obtaining the information that people are unwilling or unable to provide.

> "***Observation*** *may be structured or unstructured, natural or disguised, or direct or indirect. It may be done through human beings as well as machines.*"

The Experimentation Method Experimentation is used in research to establish cause-and-effect relationship between an independent variable and a dependent variable, by controlling the other variables. It involves manipulation of one or more independent variables to measure its effect on one or more other variables. A particular group of population taken for experimentation is called the treatment group. The changes in the dependent variable in the treatment group, caused by the independent variable, are measured. The subjects may be assigned either randomly (randomization) to the treatment group or deliberately to objects (matching) to measure the key changes.

The effectiveness of experimentation depends on how effectively the other variables are controlled or managed. The influence of other variables on the dependent variable should be at a minimum level to establish a direct cause-and-effect relation.[9]

Experimentation provides distinctive information. Its specialty is its capacity to produce realistic information. Survey research and observational research are also used in experimentation. The experimentation method is used popularly in test marketing while introducing a new service, a new marketing strategy, changes in the services product mix, price, promotional campaign and so on. Experimentation may be done in a laboratory or at field. Laboratory experiments on the treatment group are placed in an environment where the other variables are controlled to the maximum extent. Although in field experimentation the measurement is done in the presence of all other variables the efforts are made to control their influence.

> ***Experimentation*** *generates realistic information and is used to establish cause-and-effect relationship. It involves manipulation of independent variables to measure their effects on other variables.*

Selecting the treatment group and controlling variables are the major difficulties in the experimental research. Finding a typical treatment group which has homogeneity in all significant aspects is necessary, but it is a very difficult task. It is not possible to control all the variables because some variables are really uncontrollable. For example, competition, technology, and government policies are not controllable variables. A sudden change in any of these variables may spoil the entire experiment. This method is expensive and needs a thorough and careful planning to operate.

Designing the Questionnaire

> *A* ***questionnaire*** *is a popularly used research instrument. A questionnaire may be used to measure the behaviour of respondents, their demographic characteristics such as age, sex, occupation and family, the level of knowledge and the attitudes and opinions of the selected respondents.*

A questionnaire is simply a formalized set of questions for eliciting information.[10] It is a common form of measurement in marketing research. After defining the problem clearly and selecting the sources and data collection methods, the researcher should develop questions to elicit the required information from respondents.

Questions should be placed in order in the standard form to record the information. The set of these forms is called a *questionnaire*. A questionnaire may be used to measure the behaviour of respondents, their demographic characteristics such as age, sex, occupation and family, the level of knowledge and the attitudes and opinions of the selected respondents.

The development of a questionnaire is certainly a critical exercise in marketing research. The results of the marketing research mostly are influenced by the way the questionnaire is developed. It is the last comprehensive step before leaving for the field for information gathering. A questionnaire is almost a conclusive form of the researcher's decision on the requirement of information towards a particular problem. Therefore, a cautious approach is necessary in the development of a questionnaire.

The first and foremost step in this direction is the assessment of the exact information required for the problem. Questions should be developed based on such requirement. It is also necessary to know the general characteristics of respondents to whom the questionnaire is aimed. This information particularly helps in determining the language to be used, words usage, question form and so on. For example, the questionnaire should be different to literates and illiterate persons. A decision on the contact method is also necessary. For example, if the telephone interview is selected to contact respondents, the questions must be short and simple, the number of questions should be less and the questions should be capable of obtaining simple responses. If the personal interview is selected, a different structure is necessary.

> "The development of a good questionnaire requires the knowledge of exact information needs, respondents' profiles and interviewing techniques."

Development of Questions

Many issues are to be considered in the development of questions. Each question should contribute towards the objective of the research programme. First, the researchers should check that whether a question is really needed for the purpose or not. If the question is needed, then they should check the capability of the question to generate the required information and its capacity to obtain a right response from respondents. In this process the researchers can eliminate unnecessary questions and correct the questions to obtain the meaningful information.

The usage of words or phrases in the questions should be taken care of. Words should carry the same meaning for both the researcher and the respondent; otherwise the result would be misleading. For example, the question may be:"What kind of transport services do you use?". Here, the kind implies many meanings, public versus private, modes of transport, premium versus economy and so forth. If there is an improper match between the researcher's expectation and the respondent's understanding, the result will be misleading. Sometimes, the words or phrases used in a question may influence the respondent to respond in a particular way. These are called *leading questions*. Consider the following two questions: "Do you think Doordarshan really requires autonomy to improve its programmes?" "Do you think autonomy helps Doordarshan to improve its programmes?" There will certainly be some difference in the response to these two questions. The difference shows that the words "helps" and "really requires" induce some bias. The frame of reference is the other important aspect to be considered in the question development.

> "The words and phrases used in questions should carry the same meaning to the researcher and to the respondent. Leading questions should be avoided. Questions should drive respondents to the right frame of reference."

Consider the following questions:

1. What is your opinion on the LIC's promptness in payments on the maturity of policies?
2. Do you face any problem in obtaining the matured policy payment from LIC?

The first question is quite general in nature and the respondents refer their general observation. In second question the respondent's personal experience is the frame of reference. The researcher must see, therefore, the required frame of reference is used by the respondent.

The Response Format

The development of the response format is another crucial stage in the questionnaire development. The decisions relating to various measurement techniques such as attitude scales and projective techniques should be taken for

> *Respondents have freedom to answer open-ended questions as they like. However, there are some data processing problems in this type of question format.*

the development of the response format. There are three forms of questions: open-ended, closed-ended or multiple choice and dichotomous questions.

Open-ended Questions Open-ended questions offer freedom to the respondents to answer the question in their own way. However, the degree of freedom varies from question to question. An open-ended question may be completely unstructured. The respondents are free to choose any way of their interest to answer the question. For example, what is your opinion on life insurance advertisements?

Projective techniques can be used to obtain information. These techniques reduce the freedom of the respondent to a limited extent. There are many projective techniques in use. The following are the four most commonly used techniques.

1. *Word Association Technique:* This technique requires the respondents to present a stimulus with the first word that comes to their mind. For example, Give the first word comes to your mind after hearing the following:

   Railways........

   Public Sector Banks .....

   Beauty Parlours ......

   The word association technique helps know attitudes about particular services, services features such as facilitating services and support services. The analysis also may help sometimes in the development of the service positioning strategy.
2. *Sentence Completion:* The researcher develops an incomplete sentence and expects the respondent to complete it. It assists the respondent psychologically to some extent to answer the question. For example, instead of questioning directly as, "What is your opinion on TV serials?" the sentence completion technique places smoothly as, "The present day TV serials are ________."
3. *Story Completion and Picture Completion:* Story completion and picture completion are the construction techniques used to elicit information. It's an indirect way of extracting information from respondents. In the story completion technique, an incomplete story is developed and presented to the respondent to complete it. In the picture completion technique the respondent is presented a picture or cartoon wherein the researcher's intension is presented, and the respondent is asked to complete the picture or cartoon.
4. *Thematic Appreciation Tests:* In this technique, a picture is presented to respondents, and they are asked to develop a story on that.

Closed-ended Questions Closed-ended questions present possible answers to respondents as a choice to select his/her answer from one of them. These questions do not give much strain to the respondent to answer and save much time and energy of the researcher too. These questions also make tabulation and analysis much easier. In closed-ended questions, multiple choices may be given, that is, three or more choice answers or scales may be used. The following is the description of various techniques used in the closed-ended questions.

1. *Multiple Choices:* A few alternative answer choices are given to the respondent. For example:
   Who will influence your buying decisions in the purchase of healthcare services?

a) Self	b) Parent	c) Wife
d) Children	e) Relatives	f) Advertisements

2. *Semantic Differential Scale:* Between two bipolar adjectives a scale is inscribed. The respondent is required to select a point. The result indicates the direction as well as the intensity of the feelings of the respondent. For example:
   Broad band services of BSNL:

Fast	--- --- --- --- - x -- -	Slow
Expensive	--- --- --- x-- ---	Inexpensive
Accessible	--- --- --- --- - x -	Inaccessible
Good Service	--- --- --- - x - ---	Poor Service

3. *Likert Scale:* The Likert scale is by far the most popular form of the attitude scale because it is easy for researchers to prepare and interpret and simple for consumers to answer.[11] It is used to measure the degree of agreement or disagreement of the respondent. For example:
   Advertisements of X service are educative to the customers.

Strongly Agree ( )	Agree ( )	Neither Agree Nor
Disagree ( )	Strongly Disagree ( )	Disagree ( )

4. *Rating Scale:* The respondent is required to rate some attributes between excellent and poor. For example:The working of the public distribution system in India is:

Excellent ( )	Very Good( )	Good ( )
Fair ( )	Poor ( )	Very Poor ( )

5. *Importance Scale:* The respondent is required to rate some attributes between extremely important and not at all important. For example:

Extremely Important	Very Important	Somewhat Important	Not Very Important	Not at All Important
( )	( )	( )	( )	( )

6. *Dichotomous Questions*: Dichotomous questions also are part of closed-ended questions. These questions allow the respondents to

select their answer between two choices of answers. For example, Yes/No, Agree/Disagree and so forth. These two answers may be supplemented by including some neutral answers such as can't say, don't know, no opinion and neither

The Question Sequence

The arrangement of questions in the questionnaire should be made in an orderly manner so as to minimize the measurement error. There are no hard and fast rules to decide the order of questions. However, some basic principles may be followed. The first questions must be simple, introductory, objective and interesting. If the respondent gets confused or bored initially it is very difficult to obtain the qualitative information from him. Questions must be grouped according to the concerned topics, and the movement should be from one topic to the other. The previous questions should avoid the biased frame of reference to the questions followed. In other words, the answers of respondents should not be influenced by the initial questions. A proper sequence offers lot of convenience to both the researcher and the respondent.

> *The layout of the questionnaire should facilitate easy movement from one question to the other, provide adequate space for recording answers and be convenient for handling. Good layout minimizes recording errors.*

The Questionnaire Layout

The physical characteristics of a questionnaire are also an important area that requires the attention of researchers. Some errors are due to the improper physical characteristics of the questionnaire. The questionnaire must be designed in such a way that it facilitates the easy movement from one question to the other. There should be proper spacing between the questions, particularly in open-end questions, and the specification of proper places to record, so as to reduce the recording errors. Appearance and handling convenience are also important, particularly in mail surveys. Other aspects such as tabulation and computer use also should be considered.

Pre-testing the Questionnaire

After the development of a questionnaire, considering all the factors discussed above, the researcher conducts a pre-test to ensure that its design is satisfactory. Interviews are conducted by some experienced interviewers with some selected respondents generally representing variant groups in the total sample. The pre-test helps the researcher to confirm, drop, revise or add certain questions in the questionnaire.

Selecting the Sample

The next step in the marketing research process is sample selection. If it were possible to collect information from all the concerned people to a problem, there could be no need to sample. But, often it is not possible to collect information from everyone due to the limitations of time, money and so on. The study of all elements in the universe is called the *census study*. The study of a part of the universe is is called *sample study*. In marketing, census study is possible only in limited cases such as industrial consumers and distributors.

The marketing researchers should develop a sampling plan for which they develop answers for the following three questions:

1. Who should be interviewed?
2. How many should be interviewed?
3. How to select them?

> When the universe is large, a sample study is necessary to minimize cost, time and measurement errors. The sample study requires clarity on the sample unit, sample size and sampling method.

Who Should Be Interviewed?

For the purpose, the researcher should first define the population. A complete population definition consists of an element, sampling unit, extent and time. Consider the following example:

The population for a survey on the customer service in retailing may be defined as "the customer service in retail outlet in Visakhapatnam during June 1–15." In this definition, "customer service" is the element, "retail outlets" is the sampling unit, "in Visakhapatnam" is the extent and "during June 1–15" is the time.

After that, the *sampling frame* must be specified. A sampling frame may be a telephone directory, customer list, voters list, list of college students, list of business establishments and so forth. A sampling frame should ensure that all elements of the population are represented only once. The next step *sampling unit* selection is very important. A clear definition of the sampling unit minimizes sampling errors. It clarifies the investigators that whom exactly they have to interview.

How Many Should Be Interviewed?

Determination of the size of the sample involves both economic and statistical dimensions. The larger the sample, the more it costs. On the other hand, the smaller the sample, the more will be the sampling errors. The researcher has to balance these two conflicting dimensions. In fact, there is no adequate measure to arrive at an exactly required sample size. However, there are two important considerations: (1) Variations in individual items and (2) accuracy desired. If variations are more and greater degree of accuracy is required, the size of the sample should be large. Four methods followed generally are presented below:

1. *Unaided Judgement:* The researcher decides the size without having any logical reasoning.
2. *Affordable Method:* The budget allocation for the research project stands as a limitation to the sample size decision.
3. *Follow Similar Studies:* The average size of the sample in similar studies conducted by either the same company or other companies is considered.
4. *The Bayesian Statistical Model:* The model involves finding the difference between the expected value of the information to be provided by

> **Sampling methods** are of two types—probability sampling methods and non-probability sampling methods. Probability sampling methods include simple random sampling, stratified random sampling and cluster sampling. Non-probability sampling methods include convenience sampling, purposive sampling, judgement sampling and quota sampling.

the sample and the cost involves for each potential sample size. The difference is known as *expected net gain from sampling.* The sample size with the largest expected net gain is chosen.

How to Select the Sample Units?

There are a few sampling methods to follow for the selection of the required sample units. These methods may be broadly categorized into two categories: *probability sampling methods* which include simple random sampling, stratified random sampling and cluster sampling and *non-probability sampling methods* which include convenience sampling, judgement sampling, purposive sampling and quota sampling.

Probability Sampling Methods The three common methods are:

1. *Simple Random Sampling:* Each unit of the total population has an equal chance of being included in the sample. The sample may be selected either by the lottery method or by using random tables.
2. *Stratified Random Sampling:* In this method, the total population is first divided into mutually exclusive and exhaustive stratums and then simple random sampling technique is used to select the sample from each stratum. Homogeneity in one or more characteristics of the population in a stratum is the basic requirement of this method.
3. *Cluster Sampling:* It is often not possible to get the complete record of the population. Under such circumstances, the researcher makes an initial sample of groups, elements or clusters. Then from each cluster the number of elements required is selected.

Non-probability Sampling Methods There are four popular methods:

1. *Convenience Sample:* Sample units are selected as per the convenience of the sampler. The convenience sample is used often in exploratory situations when there is a need to get only an approximation of the actual value, quickly and inexpensively.
2. *Judgement Sample:* The sampler judges the sample keeping in mind various factors relating to the problem. The amount of error depends on the expertise of the sampler. However, this method is less trustworthy when the sample size is large.
3. *Purposive Sample:* The sample is selected purposefully, with some objectives in mind. The sample may be non-representation of the population. The capacity of the sample units to offer contributions is considered.
4. *Quota Sample:* This method attempts to ensure that the demographic characteristics of interest are represented in the sample selected purposely, in the same proportion as they are in the population. For example, in a TV programme evaluation survey, interviewers may be told to interview 500 people living in an area, and out of every 100 persons interviewed 25 per cent are to be businessmen, 25 per cent are to be

employees, 25 per cent college students and 25 per cent agriculturists. Within these quotas, the interviewer is free to select respondents.

Collecting the Data

The next step in the marketing research process is data collection. It is nothing but the execution of the research design. Data collection is an expensive and time-taking process. The quality of research findings mostly depends on the effectiveness in organizing the data-collection process. The primary objectives of the data collection at field are to maximize the flow of pertinent and accurate data and to minimize field errors. There are four data collection methods—observation, personal interview, telephonic interview and mail survey. Each method requires interviewers/researchers with varying degrees of skill for the collection of information. The marketing research organization should select qualified personnel and supervise and control them to maximize the benefit.

While collecting data from respondents, care must be taken to minimize field errors and maximize the flow of pertinent and accurate data. Qualified and skilled investigators as per the needs of the selected contact method should be used for effective data collection.

Minimization of field errors is a major concern of the marketing research organization. There are many areas where the scope of committing an error by the interviewer is more. Errors may be in the selection of the respondent, due to the non-response or refusal of the respondent, in communication and in recording. Sometimes, interviewers may intentionally enter false information. Appropriate steps should be taken to either eliminate or minimize errors. Simplifying procedures, selecting the right candidates as interviewers, training the interviewers, effectively supervising and controlling the researchers are some helpful measures to minimize field errors.

Analysing and Interpreting the Data

Data collection is followed by analysis and interpretation. The raw data gathered from the field is not readily usable for analysis and interpretation as it consists of bits of information in different individual forms. A lot of work goes into transforming this raw data into information as per the requirements of the research objectives.

Data analysis involves the application of several statistical techniques such as tabulation of data, summarization (e.g., measures of variation, dispersion and graphic presentation) and the selection of appropriate analytical methods such as ratios, tests of significance and correlation coefficients.

Interpretation is the conversion of mere data into information. It is the most crucial part of marketing research. It requires knowledge, good communication skills, honesty, a clear understanding of the company objectives and its position in the industry, accurate assessment of the quality of data, awareness of the general business and economic conditions and trends and so on.

***Data analysis** involves application of appropriate statistical techniques to draw useful inferences.*

Preparing and Presenting the Research Report

A report must be reader oriented. While preparing a research report the researcher should give top priority to the reader's interests and expectations.

The design of report should be based on facts. There are no specific rules and regulations that govern report preparation, but in general the following writing criteria may be followed:

- The report must ensure completeness in its form.
- The data and information presented in the report must be reasonably accurate.
- Clarity should be an important principle in writing.
- The report should be concise.

Though there is no standard form of preparing a report, many researchers follow the following format by and large with some marginal deviations.

1. Title page
2. Contents
3. List of tables, appendices, charts, figures, etc.
4. Introduction
5. Body (methodology, results, limitations)
6. Conclusions and recommendations
7. Appendices (copies of questionnaires, statistical works, tables not included in the body, and bibliography).

Diagrams and charts may be used to present a clear, quicker and comprehensive view of a few aspects. The report, thus, prepared is presented to the management.

> *"**Report preparation** is the final stage of marketing research. The report should be reader-oriented and based on factual information. The required qualities of a good report include completeness, accuracy, clarity and conciseness."*

INFORMATION ANALYSIS AND DISTRIBUTION

The information thus gathered from internal records, marketing intelligence system and marketing research requires much more analysis. The information is analysed in the light of its application to the problem. The core information is used to evaluate various alternatives and marketing opportunities.

Information has no value unless it is used by managers. Marketing information should be distributed to the concerned managers and persons for use at the right time. Effective distribution of information helps in to solve and prevent problems and contributes to organizational growth and progress.

> *"The marketing information system should ensure the process of consolidation of information from internal records, marketing intelligence and marketing research. Marketing information should be directed to the concerned personnel of the organization to support in decision making."*

SUMMARY

- The quality of managerial decision making depends largely on the quality of the available information.
- Service marketers need adequate, timely and qualitative information to handle marketing problems effectively.
- Internal records, marketing intelligence and marketing research are the three major sources of marketing information.
- Companies use marketing research when information from internal records and marketing intelligence is found to be inadequate.

- Marketing research is costly and time consuming compared to the other two sources of information.
- Marketing research provides comprehensive data and information on a specific problem and supports managers in decision making.
- Problem identification and definition is the key aspect in the marketing research process.
- Relevant data and information can be obtained through a survey, observation or experimentation research, or a combination of them.
- The selection of the contact method, the design of the questionnaire, the selection of the sample and so forth influence the relevance, accuracy, time and character of the research.
- Measures should be taken to eliminate or minimize field errors.
- The appropriate use of statistical techniques improves the quality of a research.
- Reader orientation, clarity, completeness and accuracy are the basic principles of designing a research report.

KEY TERMS

experimentation research *137*
information needs *122*
information process *121*
marketing information system *118*
marketing intelligence *121*
marketing research *121*
model development *130*
observational research *135*
problem clarification *130*
situation analysis *130*
survey method *132*
treatment group *137*

BRIEF QUESTIONS

1. Explain the three components of the MIS
2. Distinguish between the MIS and marketing research.
3. What are primary and secondary sources of data?
4. What is the process of designing a research report?
5. Explain the observation research approach.
6. Discuss the various types of interviews.
7. Explain projective techniques.

ESSAY QUESTIONS

1. What is the importance and scope of the marketing information system in an organization?
2. How do you assess the information needs of a marketing organization?
3. Define marketing research. What are the areas of its applications?
4. Explain the marketing research process.
5. How do you design a questionnaire?
6. Discuss various projective and scaling techniques.
7. How do you prepare a research report?
8. Explain the sampling techniques used for marketing research.

ASSIGNMENTS

1. Life Insurance Corporation of India, the leading public sector insurance company, has a nationwide network of branches and agencies in India. The corporation offers a wide range of insurance products. Since the insurance sector was opened to private players in 2000, LIC has been facing service competition from private insurance companies. The corporation needs information on how consumers perceive of the features of their products and quality of the services offered. It also need to know how consumers rate its services compared to the competitive private life insurance companies. You are required to:
   (a) Identify the issues to be studied.
   (b) Develop a research plan.
   (c) Design a questionnaire for the purpose.
2. Andhra University, a reputed university in India, is a multi-disciplinary university offering more than 300 courses in emerging areas. The university is strong in basic sciences and equally competent in applied sciences.

The university is unique in that it offers several innovative courses in different disciplines. A pioneer in designing and offering courses in diverse disciplines such as business management, quantitative economics, nuclear physics, parapsychology, and geo-engineering, it has earned a great reputation in humanities and social sciences as well.

Reaccredited by NAAC in 2008 and awarded an A grade with a CGPA (Cumulative Grade Point Average) of 3.65 out of 4.0, it is the first general university in the country to get the ISO 9001:2000 certificate for its quality standards. Andhra University has plans to expand its market to foreign countries to enhance the resource base, and eventually build a global image. To prepare for this transition, the university has decided to utilize the service of a research organization to identify the market potential, market expectations and the intensity of the competition. If you are given the project, how do you:

(a) Define the research problem.
(b) Identify data sources.
(c) Select a research method.
(d) Analyse the data.
(e) Prepare a report.

REFERENCES

1 Marion Harper, Jr., "A New Profession to Aid Management," *Journal of Marketing* (January 1961): 1.

2 Naresh K. Malhotra, *Marketing Research—An Applied Orientation*, 4th ed. (Delhi: Pearson Education, 2006), p. 35.

3 Donald R. Cooper and Pamela S. Schindler, *Business Research Methods*, 8th ed. (New Delhi: Tata McGraw-Hill, 2003), p. 14.

4 Ibid., p. 15.

5 Michael J. Etzel, Bruce J. Walkar, William J. Stanton and Ajay Pandit, *Marketing—Concepts and Cases*, 13th ed. (New Delhi: Tata McGraw-Hill, 2008), p. 183.

6 www.mospi.nic.in/cso_test1.htm.

7 Naresh K. Malhotra, *Marketing Research—An Applied Orientation*, 4th ed. (Delhi: Pearson Education, 2006), p. 178.

8 Ramanuj Majumdar, *Marketing Research: Text, Applications and Case Studies*. (New Delhi: New Age International Pvt. Ltd., 1999), p. 88.

9 Philip Kotler, Kevin Lane Keller, Abraham Koshy and Mitheleswar Jha, *Marketing Management—A South Asian perspective*, 12th ed. (Delhi: Pearson Education, 2007), p. 88.

10 Donald S. Tull and Del I. Hawkins, *Marketing Research—Measurement and Method*, 6th ed. (New Delhi: Prentice Hall of India, 1993), p. 330.

11 Leon G. Schiffman and Leslee Lazar Kanuk, *Consumer Behviour*, 7th ed. (Delhi: Pearson Education Asia, 2002), p. 23.

Services Strategy

7

LEARNING OBJECTIVES

After studying this chapter, you will be able to:

- Understand the importance of strategic planning
- Understand the process of strategic planning
- Identify the strategies suitable for service organizations
- Identify the components of the services marketing mix

Tech-Solutions, an early entrant in the software industry in India, was a successful company until the global meltdown of 2008. The economic downturn in developed countries, particularly USA, adversely affected its major clientele, pushing it to the brink of bankruptcy. While renegotiating the terms of business did help to a certain extent, its profits kept dropping consistently. Many customers either closed their businesses or reduced the volume of business with the company. Caught unawares with no signs of recovery in sight, the top management of the company reviewed the situation and constituted an expert committee involving members from the company and reputed management consultants from outside to suggest strategic options to overcome the current problems and to work out a future plan.

The expert committee thoroughly examined the current trends and the projections for the future. Based on this analysis, it suggested the following four strategic options to the management of the company:

1. Focus on the domestic market by introducing new service packages for small- and medium-size business concerns. The committee opined that there is an untapped huge market potential in this segment.
2. Diversify the business to minimize the risk of failure. Retailing and infrastructure development were identified as potential target areas.
3. Invest in quality enhancement to delight existing customers and to attract new customers.
4. Cut operational costs wherever possible.

The committee stated that the suggestions were not mutually exclusive but complementary in nature. The company might choose any one or a combination of a few or all depending on its executional capabilities and resource strength.

When the report was tabled in the managing board meeting, the members expressed doubts over the suitability and expected outcome of each of the suggestions made. The members wanted a detailed analysis of each of the suggestions in the light of the changing business environment before arriving at a decision.

Questions:

1. Do you think the strategies suggested by the expert committee are capable of solving the problems of the company?
2. Do you think that the key issues were either bypassed or ignored while preparing the report?
3. Which of the suggested strategies in your opinion is the most suitable? Why?
4. What kind of new problems are likely to arise if the suggestions are implemented?
5. What would be your strategy to handle the situation?

INTRODUCTION

Strategic planning was introduced in the 1970s when the industry faced several shock waves in succession due to energy crisis, inflation, severe competition, changing governments, changing approaches of companies towards resource utilization to achieve corporate goals, policies, etc. A strategy is an integrated and coordinated set of commitments and actions designed to exploit core competencies and gain competitive advantage.[1] It is the business logic employed by the company to match its competencies either with the opportunities or against threats in the business environment. To develop an effective strategy, it is necessary to assess the competencies, weaknesses and opportunities and threats either existing or emerging in the business environment. A strategy consists of a combination of competitive moves and business approaches that managers employ to please customers, compete successfully and achieve organizational objectives.[2] According to P. Kotler,[3] market-oriented strategic planning is the managerial process of developing and maintaining a viable fit between organizational objectives, skills and resources and its changing market opportunities. The aim of strategic planning is to shape the company's business and products in such a way that they yield profit and growth. Strategic planning can be defined as the approach of a company to utilize its resources to achieve its organizational goals. It is oriented to achieve the two most important objectives of an organization—growth in profits and business.

> *A **strategy** is developing the right connectivity of the company resources with emerging opportunities so as to shape the company's business and services in such a way that they bring in the desired profits and growth.*

The success or failure of a business depends not only on the management's ability to develop competitive strategic moves and approaches in view of the company's long-term plans, but also on its ability to execute the strategy effectively. The excellent execution of an excellent strategy is the best test of managerial excellence and the most reliable recipe for organizational success.[4]

THE PROCESS OF STRATEGIC PLANNING

The importance of strategic planning has been recognized by almost all companies. The success or failure in business depends on the effectiveness of strategic planning. The senior management should work to clarify issues critical from the perspective of strategic planning. At least the following 11 questions need to be answered accurately to formulate strategies:

1. What should be our business?
2. What is our business?
3. How should the business be developed?
4. How should consumers be satisfied?
5. How should competition be dealt with?
6. What should be the response to the ever-changing market conditions?
7. How should strategic and financial results be achieved?

8. How should the functional units in the organization be managed and coordinated?
9. How should relationships with customers, suppliers and other influencers be managed?
10. How can stakeholders be satisfied?
11. What is value to customers?

It is difficult to answer these questions precisely. Even if satisfactory answers are found at a given point of time, the answers may lose their validity due to the dynamic nature of the environment. Thus, organizations need to redefine their business propositions and develop new strategies to achieve the desired objective.

> *The top management of a service company should be clear on issues that are vital for strategic planning. Over the years, many developments have taken place within the business and in the business environment, resulting in conflicting interests, priorities, adjustments and directions and hence confusion.*

The Steps in Strategic Planning

Strategic planning, a necessity for each organization, can be divided into five basic steps:

1. Defining the mission
2. Carrying out a SWOT analysis
3. Formulating a strategy

India Post

India Post, a government service organization, is the largest postal system in the world with over 150,000 service outlets. The entry of technology-driven private players in the arena altered the market environment, posing serious threat to India Post. Forced to be commercially viable in a competitive environment, India Post worked out a new service strategy directed at winning over customers and increasing revenue. Technology was at the core of the new business strategy. The technology-driven improvement in service quality combined with the attempt to leverage the existing network enabled India Post to engineer a complete turnaround.

It identified two major opportunities: the direct mail of a variety of products by targeting the growing middle-income group and partnering with banks, insurance companies and other financial service providers for extending financial services to the rural population through its extensive network. It aimed to become the major player in logistics and supply-chain management by providing distribution channels, inventory management, packaging services, warehousing, transportation and time-definite distribution programmes.

India Post now plans to get into the international parcel and logistics business and function as the logistics partner to provide event-specific services for trade fairs, commonwealth games, and state-sponsored events. The plans also include official e-commerce solutions through tie-ups with suppliers, which will provide various products to customers to be delivered through posts and capacity augmentation for high-speed processing of mails and security in order to meet the challenges of the competitive market. The key change noticeable in the strategy of India Post is the shift from conventional service format to a vibrant, adaptive, technology-driven, and quality-oriented set of services through optimizing the identified core competencies such as the post office network and dedicated workforce.

4. Implementing the strategy
5. Evaluating and controlling the strategy

Defining the Mission

For every organization, the mission is a value statement, which is at the heart of the corporate strategy of an organization. According to P. F. Drucker,[5] defining the purpose and mission of a business is difficult, painful and risky. However, this alone enables a business to set objectives, develop strategies, concentrate its resources and go to work. This alone enables a business to be managed by performance. A *mission statement* defines the scope of the business and long-term vision of an organization. D. F. Abell suggested that a company define its business in terms of three dimensions: Who is being satisfied (which consumer groups), what is being satisfied (what consumer needs) and how are customer needs being satisfied (distinctive competencies).[6] According to V. McGinnis,[7] a mission statement should:

> *The **mission statement** defines the scope and identifies the priorities, distinctive competencies and future orientation of the company in a simple and understandable way to all the stakeholders of the company.*

- define what the organization is and what the organization aspires to be;
- be limited enough to exclude some ventures and broad enough to allow for creative growth;
- distinguish a given organization from all others;
- serve as a framework for evaluating both current and prospective activities; and
- be sufficiently clear to be widely understood throughout the future.

Thus, the mission statement defines the scope and identifies the priorities, distinctive competencies and future orientation of the company in a simple and understandable way to all the stakeholders of the company. The mission statement should inspire and motivate all those connected with the company.

Carrying Out a SWOT Analysis

The most popularly used analysis for relating organizational factors with environmental factors in order to develop a strategic fit between them is the SWOT analysis. The letters *S* and *W* represent the strengths and weaknesses of the organization, whereas the letters *O* and *T* represent opportunities and threats that are existing or likely to emerge in the environment in relation to the organization.

A critical review of the strengths of the organization helps identify its core competencies and define them from a proper perspective. Strengths are internal competencies, which may encompass company image, brand image and financial, personnel, marketing, production and R&D resources. The strengths of an organization are often measured against those of its competitors. Weaknesses are those competencies which the company lacks. The examples of the weaknesses of an organization include deficiencies in important skills vis-à-vis competitors and technology, poorly organized functional areas and manpower, poor financial position and weak management.

A business environment is a bundle of opportunities owing to the dynamic nature of the environment. The ability to identify and exploit an opportunity shapes the future of a company. The market opportunities most relevant to a company are those that offer important avenues for profitable growth, those where a company has the most potential for competitive advantage and those that match up well with the company's financial and organizational resource capabilities.[8] Organizations should develop a mechanism to identify, evaluate and rank the existing opportunities in the environment, in terms of business attractiveness and suitability to the core competencies.

"SWOT analysis is a widely accepted approach to analyse and understand the internal environment vis-à-vis the external environment of the organization. The analysis helps align the strengths and weaknesses of the company with the opportunities and/or threats emerging or existing in the external environment."

A dynamic business environment may pose a threat to existing businesses. The emergence of cheaper or better technologies, the entry of new and better products, new government policy initiatives and changes may spell doom to the existing business.

Every firm should develop a list of its strengths, weaknesses, opportunities and threats periodically and evaluate all of them in the light of the company's mission. The business unit should have an overall evaluation of opportunities and threats in the external environment and strengths and weaknesses of the internal environment to assess the core competencies and their adaptability to the changes in the external environment. Goal formulation for a specific period and listing the objectives in clear terms at various levels of the organization are the next steps to follow.

While goals indicate what a business unit wants to achieve, a strategy is the game plan for the achievement of the goals. The kind of approach the organization pursues towards the achievement of the goal—whether it is the overall cost leadership, product differentiation or the decision to focus to an altogether new segment—needs to be decided. Besides, the company may also think of strategic alliances with respect to a product or service, promotion, logistics and pricing, and creative thinking and innovative approach. A specific action plan needs to be developed and executed.

Formulating a Strategy

In the formulation of a strategy, it is necessary to take into consideration the full set of commitments, decisions and actions required for a firm to achieve strategic competitiveness. The SWOT analysis provides the necessary strategic inputs for effective strategy formulation and implementation. The formulated strategy should enable the organization to serve customers better than its competitors. Therefore, before formulating a strategy, an organization should scrutinize and analyse the strategies of its competitors. A company's competitive strategy consists of the business approaches and initiatives it undertakes to attract customers and fulfill their expectations, to withstand competitive pressures and to strengthen its market position.[9]

"Strategy formulation is a science as well as an art. It is necessary to analyse the environment scientifically and develop the strategy creatively by exploring artistic skills to find a distinctive and unique way of addressing the needs and wants of consumers. Competitiveness is the desired focus in strategy formulation."

According to M. E. Porter, a competitive strategy is about being different. It means deliberately choosing to perform activities differently or to perform different activities than those of rivals to deliver a unique mix of value.[10] Porter suggested five distinct competitive strategies which benefit service organizations: (1) low-cost-provider strategy, (2) differentiation strategy,

(3) best-cost-provider strategy, (4) focused strategy (market niche) based on lower cost and (5) focused strategy (market niche) based on differentiation.

The Low-cost-provider Strategy Companies that adopt the low-cost-provider strategy strive to become a low-cost provider of services as compared to the competitors to appeal to a broad spectrum of price-sensitive customers.

The Differentiation Strategy Differentiation strategies are often used by service organizations. One of the characteristics of the services—variability—provides an opportunity to the service provider to pursue a differentiation strategy for each customer, thereby providing enhanced value perceptions. It is one of the most powerful competitive strategies for service firms. The essence of a differentiation strategy is to be unique in ways that are valuable to customers.[11] The service differentiating features are generally easy to copy for competitive firms. Therefore, service organizations are at a disadvantageous position when it comes to achieving sustainable competitive advantage by way of differentiation.

Innovation is the key for service differentiation. P. F. Drucker[12] said that most innovative business ideas come from methodically analysing and listing seven areas of opportunity, some of which lie within particular companies or industries, and some of which lie in broader social or demographic trends. Astute managers ensure that their organizations maintain a clear focus on all seven areas. But analysis alone is not enough. Once an attractive opportunity is identified, it needs a leap of imagination to arrive at the right response called *functional inspiration*. Innovation requires knowledge, ingenuity and, above all, focus.

The seven sources of innovation are unexpected occurrences; incongruities; process needs; industry and market changes; demographic changes; changes in perception; and new knowledge.

New ideas are the first basic foundation for innovation. T. Levitt[13] observed that a powerful new idea lies around unused in a company for years, not because its merits are not recognized but because nobody has assumed the responsibility to convert the words into action. What is often lacking is not creativity in the idea-creating sense, but innovation in the action-producing sense, that is, ideas are not put to work effectively. All in all, the creation of ideas is relatively abundant; it is the implementation that is scarce. Service firms need to search continuously for new ideas from people within the organization and sources outside such as customers, competitors and research institutes. Firms also need to design an institutional framework with the ability to transform an idea into an innovative offer. Service firms are prone to competitive threats and surprising challenges owing to the dynamic environment they encounter. The right strategy, therefore, to reach consumers, overtaking competitors is to offer additional innovative value (AIV). When competitors are at par with the company in terms of financial, technological and human resources, it is innovation that provides the competitive edge. Thus, service firms must necessarily make innovation an institutional process on a continuous basis in order to achieve profit as well as growth objectives.

> *“Innovation is key to the success of service business. Service companies should focus on and invest in research and development to find distinctive ways of serving consumers and providing higher value. Through innovation, service firms can achieve differentiation advantage over competition.”*

The Best-cost-provider Strategy Providing more value for the money customers pay for the service is the aim of this strategy. Service firms focus on providing key service-quality features and performance attributes in such a way that they exceed customer expectations, in relation to price. Organizations should work to achieve cost efficiency in various service process attributes and better quality of service at a cost lower than its competitors. The main point here is that such internal developments have to be based on the characteristics of services, so that the relationships between the internal and external effects are taken into account. C. Grönroos emphasized that not all costs are equal. On the contrary, there is a pivotal difference between various types of costs that have to be taken into account when strategic and operational decisions about efficiency, productivity and cost savings are considered.

Jan Carlzon and his advisors classified costs into two categories—good costs and evil costs, while initiating the turnaround of the Scandinavian Airlines.[14] Good costs are those costs that are directly productive and improve the capabilities of a service organization to produce high-quality services. The focus is particularly on the improvement of buyer–seller interactions. Generally, in service organizations, the costs involved in maintaining frontline operations, support operations, training, physical goods required for service production and delivery and so on are considered good costs. Good costs are to be promoted in service organizations because the costs contribute to improved quality perceptions by consumers, resulting in consumer satisfaction. Evil costs are non-productive costs that may not improve buyer–seller interactions but may adversely affect the quality of services to customers. The costs involved in unnecessary operational and administrative routines, several heavy management levels, unnecessary bureaucracy and supervision costs are examples of evil costs in service organizations. Classifying costs by identifying them as either good costs or evil costs helps service organizations initiate cost-saving actions.

> *Consumers generally prefer quality services at a relatively low cost. Effective cost-management practices, thus, are important to service companies to follow in order to minimize costs. It is necessary to classify costs into good costs and evil costs. Good costs improve buyer–seller interactions; hence, they need to be promoted. Evil costs, on the other hand, burdensome to consumers, need to be eliminated.*

The Focused (Market Niche) Strategy Based on Low Cost The objective of focused marketing or niche marketing is to identify subgroups within a broad market segment that has a distinctive set of traits and might seek a special combination of benefits. Niches are smaller and generally attract very few competitors. Service organizations focusing on niche markets find an opportunity to direct their limited resources to provide for a relatively small group of consumers. Service firms may follow the strategy of serving consumers in a niche market at a cost lower than their competitors by providing comparable or better quality services.

The Focused (Market Niche) Strategy Based on Differentiation The aim of this strategy is to do a better job of serving buyers in the target market niche. When a company identifies a substantial group with well-defined desires, requiring special service attributes and quality levels, this strategy is capable of earning rich dividends. "Services Marketing Insight: Selecting the Right Strategy Is the Key to Success" analyses the vareables that influence strategy choice.

7.1 Services Marketing Insight | **Selecting the Right Strategy Is the Success Key**

The selection of strategies is certainly a critical decision for the companies including service companies. The choice basically depends on the type of service business and the kind of customers to be served.

The variables influencing the choice are service process (whether simple or complex) and service type (whether standardized or customized service). These two variables can combine in four possible ways to provide the following choices to the management.

1. Simple process and customized service: Companies with simple business processes tailored to customers' specific business needs such as retail sales, Web design, travel and tourism and technical support should consider strategies such as automation, self-service, end-to-end service, captive off-shoring and selective outsourcing. It is important to this set of companies to keep close tabs on the customer.
2. Simple process and standardized service: Companies using simple processes to deliver standardized services such as retail banking, data management, tele-marketing and billing want to look at off-shoring, outsourcing, globalization, one-stop shop, end-to-end service and so on. Providing complete, end-to-end services in one stop is the key strategic direction for these firms.
3. Complex process and customized service: Companies with complex processes requiring customization like personal financial planning, expert medical diagnosis, relationship marketing, engineering and design and so on may look at developing in-sourcing, on-shoring, de-integration, decoupling, selective automation, selective outsourcing and so on.
4. Complex process and standardized service: Companies using complex processes to deliver standardized services like credit analysis, technical research, content management, software development and so on may consider strategies like captive off-shoring, in-house automation, selective outsourcing, globalization, and so on.

Source: Uday Karmakar, "Will you Survive the Services Revolution?" Harvard Business Review, *(June 2004): 101–107.*

A MARKET-ORIENTED SERVICE STRATEGY

> *Traditional marketing strategies may not be suitable to service companies. They may further intensify marketing problems. If service companies follow the traditional thumb-rule strategies, they may get into the strategic management trap.*

In designing a suitable strategy, service firms need to differentiate themselves from manufacturing organizations. They have to take market sensitivities in relation to service characteristics into consideration when deciding on the strategic approach to achieve organizational goals. The conventional managerial thinking provides three thumb rules for strengthening the competitive edge of a firm. As per these rules, a firm should decrease the cost of production, enhance the promotion budget and develop new products. Manufacturing firms believed and also achieved positive results by adopting these three distinctive strategies on the marketing front. However, if the three, time-tested and proven marketing strategies are applied to the services, it is more likely the service organizations get into further trouble. C. Grönroos[15] has described this as the "strategic management trap." Service firms need to watch for the conditions that lead to the strategic management trap and develop abilities to avoid the use of traditional arsenal and design a service-oriented marketing strategy.

The Strategic Management Trap

When service firms choose to follow the traditional strategic approaches to face marketing problems, they may not be successful due to non-applicability of such strategies to the specific and distinctive characteristics of services and their marketing. Figure 7.1 illustrates the consequences of traditional strategies when used to solve services marketing problems.

Let us assume that the service organization is facing problems in marketing of a service. The first option for the management of the service organization as per the traditional input is to focus on cost-control devices and, through that, achieve internal efficiency. The decisions on internal efficiency often result in reduction of personnel, introduction of self-service, cost control in every activity, automation (replacement of personnel by machines), austerity measures and so on. In the manufacturing sector, such decisions may improve productive efficiency, reduce the cost of production, and even improve the quality of goods. But in a service organization, the chances of such happenings are rare. Of course, such decisions definitely result in some marginal cost savings, but the consequences deteriorate the service quality. Let us suppose a person in an enquiry counter of an organization is required to attend to customer calls on two telephone lines. They may have a lot of freedom and comfort in attending the calls. They may start each call with greetings, make enquiries for additional information from the caller, offer choices and suggestions and conclude with thanks. The employee has ample time to understand clearly what the consumer wants to communicate, to show empathy and to create an environment through which the

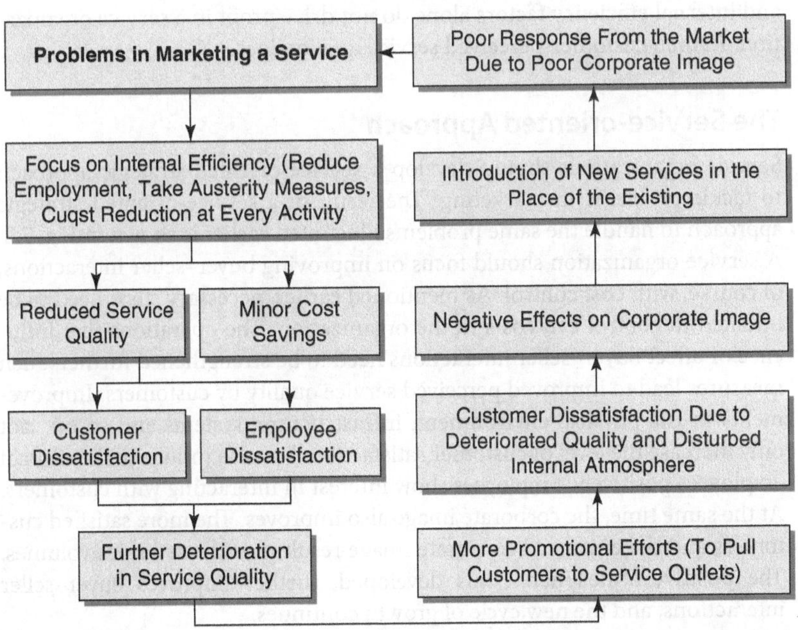

Fig. 7.1 The strategic management trap

> *Cost reduction, enhanced promotion and replacement of the product are the three traditional thumb-rule strategies. These strategies are counter-productive in services as such measures affect buyer–seller interactions negatively, leading to employee as well as customer dissatisfaction.*

consumer prefers to continue the relationship with the company. Consider, if as a cost-reduction strategy, the same employee is required to attend to five telephones lines as opposed to two. Though still capable of attending to the phones, the employee loses the freedom and comfort enjoyed earlier. Further, in a bid to reduce the call time, the quality of the interaction suffers due to insufficient information, miscommunication and other deficiencies, leaving the caller dissatisfied. The interactive personnel of a service firm who encounter comments, criticisms, aggression, irritation and unpleasant feelings of customers due to deterioration in service quality become demotivated. They cannot involve themselves in the service activity because of the unpleasant interactive environment. Consequently, the internal atmosphere of the organization deteriorates, resulting in further deterioration of service quality.

When a service organization chooses the second strategy of spending heavily on promotion to attract the market, it may succeed in increasing the demand for services. However, the reduced internal efficiency dissatisfies customers. As a result of all these activities, the corporate image of the organization weakens, and the problems of the company multiply. If the image of the organization is negative, even the introduction of a new product in the place of the existing product does not save the organization. A vicious circle is formed once the organization gets into the strategic management trap, leading to multiple problems.

Why is it that conventional wisdom and guidelines of the manufacturing sector do not help in solving the marketing problems of service organizations? The reason is obvious: Service organizations are different; they have certain characteristics of their own. The productivity of capital and labour and internal efficiency factors alone do not drive profit in a service organization. Rather, customer-perceived service quality does.

The Service-oriented Approach

> *A **service-oriented strategy** focuses on the improvement of buyer–seller interactions, when there is a marketing problem. The strategy helps enhance customers' quality perceptions and satisfaction levels to bring the business of the company back on track and make it profitable.*

Service organizations should develop a service-oriented strategic approach to tackle problems in marketing. The result of a service-oriented strategic approach to handle the same problems illustrated earlier is shown in Fig. 7.2. A service organization should focus on improving buyer–seller interactions, of course, with cost control. As mentioned earlier, necessary steps need to be initiated to control evil costs in the organization. The operations that influence or affect buyer–seller interactions need to be strengthened further. Such measures lead to improved perceived service quality by customers. Improvements in the physical environment, infrastructure, systems and so on not only increase the level of customer satisfaction but also influence the contact employees positively. Employees show interest in interacting with customers. At the same time, the corporate image also improves. The more satisfied customers and the enhanced corporate image result in increased sales volumes. The positive atmosphere, thus developed, further improves buyer–seller interactions, and the new cycle of growth continues.

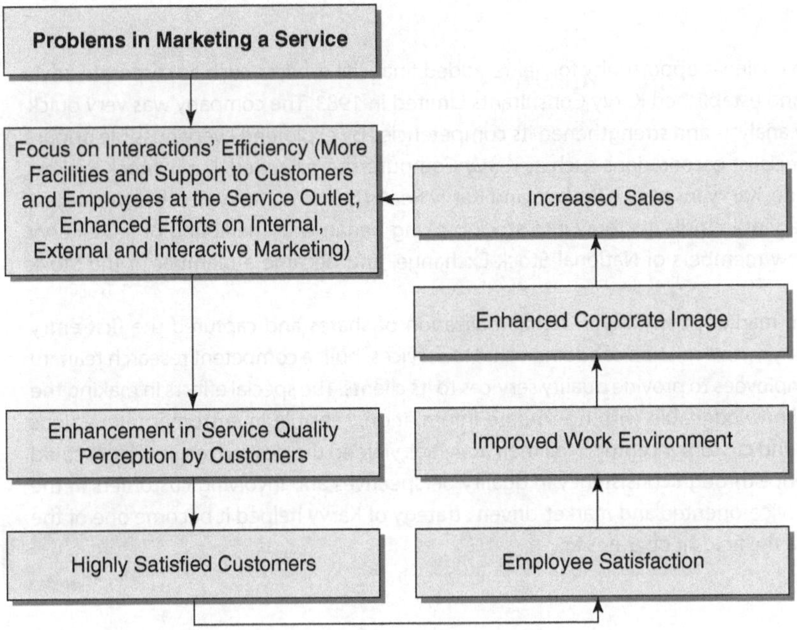

Fig. 7.2 A service-oriented approach

A Service-oriented Organization Structure

Service organizations should not have a large number of hierarchical levels or be unnecessarily bureaucratic. Market orientation requires a thorough understanding of customers and the authority to the frontline employees to take decision to serve them. The management should not be directly involved with decision making at the operational level. It should provide strategic support and the necessary resources to pursue a service strategy.

Figure 7.3 shows the desired shift in the organizational structure of a service firm. A traditional military structure keeps the top management far away from reality. Though the components of the pyramids are almost the same, the priorities are changed. Turning the pyramid upside down demonstrates the fact that the top management is not the apex level of the pyramid and the part of the organization structure that immediately determines whether

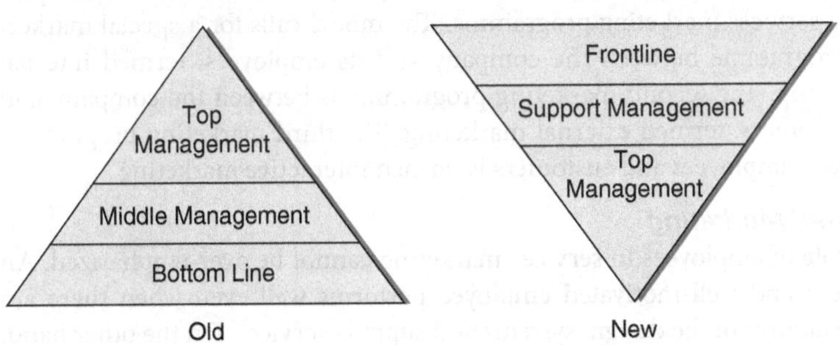

Fig. 7.3 Desired shift in the organization structure

Karvy

Karvy sensed early the business opportunity for value-added financial services such as corporate advisory services in India and established Karvy Consultants Limited in 1983. The company was very quick in market-opportunity analysis and strengthened its competencies by exploiting every possible opportunity. It promoted specialist corporations such as Karvy Computershare Limited, Karvy Stock Brokers Limited, Karvy Comtrade, Karvy Insurance Brokers and Karvy Realty Services. Karvy became the largest registrar and transfer agent in India. Its foray into stock broking began with marketing of IPOs. Karvy was among the first few members of National Stock Exchange, and became a member of the Stock Exchange, Mumbai.

Karvy identified the market potential for dematerialization of shares and captured the first-entry advantage. The company, with a mission of adding value to services, built a competent research team to support its frontline employees to provide quality services to its clients. The special efforts in making the interactive personnel knowledgeable with up-to-date information, sensible in customer interactions through varied media, and customer centric in all their activities yielded the desired results. Karvy could gain customer confidence through consistency in quality perspectives and involving customers in the service process. The service-oriented and market-driven strategy of Karvy helped it become one of the top players in almost all the fields it operates in.

the strategy of the firm will be a success or failure. It is the frontline, which includes personnel, physical resources and operational systems that interacts with customers. The frontline people take most of the decisions relating to the basic service package (BSP) to be offered to each customer against the need patterns. The performance of the frontline decides the success or failure of the organization. The other managerial parts of the organization should facilitate the frontline, for efficient performance in buyer–seller interactions.

The Service Triangle

C. Grönroos[16] developed one of the most popular strategic models for services marketing called the service triangle. Figure 7.4 presents the services marketing model. Grönroos has identified three important groups that play critical roles in successfully accomplishing organizational goals: company (top management), employees and customers. The model proposes a three-dimensional approach for the development of the overall marketing strategy. It suggests the design of three marketing programmes as the integral part of the services marketing programme. The model calls for a special marketing programme between the company and its employees, termed internal marketing. The second marketing programme is between the company and its customers, termed external marketing. The third marketing programme between employees and customers is termed interactive marketing.

Internal Marketing

The role of employees in services marketing cannot be over-emphasized. An efficient and well-motivated employee performs well even when there are some failures in the design, systems and support services. On the other hand,

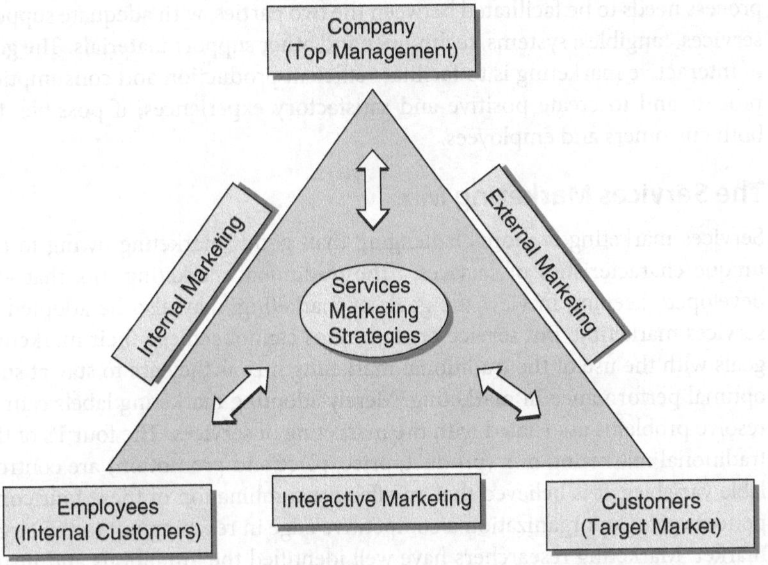

Fig. 7.4
The services marketing model (the service triangle)

an inefficient and demotivated employee may not perform well in spite of support from all departments. The concept of internal marketing suggests that the philosophy of the management should be to satisfy its employees first. The employees are viewed as the first market for the service organization to serve. Proper pay, promotion and other benefit packages are to be designed to meet their expectations. Steps should also be initiated to motivate employees and boost their morale. The ultimate goal of internal marketing is to prepare employees to serve customers with motivation and commitment.

> *A **service triangle** is one of the strategic marketing models for service companies. The model suggests that service companies should professionally manage internal marketing (between the company management and the employees), external marketing (between the company management and the customers) and interactive marketing (between the employees and the customers).*

External Marketing

Customers are co-producers of services. Without their involvement, a service output cannot be qualitative. Therefore, it is the responsibility of the service firm to prepare the customer to receive the service in the right perspective. The major tasks are consumer education about the features of the service, shaping their expectations and developing the right mind-set to participate in service production and to perceive service quality. The limitations and other problems (or possible problems) in the process of service production and consumption, if any, should also be communicated. Customers need to play an active role in the service production process. If necessary, consumers should be trained so as to promote qualitative participation and enhance consumer-perceived quality. The ultimate aim of external marketing is to prepare the customer to participate effectively in service production and consumption.

Interactive Marketing

Internal marketing and external marketing prepare the stage for the actual interaction between employees and customers. The interaction between employees and service firms and their customers are also called *service encounters*. This is an important term in services marketing. The service

> *The traditional pyramid structure of the organization is not suitable to service organizations. It is necessary to turn the pyramid upside down. The frontline contact employees of the service organizations are often required to take decisions according to the situational requirements. The management should facilitate and support the frontline to perform efficiently.*

process needs to be facilitated between the two parties, with adequate support services, tangibles, systems, techniques and other support materials. The goal of interactive marketing is to facilitate efficient production and consumption process and to create positive and satisfactory experiences, if possible, for both customers and employees.

The Services Marketing Mix

Services marketing is more challenging than goods marketing owing to the unique characteristics of services. The traditional marketing mix that was developed, keeping in view the goals of marketing, may also be adopted to services marketing. But service organizations cannot achieve their marketing goals with the use of the traditional marketing mix as they are to stay at sub-optimal performance in marketing. Merely adopting marketing labels cannot resolve problems associated with the marketing of services. The four Ps of the traditional marketing mix (product, price, place and promotion) are controllable variables. It is believed that an effective combination of these four components gives an organization a competitive edge in reaching out to the target market. Marketing researchers have well identified the limitations and insufficiencies of the traditional marketing mix if applied to services as well. B. H. Booms and M. J. Bitner[17] suggested a seven Ps marketing mix model for service firms. The seven Ps were later supported by other marketing specialists as well.

> *The conventional four Ps marketing mix is considered deficient in solving the marketing problems of service organizations. A new marketing mix with seven Ps is suggested for services, in which while retaining the old four Ps, three new Ps are added. The new additions are physical evidence, people and process.*

Components of the Services Marketing Mix

The marketing mix for service organizations are product, physical evidence, price, place, people, promotion and process. Figure 7.5 exhibits the marketing mix of services. Thus, there are three additional components—physical evidence, people and process in the services marketing mix.

1. *Product:* Service is an intangible product. It consists of a bundle of features and benefits relevant to a specific target market. As such, there is a high level of flexibility and opportunity to be innovative in designing a product offer.
2. *Physical Evidence:* Most services cannot be offered without the support of tangibles. Though consumers cannot see the service, they can

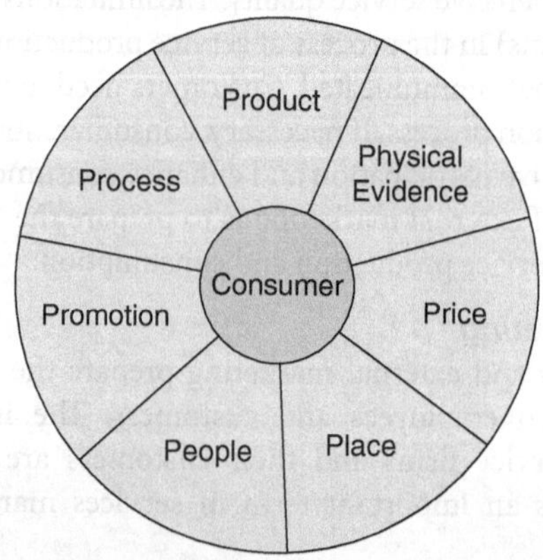

Fig. 7.5
The services marketing mix

definitely see the associated tangibles, examine them and try to form an opinion on the service provider. Thus, a passenger transport organization's promise of a safe, comfortable and timely journey from one place to another is examined by the transport vehicle's condition, seating facilities and other physical facilities, the personality of the driver and other personnel, the office furniture and equipment being used, and the way employees are responding to customers. All these physical objects are used as evidence by the consumer to assess and expect performance from the service provider. Hence, physical evidence plays a critical role in shaping consumer perceptions and expectations.

3. *Price:* The pricing decision is critical in services too, as this component of the marketing mix alone determines the revenue of the firm. Consumer sensitivity to price would be higher in services than in goods. Though the basic methods of pricing are the same as in goods, the pricing strategies for services basically depends on value perceptions of various groups of people that are targeted by the organization.
4. *Place (Distribution):* Services are intangible as well as inseparable. These two characteristics do not allow a service firm to follow the same channel options available for goods marketing. Due to the intangible character of services, traditional wholesalers and retailers cannot be used. As services cannot be stored and separated from producers, retailing cannot be an independent activity in services marketing. Production, distribution and consumption are simultaneous activities in services. However, services have an advantage in using the direct selling approach through which services can be offered to the customer at a lower cost. This does not mean direct selling is the only way of selling services. There are certainly other channels of distribution, such as agents and brokers, franchisers and electronic channels, which are used for the distribution of services.
5. *People:* Service organizations are people-oriented and people-based organizations. The employees of a service firm constitute a major competency in undertaking business operations. Every employee of the service organization is a marketing person, who undertakes either full-time or part-time marketing activity. The following have a direct influence on consumers: line of visibility, employees' direct contact with customers and their behaviour, activities and performance. Service employees are to be trained and motivated for better performance in marketing activities.
6. *Promotion:* Consumers are co-producers in the service business. The quality of services not only depends on the performance of the service provider, but also on the performance of the service consumer. Very few service organizations or service concepts can have readily available mature performers as consumers. It is the responsibility of service organizations to educate and, if necessary, train customers to make them use the services efficiently. A well-designed promotional programme is of immense help to organizations in informing, persuading and training customers to better their experiences.

7. *Process:* Process is a functional activity that ensures service availability and quality. The way the physical setting is designed technically and functions are scheduled and routed to provide promised services to customers speaks of the efficiency of the process. In simple terms, the management of process is to manage service encounters (the interaction between service employees and customers, customers and service environment, systems and other facilities) effectively. Moments of truth occurs during the service encounter. The challenges of process management are to improve the moments of truth.

The seven Ps of services marketing become the marketing offer of the organization to the target market. The marketing mix aims to achieve seven distinct goals. They are matching the offer to the consumer needs and wants, consumer quality expectations, consumer perceptions, consumer satisfaction, customer relationships, customer welfare and protection and societal well-being. The dynamic nature of the target market in all the seven distinct areas offers challenges to marketing organizations. Service firms can be successful only when they make all the marketing mix elements are dynamic and adaptable to the changes in the market environment. "Services Marketing Insight: Corporate Strategy and Social Responsibility" analyses the inside out and outside in linkages for service organisations to develop effective strategies.

STRATEGY IMPLEMENTATION

The development of a good marketing strategy alone does not yield results. The implementation of the strategy is equally important. Strategies like a blueprint indicate various courses of action to achieve desired objectives. F. R. David[18] rightly pointed out that strategy formulation is largely an intellectual process, whereas strategy implementation is more operational in character. Strategy formulation requires good conceptual, integrative and analytical skills but strategy implementation requires special skills in motivating and managing others. Strategy formulation occurs primarily at the corporate level of an organization, while strategy implementation permeates all hierarchical levels. Strategy formulation requires coordination among few individuals but strategy implementation requires coordination among many. Operationalizing the strategy requires transcending various components of the strategy to different levels; mobilization and allocation of resources; structuring authority, responsibility, tasks and information flows; establishing policies; and evaluation and control.[19]

> *"Strategy implementation requires special skills in motivating and managing others. Allocating, structuring authority, tasks and responsibilities, initiating best practices in internal management, and providing of support services help in the effective implementation of a strategy."*

Effective implementation of strategies requires resource strengths and organizational capabilities. Service firms need to link the budget to the strategy and develop strategy support to policies and procedures. The best practices in internal management need to be initiated and a commitment among all the people for continuous improvements has to be promoted. For the purpose, whatever support systems are required have to be arranged to improve the performance of the people, and reward systems should be directed for the support of strategy implementation. Above all, a right kind of corporate culture and strategic leadership need to be nurtured and developed for achieving the desired results.

7.2 Services Marketing Insight — Corporate Strategy and Social Responsibility

Business and society need each other. The interrelationship between a corporation and the society needs to be addressed in strategies and activities of a company. It is necessary to identify both positive and negative effects of the society on the company's prospects and determine the areas to be addressed. Business concerns should apply their considerable resources, expertise and insights to activities that benefit the society. Corporate social responsibility should be strategic and operational, but not cosmetic.

The proponents of corporate social responsibility have four arguments: moral obligation, sustainability, license to operate and reputation. The moral obligation is to do right things in the society. It drives the companies to achieve commercial success by honouring ethics and values of the society and by protecting the natural environment. Sustainability emphasizes environmental and community stewardship. It advocates meeting the needs of the present generation without affecting the future generations. In other words, companies should focus on long-term economic performance and avoid short-term behaviour that is detrimental to society and environment. The licence to operate means the business should identify social issues that matter to all its stakeholders. Reputation refers to the focus of companies to satisfy the external audience. Companies should work to build a reputation for social consciousness. All these four arguments focus on the tension between business and society rather than on their interdependent relationship.

M. E. Porter and M. R. Kramer focused on these interrelationships and developed a guiding model for business to promote the mutual dependence of corporations and society. The model focuses on the principle of shared values between companies and the society. The philosophy is that companies must integrate social perspectives into the core framework used to understand competition and guide the business strategy.

The interdependence between the company and the society takes place in two forms: inside-out linkages and outside-in linkages.

Inside-out Linkages: Every activity in a company's value chain touches the communities in which the company operates either positively or negatively. More specifically, companies impinge upon the society through their operations in the normal course of business. It is necessary, therefore, to map the social impact of the value chain. The impact of primary activities such as inbound logistics, operations, outbound logistics, marketing and sales, after sales services and support activities such as firm infrastructure, human relationship management, technology development and procurement should be assessed comprehensively.

Outside-in Linkages: Corporate activities affect the society; social conditions also influence the functioning of corporations. Social dimensions affect a company's ability to improve productivity and execute strategy. There are four important areas which require special attention from the company's competition point of view: (1) context for firm strategy and rivalry (the rules and incentives that govern competition), (2) local demand conditions (the nature and sophistication of local customer needs), (3) related and supporting industries (local availability of support services) and (4) factor conditions (presence of high-quality, specialized input resources)

Taking the inside-out and outside-in factors into consideration a company should select and prioritize the social issues to address and develop a corporate social agenda accordingly. The agenda must be responsive to stakeholders. Companies should move beyond responsive corporate social responsibility (CSR) to strategic CSR. Integrating business and social needs require not only good intensions and strong leadership, but also require adjustments in organization, reporting relationships and incentives. Companies should perceive social responsibility as building shared value rather than a damage control.

Source: Michael E. Porter and Mark R. Kramer, "Strategy and Society: The Link Between Competitive Advantage and Corporate Social Responsibility," Harvard Business Review South Asia, *(December 2006): 54–68.*

STRATEGY EVALUATION AND CONTROL

Strategy evaluation at various levels of its implementation is essential to identify the deviations, if any, at an appropriate time and to initiate corrective action. There may be many hurdles in the process of strategy implementation, internally and externally. Some new problems may arise due to the implementation of the strategy, and some problems may emerge due to unexpected changes in the environment. Service firms have to exercise strategic surveillance for timely detection of such developments and take the necessary corrective action. For the purpose of evaluation and control, an effective system has to be designed. This system should enable the service company to:

- establish evaluation criteria and standards;
- measure and compare performance;
- identify and analyse performance gaps; and
- initiate corrective measures.

> *Strategic surveillance for timely detection of problems and to take corrective and preventive actions is essential in evaluation and control of a strategy. It is necessary to evolve criteria and standards for evaluation to find out performance gaps and to initiate corrective measures.*

Service firms generally prefer preventive control rather than direct control of the system. Since service quality mostly depends on the quality of the service personnel, the higher the quality of the personnel, the lesser the need for direct control. Preventive control systems aim at the development of better personnel, capable of applying concepts, principles and techniques skillfully and with involvement. With the application of preventive control, support personnel and frontline employees know what is expected of them; they develop the ability to understand their levels of performance through measurement techniques and reorient themselves with the required changes in their approach.

SUMMARY

- A strategic approach is necessary for service organizations to achieve organizational goals.
- Conventional strategies used in the manufacturing sector may not be suitable to service problems.
- The use of thumb-rule strategies may lead to the strategic management trap.
- When focused on cost effectiveness, the judicious categorization of costs into good costs and evil costs is necessary.
- Good costs need to be promoted, and evil costs should be eliminated.
- There is a need to turn the conventional pyramid of organization structure upside down to facilitate effective functioning.
- Frontline employees should be empowered to take decisions on the spot effectively.
- The services marketing triangle focusing on internal marketing, external marketing and interactive marketing provides a model for designing organizational policies and practices to satisfy customers.
- A modified marketing mix consisting of seven Ps can be used as a comprehensive marketing strategy.
- Physical evidence, people, and process are the three additional components to the traditional four Ps of marketing mix.
- A marketing strategy formulated in accordance with the organizational goals needs to be implemented efficiently.
- Service firms should acquire resources and build organizational capabilities for effective implementation.
- Evaluation and control of the strategy is essential for effective execution and further development.
- Strategic surveillance is necessary for the effective execution of the strategy.

KEY TERMS

additional innovative *154*
business mission *152*
evil costs *155*
external marketing *160*
good costs *155*
interactive marketing *160*
internal marketing *160*
strategic management trap *156*
SWOT analysis *152*

BRIEF QUESTIONS

1. Discuss the various steps in the strategic planning process.
2. Explain the market-oriented service strategy.
3. What is the strategic management trap?
4. Explain the service triangle.
5. What is a service-oriented organization structure?
6. What are good costs and evil costs?
7. What are the components of the services marketing mix?
8. Explain the importance of strategy evaluation and control.

ESSAY QUESTIONS

1. What is strategic planning? Explain its importance and process in a service company.
2. How do service companies get into the strategic management trap? What suggestions can you offer to the organization for getting out of the trap?
3. What is the services marketing triangle? Explain its significance and application to service organizations.
4. Suggest a strategic approach to health services offered by the state government.
5. Illustrate the process of strategic planning by taking a service organization as a case.
6. What is the services marketing mix? Explain the components of the marketing mix.
7. Explain the service-oriented strategic approach.
8. Explain the importance of strategy implementation, evaluation and control.

ASSIGNMENTS

1. Subhiksha, the Chennai-based retail chain entered into the business to redefine and restructure conventional mom-and-pop stores into an organized format. The progress was very impressive until 2008. The number of outlets and the geographic coverage was outstanding. In 2009, the company fell into neck-deep trouble. The expansion of 1600 outlets in 2 years without adequate backup from the strategic team led to failures across all the new outlets. The company got into the debt trap. Many outlets were closed within a short period of opening. The success story became a story of failure.
   (a) Analyse the case of Subhiksha to identify strategic lapses.
   (b) If you are given a chance, how would you handle the case?
2. Indian Railways is the biggest public sector transport organization and the world's second largest rail network. Indian Railways used to take support from the Government of India for its functioning until 2005 as the revenues were not enough to meet operational and developmental expenses. During the last 5 years there has been a quantum jump in revenues as a result of the turnaround strategies adopted by Indian Railways. In 2008, Indian Railways became the major profit-making organization among all public sector enterprises.

You are required to interact with Railway officials and study the literature available to:
   (a) Find out the key factors identified by Indian Railways to design a turnaround strategy.
   (b) Study the turnaround strategy implemented by Indian Railways.

REFERENCES

1 Michael A. Hitt, R. D. Ireland and R. E. Hoskisson, *Strategic Management: Competitiveness and Globalisation*, 4th ed. (US: Thomson South Western, 2001), p. 144.

2 Arthur A.Thompson and A. J. Strickland, *Strategic Management: Concepts and Cases.* (New Delhi: Tata McGraw-Hill, 2001), p. 3.

3 Philip Kotler, *Marketing Management*, 11th ed. (Delhi: Pearson Education, 1999), p. 89.

4 Arthur A. Thompson and A. J. Strickland, *Strategic Management: Concepts and Cases* (New Delhi: Tata McGraw-Hill, 2001), p. 4.

5 Peter F. Drucker, *Management: Tasks, Responsibilities, Practices.* (Bombay: Allied Publishers, 1975), p. 89.

6 Derek F. Abell, *Defining the Business: The Starting Point of Strategic Planning.* (London: Prentice Hall, 1980), p. 17.

7 Vern Mc Ginnis, "The Mission Statement: A Key Step in Strategic Planning," *Business*, Nov–Dec. (1981): 41. Cited by Fred David, *Strategic Management* (New York: MacMillan, 1993), p. 5.

8 Arthur A. Thompson and A. J. Strickland, *Strategic Management: Concepts and Cases.* (New Delhi: Tata McGraw-Hill, 2001), p. 127.

9 Ibid. p. 150.

10 Michael E. Porter, *Competitive Strategy, Techniques for Analyzing Industries and Competitors.* (New York: Free Press, 1980).

11 Arthur A. Thompson and A. J. Strickland, *Strategic Management: Concepts and Cases.* (New Delhi: Tata McGraw-Hill, 2001), p. 163.

12 Peter F. Drucker, "The Discipline of Innovation," *Harvard Business Review*, August (2002): 95–112.

13 Theodore Levitt, "Creativity is not enough," *Harvard Business Review*, August (2002).

14 C. Grönroos, *Service Management and Marketing; Managing the Moments of Truth in Service Competition.* (Massachusetts: Maxwell Macmillan; Lexington: D.C. Heath/Lexington Books, 1990), p. 100.

15 Ibid. pp. 94–95.

16 Christian Grönroos, "A Service Quality Model and its Marketing Implications," *European Journal of Marketing*, 18, no. 4 (1984): 36–44.

17 B. H. Booms and M. J. Bitner, Marketing Strategies and Organizational Structures for Service Firms, in *Marketing of Services*, edited by J. Donnelly and W.R. George (Chicago: American Marketing Association, 1981), pp. 47–51.

18 Fred R. David, *Fundamentals of Strategic Management.* (Columbus, Ohio: Merrill Publishing Company, 1986), p. 245.

19 Francis Cherunilam, *Strategic Management.* (Mumbai: Himalaya Publishing House, 1998), p. 86.

Market Segmentation

8

LEARNING OBJECTIVES

After studying this chapter, you will be able to:

- ▶ Understand the importance of market segmentation
- ▶ Understand the bases for market segmentation
- ▶ Understand the segmentation criteria and process
- ▶ Understand the customization strategy

Soujanya Rammohan, a fresh B-school graduate, considered many options before deciding to offer "food-to-home" services. She intends to supply the three major meals—breakfast, lunch and dinner—and snacks to households. The plan is to have term-based customers by selling monthly, quarterly, half-yearly and annual cards to families. This service will help the families escape from kitchen-based investments and reduce the physical stress and strain associated with cooking.

Despite the obvious benefits and the palpable latent demand in the market, Soujanya wanted to plan her strategy to ensure the success of her business. She began by limiting her area of operations—an imperative step for her to deliver fresh food to the end customer without resorting to cold storage vans. Soujanya also worked on a viable distribution network for the delivery of the meals at the right time. Before going into the finer nuances, Soujanya undertook a quick survey to understand what sort of food items would be best received and identify the primary decision-making authority in the households. The research revealed, in the chosen area of operations, the households are affluent with a single earning member. Soujanya reasoned that the few working women in the area would welcome the idea; therefore, her strategy would have to be directed at winning over the homemakers. Aware of the fact that this segment is also representative of the existing competition to her business proposition, Soujanya hit upon the following strategy:

- ▶ Good-quality food at affordable pricing.
- ▶ Discounts for long-term customers.
- ▶ A menu that is changed every week so that customers do not get bored of the same food items.
- ▶ In addition to the standard menu, each household can order a special dish of choice, once a week.
- ▶ Each household can contribute a new recipe each week. The best recipe will be included in the menu for the following week.

The last point of the strategy was specially directed at making loyal customers of homemakers. Armed with this strategy, Soujanya gets down to the brass tacks—handling operations, managing service quality and so on.

Questions:

1. Do you think Soujanya's approach to the problem is correct?
2. Did Soujanya have all the information needed to device an efficient strategy?
3. What is your opinion of the strategy adopted by Soujanya?
4 If the area of operations comprised primarily DINKS, would the same strategy have worked?
5. How will you evaluate Soujanya's service strategy?

Companies need to find out the right way to reach the market. The three options available are to make undifferentiated , differentiated and customized offers.

INTRODUCTION

Service companies need to position themselves in order to maximize competitive advantage and to serve the target market effectively. There are basically three quite distinct approaches to marketing strategy to select a target market: undifferentiated market, differentiated market (market segmentation) and customization. A policy of undifferentiated or mass marketing emerges when a firm deliberately ignores any differences that exist within its markets and decides instead to focus on a feature that appears to be common or acceptable to a wide variety of buyers.[1] Differentiated marketing is to serve the needs of some specified homogeneous groups with specialized offers. In the changing business environment where specialization is vital to attract consumer attention, generalized market offerings may not be capable of yielding the desired results. Market segmentation, thus, is a vital strategic tool for business. Customization is one-to-one marketing. It demands the marketer to treat each customer as a market and create and deliver an exclusive offer to each customer.

*In the **undifferentiated marketing approach,** also known as mass marketing approach, the same service package is offered to the entire market. Customers' needs and wants are generalized and a service offer is developed accordingly, making many service consumers compromise on their specific desires and expectations.*

UNDIFFERENTIATED MARKETING

Under this approach, service organizations aim at capturing mass markets with a single package. Marketers pursue mass distribution and mass promotion of one product for all buyers. Only a few service organizations can depend on the undifferentiated marketing approach to maximize their financial benefits. Figure 8.1 illustrates the undifferentiated marketing strategy. Generally, public sector monopolies follow this approach. Services such as primary education, primary health, law and order services and judiciary services follow the undifferentiated marketing approach in India.

DIFFERENTIATED MARKETING (MARKET SEGMENTATION)

Market segmentation is the most popular technique to reach the markets with service packages. Modern companies seldom try to appeal to all buyers in their market in the same way. The concept of market segmentation dates back to the mid-20th century when marketers began to accept divergent demand as a fundamental market characteristic and started to adjust product lines and marketing strategies accordingly.[2] According to W. R. Smith,[3] the lack of homogeneity on the demand side can be based on different customs, desire for variety or desire for exclusiveness or may arise from basic differences in user needs. Markets generally are heterogeneous in nature, with varied

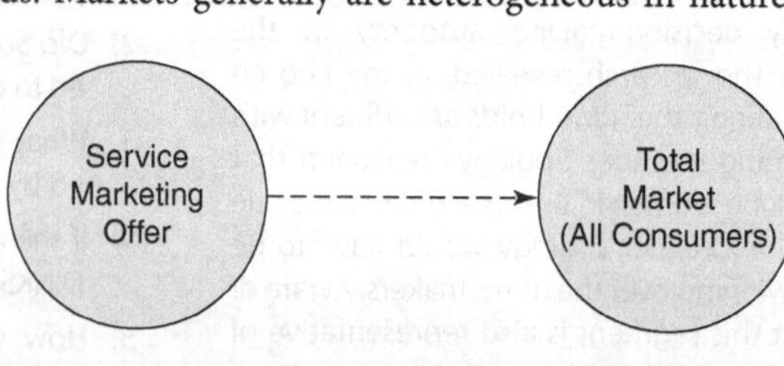

Fig. 8.1
The undifferentiated marketing strategy

cultures, lifestyles and economic backgrounds. Market segmentation is the division of heterogeneous markets into segments. It should be ensured while segmentation that each segment is homogenous in all significant characteristics. The requirements of individual customers differ greatly, and the levels of compromise and tolerance also differ. Undoubtedly, every consumer makes a compromise in satisfying a set of needs owing to a number of limitations. The limitations may be availability, personal resources, social factors and suitability. However, the level of compromise depends on the choices. If an offer from a competitor is more suitable and valuable, there is every likelihood of the customer preferring that offer. In order to reach customers by matching the service offer to the needs and wants of the consumer, market segmentation is the best approach available to service providers. Therefore, service organizations have to go for segmentation in marketing to the best possible extent. True segmentation starts with identifying the requirements and behaviour of segments, and varying marketing mixes accordingly in order to more deliberately match marketing offerings with customer behaviour.[4] A market segment should basically satisfy four important criteria: distinctiveness (each segment should have deferent needs), homogeneity (similar needs within the segment), similarity in response and possibility to reach by a market intervention.

> ***Market segmentation*** *is the process of dividing the heterogeneous market into some closely homogeneous groups or segments. It facilitates companies to develop differentiated offers. The objective is to offer service packages closely matching the needs and wants of consumers to the homogeneous segment.*

The differentiated marketing approach is illustrated in Fig. 8.2. The potential benefits of a well-developed segmentation strategy can, therefore, be considerable, since an organization should be able to establish and strengthen its position in the market and, hence, operate more effectively. Not only does it become far more difficult for a competitor to attack, but it also allows the organization to build a greater degree of market segment knowledge and customer loyalty.[5]

The need for market segmentation arises due to the necessity of balancing customers' diverse needs. Companies work to match their resources and competencies with the diverse customer needs by concentrating efforts on homogeneous customer groups. An effective segmentation process involves three distinct steps: marketing analysis to gain knowledge or competitive advantage through current marketing intelligence; strategy development to

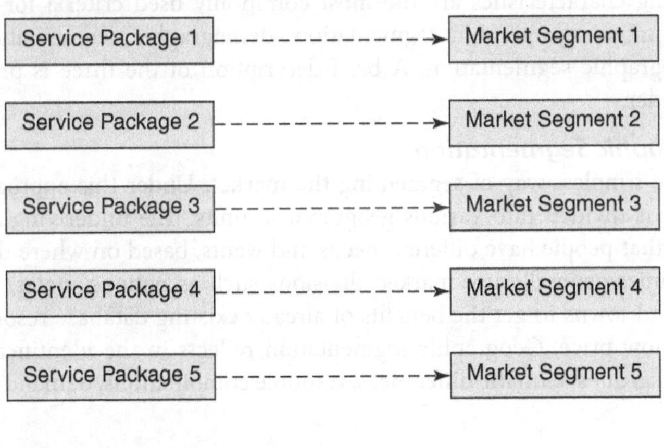

Fig. 8.2
The differentiated marketing approach

formalize ideas and marketing programmes to execute the determined revised segmentation strategy. These three stages form a loop, as the formulation of marketing strategies, segment targeting and marketing mix programmes is a never-ending cycle of revisions.[6]

BASES FOR MARKET SEGMENTATION

The basic principle of market segmentation is that markets are not homogeneous and that it makes commercial sense to differentiate marketing offerings for different customer groups.[7] Customer needs are becoming increasingly diverse. These needs can no longer be satisfied by a mass marketing approach. Businesses can cope with this diversity by grouping customers with similar requirements and buying behaviour into segments. Choices about which segments are the most appropriate to serve can then be made, thus, making the best of finite resources.[8] The selection of the right basis for dividing the market is of vital importance. Companies take into consideration the following for the selection of the right basis for market segmentation: service characteristics, the requirements of facilitating services, supporting services, the availability of service outlets and financial and other resources. The bases for segmentation can be broadly categorized into consumer characteristics and consumer responses.

> *“The segmentation of a market is based on consumer characteristics or consumer responses. Taking consumer characteristics as a base, segmentation may be done in three ways—geographic, demographic and psychographic. Taking consumer responses as a base, the market can be segmented using variables such as occasions, benefits and user status.”*

Consumer characteristics such as those related to geography, demography and psychography are used to divide the market into segments, by using either a single variable or a combination of them. A consumer response refers to the benefits sought by a consumer from a service provider. The benefits may be related to the quality–price relationship, flexibility, exceptions, usage occasions and so on. It is not necessary for service companies to choose only one of the two bases. Most service providers develop a mix of these two as their segmentation plan.

Consumer Characteristics

Many marketers use consumer characteristics as a basis for segmenting markets. It is relatively easy and also economical to use this basis. The three following characteristics are the most commonly used criteria for market segmentation: geographic segmentation, demographic segmentation and psychographic segmentation. A brief description of the three is presented hereunder.

Geographic Segmentation

It is the simplest way of segmenting the market. Under this approach, the market is divided into various geographical units. The underlying assumption is that people have different needs and wants, based on where they live. Companies generally use marked divisions such as nations, states, regions, cities and towns to get the benefits of already existing database resources at a very low price. Geographic segmentation reflects in the identification of cultural groups, climatic differences, resource combinations, demand–supply gaps, religion and race. It provides an opportunity to the service companies to explore distinctive opportunities for product development as well as product differentiation. Simple geographic segmentation is easy and relatively inexpensive way to handle a market.

Demographic Segmentation

Demography is the study of population. Under this approach, the market is divided into segments based on various demographic variables such as age, family size, gender, family life cycle, income, occupation, education, religion, race, nationality and social class. The differences in consumer responses based on demographic variables are studied and a segmentation plan is worked out accordingly. Demographics has gained popularity as a basis of segmentation since consumer needs and usage rates are closely related to it. Also, it is easily measurable. The cost of this approach is relatively low. Demographic variables, when employed properly, are capable of providing a constructive base for consumer-centric market segmentation.

Demographic and geographic variables have been combined to create a new approach called *geodemographic segmentation*. Geodemographic segmentation works by grouping together small areas with similar demographic profiles.[9] In other words, this segmentation is a combination of geographic and demographic variables. It is based on the principle that people are more similar to those who live around them than they are dissimilar.[10] Based on this assumption, customer groups with similar needs are identified to offer a distinctive set of services. These geodemographic clusters are convenient for marketers to execute their marketing programmes. Michael J. Weiss rightly pointed out that cluster-based marketing has gone mainstream and is now used by corporations, non-profit and political groups alike to target their audiences. Advertising agencies search these clusters for hot buttons on the consumer psyche. Restaurants, banks and retailers use cluster systems to identify locations in which to open new outlets or close poor performers. Direct mailers discover the best prospects from subscription lists by correlating addresses to cluster tastes and spending habits. Even health officials use clusters to correct the bad habits of citizens, earmarking funds for prevention programmes based on the profile of the community cluster.[11] The potential rating index for zip market (PRIZM) system provides the right methodology to identify and group people into segments by using geodemographic variables.[12] This segmentation approach is based on the popular philosophy "birds of a feather flock together."

Psychographic Segmentation

This approach is more focused than geographic and demographic approaches. Under this approach, consumers are divided into groups based on lifestyle, personality and values. Many a time, consumers belonging to the same geographic and demographic group may exhibit different psychographic profiles. People belonging to the same demographic group may vary in their activities, opinions, value perceptions and interests. Marketers have understood that to attract or motivate a particular group of consumers, it is necessary to know

Doordarshan

Doordarshan is the national television service of India, with a network of three national channels, 11 regional language channels, four state networks, two special interest channels and one international channel. It is one of the largest broadcasting networks in the world with 1,400 terrestrial transmitters covering more than 90.7 per cent of India's population. Doordarshan strategically used geodemographic segmentation to reach the market effectively. The states of India are divided primarily based on language. Each state, as a geographic unit, is identified with a language. The establishment of regional language channels with localized programmes helped Doordarshan have greater market penetration. All Doordarshan *kendras* produce programmes in their respective regional languages. The regional language satellite services and regional state networks broadcast a wide spectrum of programmes covering developmental news, serials, documentaries, news and current affairs programmes to communicate with the people in their own language. Programmes in regional languages are available in the respective states, terrestrially during the regional window of DD National and round the clock on the regional language satellite channels across the country. The programmes offered through these channels are focused on demographic variables of the population. Age, sex, education, occupation and so on are taken as a base for designing and transmitting various programmes.

how they think and what their values and attitudes are, as well as who they are in terms of the traditional demographic variables.[13] Psychographics helps in identifying and understanding the basic beliefs and attitudes influencing consumer behaviour in varied situations. Lifestyle variables have been used popularly in psychographic segmentation. There are basically three questions that are focused on identifying lifestyle variables: what we do, what we want, and what we think. Activities, interests and opinions, called AIO dimensions, are used to develop the lifestyle profile of consumers. Another approach to lifestyle-based segmentation is VALS (Values, Attitudes and Lifestyle Systems), developed by Standford Research International (VALS scheme is analysed in "Services Marketing Insight: Market Segmentation System"). This scheme has been applied by many marketers to predict consumer behaviour. Psychographic methods offer a new way of describing consumers. Service providers are required to develop a sound database on the psychographics of the market in order to make the service offer more focused.

Consumer Responses (Behavioural Segmentation)

Consumer responses to marketing stimulations differ significantly. It is possible to identify and group people who respond in a similar way to a marketing stimulation. Segmenting a market on the basis of consumer responses is called *behavioural segmentation*.

In this approach, consumers are divided into groups based on their knowledge, attitudes and uses or responses to a service. The variables used under this segmentation are occasions, benefits, user status, usage rate, loyalty status, buyer readiness stage and attitude towards the service. Occasion segmentation groups consumers according to special occasions and regularity. Special occasions such

Wills Lifestyle

ITC's lifestyle retailing business division promotes the Wills Lifestyle chain of specialty stores. The company aims at providing a truly international shopping experience through world-class ambience, customer facilitation and clearly differentiated product presentation. The segmentation basis adopted by Wills Lifestyle is behavioural and lifestyle segmentation. The stores are filled with a variety of products, grouped under different lifestyles for both men and women. At Wills Lifestyle, customers can browse at leisure, and shop in a relaxed and pleasing atmosphere. The use of space is refreshing, which is reflected even in the spacious changing rooms. Every store offers an international retailing ambience with the extensive use of glass, steel and granite, reflecting the most contemporary trends in store design, thereby creating a splendid backdrop for the premium offerings. Wills Lifestyle is the title partner of the country's premier fashion event—Wills Lifestyle India Fashion Week. Taking the celebration of the event to its stores, Wills Lifestyle has partnered with several leading designers including Manish Arora, Rohit Bal, Shantanu & Nikhil, Rohit Gandhi and Rahul Khanna.

as festivals, birthdays, marriage days and so on are taken as a base. Benefit segmentation divides consumers according to the benefits they seek from a given service. Some consumers may seek quality; some look for economy service and some may look at the speed at which the service is accessed. User-status segmentation divides consumers into light users, medium users and heavy users. Loyalty-status segmentation classifies consumers as non-loyal, medium loyal, strong loyal and absolute loyal. The buyer-readiness stage is another behaviour segmentation variable. According to this variable, buyers are segmented as unaware, aware, informed, interested, desirous and intending to buy. The attitude towards the service is the other variable used for segmentation in this category. Consumers are grouped as enthusiasts, positives, indifferents, negatives and hostiles to predict the buying response.

Market segmentation variables relating to geographic, demographic, psychographic and behavioural segmentation are illustrated in Table 8.1. Of late, a new basis for segmentation, called technographic segmentation, has emerged. Market segmentation based on technographic elements is discussed in "Services Marketing Insight : Technographic Segmentation".

Segmentation is fundamental to successful marketing strategies. Until competitors copy or segment the segmentation, a service firm enjoys a competitive edge, even if it serves the segment with a standard product or service. If the product or service is specific to the segment, the competitive advantage is multiplied.[14] The number of variables in respect of consumer characteristics and consumer response often makes it very difficult for the marketer to develop a market segmentation system. It is also vital to recognize the differential importance of each segment. One has to recognize the fact that not all segments are equal.

Three approaches to market segmentation can be distinguished based on the grouping of the variables:[15] forward, backward and simultaneous segmentation. The forward approach takes into consideration primarily the similarities in behavioural responses to services and later, the object or situation-spe-

Table 8.1 Market Segmentation Variables

Geographic	
Region	North, east, south, west, north-east, north-west, south-east, south-west, states and union territories
City	Towns, cities, metropolitan cities
Density	Urban, semi-urban and rural
Climate	Northern, southern, north-eastern, north-western
Demographic	
Age	Under 5, 6–10, 11–16, 17–25, 26–35, 36–45, 46–55, 56–65, 66+
Family size	1, 2, 3, 4, 5, 6 +
Family life cycle	Young, single: young, married, no children; young, married, youngest child under 6; young, married, youngest child 6 or over; married with children; older, married, no children under 18; older singles; others
Gender	Male/female
Income	Below INR 10,000; INR 10,000–20,000; INR 20,000–30,000; INR 30,000–50,000; INR 50,000–1,00,000; INR 1,00,000 and above
Occupation	Employees, businessmen, agriculturists, professionals and so on
Education	Primary, secondary, under-graduate, graduate, post-graduate
Religion	Hindu, Muslim, Christian, Sikh, Jain, Buddhist and so on
Social class	Lower-lower, lower-middle, lower-upper, middle-lower, middle-middle, middle-upper, upper-lower, upper-middle, upper-upper
Psychographic	
Lifestyle	Principle-oriented, status-oriented, action-oriented
Personality	Dogmatic, inner directed, social oriented, variety seeker, materialistic
Behavioural	
Occasions	Regular, special
Benefits	Quality, economy, speed
User status	Non-user, ex-user, potential user, first time user, regular user
Usage rate	Light user, medium user, heavy user
Loyalty status	None, medium, strong, absolute
Readiness stage	Unaware, aware, informed, interested, desirous, intending to buy
Attitude	Enthusiastic, positive, indifferent, negative, hostile

cific consumer characteristics to assign consumers into groups. The backward segmentation approach takes consumer characteristics as the primary base and consumer response variables as support to group consumers. The simultaneous analysis of both consumer characteristics and consumer response variables is done to establish the correlation between the two to group consumers into segments under the third approach—simultaneous segmentation. Segments are not homogeneous groupings of customers naturally occurring

8.1 Services Marketing Insight

Technographic Segmentation

The market for technology-related services has expanded significantly during the last one-and-a-half decades. Marketers are trying to identify the customer groups that have the willingness and the ability to use the latest technology. Forester Research Incorporation has developed a 10-category segmentation scheme, which is also called *technogrality*. The identification of segments is based on the interaction of three variables: attitude towards technology, the application of technology and the financial position of consumers. The 10 segments are as following:

1. ***Fast Forwards:*** These customers are career-oriented optimists. They are the biggest spenders and earliest adopters of new technology for various purposes at home, office and elsewhere.
2. ***Techno Strivers:*** These customers are career oriented. They use technology to gain an edge in their career. They use cell phones, Internet and so on for the purpose.
3. ***Hand Shakers:*** These customers are pessimists and, at the same time, career oriented too. These are old consumers and do not like to touch computers. They leave technology-based products to their young assistants.
4. ***New Age Nurturers:*** These customers are family-oriented optimists. They spend heavily on home-based technology products.
5. ***Digital Hopefuls:*** This group refers to families with limited budgets. They are interested in new technology and plan the resources to acquire technology-based products.
6. ***Traditionalists:*** These are family-oriented pessimists. They are willing to use technology but do not prefer to upgrade products.
7. ***Misuse Potatoes:*** These customers are optimists as well as lovers of entertainment. They spend more on online entertainment and acquire the latest technology in that area.
8. ***Gadget Grabbers:*** These customers favour online entertainment but are constrained by limited resources.
9. ***Media Junkies:*** These customers seek entertainment through low-cost sources like TV and other older media.
10. ***Sidelined Citizens:*** These individuals do not have any interest in technology.

in the marketplace. Market segments are determined by the manager's strategic view of the market. Their perspective determines the way homogenous groups of potential customers are identified by market research.[16]

Taking into consideration the bewildering array of variables, marketers look at market segmentation systems[17] to:

- identify the key consumer segments;
- recognize the varying importance of segments to the service business;
- understand individual consumers by identifying the group to which they belong, so that they can be served better;
- use that newly-gained understanding to predict how consumers will react to new services, alter brand loyalties, respond to diverse media, etc.;
- target new prospects more effectively; and
- communicate with both customers and prospects in order to establish and enhance relationships.

8.2 Services Marketing Insight **Market Segmentation System**

Any segmentation system must be restricted to the parameters set and, even given modern computing power, no methodology can begin to encompass all the variables contributing to human behaviour or psychological make-up. Ultimately, we are all different, yet share habits and attitudes with those around us. And those attitudes or preferences are also, to a significant extent, determined by the environment in which we live.[18] Until the 1970s, market segmentation was based on product-specific systems. The segmentation plan of one product is not applicable to other product categories. In 1970, William H. Tryon and Dariel Bailey developed a statistical process called cluster analysis. The researchers identified census tracks by statistically aggregating variables such as income, ethnicity, education and occupation and found a strikingly consistent behaviour on a wide variety of issues.

"Birds of a feather flock together" was the theme underlying the development of a geodemographic segmentation system (PRIZM by Claritas Corporation 1974). Geodemographics intends to identify areas of multiple needs in customer segmentation.

The growth of behavioural and lifestyle databases is another major development in the area of market segmentation. Stanford Research International introduced VALS (Value, Attitude and Lifestyle Systems). VALS is conceptually based on Abraham Maslow's hierarchy of needs. The data inventory on demographic and attitudinal issues are analysed to classify an individual into one of eight VALS types. The eight consumer groups identified are survivors, believers, thinkers, strivers, achievers, makers, experiencers and innovators. Each group is identified with certain distinctive behavioural characteristics, which are useful to marketers to identify segments and differentiate their service offers.

CRITERIA FOR MARKET SEGMENTATION

The bases for market segmentation discussed earlier help identify the segments of a market relating to a product. Whether the segment has the required characteristics or not is an important question. Service firms generally adopt the criteria described in the following sections to assess the suitability of segmentation.

Substantiality

The size of the segment is an important dimension. An identified segment should be large enough to design a distinctive marketing programme for itself. Substantiality is not only measured in size but also in terms of profitability. The benefits that are expected from segmentation should be more than the estimated expenditure from the special marketing efforts required.

Measurability

The segment identified must be amenable to measurement. Characteristics such as size, purchasing power and response rates need to be measured so as to design the appropriate marketing strategy.

Accessibility

Accessibility has a specific significance in services. The production and consumption of the service take place simultaneously during producer and consumer interaction. Therefore, the segments identified should be within the reach of service organizations.

Differentiability

The differences between segments should be substantial and measurable. For a specific service package, the response from one segment should be different from that of other segments.

> *The segments identified based on either consumer characteristics or consumer responses to be considered as suitable segments for a service company should satisfy certain criteria. The criteria generally followed include substantiality, measurability, accessibility and differentiability.*

CUSTOMIZATION

Services are delivered to people mostly by people. By its very character, services are heterogeneous and, as such, no two individuals can have the same service in the same way or can any customer have exactly the same service on two occasions. Though service providers can standardize the technical product to a great extent, it is not possible to standardize the functional part. This variability, in one way, is a blessing and, in another way, a curse. Variability provides innumerable opportunities to be innovative at every point and creates better experiences for the customer. However, it makes service delivery difficult to control and predict. As such, the inconsistencies resulting out of non-standardization may cause customers to question the reliability of the service provider. If the heterogeneity is pursued in a purposeful manner, it is possible to turn it into an effective customization standard. As the service itself is frequently delivered in real time by real people, there is an opportunity for one-to-one customization of the service offering.

> ***Customization** is to consider each customer a market and offer them a specially designed service by taking into account their specific needs, wants and expectations. This is the most desirable from the customer point of view. Though many argue that customization is not a realistic approach, companies are working towards customization with the support of technology and other resources.*

In customization, each customer is a market segment. The service offer is designed and developed to meet the needs and wants of each customer. Figure 8.3 illustrates the customization process.

Some argue that segments lone customers are practically unrealistic. It is true, of course, that in some cases segments of one or customization is practically impossible, but in many services customization to fit each individual's

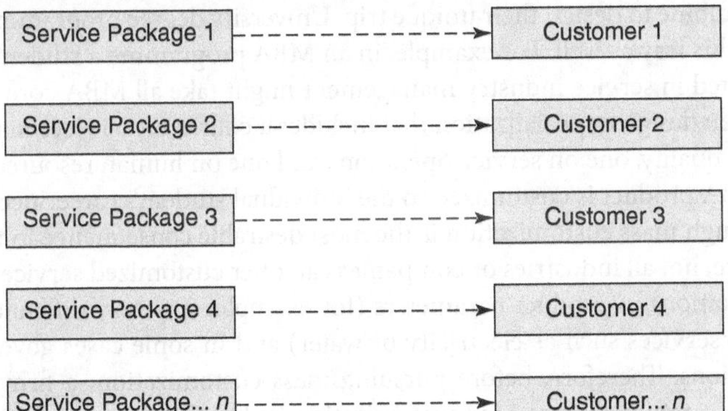

Fig. 8.3 The customization process

needs and wants should be pursued because today's consumers demand that they be treated as individuals and are very particular about satisfying a person's specific needs. Customization is not a big problem for companies that have a limited number of big customers. Even in consumer markets where a company may have millions of customers, customization is possible, if the state-of-the-art technology is used and employees are empowered. The following are some of the important approaches:[19]

Customizing the Service Around a Standardized Core

A standard core service such as airline transportation and hotel accommodation can be customized through addition of features or through creative delivery options. Hotels, for example, offer in-room variations (for example, smoking/non-smoking, size and number of beds) as well as add-ons such as office services for business travellers and exercise facilities.

Creating Customizable Services

Here the firm offers the same service to everyone, using a design that can be customized by the consumer. Interactive computer services (Prodigy, CompuServe), ATMs and automated ticketing systems are examples of this type of customization service. Other examples are self-service salad bars or entertainment environments such as Disney World.

Offering Point-of-delivery Customization

Using this option, the provider allows customers to communicate what they need or want at the point-of-service delivery. The service is customized in real time by the employee to fit those needs. Classic examples include professional services, healthcare counselling and personal care services.

Offering Standard Modules that Can Be Combined in Unique Ways

This is the approach used by tour companies that offer the traveller different vacation components (hotels, airlines, destinations, lengths of stay) that they can combine to design their unique trip. University degree programmes operate in this way as well. For example, in an MBA programme a student who is interested in service industry management might take all MBA core courses and then design a specialization that includes a course on services marketing, one on quality, one on service operations and one on human resources. Thus, the MBA product is customized to the individual student's career needs.

Though mass customization is the most desirable consequence in the marketplace, not all industries or companies can offer customized services owing to limitations in product parameters (for example, it is very difficult to customize services such as electricity or water) and in some cases government regulations. Therefore, before pursuing mass customization, a firm should analyse carefully the need for customization and its feasibility.

STAGES IN MARKET SEGMENTATION

An effective segmentation process must begin with a clear appreciation of corporate objectives.[20] It helps in identifying the broad issues to be considered, information needs and sources and the areas of priority. There are at least three stages in the process of market segmentation:
search, selection and strategy.

Search

The first step in market segmentation is to conduct a survey by using exploratory interviews and focus groups in order to have a greater insight into the motivation, attitude and behaviour of consumers. Consumer opinions on the attributes of the service package, the ratings of importance, brand awareness and ratings, attitudes, demographics, psycographics, geographics and mediagraphics are collected for a sound base for segmentation. The data collected through the survey is analysed by using statistical techniques such as correlation, regression, factor analysis and cluster analysis to identify the specific number of differentiable segments.

Selection

Based on the search information and analysis, segments are identified. Identified segments have to be given a name, based on their dominant characteristics. The identifiable characteristics may be active homeguarding, self-sufficient, socially active, passive homebody, sports enthusiast and so on. The full details of each segment relating to attitude, behaviour, demographics, psychographics and media patterns are studied. This study is helpful in the selection of the right customers.

> *The organizational process for segmentation involves three stages: search, selection and strategy.* ***Search*** *refers to information search on various issues relating to consumers.* ***Selection*** *is grouping the consumer characteristics and identifying the groups based on dominant characteristics of the group.* ***Strategy*** *is formulated based on three important issues—value maximization, capacity utilization and customer participation.*

Strategy

The formulation of a right strategy is essential to achieve success through market segmentation. While formulating the strategy, three issues are given special attention: value maximization, capacity utilization and customer participation.

Value generation by creating an adaptable service package, keeping in view the needs and wants of customers, is pivotal for service firms. Besides, they need to focus on creating value perceptions in customers in the process of service performance. The orientation of firms should be to maximize value for customers.

Capacity utilization is another dimension in the formulation of strategy. The demand and capacity management ensures quality service production at minimum cost.

Customer participation influences the value generation as well as value perception. By studying the capabilities of different customers in participating in the service production process, the right kind of approach can be designed. Every customer is distinctive in his/her ability, approach, enthusiasm and involvement in using a service. Therefore, a proper mechanism is to be evolved to make every customer participate effectively.

SUMMARY

- In the fast-changing market environment, the demand for specialized services is growing.
- Service companies have three options to reach the market: undifferentiated marketing, market segmentation and customization.
- When a service company offers only one package across its market, it is called undifferentiated marketing.
- Marketing segmentation is to divide the heterogeneous market into homogeneous segments.
- The purpose of market segmentation is to serve the needs and wants of consumers by providing differentiated offers.
- The bases of market segmentation may be based on consumer characteristics and/or consumer responses.
- Consumer characteristics include geographic, demographic and psychographic issues.
- Consumer responses are the behavioural dimensions relating to occasions, benefits, user status, loyalty, and so on.
- The heterogeneity of service offerings facilitates service providers to sell a differentiated service package to each smaller group.
- The criteria for market segmentation are substantiality, measurability, accessibility and differentiability.
- The three stages in the market segmentation process are search, selection and strategy.
- Customization means considering each customer a market and designing and offering an exclusive service package to each customer.
- Service companies can adopt customization easily since services are variable in nature.
- Though mass customization is desirable, some service companies cannot go for it due to product parameters and government regulations.

KEY TERMS

Accessibility *179*
Behavioural segmentation *175*
Customization *179*
Demographic segmentation *173*
Differentiability *179*
Differentiated marketing *170*
Geodemographic segmentation *174*
Geographic segmentation *172*
Measurability *178*
Psychographic segmentation *174*
Substantiality *178*
Technographic segmentation *173*
Undifferentiated marketing *170*
VALS *175*

BRIEF QUESTIONS

1. What do you mean by an undifferentiated market?
2. Explain technographic segmentation.
3. Discuss the applicability of customization in services.
4. Explain the criteria for market segmentation.
5. Discuss the process of market segmentation.

ESSAY QUESTIONS

1. What is market segmentation? Describe how market segmentation can be used for services?
2. What are the bases for market segmentation? Design segmentation strategies for insurance services.
3. What is mass customization? How can it be implemented for services?
4. "An undifferentiated market is not appropriate to the service business." Comment.
5. What criteria should be followed for a differentiated market? Discuss with suitable examples.
6. What are the stages in the service market segmentation process?

ASSIGNMENTS

1. Hospitality services face many marketing challenges. Market segmentation is one of the major strategic tools used by many star-rated hotels. The basis of segmentation may differ among them. You are required to study the segmentation strategy of a star-rated hotel to:
   (a) Identify the basis followed for market segmentation
   (b) Find out the results of such segmentation
2. Reliance Life Insurance is among the fastest growing life insurance companies in India. In less than three years of starting operations, it became one of the top four life insurers in the private sector—growing at upwards of 100 per cent annually. The new business premium grew over 200 per cent at INR 27.51 billion (US$ 625 million) for the financial year ended March 31 2008. The company crossed the milestone of the 1.5 million policy mark and is among the top three players in terms of the number of policies issued. Despite the growth momentum witnessed by the industry over the past few years, the potential for future expansion remains as strong as ever, due to low penetration levels, attractive demographics, robust economic prospects and increasing investor awareness. You are required to:
   (a) Find out the segmentation basis of the company
   (b) Study the merits and demerits of the segmentation
   (c) Develop an alternative basis of segmentation for the company

REFERENCES

1 Colin Gilligan and Richard M. S. Wilson, *Strategic Marketing Planning.* (Burlington: Butterworth-Heinemann Publications, 2003) p. 399.

2 Matti Uronen, Market Segmentation Approaches in the Mobile Service Business, Unpublished Thesis (Otaniemi: Helsinki University of Technology, 2008) pp. 7–8.

3 Smith R. Wendell, "Product Differentiation and Market Segmentation as Alternative Marketing Strategies," *Journal of Marketing,* 21, no. 1 (1956): 3–8.

4 Michael J. Baker, *The Marketing Book*, 5th ed. (Burlington: Butterworth-Heinemann Publications, 2003) p. 247.

5 Colin Gilligan and Richard M.S. Wilson, *Strategic Marketing Planning* (Burlington: Butterworth-Heinemann Publications, 2003) p. 399.

6 Sally Dibb and Lyndon Simkin, "A Program For Implementing Market Segmentation," *Journal of Business and Industrial Marketing,* 12, no. 1 (1997): 52.

7 Michael J. Baker, *The Marketing Book*, 5th ed. (Burlington: Butterworth-Heinemann Publications, 2003) p. 247.

8 Sally Dibb, "Marketing Segmentation: Strategies for Success," *Marketing Intelligence and Planning,* 16, no. 7 (1998): 394.

9 Charlie Nelson, Geodemographic Segmentation: Do Birds of a Feather Flock Together?, http://www.foreseechange.com/Geodemographic%20Segmentation.pdf.

10 Matti Uronen, Market Segmentation Approaches in the Mobile Service Business, Unpublished Thesis (Otaniemi: Helsinki University of Technology, 2008) p. 13.

11 Michael J. Weiss, *The Clustered World* (Boston: Little Brown and Company, 2000). Quoted in Charlie Nelson, Geodemographic Segmentation: Do Birds of a Feather Flock Together?, http://www.foreseechange.com/Geodemographic%20Segmentation.pdf.

12 www.claritas.com, dated 21-5-2009.

13 Ziff Ruth, "Psychographics for Market Segmentation," *Journal of Advertising Research,* 11, no. 2 (1971): 3–9.

14 T. McBurnie and D. Clutterbuck, *Give Your Company the Marketing Edge* (London: Penguin Books, 1988).

15 W. Fred van Raaij, "Domain-Specific Market Segmentation," *European Journal of Marketing,* 28, no. 10 (1994): 49–66.

16 M. Wedel and W. Kamakura, *Market Segmentation: Conceptual and Methodological Foundations.* (Boston, MA: Kluwer Academic Publishers, 2000) p. 336.

17 Jock Bickert, "Cohorts II: A New Approach to Market Segmentation," *Journal of Consumer Marketing,* 14, no. 5 (1997): 362–363.

18 Jock Bickert, "Cohorts II: A New Approach to Market Segmentation," *Journal of Consumer Marketing,* 14, no. 5 (1997): 378.

19 Pine B. Joseph II., "Mass Customizing Products and Services," *Planning Review,* 21, no. 4 (1993): 6–13, 55.

20 Sally Dibb and Lyndon Simkin, "A Program for Implementing Market Segmentation," *Journal of Business and Industrial Marketing,* 12, no. 1 (1997): 54.

Competition Analysis and Strategies

9

LEARNING OBJECTIVES

After studying this chapter, you will be able to:

- Identify the threats of competition
- Understand the industry and market concepts of competition
- Understand the way competitors are analysed
- Describe the competition strategies

Jacob Sarma, Managing Director, Service2Home Pvt. Ltd is working on developing a competitive strategy to ensure that Service2Home can take on the existing and the potential competition in the market.

Service2Home is in the business of providing domestic help through a network of registered maids to middle- and high-income households in urban areas. It offers different service packages at different prices. The flexibility of the service package design is such that customers themselves can formulate their service package based on their choices.

Though the rising number of working women and nuclear families in these areas increased the demand for domestic help, Sarma had to work hard to assuage customer apprehensions regarding domestic help during the initial phases. Incidents of theft, physical attack, reports of intelligence to robbers and so on were quite common, which made consumers wary of using the services of the company. Sarma assured customers that they could rely on the service personnel provided by the firm. Although some customers were unhappy about the prices of the services, the feedback on the service quality was positive from all groups of customers. Thanks to such efforts, Service2Home managed to carve a niche for itself in a very short time.

Now, it is facing competition from individual maidservants who offer the same services at lower prices and from price-sensitive customers who perform the services on their own instead of hiring any one. It had been relatively easy to capture the high-income segment as compared to the price-sensitive middle-income group. Now, Sarma wants to consolidate the position of the company in both the segments. He wants to build distinct competencies that would make it difficult for new entrants to compete with the firm. He plans to attract more independent maidservants to register with the company. He needs to work out a comprehensive strategy to establish Serve2Home as the market leader in the long run.

Questions

1. How can Service2Home gain competitive advantage in this business?
2. Do you think Sarma's strategy of attracting independent maidservants is workable? Will it eliminate competition?
3. What are the potential threats to the company?
4. What strategy would you adopt to achieve the company objectives towards competition?

INTRODUCTION

Competition is an inherent characteristic of marketing. Companies face competition from different angles and in different ways. Company strategists basically try to understand and cope with competition. Consumers' expectations from services are greatly influenced by competitive offers and communications. Companies can reach customers only by providing better value than their competitors. Thus, competition is real, and marketers should learn ways to handle it effectively. The changing economic policies and perspectives in India and the world have resulted in intense competition among many service sectors. For example, service sectors such as telecommunications, insurance, banking, post and transport with reference to road and air were opened up for the private sector after the liberalization policies were introduced in India in 1991. All these sectors have become highly competitive in recent years. The erstwhile public sector monopolies in these sectors now face severe competition in the market. Therefore, competition is dynamic and may result from several factors. Service companies should be conscious of such changes and develop the required competencies to face the challenges posed by their competitors.

> *"Service companies should equip themselves to face competition from various angles in the market. The objectives of the company can be achieved only when the company develops and executes an effective strategy to handle competition. Consumers prefer companies that offer superior value."*

COMPETITIVE THREATS

Service companies may compete with other service companies in the same or related industry such as banks facing competition from other banks, indigenous bankers and other financial institutions. Then again, service companies may have to compete with service companies from other businesses such as movies facing competition from television, stage shows, exhibitions and other forms of entertainment. At times, the competition sometimes may even be with the consumer who knows how to serve him/herself. Competition from such diverse sources makes it difficult for organizations to recognize real threats and to position their services against those of their competitors. M. E. Porter[1] identified five factors that shape the competition, (shown in Fig. 9.1):

1. *Rivalry Among the Existing Competitors:* It is the most common form of competition. The existing competitors try to gain the customer base of each other while maintaining their existing customer base. These companies also seek to expand their customer base by attracting new customers. Since the competitors are known, it is relatively easy to assess the competition and develop strategies to face them. However, each company works seriously to win over the other through several innovative approaches. This kind of market aggression enhances market costs and reduces margins, making the business segment unattractive to new entrants.
2. *The Threat from New Entrants:* New entrants generally enter the market in a big way with new capacities, technologies and other competencies. The entry of industrial giants in a service business creates a marked difference in the market and puts pressure on prices, costs and the rate of investment necessary to compete successfully. When highly successful

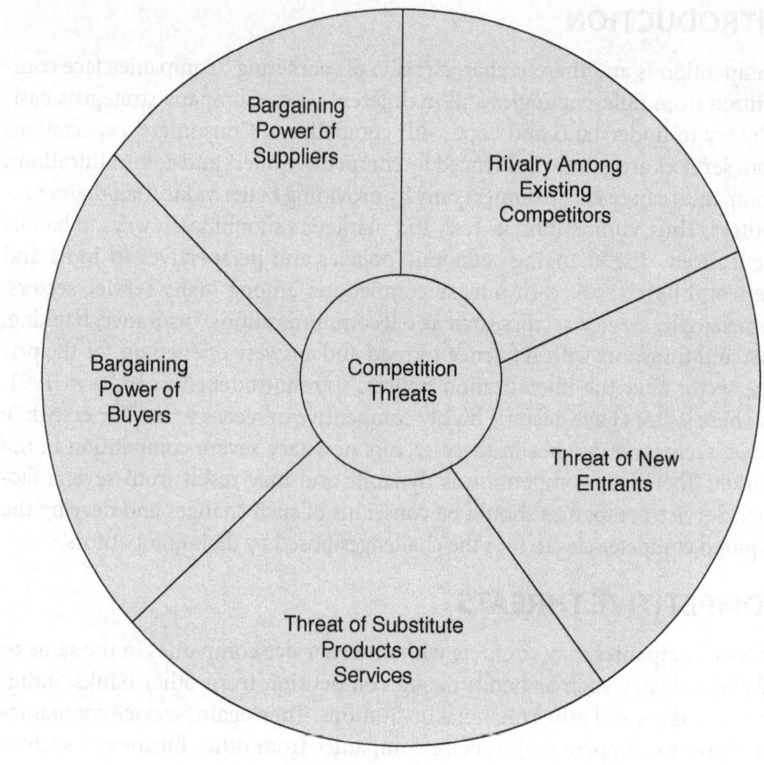

Fig. 9.1 Five factors of competition threats

companies from other sectors enter the services sector, they can leverage their capabilities and financial strength to shake up competition. For example, the entry of Reliance into the telecom as well as the retail sector posed serious threats to the existing companies. The entry of Tatas and Birlas into many service businesses also created problems for the existing companies.

3. *The Threat of Substitute Products or Services:* Substitute products are different goods or services from outside a given industry that perform similar or the same functions as a product that the industry produces.[2] For example, television channels can substitute for theatres as a mode of entertainment, direct-to-home (DTH) satellite services substitute for cable network services, mobile phones substitute for fixed-line telecom services. These substitutions significantly affect the respective markets. Adding to the competitive challenge is the fact that many entrepreneurs are forced to vie for business against firms outside the industry which offer alternative solutions to consumers' wants and needs.[3] The threat from substitute services is strong when the switching costs are low and

quality and performance factors are either equal or greater than the competing service. When service companies differentiate the service dimensions in terms of customer value, the threat from substitutes is very less.

4. *The Bargaining Power of Buyers:* Companies want to maximize their benefits. Consumers, on the other hand, try to minimize their costs and maximize transaction benefits. They demand higher quality and greater levels of service at a low price. When the bargaining power of the buyer is higher, companies get into competitive battles to acquire new customers or to defend existing customers. Buyers will have increased bargaining power when they have more choices, can place large orders, have credibility for choice making in the market, can be competitive service producers and can switch at low cost.
5. *The Bargaining Power of Suppliers:* Suppliers of tangibles required for the service and suppliers of support services required for service production are potential competitors. The bargaining power of suppliers is particularly high when a supplier has patents, satisfactory substitution is not available, the supplier is very large in size, and the service company is placing a small order and the switchover costs are very high. The suppliers are a credible threat for buyers as they may go for forward integration, thereby, entering the buyer's business segment.

> *Service companies are likely to face competition threats from five sources: existing companies that serve the same need of customers, new entrants, substitute service providers, the bargaining power of buyers and the bargaining power of suppliers.*

COMPETITION FROM THE INDUSTRY PERSPECTIVE

Industry is a group of firms offering similar or substitute products or services. From the industry perspective, competition is identified in terms of the number of sellers and the degree of product differentiation. Basically, there are four structures identified: monopoly, oligopoly, monopolistic and pure competition.

Monopoly

Monopoly is said to exist when a single seller alone provides a particular good or a service in a region. There is no direct competition. In unregulated monopoly, the monopolist may control service capacity and price and manipulate these two variables in their favour. Consumers have to oblige the monopolist in the absence of alternative measures. In regulated monopoly, the monopolist may be required to sell services at a lower price in public interest. Many services such as telecom, insurance, post, electricity, transport were public-sector monopolies in India until recently. The liberalization policies introduced in 1991 opened many service sectors for private players, ending the monopoly regime. Monopoly is still present in some forms of transport like railways, port services, roads, etc.

Oligopoly

Oligopoly involves an unspecified number of buyers but only a small number of sellers.[4] Each seller can influence the business of the other seller. Huge capital investment, entry barriers, technology, large economies of scale, mergers and acquisitions—these are some factors that promote oligopoly. A few organizations compete with each other to capture customers. This competition often leads to price wars unless there is an informal understanding or an agreement among the competing organizations. Many service businesses such as banking, insurance, telecommunications, organized retailing and post are oligopolistic.

Monopolistic Competition

This is a typical competitive situation wherein a large number of buyers and sellers are present. Product differentiation is the key characteristic of monopolistic competition, and the characteristics of both monopoly and competition are present in this competition. No single seller is in a position to control a major part of the market in terms of demand and supply positions and price determination. The sellers, however, influence the market by offering unique values related to the product as well as relationships. The switchover costs would generally keep the customers loyal to a service provider. Services such as advertising agencies, consultancy, education, small-size retailing, healthcare services and hospitality services operate under monopolistic competition.

> *The industry concept of competition is based on the number of sellers and service differentiation. The most imperfect competition structure is monopoly where there is only one seller and no competition. Pure competition is closest to perfection. Oligopoly and monopolistic competitions stand in between.*

Pure Competition

Pure competition resembles perfect competition where there are a large number of buyers and sellers in the market and no product differentiation. Here, no one can influence supply and demand, market forces decide prices, market conditions are well-organized and no entry barriers are present. It is very difficult to find pure competition anywhere. However, in some services like stock market close to pure competitive conditions can be observed.

The competition structures discussed are not permanent and subject to change with changes in the business environment. As already mentioned, many public sector monopolies turned into oligopoly due to the change in the government policy. Factors such as barriers to entry, exit and mobility, investment requirements and cost structure and mergers and acquisitions influence changes in the competitive structure.

> *From the market perspective **competition** is identified in terms of companies' focus to serve the needs of consumers. The companies serving the same set of needs of the consumers are considered competing companies.*

COMPETITION FROM THE MARKET PERSPECTIVE

Marketers focus on satisfying the specific needs of customers. Therefore, the competition is seen from the point of view of the companies serving the same need. However, the market concept of competition recognized many elements that affect, directly and indirectly, the business prospects of a company. Porter's model, presented in Fig. 9.1, changed the conventional perceptions of competition. The five levels of competition broadened the framework of competition. Marketers identify the set of actual and potential competitors. The healthcare services provided by hospitals (allopathy) face competition from the similar form of hospitals and also from ayurvedic, aroma and homeopathy services.

The fitness centres and yoga centres also affect the business significantly. Therefore, an analysis of competitors based on certain parameters is important to marketers to understand the competition situation properly and to design effective strategies to face the competition. The impact of competition in the life insurance business in India is analysed in "Services Marketing Insight: Competition Leads Life Insurance Market Development in India".

9.1 Services Marketing Insight

Competition Leads Life Insurance Market Development in India

The insurance sector entered in a phase of intense competition in India. The private sector insurance companies came out of their teething troubles to offer viable competition to the public sector giants. Both in life and non-life insurance segments, a large number of private players entered and each company could carve a niche for itself, posing threats to the competing insurers. Most of the private insurance companies were joint ventures with recognized foreign players across the globe. Competition brought more product innovation and better customer servicing.

Growth in life insurance was spurred by product innovation, vibrant distribution channels, coupled with targeted publicity and promotional campaigns by the insurers. Innovations came not only in the form of benefits attached to the products, but also in the delivery mechanism through various marketing tie-ups both within the realm of financial services and outside. The insurance companies were increasingly tapping the semi-urban and rural areas to take across the message of life protection through insurance cover. The insurers also introduced special products aimed at the rural markets. One of the most significant outcomes of the enhanced competition was the reduction in the rates of pure protection plans. During 2001–2008, the rates were revised downwards, and were significantly lower than those that prevailed prior to opening up of the sector. The life insurance market became competitive, benefiting the policyholders. Simultaneously, the insurance industry was evolving and improving its underwriting and risk management abilities. The reduction of term rates facilitated the increase in the level of sum assured for policies. This higher level of protection implied that customers were more conscious of the need for risk mitigation and greater security and about the future of their dependents.

New Policies: New policies underwritten by the industry were up by 10.23 per cent in 2007–2008. While the private insurers exhibited a growth of 67.40 per cent, the LIC showed a decline of 1.61 per cent. The market shares of private insurers and the LIC, in terms of number of policies underwritten, were 26.07 per cent and 73.93 per cent, respectively.

Premium: The life insurance industry recorded a premium income of INR 2013514.1 million during 2007–2008, recording a growth of 29.01 per cent. In 2000–2001, when the industry was opened up, the life insurance premium was only INR 348984.8 million. The LIC reported the growth of 24.17 per cent in single premium individual policies and decline of 6.48 per cent in non-single premium individual policies. As against these, private insurance companies reported the growth of 39.45 per cent and 69.93 per cent in individual single and non-single policies, respectively.

The facts presented above drives to the conclusion that the insurance market expanded significantly after it opened up to competition. The private companies could achieve greater penetration into the market. The LIC was also benefited from the sectoral growth, but faced a threat to its leadership.

Source: Annual Report 2007–2008, Insurance Regulatory and Development Authority, and www.irda.gov.in

COMPETITION ANALYSIS

Competition analysis is one of the key inputs in deciding a competitive strategy. To this end, it is necessary to study and interpret data from various sources. In the context of globalization, it is necessary for a company to understand the competitive competencies of multinational giants to shield itself. In some service sectors, international variables are more important than the domestic ones.

To analyse competition, it is necessary for the service firm to identify the strategic group that it belongs to. A *strategic group* is a group of firms in an industry following the same or similar strategy along the same strategic dimensions.[5] The dimensions may be technology, service quality, pricing, distribution system or the consumer segment. According to H. R. Greve,[6] an organization in a strategic group occupies a similar position in the market, offers similar services to customers and may also make similar choices about the production technology and other organizational features. The competition among the firms in the strategic group is likely to be intense. Since the resources, markets and environmental factors are similar to each other, they fight for winning over each other. When the strategies followed to reach target customers are also similar, the rivalry is likely to be much greater.

Competition analysis basically focuses on understanding, interpreting and predicting the actions and initiatives of the direct competitors. It involves analysis of four[7] important aspects:

1. What drives the competitor, as shown by its *future objectives*?
2. What the competitor is doing and can do, as revealed by its *current strategy*?
3. What the competitor believes about itself and the industry, as shown by its *assumptions*?
4. What the competitor's capabilities are, as shown by its *capabilities*?

Future Objectives

Further objectives are the driving forces. The activities of a company are oriented towards achieving the set objectives. Their stand against competition is based on the kind of objectives set for a period. It is necessary to know the future objectives of the competitors to compare them with the future objectives of the company. It is also important to know the emphasis of the competitor and its attitude towards risk. Understanding the future objectives of the competitors helps predict the actions of the competitors in future. When the future objectives of the competitors match closely with the company's objectives, the competition is likely to be face to face and severe.

Current Strategy

The analysis of the current strategy of the competitor helps ascertain the competitive advantage of the company. It helps find out the strategic orientation of the competitor, the levels of aggression, defence, abilities and relative success in the market. The current strategy reveals the strategic priorities, focussed dimensions and also the risk-taking abilities of the competitor. The service company can assess the competitor well through current strategy analysis as it is relatively easy to obtain accurate information and reliable data.

Assumption

Though it is very difficult to obtain information on assumptions of the competitors, if obtained, it serves as a very important input for the competition strategy. The strategy of any company involves the facts of the current status and assumptions of the future. When the company knows the assumptions of the competitors, it can predict their strategies with reasonable accuracy.

Capabilities

Competitors' actions and reactions basically depend on their capabilities. It is necessary to have information on the strengths and weaknesses of the competitors. According to P. Kotler and co-workers.,[8] a company should monitor three variables when analysing competitors:

1. *Share of Market:* the competitor's share of the target market.
2. *Share of Mind:* the percentage of customers who named the competitor in responding to the statement, "Name the first company that comes to mind in this industry."
3. *Share of Heart:* the percentage of customers who named the competitor in responding to the statement, "Name the company from which you would prefer to buy the service."

The analysis of these three shares helps in understanding how strongly the competitor could establish itself in the market. The strengths and weaknesses of the competitors are very difficult to assess as they vary from company to company, region to region and also from time to time. However, it is possible to have a fair understanding by assessing the competencies in terms of:

> *Competition analysis is the key input for developing a competitive strategy. The companies should collect data and information related to the competitor's future objectives, current strategy, assumptions and capabilities.*

- The ability to develop new services offerings
- The ability to design and execute service processes
- The ability to generate financial and other resources
- The ability to market services
- The ability to build and retain competent human resources
- The ability to develop networks and build partnerships
- The ability to manage consistency in service quality
- The ability to innovate
- The ability to build, maintain and enhance customer relationships

The analysis of strengths and weaknesses of the competitors is useful to rate the competitors against the position of the company. It also helps decide the kind of relationship the company will establish with each competitor. The companies generally classify the competitors to decide their strategy. Between strong and weak competitors, a company generally chooses to attack weak competitors as it requires very few resources. When it is necessary to attack strong competitors, the company tries to attack the weaknesses of strong competitors. Some companies may be good, and some may be bad. A company tries to support good competitors and attack bad competitors. In the market some competitors are very close, resembling similar strengths and weaknesses, and some are distant. The distant competitors do not have immediate or direct impact on the business of the company unlike close competitors. However, company should recognize the distant competitors as they may create problems in future. It is, therefore, necessary to have a fair understanding and up-to-date information on these four types of competitors. Service companies should design a marketing information system that ensure the supply of data and information continuously on these aspects. The data and information from primary as well as secondary sources may be necessary. The secondary sources of data for competition analysis include internal sources, newspapers, journals and magazines, annual reports, patents filings, government, trade association reports, consultants, promotional literature and websites. The primary sources include sales force, suppliers, customers, employees and bankers.

COMPETITION STRATEGIES

The strategies followed by an organization to tackle competition depend on its role in the target market. A company may function as one of the following: leader, challenger, follower and nicher. In any industry, one company will be recognized as the market leader. A company is recognized as the market leader if it has a major market share in the respective service and it is a front runner in introducing changes in service packages and other marketing mix elements.

Market Leaders

The top position in a particular service business is a privilege to the service company, and this position is always subject to attack by close competitors. To retain its position, the company may adopt three strategies directed at expanding the market, defending the market share and expanding the market share.

Market Expansion

The strategy of market expansion is designed to add new customers to the existing customer base to gain maximum market share. The company tries to identify and acquire those customers who are either unaware of the service or carry some negative perceptions about the service in an attempt to improve its market penetration and expand its customer base. The company may also enter new market segments. Another strategy to expand the market is to influence the existing consumers to use the service more frequently by communicating the new applications of the service.

Defending the Market Share

Market leaders may adopt a variety of strategies to defend their market share from potential sources of competition. The six[9] popular defence strategies are:

1. *Position Defence:* The leader works to build a superior brand power, leaving no scope for the competitors to attack.

2. *Flank Defence:* The leader works to protect its weak points from its competitors.
3. *Pre-emptive Defence:* The leader attacks the competitor before the competitor makes an attack. This is an aggressive action of the leader to eliminate competition.
4. *Counteroffensive Defence:* The leader chooses to attack only after the company is attacked by the competitor.
5. *Mobile Defence:* This strategy defuses the powers of the competitors indirectly. The leader works to broaden the market by shifting the focus from the current service to the core need of the consumers. By strengthening research and development and designing creative offerings, the leader tries to gain a psychological advantage.
6. *Contraction Defence:* The leader realizes its inability to defend the entire market territory. It closes weak territories and focuses on strong territories to retain its leadership in such territories.

> "***Market leaders*** *are generally identified in terms of market share holding, and innovation. Market leaders focus on expansion of market, defending market share and expansion of market share.*"

Expanding the Market Share

This is an attacking strategy of the market leader. It tries to encourage switchovers from competing service producers by offering additional values to the customers. This approach may lead to a marketing warfare.

Market Challengers

Companies ranking second or lower in the market have to decide their relationship with the market leader and other competitors. There are two alternative options for the company: to either be a challenger or a follower. If the choice is to be a challenger, the company may choose to attack the market leader or the companies of its size or the small firms in the business. The choice depends on the objective of the company. The challenger may use any one of the following five[10] strategies:

1. *Frontal Attack:* This strategy is to attack all strategies of the opponent. The challenger works out a matching strategy for the opponent's product, price, promotion, distribution and other attacking strategies.
2. *Flank Attack:* The challenger targets weak areas of the opponents, either in terms of geographic coverage or segmentation.
3. *Encirclement Attack:* This strategy is to carry out a grand offensive on several fronts of the opponents.
4. *Bypass Attack:* This is an indirect attack by the challenger. Through this strategy, the challenger enters into new service businesses or new geographies or expands to new market segments or adopts leapfrogging into new technologies to broaden the resource base.
5. *Guerrilla Attack:* This attack would be in random corners of the larger opponents market with an intention to weaken the opponent.

> "***Market challengers*** *are basically attackers. They attack the leader or other opponents whenever or wherever they feel necessary. They eye market leadership.*"

Market Followers

Market followers do not challenge any competitor but exploit the strengths of the competitors by imitation. It is common to find many followers in the market. The follower can achieve higher profits since the firm does not incur the cost of innovation and the cost of attacking others. Market followers capture their market share by projecting some distinct advantages to target customers in terms of location, support services and other promotional measures.

Market Nichers

Market nichers capture a small market by way of specialization. The specialization may be in catering to specific geographies, channels, customer services, support services or service lines. The tasks of the nicher are to create, expand and protect market niches. Competition in some service businesses is regulated to protect the interests of consumers. For such services, market competition is regulated by the Government of India. "Services Marketing Insight: Regulated Competition in the Indian Telecom Sector" details the competition scenario in the telecom sector.

ACHIEVING COMPETITIVE ADVANTAGE

Service companies need to conduct internal analysis to better assess their competencies. Critical to the required mindset is the view that a firm is a *bundle* of heterogeneous resources, capabilities and core competencies that can be used to create an exclusive market position.[11] This view suggests that individual firms possess at least some resources and capabilities that other companies do not have—at least not in the same combination.

Reliance Communications

Reliance Communications is the flagship company of the Anil Dhirubhai Ambani Group (ADAG) of companies. The company, started in 2002, is one of India's leading integrated telecommunication companies in the private sector today with over 80 million customers. Reliance Communications has a reliable, high-capacity, integrated (both wireless and wireline) and convergent (voice, data and video) digital network. It is capable of delivering a range of services spanning the entire infocomm (information and communication) value chain, including infrastructure and services for enterprises as well as individuals, applications and consulting. The business encompasses a complete range of telecom services covering mobile and fixed-line telephony. It includes broadband, national and international long-distance services and data services along with an exhaustive range of value-added services and applications. The company endeavours to delight its customers by enhancing the productivity of the enterprise and individual customers.

The company has continued to challenge and attack the market leaders (BSNL and MTNL in wireline and Bharti Airtel in wireless) and other competitors by using appropriate challenger strategies. Reliance does not allow the consumers and competitors to ignore its presence in any business.

Resources are the source of capabilities, some of which lead to the development of a firm's core competencies.[12] Core competencies are resources and capabilities that serve as a source of competitive advantage for a firm over its rivals.[13] The clear identification of core competencies helps the company to use them better than competitors. Service companies should promote strategic capabilities that are valuable, rare, costly to imitate and non-substitutable.

In order to build a competitive advantage, companies use two important approaches: benchmarking and value-chain analysis.

9.2 Services Marketing Insight | **Regulated Competition in the Indian Telecom Sector**

The Indian telecom sector was opened up to private players in 2001–2002. In the pre-reforms era (prior to 1991), the telecom sector was entirely in the hands of the central government, and due to lack of competition, the call charges were quite high. Further, due to insufficient funds the public sector companies could never meet the demand for telephones. In fact, individuals seeking telephone connections had to wait for years before they could get a telephone connection. The service rendered by the government monopoly was also very poor. Wrong billing, telephones lying dead for many days continuously due to slackness on the part of the telecom staff to attend to complaints, cross connections due to faulty/ill-maintained telephone lines, obsolete instruments and machinery in the telephone department were the order of the day in the pre-reforms era.

The entry of private players increased the teledensity in the country substantially. Due to the competition, the tariffs dropped and service coverage extended to almost all parts of the country. The flow of investment into this sector was very high. In the wire line segment, there are eight companies competing for the top spot. BSNL and MTNL are public sector companies. BSNL covers the entire country, except Delhi and Mumbai, while MTNL operates in these two metros only. The private companies in fixed line are Bharti Airtel Ltd., Tata Teleservices (Maharashtra) Ltd., Tata Teleservices Ltd., HFCL Infotel Ltd., Shyam Telelink Ltd. and Reliance Communications Ltd.

The Government of India has established the TRAI (Telecom Regulatory Authority of India) to ensure technical compatibility and effective interconnection between different service providers; to regulate arrangement among service providers for sharing the revenue derived from providing telecommunication services; to lay down the standard of quality of service to be provided by the service providers; and to ensure the quality of service and conduct the periodical survey of such service provided by the service provider to protect the interest of the consumers of telecommunication services.

In the fixed-line segment, public sector companies are the market leaders in both urban as well as rural areas. In 2007–08, BSNL alone accounted for 80.05 per cent of the total market share. In stark contrast, all the six private companies, put together, held a share of 10.62 per cent only. MTNL accounted for the remaining 9.33 per cent.

The wireless segment has witnessed intense competition between 12 companies including BSNL and MTNL. Here, Bharti is the market leader with 23.74 per cent market share followed by Reliance, Vodafone and BSNL. In the CDMA segment, however, Reliance Infocom was the leader with 56.71 per cent, and Tata Teleservices occupied second position with 35.58 per cent market share in 2007–08.

Source: Telecom Regulatory Authority of India, The Indian Telecom Services—Performance Indicators, January–March 2008.

redBus

Phanindra Sama hit upon the idea of providing an online reservation system for bus services when he himself ran from pillar to post trying to book a bus ticket from Bangalore to Hyderabad.

Sama's idea became a reality in 2006. It was not easy to market the concept; it needed time and money. Those who used the service liked it and told others and the chips started to fall in place gradually. redBus has come a very long way from the days of struggle to the days of growth. Currently, it has the largest number of tie-ups (and growing) with bus operators and a large and satisfied customer base. redBus has moved beyond providing value over the Internet by reaching out to customers using all media that provide them convenience—be it the phone, home delivery, physical outlets or even SMS. Aggregating online booking for bus tickets across the country has provided great value to bus travellers as well as to redBus. With the Internet becoming the preferred medium, it is expected that more than 50 per cent of the bookings will be done online by the end of 2010. redBus is set to get a large slice of this huge pie. redBus is competing with ticketval.com and abhibus.com.

Benchmarking involves the study of company performance compared with the standards of the best-performing organizations in different facets of business. The objective is to find the areas where improvement is required. The broader objective is not only to catch up with the performance levels of the best companies but also to create higher benchmarks in performance. The benchmarking approach requires organizations to carry out systematic search for best practices within and outside the industry. Benchmarking can be done at three distinct levels:

1. *Internal Benchmarking:* The best-performing departments are shown as benchmarks for comparatively low-performing departments within the organization.
2. *Competitive Benchmarking:* The best-performing competitors are taken as benchmarks.
3. *Comparative Benchmarking:* The best practices across industries are identified to achieve excellence.

> *"Companies should develop a competitive advantage to win over the target customers. Internal analysis of resources is critical to find out core competencies and to position them against competition. Benchmarking and value chain analysis are the two valid approaches that help companies sharpen this competitive advantage."*

Value chain analysis helps the organization understand its cost position and identify the multiple needs that might be used to facilitate the implementation of its business-level strategy.[14] The value chain involves facilitating services and support services. It is obvious that competitive advantage stems from the superior value a firm is able to create for its buyers vis-à-vis its competition. The superior value may be in the form of lower prices for equivalent benefits or unique benefits that more than offset a premium price. The objective is to enhance value relative to competition, in the vast matrix of value-creating activities performed by the firm and develop a value chain that is superior to that of the competitors.[15] Service firms need to develop a durable competitive advantage. The durability results from building unique strengths and competencies that provide a sustained gap between the company and its competitors.

SUMMARY

- Service companies face competition from different angles and in different ways.
- Competitive threats may arise from existing companies in the same business, new entrants, substitutes, and the bargaining power of both suppliers and buyers.
- Service buyers can also be potential competitors in case of services offered to the household sector and the organized sectors.
- The industry concept of competition is to identify competition in terms of the number of sellers and the degree of differentiation.
- From the industry perspective, competition is identified in four structures: monopoly, oligopoly, monopolistic and pure competition.
- Monopoly results when a single seller offers services to the buyers in a region. The presence of few sellers offering services to large number of buyers is called oligopoly. In monopolistic competition, sellers and buyers are present in large number. Service differentiation is the key characteristic. In pure competition, almost all characteristics of perfect competition exist with marginal variation.
- The market concept of competition refers to the companies serving the same need of consumers.
- For the design of a competitive strategy, marketers need to analyse competitors.
- The competition analysis covers future objectives, current strategy, assumptions and capabilities of competitors.
- The strengths and weaknesses of the competitors should be analysed carefully to arrive at a competitive strategy.
- An effective market intelligence system and the flow of right information from both internal and external sources are necessary for competition analysis.
- Competition strategies depend on the roles the company plays in the market. The four roles are market leader, market challenger, market follower and market nicher.
- A market leader focuses on market expansion, defending market share and expanding its market share.
- A market challenger chooses to attack the leader and other competitors.
- A market follower tries to imitate the best of competitors to gain advantages.
- A market nicher selects an area to specialize and carve a niche for itself.
- Service firms should carry out internal analysis to know their competencies and to identify the resources that can help it gain a competitive advantage.

KEY TERMS

benchmarking *196*
competitive advantage *190*
competitive threats *185*
core competencies *196*
market challenger *193*
market follower *194*
market leader *192*
market nicher *195*
monopolistic competition *188*
monopoly *187*
oligopoly *187*
pure competition *187*
strategic group *190*
value chain analysis *196*

BRIEF QUESTIONS

1. What are competitive threats?
2. What is competitive advantage?
3. What is benchmarking?
4. Explain niche marketing.
5. What are market follower strategies?

ESSAY QUESTIONS

1. Explain Porter's five threats of competition and their applicability to services.
2. What is the importance of competition analysis? How is it done?
3. Discuss market leader strategies with special reference to services.
4. Analyse market challenger strategies.
5. Explain the industry perspective of competition.
6. Explain the market perspective of competition.
7. How to build competitive advantage?

ASSIGNMENTS

1. Primary education in the country is offered by government schools, private entrepreneurs and large-size companies. The competition is multi-dimensional. There exists a very wide gap between the three types of schools in terms of resources, controls and competencies. You are required to:
   (a) Study the competitive threats of the three types of schools.
   (b) Suggest measures to build competitive advantage.
2. Ever since organized retailing came to India on a large scale, small- and medium-size retailers are facing serious threats to their businesses. In many parts of the country, small-size agricultural retailers agitated against the entry of corporations into the business. In this situation, you are required to:
   (a) Study the competition scenario in retailing in your locality.
   (b) Study the prospects of the small retailers by interviewing a few of them.

REFERENCES

1 Michael E. Porter, "The Five Competitive Forces that Shape Strategy," *Harvard Business Review, South Asia*, January (2008): 65.
2 Ibid., p. 74.
3 Amy Risch Rodie and Charles L. Martin, "Competing in the Service Sector—The Entrepreneurial Challenge," *International Journal of Entrepreneurial Behaviour & Research*, 7, no. 1 (2001): 13.
4 H. Craig Peterson and W. Cris Lewis, *Managerial Economics* (New Delhi: Prentice Hall of India, 1996) p. 339.
5 M. E. Porter, *Competitive Strategy* (New York: Free Press, 1980) p. 129.
6 H. R. Greve, "Managerial Cognition and the Mimetic Adoption of Market Positions: What You See is What You do," *Strategic Management Journal*, 19 (1992): 967–988.
7 M. E. Porter, *Competitive Strategy* (New York: Free Press, 1980) p. 49.
8 Philip Kotler, Kevin Lane Keller, Abraham Koshy and Mithileshwar Jha, *Marketing Management—A South Asian Perspective*, 12th ed. (New Delhi: Pearson Education, 2007) p. 235.
9 Ibid.
10 Philip Kotler, *A Frame Work of Marketing Management* (New Delhi: Pearson Education Asia, 2002) p. 136.
11 V. P. Rindova and C. J. Fombrun, "Constructing Competitive Advantage: The Role of Firm-Constituent Interactions," *Strategic Management Journal*, 20 (1999): 691–710.
12 T. H. Brush and K. W. Artz, "Toward a Contingent Resource-Based Theory: The Impact of Information Asymmetry on the Value of Capabilities in Veterinary Medicine," *Strategic Management Journal*, 20 (1999): 223–250.
13 Michael A. Hitt, R. Duane Ireland and Robert E. Hoskisson, *Strategic Management—Competitiveness and Globalisation*, 4th ed. (Singapore: South Western College Publishing, 2001) p. 26.
14 G. G. Dess, A. Gupta, J. F. Hennar and C. W. L. Hill, "Conducting and Integrating Strategy Research at the International Corporate and Business Levels: Issues and Directions," *Journal of Management*, 21 (1995): 376.
15 V. S. Ramaswamy and S. Namakumari, *Marketing Management*, 4th ed. (New Delhi: Macmillan Publishers India Ltd., 2009) p. 227.

Service Demand Management

10

LEARNING OBJECTIVES

After studying this chapter, you will be able to:

- Understand service demand situations and patterns
- Identify variations in the demand for services
- Understand how strategies are formulated for demand management
- Describe strategies to manage waiting lines

A special workshop was organized to promote tourism in the country by the Union Minister of Tourism, Government of India. The managing directors of all state-level tourism corporations attended it. The minister highlighted the need for a coordinated effort and holistic approach to marketing tourism in the country. All the participants agreed that there were no strategic relationships among them. Most of them just reacted instead of managing the demand effectively. The potential was substantial, but none could confidently claim that they had exploited the demand potential optimally. The deliberations led to the identification of the following issues:

- In some destinations, there was negative demand mostly due to security reasons.
- Some destinations had potential, but there was no demand.
- Latent demand existed in many areas connected to tourism.
- Many destinations had only seasonal demand.
- The demand patterns of domestic tourists and foreign tourists were not similar.
- Excess demand during seasons and low demand for the rest of the period was a common feature.
- Due to inconsistent and unexpected demand patterns, tourism corporations were facing problems in offering quality services.
- More complaints were made by foreign tourists as well as domestic tourists during peak periods.

The list of problems aired by the participants was not exhaustive. The minister intervened and requested them to work out a plan to handle all these problems relating to demand and capacity management. The participants opined that tourism marketing is a complex process involving many support and facilitating services. Therefore, it was appropriate to refer the problem to a professional market research company. The minister agreed to the proposal.

Questions:

1. Do you think the demand for tourism is manageable?
2. What are the appropriate demand forecasting methods for tourism?
3. Is it appropriate to refer the problem to a professional marketing research firm or is it good to leave the problem to concerned state-level tourism corporations?
4. Will coordination among state tourism corporations serve as a remedy for demand and capacity management problems?
5. What do you suggest to solve the problem?

> *Every service product has the capacity to generate demand. Such demand is often insufficient to achieve organizational objectives. Service companies need to manage demand to the level of its optimum capacity. The perishability character of services intensifies the problems of demand management.*

INTRODUCTION

Three characteristics are needed in a society to generate demand for a service—desire, affordability and willingness to purchase. Every product, including services, will have a minimum demand which may or may not be adequate enough for the organization to achieve its objectives. One of the primary responsibilities of a marketing organization is to manage demand such that it stays at a desirable level. Thus, demand management has become one of the major challenges for marketing organizations. Though demand for a marketing offer is not a controllable factor, it is definitely possible to manipulate demand. Very few organizations have adequate and positive demand for their new products. Most organizations have to face varying demand situations, which may not even be favourable for them.

Services are perishable and, therefore, cannot be inventoried. This characteristic multiplies the problems of demand and capacity management. Any unserved demand and unutilized capacity are lost forever. The challenge, therefore, is to match the demand to the service production capacity of the company consistently. The unutilized capacity will have serious effects on the profitability of the organization. Fixed costs are significantly higher in services. When demand falls short of capacity, the per-unit cost of service production increases resulting in either losses or reduced margins. A careful study and analysis of demand, thus, is critical to appropriate and timely marketing decisions.

DEMAND SITUATIONS

Service companies experience different demand situations in different market segments at different times. Changes in demand are quite common. It is necessary to study the situations and develop appropriate strategies to face the situations; else, it may prove fatal to the future of the organization. The possible demand situations are negative demand, no demand, latent demand and seasonal demand.

Negative Demand

The market response to a service offering can be negative, as shown in Fig. 10.1. Though people may be aware of the features and benefits of the service, they might decide against the service offer on the basis of their evaluation. In such circumstances, the marketing unit of a service firm has to understand the evaluation process of potential buyers to find out the prime reasons for rejection. An appropriate strategy needs to be designed to diffuse the misunderstandings of potential buyers and transform the negative demand into a positive demand.

No Demand

The situation of no demand (see Fig. 10.2) exists either due to unawareness or insufficient information about the service or due to consumers' indifference. Marketers should focus on promotional campaigns and communicating the

Fig. 10.1
Negative demand: Passengers refuse a bus conductor's call to board the bus

Fig. 10.2
No demand: A bus with no passengers

right reason for preferring the services offered by the firm. Service differentiation is a popular strategy used to face the no-demand situation in the market.

Latent Demand

In any given environment, it is impossible to have a set of products capable of satisfying all the needs and wants of a society. There always exists a gap between the desired and the available. The market always looks for better and new offers that bridge this gap. Latent demand is nothing but this gap between desirability and availability (see Fig. 10.3). Thus, it is a live phenomenon of any economy at any given point of time and is a business opportunity. Service firms should orient themselves to identify such opportunities and exploit them at the right time.

Seasonal Demand

Some services are in demand only during a particular season of the year. Seasonal demand creates many problems for service organizations, including idle capacity, fixed cost and excess expenditure on promotion. Generally, service firms nurture the service consumption habit of

Fig. 10.3
Latent demand: A passenger travelling in an ordinary bus dreams of travelling in a luxury bus

customers in order to make the demand unseasonal. Another strategy is to identify markets elsewhere in the world during the off-season period in a market. Seasons in various parts of the world are diverse. Hence, there will be opportunities to find a market with the appropriate season in different parts of the world.

Service organizations need to study the service demand patterns over various time periods. The demand levels should be charted on daily, weekly and monthly basis. Where the demand is seasonal, graphing should be done to identify fluctuations. The charting and graphing of demand patterns help service organizations predict demand cycles and identify random demand fluctuations. Further, this effort helps study the demand pattern in each segment of the market.

> *"Service companies may face different demand situations in different markets or segments. Situations such as negative demand, no demand, latent demand and seasonal demand create distinct problems for marketers, necessitating unique demand management solutions for each."*

DEMAND PATTERNS

The study of the status of demand and its behaviour in relation to a service is important for marketers to take appropriate strategic decisions. The demand may fluctuate between below the capacity level to above the capacity. These patterns of demand fluctuation need to be analysed carefully to identify demand behaviour. A proper understanding of demand patterns enables marketers to handle demand problems effectively through advance planning and adopting strategic measures.

Irregular Demand

A fluctuating demand curve creates (see Fig. 10.4) many capacity-management problems for service organizations. Demand fluctuations are undesirable that warrant a right strategy. Service firms should endeavour to influence customers and shift the demand of peak periods to slack periods.

Falling Demand

A falling demand curve is a danger signal to service firms. The reasons leading to a fall in the demand are to be identified and analysed to take corrective actions. When a service firm notices a fall in demand, it should take corrective measures to arrest it immediately. Following this, it should devise a strategy to enable it to reclaim its position.

Fig. 10.4(a)
Irregular demand: A bus full of passengers during peak hours

Fig. 10.4(b)
Irregular demand: A bus that is not quite full during "off-peak" hours

Demand to the Level of Optimum Capacity

The situation when demand matches the optimum capacity of a firm is called a *full demand situation* (see Fig. 10.5). Service firms that become complacent during this time risk the danger of competition or an altered marketing environment adversely affecting their performance.

Demand Exceeds Optimum Capacity

Optimum capacity is the ideal capacity at which service firms can offer quality service to their customers. When demand exceeds capacity, as shown in Fig. 10.6, service firms have two options: stretching the capacity to accommodate maximum number of customers or rejecting the demand. In the first option, there is a likelihood of dilution of the service quality, leading to customer dissatisfaction. Customers may then switch to other competitive offers. If the situation of increased demand lasts for a very short period, service firms can take temporary measures to stretch the service capacity. When it is likely to continue for a long period, service firms should make arrangements for capacity expansion in order to serve customers better. Thus, whenever

Fig. 10.5
Demand to the level of optimum capacity: A bus filled to capacity

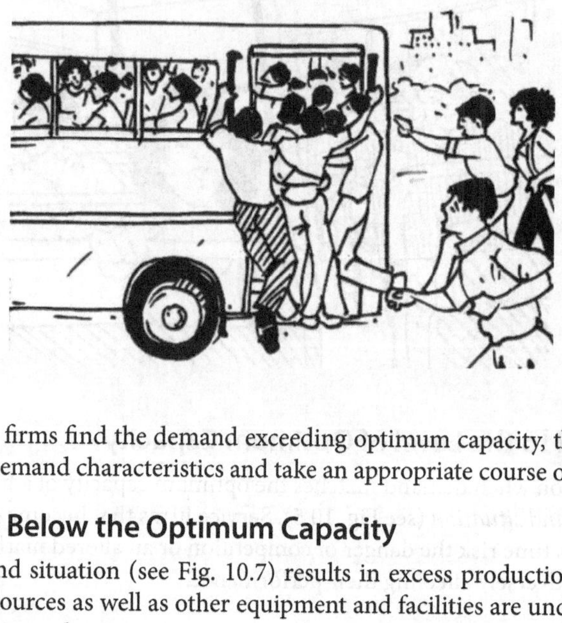

Fig. 10.6
Demand exceeds optimum capacity: An overcrowded bus

the service firms find the demand exceeding optimum capacity, they should study the demand characteristics and take an appropriate course of action.

Demand Below the Optimum Capacity

This demand situation (see Fig. 10.7) results in excess production capacity. Human resources as well as other equipment and facilities are underutilized. The per-unit production cost in service firms is higher on account of higher fixed costs. The high cost coupled with low revenues may lead to either a decline in profits or the incurrence of losses. Though customers may receive high-quality service—full use of the available facilities, no waiting time and the total attention of the employees—the absence of an adequate number of service takers may disappoint them.

Excess Demand

When the demand exceeds the maximum capacity of a service firm, it results in excess demand situation (see Fig. 10.8). The possible consequences of excess demand is that some customers will not be served because of which the business

Fig. 10.7
Demand below optimum capacity: a bus with few passengers

opportunity is lost. The customers served by the firm may not receive the promised quality due to overcrowding and excessive use of human and other resources.

The status and behaviour of demand such as irregular, falling, or below or above the optimum capacity should be understood to develop an action programme. The study helps the marketers strike an equilibrium between demand and capacity of the service firm.

DEMAND VARIATIONS

Service firms often encounter demand variations for two major reasons. The first reason is that services are perishable; they cannot be stored or inventoried, which puts service firms at a serious disadvantage vis-à-vis manufacturing firms. Since services production and consumption are simultaneous, any unutilized capacity is lost forever. Further, services also cannot be transported from one place to another or transferred from one person to another person. Thus, service firms are left with no option but to buffer the service delivery system against demand variations.

The second reason for sustaining systematic imbalances in supply and demand is the fact that the service-sector productivity is improving slower than the manufacturing sector productivity, resulting in increasing costs for the service sector.[1] Increasing operating costs translate into financial

Fig. 10.8
Excess demand: some persons are left behind at the bus station because the bus is full

pressures that drive service organizations to process improvement and cost-containment initiatives to seek efficiency gains. This continuous search for productivity gains might be the only way for service organizations to remain viable in a highly competitive environment. These initiatives, however, also ensure that service organizations operate close to the balance point between supply and demand, thus increasing the risk of temporary imbalances or even systematic underinvestment in service capacity.[2]

The imbalances in supply and demand situations eventually translate into consequences for customers as well as for the profitability of service organizations. Customers may face long waiting times or reduced attention from service personnel when demand exceeds capacity. Service enterprises may get affected due to unattended and dissatisfied customers. Demand over optimum level and excess demand situations increase the work pressure on servers. Service personnel perceive work pressure as the difference between the amount of work that can feasibly be done and the amount of work that needs to be performed. With increased work pressure, service personnel struggle to keep a balance between the flows of incoming and outgoing orders while maintaining reasonable working hours and sustaining service quality. How a service organization responds to work pressure is a critical determinant of service quality, employee satisfaction and the overall profitability of the service firm.

Management challenges relating to supply and demand are not similar to all service organizations. The gravity of the problem depends on the extent of demand fluctuations over a period of time, and supply flexibility. Demand will be highly flexible for some organizations such as transportation and telecommunications. Some service firms may experience narrower fluctuations (e.g., insurance and banking). It is important, therefore, to understand the demand patterns and also the supply constraints in order to develop demand management strategies. The methods of demand forecasting are discussed in "Services Marketing Insight: Demand Forecasting Methods".

> *"The capacity of a service firm refers to the maximum output possible in a given period with pre-determined resources such as employees, equipment, systems and facilities. Variations in demand affect work processes and result in variations in capacity utilization. Efficient performance of external and internal jobs with coordination is the critical task of service companies. Adjustments in capacity to match demand variations are the internal job, whereas adjusting the demand to the level of capacity is the external job."*

The production capacity of the service organization also influences the demand management of the services. The production capacity of service firms can be flexed in the short period and in the long run. However, at a given point of time, the capacity would be more or less fixed or can be expanded a little. The major limiting factors of capacity are time, labour, equipment and other facilities. Time is the primary constraint for any service provider. A doctor, a teacher, a lawyer and a consultant primarily sell their time. In case of excessive demand, time cannot be created, or when there is less demand, time cannot be saved for the next day. Time definitely is a major constraint from the individual point of view. For large organizations, employees, labour or staffing levels are the major time constraints. When the staff is operating at peak capacity in a service organization, such as accounting service, college department or law consultancy, it cannot meet the excess demand. However, they can hire temporary or part-time employees for service production. Often, such efforts lead to deterioration in service quality and affect the image of the organization. Lack of equipment is also a critical constraint for organizations where the support of tangibles is essential for service production

10.1 Services Marketing Insight

Demand Forecasting Methods

Opinion polling methods and statistical methods are the two types of forecasting methods. By using opinion polling methods, business organizations aim to obtain information about the intensions of present and potential buyers or consumers through the means of marketing research, survey, economic intelligence and so on. Statistical methods, on the other hand, use past experience as a guide to estimate the future.

Opinion Polling Methods

1. ***Consumers' Survey Method:*** It is the most direct method of estimating demand in the short run. Consumers are contacted personally to know their future purchase plans relating to a specified service for a specific period. The consumers' intentions can be collected either with the help of a complete enumeration survey of all consumers or by selecting a sample of the total universe of consumers.
2. ***Sales Force Opinion Method:*** Under this method, the salesmen of a company are required to estimate expected sales in their respective sales territories. Since the salesmen are the closest to customers, it is believed that they can have the first-hand information relating to customers' actions and reactions and relating to services of the company and their sales trends. Each salesman is asked to estimate sales, and the estimates of all the salesmen are consolidated to find out the total sales estimate.
3. ***Experts' Opinion Method:*** The views and opinions of the experts outside the organization are obtained for the purpose of forecasting demand. Since the outsiders do not succumb to any sort of pressure relating to the concern, they can be unbiased in estimating the future. The Delphi technique is generally used for the purpose.

Statistical Methods

1. ***Mechanical Extrapolation or Trend Projection Method:*** A firm that has been in existence for some time will have accumulated data on different aspects pertaining to different time periods. The mechanical extrapolation or trend projection method takes past data as a basis for forecasting future happenings, particularly, in the case of sales forecasting. The five important techniques of mechanical extrapolation are fitting a trend line by observation, trend through least-squares method, time-series analysis, moving averages method and exponential smoothing method.
2. ***Barometric Techniques:*** Mechanical extrapolation basically implies that the future is an extension of the past. In contrast, barometric techniques are based on the assumption that future can be predicted from certain events accrue in the present. Barometric techniques use statistical techniques such as time series, statistical indicators to measure or ascertain the direction of change and its impact on the business in the future. The three indicators prominently used in forecasting are leading indicators, coincident indicators and lagging indicators.
3. ***Regression Analysis:*** This analysis helps the forecaster estimate unknown values of one variable from the known values of another variable. The analysis is designed to examine the relationship between two or more variables.
4. ***Simultaneous Equation Method:*** This method involves considering all variables that influence the decision environment. The simultaneous equation method believes that every variable like price, competition, promotion, income, and so on will influence the other variables. The method equates the number of dependent variables (controllable variables) by setting equations.

and delivery. Thus, a transport organization, either passenger or goods traffic, cannot meet the excess demand at a given point of time. Similarly, a hotel with a fixed number of rooms cannot meet demand beyond its capacity.

DEMAND MANAGEMENT

Service organizations, generally, follow two alternative strategies for balancing supply–demand positions. One alternative is to shift the demand to match the capacity, and the other alternative is flexing the capacity to match the demand. These alternative strategies are not mutually exclusive but complementary in nature. Table 10.1 outlines the strategies for shifting demand to match the service capacity and strategies for increasing demand to the level of optimum capacity.

Shifting Demand to Match Service Capacity

When the demand does not match the optimum level of capacity, two situations are likely to occur—more demand than the optimum level of capacity and less demand than the optimum level of capacity. When demand exceeds the optimum level of capacity, it has to be shifted to the periods during which the demand is low. The point to be noticed here is that the shift should not be by force but by convincing customers. The following are the approaches useful in handling situations when demand is more than the optimum level of capacity:

- *Identify Peak Periods and Communicate it to Customers:* When customers are informed of the peak business hours or peak business days by the service organization well in advance, some customers, who do not have an urgent need or want to avail of the service in a pleasant form, may prefer non-peak hours and days. Thus, the problem gets solved automatically. Further, those customers who seek the service during peak hours or days do not have high expectations of service quality. As such, the diluted quality of service due to work pressure from the organization may not create any serious negative feelings in the customers.

Table 10.1 Strategies for Demand Management

Strategies for Shifting Demand to Match Service Capacity	Strategies for Increasing Demand to the Level of Optimum Capacity
Identify peak periods and communicate to customers	Promote services aggressively
Offer incentives during low-demand periods	Search for new segments and enter
Charge premium during peak periods	Offer price incentives
Recognize regular customers and serve them first	Schedule services as per customer convenience
Schedule service segment wise	Provide service convenience better than competitors
	Focus on word-of-mouth communication
	Bundle services
	Position services differently during slow periods

- *Offer Incentives During Low-demand Periods:* This is a very popular strategy adopted by many service firms to shift the demand from peak periods to non-peak periods. Customers who opt for non-peak periods are offered special benefits either in cash, in kind or both.
- *Recognize Regular Customers and Serve them First:* Sometimes, it is not possible for organizations to shift all service seekers over the production capacity to non-peak periods. A sudden rise in demand may not leave any option to the service firm, except to face the situation. Under such circumstances, the most important issue is to prioritize by dividing the service seekers into groups. Most service firms survive and grow on loyal customers. Therefore, the interests of the loyal group of customers should be protected by recognizing them separately and offering them some special treatment over others.

> *When demand exceeds capacity, strategies such as communicating peak service periods, offering incentives during low-demand periods, discouraging customers by charging a premium during peak periods and so on may be employed by service firms to save the situation and to reduce the customer displeasure.*

Tata Power

Tata Power is the largest private power company in India. The company is well known for its operational efficiencies and innovative programmes in the power sector. One of the key functions of the company is demand side management (DSM). DSM refers to cooperative activities between the utility and its customers to implement options for increasing the efficiency of energy utilization, with resulting benefits to the customer, utility and society as a whole. DSM follows five steps in its operations:

1. ***Load Research:*** Assessment of customer base, tariff, load profile on an hourly basis, identification of sectors contributing to the load shape and identification of peak load contributors.
2. ***Define Load-shape Objectives:*** DSM teams define the load-shape objectives for the current situation, as shown in the following:
   - *Peak Clipping:* The reduction of utility load, primarily during periods of peak demand
   - *Valley-filling:* The improvement of the system load factor by building load in off-peak periods
   - *Load Shifting:* The reduction of utility loads during periods of peak demand, while at the same time building load in off-peak periods
   - *Conservation:* The reduction of utility loads, more or less equally, during all or most hours of the day
   - *Load Building:* The increase of utility loads, more or less equally, during all or most hours of the day
   - *Flexible Utility Load Shape:* Programmes that set up utility options to alter customer energy consumption
3. ***Assess Programme Implementation Strategies:*** This stage identifies end-use applications that can be potentially targeted to reduce peak demand, specifically in sectors contributing to system peak. This step will also carry out a detailed *cost– benefit analysis* for the end users and the utilities, including analysis of societal as well as environmental benefits.
4. ***Implementation:*** This stage includes the programme design for specific end-use applications, promoting the programme to the target audience through marketing approaches.
5. ***Monitoring and Evaluation:*** This step tracks the programme design and implementation, and compares the same with the proposed DSM goal.

- *Schedule Services Segment-wise:* This approach divides markets segment-wise and schedules the service offering to each segment separately. This helps cover as well as give representation to all segments of the market. The unserved demand in a particular segment during the scheduled period will be served in the next scheduled period reserved for the segment.

Increasing Demand to the Level of Optimum Capacity

There are six distinctive approaches intended to increase the demand when service firms have demand below the optimum level of capacity.

- *Promote Services Aggressively:* Often, aggressive promotion through advertising, personal selling, sales promotion, publicity and public relations using varied media is a competent strategy to attract the market or increase the consumption levels of the existing customers. An effective communication campaign with a positioning strategy is likely to generate positive responses from the target market.
- *Search for New Segments and Enter:* When demand generated from the market segments being served is less than the optimum level of capacity, market expansion would be a sensible strategy. Identifying the new segments and serving them with a new service package or a modified offer may push the demand upwards.
- *Offer Price Incentives:* The strategy of offering incentives to increase the demand is workable when the market is price sensitive. Price may be reduced, either directly or indirectly, through discounts, gift offerings, free services and so on. Such price changes are likely to change the demand positively. Freebies may create a snowball effect that increases sales. A customer who is given a loyalty-driven voucher may purchase additional services from the firm. However, price reductions should not generate a feeling in the market that the producer is desperate or that the service quality will be compromised for a low price.
- *Schedule Services as per Customer Convenience:* The contact timings scheduled by the service organizations may not be convenient to some sections of the potential market. Therefore, modification of timings by the service firm may increase the convenience, thereby resulting in an increase in demand. Thus, many banks in India could increase their customer base by changing the hours of operation. The examples include 7-day banking, 24-hour banking, morning schedule, night schedule and extended hours of operation.
- *Provide Service Conveniences Better than Competitors:* When customers are provided better service conveniences such as decision convenience, access convenience and transaction convenience, they are likely to respond positively. Internet shopping, tele-banking and Internet banking are a few examples of service convenience.

- *Focus on Word-of-mouth Communication:* Word-of-mouth communication plays a vital role in influencing consumers. The role of reference groups in promoting word-of-mouth communication is quite significant. Service firms need to identify opinion leaders and exert their influence on consumers to create or increase demand.
- *Position Service Offers Differently during Slow Periods:* A typical marketing tactic is to position the service differently for a short period. Consumers should identify the distinctive value of the service if availed during the low-demand periods from a service company.
- *Bundle Services:* Service companies have been practising this strategy for a long time. For example, airline sales are bundled with tours and hotel accommodation and advertising agencies bundle their creative talents with media services. Bundling is the offer of two or more services at a package price. Consumers do not have an option of purchasing individual services separately. Bundling less-demanded service with highly demanded service may have positive and sometimes negative effects. Marketers should work out customer benefit in monitory and non-monitory terms while bundling services.

> *"Demand below the capacity not only affects the profitability of the service company but also the company image and the morale of the employees. Strategies like aggressive promotion, incentive offers, serving new segments, improving quality and so on are employed by service marketers to raise the demand."*

CAPACITY MANAGEMENT

Another approach to either eliminate or to reduce the imbalance between supply and demand of services is to flex the capacity beyond the optimum level when the demand is more and reduce the capacity when the demand is less. Capacity among service firms has one commonality. Every day if a service is not put to profitable use, it cannot be saved.[3] This perishability suggests a need for careful planning and management, as idle capacity due to slack demand, as well as turning away customers due to insufficient capacity, are serious problems critical to the success of many service firms.[4] V. A. Zeithaml and M. J. Bitner[5] suggest several strategies for flexing capacity. Table 10.2 illustrates the strategies for flexing capacity to match the demand.

Table 10.2 Strategies for Capacity Management

Flexing Capacity when Demand Is High	Flexing Capacity when Demand Is Low
Add physical infrastructure	Perform maintenance and renovations
Increase working hours of employees	Schedule vacation
Cross-train employees	Schedule employee training
Hire temporary workers	Lay off employees
Motivate employees to work overtime	Take on sub-contract jobs
Rent or share facilities	Rent equipment and space
Rent or share equipment	
Outsource support services	

> Stretching capacity to accommodate more customers is the strategy used when demand is high. Capacity flexing is a very hard task and needs advance planning. Extracting more work from employees or making them work for longer hours may lead to dilution of quality and may affect buyer–seller interactions, so care should be taken to ensure customer quality while using stretching strategies.

High Demand

There are several strategies, complementary in nature, which are useful for flexing the capacity when the demand is more than the optimum level of capacity. The following are the useful strategies for service companies to save the situation:

- *Add Physical Infrastructure:* The facilities can be expanded to accommodate more customers. In a restaurant, space can be expanded temporarily by adding a few tables and chairs during peak times.
- *Increase Working Hours of Employees:* During peak seasons, the working hours can be extended by the service firms. Employees may be asked to work longer and faster.
- *Cross-train Employees:* This strategy is to make use of supporting staff as frontline employees for service production and employees of less-demanded service packages of the company. When all employees are trained to perform each and every function, the manpower can be utilized to increase the capacity during times of special requirement. This will improve the efficiency of the whole system and reduce underutilization of employee time.
- *Hire Temporary Workers:* Temporary or part-time workers either support the organizational employees or may perform frontline activities. However, while using part-time employees, care should be taken with respect to quality of service.
- *Motivate Employees to Work Overtime:* Employees may be asked to work more number of hours on additional payment. Employee fatigue and lower involvement are the problems arising from this strategy, if implemented.
- *Rent or Share Facilities:* In case of inadequacy of facilities for the performance of service, one viable alternative is to get them on rent. Sometimes, organizations with complementary demand patterns can share facilities.
- *Rent or Share Equipment:* Equipment can be obtained for rent in case of insufficiency.
- *Outsource Support Services:* Some of the support services of a service package can be performed by outsiders on a sub-contract, or the service firm may buy specialist services from outside for servicing their customers, as part of the service package.

> When demand is low, idle capacity exists. It costs the service companies dearly due to the high proportion of fixed costs. Strategies such as scheduling vacations and, training and maintenance activities; laying off employees, subcontracting, renting equipment and space reduce the negative effects of the situation.

Low Demand

The following are the strategies frequently used by service companies for flexing the capacity during low-demand situation:

- *Perform Maintenance and Renovations:* Slack seasons (of demand) are the best periods for service firms to perform maintenance work for equipment and other infrastructure. As such, service firms schedule down time during non-peak seasons.
- *Schedule Vacations:* Scheduling the vacation of employees during the period of low demand helps the organization have continued service of employees during peak periods of demand.

- *Schedule Employee Training:* Employee training is a very important activity. The time period during which demand is low can be used effectively by deputing some employees for training.
- *Lay off Employees:* This is the last resort available to service organizations to reduce costs during non-peak periods. However, the labour laws of respective countries should permit such an exercise by service firms.
- *Take on Sub-contract Jobs:* During slack seasons, the service company may accept contract works from other companies within and outside the country.
- *Rent Equipment, Space and so on:* A part of the office space, warehouse space, may be given for rent. The equipment unused also may be given for rent during low-demand periods.

Idle capacity can also be used to differentiate on quality. Customers enjoy greater comfort when consuming a service when some part of the capacity is idle. It is not always possible to eliminate imbalances between demand and supply by shifting the demand, flexing the capacity or both. These may be too costly and time consuming. Demand patterns may be highly unpredictable for service firms to take up any approach of shifting demand when there is an excess flow. During peak periods, even when service firms are geared to serve to their full capacity or stretched capacity, consumers may have to wait. Waiting customers is a common feature for most service organizations, either due to excess demand over capacity or variability in the length of time for services. Service firms use the reports of credible research organizations to understand demand patterns related to the services offered and to develop strategies to face them. "Services Marketing Insight: Top Ten Predictions for the IT/ITeS Sector in India presents some predictions for the IT/ITeS sector in India.

WAITING-LINE MANAGEMENT

Waiting, generally, is not a pleasant experience for most people. People look for efficient and quick service. When customer waits are inevitable, service organizations should deal efficiently by employing a variety of waiting-line strategies. Although waiting for service delivery has been treated as an economic (or time) cost, the psychological cost of waiting also has been documented by consumer researchers. Stress, boredom, anxiety and annoyance are often triggered by waiting influence consumers' service evaluations and satisfaction with the firm.[6] The most important factors that influence the perceptions of the consumers on waiting include the intensity of the need of the service facility, customer characteristics, perceived fairness of the wait and information provided by the firm. The following are the four strategies to manage waiting.

Developing Operational Logic

When consumer waits are common, the service firm should first analyse the operational process to locate any loopholes in the system and initiate corrective measures to plug them. Efforts also can be directed at innovating better

10.2 Services Marketing Insight — Top 10 Predictions for the IT/ITeS Sector in India

IDC India, the global information and communication technology market intelligence firm, predicted that the domestic Indian IT/ITeS market would grow at 13.4 per cent in 2009, the slowest since 2003. The first growth phase for this sector was over (2008–2009). The second growth phase began quite differently from the earlier phase. The unprecedented growth during the first phase, nearly tripling the market size from INR 340 billion in 2003 to INR 1020.31 billion in 2008, was a blessing to this sector. The second phase was built on the strength of new and innovative services sought by consumers and enterprises alike. IDC expected the Indian domestic IT/ITeS market growth rate to come down from an average of 24.3 per cent recorded during 2003–2008 (the first growth phase 1.0) to 16.4 per cent by 2013. This relatively slower growth will see an enhanced competition, leading to a rapidly changing strategy and continuous market re-alignment on the part of ICT market participants. The domestic IT market was expected to grow at 11.4 per cent in 2009 to post revenues of INR 1049.37 billion, and the domestic ITeS market would post revenues of INR 96.37 billion, a growth of 40.8 per cent.

The Top 10 Predictions

1. Slowdown to accelerate IT/ITeS market transformation from growth phase 1.0 to growth phase 2.0: The transformation of the Indian domestic IT/ITeS market has already started, with market players preparing for a new landscape. They need to innovate, leverage the existing infrastructure and align continuously with market opportunities. Growth phase 2.0 will be an era of following dynamic strategy as any existing strategy will not remain effective for long and would need to be re-constructed. The economic slowdown will only accelerate this transformation, which would manifest itself in terms of cost savings, productivity enhancement and customer retention in the short run, giving way to new engagement and delivery models in the long run.
2. India to be the fastest growing market in APAC. The top five growth markets in the APAC region are India, China, Vietnam, Thailand and Philippines. India will continue to lead the pack with 11.4 per cent growth in domestic IT spending.
3. IT optimization technologies adoption and usage will grow.
4. Telecommunications sector's IT spending growth will be the fastest.
5. The outsourcing services market will move towards consolidation in favour of larger players.
6. Experimentation with "cloud computing" model will increase but will not become mainstream.
7. The stage would be set for new channel forms to evolve.
8. Consumer 2.0 elusive! Delay in orchestration of content, convergence and connectivity.
9. Enterprises to look at an integrated security approach, revamp their business continuity plans.
10. Global IT growth will be halved.

These 10 predictions help service companies in IT/ITeS to prepare in advance for the likely changes in demand for services. They can plan changes in capacity to exploit the emerging opportunities and face threats effectively.

systems that can either reduce the wait lines or reduce the pressure of customers. *Tirumala Tirupathi Devasthanam* has introduced *Sudarsanam* token system[7] to minimize waiting time for pilgrims. Under this system, tokens indicating the time of *darshans* is given free of cost for different types of *darshans* and *sevas*. Pilgrims can have *darshan* within two hours of the time indicated on the token after entering the queue complex. As this system saves on waiting time, it provides pilgrims with enough time to visit temples in the vicinity. This approach has reduced several managerial problems as well as the burden of consumers. Though consumers cannot have *darshan* early due to this system, they are satisfied because of the reduced burden. This system contributed to the growth in demand for various tourist locations in and around Tirumala.

When queues are inevitable, the service firm should decide upon issues such as the number of queues, their locations, reservation to special segments and their effect on consumer behaviour. Thus, Indian Railways operates a number of terminals at the railway reservation complex and allocates some queues for women, some for physically handicapped, some for senior citizens, some for foreigners and many for the general public. This arrangement not only reduces waiting time but also satisfies some market segments that expect special recognition and privilege.

Establishing a Reservation Process

While service enterprises cannot inventory supply processes, they can inventory demand by creating reservation systems.[8] In case of unavoidable waiting, an advance reservation system can be used to reduce customer panic during the wait and to increase the certainty of having the service at a designated time. The reservation system not only reduces the waiting time but is also useful in shifting the demand to less-demanded time periods. Reservation systems provide specific intelligence about demand trends. Organization can gain time to make all necessary arrangements for service production. Reservation trends are useful to enhance marketing and managerial decision making. Consumers also find values in this system since it eliminates uncertainty. When demand is inventoried by making customers wait, service firms can recover from consumers' perception of dissatisfaction.

Tirumala Tirupati Devasthanam

Lord Venkateswara temple, located at Tirupati, Andhra Pradesh, is one of the most famous temples of the world. Nearly 40,000 pilgrims visit the temple daily to offer prayers to Lord Venkateswara. Waiting lines are common in all seasons. Since the capacity is limited and further stretch is not possible, the management of TTD introduced advance reservation system for many services. The temple offers 10 types of *seva* services including *archanananthara darshanam, suprabhatam, nijapada darshanam, thomala seva, archana, visesha pooja, astadala pada padmaradhanamu, sahasra kalasabhishekam, tiruppavadai* and *kalyanotsavam*. e-*seva* booking is offered to pilgrims to have any of the *sevas* at a designated time. One can book a minimum of 3 days in advance and up to 90 days. Accommodation services are offered in five categories ranging from INR 100 to INR 2,000. One can use e-accommodation service to reserve a maximum of two rooms each. To reduce waiting time in queue lines, TTD has introduced e-*darshan* facility wherein the pilgrim is provided with the *darshan* slot remotely before actually the pilgrim reaches Tirumala. This system was started with the token system and replaced with the biometric system. Pilgrims are permitted to enter the Vaikuntam Queue Complex-I, according to the time slot provided to them.

> "Services cannot be inventoried, but demand can be inventoried through a properly executed reservation system. Though waiting is inevitable during peak periods, the reservation system facilitates customers to gain confidence of getting the service, and that too at the designated time and through defined processes."

Differentiating Waiting Customers

This strategy is to differentiate customers based on needs or customer priority. Some service organizations follow a popular discipline called first-come–first-serve for this purpose. C. Lovelock suggested four approaches to differentiate customers[9]:

- *Importance of the Customer:* The importance may be attached to a customer by taking into consideration the variables such as loyalty, order volume, position and status in the society, connectivity with the company and expected positive or negative effects of the actions of the customer.
- *Urgency of the Job:* Customers are prioritized based on urgency of the service requirement.
- *Duration of Service Required:* Short service jobs are given priority so that more number of customers can be served.
- *Payment of a Premium Price:* The customers who paid or are ready to pay higher price are served first.

Making Waiting Fun

> "Waiting is not desired by either customers or service companies. However, it happens due to mostly uncontrollable variables. Customer dissatisfaction can be avoided by making waiting fun. Entertainment programmes diffuse the tension of service consumers and keep them in right condition and spirit to participate in the service process."

All waits need not be boring to customers. Organizations can make waiting a value received by the customers. Customers can be satisfied by making waiting fun or at least tolerable. D. A. Maister[10] proposed several principles in his work *The Psychology of Waiting Times*. The following are the observations relating to psychology of people in waiting lines:

- Unoccupied time feels longer than occupied time.
- Pre-process waits feel longer than in-process waits.
- Anxiety makes waits seem longer.
- Uncertain waits are longer than known waits.
- Unexplained waits are longer than explained waits.
- Unfair waits are longer than equitable waits.
- The more valuable the service, the longer the customer will wait.
- Solo waits feel longer than group waits.

These principles are highly useful to service organizations in designing wait-line strategies and manage the waiting time of the customers efficiently.

SUMMARY

- Demand management is critical for service companies because services are perishable.
- Service marketers may face different demand situations such as negative demand, no demand, latent demand, seasonal demand, irregular demand, excess demand and falling demand in the market.
- Each situation has to be handled strategically.
- Capacity utilization and demand management are to be coordinated effectively.

- If some capacity is unutilized, it is lost forever.
- Demand below the optimum capacity or above the maximum capacity is undesirable.
- A proper strategic system should be used to manage demand and capacity.
- When demand is more than the capacity, service providers should work out strategies to shift demand or to stretch the capacity.
- When demand is lower than the optimum capacity, strategies should be worked out to increase the demand or to reduce cost of having idle capacity.
- Inventorying demand by creating reservation systems is one popular strategy being adopted by service providers when demand is more.
- Waiting-line management is one of the approaches that helps in reducing consumer dissatisfaction.

KEY TERMS

Excess demand *204*	Irregular demand *202*	No demand *200*
Falling demand *202*	Latent demand *201*	Optimum capacity *203*
Flexing capacity *212*	Negative demand *200*	Seasonal demand *201*

BRIEF QUESTIONS

1. Explain various demand situations.
2. Discuss various demand patterns.
3. How do demand variations take place in services?
4. What are the strategies to shift demand?
5. How can demand be promoted in services?
6. How can capacity be matched to demand fluctuations?
7. Explain the importance of waiting-line management.

ESSAY QUESTIONS

1. Why do service companies show greater concern for demand management?
2. Explain various demand situations and suggest suitable management approaches to tackle them.
3. How do you study demand fluctuations and capacity constraints of service firms? What strategies do you suggest for balancing the supply-demand position?
4. How can waiting customers be managed? Take an example of a service organization that often faces excessive demand over capacity and suggest measures.
5. "When waiting is unavoidable make it at least tolerable." Comment.
6. "Capacity and demand management is a major challenge for service firms." Why? Discuss.

ASSIGNMENTS

1. Passenger transport organizations in India—road, rail and air—face excess demand situations during summer, festivals and other seasons. Seasonal variations in demand are one of the major problems for the organizations in the sector. You are required to:
   (a) Select one transport organization of your choice and study demand variations for the last 3 years.
   (b) Study the demand and capacity-management strategies to find out their effectiveness.
2. A healthcare centre has been facing fluctuating demand for the last 5 years. The capacity utilization is about 60 per cent on an average. During peak times, the centre is losing customers to competitors. The demand is not up to the desirable level during other times. You are required to:
   (a) Study the demand patterns for the services of healthcare centres.
   (b) Work out a plan for demand forecasting.
   (c) Select appropriate strategies to manage demand and capacity.

REFERENCES

1 W. Baumol, S. B. Blackman and E. Wolf, *Productivity and American Leadership.* (Cambridge, MA: MIT Press, 1991).

2 Roelio Oliva, "Tradeoffs in Responses to Work Pressure in the Service Industry," *California Management Review*, 43, no. 4 (2001).

3 D. R. E. Thomas, "Strategy Is Different in Service Business," *Harvard Business Review*, 56, July–August (1978): 158–65.

4 F. H. D. Harris and P. Peacock, "Hold my Place, Please," *Marketing Management*, 4, no. 2 (1995): 34–46.

5 V. A. Zeithaml, D. D. Gremler, M. Jo Bitner and A. Pandit, *Services Marketing*, 4th ed. (New Delhi: McGraw-Hill, 2008) pp. 462–494.

6 Leonard L. Berry, Kathleen Seiders and Dhruv Grewal, "Understanding Service Convenience," *Journal of Marketing*, 66, July (2002): 1–17.

7 http://www.tirumala.org/darshan.htm.

8 Donald J. Shemwell, Jr. and J. Joseph Cornin, Jr., "Services Marketing Strategies for Coping with Demand/Supply Imbalances," *Journal of Services Marketing*, 8, no. 4, (1994): 14–24.

9 Christopher Lovelock, Jochen Wirtz and Jayanta Chatterjee, *Services Marketing*, 5th ed. (New Delhi: Pearson Education, 2009) pp. 246–267.

10 David A. Maister, "The Psychology of Waiting Lines" in *The Service Encounter: Managing Employee/Customer Interaction in Service Businesses*, edited by John A. Czepiel, M. R. Solomon and C. F. Surprenant, (Lexington, MA; Lexington Books: D.C. Heath and Company, 1985).

The Service Product

11

LEARNING OBJECTIVES

After studying this chapter, you will be able to:

- Understand the concept of service product
- Understand the process of development of a basic service package
- Understand the process of new service development
- Describe the concept of service blueprinting
- Understand the service product mix and service differentiation
- Understand service life-cycle management

Manas Market Research Solutions (MMRS) Pvt. Ltd. is a five-year-old company providing a full range of market research and data-analysis solutions to clients within and outside India. The specific services offered by MMRS include research design, survey programming, data collection, project management, data processing and analysis and research report preparation. Within a short span of five years, MMRS has created a reputation for itself in the market. It is known for its comprehensive research capabilities, proactive client service and accurate and actionable results.

MMRS evolved itself as a state-of-the-art research unit with advanced technology, sophisticated tools, experienced and talented experts, technocrats, data analysts and professionals. The company management, though satisfied with the internal strengths, is somehow not satisfied with the company's performance in business. The management strongly feels that the company potential is yet to be exploited completely. It has not earnt a distinctive place in terms of value creation and delivery in the minds of prospective buyers. The management of the company is convinced that product management is the area that needs immediate attention. The management aims to remedy the situation at the earliest.

To achieve this, it has identified innovation and high-quality performance as critical to its long-term success. Aware of the fact that the market is highly competitive and the needs of the clients are dynamic and ever-changing, MMRS knows that sticking to the conventional track of research process will not help it attain its long-term goals. To achieve its goals, MMRS has to have a system to develop new service products in a systematic and organized manner so that it can implement a dynamic product mix.

Questions:

1. Do you agree that the company management's assessment is right?
2. What should be the management system for new service development in this case?
3. How to make the product mix of the company dynamic?
4. What action programme do you suggest the management to solve the problem?

INTRODUCTION

A service is an intangible product. It cannot be photographed, touched and verified. It can only be experienced. A service product is a bundle of features and customer benefits. It is very difficult to describe what a service product is. According to Lynn Shostack,[1] there are four risks of attempting to describe services in words alone. They are (i) oversimplification, (ii) incompleteness, (iii) subjectivity (based on personal experience and exposure) and (iv) biased interpretation. Service consumers generally tend to express the service experience in a simple form. It is often incomplete because customer experiences cannot be translated into words. Differences in attitudes, exposure, perception, participation make consumers subjective and biased while describing a service. When asked to describe the experience of a two-and-a-half hour motion picture, no customer can describe every movement in detail. While designing the product, service organizations have to consider these four risks which influence both the customers and the service providers (contact employees). Unless both the customers and the employees of an organization understand the service product properly, it is not possible to produce quality service. Designing new services is a challenging task because it requires thinking about processes, people and experiences as well as outputs and benefits.[2] The understanding of these portrays the wider scope of a services product and its management.

> *A service product is complex and very difficult to describe. The four risks in describing a service are oversimplification, incompleteness, subjectivity and biased interpretation. It is necessary to put serious efforts to find clarity on features and benefits of a service product.*

THE BASIC SERVICE PACKAGE

A service product is a package comprising a series of service elements executed in proper order in keeping with the needs and wants of the consumer, with the intention of maximizing consumer satisfaction. The concept of a basic service package[3] (BSP) helps to completely understand a service product. Figure 11.1 presents the basic service package. There are three elements in a BSP—core service, facilitating services (and goods) and supporting services (and goods).

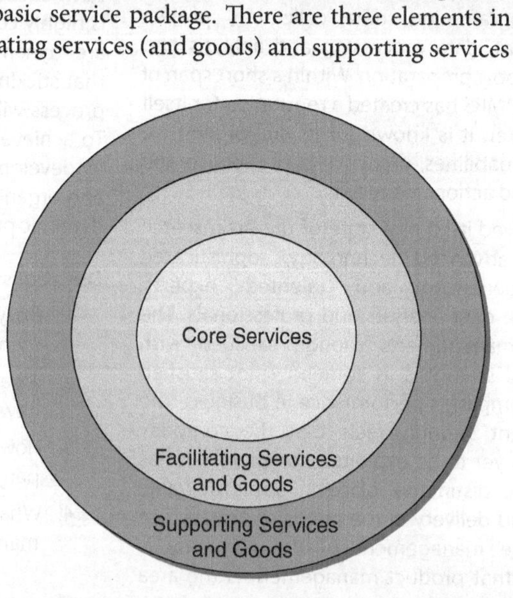

Fig. 11.1 The basic service package

The core service is the reason for the service firm's existence in the market. Thus, a hospital is for healthcare, a hotel is for lodging and an airline is for transportation. Facilitating services are those services without which core service cannot be performed. They make it possible for customers to use a core service. Thus, a hotel requires a building consisting of rooms, cots, toilet, and so on to provide lodging services. Similarly, a hospital requires doctors, nurses, medical equipment, medicines, and so on to offer healthcare services. Supporting services do not facilitate the consumption or use of a core service, but increase the value of the service offering. Thus, a hotel can run a restaurant, operate transport services for local visits, offer reservation and shopping facilities, etc. as auxiliary services which enhance value of the total offering. As far as the core service and facilitating services are concerned, there is not much scope for a competitive edge. But in case of supporting services, a high level of differentiation is possible, and, as such, the firm can enjoy a competitive edge by being up to date, innovative, fast, bold and flexible.

*The **basic service package** consists of three important components: core service, facilitating services and goods and supporting services and goods. A service cannot be performed without facilitating services and goods. Support services and goods augment the service product.*

For a better understanding, let us analyse the BSP of a tourism product. Suppose that the core service of a tourism product offers destination experiences. The facilitating services include

- *Natural Places*: Waterfalls, rivers, islands, caves, hills and landscapes, seashores and villages
- *Historical Places:* Monuments, museums, mythological places, archaeological sites and temples
- *Designed Environments:* Man-made environments such as parks, entertainment and fun-related environments and events

The supporting services include

- Transportation
- Hospitality (lodging)
- Healthcare
- Education, information and training
- Communication and guidance
- Security
- Need-based special packages

A proper mix of the three components of the BSP is to be developed. The facilitating and supporting services, which include a number of variables, provide an opportunity to the service provider to develop various combinations and to offer them to various market segments. The most important understanding the service provider should have is the ability to relate to the need set of target markets. The need set of a tourist comprises primary needs and supplementary needs. The primary need of a tourist is to satisfy leisure-time needs. The supplementary needs, generally are many in number, include economy needs, social (family/relations/friends) needs, security needs, safety needs, entertainment and fun needs, adventure and non-routine exercises and other person-specific needs.

The selection of a tourism product by a customer or a group of customers depends upon their evaluation of the sacrifices they make against the benefits they receive. Generally, there are three sacrifices a customer makes while purchasing a tourism product—money, time and an alternative opportunity. The benefits are ascertained as per the perceived value of various components of the offering against the need set. Therefore, the most important task for a tourism provider is to develop value offerings. The design of customer-oriented service packages is the first step in the process.

11.1 Services Marketing Insight — Service Product Classification: The Consumer's Perspective

Service classification from the point of view of customers is useful to marketers. It provides new insights into service offerings. R. Stell and C. L. Donoho examined eight different services to gain insight into customer perceptions of services and classified the services using well-known taxonomy which includes convenience, preference, shopping and specialty categories. The key variables used in the study included consumer perception of risk, purchase effort and consumer involvement. Risk is the pre-purchase concern that the service may not deliver the expected benefits. Purchase effort is the amount of money, time and energy which the buyer is willing to expend to consume the service. Involvement refers to the interest and importance the consumer attaches to a service. They classified services into convenience services, preference services, shopping services and specialty services.

Convenience Services: These services are relatively inexpensive and frequently purchased. Consumers perceive lowest risk and put minimum purchase effort in using these services. The consumer involvement is also very low for this category of services. Postal services, mom-and-pop stores, film processing are examples of such services. Thus, low risk, low effort and very low involvement are the characteristics of convenience services from the consumer's point of view.

Preference Services: A convenience service differentiated through branding is termed as a preference service. Characterized by higher risk perception, purchase effort and involvement, services in this category also benefit from brand loyalty. Fast-food restaurants, Internet cafes and local transport fall under this category. Thus, low risk, medium effort and low involvement are the characteristics of preference services.

Shopping Services: High risk, medium effort and high involvement are the characteristics of shopping services. Consumers perceive higher risk in these services. Therefore, they are willing to put up greater amount of purchase effort with high involvement in searching for and evaluating the services. Healthcare centres, beauty shops, tailors, etc., are examples of shopping services.

Specialty Services: A specialty service is a shopping service that reaches the ultimate in differentiation and brand loyalty, where only the chosen service company or service provider is acceptable to the consumer. The compromise levels are at the lowest in this category of services. Very high perceived risk makes the consumers put in very high purchase efforts, with grater involvement. Examples include tourism, entertainment concerts and financial products.

Source: Roxanne Stell and Casey L. Donoho, Classifying Services from a Consumer Perspective, The Journal of Services Marketing, *10, no. 6 (1996): 33–44.*

THE CUSTOMER VALUE HIERARCHY

Any service product is ultimately assessed in terms of customer value. Therefore, defining customer value from different perspectives and creating and offering the same are critical in services marketing. "Services Marketing Insight: Service Product Classification: The Consumer's Perspective presents a brief analysis of the consumer preferences.

According to P. Kotler,[4] a marketer needs to think through five levels of the product: core benefit, basic product, expected product, augmented product and potential product. These five levels of the product constitute a customer value hierarchy (CVH) (see Fig. 11.2). Each level of hierarchy progressively adds customer value. The product level and the customer value of the hospitality service are presented in Table 11.1.

From the consumer's perspective, the core benefit represents the essentials of the service product for which the customer is purchasing it. This consumer need has to be met by the company. Thus, the core benefit offered by a life insurance policy is an assurance in the face of risk to life. For the same service, the core benefit is similar across competing organizations. The basic product represents the tangibles and processes that facilitate service production and

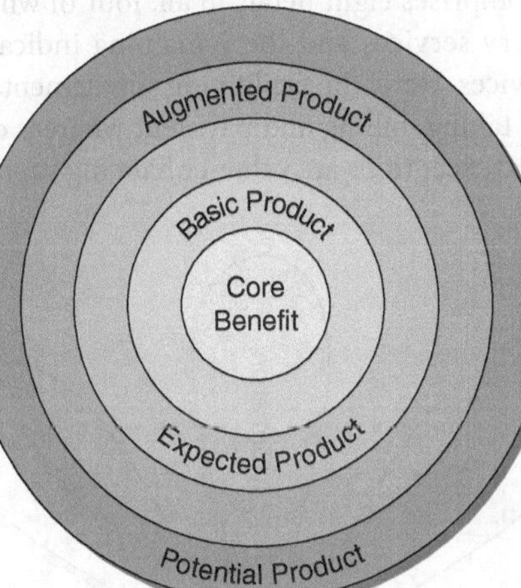

Fig. 11.2
Customer value hierarchy
Source: Philip Kotler, Kevin L. Keller, Abraham Koshy and Mithileshwar Jha, *Marketing Management* 13th ed. (New Delhi: Pearson Education, 2009) p. 309. Reproduced with permission.

Table 11.1 Product Level and Customer Value of the Hospitality Service

Product Level	Customer Value
Core benefit	Rest and sleep (It is the most fundamental benefit the customer purchase.)
Basic product	Hotel room, bed, bathroom, towels, desk, closet and so on (It is how a marketer translates the core benefit into a service package.)
Expected product	Clean bed, fresh towels, working lamps and the relative degree of quiet (A set of attributes buyers normally expect while purchasing a service.)
Augmented product	Supply of food that suits customer health, anything that surprises and delights the consumer
Potential product	New ways of satisfying customers

"Customers perceive the value of a service product based on which they judge whether or not to buy it. The customer value hierarchy provides a hierarchical value-perception process of consumers. The five layers in the value hierarchy are core benefit, basic product, expected product, augmented product and potential product."

consumption. Service providers find opportunities to differentiate their processes and tangibles from that of their competitors. The expected product refers to the understanding and assessment of consumer expectations vis-à-vis the service offer. For a service offer to satisfy the consumer, the expected product should match consumer expectations. At the "product-augmentation" level, service firms face severe competition on several counts. Each augmentation adds to the cost. The augmented benefits very soon become expected benefits to the customer. Creative and innovative BSPs represent the key strength of service providers. As the BSP is easy to copy and the chances of legal protection remote, service firms have to innovate continually to provide better value than their competitors to customers. The "potential product," which encompasses all possible augmentations that a product might undergo in the future, needs to be developed carefully. Successful companies add benefits to their offerings to not only satisfy, but also surprise and delight their customers. In other words, they strive incessantly to surpass customer expectations in a variety of ways.

THE FLOWER OF SERVICE

C. Lovelock[5] developed the flower of service (shown in Fig. 11.3) which indicates the core service surrounded by a cluster of facilitating and support services. The flower comprises eight petals in all, four of which represent facilitating supplementary services and the remaining indicate value-enhancing supplementary services. Here, the facilitating supplementary services include information, order taking, billing and payment whereas consultation, hospitality, caretaking and exceptions are value-enhancing supplementary services.

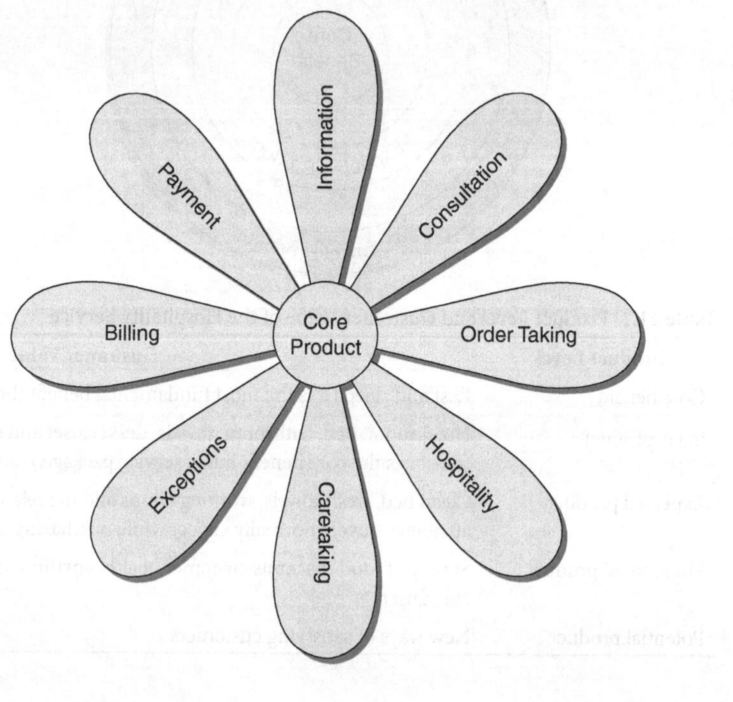

Fig. 11.3
The flower of service
Source: Christopher Lovelock, Jochen Wirtz and Jayanta Chatterjee *Services Marketing* (New Delhi: Pearson Education, 2003) 5th ed., p. 96. Reproduced with permission.

BSNL Mobile

Bharat Sanchar Nigam Limited (BSNL), the leading public sector company in telecommunications, launched BSNL Cellular services "CellOne" (renamed as BSNL Mobile in 2009) in 2002. By then, private sector companies had penetrated the market. In spite of its huge presence in the telecom sector for decades, BSNL could not exploit the early entrant opportunity. Hence, BSNL Mobile incorporated many unique features. The services use state-of-the-art GSM technology to attain global excellence. As the core benefit is common among all the competing brands, BSNL took care in developing the basic product with many additional and unique value-added services and features, compared to competitors' offers. The mobile subscribers were offered benefits such as no security deposit to the existing BSNL subscribers, no security deposit or monthly rental for national roaming , free voice mail recording and receiving, free CLIP, free call waiting and call holding, free missed call alerts by SMS, online bill payment, recharging facility, etc. The service packages included voice mail service, short message service, group messaging, national and international roaming, call forwarding, corporate virtual private network, call conferencing, friėnd and family talk, call waiting and call holding facility, in services like prepaid cards, universal, access no. split charging, VPN, etc., wireless application protocol (WAP) and unified messaging services. The expectations of the consumers regarding voice clarity, network connectivity, service support and low-cost service were also taken care of. The service was augmented with promos to build a brand image and with special schemes to existing BSNL customers. The composition of service package and efficiency in leveraging the corporate competencies in marketing the service are the reasons behind the success of the product.

Information

Customers need information on various elements of a service for evaluation and decision making. Service firms also need to educate the market and prepare and persuade potential buyers to take purchase decisions in favour of the service provider. Sometimes information is required by the law; for example, conditions of sale, warnings, reminders and notification of changes. The examples of information elements are signboards to the service site, service performance hours, charges for services, directions on using core and supplementary services, alerting people, notices, conditions of sale/service, indicating the changes, documentation, reservation information, activity summaries and bills and receipts.

*"The **flower of service** indicates a cluster of facilitating and supporting services surrounding the core service. The eight petals of the flower are information, consultation, order taking, hospitality, care taking, exceptions, billing and payment. The flower of service helps in visualizing the service product comprehensively."*

Consultation

Consultation involves a dialogue with customers, which is directed at identifying and understanding their requirements so as to design and develop a tailored solution. Consultation often helps customers understand their own situation better and encourages them to come up with their own solutions and action programmes. Consultation is offered generally to help customers use the service, clarify doubts, and offer management/technical consultancy.

Order Taking

Order taking is the first step in transaction. Some organizations such as banks and insurance companies require prospective customers to fill out an application form. Some organizations make order entries and some others make advance reservations. The examples of order-taking elements are filling out applications for membership of associations, subscription to a service, reservation of seats, tables, rooms and rentals and entry of orders—online, postal or telephonic order.

Hospitality

Customers may be required to stay at the service outlet for a long time due to the nature of the service process. Hence, hospitality becomes a part of the service offering. The hospitality extended to the customer during the service process contributes significantly to quality perceptions. Many services companies treat their customers as guests and provide facilities to make customers comfortable. Hospitality includes greeting, enquiry and reception, waiting facilities, bathroom kits, food and beverages and transportation.

Safekeeping

It is likely that service customers may carry personal possessions to the service outlet and participate in service production process. Service organizations have to make arrangements for the safekeeping of customer property. This support service is capable of adding value to the service package. Safekeeping includes childcare and pet-care services, parking facilities, storage and baggage handling services, security and safe-deposit boxes, goods packaging, transportation, delivery, installation of goods, etc.

Exceptions

Service providers may be required to provide supplementary services—that are not routine—to the customers on special considerations. Exceptions may be allowed on special requests by the customers for the advance delivery of service under special circumstances. Exceptions also need to be granted to facilitate problem solving. Many a time, service firms face unexpected situations. Frontline employees of the service firm should respond quickly by deviating from the normal procedures to handle such a situation. In case of accidents and emergencies, exceptions need to be granted.

Billing

Billing is important from the company's as well as the customer's point of view. Customers expect accuracy, completeness and legibility in bills prepared by service providers. Companies may provide periodic statements of account to customers or allow customers to complete bills by themselves (self-billing) for greater transparency in the process.

Payment

After billing, customers have to take action on payment. Activities such as cash handling, cheque handling, credit system and coupon system are part of the payment system. The payment system should facilitate easy and convenient payment of dues.

Service marketers can make use of the flower of service to develop a comprehensive product, to check the value-generating abilities of each petal and to carry out continuous improvements. It also helps to communicate and create value perceptions to consumers.

THE DEVELOPMENT OF A NEW SERVICE

One of the serious challenges service firms face in recent times is new service product development. According to P. Kotler,[6] every company must develop new products. New product development shapes the future of the company. The development of a new service can lead to a better understanding of a market's particular requirements, making it easier to spot further opportunities.[7] Customers want new products, and competitors do their best to surpass the company. The increased level of competition, the rapid pace of change in technology and innovations, growing consumer awareness and heightened consumer expectations, established, beyond doubt, the need for introducing new services much faster than the competitors in the market. The faster offer provides greater mileage for firms to face competition and win consumers.

> *Developing successful new services is critical for many companies. To have a competitive edge in the market, the introduction of new services that too faster than its competitors is essential. An effective organizational mechanism is necessary for new service development.*

A constructive organizational mechanism is necessary to facilitate new service development in service companies on a continuous basis. Research studies suggest that services that are designed and introduced by following a structured planning framework have a greater likelihood of success than those that are not developed in a structured framework. "The technical infrastructure for the development and production, that is to say, the hardware, software and delivery systems of one new product, can provide a platform for new services."[8] It is important to develop human resource infrastructure for various stages of a new service development process to improve design, production and marketing operations and also to face challenges of new service development in the future.

What Is a New Service Product?

A service can be termed as a new service when it is innovative, created and offered by the company to the world for the first time. Some new services are adaptive replacements. They are the improved versions of the existing service products either in technology, style, status or performance. According to Booz Allen Hamilton,[9] there can be six categories of new products.

1. *New-to-the-world Products.* The products are really innovative, and the world has not witnessed such products earlier. These products create an entirely new market.
2. *New Product Lines:* The products are not new to the market but new to the company. A company may add a new business to the existing one and enter an established market for the first time.

> New products can be broadly classified into three classes; products that are really innovative and first of their kind to the world, superior offers to replace the existing and imitative products.

3. *Additions to the Existing Product Line.* A company may add new products to the established product lines in order to strengthen the product lines
4. *Improvements and Revisions of Existing Products.* A company may modernize its products by adding new values or replacing the existing products with improved ones.
5. *Re-positionings:* The existing products of a company may be targeted to new markets or new market segments.
6. *Cost Reductions:* Companies may develop new products that are capable of providing similar performances at a lower cost than that of earlier products.

Steps in the Development of a New Service

New service development has a similar development process to product development, but there are significant differences in the activities and the research techniques.[10] One of the distinctive characteristics of service is that the production and consumption of a service takes place simultaneously. The production process is done at a point where the service provider encounters the service customer. The most significant aspect in service production is that the customers are the co-producers. The production performance and the service quality depend not only upon the infrastructure, service environment and the ability of the service provider but also on the ability, attitude and involvement of the customer. Service firms may offer the service product in three different forms.

> Service companies may offer a generalized fixed service package, a generalized flexible service package or customized service package. The choice depends upon several factors including the nature of the service, the technology used, market needs, cost and competition.

1. *Generalized Fixed Service Package*: The company may choose to offer a generalized service product on fixed parameters to the customers. The customers do not have the freedom to choose a part of the service or select a few items of the total package. They have to either take the service as is or reject it.
2. *Generalized Flexible Service Package:* The company offers a limited choice to the customer on various features of the service and offers the customer a partially customized service product. The vast majority of service firms the world over make such offers to customers.
3. *Customized Service Package:* This is the most desirable package from the customers' point of view, as the customers have a choice in designing a service which suits their needs and wants. On the other hand, this is the most complex proposition for companies to offer. It takes more time to design and produce the service and also requires a high-level support mechanism. The company may not be confident of the quality of service and, if at all a service turns out to be of low quality, companies may fear that customers will blame them for no fault of their service personnel.

The realization that customers may be attracted by more than core performance attribute has important practical implications for service providers. Operationally, it requires a wider set of variables to be brought into play for service development than has traditionally been the case.[11] Whatever be the package service firms choose to offer, they need to follow a process for the development of a new service. There are eight steps in developing a new service. Figure 11.4 outlines the steps in the new service development process.

Idea Generation

The first step in developing a new service is the generation of new ideas. The most scarce product in today's competitive world, undoubtedly, is a good idea. In themselves, ideas are neither good nor bad; it is their application and execution that make them so. The frontline people, in direct contact with customers and involved in service production, are a critical factor to the development of new ideas. Given the physical and psychological proximity of frontline personnel to customers, steps should be taken to establish a mechanism to solicit and reward new service ideas from contact personnel.[12] Next to these sales personnel, customers occupy the chief position as sources of ideas. Generally, customers buying services are more expressive than those buying manufactured goods because they interact directly with the service provider and participate in service production. Relationship marketing contributes a lot in this direction. The other sources of ideas include

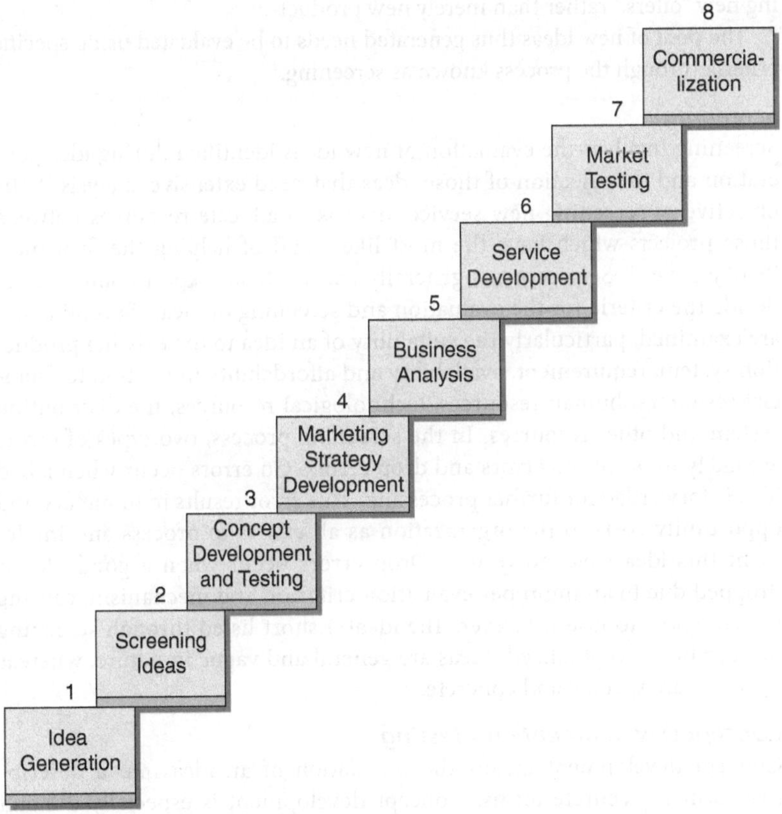

Fig. 11.4 The new service development process

support personnel, competitors, professional organizations, researchers and social organizations.

Service firms should focus on gathering new ideas from various sources. They should establish channels to this end and motivate employees and customers through incentives and reward schemes. While collecting ideas, the concerned managers should have an open mind and not be evaluative at this point. They should look for the maximum number of ideas from various sources; pooling of ideas should be the only objective. Very often, it is difficult to get breakthrough ideas. Service firms are pressurized to introduce new service packages. Therefore, quite often, they have to depend upon ideas that improve existing offerings.

*An **idea** is a new way of solving a problem; it is at the core of new service development. The inflow of ideas needs to be channelled. The important sources are frontline people, sales personnel, customers and competitors.*

Service attribute analysis is one technique that helps service organizations improve the existing processes. Under this approach, each of the attributes—facilitating service attributes and supporting service attributes—is scrutinized for any possible improvements. A combination of changes in a few attributes of a service package generates a noticeable difference in consumers' value perception. In many financial services markets, it has been found beneficial to "augment" the core service product attributes with appropriate support in order to achieve differentiation from competitors' offerings.[13] As a result, some innovative financial service providers now routinely speak of developing new "offers," rather than merely new products.[14]

The pool of new ideas thus generated needs to be evaluated using specific criteria through the process known as screening.

Screening

Screening involves the evaluation of new ideas identified during idea generation and the selection of those ideas that need extensive analysis.[15] The objective of screening new service ideas is to allocate resources between those projects which have the most likelihood of helping the firm meet its objectives.[16] Service firms generally constitute an expert committee to decide the criteria for the evaluation and screening of ideas. Several issues are examined, particularly the suitability of an idea to the existing production system, requirement, availability and affordability in relation to financial resources, human resources, technological resources, the distribution system and other resources. In the screening process, two types of errors are likely to occur: go errors and drop errors. Go errors occur when a bad idea is forwarded for further processing. This error results in monetary and opportunity costs to the organization as all efforts to process and implement this idea yield no results. Drop errors occur when a good idea is dropped due to an improper evaluation criterion and mechanism, causing the company to lose it forever. The idea(s) short listed through screening need to be conceptualized. Ideas are general and vague in nature, whereas concepts are specific and concrete.

***Screening** ideas is a critical exercise, with two possible types of errors: go errors and drop errors. It is necessary to find out the match between company resources and the demanded resources of the new idea.*

Concept Development and Testing

Concept development means the translation of an idea into a descriptive form in accurate terms. Concept development is especially difficult for service firms because of the specific characteristics of services such as intangibility and simultaneous production and consumption. A clearly defined service concept includes the elements of a BSP, customer–employee interaction and the service design document. A service design document describes:

- The problem to which the solution is offered in the form of service
- Reasons for offering a new service
- List of sequential service processes and its benefits
- A rationale for the consumer as to why he/she should have the service

Service Blueprint A popularly used technique for the development of a service concept is "service blueprinting." A service blueprint is a picture or map that portrays the service accurately. It is intended to provide a clear picture of the service process to different people involved in service production and consumption. It helps the people involved in understanding the processes of a service without any confusion or ambiguity and enables them to act accordingly. The blueprint visually depicts the roles of customers and employees. It also depicts a systematic arrangement of different service touch points and the means by which services are performed. A service blueprint also provides evidence to the customers on the basis of which they develop service expectations.

In designing a service blueprint, managers often make use of the decision theory. The decision theory provides an analytical approach to describe such processes that require judgment in relation to choices to be provided for personalized or customized services. A model service blueprint of a bank branch

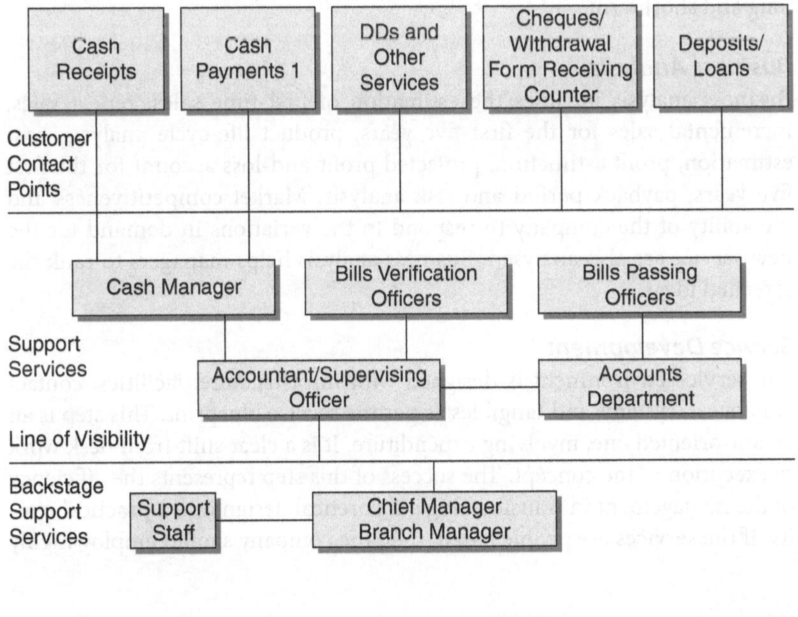

Fig. 11.5 A model service blueprint of a bank

> A **service blueprint** is a picture or map that portrays the service accurately. It exhibits clearly the service processes, employee actions, backstage and technology actions and the linkage of various processes of the service.

is presented in Fig. 11.5. V. A. Zeithaml and M. J. Bitner[17] have listed six steps for building a service blueprint:

1. Identify the process to be blueprinted.
2. Identify the customer or customer segment.
3. Map the process from the customer's point of view.
4. Map the employee actions, onstage and backstage and/or technology actions.
5. Link contact activities to needed support functions.
6. Add evidence of service at each customer action step.

Concept Testing

A new service concept developed is tested by presenting the concept to target consumers and seeking feedback. Besides customers, the concept has to be tested with the employees of the organization, so as to assess their understanding, ability and willingness in performing the service. The results of the concept testing help the management find out the need-gap level, purchase-intention level, the broad and strong consumer appeals, the shortcomings in the concept, the preferential order of influence of various processes and so on. It provides an opportunity to develop a service package that matches closely with target consumer expectations.

Marketing Strategy Development

After the successful testing of the concept, a preliminary marketing strategy has to be developed. The strategic plan should clearly identify the target consumers, the market size and the competitors. The plan should also outline the positioning, pricing and distribution strategies. The strategic plan should also set targets for long-term sales, the expected market share and profit—both long and short term.

Business Analysis

Business analysis includes the estimation of first-time sales, repeat sales, incremental sales for the first five years, product life-cycle analysis, cost estimation, profit estimation, projected profit-and-loss account for the first five years, payback period and risk analysis. Market competitiveness and the ability of the company to respond to the variations in demand for the new service are also analysed. Business analysis helps managers to rank the screened ideas.

Service Development

The service environment is designed with infrastructure, facilities, contact employees, systems and tangibles as per the service blueprint. This step is an action-oriented one, involving expenditure. It is a clear shift from desk work to execution of the concept. The success of this step represents the efficiency of the management in transforming a theoretical design into a practical reality. If the services are people based, then the company should employ highly skilled or professional personnel to play a critical role in producing and delivering services to the clients. If the services are equipment based, it involves significant investment in capital facilities.

Market Testing

Now the services are ready for sale. To know how the service offer could really provide satisfactory experiences, it is necessary to test it among different groups of customers. Based on the early responses, appropriate changes can be made to make the offer more qualitative. Service firms generally invite employees' families and select customers to know their responses. A careful evaluation of the logical process of operational functions is very important at this stage.

Commercialization

The new service developed is now offered for sale. At this stage, service firms have to incur huge costs, particularly in external marketing. The major task is to create awareness in the market and persuade the target market to use the service. Consumer education, guidance and training, if necessary, are to be organized to make the consumers participate well in the service process and also to make them perceive the quality of service. At this stage, the following four decisions are of utmost importance:

1. When should the service be offered?
2. Where should the service be offered?
3. To whom should the service be offered?
4. How should the service be offered?

Continuous process review to introduce the necessary changes to offer quality services from the customer's point of view is needed at this stage. "Services Marketing Insight: Success Factors for New Products" describes seven factors necessary for a product to become a superior, unique product in the market. Companies need to develop expertise in creating new services. To achieve proficiency in this process, companies should develop a formal organizational system for new services development process. It includes a detailed study of market needs, customer research, concept descriptions and the eight-step systematic process outlined above. "Corporate synergy is so important for sales and competitive performance. Since new services can be difficult for customers to evaluate and to differentiate from competing services, it is often the firm's expertise and facilities for performing the service that become the essence of the service being purchased."[18]

"Service companies must be either market driven or market driving in their new service development efforts. The new product should reflect service innovativeness, quality of service experience and customized features. It should be capable of achieving high performance in sales, competitiveness and cost efficiency. Corporate synergy is very important in achieving such performance."

New service development requires management commitment and support. The commitment of the management is reflected in corporate strategy and its concentration on managing key activities in the new service development process or creating a climate for continuous innovation. "Managing key activities enhances an effective implementation of new services. It includes different organizational characteristics that directly improve the development of services. Some of the organizational characteristics aim at the role of key people and formal structures that are most suitable for new service development."[19]

11.2 Services Marketing Insight | **Success Factors for a New Product**

Product innovation is central to business prosperity. In the era of rapidly progressing technologies, intense competition, evolving market places and spaces, companies need to restructure and re-strategize to cope with the changing times. The companies that strive to continually improve the effectiveness and the time efficiency of their new product development efforts are the ultimate winners.

R. G. Cooper has identified seven success factors for a product to become a unique superior product—a differentiated product that delivers unique benefits and superior value to the customer.

1. Unique attributes and characteristics for the customer, not available from competitive products
2. Good value for money for the customer (positive economic impact on the customer)
3. Superior to competing products in terms of meeting customer needs
4. Excellent relative product quality, relative to competitors' products, and in terms of how the customer measures quality
5. Superior price/performance characteristics for the customer relative to competitors' products
6. Product benefits or attributes easily perceived as being useful by the customer
7. High visible benefits, very obvious to the customer

Cooper observed that product superiority separated winners from losers and emerged as the key determinant of success. The research carried out by him proved that superior products had significantly higher success rates, achieved greater market shares, had higher profits and met company sales and profit objectives.

Source: Robert G. Cooper, New Products: The Factors that Drive Success, International Marketing Review, *11, no. 1 (1994): 60–76.*

THE SERVICE PRODUCT MIX

A service product mix is a set of services offered for sale by a company. The service mix of a company can be assessed in terms of width, length, depth and consistency. The width of the service mix refers to the number of different service lines offered by the company. The length of a service product mix refers to the total number of service items in the mix. The depth of the service product mix refers to the number of variants offered in each service line. The consistency of the service product mix refers to how closely the service lines are related in consumer perception, distribution channels and so on. The service product mix of State Bank of India is presented in Fig. 11.6.

The service product mix can be expanded in four ways. Service firms can add new service lines; they can expand each service line; they can add more variants to each service and they can improve service-line consistency.

Service-line Decisions

A service line consists of a number of related services. Companies divide the service product mix into service lines for administrative convenience. Each line can be assessed from the points of view of competition and profitability, and appropriate strategic approaches can be followed to achieve organizational

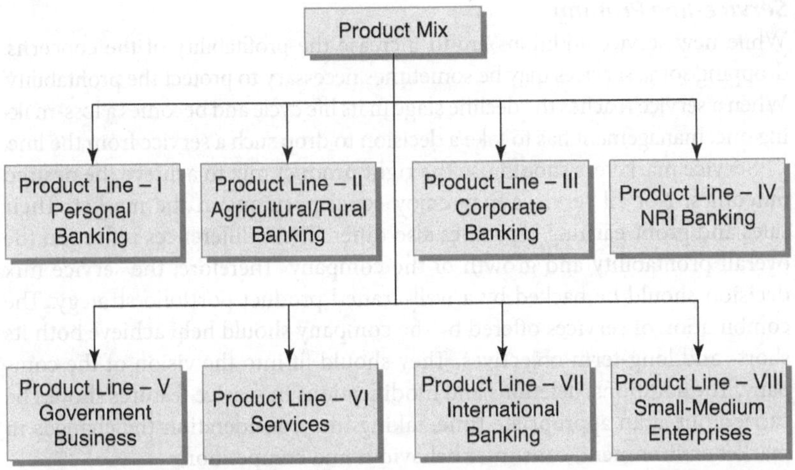

Fig. 11.6 Service product mix of the State Bank of India

objectives. Service-line managers have to take decisions on service-line length, service-line modernization, service-line featuring and service-line pruning.

Service-line Length

Keeping profit maximization as one of the key objectives, service firms decide the length of each service line. For building a service line, companies adopt the following different strategies:

- *Downmarket Stretch*: A company may begin by offering service at upper or middle markets and then add services down the line.
- *Upmarket Stretch:* A company may begin by offering service at low or middle markets and then add upmarket services.
- *Two-way Stretch:* A company may offer service at middle markets and then add services in both upward and downward directions.
- *Service-line Filling:* A company may develop a master plan of a particular service line and may strategically introduce services, leaving some gaps in between. Over a period of time, the company fills such gaps to build a total service line as per the master plan.

Service-line Modernization

Service packages, once introduced, cannot be continued as they are for a long time. On one side, competitors try to overtake in value offering, and, on the other side, consumers expect improved value perceptions. Service firms need to modernize the service lines continuously adapting themselves to the changing environment. Successful companies make a run ahead of competitors and consumer expectations in modernizing service packages and thus delight their customers.

Service-line Featuring

Not all services of a service line can be campaigned to target consumers due to economic reasons. Companies may select one or two service packages of a service line, capable of creating demand for themselves as well as the other service packages on the line.

> *Service product lines are classified for the purpose of administrative convenience. It helps to focus on the development of individual lines and strengthening them. Service-line development, modernization, featuring, pruning are the important decisions.*

Service-line Pruning

While new service additions are to increase the profitability of the concerns, dropping some services may be sometimes necessary to protect the profitability. When a service reaches the decline stage in its life cycle and becomes a loss-making one, management has to take a decision to drop such a service from the line.

Service marketers should use the right product mix to achieve the desired outcomes. Not all services may enjoy equal positions in the market. Their sales and profit-earning capacities also differ. These differences reflect on the overall profitability and growth of the company. Therefore, the service mix decision should be backed by a well-crafted product portfolio strategy. The combination of services offered by the company should help achieve both its short- and long-term objectives. They should fit into the vision of the company. The additions, deletions and modifications in service features should be carried out at an appropriate time, taking into consideration the changes in market environment, consumer behaviour and competition.

SERVICE DIFFERENTIATION

Service differentiation means providing meaningful changes in a service offer, which add value to it from the customer's perspective. It is capable of generating quality perceptions distinct from competitive offers. Service companies can go closer to the customer through service differentiation and can offer delightful experience. In many cases, it is extremely difficult to identify features that differentiate a product from all the similar ones on the market. So, it is difficult to make the service offering stand out from the crowd. Endearing the service to customers, motivating them to choose it instead of the competition are critical and challenging tasks. Generally, the major service differentiators are the BSP, accessibility, interaction, customer participation, tangibles used, service personnel, service channel, service image and service recovery (see Table 11.2).

- *Basic Service Package:* One of the key areas of service differentiation is the design of the BSP itself. There is an enormous scope for differentiating the facilitating services as well as supporting services from those of the competition. By introducing small changes in the BSP, consumers can be made to perceive differentiated value.
- *Accessibility*: Improving the accessibility to a service generates a differentiated value perception. The commonly used variables to differentiate service offerings include the number of contact personnel, service contact hours, time taken to perform tasks, location of the outlet, exterior and interior of service outlet, tools, equipment and documents used and co-customers.
- *Interaction*: Yet another area of differentiating service is the design and process of customer interaction. Service firms have several opportunities to differentiate and excel. These can be identified by seeking answers to questions such as how well received customers are, how involved they are in the service production and consumption, how detached they are from the service outlet after production and consumption process, who they interact with and how organized the interactions are.

- *Customer Participation:* Customers differ in their knowledge, ability and willingness to participate in service production. The responsibility of the service firm lies in ensuring the total, able and involved participation of customers. Service firms can differentiate themselves in their approach to educate, train and convince the customers. Unique values can be generated in providing customer knowledge, building participative abilities, persuasiveness and supporting in relational purchase decision making.
- *Tangibles Used:* The quality, adequacy, maintenance, technology and suitability of various tangibles required for service performance can be used to create differentiated value perceptions.
- *Service Personnel:* Human resources play a pivotal role in service production. Though some services can be provided through machines, they cannot be viewed as perfect substitutes to human resource. The differentiating variables that build or are capable of building a distinctive image of the organization include competence, courtesy, credibility reliability, responsiveness, communication and empathy.
- *Service Channel* The choice of channels such as agents, brokers, franchisees or electronic channels; the extensive, exclusive and selective coverage of the channel; the skill and expertise of channel members and their performance are the areas where differentiation is a possibility.
- *Service Image:* The image of the company at the corporate level and also at the local level differentiates in value perception by the customers.
- *Service Recovery* In spite of a careful and cautious approach, deficiencies in service are not an exception to any service organization. Successful companies adopt recovery strategies to win customers and also use such strategies to differentiate their service offerings from that of their competitors.

"*__Service differentiation__ means providing meaningful changes in the service offer, which add value to the customer and are capable of generating quality perceptions distinct from competitive offers. The major service differentiators are basic service package, accessibility, interaction, customer participation, tangibles, service personnel, service channels, service image and service recovery.*"

Apollo Pharmacy

Apollo Pharmacy is a part of Apollo Hospitals. This pharma retail network development is the key forward integration strategy of Apollo. As Apollo Hospitals became the largest healthcare group in Asia by transforming the medical landscape in India, the pharmacy network developed distinctive service offers for consumers. Apollo Pharmacy introduced schemes like free health insurance, free delivery of prescriptions, 24-hour service, free reminder service, helpline service, free health camps, etc., as support services to enhance the customers' value of the services. The target groups of customers served include a large number of individual consumers, leading hospitals and clinics, corporations and government bodies across the country. It has established the largest pharmacy chain of over 300 outlets in the country. Quality standards are followed in all key areas of product development. Genuine medicines, well-stocked pharmacy, competent staff, computerized systems, cold chain maintenance, personalized pharmacy refilling services, controlled temperature to maintain quality of medicines and their efficacy on consumption are the features which keep the pharmacy network distinctive. The professionalism in service product management through multiple selling propositions enhanced the brand value of Apollo Pharmacy.

SERVICE LIFE-CYCLE MANAGEMENT

Marketers believe that every service product eventually dies, though there is no universal possible lifetime (as in case of human beings) for any service. Marketers also believe that the life of a service product passes through different stages. There are four identified stages in the life cycle of a service: introduction, growth, maturity and decline, depicted in Fig. 11.7. Companies use sales and profit to identify the stages in a life cycle.

1. *Introduction:* At the introductory stage, companies enjoy the benefit of novelty if the service introduced is really innovative. Such an advantage is not available to all products. The initial expense of promoting the brand is very high; the focus is on creating awareness and knowledge of the service among the target customers. The sales increase slowly. Service firms generally do not expect profits at this stage. Service firms make efforts to reduce this stage to the shortest time period possible.
2. *Growth:* The company sees the results of its efforts at this stage. The sales grow at a faster rate, and the promotional focus is on persuading target customers. Word-of-mouth communication plays a significant role in image building. This is a profit-generating stage, characterized by high turnover and low promotional expenditure. The profit curve peaks during the period. The end of the period indicates declining growth rate of sales and increased intensity of competition. Profit starts declining at the end of the period. Service firms strive hard to stretch this period to the longest possible.
3. *Maturity:* This stage of the service life is marked by stabilization in turnover and a downward tendency of the profit curve. Competition is severe, and firms need to invest heavily to match up to competitive

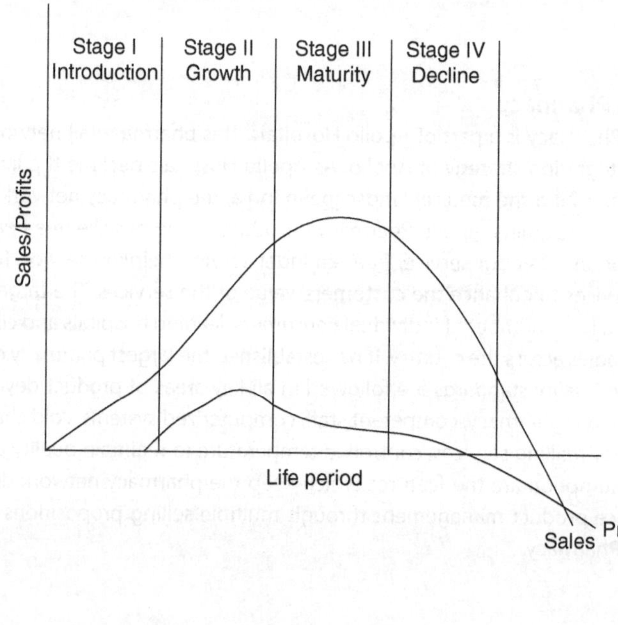

Fig. 11.7
The service product life cycle

threats in the area of service modernization and sales promotion. The increased expenses reduce the profit margin, and, as a result, the profit curve experiences a downward slide. The sales peak at the beginning of this stage, gradually declining thereafter. The end of the period is marked by an increased rate of decline in sales; the profit curve reaches its lowest level. Service firms try to prolong this stage in a bid to generate the maximum possible profit.

4. *Decline:* During this stage, the sales curve slides down at a faster rate, profits evaporate and soon the service becomes a loss-generating one. As soon as the service product reaches this stage, service firms seriously consider dropping the service product.

Life-cycle management means learning to deal with changing technologies and systems, initiating quality leadership, process management, shaping direction for the change, taking control and establishing the improvement process. With the advent of new process and design techniques, current processes may need to be restructured, reprocessed or renovated to exploit their maximum potential on product life cycle.[20]

> *Just like human beings, services also follow a life cycle. The stages in the service life cycle are introduction, growth, maturity and decline. The stages are identified based on the two variables, that is, sales and profit. Each stage needs to be managed using appropriate strategies.*

Although service life-cycle concepts help in planning and controlling the life of a service, they have very limited application in formulating a future-oriented service strategy. The pace of change in the environment and market dynamics do not permit any service organization to plan and manage the various stages in the service life cycle. Consequently, the life of a service is becoming shorter and shorter. Most service firms try to terminate service packages in the shortest possible time frame, replacing it with a new service. The software industry is a case in point. The concern of firms now is to maximize the benefits from a new product in the shortest possible time rather than to visualize or to work on strategies for an extended life.

SUMMARY

- A service product is a package of a series of service elements executed in a proper order against the needs and wants of consumers.
- The service product is a bundle of features and benefits.
- The basic service package (BSP) comprising the core service, facilitating services and supporting services needs to be designed effectively.
- The BSP should be capable of offering satisfactory services to the customers.
- Customer value expectations are important in the design of basic service package.
- The service flower approach provides a comprehensive view of service product management.
- The service product mix is a critical strategic decision area that influences the profitability and growth objectives of the company.
- The service product mix decisions and service-line building and management decisions prove vital in this respect.
- Service differentiation is one of the key competitive strategies.
- The major service differentiators, which include BSP, accessibility, interaction, customer participation, tangibles, service personnel, service channel, service image and service recovery, are useful for creating different value perceptions to service consumers.
- The service life-cycle analysis helps companies formulate an effective strategic framework to manage the life of a service.

KEY TERMS

basic service package (BSP) 220
business analysis 232
concept development 230
core service 221
customer value hierarchy (CVH) 223
customized service package 228
drop errors 230
expected product 223
facilitating services 220
generalized fixed package 228
generalized flexible package 228
go errors 230
market testing 233
new service product 227
potential product 224
product augmentation 224
service attribute analysis 230
service blueprinting 231
service differentiation 236
service flower 224
service life cycle 238
service line 234
service product mix 234
supporting services 220

BRIEF QUESTIONS

1. What is a new service product?
2. Explain service-line decisions.
3. What is service differentiation?
4. What is service blueprinting?
5. Explain the concept of the service flower.

ESSAY QUESTIONS

1. What is a basic service package (BSP)? Explain the issues involved in the development of BSP.
2. Critically evaluate the BSP of a service company you know.
3. What is customer value hierarchy (CVH)? Explain the five levels of the hierarchy.
4. Explain the concept of the flower of service using a service of your choice.
5. What are the steps in the development of new services? Explain.
6. What is service blueprinting? Explain its importance in services marketing.
7. What is service–product mix? What are the decision areas in developing service lines?
8. What is service differentiation? Explain the service differentiators.
9. What are the stages in a service life cycle? How can they be managed?

ASSIGNMENTS

1. New India is a leading global insurance company with a wide network of service outlets within and outside the country. The company offers non-life insurance services in different categories including personal, commercial, industrial, liability, social and credit insurance. This public sector company is facing competition from several private non-life insurance companies established in India after this sector opened up in 2000 to private players by the Government of India. In the light of changing competitive environment, product-mix management and new service development assumed significance. You are required to:
   (a) Study the product-mix management of the company
   (b) Study the process of new product development in the company
2. YOU Telecom India Pvt. Ltd., was set up in 2001. The company emerged as one of the leading independent Internet service providers in India by offering high-speed Internet, VoIP, wireless (WiFi) broadband, digital cable and online value-added services, etc., across 12 cities in India. It is one of the few companies offering triple-play services. Using this service, customers can access broadband, make voice calls though the Internet (VoIP) and watch videos (digital cable TV) through one connection. You are required to:
   (a) Study the product differentiation strategies of the company
   (b) Study the value-added services offered to the consumers

REFERENCES

1 G. L. Shostack, Understanding Services Through Blueprinting, in *Advances in Services Marketing and Management,* Vol. 1, edited by T. A. Swartz, D. E. Bowen and S. W. Brown (Greenwich, CT: Jai Press, 1992) pp. 75–90.

2 Christopher Lovelock, Jochen Wirtz and Jayanta Chatterjee, *Services Marketing,* 5th ed. (New Delhi: Pearson Education, 2009) p. 216.

3 C. Grönroos, *Service Management and Marketing; Managing the Moments of Truth in Service Competition.* (Massachusetts: Maxwell Macmillan; Lexington: D.C. Heath/Lexington Books, 1990) p. 74.

4 Philip Kotler, *Marketing Management,* 11th ed. (New Delhi: Pearson Education Asia, 2003) p. 408.

5 Christopher Lovelock, Jochen Wirtz and Jayanta Chatterjee, *Services Marketing,* 5th ed. (New Delhi: Pearson Education, 2009) p. 233.

6 Philip Kotler, *Marketing Management,* 11th ed. (New Delhi: Pearson Education Asia, 2003) p. 348.

7 C. J. Easingwood and J. Percival, "Evaluation of New Financial Services," *International Journal of Bank Marketing,* 8, no. 6 (1990): 3–8.

8 G. L. Shostack, "Designing Services that Deliver," *Harvard Business Review,* (January–February, 1984): 133–139.

9 Booz Allen Hamilton, *New Products Management for the 1980's* (New York: Booz Allen Hamilton, Inc. 1982).

10 A. Johne and C. Storey, "New Service Development: A Review of the Literature and Annotated Bibliography," *European Journal of Marketing,* 32, no. 3/4 (1998): 186.

11 Ibid.

12 M. R. Bowers, "Developing New Services: Improving the Process Makes it Better," *Journal of Services Marketing,* 3, Winter (1989): 15–20.

13 C. Storey and C. Easingwood , "New Service Success and the Augmented Service Offering," *Proceedings of Product Development & Management Association 18th International Conference,* (Boston, 5–10 November 1994) 178–189.

14 A. Johne, "Developing New Products: Marketing for Success," *Capital Market Strategies,* 94, no. 1 (1994): 41–46.

15 L. Rochford, "Generating and Screening New Product Ideas," *Industrial Marketing Management,* 20, no. 4 (1991): 287–296.

16 David Kelly and Chris Storey, "New Service Development: Initiation Strategies," *International Journal of Service Industry Management,* 11, no. 1 (2000): 47.

17 V. A. Zeithaml, D. D. Gremler, M. J. Bitner and A. Pandit, *Services Marketing,* 4th ed. (New Delhi: McGraw-Hill, 2008) p. 281.

18 Ulrike de Brentani, "Success Factors in Developing New Business Services," *European Journal of Marketing,* 25, no. 2, (1991): 52.

19 J. De Jong and P. Vermeulen, "Organizing Successful New Service Development: A Literature Review," *Management Decision,* 41, no. 9 (2003) 844–858.

20 Biren Prasad, "A Structured Approach to Product and Process Optimization for Manufacturing and Service Industries," *International Journal of Quality & Reliability Management,* 12, no. 9 (1995): 123–138.

Service Branding and Positioning

12

LEARNING OBJECTIVES

After studying this chapter, you will be able to:

- Understand the importance of branding services
- Describe the criteria for choosing brand elements
- Understand the brand equity
- Understand the importance of service positioning and positioning strategies

Good Health, a pharmaceutical company specializing in vitamin-based syrups, capsules and tablets, has a significant market in South India. In North India, its presence is limited only to the major cities. Though an established company, Good Health has not been able to increase its profits owing to intense competition and wafer-thin margins in this segment. Now the company management wants to diversify into a new business. To this end, it has analysed current business trends and identified grooming services for men as the next big thing. This is a niche market with no big players. The company wants to target the middle-income youth, employees and business segments. It wants to leverage its position as a corporate and make a big entry into this segment. The management plans to open exclusive boutiques for men in all the major cities in the first phase. After consolidating its position, it plans to extend its services to smaller cities and towns in the second phase.

Having identified the business segment and the target market, the management wants to decide on a suitable brand name for its range of services. The managers are divided in their choice of a brand name. Some managers argue that the existing corporate name could be projected as the brand name so that there is no confusion. According to them, the name *Good Health* also suits the business as health and beauty are correlated. Some managers maintain that consumers may perceive it as a medical treatment if the company name is used while others claim that people may not relate to the name *Good Health* as it is generic.

Brand positioning is identified as the next major problem. How to ensure that this unconventional range of services appeals to the males in the target segment? The positioning has to be such that it stimulates the latent need among males and generates social pride. The management has assigned the task to a consultant to suggest a business plan particularly for branding and positioning.

Questions:

1. Do you support the idea of business diversification to male grooming services?
2. Is it proper to use the company name as the brand name for the proposed business?
3. What should be the criteria for selecting brand elements in this case?
4. What positioning strategy would work for the new business?

INTRODUCTION

Branding is nothing but providing an identity and building a distinct image of a product or a service. It is all about differentiating an organization from its competitors. Branding involves creating mental structures and helping consumers organize their knowledge about products and services in a way that clarifies their decision making, and in the process it provides value to the firm.[1] In other words, branding is endowing products and services with the power of a brand. The American Marketing Association defines a brand as "a name, term, sign, symbol, or design, or a combination of them, intended to identify the goods or services of one seller or group of sellers and to differentiate them from those of competitors."[2] Branding has now become one of the strategic weapons of business. Brand building though expensive is profitable to the companies.

Marketers believe that branding is not simply the naming of a product but something beyond that. The visual distinctiveness of a brand may be a combination of any of the following: name, letters, numbers, a symbol, a signature, a shape, a slogan, a colour, a particular typeface. But the name is the most important element of the brand as its use in language provides a universal reference point.[3] The name is such an element of a brand that should never change unless some extraordinary conditions demand the change. The key to creating a brand is the ability of a service company to choose attributes such as name or logo that identify the service and distinguish it from others. These different components of a brand are called brand elements. Creating a successful brand entails blending all these brand elements together in a unique way—the product or service has to be of high quality and appropriate to consumer needs, the brand name must be appealing and in tune with the consumer's perceptions of the product, the packaging, promotion, pricing and all other elements must similarly meet the tests of appropriateness, appeal and differentiation.[4] Consumers view brands beyond their functional attributes and benefits. They also look for non-functional and symbolic qualities. Such perceptions are often referred to as brand image.

> “*Branding* is providing an identity and building a distinct image of a product or a service. A brand represents several values of the company and the service package to the customers; it is more than a name for marketers and consumers.”

The brand image, of course, includes more than the name, logo and advertising appeal. The quality of the service determines the success of the image. If you don't satisfy customers, the name won't help. But of course, if you combine good performance with a good name, you will generate the most powerful branding effect for your services.[5]

SERVICE BRANDING

Service branding is critical to the total marketing strategy, particularly for new companies facing severe competition and for companies expanding their range of services or operations. Strong branding can accelerate market awareness and acceptance of high-quality services, while weak branding can accelerate failure for poorly conceived or delivered services.[6] Service companies generally do not lend themselves to product-specific branding as tangible goods. Though, a service provider may have a variety of offerings, consumers tend to perceive all of them as components of a single brand. Therefore, in the case of services, mostly, the company name is either the total or the dominant part of the brand name. A well-chosen name can give a company a decided marketing edge over comparable competitors, and that the branding effect of a strong corporate name can be especially important for service companies.[7]

Goods Branding Versus Services Branding

The definition of *brand* does not distinguish goods branding from services branding. But, the executional strategy of branding goods and services differ.[8] Because of the intangible character of services, consumers try to identify and assess functional and emotional values in service brands. Service companies need to identify the differences in brand-value perception of the consumers between goods and services and work for capitalizing on clues associated with physical evidence. They can use physical evidence effectively as a vehicle for communicating their brand values.

Though service brands are rewarded as clusters of functional and emotional values, nevertheless because of their intangible nature, it is especially important to capitalize on clues associated with their physical evidence as a vehicle for communicating their values.[9] Services branding differs from goods branding due to the following reasons:

> “***Services branding** is not similar to goods branding. The service characteristics influence the branding process, priorities, value propositions and value consistency factors. Identification and bridging of service quality gaps, integrating the interests of internal and external stakeholders, and promoting strong organizational values besides monitoring the service delivery process are hot issues.*”

- Goods branding assumes an internal quality-controlled, value-delivery system which is not seen by consumers. In contrast, the value-delivery system for service brands is visible to consumers who are active participants of the system.
- Branding activity concentrates on the technical product in the case of goods. Service branding takes into consideration technical product as well as functional performance.
- The contact points between brands and stakeholders are limited in goods branding. The number of contact points is more in services marketing, making it necessary for service brands to focus on their internal and external communication strategies.
- In the case of product-based branding, the cluster of values can be tightly controlled by production, communication and distribution systems. While these are important in services branding, albeit more difficult to control, corporate culture plays a critical role through its potential to influence staff behaviour.
- Many services branding issues require a company-wide approach to their solution and implementation. Such issues include identifying and cementing service quality gaps, focus on internal and external stakeholders, including staff, and monitoring the whole service delivery process and promotion of strong organizational values in motivating staff to deliver the services brand.

CHOOSING BRAND ELEMENTS

A service is a complex product with distinctive characteristics compared to tangible goods. Since the value perceptions of consumers of services are linked with many performance attributes, it is very difficult to judge service brand names isolating the performances of the service company. However, some characteristics can be identified based on their potential to be a part of a successful brand. The following eight criteria are the most used for selecting a brand:

1. *Distinctiveness:* It is the fundamental quality of a brand. The consumer should be able to identify a service provider and distinguish it from its competitors. The brand should facilitate this. To be distinctive, service providers use word(s) that are uncommon to the service category. Usually, generic names are avoided in branding. Some companies such as Airtel, Tata Indicom, ING Vysya and Bajaj Allianz use fabricated words to establish a distinct identity.
2. *Memorability:* One of the key objectives of branding is to occupy a space in consumer memory. Several factors affect memorability. A name that is easy to understand and pronounce is likely to get memorized. Short and simple words are also easy to memorize. Idea, for example, is an uncommon brand name and enjoys a high level of memorability. Similarly, Hutch and its transform Vodafone are new terms to Indians and, therefore, could gain memorability.
3. *Likeability:* The brand should be likeable visually, emotionally and in other ways. Consumers are co-producers of service and, therefore, associate brand names to themselves as the partners of a relationship with the service provider. The brand should have an aesthetic appeal taking into consideration consumers' behavioural dimensions and cultural background. The likes and dislikes of people are influenced by their beliefs, attitudes, culture, traditions, habits, lifestyles and personality factors. Corporate brands such as SBI, LIC, Airtel, Reliance, Tata and Idea are high on likeability.
4. *Relevance:* The name that conveys the essence of a service has the ability to position the company clearly in the minds of consumers. Brands such as Lifestyle, Indian Airlines, Music World and Café Coffee Day are examples of successful brands that have used this principle.
5. *Meaningful:* The ability of a brand to communicate credibility, corresponding category, and benefits to customers and so on is assessed to find out the meaningfulness. The brand may suggest a product ingredient or the target market either directly or indirectly. Brands such as Speed Post, more. for you and Kalanjali convey the features of the services meaningfully.
6. *Flexibility:* Many companies grow over the years in size and also in terms of the scope of the business. The companies may in some cases

outgrow their original names. The big brand names in India such as TATA, Reliance and Wipro started their businesses in the manufacturing sector and later entered the services sector in a big way. They did not face any branding problems as they could promote sub-brands with the corporate name wherever necessary and maintain their legacy. This may not be the case with every company. Brand names in regional languages, region names, names from epics and local literature, etc., will have very less or no flexibility. The brand names of dailies such as *The Times of India*, *The Hindu* and the *Indian Express* have less flexibility to become international brands.

> *The criteria for selecting brand elements are based on several issues including the target market, service category, competition intensity and branding objectives. The general criterion includes distinctiveness, memorability, likeability, relevance, meaningfulness, flexibility, adaptability and protectability.*

7. *Adaptability:* The brand elements should have the potential to adapt to changes in the environment and be updated. Sometimes, more than 50 per cent of the service package might get altered over the years. The name, however, should be capable of converging the core value consistently to the consumers. For example, the service package of Apollo Hospitals has been changing over the years. The brand value of the group is getting enriched due to the changes. The adaptability of the brand enacted no confusion over the core value of the brand in the market.
8. *Protectability:* Brand elements should be legally protectable. The Trade Marks Act, 1999 provides legal protection for the brand elements, if registered properly. Generic names are not given legal protection.

Which brand becomes strong or weak is a debatable question always. The theories do not work exactly to get desired results. Branding is more an art than science. However, lessons from successful brands and failure ones always provide useful input for marketers in branding. K. L. Keller[10] identified 10 attributes of strong brands in the world, which are as follows:

1. The brand excels at delivering the benefits consumers truly desire.
2. The brand stays relevant.
3. The pricing strategy is based on consumer perceptions of value.
4. The brand is properly positioned.
5. The brand is consistent.
6. The brand portfolio and hierarchy makes sense.
7. The brand makes use of and coordinates a full repertoire of marketing activities to build equity.
8. Brand managers understand what the brand means to consumers.
9. The brand is given proper, sustained support.
10. The company monitors sources of brand equity.

Service brands should possess, if not all, many of the above-listed qualities. Brand elements have the potential to play a number of brand-building roles. They facilitate consumers to recognize, recall and memorize brand names and features. The brand value stages from the customer's point of view are discussed in "Services Marketing Insight: The Brand Value Chain". A powerful—but sometimes overlooked—brand element is a slogan. Like brand names, a slogan is an extremely efficient means to build brand equity. Slogans can function as useful "hooks" or "handles" to help consumers grasp what the brand is and what makes it special.[11]

BENEFITS OF BRANDING

Branding offers many benefits to service providers as well as service consumers. The following are the benefits of branding services:

1. Provides corporate identity and recognition
2. Provides an opportunity to distinguish the service from that of competitive services
3. Helps customers develop value perceptions
4. Helps in developing customer relationships
5. Builds up long-term equity to the concern
6. Makes market penetration easy
7. New service offers get quick responses.

12.1 Services Marketing Insight — The Brand Value Chain

K. L. Keller has identified value stages and multipliers to develop the brand value chain. The brand value chain is a structured approach to assess the sources and outcomes of brand equity. It assumes that the value of a brand ultimately resides with customers. Another assumption is that a number of linking factors intervene between the value stages. The model recognizes four value stages. The first stage is market programme investment. The value of this stage is influenced by the composition of the product, communication, trade, employees and other factors. The second stage of value is customer mindset, which is influenced by the awareness, association, attitudes, attachment and activity of the consumers in relation to the first value stage. The intervening multiplier variable between the two stages is programme quality. The four attributes that influence programme quality are: clarity, relevance, distinctiveness and consistency. The third value stage is market performance, which is based on price premiums, price elasticities, market share, expansion success, cost structure and profitability. Market place conditions—the intervening multiplier between stage two and three—are influenced by competitive reactions, channel support and customer size and profits. The fourth value stage is shareholder value. This value is the reflection of stock price, P/E ratio and market capitalization of the brand. The intervening multiplier between stage three and four is investor sentiment. The sentiment is influenced by market dynamics, growth potential, risk profile and brand contribution.

The brand value chain is a comprehensive model that guides managements to identify critical links in building brand value and take appropriate measures for promoting value at every stage of the value chain.

Source: Kevin Lane Keller, Strategic Brand Management: Building, Measuring, and Managing Brand Equity, *2nd ed. (New Delhi: Prentice Hall of India Pvt. Ltd., 2003), p. 391.*

CORPORATE BRANDING FOR SERVICES

Service characteristics such as intangibility, variability and perishability make branding a strategic requirement to promote beliefs and values in the target market. Most service companies promote product brand names along with corporate branding. Telecom companies (BSNL, Airtel, Vodafone, Idea Cellular and Reliance Infocom), banking companies, insurance companies, transport companies and courier services promote corporate branding along with individual names to specific service packages.

Successful corporate brands are valuable assets. M. J. Hatch and M. Schultz[12] found, through their research across 100 companies, that a company must align three essential, interdependent elements—they called them strategic stars—to create a strong corporate brand: vision, culture and image. *Vision* refers to the aspirations of the top management of the company; *culture* refers to values, beliefs and attitudes of the people in the organization and *image* refers to the impression of the outside world especially the stakeholders of the company. In order to build corporate brand effectively, the management should look at the relationships between vision and culture, vision and image, and image and culture. If gaps are found in any of the three relationships, such as vision–culture gap, vision–image gap and culture–image gap, appropriate and timely measures need to be initiated to bridge the gaps. Such gap analysis should be carried out continually as there is a likelihood of emergence of such gaps due to the dynamic nature of the business, social and other environments in which the business is operated. "Services Marketing Insight: Indian Consumers' Brand Loyalty and Performance Rating of Select Service Brands" highlights the top-rated companies in various industries in India.

"Most service companies promote corporate brands to gain on some specific fronts such as cost advantage, building a sense of community in customers and a seal of approval for all the services offered. A corporate brand provides an umbrella image and becomes a valuable asset to the company."

Creating a corporate brand—an umbrella image that casts one glow over an array of products—is a relatively new approach to integrating a company's stakeholders.[13] Corporate brands offer essentially four important benefits: They reduce cost of branding; give customers a sense of community; provide a seal of approval from customers to all the services offered by the company,

Infosys

Infosys Technologies Ltd is one of the fascinating success stories of India. Started in 1981 by seven people with USD 250, the company has emerged as a global software giant. The corporate brand reflects well-honed competencies and business values. The brand symbolizes the values of customer delight, leadership, integrity and transparency, fairness and pursuit of excellence. The company provides a complete range of software services by leveraging the chosen business domain, business expertise and strategic alliances with leading technology providers. Infosys defines, designs and delivers technology-enabled business solutions that help Global 2000 companies win a flat world. As a pioneer in the Global Delivery Model (GDM), Infosys builds strategic long-term relationships with clients. The revenue share of existing customers standing at 97 per cent is a testimony for very strong brand loyalty. The company further strengthened its brand equity by winning several awards and recognitions through performance and innovativeness. Thus, Infosys emerged as a strong corporate service brand in the international market.

12.2 Services Marketing Insight

Indian Consumers' Brand Loyalty and Performance Rating of Select Service Brands

Customer Satisfaction Management and Measurement (CSMM), a Delhi-based specialist unit of IMRB International, conducted a study on customer experience which reflects how customers rate a brand's performance and customer loyalty. The findings of the study in services such as airlines, insurance, credit cards, retail banking, housing loans and lifestyle stores provide useful insights to marketers.

Airlines: The airlines sector is witnessing fierce competition. Kingfisher Airlines occupied the top position in consumer rating followed by Jet Airways and Air Sahara. Kingfisher, with 56 per cent of true loyals, secured the top slot in customer loyalty. Jet Airways and Air Sahara secured second and third positions, respectively. Kingfisher was rated the best in terms of in-flight experience, boarding experience, pre-boarding experience, ticketing and purchase experience, advertising and communication and schemes offered. Indian Airlines scored high in call centre/helpline performance. Air Sahara rated high in terms of the offered tie-ups. Kingfisher, with its mix of comfortable and spacious seats, special services such as in-flight television entertainment for every seat, managed to impress the customer.

Insurance: Life Insurance Corporation of India (LIC) secured first position in consumer rankings followed by ICICI Prudential and HDFC Standard Life. Though LIC enjoyed the confidence of two-thirds of the customers, it failed to secure the first position in any one of the measures. ICICI Prudential emerged at the top in the application approval process, post-purchase experience and insurance agent/advisor performance. TATA AIG was voted the best in the medical exam process, communications on new policies and schemes and call centre/helpline performance. HDFC Standard Life secured a high rating on insurance policy and advertising and promotion.

Credit Cards: American Express secured top ranking followed by HDFC and SBI credit cards. Customer loyalty is the lowest for credit card services. One out of every five credit card customers feels trapped. American Express dominated in many performance measures—the application and approval process, the payment process, schemes and promotions, and call centre services. ICICI was ranked number one in advertising and communication.

Housing Loans: The State Bank of India was at the top followed by HDFC and Citibank at the second and third positions, respectively. In this sector, customer loyalties are low as one out of every three customers feels trapped. Ranked the best in terms of performance, SBI shares the top slot with Citibank which was voted to be the best in terms of advertising and promotion. HDFC Bank is scored high in the repayment process and call centre performance.

Lifestyle Stores: Allen Solly, voted the best in terms of store experience, merchandise, sales personnel, billing, additional services, schemes and promotions and advertising and communications, emerged as the clear winner in this segment followed by Provogue and Louis Philippe. Brand loyalty is very high in this segment. Louis Phillippe scored marginally better over Allen Solly in packaging performance.

Source: M. Anand and Alokesh Bhattacharyya, The Consumer Enigma, Businessworld, *(April 2007): 24–40.*

even if in different areas and create a common ground for the customers to symbolize or label a company.

As shown in Fig. 12.1, S. Knox and D. Bikerton have identified six conventions of corporate brand management:[14] brand context, brand construction,

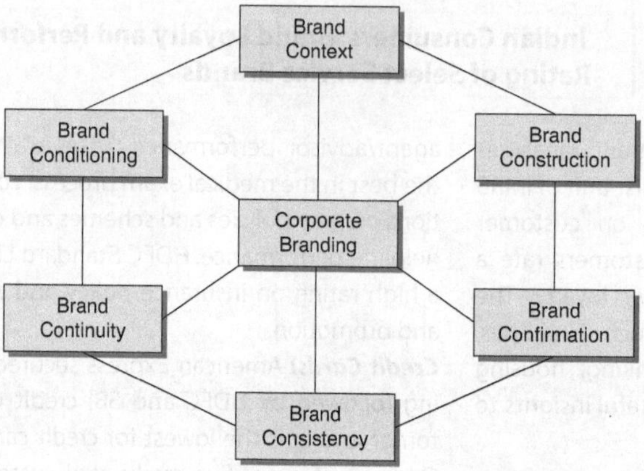

Fig. 12.1 The six conventions of corporate brand management

brand confirmation, brand consistency, brand continuity and brand conditioning. These six conventions are discussed as follows:

1. *Brand Context:* The focus is on establishing the coordinates with the philosophy that corporate branding is multi-disciplinary, combining elements of strategy, corporate culture and communications. The corporate brand is developed based on two relationships—the current image of the organization and its future competition, and the current culture of the organization and its vision for the future.
2. *Brand Construction:* The central values of an organization are the starting points of brand construction. Organization attributes such as purpose, commitments and values, performance benefits which refer to the way services are created and delivered, portfolio benefits relating to customer groups and other brands of the company and network benefits such as contacts and mechanisms are taken as the base for brand construction.
3. *Brand Confirmation:* The brand positioning developed during the brand construction phase should be consolidated and communicated to the rest of the organization as well as to the external audiences.
4. *Brand Consistency:* It is the core principle of successful corporate brand development. The role of corporate communication in creating consistency is significant. The communications should be consistent in promoting core values of the company.
5. *Brand Continuity:* Continuity of the brand is an important consideration for service companies. Managements should adopt a holistic approach to corporate branding, which encompasses all the business processes associated with value delivery. The brand confirmation can be reinforced throughout the organization through the holistic approach.
6. *Brand Conditioning:* Brand conditioning refers to the ability of the organizations to review its corporate brand on a regular basis. Management should ensure the relevance and distinctiveness of the brand in respect of customer value hierarchy. This requires communication of

key aspects of the brand proposition and reinforcement of organization behaviours and processes which deliver superior customer value. The top management should exhibit commitment to the brand values and proactivity in communicating such values.

BRAND EQUITY

Brand equity represents the value of the brand in the market. This value is an outcome of several variables and behavioural attributes of consumers. It may be consumer responses to brand attributes—how they think, feel and act and/or others such as price, market share, profitability, growth rate and innovativeness. A company gains added value with brand equity to its products and services. Brands with strong brand equity can command premium prices, capture and maintain market share, support new line extensions, attract investors and fend off new competitors.[15] Brand equity results from all the activities needed to market the brand.[16] It is considered an important intangible asset of a company. Thus, brand equity is the financial as well as psychological value to a company.

> **Brand equity** *represents value of the brand in the market and is the financial and psychological value of the company. Brands with a strong brand equity command premium prices, capture and maintain market share, support new line extensions and attract investors.*

Branding is more critical for services than goods because many services are seen as commodities by consumers.[17] Branding services is considered difficult than branding goods because of the complexity faced by consumers in assessing the value of services and taking purchase decisions. All products, whether goods or services, possess search, experience and credence attributes.[18] Experience and credence attributes dominate in services while search and experience attributes play a key role in goods value assessment. Most service characteristics are determined and evaluated by consumers only during or after the consumption of service. The dominance of search attributes in services is rarely found. When credence attributes dominate the service offering, consumers are even more likely to rely on external cues, such as brand name, to aid in their buying task. This occurs because consumers cannot judge the performance of credence-dominant services even after consumption. As a result, it is expected that branding would be more important in services dominated by credence attributes than those dominated by search or experience attributes.[19]

K. L. Keller proposed a customer-knowledge-based framework for creating brand equity based on two dimensions—brand awareness and image. According to him, "Customer-based brand equity occurs when the consumer has a high level of awareness and familiarity with the brand and holds some strong, favourable, and unique brand associations in memory."[20]

Brand awareness refers to the memory and recall ability of the consumer. Consumers are exposed day in and day out to a number of marketing stimulations through advertisements in various media, word of mouth and other promotions. If a consumer can recall a brand without any cue, the brand awareness is said to be high in them. When the brand is recognized and recalled with the support of a cue, it is called aided recall, indicative of low levels of brand awareness. Brand awareness is important for other reasons besides its role in generating a consideration set. For some low-involvement products, brand awareness is sufficient to create sales. Since consumers spend little time or effort on the consumption decision of low-involvement products, familiarity with the brand name may be enough to determine purchase. The most important aspect of brand awareness is the formation of information in the memory.[21]

Brand image refers to the perceptions about a brand in the consumers' mind. It is generally reflected by the brand associations held in the memory of the consumer. A positive brand image is vital for defining a target market, determining a product's position, and measuring market response.[22]

> ***Search attributes,*** *such as brand name and price, are product characteristics that consumers can determine and evaluate prior to purchase. Experience attributes, such as fun, emotion or entertainment value, are product characteristics that can be discerned and evaluated only after purchase or during consumption. Credence attributes include any product characteristics that consumers cannot determine or evaluate even after purchase or during consumption.*

The concept of brand equity can be better understood with the help of the customer-based brand equity pyramid developed by K. L. Keller (as shown in Fig. 12.2), which contains six brand-building blocks arranged sequentially to create the right brand identity, brand meaning, brand responses and brand relationship. The six brand-building blocks are described as follows:

1. *Brand salience* refers to consumers' awareness of brands.
2. *Brand performance* refers to the way the product or service meets the needs, wants and expectations of consumers.
3. *Brand imagery* refers to how people think about the brand.
4. *Brand judgements* refer to the customer's personal opinions and evaluations of quality, credibility, superiority and other characteristics of the brand.
5. *Brand feelings* refer to the customer's emotional responses such as warmth, fun, excitement, security, social value and self-respect relating to the brand.
6. *Brand resonance* refers to the nature of the relationship of the customer with the brand. It may reflect in loyalty, attitudinal attachment and sense of community.

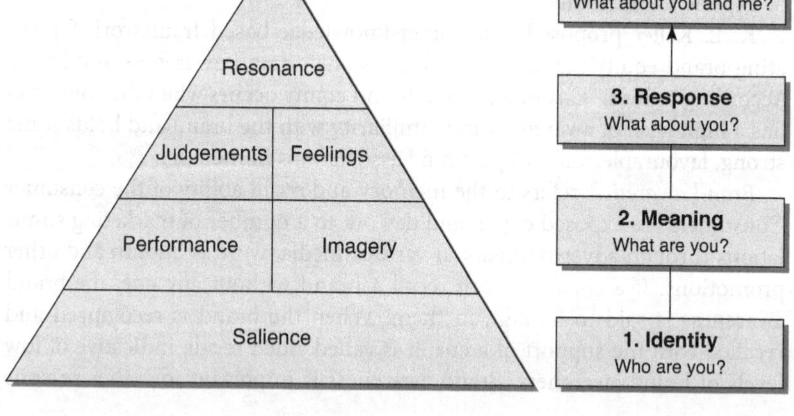

Fig. 12.2 Customer-based brand equity pyramid

Brand equity signifies the status of the brand in the consumer's mind. Positive brand equity indicates the success of marketing mix elements. Building brand equity, thus, is a major challenge to marketers.

> **Positioning** *means projecting the image of a product or a service in such a way that consumers perceive its value distinctively from that of competitive offers. In other words, positioning intends to influence the perceptual process of consumers against a product or a service.*

SERVICE POSITIONING

Positioning refers to the projection of an image of a product or a service that enables consumers to distinguish it from competitive offers within a defined space. In other words, positioning intends to influence the perception of consumers. Studies on consumer behaviour reveal that consumers do perceive against a marketing stimulation and identified that consumers may not respond to all marketing stimulations through a perceptual process as they expose to many stimulations day in and day out. Thus, correct brand positioning is required not only to attract consumer attention, but also to influence the final decision—purchasing the service.

Good brand positioning helps guide marketing strategy by clarifying what a brand is all about, how it is unique and similar to competitive brands, and why consumers should purchase and use the brand.[23] Positioning, a critical factor in brand building, starts with a product—a piece of merchandise, a service, a company, an institution or even a person. However, as pointed out by Al Ries and Jack Trout in *Positioning: The Battle for your Mind*, "Positioning is not what you do to a product. Positioning is what you do to the mind of the prospect. That is, you position the product in the mind of the prospect." Service marketers should work out an effective brand positioning strategy to influence the minds of the people to develop positive perceptions towards the service brand. The identified brand attributes for positioning should be capable of communicating specialized brand values and image identity of the service company.

> **Brand communication** *refers to the communication campaign taken up by the company to propagate brand attributes selected for positioning it in the minds of target consumers. The success of any brand depends on the effectiveness of the brand communication campaign.*

Brand positioning and brand communication are critical to success and, often, most challenging for marketers. Marketing strategies focus basically on three vital issues—segmentation, targeting and positioning, popularly called STP (discussed in Chapter 2). Based on the needs and wants of consumers, marketers segregate them into various segments. They select the segment to be served; target its needs and wants so as to satisfy them. The offer is then so positioned so as to enable the target consumers to perceive it as being distinct from the existing offers. Various features may be used to position a product or a service. These include attributes or benefits; uses or applications; and user class, price or level of quality. Positioning is essentially directed at aligning what the brand can deliver with the needs and wants of the target market.

Frame of Reference

The positioning of the brand requires identification category membership of the brand. Identification category is the group of competing brands to satisfy a consumer need. For example, Lifestyle is in the retail category and Idea is in the telecom category. A brand is positioned keeping in view the target market and the competition in that segment. This constitutes the frame of reference. In other words, the frame of reference refers to the set of brands with which the company brand competes and the service brands which the consumers consider close substitutes. The determination of category membership helps identify the scope of competition and finalize the positioning strategy to get into the consumer's mind. From the competitors' perspective, service companies need to define two important issues in a corporate brand. They are points of difference and points of parity and are described as follows:

- *Points of Difference:* Consumers of a service brand may identify certain attributes or benefits of the brand as exclusive, not found to the same extent in any other competitive brand. These brand benefits establish a distinct brand identity in the minds of the consumer.
- *Points of Parity:* The points of parity, as the name suggests, refer to those attributes and features that a product or a service necessarily shares with its competing brands. Representative of the needs of the target segment, these are also referred to as the minimum expectations of service features in a brand.

Service companies need to establish category membership to set up the right frame of reference. It is necessary to inform the consumers the category membership of the brand before stating its points of difference. As the points of parity are driven by the needs of category membership, it is vital to focus on points of difference. The selected points of difference should be relevant and important to the target consumers. They should convey the superior distinctive factors and also the believability to develop consumer confidence on the ability of the service providers in providing superior distinctive benefits.

Positioning Strategies

Consumers are excessively influenced by many marketing stimulations. The pressure in performing a variety of roles in daily life is not leaving much time and energy for people to go through the details of every offer leisurely. Psychologists found that consumers try to make the processes in the mind simple by not allowing every stimulation into the mind. Selective attention and selective retention are the key strategic moves of the consumers to defend themselves from the high pressure stimulations of the marketers. This type of behaviour requires the marketers to be simple in their message. It's really a big challenge to use a very simple yet effective message to convey what the company wants. Positioning strategy really works in this perspective.

There is no standard rule on how to position a product or a service. The only guiding principle is providing a simple and precise answer to the very basic and fundamental question of the consumer, "Why should I choose your offer?" This may be against a need, value or competition. Smart positioning is that which imprints the brand in the consumer's mind. Further, products and services need to be repositioned to keep up with the dynamic marketing environment. A common framework for product positioning can be taken from a series of questions such as the ones listed here.

Virgin Mobile

Virgin Mobile entered India in partnership with Tata Teleservices. This brand is India's first youth-focused mobile service. It is directed at the youth is evident not only from the brand name, but also from its positioning and service portfolio. Even the tag line—Think *hatke*—is a combination of English and Hindi, which is used by the youth of the country in all their communication, whether verbal or written. Its services are offered through a brand franchise with Tata Teleservices. Virgin Mobile looks into designing, marketing and servicing of the brand. A well-crafted brand communication strategy and correct positioning enabled it to reach out to its target market in a very short time span.

- Who are target customers?
- What is the relevance of our service to their lives?
- What is the key benefit offered?
- How will it fits into their lifestyle?
- How is the service different from that of competitor offers?
- What experience is the brand promising?

A service company may use any of the following themes for positioning of services.

- *Service Attributes:* A company can position the service attributes such as facilitating services and supporting services. State Bank of India positioned its services stating the product attributes as "Pure banking, nothing else" The tag line "With you—all the way"' emphasizes the association of the bank for a long time with the customers and gives an assurance for the future. India Infoline, with the motto "It's all about money, honey!" clearly projects the category membership and its relationship focus with its customers.
- *Service Benefits:* This strategy focuses on the distinctive benefits of using the service to the consumer. ICICI Prudential, for example, used a very powerful metaphor in the Indian context—*sindoor*—for concept selling in life insurance and communicating the generic benefit of protection. The use of the Indian cultural symbol *sindoor* helped the company score high on image parameters such as safety, services and good returns. ECGC's "Don't lose sleep. Dream of the gain." campaign with the message "You focus on exports. We cover the risks." effectively reached out to its target market—exporters. The line "An idea can change your life" used by IDEA cellular projects the company's focus on consumer benefit, thereby endearing itself to the consumer. This was a simple yet powerful statement that enabled IDEA to reach out to millions and create a positive brand image. Another tag line that found its way into the minds of consumers is the Hutch (now known as Vodafone) campaign—Wherever you go, our network follows. Together with highly creative advertisements, this tagline added significant value to the brand, making it one of the top players in the telecom segment.

- *Service Application Positioning:* The service company makes the consumer identify the service need or desire and the suitability of the service offered to satisfy his/her need or desire. For example, naukri.com successfully positioned itself as the best job portal in India by taking up a humorous campaign based on the consumer insight that people do not quit their jobs, but their bosses. The message was clear to the bosses: treat your employees well or Naukri is on the prowl. The focus on empowering employees by offering them more choices attracted the existing employees along with the unemployed youth as well.
- *Service User Positioning:* A service company may identify the target group and position the service as the best for them. For instance, Virgin Mobile positioned its services for the youth of the country. Idea cellular positioned the services for different segments across the society. Banks are positioning many of their services to suit the requirements of specific consumer segments. For example, Andhra Bank offers the Kiddy bank deposit scheme to encourage the saving habit in children. Vanitha Vahan is a loan scheme aimed at women. It has designed priviledge corporate salary savings accounts for salaried individuals.
- *Competitive Positioning:* The positioning may be against the competition or away from the competition. The positioning of IIPM—"Dare to think beyond the IIMs"—helped the institute grow 50 times in turnover in just seven years. This unconventional positioning of educational institutions of the country attracted many management course aspirants.
- *Quality Positioning:* The positioning focuses on quality leadership of the firm. For example, CRISIL, India's leading credit rating company positioned its brand with the value of "unimpeachable credibility and unmatched analytical rigour."
- *Price Positioning:* The positioning is to communicate the best value for the price the consumers pay. The positioning of Big Bazaar—"*Is se sasta aur achha kahin nahi*"—signifying the lowest prices, reached to millions and helped in increasing the sales.
- *Leadership Positioning:* This communicates to the consumers that the service company is a major shareholder in the market and enjoys the acceptance of the majority. Some companies may focus on innovation leadership. At a time when its competitors' strategies focused on network coverage and tariff, Airtel's tagline—"Barriers break when people talk"—helped position it as a company that was willing to be different despite being the leader in the category.
- *Excellence Positioning:* The positioning is on the performance and the efficiency of the firm. Premium hotel groups including the Taj, the Oberoi and ITC use excellence in services as their positioning strategy.

> **Service positioning** *should be very simple in message yet effective enough to convey what the company wanted. Service companies may use service attributes, benefits, applications, quality, leadership or any other feature that has the potential to influence the target consumers to prefer the service.*

Service firms should study, time and again, the effectiveness of their positioning strategy in influencing the consumer's mind. Based on the results they need to initiate appropriate changes in the positioning strategy.

SUMMARY

- Branding is nothing but providing an identity to a service.
- A brand is a name term, sign, symbol or design or a combination of them.
- Different components of a brand are called brand elements.
- Branding is not simply naming a service but providing value beyond normal utility.
- Service branding is different from that of goods branding due to a variety of service attributes that demand a different process.
- The criteria for choosing brand elements include distinctiveness, memorability, likeability, relevance, meaningful, flexibility, adaptability and protectability.
- Service companies generally prefer corporate branding to individual branding.
- Corporate brands reduce the cost of branding, provide a sense of community to the customer, provide a seal of approval and help in symbolizing or labelling the company.
- The six conventions of corporate brand management are brand context, brand construction, brand confirmation, brand consistency, brand continuity and brand conditioning.
- Brand equity is the value of the brand in the market.
- Brand awareness and brand image are the two dimensions of brand equity.
- Positioning means projecting the image of the service distinctively to that of competing brands in the minds of consumers.
- The positioning of a service brand requires identification of category membership of the brand.
- Service companies should identify points of difference and points of parity in their service offer as compared to competitive offers.
- Service companies focus on various factors like service attributes, service benefits, service applications, service user status, competition, quality, price leadership, excellence, etc., for developing positioning strategy.

KEY TERMS

Brand elements *243*
Brand equity *250*
Brand image *252*
Category membership *253*
Corporate branding *248*
Points of difference *254*
Points of parity *254*
Positioning *253*

BRIEF QUESTIONS

1. Explain the importance of branding services.
2. What are the differences between goods and services branding?
3. What is corporate branding?
4. What is brand equity?
5. Explain the concept of service positioning.

ESSAY QUESTIONS

1. "All service brands are corporate brands." Discuss.
2. How do you select the brand elements for service branding?
3. "Building brand equity is critical for service companies." Discuss.
4. Explain the importance of service positioning and various service positioning strategies with examples.
5. "Branding and positioning should go together." Comment.

ASSIGNMENTS

1. Mobile services companies are very active in brand building and positioning. Companies such as Airtel, Idea, Vodafone, BSNL are highly focused on this. You are required to study:
   (a) The positioning strategies of any two companies.
   (b) The consumer perception of such positioning by interviewing 25 customers of these services.
2. Public sector as well as private sector banks promote many financial service products individually with a brand name under the umbrella of the corporate brand name. Whether this move has really helped the banks or not has not been studied so far. You re required to find out the opinion of employees as well as customers:
   (a) Do they perceive distinctive values for individual brands?
   (b) Is there any difference in opinions of employees and customers on value perceptions?

REFERENCES

1 Philip Kotler, et al., *Marketing Management—A South Asian Perspective*, 12th ed. (New Delhi: Pearson Education, 2007) p. 255.

2 Ibid., p. 254.

3 Tom Blackett, "What is a Brand?" in *The Economist: Brands and Branding*, 2nd ed. (New York, NY: Bloomsbury, 2004) p. 3, www.interbrand.com.

4 John Murphy, *Brand Strategy* (New York: Prentice Hall, 1990) p. 4.

5 Leonard L. Berry, et al., "In Services, What's in a Name?" *Harvard Business Review*, (September-October, 1988): 28.

6 Ibid.

7 Ibid.

8 L. de Chernatony and Dall'Olmo Riley, F., "Experts' Views about Defining Services Brands and the Principles of Services Branding," *Journal of Business Research*, 46, no. 2 (1999): 181–192.

9 S. Onkvisit and J. Shaw, "Services Marketing: Image, Branding and Competition, *Business Horizons*, (January–February, 1989): 13–18.

10 Kevin Lane Keller, "The Brand Report Card," *Harvard Business Review*, (January 1, 2007): 147–157.

11 Philip Kotler et al., *Marketing Management—A South Asian Perspective*, 12th ed. (New Delhi: Pearson Education, 2007) p. 264.

12 Mary Jo hatch and Majken Schultz, "Are the Strategic Stars Aligned for Your Corporate Brand?" *Harvard Business Review*, (February, 2001): 130.

13 Ibid., p. 133.

14 Simon Knox and David Bikerton, "The Six Conventions of Corporate Branding," *European Journal of Marketing*, 37, no. 7/8 (2003): 998–1016.

15 Rebecca Colwell, "A Conceptual and Measurement Model for Brand Equity Research," http://www.qsaresearch.com/images/equity.pdf, dated 3-6-2009.

16 Dennis A. Pitta and Lea Prevel Katsanis, "Understanding Brand Equity for Successful Brand Extension," *Journal of Consumer Marketing*, 12, no. 4 (1995): 52.

17 Onkvisit, S. and Shaw, J. J., "Service Marketing: Image, Branding, and Competition," *Business Horizons*, 32, (January–February, 1989): 13–18.

18 M. R. Darby and E. Karni, "Free Competition and the Optimal Amount of Fraud," *Journal of Law and Economics*, 16, (April, 1973): 67–88.

19 Balaji C. Krishnan, "Brand Equity: Is It More Important in Services?" *Journal of Services Marketing*, 15, no. 5 (2001): 328–342.

20 Kevin Lane Keller, *Strategic Brand Management: Building, Measuring, and Managing Brand Equity*, 2nd ed. (New Delhi: Prentice Hall of India Pvt. Ltd., 2003) p. 67.

21 Dennis A. Pitta and Lea Prevel Katsanis, "Understanding Brand Equity for Successful Brand Extension," *Journal of Consumer Marketing*, 12, no. 4 (1995): 53.

22 Ibid., p. 54.

23 Kevin Lane Keller, *Strategic Brand Management: Building, Measuring, and Managing Brand Equity*, 2nd ed. (New Delhi: Prentice Hall of India Pvt. Ltd., 2003): 119–120.

Physical Evidence

13

LEARNING OBJECTIVES

After studying this chapter, you will be able to:

- Understand the importance of physical evidence in services marketing
- Understand the servicescape and its dimensions
- Describe the effects of servicescape on behaviour
- Describe the guidelines for physical evidence strategy

Vidyadhar, a retired employee from a middle-income household, was diagnosed with atherosclerosis. His physician referred him to Sindhu Cardiac Care Centre for a bypass surgery. Considering his economic status, some friends advised him to go to a government hospital where speciality services are offered free of cost for cardiac diseases. Conscious of his constraints, he decided to put in considerable efforts to find evidence that would minimize the inherent risk in choosing a hospital.

Vidyadhar started searching for information on the Web sites of hospitals. He found very little desired information on the government hospital Web site. In contrast, he found the Web sites of the corporate hospitals to be very attractive and informative. The patient feedback was also very useful. Conventional wisdom led Vidyadhar to conclude that the private hospitals provide superfluous information while government hospitals are conservative in communication. Therefore, this information could only be taken as base clue but not as concrete evidence. He decided to visit all these hospitals.

Vidyadhar found the government hospitals to be lacking in hygiene. The buildings, rooms, furniture, walls, inside decors, etc., were in a very bad shape. Employees functioned mechanically, without any concern for the patient. They were simply not involved; their focus was on dispensing with the patients in the least possible time. He noticed that the family of a heart patient admitted to the hospital was quite tense on account of a change in the doctor who had changed all the medicines and the treatment process. Based on this observational experience, Vidyadhar did not opt for the government hospital. A visit to Sindhu Cardiac Care Centre on the following day revealed a completely different scenario. There, every thing was clean and arranged properly. All support facilitates such as medical store, diagnostic services, canteen and lodging were available and well maintained. During his two-hour visit, at least five persons offered help. The family and friends of patients appeared relaxed. The signage was appropriately placed and the ambience was comfortable and pleasant.

Vidyadhar calculated all the factors by evaluating the input variables and finally decided to join Sindhu Cardiac Care Centre for treatment.

Questions:

1. What were the physical evidence clues identified by Vidyadhar before arriving at the purchase decision?
2. Where did the government hospital fail to convince Vidyadhar through physical evidence?
3. Is it necessary to provide evidence to the patients of government hospitals?
4. How can the physical evidence clues be tactically communicated to the consumers?

INTRODUCTION

Every individual considers many variables before taking a purchase decision. The variables that influence a purchase decision vary from product to product, situation to situation and individual to individual. In case of tangible goods, buyers can physically examine the product to assess the quality and suitability; they may also opt for a trial to test the functioning of the product. The purchase decision is taken only after a thorough assessment of the product. In the case of services, such a process is not possible. Services are intangible and also variable. Consumers cannot see, touch or try the service before the purchase. Consumers have to depend upon search quality and experience quality for the assessment of a service. Often, service consumers entertain doubts and suspicions while taking purchase decisions related to services. A salesman of a new company carrying a household article for a door-to-door sales campaign may be received by many and may make good sales. Consumers, who are convinced of the utility of the product, after examining the tangible product, may seek some additional information and negotiate with the salesman regarding the offers proposed by the salesman. However, when a salesman of a new service company goes for a door-to-door sales campaign, his job is far tougher. Consumers may not find it possible to trust the company or the seller sufficiently to get into an agreement. In the service sales deal, nothing is transferred physically and no ownership results. Therefore, physical evidence plays a key role in creating confidence in the consumers of the service. Service companies should use physical evidence as a strategic weapon to convince the customer.

> *"Service consumers search for clues of evidence in the service offer as services are intangible. Service companies should find right means to communicate evidences of service."*

THE CONCEPT OF PHYSICAL EVIDENCE

Physical evidence is everything that a company physically exhibits to the customer. It includes the physical environment of the service outlet, the exterior, the interior, all tangibles such as machinery, furniture, vehicles, stationery, signboards, communication materials, certificates, receipts, service personnel and so on. Physical evidence provides tangible cues to customers to develop service quality expectations. "Physical evidence is often referred to as the environment that facilitates the performance and the communication of the service."[1] It is a fact that service consumers cannot see a service but they can visualize various tangibles associated with the service. These tangibles serve as clues for the service that is invisible and help the consumers to grasp various aspects of the service. Particularly, tangible cues help in assessing the quality of the service provided. Thus, individuals' perceptions of a hotel lobby tend to be based on not only the front desk, but also many other elements such as the employees and customers, the lighting, floors, furniture, artwork and colour of the walls. The lobby is also assessed on the basis of sensory inputs such as music and fragrance. All these elements contribute to the formation of customers' image of the lobby. Furthermore, in evaluating the entire property, individuals also include the exterior architecture, as opposed to only the interior decor. Both the exterior and interior of the hotel reflect the style and image of its physical environment and influence customers' evaluations.[2]

> **Physical evidence** *is what a company physically exhibits to customers. It includes the physical environment of the service outlet, the exterior, the interior, all tangibles such as equipment, furniture, vehicles, stationary, signage, certificates, receipts, service personnel and so on.*

ELEMENTS OF PHYSICAL EVIDENCE

The elements of physical evidence can be broadly referred to as the physical environment of the service unit and other tangibles. Services are predominantly intangible processes, and consequently, service consumption is an experiential phenomenon. The environmental conditions of the service location facilitate consumption experience to service consumers. "Psychologists began to study during early 20th century the human perception of environmental stimuli such as light, sound, weight, and pressure. The study of the interrelationship between physical environment and human behaviour advanced with the emergence of environmental psychology."[3] The environmental design needs to be neutral enough to please everybody as the service outlet is meant to serve a wide variety of people. The spatial dimensions of a physical setting are capable of creating moods and influencing behavioural intentions. The internal layout of the physical space, for example, may either ease or restrict the movement of the consumers. It may evoke a sense of either crowding when the space is conservatively designed or spacious when it is liberally designed. The conservatively designed space layout often creates confined conditions and makes customers feel uncomfortable. The physical environment of a service unit is popularly called *servicescape*."

The Concept of a Servicescape

A servicescape represents the physical environment designed in a service outlet. Research studies have proven that the design of the servicescape influences customers' choice, expectations, satisfaction and other related behaviour. The nature of the service activity and the service-consumption experience sought by consumers influences the design of a servicescape. The concept of a servicescape was first developed by B. Booms and M. J. Bitner.[4] They defined *servicescape* as "the environment in which the service is assembled and in which seller and consumer interact, combined with tangible commodities that facilitate performance or communication of the service". "The servicescape is the outward appearance of the organization and thus can be critical in forming initial impressions or setting up customer expectations—it is a visual metaphor for the intangible service."[5]

The term *servicescape* is widely used to describe physical surroundings of a service company. The exterior and interior design of the service outlet, the ambience which includes temperature, tangibles, noise, odour and the signage used for communication are parts of the servicescape. The perceived servicescape can have an effect on people's beliefs about a place and about the people and products found in that place. In a sense, the servicescape can be viewed as a form of non-verbal communication, imparting meaning through

The Taj Lake Palace

The Taj Lake Palace located at Udaipur is reminiscent of the world-famous Taj Mahal with white marble and mosaic. All care has been taken to design the servicescape of this five-star, deluxe hotel right from the choice of location to the design of exterior, interior and many facilities and services to create delightful experiences to consumers. With the Aravalli mountains on the one side of the lake and lofty palaces on the other, the location gives the hotel a feel of royal elegance. The design of rooms and suites, with richly coloured murals and ornately carved wood furniture, is opulent. A variety of dining experiences in different restaurants is offered to the customers. The physical environment and other tangibles of the hotel have been designed not only to facilitate the service processes but also to create right frame of mind in the consumers to perceive quality of the service. The ambience, elegance, style, furnishings, spatial comfort and signage are perfectly blended to create a holistic quality experience to the customers.

what is called "objective language."[6] Servicescape, thus, is a man-made built environment to facilitate service processes to take place smoothly and effectively. The design of servicescape basically should take into consideration two important aspects: spatial layout and functionality, and aesthetic appeal. Spatial layout and functionality refer to the ways in which seats, equipment, furnishings and entrances and exits are designed and arranged. Aesthetic appeal refers to factors such as the surrounding external environment, architectural specialities, cleanliness and upkeep of facilities, signage, etc., that influence customers' perception and evaluation. These two sets of factors will influence the thoughts and feelings (emotional and physical) which ultimately lead them to display the behaviour of either approach or avoid the service outlet.

> *A* ***servicescape*** *is the man-made physical surrounding where service production and consumption processes take place. Spatial layout and functionality, and aesthetic appeal are the two critical factors in its design*

"Perceived quality of the servicescape is an issue that should be of concern (at least to some degree) to most service marketers. On the vertical axis, this typology of services proposes that, the longer one spends in a facility, the greater the likelihood that the perceived quality of the servicescape will play an important role in determining satisfaction with the service. The perceived quality of the servicescape may be an important determinant of customer satisfaction in situations where the customer spends an extended period of time observing and experiencing the servicescape."[7]

Types of Servicescapes

Service companies design servicescapes based on the nature of interactions required for the service production and delivery. The basic principle that guides the design is user friendliness. Therefore, service companies should first identify the users of the servicescape. Based on usage, servicescapes can be classified into three types—self-service, interpersonal service and remote service.

1. *Self-service:* In a self-service environment, the customer performs most of the activities, and very few employees are involved. ATMs, fast-food centres and movie theatres are examples of self-service environments. If the service firm is focussing on a self-service environment, it has to attract the right market segment and offer easy-to-use facilities.

2. *Interpersonal Services*: In this type of servicescape, both employees and customers are given adequate importance. In the case of hospitals, educational institutions and banks, the servicescape must be planned to attract, satisfy and facilitate both employees and customers simultaneously. The servicescape should contribute to social interactions between and among customers and employees.
3. *Remote Service*: In some services, the customer's physical involvement in the servicescape may be very little or even absent. Mail order services, consultancy services, telecommunications and the like can be provided without the customer ever seeing the service facilities. In such servicescape designs, only employees' needs and preferences are considered. The goal of the servicescape is to keep employees motivated and to facilitate productivity, team work and operational efficiency.

> *Servicescapes can be classified into three categories. In a self-service environment, customers use more space of the servicescape. In interpersonal services, both the employees and customers use more space. In remote services, more space is provided for employees' operations.*

The design of a servicescape has a lot of implications on organizational performance. The servicescape is the appearance of the organization. It has a critical role to play in forming initial impressions and in setting up customer expectations. It also serves as a facilitator in supporting the performance of a person in the environment. The influence of physical environment on consumer behaviour and in creating image is apparent in services such as hotels, restaurants, banks, retail stores, hospitals, professional offices and beauty centres. Since consumers participate in service production at the service outlet, they experience the total service within the firm's physical facility. A well-designed servicescape can make the service easier for both customers and employees to achieve their respective goals. It facilitates the smooth flow of service processes, speedily and efficiently. It also makes work a pleasure to perform for both. The socialization process for both employees and customers can also be achieved through the servicescape as it helps to convey expected roles, behaviours and relationships. Servicescape can also be used as a differentiator to position the service in the market as against competition.

Servicescape Dimensions

Service companies often introduce changes in physical surroundings to create an impression of newness. Many companies, however, initiate changes without properly understanding the impact of changes in design of servicescape on the ultimate users of the service facility. Critical analysis of various dimensions and a strategic approach are necessary to design servicescape to achieve desired results. Figure 13.1 presents a list of servicescape dimensions that will influence the behaviour of people involved in the service process. Broadly, three dimensions[8] are identified in the physical environment, which are capable of influencing the customers as well as employers for approach or avoidance behaviours. The three dimensions are:

> *The three dimensions of servicescape are ambience, space and functional conditions and signs, symbols and artefacts. A critical analysis of these three dimensions and a strategic approach is necessary to design servicescape in order to achieve desired results.*

1. Ambient conditions
2. Space/function
3. Signs, symbols and artefacts

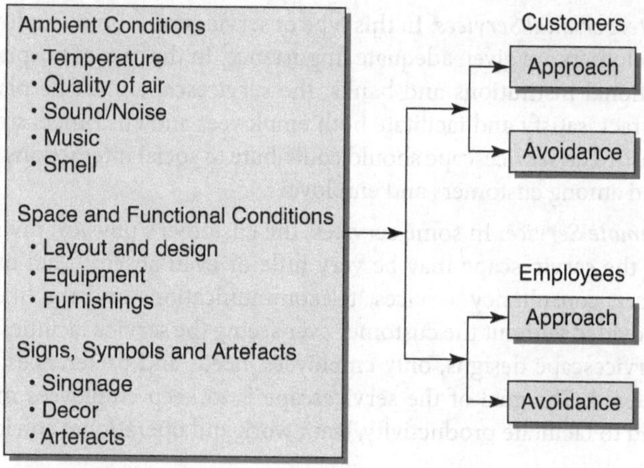

Fig. 13.1 Servicescape dimensions

Ambient Conditions

Ambience represents the surrounding or persuading atmosphere of a servicescape. Ambient conditions are those characteristics of the environment pertaining to our five senses. Even when not consciously noted, they may still affect people's emotional well-being, perceptions and even attitudes and behaviours. "The ambient environment, or atmosphere, composed of literally hundreds of design elements and details that have to work together to create the desired service environment."[9] The following are the important ambient conditions that may influence human behaviour at the service environment:

- *Temperature:* The temperature that exists in service environments has the capability to influence behaviours. In an air-conditioned environment, both employers and customers feel comfortable. In a non-air-conditioned environment, seasonal influences on temperature affect the behaviour. In summer, the temperature would be above normal and during winter it is below normal in many parts of India. The variation in temperature creates inconvenience to the consumers and employees. It influences the approach, stay, waiting and also social interactions.
- *Quality of Air:* The quality of service interaction will be greatly influenced by the quality of air. No smell, foul smell, dust and fresh air will attract different reactions from the people. An assurance of pollution-free air can also become a selling proposition for service companies.
- *Noise:* The noise level ranging from absolute silence to high-decibel sounds will have an influence on the behaviour. Noise may be internal or external. If the noise is internal, but unavoidable (noise generated in operating machines for service processes), care must be taken to reduce the effect by using sound-proof material or keeping the customer contact point away from the sound generator place. If it is from outside, it is better to avoid such a location or to use sound-proof material to minimize the disturbance. "Noise and loudness of sound have usually been

perceived as irritating and annoying. Two components of sound are volume (loudness), which relates to amplitude or height of sound waves, and pitch, which is the frequency of sound waves. Loudness is perceived as negative stimulation, especially when the sound is unexpected or is subjectively perceived as undesirable. Too much sound may result in decreased concentration, increased activity, irritability and tension."[10]

- *Music:* Music is a very powerful stimulator of feelings in human beings. People have different preferences in music. Some like classical, some like western, some like old and some like new. If music is arranged, while taking into consideration the preferences of the customer groups, positive behaviour can be expected. In a servicescape, guests take note of music and noise as auditory components of their evaluations. "Studies on music and consumer behaviour have demonstrated that music can be used as an effective tool to minimize the negative consequences of waiting in any service operation."[11]
- *Smell:* People have different likings as far as smell is concerned. A right combination makes the environment pleasant.

Space/Function

The living space and functional support facilities form an important part of the servicescape. The following are the influencing factors with regard to space/function on the behaviour of employees and customers:

- *Layout and Design:* The service environments are intended to fulfil the needs and specific purposes of the customers. Therefore, spatial layout that facilitates functionality is an important requirement. Spatial layout refers to the ways in which machinery, equipment and furnishings are arranged and the size and shape of those items and the relationship among them.
- *Equipment:* Service firms should acquire such equipment that facilitates the accomplishment of customer and employee goals. In self-service environments, particularly, the equipment should be of state-of-the-art technology and customer friendly.
- *Furnishings:* The provision of furnishings, their quality and maintenance has an impact on the behaviour of the people who use them. "The furnishings in a servicescape link the space with its occupants and convey the personality of the servicescape through form, line, colour, texture and scale. The furniture placement may convey a sense of enclosure, define spatial movement, function as walls and communicate visible or invisible boundaries. Recognizable changes in ceiling heights affect spatial perception more than a similar change in room width or length. High ceilings convey feelings of spaciousness, whereas low ceilings are associated with coziness and intimacy."[12]
- *Colour*: "Colour is one of the important visual cues in a servicescape. Colour is stimulating, calming, expressive, disturbing, impressionable, cultural, exuberant and symbolic. It pervades every aspect of our lives, embellishes the ordinary and gives beauty and drama to everyday

objects."[13] Colour influences the moods and emotions of the service consumers and thereby their attitude towards the service and their perceptions of service experiences. "Research has shown that different colours stimulate varying personal moods and emotions. In evaluating a servicescape, this visual sensory input includes forming a mental picture through cognitive processing prior to affecting individuals' personal moods and emotions."[14] "Services Marketing Insight: Impact of Colour on Consumer Behaviour" provides more details on this topic.

- *Lighting*: Lighting is yet another influencer of consumer perception. It provides cues for defining and perceiving the quality of space and influence consumers' awareness of physical, psychological and spiritual aspects of servicescape. "Environmental psychology has assessed the relationship

13.1 Services Marketing Insight | **The Impact of Colour on Consumer Behaviour**

A popular strategy for the influence of consumer choice is the colour. Colour can stimulate interest and subsequently increase the saleability of services. White has been associated with peace and purity and red the colour of blood representing strength, health and passion. Light blue of the sky is the colour associated with calmness and with healing. Purple is the colour associated with royalty for its rarity and expense. Green is cool. Yellow is the feeling of joyousness and brightness. Colours have both scientific significance and relevance to service providers.

Perception of the relative size and appearance of a space is often related to colour. The following are some generalities to remember about colour, human perception and aesthetics.

- Certain colours may make a space appear larger than it actually is, while others cause spaces to appear smaller.
- Certain colours may cause a space to seem warm, while others may make it seem cold.
- Colours have a definite effect on the mood of the observer. Some colours are stimulating, others are relaxing.
- Colours that clash with each other may produce feelings of irritation or uneasiness.

Light affects the perception of colours. Whether it is the colour of walls in a restaurant or retail stores, it is usually electrical lighting that allows colours to be seen. Colour is related to culture and religion. Orange is the most sacred colour in Hindu religion in India. Muslims view green as a sacred colour.

There are differences in the perception of colours between genders. Research suggests that men were more tolerant of grey, white and black than women. Women reacted to the combination of red and blue more frequently and got confused and distracted more than men. The combination of red and blue was the most preferred colour by adults.

The red colour stimulates appetite because of its effect on our metabolism, making red a popular colour choice among fast-food restaurants. The yellow colour is also employed by fast-food moguls to hijack customers' interests—they gain customers' attention, increase their appetite, and encourage them to eat. This is the best way for fast-food companies to generate sales. By contrast, formal restaurants use blue colour to calm and relax their customers.

Source: Satyendra Singh, Impact of Colour on Marketing, Management Decision, *44, no. 6 (2006): 783–789.*

between light intensity and task productivity, revealing that people's perceptions of light influence their perceptions of the environment."[15]

> Colour is one of the key visual clues. Different colours stimulate different moods and emotions. Lighting also impacts the human behaviour. The perception of light by the consumer influences their perception of the environment.

Signs, Symbols and Artefacts

Sign boards displayed on the exterior or interior provide explicit communication. These can be used to communicate rules, directions, cautions, processes, layout details and so on. Signs provide relief to such customers who are poor communicators or are not comfortable interacting with others. Signs can also be used to reduce perceived crowding.

The quality of the materials used in the construction of physical structures at work, the presence of certificates and photographs, the floor coverings and architectural values communicate symbolic meanings and create an aesthetic impression. Signs, symbols and artefacts influence the formation of the first impressions of customers. Sign boards displayed on the exterior or interior provide explicit communication. When customers are not familiar with the service environment, they look for environmental clues for initial help.

Servicescape Effects on Behaviour

"Customers frequently use the service environment as an important quality proxy, and service firms take great pains to signal quality and to portray the desired image."[16] A servicescape design influences human behaviour. Psychologists have established relationships between human beings and built environments. "Environmental psychologists suggest that individuals react to places with two general, and opposite, forms of behaviour: approach and avoidance. Approach behaviours include all positive behaviours that might be directed at a particular place, such as desire to stay, explore, work, and affiliate."[17] Avoidance behaviours on the other hand reflect negative orientation towards service organization. In other words, they reflect in behaviours like a desire not to stay, explore, work, affiliate, etc. Service firms want to encourage approach behaviour by creating a nice environment for both customers and employees to carry out their plans. It is necessary at the same time to discourage avoidance behaviours.

> A servicescape affects the behaviour of consumers as well as employees. Individuals react to places with two opposite forms of behaviour—approach and avoidance. Service firms encourage approach behaviour and discourage avoidance behaviour.

Stimulus–Organism–Response (SOR) Model

A. Mehrabian and J. A. Russell's stimulus-organism-response (SOR) model[18] establishes the relationship between environmental factors and consumer response. Specifically, environmental stimuli are said to affect the emotional states of pleasure and arousal, which, in turn, affect approach/avoidance behaviours. Pleasure is a feeling state that is similar to liking but also correlates with arousal. Arousal is also conceptualized as a feeling state varying along a single dimension ranging from sleep to frantic excitement. The stimulus factors are physical features (e.g., colour, store layout, lighting, music, ambient factors). The emotional states are induced by the physical environment in terms of pleasure or arousal. Approach behaviours include a willingness—or desire—to move around and explore the store (e.g., propensity to buy). Contrary to approach responses, avoidance behaviours are an outgrowth of negative feelings about a service place, manifested by an unwillingness to purchase. The physical environment has an impact on the behaviour of both customers and employees. Interestingly, in service organizations, the same physical setting that communicates with and influences customers may affect employees of the firm.[19] Three kinds of internal responses get generated in employees and customers while interacting. They are cognitive, emotional and physiological responses. Cognitive responses are influenced by beliefs. In other words, they are influenced by the way in which an individual categorizes the stimulation and develops symbolic meanings for the stimuli. Emotional responses are influenced by the moods and attitudes of the individual against the service firm. "Physiological responses include pain, comfort, movement and physical fitness. The interplay of these factors finally results in customer response or employee response. Environmental psychology has made a valuable contribution to the investigation of service places, and the role of physical settings on the customers' behaviours and attitudes."[20] The physical environment plays an instrumental role in the assessment of the quality and level of service expected by consumers. Therefore, physical environment is crucial in customer satisfaction, particularly, in the case of restaurants, retail stores and banks. The influence of visual merchandising in retail service outlets is discussed in "Services Marketing Insight: Using Visual Merchandising to Influence Customer Perceptions at Retail Service Outlet".

Socialization of Servicescapes

Social interaction is a critical dimension of physical environment. The servicescape influences the nature and quality of customer–employee interactions. Physical environments represent a subset of social rules, conventions and expectations of consumers as well as employers and provide a social platform for interactions. Environmental variables such as physical proximity and seating arrangements have an influence on customer–employee interactions and also customer–customer interactions. Individual behaviours are seen as the interaction with the customer's physical environment and that occurring between employee and customers, known as social interactions. "The dimensions of the physical surroundings include all the objective physical factors that can be controlled by the firm to enhance (or constrain) employee and customer actions."[21] Research studies have confirmed that the environmental conditions influence such social behaviours as small group interactions, friendship formation, participation, aggression, withdrawal and helping. A sociological perspective also offers potential advancement in understanding service settings. Various factors including the number, appearance and behaviour of employees, and the quality and number of other customers have a psychological impact on the social behaviour of the customers.

The issues identified above suggest the importance of physical environment and emphasize the need for the development of an ideal environment. Servicescapes are not only an important component of a customer's impression formation but also serve as evidence in the overall evaluation servicescape and service organization in general. Evaluation and prediction of what the consumer will think or feel and how they will behave in response to the stimuli of the physical environment is important in designing the physical environment.

13.2 Services Marketing Insight

Using Visual Merchandising to Influence Consumer Perceptions at Retail Service Outlets

Visual merchandising is the art and science of presenting the service package in the most attractive way possible. It is everything the customer sees, both exterior and interior, that creates a positive image of a business and results in attention, interest, desire and action on the part of the customer. It includes the dramatic presentation of merchandise and other features to create the store's overall atmospheres. Eighty per cent of our impressions are created by sight; that is why one picture is worth a thousand words. Each customer has a mental image of a store and its merchandise. An inviting appearance of a store makes the customer feel comfortable and yet eager to buy. The interior and exterior of the store should be coordinated according to the overall theme of the store. It is necessary to continually determine what the customer sees for creating and maintaining a store's visual merchandising plan. Evaluation from the customer's perspective should start on the exterior and work completely through the interior of the store.

The 12 ideas for visual merchandising:

1. ***Take It Outside:*** Set up a display of merchandise outside the store to create a sense of excitement. A street faire environment with flags and balloons attracts customers.
2. ***Identify Everything:*** Use signage to identify departments and categories to facilitate customers to identify easily the desired products and inspire additional purchases.
3. ***Set the Mood with Your Windows:*** Use store windows to set the mood of the customers according to the event like excitement, family fun, romance, etc.
4. ***Embrace all the Senses:*** Send right messages through music, scents and other environmental factors either directly or indirectly.
5. ***Show Them How it Will Look at Home:*** Demonstrate the merchandise with natural settings to create a home atmosphere to the customer.
6. ***Group Like with Like:*** Organize the store logically. Create grouping with categories based on colour, types, price or size.
7. ***Group by Lifestyle:*** Categorize and display using lifestyle-based themes.
8. ***Use the Spotlight:*** Use lighting to attract customers to key pieces of merchandise.
9. ***Change Your Displays often:*** Customers don't comeback to boring stores. Plan to change displays once in a week.
10. ***Don't Be Afraid of Colour:*** Plan displays around a central colour that captures attention of customers. Change colours every week.
11. ***Integrate Motion:*** Merchandise that moves will catch the eye. Let customers observe the working of the merchandise.
12. ***Remember the Rule of Three:*** Create a display in sets of three, which may be in the order of size, price, width, length, quality, etc.

Source: www.theretailersadvantage.com

Other Tangibles

The tangibles used in service processes have the potential to influence the quality perceptions of the consumers. The stationary used, the reports, brochures, billing statements, etc., are usually the parts of a service. These tangibles though look very simple and constitute a minor part of a service, play an important role in creating perceptions in the consumers either directly or indirectly. The presentability of the employees is another important factor.

SBI

The State Bank of India took up business process reengineering in 2005 to simplify transaction processing and administration work load at branch level. The branch redesign involved a change in roles of various functionaries and changes in the internal layout with the objective of providing multiple benefits to customers and employees. Clear communication of roles of the employees, increased focus on sales and shifting of non-customer facing activities out of the branch were the three major principles of the redesign. The measures included the introduction of:

- Single-window operators (SWOs) to handle all service transactions where transaction time is of prime importance
- Customer relations officers (CROs) to handle transactions with significant interaction and opportunity to cross-sell
- Service manager (upgraded role of accountant) in charge of the service section of the branch, Case managers added if the work of service manager exceeds one man-day
- Full-time cash officer in currency chest branches. In hand balance branches, role to be played by the senior SWO
- Grahak Mitra as first touch point for customers

The changes initiated in the redesign process were intended to benefit all the three important pillars of bank marketing—customers, employees and the bank. Customers benefited from the help and guidance offered by the Grahak Mitra at the entry point, the reduced waiting time, the convenience offered by single-window operators, the enlarged and friendlier customer area and the improved ambience. The employees benefited by way of greater specialization of skills, fewer roles and better team spirit. Following the completion of the reengineering process, the impact of sudden absenteeism of the staff members on customer service has been significantly reduced as the multi-skilling of staff helps in balancing the work load and improving productivity.

The dressing pattern, appearance and interactions of the employees provide vital clues to the consumers on physical evidence. To have an identity and to ensure presentability, some service companies prescribe uniforms to their employees. The employees of airline services and hospitality services generally use uniforms.

ROLE OF EVIDENCE IN SERVICES MARKETING

In services marketing, physical evidence plays a definitive role in influencing the perceptions of customers and employees by exposing them to the critical objects of the servicescape. Individuals do not evaluate a specific servicescape based on only one environmental stimulus. They combine all discrete pieces to form a holistic picture. A. Parasuraman and L. L. Berry[22] identified six specific roles of evidence as presented in Fig. 13.2.

1. *Shaping First Impressions:* Consumers form initial impressions once they are exposed to the exterior and interior of a service outlet. The first flash quickly creates an impression on the service provider. Such first

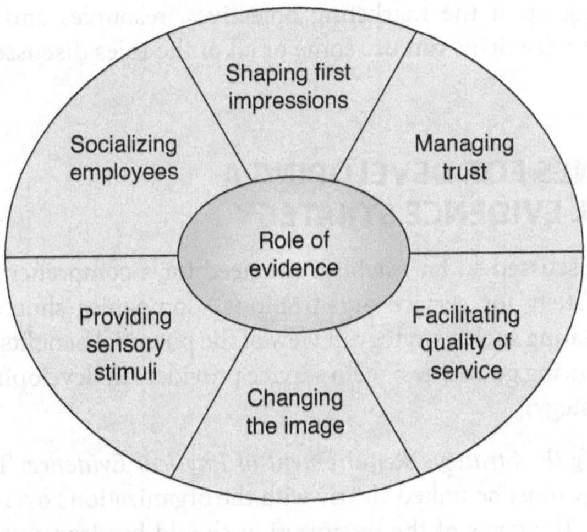

Fig. 13.2
Roles of evidence in services marketing

impressions condition the mind and influence perception of the situations that follow in the service process. The service provider, thus, finds an opportunity to shape the first impressions of the consumers through the physical settings of the service outlet.

2. *Managing Trust:* Physical environment and the tangibles used in service processes stand as clues to consumers. The positive clues will clarify the doubts and suspicions of the consumers and build trust. The consistency in quality of the physical settings will help in managing the consumer trust.
3. *Facilitating Quality of Service:* A good servicescape facilitates employee–customer participation in the service production, delivery and consumption process. It makes sure all kinds of support facilities are present in the order and function as desired. The ambience itself has the capacity to stimulate positive moods and emotions to people engaged in service process.
4. *Changing the Image:* A change in the physical environment has the potential to change the image of the service outlet and the service provider. The up-scaling of facilities and structures like conversion of non-A/C to A/C, additional moving space to customers, new decors, new lighting systems, new dress code to contact employees, new systems, new way of reception, new machines, etc., contributes for the change of the image of the service provider.
5. *Providing Sensory Stimuli:* The aesthetics of the service environment has the potential to stimulate the senses. Such stimulations support the customer in participation of service production and in quality perceptions.
6. *Socializing Employees:* Many services need employee–employee cooperation and coordination in creating quality experiences to the customers. Servicescape facilitates employee interactions formally and informally and helps in developing social bondage among them.

> *Physical evidence shapes first impressions of consumers, manages trust between the service provider and customers, facilitates quality service processes, contributes towards changing the image of the service provider, provides sensory stimulations and creates a sociable environment.*

Depending upon the marketing objectives, resources and competitive situations, service firms can use some or all of the roles discussed earlier for evidence.

GUIDELINES FOR DEVELOPING A PHYSICAL EVIDENCE STRATEGY

> *The management should identify the strategic requirement of physical evidence while designing the physical evidence strategy. Service blueprinting provides absolute clarity to identify the areas wherein physical evidence attributes can be incorporated effectively.*

The issues discussed so far establish the need for a comprehensive physical evidence strategy for service organizations. Companies should be careful while formulating such a strategy in view of the potential benefits of this strategy. The following guidelines[23] help service providers in developing a physical evidence strategy:

1. *Identify the Strategic Requirement of Physical Evidence*: The evidence strategy must be linked clearly with the organization's overall goals and vision. The goals of the organization should be clearly understood so as to determine the kind of support that can be built through evidence strategy. The vision of the firm provides an understanding of the future. Most of the evidence decisions are costly and have long-term consequences. Therefore, the vision of the organization should be kept in mind.
2. *Decide the Kind of Physical Evidence Required*: Prior to designing the servicescape, it is necessary to decide what kind of physical evidence is required and what its role in services marketing is. Service blueprinting should be carried out to have absolute clarity over organizational service process, placement of equipment, furniture and other support material, people and other environmental features.
3. *Clarify Roles of Employees and Customers in the Servicescape*: The identification and definition of the roles to be played by employees and customers, machines and other elements in the servicescape aid in identifying opportunities and deciding who needs to be consulted in making decisions.
4. *Identify and Assess Physical Evidence Opportunities*: All service firms need to look for possibilities of introducing changes and improvements in the forms of evidence and the roles of the servicescape. What are the perceptions of the customers and employees on the physical evidence? What are missed opportunities? What are the defects in the present evidence strategy? Such questions need to be answered periodically to identify the opportunities that can be exploited.
5. *Update and Modernize Evidence:* Some aspects of evidence require frequent or periodic updating and modernizing. Service firms should be prepared to introduce changes as per the requirements of the market. The orientation to change makes the service firm innovative and capable of influencing the perceptions of the customers much better than its competitors.

SUMMARY

- Service companies should provide physical evidence to build confidence in consumers with respect to quality, reliability and other parameters.
- The absence of physical evidence is likely to create doubts and suspicions in the minds of consumers.
- The physical environment, the social environment and the tangibles are important constituents of physical evidence.
- Designing a servicescape, taking into consideration all the three parameters, will have an impact on consumer as well as employee behaviour.
- Servicescapes are of three types: self-service, interpersonal service and remote service.
- Ambient conditions, space/functionality and signs, symbols and artefacts are the three dimensions of a servicescape.
- Environmental psychologists found that service environments influence the behaviour of employees and consumers either positively or negatively.
- Social interaction is an important dimension of the physical environment.
- The nature of business, the mode of operations, the target market, the positioning strategies and the marketing objectives are the inputs for developing a physical evidence strategy.

KEY TERMS

Ambient conditions *264*
Cognitive responses *268*
Emotional responses *269*
Physiological responses *268*
Servicescapes *262*

BRIEF QUESTIONS

1. What is physical evidence?
2. Explain the influence of ambient conditions on behaviour.
3. What is the role of physical evidence in services marketing?

ESSAY QUESTIONS

1. What is the importance of physical evidence in services marketing?
2. What are the behavioural influences of servicescapes on employees and customers?
3. How can physical evidence be managed?
4. What are the guidelines for the development of a physical evidence strategy?

ASSIGNMENTS

1. Physical environment plays an important role in the hospitality industry. The guests' experience and quality perceptions are influenced by several features of the physical environment. You are required to select a star-rated hotel to:
   (a) Study the physical environment design and critical points of consumer interaction with the environment
   (b) Collate and analyse the opinion of a few customers of the hotel on the physical environment
2. DLF is India's largest real estate company in terms of revenues, earnings, market capitalization and developable area. In line with its current expansion plans, DLF has over 425 million sq. ft. of development across its businesses, including developed, on-going and planned projects. This land bank spans 32 cities, mostly in metros and key urban areas across India. DLF, with over six decades of experience, is capitalizing on emerging market opportunities to deliver high-end facilities and projects to its wide base of customers.
   (a) What are the evidences the company is communicating to the customers?
   (b) What are the sources of evidence to the consumers?

REFERENCES

1 P. Eiglier and E. Langeard, *Servuction, Strategie et Management,* (Paris: McGraw-Hill, 1987).
2 Ingrid Y. Lin, Evaluating a Servicescape: The Effect of Cognition and Emotion, *Hospitality Management,* 23 (2004): 165.
3 F. Gulliver, Orientation of Maps, *Journal of Geography,* 7 (1908): 55–58.
4 B. Booms and M. J. Bitner, Marketing Strategies and Organization Structures for Service Firms, in *Marketing of Services,* edited by J. H. Donnelly and W.R. George, (Chicago, IL: American Marketing Association, 1981) pp. 47–52.
5 V. A. Zeithaml et al., *Services Marketing,* 4th ed. (New Delhi: McGraw-Hill, 2008) p. 334.
6 Ibid, p. 340.
7 Kirk L. Wakefield and Jeffrey G. Blodgett, "The Importance of Servicescapes in Leisure Service Settings," *Journal of Services Marketing,* 8, no. 3 (1994): 66–76.
8 Mary Jo Bitner, "Servicescapes: The Impact of Physical Surroundings on Customers and Employees," *Journal of Marketing,* 56 (April 1992): 57–71.
9 Patrick M. Dunne, Robert F. Lusch and David A. Giffith, *Retailing,* 4th ed. (Orlando, FL: Harcourt, 2002) p. 518.
10 K. D. Kryter, *The Effect of Noise on Man,* 2nd ed. (Orlando, FL: Academic Press, 1985).
11 M. K. Hui, L. Dube, J. Chebat, "The Impact of Music on Consumers' Reactions to Waiting for Services," *Journal of Retailing,* 73, no. 1 (1997): 87–104.
12 F. Ching, *Architecture: Form, Space, and Order* (New York: Van Nostrand, 1996).
13 Linda Holtzschuhe, *Understanding Colour – An Introduction for Designers,* 2nd ed. (New York: John Wiley, 2002) p. 1.
14 Ingrid Y. Lin, "Evaluating a Servicescape: The Effect of Cognition and Emotion," *Hospitality Management,* 23 (2004): 168.
15 Ibid.
16 Christopher Lovelock, Jochen Wirtz and Jayanta Chatterjee, *Services Marketing,* 5th ed. (New Delhi: Pearson Education, 2009) p. 269.
17 A. Mehrabian and James A. Russel, *An Approach to Environmental Psychology* (Cambridge, MA: Massachusetts Institute of Technology, 1974).
18 Ibid.
19 Barker, Leonard L. Berry and A. Parasuraman, "The Marketing Impact of Branch Facility Design," *Journal of Retail Banking,* 10, no. 2, (1988): 33–42.
20 Véronique Aubert-Gamet, "Twisting Servicescapes: Diversion of the Physical Environment in a Re-appropriation Process," *International Journal of Service Industry Management,* 8, no. 1 (1997): 26–41.
21 M. Bitner, "Servicescapes: The Impact of Physical Surroundings on Customers and Employees," *Journal of Marketing,* 56 (1992): 57–71.
22 A. Parsuraman and Leonard L. Berry, *Marketing Services: Competing Through Quality* (New York: Free Press, 1991) p. 94.
23 V. A. Zeithaml, M. J. Bitner, D. D. Gremler and A. Pandit, *Services Marketing,* 4th ed. (New Delhi: McGraw-Hill, 2008) pp. 348–350.

Pricing

14

LEARNING OBJECTIVES

After studying this chapter, you will be able to:

- Understand the distinctions between goods and services pricing
- Understand the objectives of pricing
- Understand the pricing approaches
- Understand value-based pricing strategies

Alfa Academy is a private educational institute offering short-term training, counseling programmes and placement services to students. The institute was established in 2000 and expanded its network of institutions to various places. Seventy-five franchisee institutions offer programmes under the brand of Alfa Academy. Many programmes are customized, and some programmes are standardized. The institution has earned a reputation for the quality of its programmes. However, competition from various institutions in all the places where the institution or its franchisees are present is creating marketing problems. The background of customers and the intensity of competition have compelled the institute to follow variable pricing. The fee is decided based on negotiations with the service seeker, making fee finalization an important process both for the manager of the institute and the students. The close ones of many students also participate in the negotiation process. Further, the variations in fees for different students of the same programme have resulted in mixed perceptions of the institution.

The manager of one of the branches of the Alfa academy, Mr. Joseph is not happy with this system of pricing. Sometimes the institute accepts students at a low fee with a lot of vacancies left over; at other times, when negotiations fail, people bad mouth the pricing system . Many a time, despite the fact that students turn up in sufficient numbers by the end of the closing date of the programmes, the services are sold at very low prices on account of the uncertainty in demand. Franchisee institutes pose another problem. Alfa takes the records of fee of the franchisees as true statements to calculate its share in the profits. Informal enquiries have revealed that many franchisees take advantage of this pricing policy and submit false reports. Joseph has decided to change this pricing system. He has called for a meeting of the Board of Management to discuss and finalize the new pricing policy of the institute.

Questions:

1. What are the factors influencing the pricing of the services offered by the institute?
2. Is the problem related to the pricing policy or execution of the pricing system?
3. What are the alternative pricing strategies available to the institute?
4. Do you think discriminatory pricing is suitable for this institute?

INTRODUCTION

Price is the medium for exchange of value between a buyer and a seller. It is an influencing factor in consumer decision making, related to a purchase. Whether it is a high- or low-priced good or service or whether the customer belongs to high-income group or to middle- or low-income group, the influence of price in a purchase decision cannot be overemphasized. The only difference is in the degree of its influence. Several services use a different terminology to denote price. For educational institutions, it is tuition fees; for professional organizations, it is fees; in banks, it is interest and service charge; for transporters, it is fare; for bridges and highways, it is toll and for libraries and clubs, it is subscription. We pay commission to brokers, rent to landlords, tariff to utilities and hotels, premium to insurance companies and so on.

Service organizations should have strategies for arriving at pricing decisions. In services marketing mix, price is the only "p" that generates inflow of revenues to the company while all others are associated with costs. "If effective product development, promotion and distribution sow the seeds of business success, effective pricing is the harvest."[1] According to D. D. Shipley and D. Jobber, price management is a critical element in the marketing and competitive strategy and a key determinant of performance. Price is the measure by which customers judge the value of an offering, and it strongly impacts brand selection among competing alternatives.[2] "Pricing is a bit like the weather. People complain about it; they worry about it; and in the end they feel there is not much they can do about it. But unlike the weather, pricing can in fact be controlled. It can be managed. And it can be a powerful tool for business."[3] The revenue of the company is greatly influenced by the pricing decision. Traditional approaches of pricing have some problem when applied to services. Taking into consideration the service characteristics and consumer perceptions, service firms should take the right decision relating to the pricing of services.

> "***Price is*** *the medium for exchange of value between buyers and sellers. It is the only element of the marketing mix that ensures inflow of revenues while all others are associated with costs.*"

THE PRICING OF SERVICES

Several factors make the pricing of services different from the pricing of goods. These differences influence the acceptable price and purchase decisions. In terms of customer need fulfilment and satisfaction, the importance and the elements of risk also vary for goods and services. "In case of services, a greater proportion of the perceived value hinges on the uncertainty the consumer discerns in the delivery and fulfilment of his/her expectations compared to goods."[4] The service attributes that influence pricing decisions are discussed in "Services Marketing Insight: Service Attributes that Influence Pricing Decisions". The following three factors make services pricing different:

1. *No Ownership of Services:* It is more difficult to calculate the costs involved in creating an intangible service than in producing a physical good. The absence of ownership transfer compels the customer to assess the value of the service before its production and consumption. In the case of goods, consumers can leisurely verify and compare with substitutes and can take a purchase decision after production.

14.1 Services Marketing Insight | **Service Attributes that Influence Pricing Decisions**

Service pricing demands unconventional approaches due to a variety of service attributes and dynamic changes in the market environment. Many researchers focused on this issue and found useful points to consider in service pricing. George J. Avlonitis and Kostis A. Indovnas reviewed the research on service pricing and developed the following list of service attributes that influence service pricing.

Cost of the service	**All the fixed and variable expenses associated with production and delivery of services**
▶ Type of the service	▶ Customer services or industrial services
▶ Timerequiredforcompleting the service	▶ Time horizon required for performing service processes
▶ Risk associated with the service	▶ The potential loss (in monetary, psychic, energy or time terms) that customers must incur in order to purchase the service
▶ Service quality	▶ A number of quality factors (e.g., price, staff appearance, equipment, premises) that determine the total outcome of service delivery to customers
▶ Service automation	▶ The extent to which the service can be delivered without human interaction
▶ Service standardization	▶ The extent to which the service is offered in exactly the same way to all customers
▶ Service availability	▶ The extent to which customers can find the service easily
▶ Service innovation	▶ The extent to which the service satisfies a unique need
▶ Service differentiation	▶ The extent to which the service is different from the competing ones
▶ Service testing	▶ The extent to which customers can try the service before using it
▶ Service customization	▶ The extent to which the service can be adapted to customers' individual needs
▶ Human or capital base	▶ The extent to which the service requires labour- or asset-based elements in order to be produced

Source: George J. Avlonitis and Kostis A. Indounas, An Empirical Examination of the Pricing Policies and their Antecedents in the Services Sector, European Journal of Marketing, *41, no.7/8 (2007): 740–764.*

2. *Input and Output Variability:* The invariable change in the combination of service provider, customer, tools and equipment used, time taken and so on makes the output of the service variable. Therefore, price output relations vary significantly.
3. *Price–Value Relations*: Often customers are not aware of costs of services and are unable to assess price–value relationship. Generally, customers use personal reference prices. Personal reference price consists of the price last paid, the price most frequently paid or the average of all prices paid for similar service offerings. Service firms generally

ISB

The Indian School of Business (ISB) established in Hyderabad, Andhra Pradesh, has become one of the top business management schools in the world in a short span of time. The service package, design of processes, world-class ambience and experiential and skilled man power are the key strengths of the school. The one-year postgraduate programme offered by the school is unique in itself as per the Indian management education standards. The pricing policy of the school focuses on establishing a healthy price–value relationship. The fee of the course in terms of Indian rupees stands at the top of all premium B-schools of the country. However, ISB tried to touch the global manager aspirations among the prospects and communicated the price in USD but not in Indian rupees. Further, the school positioned the price as the lowest compared to top B-schools of the world and the average cost of any good U. S. school. The tagline, "Great Value for Money", signifies more customer delivered value offering from the school.

explore the variable nature of the services to have greater flexibility in the configurations of services. A large number of varieties, combinations and permutations lead to complex price structures. LIC agents cannot quickly tell you the premiums of various policies without referring to the price table. Railway clerks cannot immediately tell you the cargo tariffs for various goods. They have to refer to the price list of the Indian Railways. Under these circumstances, reference prices cannot provide adequate clues to the customer. Reference prices may not be accurate for the customers due to the following reasons:

- The needs of individual customers vary from time to time, place to place and situation to situation. As such, accuracy of reference prices is not possible.
- Unlike goods, similar services cannot be offered at a single outlet. If customers want to compare prices, they must go to individual outlets. Alternative services cannot be compared simultaneously.

Influence of Non-monetary Costs

The role of non-monetary costs is very significant in services. Non-monetary costs are the sources of sacrifices perceived by customers. They include time costs, search costs and psychic costs, which may sometimes become more important for the customers than monetary costs. Time costs refer to the spending of time by the service customer on travel to reach the service outlet, waiting time, service process time and so on. Search costs refer to the efforts put in by the service customer in collecting information relating to the service and the service provider in making a correct decision. Psychic costs refer to the psychological pressure the service customer undergoes in selecting a service provider.

Price–Quality Relations

Buyers are likely to use price as an indicator of both service cost and service quality. In the absence of complete information on the service, price provides clues with regard to the quality of the service. In credence services such as medical treatment or management consultancy, price is the surrogate for quality. As price is viewed as an indicator of the quality of the service, service providers should be careful in fixing prices. Apart from covering service costs and matching competitors, the price should also convey quality. "If the prices are too low, it might indicate low quality of the service to the consumer. On the other hand, high prices may raise consumer expectations on quality, making it difficult to match service delivery with service expectations. From a strategic marketing perspective, knowing the extent by which consumers use the price–quality cue in their decisions is critical to optimal positioning of the brand."[5] Price can serve dual roles in the consumers' decision process. Higher price may either serve as a deterrent to consumer purchase or it may help motivate consumer purchase. It all depends on consumers' inference formation processes. Many consumers interpret higher prices as indicative of higher quality levels and vice versa.

> *Some characteristics of services demand a different approach for the pricing of services. Consumers consider no ownership of services, input and output variability and price–value relations in assessing value of services. Also, the influence of non-monetary costs is significant in services.*

THE OBJECTIVES OF PRICING

The first step in the pricing process is to decide the objectives of pricing. Although pricing objectives of a service concern depend on the vision, mission, corporate objectives and business situations—all of them being company specific, but not universal—a discussion on pricing objectives provides guidelines to the companies to formulate appropriate objectives at an appropriate time. Pricing objectives provide direction for action when setting prices. "Empirical research has indicated that the objective functions of companies are multifaceted in that the viability of companies rests on a combination of different pricing objectives."[6] Pricing objectives should be flexible and change over time in tune with environmental or organizational conditions.

> *Consumer perceptions of price–quality relationship have been well established over the years. In the absence of total information on the quality of a service, consumer finds a clue in price to estimate quality. High price is generally associated with high quality and vice versa.*

Christopher Lovelock[7] classified the pricing objectives of service organizations into the following three basic categories: Revenue-oriented, operation-oriented and patronage-oriented objectives.

1. *Revenue-oriented Objectives:* Profit making is one of the goals of business concerns. Companies are responsible for satisfying the stake of stockholders and also for expanding the business as per the expectations of the stock holders. Firms aim at a target return on investment to meet their priorities. Even non-profit organizations look for revenues that at least breakeven.
2. *Operation-oriented Objectives:* Some service organizations are constrained by capacity. They try to match demand and supply in order to ensure optimum use of their productive capacity at any given time. Hotels, transport vehicles and other such services seek to fill vacancies because the unfilled position becomes an unproductive asset. Service firms may need to change prices frequently to match demand and supply. However, it may be noted that frequent variations in pricing may confuse or irritate the customers.
3. *Patronage-oriented Objectives:* Price may be used effectively to develop loyalty and relationship with customers. Many companies now prefer patronage building to profit maximization as a future-oriented strategic option. Companies can accrue multiple benefits through relationship building.

> *Pricing objectives show the way for fixing prices. Market conditions, company vision and priorities and consumer expectations are needed to be considered in the formulation of objectives. Service companies broadly categorize pricing objectives as revenue-oriented, operation-oriented and patronage-oriented objectives.*

Different characteristics of the market structure may lead to differences in price settings. The following elements of the market structure[8] are likely to impact pricing objectives:

- Extent of differentiation
- Level of concentration
- Size of the market (number of customers and competitors)
- Existing profit margins
- Form of competition (perfect competition, oligopoly, monopoly, monopolistic competition)
- Degree of governmental intervention
- Customers' price elasticity
- Extent to which customers are informed about the existing prices
- Extent to which customers are informed about the existing products or services offered in the market
- Barriers to entry and exit from the market
- Rate of technological change

APPROACHES TO PRICING

The approaches for services pricing are more or less the same as that of pricing of goods. The three recognized pricing approaches are:

- Cost-based pricing
- Competition-based pricing
- Demand-based pricing

Each of these pricing approaches for services needs to be adapted to the conditions of the services and the market sensitivity. Let us examine the adaptability of these three approaches to services.

Cost-based Pricing

Cost-based pricing is a traditional approach and a simple method. The company determines the expense incurred—either direct or indirect—on production and adds a desired profit margin to arrive at a price. Empirical research has shown that the cost-plus method is the most widely used one for pricing. "The popularity of this method might be attributed to the simplicity of its application, the fact that it is considered fair by both customers and competitors, and the price stability that it tends to establish in an industry. The rationale of this method is to add a percentage mark-up to the cost of producing and delivering a service."[9]

When the demand for a service does not fluctuate and when there is supply–demand balance at optimum capacity of the firm, this approach of pricing is convenient to the service provider. Those service firms that face fluctuating demand trends cannot use this method as the fixed-cost component will be very high in proportion to the total cost. When the demand is low, the unit cost of production will be very high, and when the demand is high, the per-unit cost will be low. A high price, when the demand is low, proves disastrous to the firm, and in the same way a low price when the demand is high results in the loss of marketing opportunities. In addition, there are a few more problems of cost-based pricing. The major problem is that it is very difficult to trace the cost of each unit of a service. Consultancy services, legal services, education services and so on are sold in terms of time in many markets. For example, a railway station is used for a variety of passenger trains, goods trains and a number of auxiliary services offered by railways; finding the exact cost incurred on each and every service is close to impossible. The other problem is that labour is more difficult to price than materials. The value of an employee's time, particularly non-professional time, is not easy to calculate. Cost-plus pricing has been criticized on the following fronts:

> **Cost-based pricing** is followed by many service companies due to its simplicity in application. They cannot depend on this method when the demand for the service is highly fluctuating. When demand is stable, predictable and exceeds capacity, this method yields good results.

- Cost-plus pricing ignores the image and market position aimed at.
- Cost-plus pricing ignores demand–price relations.
- Some hidden costs are usually forgotten. Therefore, true margins may be lower than what are realized.
- Common oversights include holiday pay, depreciation and costs of handling waste.
- Cost-plus pricing assumes that the company will achieve/exceed the sales target to break even.
- Competitors can lower prices to win business by having a lower cost base or working with lower margins.

Competition-based Pricing

Competition-based pricing uses anticipated or observed price levels of competitors as the primary source for setting prices.[10] There are two situations in which competition-based pricing is most suitable—when all the service providers offer services more or less of the same standard such as in the dry cleaning sector, or when the oligopoly competitive situation is present in the market wherein a few large service providers have control over the market. "In competition-based pricing, competitors' prices and actions are the main characteristics that trigger pricing decisions."[11] Companies have three main choices under this approach: pricing above the competition, below the competition or at par with competition. The decision depends on the extent to which their services differ from those of their competitors, the intensity of competition and the company's position in the market. "Generally, big companies set the rules of the game, leaving smaller companies with small price discretion and no other option than to follow the leaders' pricing initiatives."[12]

> **Competition** is used as a base for pricing when the market is highly competitive. Service companies have three options: follow competition, fix the price above the competition level or fix it below the competition level. When services are highly differentiated, competition-based pricing may not be a logical decision.

Firms generally follow the live-and-let-live policy. Prices will be more or less stable. However, some small firms may charge too little to be viable and create problems to the competitors. The heterogeneity of services does not allow customers to compare closely the service of a firm to that of another firm. Therefore, competition may not have much significance in pricing. Customers may not be sensitive to minor variation in prices unlike in the case of goods.

Demand-based Pricing

Cost-based pricing is oriented to ensure adequate returns to the service provider, and competition-based pricing aims to attack competition or to defend the company from competitive attacks. But neither of the two is customer oriented. Demand-based pricing is customer-oriented pricing. This approach takes into consideration the customer's sensitivity to non-monetary costs, the customer's perception of value and the customer's acceptability of a service at a price. Demand-based pricing promotes the most important pricing concept for services, that is, "value pricing." Value pricing uses the value that a service delivers to customers as the main factor for setting prices.

> ***Value pricing*** *is the most suitable pricing concept for services. Customer value assessment is taken as the base to fix the price under this method. It is also necessary to understand value perceptions of the consumers against price. Companies should plan to offer more customer delivered value.*

The value perceptions of a service vary among different groups of customers. Service customers generally perceive the following four important value perceptions:

1. *Low or Reduced Price Is Value:* In a market, some customers may perceive value when services are available at a reduced or low price. Money is the most important limitation for them in purchasing services.
2. *Value Is Everything Expected in a Service:* Some customers may consider the benefits that they receive from the service as the most important component in assessing value of the service. This group with a high level of discretionary money does not give more weightage to price. These customers give value to the suitability, quality or features of services.
3. *Value Is Price Versus Quality Relationship:* This group of customers see a trade-off between the money they pay and the quality of the service they receive. They evaluate alternatives rationally and try to optimize their benefits from every transaction.
4. *Value Is Special Packages Offered by the Company:* This group of customers considers the total benefit received and the total sacrifices made by them, including money, time and effort, when assessing value of services. The special packages offered by the company attract this type of customers. This group of customers are critical assessors and less loyal. They prefer those service providers who can give more customer delivered value.

> *Consumers' purchase decision making is generally based on a cost–benefit analysis. The value assessment of a service product is seen from the perspective of core service value, support services value, personal value and image value.*

Whatever the approach, the customer relates value with the benefits from the service offer. It is a certain fact that every consumer does analyse consciously or subconsciously various monetary and non-monetary costs before arriving at a purchase decision. The amount of sacrifice is generally compared with the benefits they receive by using a service. The costs and benefits of a service differ from individual to individual. However, service companies can broadly identify the recognized costs and benefits by the customers and their sensitivity to each cost and benefit. Figure 14.1 illustrates the components of customer values and customer costs. Service firms can use them as a guide to understand the customer assessment process and to develop a right policy for service pricing. The components of customers' assessment in terms of value and cost in arriving customer delivered value are discussed in detail hereunder.

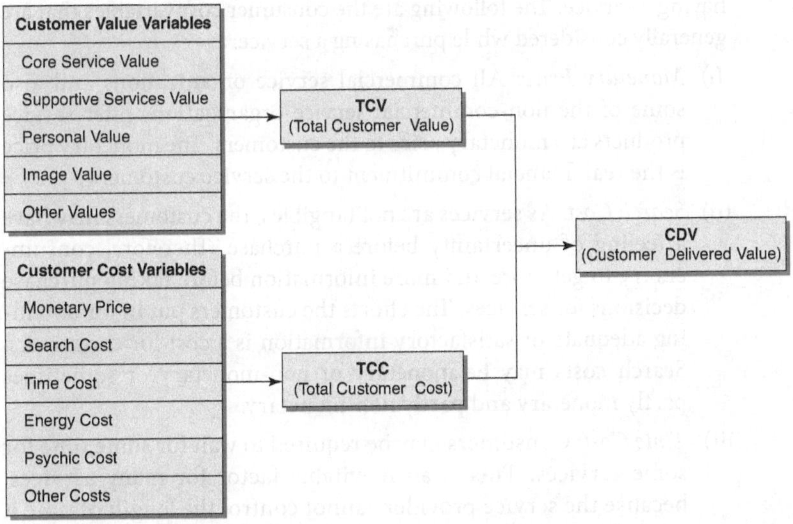

Fig. 14.1: The components of customer delivered value

> *The total customer cost consists of monetary and non-monetary costs and is the sum of all consumer cost variables such as monetary price, time cost, search cost, energy cost and psychic cost.*

1. *Total Customer Value:* The total customer value (TCV) is the sum of variables that the customers attach to specific values in relation to a service. The following are some of the values consumers generally try to measure in a service:
   (i) *Core Service Value:* This value is commonly assessed in every service. It signifies the relevance and suitability of the service to the prime need of the customer. The assessment of the value depends on the intensity of the need of a customer or a group of customers at a given situation.
   (ii) *Supporting Services Value:* Customers also assess the additional services associated with the core service and their capacity to enhance value of the service. Support services provide an opportunity to gain competitive advantage for service providers.
   (iii) *Personal Value:* The suitability of a service to the customer can be a measure for value assessment. As the physical conditions, lifestyle and personal goals vary from customer to customer, it becomes difficult to generalize this value. Some service companies use customization as a way to maximize this value.
   (iv) *Image Value:* The corporate image and the local image of the service provider influences value perceptions of customers. The social status and the ego system of the customer are the inputs for image value assessment.
   (v) *Other Values:* Consumers may perceive some additional values in such cases as emergency, impulse and other emotional and psychological values which may be associated with a service offer.
2. *Total Customer Cost:* The total customer cost (TCC) is the sum of the cost, both monetary and non-monetary, that a customer incurs in

having a service. The following are the consumer cost variables that are generally considered while purchasing a service:

(i) *Monetary Price:* All commercial service organizations and also some of the non-commercial service organizations offer service products at a monetary price to the customers. The monetary price is the real financial commitment to the service customer.

(ii) *Search Cost:* As services are not tangibles, the customers may have a feeling of uncertainty before a purchase. Therefore, consumers try to get more and more information before taking purchase decisions for services. The efforts the customers put in for obtaining adequate or satisfactory information is a cost for consumers. Search costs may be monetary or non-monetary or sometimes partly monetary and partly non-monetary.

(iii) *Time Cost:* Consumers may be required to wait for some time for some services. This is an inevitable factor for many services, because the service provider cannot control the length of time it takes for a customer to be serviced and the number of customers to serve. Time definitely carries some opportunity cost. The total waiting time of customers adds to the cost of the service from the customer's point of view. Time costs also vary from customer to customer.

(iv) *Energy Cost:* The energy costs include the loss of physical energy in travelling to the service outlet, waiting, participating in a crowd of other customers, weight being carried and so on. Service customers may add energy cost as non-monetary cost to the total customer cost.

(v) *Psychic Cost:* Psychological costs are the most painful non-monetary costs incurred while receiving services. While selecting a service, consumers may have some fears—fear of not understanding the service, fear of rejection, fear of uncertainty and so on. All these anxieties constitute psychic costs. When vending machines were introduced by the Metro Railway of Kolkata, most people preferred to obtain tickets by waiting in a queue at manned counters due to the psychological fear relating to operations, accuracy of result, and the image cost (in case of failure, how will the other customers rate their abilities?) in operating the machine.

(vi) *Other Costs:* Apart from the above, consumers may perceive other non-monetary costs related to a specific service. For example, the convenience costs may be more in a particular means of the transport service when compared to other means of transport.

The TCV is compared with the TCC by each and every customer. Though customers may not know or have the methodology to measure the cost items as well as value items in accurate terms, the assessment will be automatic for them. Customers may not identify all the items of costs and values or may not use the same measurement techniques against each service. Therefore, service firms should assist their customers through their communication campaigns in assessing values and costs of a service.

Customer delivered value (CDV) is the value customers obtain over and above the cost they incur in obtaining a service. Consumers naturally prefer those service providers who offer more CDV. In other words,

Customer delivered value = Total customer value − Total customer cost

The TCV and the TCC can be managed by service organizations. Without changing the monetary price, the total cost can be reduced and the total value can be enhanced for a service. By reducing waiting time or adopting effective wait-line strategies, the time cost can be reduced significantly. By educating and training the customers and by managing evidence, psychic costs can be reduced. Similarly, other costs also can be reduced by pursuing appropriate strategies. On the other hand, the value of supporting services can be enhanced through innovation. Similarly, other values such as personal value and image value also can be enhanced by pursuing customer-oriented strategies.

> ***Customer delivered value*** *is the value over total customer cost. This surplus value is the value delivered by the service provider to the service consumer. CDV should be superior to competitive offers in order to get the consumer preference.*

The buyer's perception of the total value prompts their willingness to pay for a service. Therefore, value pricing is the most suitable pricing approach for most services. Service companies need to develop appropriate pricing strategies based on value perceptions of the consumers.

PRICING STRATEGIES LINKED TO VALUE PERCEPTIONS

As mentioned already, there are four identified value perceptions that the consumers may develop in relation to a service. The following are the pricing strategies that can be adopted effectively against the four different perceptions of value by customers (see Fig. 14.2). Price discrimination is yet another strategy followed by many service companies. The details are discussed in "Services Marketing Insight: Price Discrimination in Services".

Low or Reduced Price Is Value

When customers perceive value is low price, the following pricing strategies are more effective:

Low or Reduced Price is Value • Discounts • Psychological Pricing • Penetration Pricing	**Value is Everything Expected in a Service** • Prestige Pricing • Skimming Pricing
Value is Price Versus Quality Relationship • Value Pricing • Market Segmentation Pricing	**Value is Special Packages Offered by Service Company** • Price Framing • Price Bundling • Complementary Pricing

Fig 14.2
Pricing strategies based on value perceptions of customers

14.2 Services Marketing Insight | **Price Discrimination in Services**

Price discrimination occurs wherever identical goods or services are sold to different consumer segments at different prices. Discriminatory pricing is one of the pricing strategies widely used by service organizations. The purpose is to compensate for fluctuations in demand and to exploit the market potential. The factors influencing price discrimination can be categorized into two types: service intrinsic factors and extrinsic/environmental factors.

Service Intrinsic Factors: The intrinsic factors include criticality of service, customization, demand fluctuations and service characteristics. *Criticality* refers to three important issues from the point of the consumer: the essentiality of the service, consumer involvement and the importance of service failure. The more essential the service, the higher the price demanded. The more the involvement, the more the consumer is willing to pay for the service. When the consumer doesn't want service failures, he/she will be ready to pay higher price. Customization is possible in many services such as legal, medical, financial, restaurants, teaching and consultancy. Depending on the levels of service customization, price differentials can be offered in the market place.

Demand fluctuations may be wide or narrow for services. Price discrimination is used when fluctuations in demand are to be managed. The nature of service characteristics also shapes the degree of differential pricing. Firms offering services salient in credence/experience attributes are more likely to command higher and differential prices whereas in search-based services competitive pricing is mostly followed.

Extrinsic/Environmental Factors: The nature of the market and the degree of competition are the two factors under this head influence price discrimination. The nature of market segment and the elasticity of demand are the key influencers of price differentiation. When demand is less elastic the service provider can charge higher price and vice versa.

The degree of competition may influence the magnitude to which one can charge different prices. The more the competition, the less the chances of price discrimination, and vice versa. A monopolist is free to charge higher prices but in other competitive structures price discrimination depends on the ability of the firm in providing differential value to the customers.

Source: Kaushik Mitra and Louis M. Capella, Strategic Pricing Differentiation in Services: A Re-examination, The Journal of Services Marketing, *11, no. 5 (1997): 329–343.*

Discounts

Consumers belonging to this group can be attracted by offering price discounts. This strategy is useful when demand for the service is low or when it is required to shift demand from peak periods to slack periods.

Psychological Pricing

This strategy is used to influence the consumers psychologically by fixing the price in odd numbers like INR 6,999, 199 and so on. The intention is to create a psychological feeling in customers that they are offered services at a low price.

Penetration Pricing

Introducing a service at low initial price is called penetration pricing. This strategy is to attract the price sensitive market.

Value Is Everything Expected in a Service

For a customer group that perceives value to be everything, the following strategies are suitable.

Prestige Pricing

This pricing intends to attract premium segments of the market. The price of the service reflects the status of the target market. Customers attach more value to high price of the service.

Skimming Pricing

This strategy involves introducing the service at a high initial price. Service companies look for exploiting the opportunities in the premium segment at the first phase. After the premium segment is exploited, companies may focus on other down-the-line segments of the market.

> *Price–value perceptions are broadly categorized into four categories. Some segments consider value is low price. Some premium groups of consumers perceive "value is everything I want in a service." Rational consumers assess it as "value is the quality I get for the price I pay." Some other segments consider "value is all that I want for all that I give."*

Value Is Price Versus Quality Relationship

The customers, who have this kind of perception, are more rational in the decision-making process. The following strategies are suitable for this segment:

Value Pricing

Offering higher CDV can be a right strategy for this group. Since the customers are rational in their approach, focus on reduction in customer costs and enhancement of customer value will yield positive results.

Segmentation Pricing

This strategy involves separating these customers from the rest of the market by offering a separate package. The customers are likely to perceive more value in distinctive identity.

Value Is Special Packages Offered by the Company

This group consists of consumers who are highly evaluative and look for beneficiary service packages. The following strategies are suitable for this group:

Price Framing

Price framing means providing total information on pricing of various service packages so that the customers can group the desired services at a price to place an order. A detailed list of prices should be communicated through an appropriate media, for example, by using a price anchor.

Price Bundling

When customers find value in packaging of interrelated services, price bundling is an appropriate strategy. Price bundling means pricing and selling services as a group, not individually.

Complementary Pricing

Under the head of complementary pricing, the following three closely related pricing strategies can be adopted:

Sun Direct

Sun Direct is one of the few companies into DTH services. As an alternative service to the highly unorganized cable services in the country, DTH is fast emerging and has carved a niche in the urban market. While technology-driven quality services are the strong differentiator against the cable services, it is not at all a factor that provides identity among DTH companies. Pricing is considered the major factor that provides competitive advantage. Sun Direct began with a very low subscription offer of INR 499 for five months and INR 999 for 10 months along with free installation and activation offers. The recharge vouchers are offered at INR 25, 100, 200, 300, 400, 500 and 1000, taking into consideration the consumer affordability and willingness to have term commitment. The channel packages are specially developed for South Indian and North Indian customers, taking into consideration the regional language channels. The two-part pricing strategy provides optional service enrichment. The add-on pack offers a variety of national and international channels specializing in various fields of interest at a price varying from INR 6 to 300. Sun Direct offers a jumbo pack to those customers who perceive value as everything they want in a service. The pack offers wholesome entertainment across all genres at INR 300 per month. The pricing strategy helped the company find a respectable place in the market.

1. *Captive Pricing:* Under this pricing scheme, the service firm offers a basic service or product and continues supplies or peripheral services that are needed. In case of a cable network firm, the first cable connection is provided for a price or a deposit and later monthly or bi-monthly payments are collected for a long period.
2. *Two-part Pricing:* Under this strategy, the price of the services is divided into two parts. The first part may be compulsory and the second part depends on the usage of the service. The telecommunication industry adopts this pricing strategy. The rental charges and a fixed number of free calls constitute the first part. The second part of pricing depends on the level of usage of the service.
3. *Loss-leader Pricing:* The objective of this strategy is to attract a large number of customers to the service outlet. Some supplementary services, generally, are offered at a very low price for attracting customers to the business service provider. The loss incurred on some offers is recovered with the additional turnover generated due to this strategy.

SUMMARY

- Price is the medium for exchanging value between buyers and sellers.
- Price is the only element of marketing mix that is associated with revenue.
- Service characteristics and consumer-value perceptions influence pricing decisions.
- Service attributes such as no ownership, output variability and consumer perceptions of price–value relations influence pricing.
- The influence of non-monetary costs is significant in service pricing.
- Consumers do establish price–quality relationship in services due to its intangibility and variability characteristics.
- Pricing objectives may be revenue oriented, operation oriented and patronage oriented.

- The three approaches to pricing are cost-based pricing, competition-based pricing and demand-based pricing.
- Cost-based pricing is useful when demand is stable and predictable.
- Competition-based pricing is used when the competition is intense in the market.
- Value pricing is considered more suitable for services as consumer assessment of value forms the basis for pricing decisions.
- Consumers take purchase decisions based on cost–benefit analysis against a service offer.
- The service provider who offers more customer delivered value is preferred by consumers.
- Consumers' price–value perceptions are important for formulating pricing strategies.
- Value is low or reduced price, value is everything expected in a service, value is price versus quality and value is special packages offered by the service companies are the four different value perceptions used to categorize customers and differentiate pricing strategies.

KEY TERMS

Captive pricing *287*
Customer delivered value *285*
Loss-leader pricing *288*
Non-monetary costs *277*
Penetration pricing *286*
Personal reference price *277*
Price bundling *287*
Price framing *287*
Psychological pricing *286*
Segmentation pricing *287*
Skimming pricing *287*
Total customer cost *283*
Total customer value *283*
Two-part pricing *288*

BRIEF QUESTIONS

1. Explain price–quality relations.
2. Discuss the suitability of cost-plus pricing for services.
3. Suggest pricing strategies for segments that perceive value is low price.
4. What is psychological pricing?
5. Explain contemporary pricing strategies of service companies with suitable examples.

ESSAY QUESTIONS

1. Companies often find pricing of services more difficult than pricing of goods. Why?
2. What is value pricing? How can markets be divided, based on value perceptions?
3. Discuss the pricing strategies applicable for services with suitable examples.
4. What is CDV? How can CDV be calculated?
5. Critically examine the pricing policies and strategies of a service company of your choice.
6. Explain the approaches for pricing of services.
7. What is the role of non-price factors in influencing the demand of services?

ASSIGNMENTS

1. Price plays a very significant role in the marketing of prepaid mobile services. BSNL, Airtel, Vodafone, Reliance and Tata Indicom are keen on attracting customers through various pricing strategies. You are required to:
   (a) Study the pricing objectives and pricing strategies of prepaid mobile services of any two competing companies.
   (b) Interview 25 mobile users and study price–value relationship.
2. The Insurance Regulatory and Development Authority (IRDA, which was constituted by an act of parliament in 1999) takes care of protection of the interests of the policy holders in matters concerning assigning of policy, nomination by policy holders, insurable interest, settlement of insurance claim, surrender value of policy and other terms and conditions of contracts of insurance. Regulating investment of funds by insurance companies; regulating maintenance of margin of

solvency; specifying the percentage of premium income of the insurer to finance schemes for promoting and regulating professional organizations; supervising the functioning of the Tariff Advisory Committee and specifying the percentage of life insurance business and general insurance business to be undertaken by the insurer in the rural or social sector are the major functions of the authority. You are required to study:

(a) The role of the regulatory body in insurance pricing
(b) The positive and negative consequences of such a regulatory body

REFERENCES

1 T. T. Nagle and R. K. Holden, *The Strategy and Tactics of Pricing* (Englewood Cliffs, NJ: Prentice Hall, 1995).
2 D. D. Shipley and D. Jobber, "Integrative Pricing via the Pricing Wheel," *Industrial Marketing Management*, 30, no. 3 (2001): 301–314.
3 R. A. Garda, "Use Tactical Pricing to Uncover Hidden Profits," *Journal of Business Strategy*, 12 (1991): 17–23.
4 John Groth, "Important Factors in the Sale and Pricing of Services," *Management Decision*, 33, no. 7 (1995): 29–34.
5 Hooman Estelami, "Consumer Use of the Price-Quality Cue in Financial Services," *Journal of Product & Brand Management*, 17/3 (2008): 197.
6 D. Diamantopoulos (1991), "Pricing: Theory and Evidence—a Literature Review," in Baker, M. J. (ed.), *Perspectives on Marketing Management*, (Chichester: Wiley, 1991) pp. 61–193.
7 Christopher Lovelock, Jochen Wirtz and Jayanta Chatterjee, Services Marketing, 5th ed. (New Delhi: Pearson Education, 2009) pp. 143–144.
8 George J. Avlonitis and Kostis A. Indounas, "The Impact of Market Structure on Pricing Objectives of Service Firms," *Journal of Product & Brand Management*, 13, no. 5 (2004): 345.
9 Kostis Indounas, "Successful Industrial Service Pricing," *Journal of Business & Industrial Marketing*, 24/2 (2009): 88.
10 Andreas Hinterhuber, "Customer Value-based Pricing Strategies: Why Companies Resist," *Journal of Business Strategy*, 29, no. 4 (2008): 41–50.
11 A. C. B. Tse, "How Much More Are Consumers Willing to Pay for a Higher Level of a Service? A Preliminary Survey," *Journal of Services Marketing*, 15, no. 1 (2001): 11–17.
12 O. P. Heil and K. Helsen, "Toward an Understanding of Price Wars: Their Nature and How They Erupt," *International Journal of Research in Marketing*, 18, no. 1/2 (2001): 83–98.

Distribution

15

LEARNING OBJECTIVES

After studying this chapter, you will be able to:

- Understand the challenges in the distribution of services
- Describe the distribution flows for services
- Identify the intermediaries for service distribution
- Describe the strategies for channel management

Vijay Agarwal, the senior marketing manager of Blue DTH services, organized a meet of franchisees to review the marketing performance of the company. The meeting began with exchanging pleasantries but became heated gradually as the franchisees began to describe their problems regarding the distribution of services. The participants from franchisee companies identified some positives and several deficiencies. Vijay noted down all the opinions and identified three major grievances of the franchisees.

1. ***Poor External Marketing Support by the Company:*** In the absence of proper support from Blue DTH, the franchisee organizations were struggling to communicate with the market—right from creating awareness to persuading consumers to buy the service.
2. ***Irregular Supply of Set Top Boxes and Dish Antennas:*** The franchisees rued the fact that the supply was erratic and irregular on account of which the contact employees of the franchisees were unable to keep up their promises to customers.
3. ***Poor Response from the Company to the Calls of Franchisees:*** According to the franchisees, Blue DTH failed to respond to their queries and calls on time. This lack of response had created several problems for the franchisees on numerous occasions

Vijay Agarwal was shocked to learn this information. His subordinates had always assured him that things were going on very well for the company and the sale was growing at a satisfactory rate. Till then, neither had he received a direct complaint from any franchisee nor had he made any attempts to know the problem. As the meeting progressed, Vijay felt that he had been kept in the dark. He concluded the meeting with the promise to take care of all the issues raised in the meeting. Aware of the fact that franchisee dissatisfaction could be detrimental to the business in the long run, Vijay decided to take immediate measures to gain their confidence. He started working on developing an action plan to address the key issues.

Questions:

1. In your opinion, what are the possible lapses in franchisee management?
2. What would be the negative effects on the business if franchisees continue to be dissatisfied?
3. What action plan would you suggest for Vijay Agarwal?
4. What are the key issues for successfully managing the franchisee system of Blue DTH services?

INTRODUCTION

The factors influencing the distribution of services differ significantly from those of goods. In the case of goods, production is separate from consumption. But in services, production and consumption take place simultaneously. The service provider and consumer participate in service production at a specified location. Linking production with distribution makes services distribution more complex than goods distribution. "The intangible nature of services would appear to make the idea of distribution inapplicable to services. But there are more than enough similarities to make distribution relevant and important to service firms."[1]

Business firms or social organizations measure their growth in terms of market expansion. When service providers intend to expand their market operations, they have two options: to start service outlets at various places offering the same package and quality, or to use private distributors for the purpose. Basically, the quality of the service is reflected in the encounter between customers and employees of the service firm. It is a challenge for the service provider to maintain standards of performance at the service outlet. If this job is assigned to middlemen, there may be a danger of a decrease in the value of offering, which brings bad reputation to the organization. However, if the distributors are able and willing to offer such services, the risk of failure and damage to the company image is minimized.

> *"The distribution of services is more challenging than the distribution of goods due to their inherent characteristics such as intangibility, inseparability, variability and perishability. These characteristics and more particularly customer participation in the service process make service distribution critical in shaping customer perception."*

The basic objective of the distribution of services is to make services available at the right time and place and accessible to consumers with ease and convenience. All characteristics of services influence the distribution of services. If the services—such as education, consultancy and so on—do not involve significant tangibles, the service provider needs to have more direct contact with the customer. However, this contact may be reduced or avoided all together in those services—such as ATMs in banking services—in which tangibles play a significant role in service production and delivery. The inseparability characteristic of services limits the scope of market expansion. The variability characteristic of services limits the chances of standardization and creates frontline management challenges. Due to the perishability characteristic of services, demand and capacity management at every service outlet becomes critical. Customer participation demands a customer-friendly environment and equipment at the service distribution outlet. As services cannot be owned, the job of frontline employees becomes more critical in classifying and convincing customers.

SERVICE TRANSACTIONS

Transactions in services can be broadly categorized into three groups: customers calling service outlets; service firms calling customers; and service firms transacting witn consumers at an arm's length.

1. *Customers Calling Service Outlets:* In such transactions, customers have to go to service outlets to avail of the service. The service provider creates an environment conducive to the production and consumption of the

service with good service care and infrastructural facilities, for example, educational institutions, theatres, beauty parlours, health clubs and so on.

2. *Service Firms Calling Customers:* In such transactions, consumers need not move from their premises whether it is home or office to avail of the service. The employees of the service organization call on the customers and perform the service at the desired location. For example, postal services, security services, personal services and so on.
3. *Service Firms Transacting with Consumers at an Arm's Length*: In such transactions, there is no need to for service providers to have personal contact and face-to-face encounters with the consumers. Services can be produced and consumed with the help of tangibles and equipment provided for the purpose, for example, telecom services, cellular services, credit card services and so on.

Service companies may adopt different strategies depending on the service product, the market and the objectives of the company. There are three distribution strategies available to service organizations: extensive distribution, selective distribution and exclusive distribution.

Extensive distribution makes the services available to as many as possible through a wider distribution network. It is suitable for mass consumption services such as transportation, electricity, telecommunications and primary education.

Selective distribution offers services to an identified target segment through a limited number of distribution outlets selected for the purpose. Selective distribution is suitable for services that have to follow specified conditions and regulations and special skills to the service provider. This type of distribution may be more suitable to services such as higher and technical education, tourism and courier services.

Exclusive distribution offers services to focused segments through distribution outlets established exclusively for the purpose. Exclusive distribution can be used for services that reflect the corporate brand image and exclusivity in many dimensions of the service package. This distribution may be suitable for healthcare services, hospitality services, retail networks and so on.

> *"Services may be distributed through customer contact service outlets, service firms calling customers at their door steps or non-personal interactions. Service companies may opt for exclusive, selective or extensive distribution."*

SERVICE LOCATIONS AND SERVICE PROVIDERS

The basic strategic issues in services distribution are two dimensional. One is the service location and the other is the service provider.

Service Locations

Where to locate a service outlet is a critical decision, which is influenced by many factors. The target consumers, the degree of interaction required with them and accessibility are the major influencing factors. Location is typically the prime consideration in a customer's choice of a service outlet. Location decisions have strategic importance because they can be used to develop a sustainable competitive advantage. They are harder to change due to the fact that a change requires substantial investments.[2] While selecting a location for service outlets, the following factors are to be considered:

- *Proximity:* The location of the service outlet should be as close to the target market as possible. The proximity of the service outlet saves time and energy costs and also develops affinity among the consumers.
- *Image*: The image of the location should match the corporate image of the service company. The level of acceptability of a location by the consumers varies. If an air-conditioned restaurant is established in a slum area, the proximity factor does not work to attract customers.
- *Parking Facility:* Parking facility is becoming an important factor, particularly in cities and metros. A service outlet without adequate parking facilities is less likely to attract customers.
- *Convenience:* The location of the service outlet should be convenient for customers. Convenience is often measured in terms of public transport, other shopping facilities, safety and security and so on.
- *Accessibility to Other Services:* A service outlet requires a host of other services and infrastructural facilities such as electricity, telecommunications, water and sanitation. The location that provides an adequate qualitative supply of these services is more suitable for service organizations.
- *Competitive Advantage:* The effect of the competition cannot be ignored while taking any decision in services. The location that provides competitive advantage can be preferred.

> *A **service location** is an important value for both the company and the customer. The selection of the location is based on the target customers, the degree of interaction required and the required accessibility.*

Service Providers

Service firms need to select those service providers who are capable of managing service outlets efficiently and provide quality services to the customers. Service firms may opt for direct distribution or private channels, or they may use both to reach the target market.

In case of service distribution through a middleman, there are two marketers—service principal and service deliverer. The service principal is the service originator and the service deliverer is the distributor. The service deliverer becomes the co-producer of the service and fulfils the promises of the service principal to customers. The service intermediaries, apart from fulfilling promises, also provide time, place and convenience utilities to the target customers. The intermediaries may perform services of many service principals, thereby providing a retailing function for customers.

DISTRIBUTION FLOWS OF SERVICES

The distribution flows of services are shown in Fig. 15.1. There are four choices available to any service provider. The first option is direct marketing, wherein services are provided directly through the employees of the service organization. The second option is to use agents/brokers as distributors of service. In

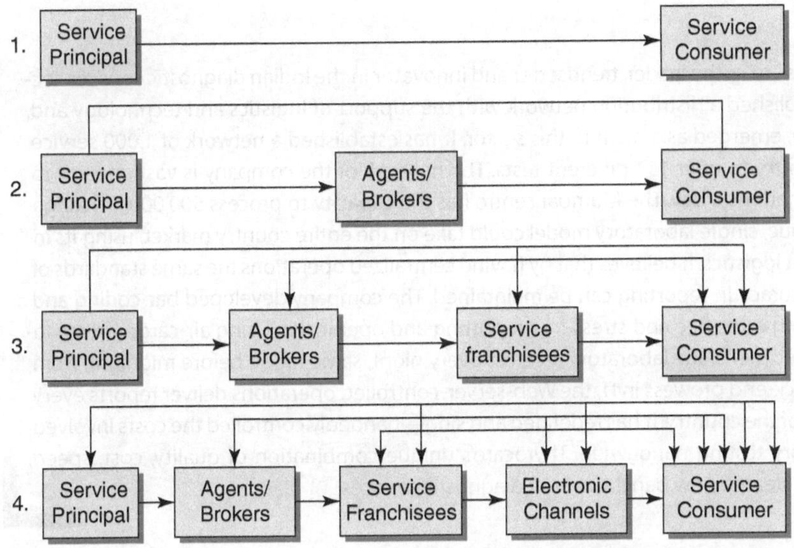

Fig. 15.1: Flowchart of services distribution

this option, two flows are possible: direct channel and through agents. The third choice involves two types of intermediaries: agents/brokers and service franchisers. Four distribution flows are possible in this choice, as indicated in the figure. The fourth choice involves three types of intermediaries: agents/brokers, service franchisers and electronic channels. Seven distribution flows are possible in this choice, as indicated in the figure.

Distribution by Company-owned Channels

The service company develops national chains with multiple service outlets at various locations. Company-owned channels such as the branch network of banks, insurance companies, postal services and retail chains are common in service distribution. Company-owned outlets offer many benefits to the company in the form of control, consistency and maintenance of image. The specific benefits are:

- Service delivery quality standards are easy to maintain
- Employees own the service
- Zero gap between promise and delivery
- Flexibility in operation
- Creativity through empowered employees
- Greater control over operational processes
- Direct feedback from contract employees
- Freedom to introduce improvements in the service outlet wherever and whenever wanted
- Opportunity to establish direct relationship with customers
- Speedy recovery for the service deficiencies

Thyrocare

Thyrocare Technologies Ltd. is the leader, trendsetter and innovator in the Indian diagnostic services sector. The company established a distribution network with the support of logistics and technology and, in a short span of time, emerged as a giant in this sector. It has established a network of 1,000 service centres across the country to offer 134 different tests. The network of the company is vast enough to process 50,000 investigations a day. The Mumbai centre has the capacity to process 500,000 investigations per day. This unique, single laboratory model could take on the entire country market, using its innovative and intelligent logistics. It believes that by having centralized operations the same standards of quality control and accuracy in reporting can be maintained. The company developed bar-coding and bi-directional interfacing error-free and stress-free reporting and operations. Using air-cargo-driven logistics for incoming specimens, the laboratory receives every night, same night, before midnight, from 90% of India. With a back-end prowess in IT, the Web-server-controlled operations deliver reports every morning in every part of the country. It has redefined and single-handedly controlled the costs involved in specialized laboratory testing nationwide. Thyrocare's unique combination of quality, cost, speed, reach and systems has created new benchmarks in diagnostic services.

Besides several advantages, the company-owned channels also have certain disadvantages. "Huge investment requirement and financial risk are the major problems. Market expansion is difficult. When adjustments are needed in business formats for different markets they may be unaware of what these adjustments should be. This disadvantage is especially evident when companies expand into other cultures and other countries. Partnering or joint venturing is almost always preferred to company-owned channels in these situations."[3] A failure at some locations may affect corporate image. Considering the benefits and problems of relying on company-owned channels, many service companies prefer a mix of owned and private channels. Electronic channels are being used by many service companies to maximize direct channel benefits and minimize the problems of physical distribution units. Intermediate e-channels are also available for service companies.

CHANNELS FOR SERVICE DISTRIBUTION

Service distribution deals with the means that service firms use to provide services to the consumers. The distributors of services need to play a critical role before and after the sale of the service. This is because distribution becomes a potent competitive weapon for service firms. What channel to use for service distribution is a critical decision. The popularly used channels for the distribution of services are franchising, agents and brokers and electronic channels.

Franchising

Franchising is the most-often used channel for the distribution of services. It is like the retail selling of services. The franchisers are authorized to distribute services to the end customers, on behalf of the service principal. The importance of franchisees has been discussed in "Services Marketing Insight: Franchisee Satisfaction Is the Key". Franchising involves a contractual arrangement between a franchiser (service principal) and a franchisee. It allows the franchisee to conduct service business under the established brand name of the service company, following guidelines. In service franchising, there is more interactive relationship between a franchiser and a franchisee. "The franchisee receives assistance on site location, quality control, accounting systems, start-up practices, management training, and responding to problems besides the right to sell services."[4] Franchising is mostly used in service businesses such as educational institutions, film-processing companies, hotels and restaurants. Agreements and contracts are essential documents in franchising. Generally, agreements and contracts include a clear description of the following:

- Nature of the service
- Geographic territory
- Percentage share to be paid to the franchiser on the revenue of the franchisee

15.1 Services Marketing Insight | **Franchisee Satisfaction Is the Key**

Franchisee satisfaction is the key to franchise management. It is important to have long-term relationship and continuance of the franchisee networks. Generally, franchise agreements are term-based. On the expiry of the term franchisee decides whether to continue with the same principal or to switch over to a new one. If the franchisee decides to quit, it is critical for the principal to recruit new franchisees. If the franchisee is a poor performer, it is good to the company to get out of that franchisee. When the good performers leave the company it raises danger alarms. The franchiser must acquire the means to evaluate candidates, and to stimulate internal relations in the network. The franchisees' satisfaction must be considered the most directly influential variable.

Satisfaction of channel members is central for more than one reason. Satisfaction increases morale of the channel members and motivate them to work for the principal organization with involvement and commitment. It protects the relationships and prevents conflicts within the organization system. The basic determinants of franchisee satisfaction are the administration of the franchise (satisfaction as to interaction with the franchiser); the support and service that are provided; and the arrangements for extrinsic rewards (profits, inducements within the context of promotions) and intrinsic ones (status, the sector's public image, sales awards, etc.)

Service companies need to develop the mechanism to measure franchisee satisfaction in order to strengthen their distribution system. As franchisee organizations are having direct contact with customers, the dissatisfaction of the franchisee may lead to customer dissatisfaction. Such potential danger can be prevented through strengthening franchisee–franchiser relationships.

Source: Claire Gauzente, "Measuring Franchisees' Satisfaction: Theoretical Considerations and Empirical Testing", Journal of Retail & Distribution Management, *31, no. 10 (2003): 508–517.*

- Time period of agreement
- Instructions, interactions and conditions
- Support to be provided by the franchiser
- Roles and responsibilities of franchisee
- Rules and regulations of termination of agreement

The following are the benefits of franchising:

- *Business Expansion and Revenue Gains:* Service companies (franchiser) can reach more markets without much effort through franchisees. The wider distribution, thus achieved, results in increased revenues, larger market share, brand name recognition as well as economies of scale.
- *Consistency in Outlets*: Service companies can ensure consistency in performance of the franchisees with the help of agreements and contracts. By way of providing standard specifications relating to exterior, interior and process of service production, it is possible to maintain consistency in outlets.
- *Knowledge of Local Markets*: Greater reach of the market provides adequate information back through the franchisee, relating to specific issues of local markets. This information helps the organization develop market-oriented service packages. Also, service companies can get feedback quickly and with useful interpretation from customers through franchisees on various dimensions of service quality. Such feedback helps improve the performance of the company.
- *Shared Financial Risk and Investment Burden:* Franchisees invest money and other resources to arrange for the required equipment and personnel for performing services as per the specifications of the franchiser. Therefore, the franchiser's investment burden gets reduced significantly.

> *“**Franchising** is the most often used channel for the distribution of services; it is like the retail selling of services. The franchisees are authorized to distribute services to the end customers, on behalf of the service principal.”*

In spite of the benefits, there are also some challenges associated with distribution through franchising. Service companies should be ready to face such challenges, when they opt for franchising. Some of the major challenges associated with franchisers are:

- *Problems in Maintaining and Motivating Franchisees:* Most service companies face problems in motivating their own employees. When it is the case of outside independent operators, it is a more difficult task to motivate them to perform the service as per specifications. Maintaining franchisees during slack periods may be very hard, as there is frustration due to fall in revenues.
- *Quality Inconsistency May Affect Company Image*: Many a time, the quality of services offered by franchisees vary from the service specifications. Exercising quality control devices by the service company may not yield good results in the case of private operators. Even though the

company is making money from such a franchisee, there is a danger that the company may be losing future business due to a negative market image. Therefore, the service firm should be cautious in selecting and maintaining franchisees.

- *Control of Customer Relationship by the Franchisee*: Since franchisee organizations are involved in managing service encounters they have a chance to build relationships with the customers. Total customer information will be in the hands of the franchisee organizations and the service firm becomes dependent on franchisees for such information.

Agents and Brokers

An agent is an intermediary who is authorized to negotiate on behalf of the service principal with the customers. Brokers are middlemen who bring buyers and sellers together and assist in negotiation. Either a buyer or a seller can hire a broker. Although brokers and agents are two different kinds of intermediaries, both of them perform similar functions in service distribution.

Service companies have some special benefits in using agents and brokers as intermediaries for service distribution. The benefits of using agents and brokers are as follows:

- *Low Selling and Distribution Cost:* Agents and brokers work on commission basis. Service companies need not employ permanent sales force for the purpose. Selling and distribution costs are directly linked with sales revenue when agents and brokers are used.
- *Specialized Skills and Knowledge of the Agents and Brokers:* Persons who choose to be agents and brokers generally possess specialized skills in persuading people. Such skills are mostly inherent and inherited. Service companies can exploit those skills in their favour without any additional cost.
- *Wider Representation in the Market:* Service companies can appoint many brokers and agents and can have a wider representation in the market. The agency network of LIC of India is an example of this.
- *Knowledge of Local Markets:* Agents and brokers operate within specific locations, have knowledge on various local issues and possess the talent to exploit their knowledge for making sales. Through agents and brokers, the company can get required information relating to local markets. The information provided by these intermediaries, naturally, is more reliable.
- *Customer Choice:* There may be a number of authorized agents and brokers relating to a service in a location. Customers may choose known intermediaries for providing the service. Customer confidence will be high when they take service through a known broker or agent.

> *"Agents and brokers are widely used as intermediaries, particularly in insurance, transport and tourism services. An agent is an intermediary who is authorized to negotiate on behalf of the service principal with the customers. Brokers are middlemen who bring buyers and sellers together and assist in negotiations."*

However, there are some challenges service organizations have to face in using agents and brokers as intermediaries. There is loss of control, in pricing and other aspects of marketing when the agents and brokers interfere and prevail over the producers as well as consumers (for example, real estate business). Some brokers and agents, generally, represent multiple service principals, and special focus may not be provided to any one of the service principals.

Electronic Channels

Electronic channels are becoming more and more popular in the distribution of services. They do not require direct human-to-human interactions. The examples of the electronic channels are television, telephone, Internet, e-commerce and so on. The Internet has rapidly developed as a commercial medium for retailers to do business. "Electronic home shopping via the Internet is referred to as business-to-consumer (B2C) e-commerce, which is all about speed, connectivity, information sharing, goods exchange and service."[5] The Internet continues to offer more efficient distribution options. Distance is unimportant in an economy dominated by electronic activities, and industries such as financial services, software, and data processing are, in effect, "weightless." Thus, they all can explore strategic alliances in the rights-of-way of cyberspace.[6] Through electronic channels service firms are able to provide movies on demand, banking and financial services, multimedia libraries, database, distance learning modules, video conferencing facilities, remote health services and so on.

"The use of the Internet within the business context has offered organizations a new global marketing platform, through which businesses and consumers have the opportunity to exchange not only information but also all kinds of products and services."[7] M. L. Meuter et al. define the Internet market as "a virtual realm where products and services exist as digital information and can be delivered through information-based channels."[8] The potential for global connectivity on the Internet empowers customers by providing necessary information and a medium to convert the purchase intentions into purchase.[9]

Yatra Online

Yatra Online Pvt. Ltd. is a smart travel company serving as an intermediary channel for air travels, railways, hotels, buses and car rentals. The company provides information to the customers on choices, pricing and availability and provides booking facility. It has established a multi-language customer service centre to facilitate comfortable and clear interactions with the company. The centre enables business and leisure travellers to make well-informed and cost-effective bookings any time.

Yatra Online started off as an online booking company. Now, it offers its services through retail partners as well. It has managed to create a niche for itself in the industry within a very short time. This may be attributed to its focus on accessibility, fast turnaround time, responsive team, customization and dynamic modifications. Yatra.com is an example of successful e-channel operations.

The World Wide Web offers service firms the opportunity to meet the growing customer expectations particularly in speed, comparability and price. The global marketplace makes it imperative that service companies improve their quality in all dimensions and compete with others regardless of their size. Technology has, therefore, become increasingly important in the direct and indirect distribution (retailing) of services, and has assumed a central role in the crucial links among service providers, distributors and consumers. "Given the rapid development of the Internet market, and its acceptance by the consumers, it is likely that electronic distribution will gain

15.2 Services Marketing Insight | **Services e-Retailing**

The e-commerce retail market has grown significantly during the last decade. Service companies found e-retailing as an excellent business opportunity to provide accessibility to millions of customers at a very low cost. The banking, insurance, transport, hospitality, tourism, communications, financial services and many other services have entered in a big way in e-retailing. E-retail sites try to attract consumers by offering greater utility compared to the shopping formats. The consumers can have greater search facllity, evaluation facility and on-line purchase facility. Consumers can save a lot of time and effort. The Internet affords e-retailers with a unique opportunity to provide on-line experiences that can be renewed and potentially customized to a customer's own interests and preferences. To the extent that e-retailers can leverage these opportunities to engage shoppers in positive experiences, the more likely shoppers will be to value the e-retail experience and return.

Service e-retailers face unique challenges in providing service quality perceptions to consumers. The task of providing adequate information sources is complicated due to the heterogeneity of consumer information requirements. E-retail consumers are required to play an active role in the service process. They have to engage in search and evaluation by performing such tasks as filling e-shopping carts electronic payment and providing delivery information according to the script set out by the Web designer. The effective participation of the consumers in these roles depends on the consumer knowledge capabilities and self-image. Physical evidence is another important consideration. The consumer evaluates search properties of the Web site. The fundamentals such as speed-up response and ease of negotiation in the Web site influence customers' perception of the overall experience. The value of the e-retailer is assessed by the ability to demonstrate willingness to respond to the consumers' specific needs. In a computer-mediated interaction over the Internet, demonstrating these challenges present unique challenge to the service provider.

The challenge for e-retailers is to encourage customers to modify their current shopping habits in favour of Internet shopping. A successful service e-retailer tries to use new motivators to encourage consumers to change their traditional shopping behaviour towards purchase over the Internet. The Internet-based retail channels offer convenient ways to explore a range of services and service attributes and support the consumers to compare features and prices of different offers.

Source: Mark B. Kolesar and R. Wayne Galbraith, "A Services-Marketing Perspective on E-retailing: Implications for E-retailers and Directions for Further Research," Internet Research: Electronic Networking Applications and Policy, *10, no.5 (2000): 424–438.*

a very high market share compared with traditional methods."[10] The on-line shopping market is shared by pure players and multi-channel retailers. Pure players are companies that do not have an upfront store presence and sell products only via the internet.[11] Multi-channel retailers, also called "bricks and clicks" retailers, supplement conventional stores with on-line services.[12] The challenges of e-retailing are presented in "Services Marketing Insight: Services e-Retailing".

Electronic channels are useful for service companies in many ways. The following are the major benefits:

- *Quality Control:* Service firms can reach customers without any variation in the standard package through electronic channels. Unlike delivery through human beings, electronic channels do not interpret the service and execute it according to that interpretation. It transmits exactly what is designed. Also, the channels facilitate the centralized design of the service package and thereby, better quality control.
- *Cost:* The cost incurred for reaching each buyer is lowest through electronic media when compared to distribution through human resources.
- *Customer Convenience:* One of the important benefits of using the electronic channels is customer convenience. Whenever and wherever customers want the service, they can access it through the electronic media.
- *Distribution:* Cost-effective extensive market coverage is possible through electronic channels.
- *Customer Choice:* Through electronic channels a wide variety of services can be offered as choice to the customers. Movies, cable programmes, education modems and music are some electronic channels used by service firms.

Besides many benefits, there are some challenges in using electronic channels for the distribution of services.

- *No Control on Electronic Environment:* The electronic media, of late, has become a subject of controversy due to lack of proper regulation. Once a network becomes popular some controversial material starts appearing, and results in a negative effect, in some cases, on service quality. The effectiveness of the channel depends on many factors such as power, signal, satellite linkage, weather conditions and so on. Most of them are beyond the control of a service company.
- *Inability to Customize:* Adaptability to the local needs is not possible through electronic channels. If service personnel are used for delivery, there is a chance to modify the business systems planning (BSP) on the spot, according to the needs of each customer. But electronic channels cannot provide such facilities. However, interactive mechanisms in the electronic channels provide customized service to some extent.

- *Customer Involvement:* The need for customer participation is very high in the case of electronic channels. Customers should know how to operate the electronic media. Therefore, technology should be highly user friendly. Any complexity keeps the customers away from using the service.

> *The IT revolution and the growth of Internet users have provided an opportunity to use electronic channels for service distribution. e-channels provide a lot of flexibility to both the service provider and the consumer at a very low cost of distribution. Some service companies are depending totally on e-channels and many companies are using e-channels as a support to other channels.*

THE DESIGN OF A SERVICE DISTRIBUTION SYSTEM

While designing a distribution system for services, it is necessary to take care of effectiveness of its execution. A sound design of the system with poor execution will certainly yield poor or sometimes negative results. If the distribution system is designed properly, it can be used as a truly effective competitive weapon. Donald H. Light[13] has suggested the following seven points that help in making the distribution system work.

1. *Align the System Properly:* An indirect distribution system involves service principals, intermediaries and customers. The BSP designed by the service principal has many dimensions. The channel member's personal and business dimensions and the customer's personal and social dimensions also play an important role in the process of service production, delivery and consumption. A proper alignment of the dimensions of the service firm, intermediaries and customers is important to make the distribution system work. It is also necessary to align the goals of the distribution with corporate goals.
2. *Remember Each Part of the Sales Cycle:* The sales cycle of any service product has three phases: "before the sale," "during the sale" and "after the sale." The initial contact between the service sales employee and the customer occurs "before the sale." Service companies should focus on accessibility and location to ensure that locating the service provider is convenient for the customer. The design of the service process and the promotional campaigns by service companies has a greater influence at this stage. "During the sale" the focus should be on quality performance and performing right at the first time. Service companies need to facilitate customer participation. During the "after-the-sale" phase, efforts are directed towards customer retention through customer relationships, customer complaint handling, service recovery strategies, promoting customers to a higher stage in the relationship ladder. The efficient management of these three phases has a positive influence on quality perception of consumers.
3. *Balance Retail and Wholesale Intermediaries:* Retailers interact directly with service customers whereas the wholesale intermediaries work with retailers. Wholesalers and retailers require different skills and techniques and need to perform distinctive functions. Service companies should ensure that the activities of wholesalers and retailers are balanced properly and there is no ambiguity. The coordination of these two levels in the distribution channel is important for the efficient functioning of service organizations.

4. *Make Wholesale Intermediaries Effective Product Managers:* Proper delegation is necessary when intermediaries are used in service distribution, particularly, when wholesalers function as product managers. The idea is that the wholesalers be made responsible for production and further distribution of the service. They should be encouraged to develop an overall plan for the product in the distribution area and also to develop the ability to meet the technical needs of the functional departments at service production outlets.
5. *Keep Intermediaries Loyal:* Intermediaries are the link between the customers and the service company. The image of the company depends on the performance of intermediaries. Selection of intermediaries, who can deliver the desired results, is important. They should be encouraged to have a continued and loyal relationship with the service principal. This is possible through cooperation, extending support services and exercising control in service processes by involving the intermediaries.
6. *Pay the Price to Do Multi-marketing Correctly:* Multi-marketing means using more than one distribution channel to serve the customers. Most companies use multi-marketing to provide greater accessibility to the customers and for market expansion and penetration. For example, banking services are offered through a branch network, ATMs, electronic channels and agents and brokers. Multi-marketing requires more investment and also incurs more cost. Yet, the benefits are many. Therefore, service companies should be prepared to incur additional costs for efficiency in distribution.
7. *Control the Pace of Change:* The distribution system of any company should not be rigid. Flexibility is necessary in order to make the system adaptable to changes in the business environment. Besides good planning and execution, good luck is also necessary for making a service distribution work. It is necessary to restructure intermediary relationships, time and again, and shift towards new channels by taking into consideration external forces such as competition, technology, regulation and so on.

> *"A sound design of the system with poor execution certainly yields poor or sometimes negative results. If the distribution system is designed and executed properly, it can be used as a truly effective competitive weapon."*

THE STRATEGIES FOR CHANNEL MANAGEMENT

Channel management is critical in service companies as the quality perception of customers depends on the performance of distributors. The characteristics of services stand as limitations on many fronts of channel operations. Unless companies follow effective strategies for channel management, it is not possible to achieve the desired marketing objectives. The following three strategies are vital in this respect:

Control Strategies

The basic issue of control by the service principal is service quality. It is possible only when a standard measurement programme on service performance by the intermediary and a feedback system to the service principal is designed and executed. Organizing customer surveys on key points of service encounter is necessary to measure the performance. It is also possible to control the intermediaries through punishment strategies, which include terminations, non-renewals, quotas and restrictive supplier sources.

> *Control, empowerment and partnering are the three strategies useful for **service channel management**. The channel members need to be controlled to ensure delivery of the service as per the standards. Empowerment is necessary as the services cannot be totally standardized. Partnering is intended to include the intermediaries in the vision of the company.*

Empowerment Strategies

This approach provides greater flexibility to intermediaries to exhibit their talents in making the service offering more beneficial to the customers. The service principal helps the intermediary to develop customer-oriented service processes, support systems, efficiency in delivering service quality and so on. A cooperative management structure can be designed to manage and motivate intermediaries.

Partnering Strategies

Service firms, of late, are increasingly adopting partnering strategies, which have the highest potential for effectiveness in relationship with intermediaries. Partnering with intermediaries is to learn together about end customers, set specifications, improve delivery and communicate honestly. This approach depends on the skills and strengths of both the service principal and middlemen, and develops a sense of trust between the parties. The alignment of goals of the service principal and the intermediary firms is one of the most successful approaches to partnering. When channel members believe that they benefit the ultimate consumer of service and in the process optimize their own revenues and profit, they begin the relationship with the service principal.

SUMMARY

- The distribution of services is a difficult proposition, due to the fact that services are intangible, inseparable and variable.
- When service providers want to expand their market to other locations, they should either open branches or use middlemen for the purpose.
- The major challenge is to provide the same quality specifications in all the service outlets. In case of any deviation, the marketing consequences are very serious.
- The middleman becomes a co-producer of the service.
- Service companies may opt for extensive, exclusive or selective distribution.
- The location of the service outlet and the service deliverer are the two critical issues in service distribution.
- There are three kinds of channel options to a service provider: agents and brokers, franchisees and electronic channels. Each and every channel has its own benefits and limitations.
- Electronic channels are becoming highly potential for service distribution due to the advancements in IT and expanded base of Internet users.
- The decision on the selection of a channel should be based on the nature of services, customer groups and the availability and capability of service distributors.

KEY TERMS

Electronic channels *300*	Franchising *297*	Service deliverer *294*
Exclusive distribution *293*	Multi-marketing *304*	Service principal *294*
Extensive distribution *293*	Selective distribution *293*	

BRIEF QUESTIONS

1. Explain service transactions.
2. Discuss the importance of service locations and service providers for the distribution of services.
3. What are the uses and limitations of electronic channels?
4. Explain empowerment strategies for channel management.
5. What are the benefits in using franchisees for service distribution?

ESSAY QUESTIONS

1. What are the challenges to service firms in designing a distribution system?
2. Evaluate the suitability of different types of intermediaries for services distribution.
3. Suggest measures for the efficient functioning of a service distribution system.
4. Discuss various strategies for channel management.

ASSIGNMENTS

1. Private sector insurance companies in India are recruiting insurance advisors in large number to build their agency network. They are also expanding their branch network to many parts of the country. You are required to study:
   (a) The interrelationship and interdependency of branches and advisors
   (b) The role of agents in the distribution of insurance services
2. e-channels are used prominently by airlines and railways for the distribution of their services. You re required to study:
   (a) The special benefits to consumers in this sector from e-channels
   (b) The problems of using e-channels for transport services

REFERENCES

1 Donald H. Light, Marking Service Distribution Work, *The AMA Hand Book of Marketing for Service Industries*. (New York: American Marketing Association, 1991), pp. 323–342.

2 Michael Levy and Barton A. Weitz, *Retailing Management*. (New Delhi: McGraw-Hill, 2002), p. 233.

3 Valarie A Zeithaml, et al., *Services Marketing*, 4th ed. (New Delhi: McGraw-Hill, 2008), p. 438.

4 Barry Berman and Joel R. Evans, *Retail Management: A Strategic Approach*. (New Delhi: Pearson Education, 2007), p. 111.

5 R. Javalgi and R. Ramsey, "Strategic Issues of E-commerce as an Alternative Global Distribution System", *International Marketing Review*, 18, no. 4 (2001): 376–391.

6 Edie Weiner and Arnold Brown, "A Right-of-Way Strategy," *Strategy & Leadership*, 3, no. 6 (2005): 22.

7 Khanh V. La and Fay Kandampully, "Electronic Retailing and Distribution of Services: Cyber Intermediaries That Serve Customers and Service Providers," *Managing Service Quality*, 12, no. 2 (2002): 100.

8 M. L. Meuter, A. L. Ostrom, R. L. Roundtree and M. J. Bitner, "Self-service Technologies: Understanding Customer Satisfaction with Technology-based Service Encounters," *Journal of Marketing*, 64, no. 3 (2000): 50–64.

9 C. Wymbs, "How E-commerce Is Transforming and Internationalizing Service Industries," *Journal of Service Marketing*, 14, no. 6 (2000): 463–478.

10 Khanh V. La and Fay Kandampully, "Electronic Retailing and Distribution of Services: Cyber Intermediaries That Serve Customers and Service Providers," *Managing Service Quality*, 12, no. 2 (2002): 101.

11 K. K. Boyer, "E-operations: A Guide to Streamlining with the Internet," *Bus Horizon*, 44, no. 1 (2001): 47–54.

12 S. Burt and L. Sparks, "E-commerce and the Retail Process: A Review," *Journal of Retailing and Consumer Service*, 10, (2003): 275–286.

13 Donald H. Light, Marking Service Distribution Work. *The AMA Hand Book of Marketing for Service Industries.* (New York: American Marketing Association, 1991), pp. 323–342.

Internal Marketing

16

LEARNING OBJECTIVES

After studying this chapter, you will be able to:

- Understand the importance of internal marketing
- Understand the various roles of employees in a service organization
- Describe the strategies for internal marketing

Sharada Management Institute, established in the early 1960s in India, is regarded by many as one of the premier management institutes in the country. The old students of the institute occupy very important positions in government and private enterprises, both within and outside the country. Good infrastructure and a highly qualified staff have been the strengths of the institute from the very beginning. The established image of the institution draws crowds for admission into the course.

Mr Parasuraman, the newly appointed director of the institute, is not happy with the happenings in the institute. In spite of the mushrooming of government and private institutes at the undergraduate and postgraduate levels, demand management has never been a problem—the number of candidates seeking admission exceeds the number of available seats. However, Parasuraman has noticed that the number of applications has been steadily declining over the last five years. Though the senior members of the faculty attribute this to the increased competition, Parsuraman has his reservations. In addition to this, Parsuraman has observed several trends:

1. The class work is not properly conducted.
2. Absenteeism among students is high.
3. Teachers give more importance to personal and private jobs.
4. The placement cell has been unable to network with established companies for the last few years.
5. Enthusiastic participation is absent, both from faculty and students.
6. Teacher–student relationships are neither positive nor negative.
7. The facilities offered by the institute are not being optimally utilized by the faculty and students.

Unhappy about these trends, Parasuraman has realized that it is necessary to take constructive action to rebuild the institute. If the management does not take any steps to this effect, the institute is likely to face severe problems in the future. He strongly feels that all the problems he has noticed can be solved if the members of the faculty are committed and get involved with their work. Since he is undecided on the best way solve the problem, he has hired a consultant to tackle the situation at hand.

Questions:

1. What, according to you, ails Sharada Educational Institute? Do you think the problem lies with the faculty and support personnel?
2. What kind of HR strategies will be useful for an institution like this?
3. In your opinion, is it correct to hire a professional consultant to solve this internal problem?
4. How would you handle this if the problem were referred to you?

INTRODUCTION

More than 20 years ago, internal marketing (IM) was first proposed as a solution to the problem of delivering consistently high service quality by L. L. Berry et al.[1] The concept of internal marketing signifies the role of employees in achieving organizational objectives. Employees are a critical resource for any service organization. Internal marketing states that the employees of the organization are the first market, and the final consumers are the second. It is essential to understand and satisfy the needs and wants of the employees in order to serve the consumers better. It is a proven fact all over the world that only satisfied employees can deliver quality services to the customers. Employees should be fast and efficient at executing operational tasks, as well as courteous and helpful in dealing with customers. Many service encounters have the potential to be a three-cornered fight regarding the needs of partially conflicting parties: the customer, the server and the service firm. The role of the employee as the service provider is critical in this proposition, if the right people are not assigned to the right job, the employees become stressed and less productive. L. L. Berry[2] defined internal marketing as "viewing employees as internal customers, viewing jobs as internal products that satisfy the needs and wants of these internal customers while addressing the objectives of the organization."

Specialist employees of the marketing department are not the only human resource in the marketing of services. Quite often, these personnel are considered the most important resource. But during service production and delivery, marketing specialists are often outnumbered by a variety of employees who perform such duties as production, delivery, client handling, technical service and other activities that are traditionally considered non-marketing activities. To perform these activities, employees must be skilled, have customer orientation and be service minded so that they can influence customer perceptions positively in interactions. Internal marketing is a management strategy that focuses on how to develop customer-conscious employees.[3] According to Christian Grönroos,[4] the concept of internal marketing states that the internal market of employees is best motivated by an active, marketing-like approach, where a variety of activities are used internally in an active, coordinated way. Treating every employee as a valued customer is the focus of the new discipline of internal marketing.

Internal marketing is attracting, developing, motivating and retaining qualified employees through job products that satisfy their needs.[5] It includes aligning, educating and motivating employees towards institutional objectives. Internal marketing process should ensure personnel understand and recognize the value of the marketing programme and their place in it. Five[6] main elements of internal marketing are identified from the analysis of the key conceptual and empirical literature. These are:

- Employee motivation and satisfaction
- Customer orientation and customer satisfaction
- Inter-functional coordination and integration

> *"**Internal marketing** refers to identification of employees as market and serving them as final customers. The concept believes that satisfaction of internal customer is the prerequisite for satisfying the external customer."*

- Marketing-like approach to the above
- Implementation of specific corporate or functional strategies

Service companies in businesses like hotels, insurance, banking, retail, etc., are increasingly paying attention to frontline customer–contact employees to achieve the desired profit and marketing goals. Companies are preferring a people-oriented approach as compared to a profit-oriented one. "Successful service managers recognize the importance of crucial factors that drive profitability in this new service paradigm: investment in people, technology that supports frontline workers, revamped recruiting and training practices, and compensation linked to performance for employees at every level."[7]

EMPLOYEES CAUGHT IN BETWEEN

The importance of employees in marketing of services is well recognized and captured in the "people" element of the marketing mix. Service employees have to face customers on one end and the organization on the other. Customers demand attention and service quality while the organization demands efficiency and productivity. This apparent tension of satisfying management and customers and of meeting productivity and quality goals is an important area to be considered by the managements of service companies. Employees need to be relieved of this tension to deliver better performance. In case of personal and professional services such as beauty care, consultancy, legal services and so on, contact employees are viewed as service. In the eyes of the customers, employees are the service organization. The contact employees directly influence customer satisfaction by performing the role of marketers. Consumer expectations in such cases would be very high. Therefore, service organizations should take into consideration the critical functionality and the work pressure involved for the employees in designing internal marketing processes.

> *"Service employees have to satisfy the needs of the employer as well as customers, which are often conflicting. Employer demands productivity and efficiency while customer demands more attention and service quality. Thus, the service employees are caught in between."*

The purpose of internal marketing is to integrate multiple functions of the firm and operate the service firm as a holistic management process. Internal marketing ensures that all employees understand and experience various business activities and campaigns and are also prepared and motivated to act in a service-oriented manner. The necessary condition is that the internal exchange between the organization and its employees should operate effectively before facing external markets. The employees should be given right kind of support at the right time.

EMPLOYEE SATISFACTION

The marketing goal of every service organization is to achieve customer satisfaction and customers' retention. Research studies prove beyond doubt that the marketing goal can be achieved only when employees are satisfied. Service organizations should study employee expectations, time and again, and gear up the policy framework to satisfy them. Employee satisfaction will not only increase employee productivity but also result in employee retention. The performance of a satisfied employee results in customer satisfaction,

ICICI Infotech

ICICI Infotech Services Limited, the leading software solutions and services provider based in India, was established in October 1993. The company presently focuses on software development and Web-enabling businesses, IT-enabled services and IT infrastructure, communications and related services. ICICI Infotech employs about 750 professionals of which about 120 are employed in the USA. The company conducts employee satisfaction surveys twice a year to assess job satisfaction, overall work place productivity and work culture. It also analyses the employees' perceptions and attitudes towards the job as well as the organization through these surveys. These surveys are conducted by a team consisting of MD core group and the HR team. The team identifies the core parameters for the survey and accordingly questions are formulated. The parameters generally include organization and strategy, corporate culture, employee role, team work and cooperation and internal support services. The structured questionnaires are made open to the employees online, and the employees are asked to respond within a specified time frame. The findings of the surveys are analysed to identify areas of concern and to initiate measures to fill the gaps. The company finds these surveys useful for internal marketing management.

and the satisfied customer becomes loyal to the service organization. A loyal customer base increases revenue as well as profitability of the organization. Therefore, employee satisfaction has a chain of positive effects to the service firms. Quality perceptions of customers are greatly influenced by employees' behaviour. Service quality dimensions such as reliability, responsiveness, assurance, empathy and appearance, affect the customer perceptions positively or negatively.

EMOTIONAL LABOUR

Employees of service organizations have to stretch their physical or mental skills to the utmost to deliver quality service. This is why they are called "emotional labour." They are also known as "boundary spanners" because they operate at the boundary of the organization. They have to interact with external as well as internal environments. Frontline employees require extraordinary ability to handle interpersonal and inter-organizational conflicts. While participating in service encounters, they need to be cheerful, make eye contact, show interest and engage in friendly conversation with customers. The performance of this service function requires the emotional involvement of the employee. The functional quality of the service mostly depends upon the emotional labour.

> *"Employees are required to handle a variety of consumers and share their emotions in the service production process. The functional quality of the service depends upon how the employees manage their emotions in customer interactions."*

OBJECTIVES OF INTERNAL MARKETING

Service companies strive to achieve customer satisfaction through employee satisfaction. Christian Grönroos[8] suggested two internal marketing objectives. They are:

- To ensure that the employees are motivated for customer-oriented and service-minded performance and, thus, successfully fulfil the duties as "part-time marketers" in their interactive marketing tasks
- To attract and retain good employees

The employees of a service organization are broadly categorized into two groups.

1. Full-time marketers
2. Part-time marketers

Full-time marketers are specialist functionaries in the marketing department, and part-time marketers are those who are involved in various service activities either on the line of visibility or below the line of visibility.

ROLES OF A SERVICE EMPLOYEE

Service employees are required to perform a variety of roles in a service organization. Employees who are involved in the service production process need to perform the following roles effectively (see Fig. 16.1):

- *Product Designer:* The basic service package (BSP) formulated by the service organization serves as a basic input for the contact employee. Each and every customer requires a different service for solving their problems. Service employees should ascertain each customer's specific service requirements and design a distinctive service product by taking into consideration the resources and competencies of the service organization.
- *Performer:* Service employees are the performers in the service production process. They have to interact with uncontrollable elements (consumers) and extract quality performance by influencing the customers to get involved in the process.
- *Technician:* Some services require the use of equipment and tools. The service employee who possesses the skills to operate such equipment is required for such purposes.
- *Associate:* Service employees and service consumers together produce service. The expected role of an employee is to associate with the consumer and produce quality service. Further, some services may need

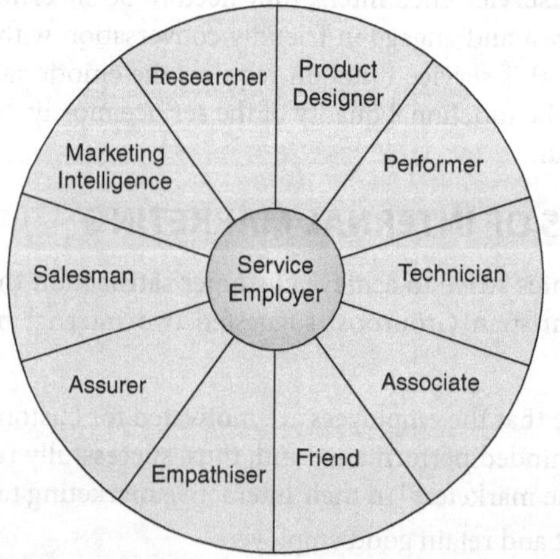

Fig. 16.1
Roles of a service employee

group involvement. Then it may be necessary for a service employee to associate with the group members for performing the service.

- *Friend:* A service employee has to play the role of a friend with consumers as well as co-employees in a team. Co-employees and customers look for help, cooperation, guidance and support from others on various issues. Every employee of the service organization should respond to such needs positively.
- *Empathiser:* Empathy is the key quality parameter in service. Service consumers feel comfortable and perceive better quality when contact employees are empathetic. Service employees should have the patience and inclination to be empathetic towards customers.
- *Assurer:* Service employees' words and actions should reflect assurance to customers. As services are intangible, variable and perishable, customers seek assurance in every production process. For the consumer, contact employees are the representatives of the service company. This is why a contact employee needs to perform the role of an assurer.
- *Salesman:* The performance of a service employee builds a positive image for the service company. The customers of a service are likely to become consumers of other services offered by the company. Contact employees will have an opportunity to interact closely and intimately with customers. Therefore, their role in influencing and persuading the customers to buy other services of the company is vital. Service companies can use their contact employees as sales personnel.
- *Marketing Intelligence:* One of the most prominent sources of marketing intelligence is contact employees. They are the right personnel to assess response of the customers on company policies and quality specifications. The feedback from contact employees proves to be very valuable.
- *Researcher:* Innovation is the key to success in service business. Employees of the service companies are the real innovators in many respects. As variability is the key character of services, continuous improvements, whether minor or major, provide a competitive edge in the market. Employees, with their continuous involvement in work and interactive experience with varied customers, with a distinctive knowledge base, are capable of bringing innovation in work. There is a lot of scope to exploit the creativity of employees in service business.

> "*Service employees perform multiple roles in a service process. A contact employee is expected to play the roles of a service designer, performer, technician, friend, associate, empathizer, assurer, salesman, intelligence and researcher.*"

THE INTERNAL MARKETING PRODUCT

Service companies need to put in almost equal effort in designing "products" for external as well as internal markets. While customer satisfaction is the orientation for external market, employee satisfaction is the orientation for internal market. Employees' needs and wants should be studied carefully along with their expectations to design a package of benefits that is capable of satisfying them. According to C. Grönroos,[9] "The internal product consists of a job and a work environment that motivates the employees to respond favourably to the management's demands for customer orientation and good interactive marketing performance as part-time marketers and which moreover attracts and retains good employees." In order to ensure proper design of an internal service product, there is a need to make the concept of internal marketing a part of the strategic management philosophy. A practical approach for internal marketing is presented in "Services Marketing Insight: Employee Development—Facilitating Practices".

STRATEGIES FOR INTERNAL MARKETING

Internal marketing is a philosophy of managing personnel and developing and enhancing a service culture systematically. The activities of internal marketing should promote service mindedness and customer orientation. Most

16.1 Services Marketing Insight | **Employee Development—Facilitating Practices**

Employee development is one of the top priority areas of service management. The theme of internal marketing revolves around employee skill development and empowerment. The following guidelines for practising employee development are useful to service companies:

1. Share the organization's mission and the roles to be played by the employees.
2. Make sure the communicating channels within the organization work effectively to sell ideas and services internally.
3. Recognize frontline personnel as critical means of facing competition and motivate them.
4. Bridge gap between internal customer expectations and performance.
5. Facilitate employees to play an active role in all aspects of work life.
6. Review employer–employee interactions periodically.
7. Identify performance gaps in internal service through internal audits.
8. Apply the marketing concept to manage employees.
9. Ensure all managers properly understand the employees' skill package and participate in the employee development process.
10. Create a conducive environment for employee–customer interactions.
11. Establish channels for interpersonal interactive communications.
12. Provide access to mass communication media.
13. Organize programmes to educate employees on important organizational issues.
14. Consider the development of knowledge and skills as an investment rather than as a cost.
15. Teach employees "why they should do things" and not simply "how they should do things."
16. Reward the employees for excellence in service.
17. Undertake internal market research.
18. Inform employees all the new developments within the organization.
19. Encourage employees to innovate without fear.
20. Encourage employees to participate in quality management techniques across the organization.
21. Listen to employees' ideas and problems.
22. Seek suggestions from employees for improvement and quality enhancement.
23. Communicate with employees the expectations of the management.
24. Be realistic in dealing with employees.

Source: Tony Proctor and Ioanna Doukakis, "Change Management: The Role of Internal Communication and Employee Development," Corporate Communications: An International Journal, *8, no. 4 (2003): 271–272.*

of the internal marketing activities are part of human resource management and development. A combination of management and development strategies is needed to ensure that right kind of people are entrusted with the right kind of jobs. They must have customer orientation, service mindedness and the capacity to stay motivated to perform services. Figure 16.2 shows various strategies for internal marketing. The strategies presented in the figure are organized around eight basic themes. They are staffing, training, organizing, supporting, motivating, evaluating, rewarding and retaining. The central theme of internal marketing strategy is to make the employees involved in the service process. The challenges of internal marketing are discussed in "Services Marketing Insight: Internal Marketing Challenges".

> *Internal marketing activities should ensure right people are taken for the right jobs. The employees need to be trained, supported, rewarded, empowered and provided with all necessary inputs for quality performance.*

Staffing

A proper assessment of what kind of people are required and how many is the starting point in human resource policy of any service organization. The three important issues in staffing are manpower planning, recruitment and selection.

1. *Manpower Planning:* In service business, manpower often becomes the core competence for companies. To build the organization with competent personnel, it is necessary to have a proper manpower planning. Besides planning the right size of employment at various service points, manpower planning ensures that the right people occupy positions. It also develops supplementary plans for manpower expansion and contraction, according to demand fluctuations.

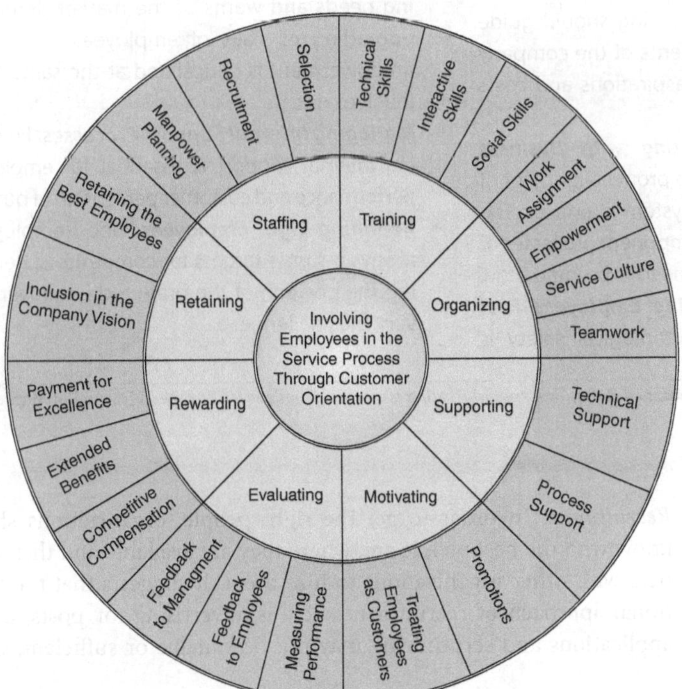

Fig. 16.2: Strategies for internal marketing

16.2 Services Marketing Insight — Internal Marketing Challenges

Managing human resources is always a challenging task. Particularly, when business performance depends significantly on the performances of employees, for example, services business where the tasks are critical and ever challenging. The major challenges of internal marketing are:

- ***Satisfying Employees:*** Fulfilment of employee needs, wants and expectations results in employee satisfaction and loyalty. Service companies should exhibit their commitment towards employee satisfaction.
- ***Building Multiple Skill Sets for Performing Cross-functional Roles:*** Multiple operations of service production require people with multiple skill sets. The performance of people in cross-functional activities has a major influence on the final outcome.
- ***Building Internal Relationships:*** The success of service operations is driven by integrating related functions such as production, sales, advertising, marketing research and finance within the organization. Internal marketing should guide all functions and departments of the company to appreciate the needs, aspirations and costs of each.
- ***Aligning Internal Marketing with Business Strategy:*** There should be a proper alignment of systems, subsystems and system interfaces. The specific capabilities and component processes of each system or sub-system need to be integrated.
- ***Building Trust and Making Employees Feel Psychologically Safe:*** Psychological safety is a state in which people feel safe to be candid in what they think and how they feel. Trust and psychological safety develop creative personnel in the service organization.
- ***Developing Service Culture in the Organization:*** Service cultures among employees builds relationships, enhances mutual understanding and inter-personal support.
- ***Planning and Execution of Effective Internal Communications:*** Internal communications should aim at filling knowledge gaps and a proper understanding of company philosophy, business mission, policies, procedures, internal developments, company's market strategy, research output, promises and performances and so on.
- ***Motivating Employees:*** The stressful and emotional nature of a service job requires highly motivated employees.
- ***Building Employee Competencies and Promoting Employee Empowerment:*** The changing needs and wants of the market demands upgrading of skills of employees. Employee empowerment is critical and at the same time involves risk.
- ***Managing Internal Support Processes:*** Perfecting internal support is essential for employee performance and customer perception of quality.
- ***Retaining Right Employees:*** Good employees always become targets for competitors. Retaining the position of the preferred employer is a very big challenge.

Source: Pervaiz K. Ahmed and Mohammed Rafiq, "Internal Marketing Issues and Challenges," European Journal of Marketing, *37, no. 9 (2003): 1177–1186*

2. *Recruitment*: In order to get the right people, organizations should know who the best people are, where they are available and then compete with other organizations to hire them. It suggests that the traditional approach of recruitment such as advertising for posts, calling applications and scrutinizing may not be suitable or sufficient. Other

recruitment ideas such as campus interviews at reputed universities and institutions, career fairs and encouraging current employees to identify potential employees can be used. Service firms should be prepared to spend time, energy and money to get the best people. It can be said that spending money and time is worth it when finding a right person, rather than losing millions of rupees because of the entry of a wrong person in the organization. Ensuring that employees are highly motivated, customer oriented and sales minded requires recruitment practices that attract and select employees with the requisite attitudes.[10]

3. *Selection*: Internal marketing is aimed at attracting, retaining, and motivating "service-minded," "customer-conscious" employees capable of generating customer-perceived service quality and provide competitive advantage. Service providers, by the nature of the service business, are very dependent on their employees to achieve customer satisfaction.[11] For performance of some services, employees must be professionally qualified. Thus, a medical degree for doctors in a hospital, a law degree for advocates in a legal service firm, specialized postgraduate and doctorate degrees for teachers in universities and institutes are the basic minimum requirements. Service competencies include skill and knowledge of the employees. Some services do not require knowledge and skill in a specific discipline, or trained people may not be available. In such cases, the companies have to prescribe minimum qualifications and identify those having the best credentials. A proper selection process needs to be designed. The selection process may vary according to the needs of the service organization.

"***Staffing*** *is one of the critical parts of internal marketing. Service companies should take up manpower planning and search for right sources of recruitment to get the best people, with not only technical skills but also service inclination.*"

Besides finding qualified people, it is necessary to examine whether they have an inclination to the service or not. People in service firms should have an interest to serve. The attitude towards the service job and orientation to serve people are important criteria to test. Although all the applicants for service jobs may have some level of service inclination, some will be more service driven. Such people must be spotted and selected for the service. The employer should look for people who have both the qualifications and the inclination. A variety of tests and interviews may be designed to identify the right candidate for the job. In customer-contact businesses, the quality of service delivered cannot be separated from the quality of the service provider.[12] Because service delivery occurs through human interaction, customer-contact personnel during the service encounter largely determine the level of service quality delivered. All kinds of behaviour and actions on the behalf of customer-contact employees during the service encounter cannot be directed and controlled by the management.[13]

"***Training*** *is an important input for employee performance. The inducted employees and experienced employees also should be given training as per the needs. The training should focus on building technical, interactive and social skills in employees.*"

The ability to attract the right people depends upon, among other things, the image of the organization as an employer. The internal marketing efforts, the satisfaction of the existing employees, the employee turnover, the growth prospects of the firm and career prospects of employees are some of the measurement points used by the people to join an organization. Therefore, to

New India Assurance

New India Assurance is a leading non-life insurance company in India. The company has approximately 21,000 specialist and technically qualified personnel at all levels of service operations. The company established a corporate training college, regional training centres and zonal training centres to train and upgrade the skills of employees at different managerial levels. The training programmes focused on information technology, computer literacy, new product development, insurance laws and new forms of distribution like bancassurance. In addition to the employees, the company provides training to its agents. The company promotes training centres of agents at various locations in the country.

The objective of training employees is to make them efficient functionaries in operational processes, creative in introducing improvements in interactive processes and new product development and contributive for organizational development in all possible areas. The agents are provided training not only to satisfy the regulation of IRDA but also to strengthen their selling and service skills. The company's success is attributed to the proactive support of the employees and agents of the company.

attract people, service firms should develop a positive internal environment that ensures employee prosperity.

TRAINING

Service firms may have a training system and infrastructure or may hire a specialist organization for its training needs. Training employees on relevant aspects is an absolute necessity for service firms. Christian Grönroos[14] has identified the following three kinds of training tasks:

1. Developing a holistic view of how a service strategy works and what is the role of each individual in relation to other individuals, functions within the firm and relations with customers.
2. Developing and enhancing a favourable attitude towards a service strategy and part-time marketing performance.
3. Developing and enhancing communication skills and service skills among employees.

The training programme should aim at basically three important skills for employees. They are

1. *Technical skills* relating to job specification and expected role performances.
2. *Interactive skills* relating to providing courteous, caring, responsive and empathetic service. It includes communication, listening, problem-solving and interpersonal skills.
3. *Social skills* relating to building personal relationships and recognizing and treating regular customers differently.

Training in service organizations should not be limited only to new employees. It should be an ongoing process. The ever-changing market environment necessitates change in service organizations and the need for improved service skills. Continual training of employees is important for firms to offer better quality service.

ORGANIZING

Employees of service organizations need to be organized properly to achieve better results. The following are the four important dimensions of organizing employees:

1. *Work Assignment:* Classification of service jobs and assigning them to such personnel who have the capability as well as willingness to serve is a critical task. The qualities, qualifications and interests of the employee have to be thoroughly assessed before assigning a service job. A wrong assignment not only makes the service a failure, but also causes loss of customers. There is a lot of difference between handling a job and handling a job efficiently. Consumers normally possess the ability to perceive the difference in handling.
2. *Empowerment:* In service production and delivery process, frontline employees have to assess the exact needs of the customer and develop a customized service product within the framework of the BSP. To perform these activities on the spot effectively, frontline employees need to be empowered. Empowerment is recognizing and releasing into the organization the power that people already have in their wealth of useful knowledge, experience and internal motivation.[15] According to V. A. Zeithaml and M. J. Bitner[16], "Empowerment means giving employees the desired skills, tools and authority to serve the customer." Empowerment is more than just giving employees limited and conditional authority and/or responsibility. It involves enabling employees to recognize their own power and the significance of their role in the service process. Delegation of authority is the key factor in empowerment. It is particularly necessary to allow contact employees to take decisions at interaction points. Employee empowerment creates a free environment where every employee feels free to perform service functions that are mostly non-routine and often unpredictable. It motivates employees to modify and create processes. Even minor improvements in service processes are capable of generating major responses from customers. Frontline employees, when empowered, emerge as a major source for minor improvements. "In a competitive environment in which organizations must be faster, leaner, provide better service quality, be more efficient, and more profitable, an empowered and proactive service worker is thought to be essential."[17]
3. *Service Culture:* Culture is a broad term that reflects the norms and values of a society. Culture explains why people do certain things, think in common ways and appreciate similar goals, routines, even jokes, just because they are members of the same organization. S. M. Davis[18]

defined corporate culture as the pattern of shared values and beliefs, which give the members of the organization meaning and provide them with the rules for behaviour in the organization. A strong corporate culture empowers the people to act in a specific manner and to respond to various stimulations in a uniform way. A strong service-oriented culture in an organization gets easily picked up by new employees. It helps the existing employees by way of sharing the norms and values. On the other hand, a weak corporate culture creates an insecure feeling for the new incumbent of the organization. He or she may be under confusion as to how to respond to various clues and how to react in different situations. "Empowering employees to provide differentiated services requires a culture that values, trusts and provides them with the flexibility to make decisions that impact on the customer."[19]

A service culture cannot be developed overnight. Continuous and sustained efforts of the management over a period of time in designing work environment, human resource policies and efficiency of execution naturally result in the development of a service culture. Good culture once developed becomes the core competency of the organization.

> *Assignment of jobs as per the suitability of individual employees, empowering them to perform freely and creatively, promoting service culture and team work are the critical areas of internal marketing management.*

4. *Team Work.* Customers often perceive better experiences when employees work together as teams. Due to the nature of service jobs, which is sometimes frustrating, demanding or challenging, team work reduces the stress and strain of individual employees and helps them to maintain enthusiasm in work. Team work, therefore, should be developed and promoted. It may require restructuring the organization to develop market-based groupings. Creating teams and supporting effective team work, especially across functions, is important. Individuals skilled in interpersonal facilitation often work behind the scenes to keep their colleague committed and engaged, so projects do not get derailed.[20]

   There are many barriers and obstacles to overcome while implementing team work strategies in most traditional organizations. However, if this exercise is done well, the benefits to both employees and customers are tremendous.

SUPPORTING

Service employees need support systems to be efficient and effective in their jobs. If everybody strives to provide their "internal customer" with better service, then the end customer will receive higher quality service.[21] The quality of service provided will be greatly dependent on the adequacy of support systems. A medical practitioner requires a system that provides information relating to the patient, testing facilities, equipment to handle and support services to perform effectively. Similarly, a professor requires a good library, teaching aids, supply of student information and feedback, secretarial assistance to develop notes and reading material and facilities to counsel students in order to perform well. Organizational units should provide a high level of service quality to internal customers for some of the same reasons they provide to external customers—more effective performance, lower waste and lower costs.[22] Looking at it from the employees' perspective, a systematic understanding of requirements, expectations and satisfaction is essential to design internal processes to meet employees' needs. With internal cooperation and collaboration, it is easier to focus on delighting the external customer.[23] To transform the vision of delighted customers into reality requires organization structure, management practices and business systems, which encourage and permit employees to provide exceptional customer service. Providing an infrastructure that supports, rather than impedes, employee motivation is an absolute requirement.[24] Therefore, service firms should design effective support systems for their employees.

Basically, service employees require two types of support—technical support and process support.

1. *Technical Support:* The quality of the work by the employees gets enhanced with the support of technology and equipment. Tools, machines, other tangibles and systems provided to the employees not only increase speed and accuracy but also provide comfort and convenience in service performance. The EPBAX system, computerization and other instruments in a service outlet would certainly provide convenience to both employees and customers. A teacher's classroom performance would be greatly influenced by the quality of support systems such as audio visual equipment, multimedia system, supply of support material to the students and the like provided to him. Involvement and commitment coupled with clear sense of purpose are pre-requisite for the much-needed coherence and focus that are ultimately required to produce successful outcomes. Involvement concerns not only people, but also include all organizational resources such as systems, equipment and information.[25]
2. *Process Support:* Support services are necessary to service employees and customers for their efficient functioning in service production and consumption. Secretarial assistance, documents, information networking, communication system, mobility, scheduling and routing, influence the performance of employees and customers in the service process.

> *"Frontline employees need institutional support for better performance. The support may be technical or related to internal processes. The internal processes should facilitate the frontline employee's work. The services to the internal customer should be planned and well managed."*

MOTIVATING

Employee motivation is the key element for internal marketing. Employee motivation is particularly significant in services because of the human impact on buyer–seller interactions. Employees are often required to respond to new situations, unforeseen or even awkward to them. A motivated person alone can handle such situations properly and, thus, build the reputation of the organization. What motivates an employee to perform quality service and to continue with the service organization is the question for which the management has to search an appropriate answer. There are two important issues the management has to take care of particularly in motivating employees: promotions and treating employees as customers.

> *Several researchers established positive correlation between employee motivation and performance. Service employees need to be motivated by way of providing them enhanced benefits, promoting to high positions and in all treating them in real sense as internal customers.*

1. *Promotions:* All employees look for improvement in rank within an appropriate time span of their career. If an organization does not provide opportunities to move forward in their careers, employees get frustrated and de-motivated. If they find opportunity elsewhere, they quit the organization. Service companies should realize the need for creating promotional opportunities for employees. If promotion is purely given by merit, the management can create a healthy competitive environment among the employees and motivate them to perform better.
2. *Treating Employees as Customers:* The basic concept of internal marketing propagates the theme of treating employees as customers. Employee–employer relations play a vital role in service performance. When employees are considered important by the management which understand their needs and wants and offer value satisfaction, employees are more likely to stay with the organization. An organization can become the best place to work if the following four important principles are followed: (i) treating employees as customers, (ii) involving employees in decision making, (iii) ensuring employee satisfaction and (iv) benchmarking and incorporating the best practices of human resource management.

In order to design programmes to satisfy the needs of employees, internal research and employee segmentation are useful approaches. Advertising and other forms of communication directed at employees can also increase their sense of value and enhance commitment to the organization.

EVALUATING

Evaluation of performance of the employees is vital in internal marketing. It is necessary to develop systems that measure the performance of the employees.

1. *Feedback to Management:* Management of service firms should collect feedback on employee performance regularly for several purposes. The feedback helps the management identify areas for improvement, defects and deviations from the quality specifications and initiate appropriate corrective action.
2. *Feedback to Employees.* In the service industry, direct supervision may not be effective in assessing the performance and such measures, sometimes, become counter productive. Employees of service firms need to be provided support systems that can help evaluate performance by themselves and also report such performance to the top management. Therefore, the evaluation system not only has the capability of measuring performance but also has the capability of providing timely feedback to employees and management. Corrective actions can then be initiated when something is not in the order. A survey by internal employees, customer feedback surveys and so on are useful in designing and evaluating the system.

3. *Measuring Performance:* Service firms need to develop an acceptable methodology for measuring the performance of employees. The measures should help employees know their level of performance so that they can plan for further improvement. The performance measures help the management recognize the merit, to identify training needs and to develop plans for motivating employees, if necessary.

REWARDING

One of the prime concerns of any employee is the reward that he or she gets for the service rendered to the organization. The rewarding system primarily should contain the following three dimensions to be effective in service business:

1. *Competitive Compensation:* The compensation offered to service personnel—brokerage, salary, commission or wages—should be competitive. Since employees acquire distinctive identities in service performance, which are linked to a company's capability, credibility, reliability and responsiveness, competitors always try to attract the employees of other organizations. During the software boom of the 1990s, software companies faced a severe threat of employee turnover. The only approach that helped organizations retain software experts was a competitive compensation policy. Service firms need to review their compensation package periodically to motivate the employees and promote morale in them.
2. *Extended Benefits:* Besides direct compensation, service firms provide extended benefits to the employees. The extended benefits include employee welfare measures within the organization, employee family welfare measures, employee children education, functions and social interaction. Managements can be innovative in providing extended benefits. They can touch upon the sensitivities of employees and can create a positive inner feeling among employees for the service organization. Such benefits promote the sense of belongingness among employees and help build a strong morale.
3. *Payment for Excellence:* A rewarding system, to be effective, should be capable of identifying the best performers and rewarding them to the level of their excellence. The measures adopted to identify the performers are often subjected to severe criticism by employees. If the system is not properly received by employees, it may prove harmful to the organization. It is necessary, therefore, to involve the employees in developing the measurement system and the related reward policy.

> ***Compensation** is an important dimension in management of human resources. Service employees need to be provided more than the competitors offer to motivate and retain. It is also necessary to recognize excellent performers and pay them for their excellence.*

RETAINING

Hiring the right people is the beginning of a human resource policy. Retaining them is the real essence of the policy. When experienced and efficient personnel move out of the service organization, the reputation, image and performance of the company suffer. Service companies have to develop the following strategies to retain employees.

1. *Inclusion in the Company Vision:* One of the key elements of the retention strategy would be inclusion of employees in the "company's vision." When the employees are made part of the company's vision, they share not only the present benefits but also the benefits to be generated in future. This step helps employees relate their personal goals with organizational goals. They try to share an understanding of the organization's vision. They feel motivated and committed to the organization, when they understand how their work fits into the big picture of the organization and its goals. Service companies should prepare a vision document and communicate it to all employees frequently to reorient them to achieve their organizational goals. In other words, the same marketing tools used to attract customers can also serve to attract and retain the best employees, who can be thought of as internal customers.[26]

> "***Employee retention*** *is one of the benchmark performances of a service organization. Not all employees need to be retained. Only the performers need to be retained. Poor performers should be sent out of the organization.*"

2. *Retaining the Best Employees:* In spite of an efficient process of recruitment, selection and training, it is impossible for any organization to find that all the people hired are good and efficient. However, service firms cannot afford to retain inefficient and incompetent people in the organization. It is important to retain the best employees and keep away unwanted employees. The employee retention strategy is applicable only to the best performers.

SUMMARY

- Internal marketing is a new approach to handle human resources in an organization.
- It applies the marketing concept to human resource management and development. In service business, employees are categorized into full-time marketers and part-time marketers.
- Customer orientation is necessary in every activity of a service organization.
- Service quality can be achieved only when employees are well organized and well managed.
- Employee satisfaction is the only route through which service companies can satisfy their customers.
- Service employees play varied roles in the service production process and as an employee of the organization.
- Roles such as product designer, performer, associate and friend to the customer, assurer and salesman require total commitment and involvement of employees.
- Service companies need to develop effective human resource policies and strategies. There are eight basic themes in internal marketing: staffing, training, organizing, supporting, motivating, evaluating, rewarding and retaining.
- All HR policies and strategies focused to make every employee involved in the service process with customer orientation.

KEY TERMS

Emotional labour *311*
Empowerment *318*
Full-time marketers *312*
Interactive skills *317*
Manpower planning *315*
Part-time marketers *312*
Service culture *319*
Service inclination *316*
Social skills *317*
Technical skills *317*
Work assignment *317*

BRIEF QUESTIONS

1. What is an internal marketing product?
2. What are the objectives of internal marketing?
3. What is emotional labour?
4. How does employee behaviour influence service quality?
5. Explain various employee roles in service performance.
6. How can employees be retained?
7. How do you motivate service employees?
8. What is service culture?

ESSAY QUESTIONS

1. Explain the concept of internal marketing and analyse different roles played by employees in the service process.
2. What is employee empowerment? Why is empowerment essential in services?
3. What are the human resource strategies that service companies need to follow?
4. Discuss internal marketing strategies of a service company of your choice.
5. How to make internal marketing a successful one? Discuss.
6. "All service employees are either full-time or part-time marketers." Comment.

ASSIGNMENTS

1. Study the recruitment and selection process of a public sector bank and a private sector bank and find out :
   (a) The differences in the strategy and approach
   (b) The impact of the recruitment and selection process on building the desired workforce
2. Call centres are used by many service companies as a support to customer service. The employees of call centres should contact customers and attend to complaints and enquiry calls. Training plays a vital role in the performance of call centre employees. You are required to:
   (a) Study the training methods used to train call centre employees by selecting a call centre
   (b) Find out positive and negative factors in the training process

REFERENCES

1 L. L. Berry, J. S. Hensel and M. C. Burke, "Improving Retailer Capability for Effective Consumerism Response," *Journal of Retailing*, 52, no. 3 (1976): 3–14.

2 L. L. Berry, "The Employee as Customer," *Journal of Retail Banking*, 3, no. 1 (1981): 25–28.

3 W. R. George, "The Retailing of Services—A Challenging Future," *Journal of Retailing*, 53, (Fall, 1977): 85–98.

4 C. Grönroos, *Service Management and Marketing; Managing the Moments of Truth in Service Competition*. (Lexington, D. C.: Maxwell Macmillan, Heath/Lexington Books, 1990), p. 223.

5 L. L. Berry and A. Parasuraman, *Marketing Services: Competing through Quality*. (New York, NY: Free Press, 1991).

6 M. Rafiq and P. K. Ahmed, "Advances in the Internal Marketing Concept: Definition, Synthesis and Extension," *Journal of Services Marketing*, 14, no. 6 (2000): 453.

7 J. L. Heskett et al., "Putting the Service Profit Chain to Work," *Harvard Business Review*, (March–April, 1994): 164–174.

8 C. Grönroos, *Service Management and Marketing; Managing the Moments of Truth in Service Competition*. (Lexington, D. C.: Maxwell Macmillan, Heath/Lexington books, 1990), p. 225.

9 Ibid., p. 230.

10 L. L. Berry and A. Parasuraman, *Marketing Services: Competing through Quality*. (New York, NY: Free Press, 1991).

11 C. Sanes, "Employee Impact on Service Delivery," *Management Development Review*, 9, no. 2 (1996): 17.

12 B. R. Lewis, "Customer Care in Service Organizations," *Marketing Intelligence & Planning*, 7, no. 5/6 (1989): 18–22.

13 N. Malhotra and A. Mukherjee, "The Relative Influence of Organizational Commitment and Job Satisfaction on Service Quality of Customer-Contact Employees in Banking Call Centres," *Journal of Services Marketing*, 18, no. 3 (2004): 163.

14 C. Grönroos, *Service Management and Marketing; Managing the Moments of Truth in Service Competition*. (Lexington, D. C.: Maxwell Macmillan, Heath/Lexington books, 1990), p. 231.

15 W. A. Randolph M. and Sashkin, "Can Organizational Empowerment Work in Multinational Settings," *Academy of Management Executive*, 16, no. 1 (2002): 102–115.

16 V. A. Zeithaml, M. J. Bitner, D. D. Gremler and A. Pandit, *Services Marketing*, 4th ed. (New Delhi: McGraw-Hill, 2008) p. 380.

17 D. E. Bowen and E. Lawler, "Empowering Service Employees," *Sloan Management Review*, (Summer, 1995): 73–83.

18 S. M. Davis, *Managing Corporate Culture*. (Cambridge, MA: Ballinger, 1985).

19 C. Sanes, "Employee Impact on Service Delivery, *Management Development Review*, 9, no. 2 (1996): 18.

20 T. Butler and J. Waldroop, "Understanding 'People' People," *Harvard Business Review*, (June 2004): 80.

21 S. Farner, F. Luthans and S. M. Sommer, "An Empirical Assessment of Internal Customer Service," *Managing Service Quality*, 11, no. 5 (2001): 350.

22 G. W. Marshall, et al., "Exploring Internal Customer Service Quality," *Journal of Business & Industrial Marketing*, 13, no. 4/5 (1998): 381.

23 M. K. Vora, "Creating Employee Value in a Global Economy through Participation, Motivation and Development," *Total Quality Management*, 15, no. 5–6, (July/August, 2004): 795.

24 C. Sanes, "Employee Impact on Service Delivery," *Management Development Review*, 9, no. 2 (1996): 18.

25 P. K. Ahmed and M. Rafiq, "Internal Marketing Issues and Challenges," *European Journal of Marketing*, 37, no. 9 (2003): 1179–1180.

26 L. L. Berry, "The Employee as Customer," *Journal of Retail Banking*, 3, no. 1 (1981): 33–40.

External Marketing

17

LEARNING OBJECTIVES

After studying this chapter, you will be able to:

- Understand the importance of external marketing
- Understand the design of integrated marketing communications
- Identify the decision areas in designing communication campaign
- Understand the impact of word-of-mouth communication
- Understand the success strategies of external marketing

Each time there is a bomb blast, there is a 10 per cent increase in demand for security systems and a substantially higher increase in the demand for physical security services. The demand is from government offices to corporate facilities, private homes, neighbourhoods and shopping centres; virtually every organization is looking for ways to protect itself from the terror threats, street crime and corporate espionage that are increasingly plaguing India.

The series of bomb blasts that have rocked India over the past decade has precipitated the demand for private security services. India has the largest private security force in the world with 5.5 million guards across the country, with one million being added to this number each year. The market growth rate is about 35 per cent. The fact that in the year 2008 alone, 200 new security service companies have came into being is an indicator of the growth in business as well as growth intensity of competition. The services range from man guarding to background checks for employees and espionage operations. Malls, hotels, educational institutions, hospitals, IT and finance companies are demanding these services in the form of guards, electronic surveillance, detective services and so on.

Kapil, a former military officer, promoted a security services company called Kapil Security Services (KSS) five years ago. KSS has a workforce of 5,000 security guards. Currently, the operations of the company are limited only to Delhi and Uttar Pradesh. Considering the recent growth in demand, Kapil plans to extend the services to 10 more states. Financial resources and human resources do not pose serious problems to Kapil. With his military background, he is confident of offering quality services, irrespective of the size of operations. The problem that faces Kapil is not of size or human resource; rather it is customer perception. According to Kapil, selling the services successfully to business houses and individuals alike is the actual problem. Most household customers feel insecure when it comes to security services. In fact, many prospects are not even familiar with the concept! Concept selling is needed in this case. Further, new users need to be trained to use the systems effectively.

Questions:

1. What are the communication needs of the consumers that are related to security services?
2. What should be the communication campaign strategy that addresses the problems of the firm?
3. Do you think external marketing alone ensures market acceptance?
4. How can Kapil proceed further in handling the problem?

INTRODUCTION

External marketing is the interaction of the service company with the target market. There is a saying that "nothing happens until somebody sells something in the market." Unless and until a marketing organization comes with a proposal, there is no response from the market, either positive or negative. A marketing stimulus, therefore, is necessary to generate responses in the form of demand. External marketing includes all such communication campaigns by the service provider which inform, educate, persuade, train and influence the customers to purchase services.

THE NEED FOR EXTERNAL MARKETING

Services are intangible. Therefore, the psychic costs of the consumers are high in services. In the absence of relevant and effective communication campaigns, consumers have doubts and suspicions about a service and look for proper evidence. Campaigns through appropriate media provide the customers with evidence. Service quality depends, to a large extent, on the ability and effective participation of customers. Participation ability, skill, involvement and moods and emotions depend upon the way the consumers are informed, educated and trained through external marketing. Thus, external marketing influences customer-perceived quality. In the absence of proper communication, most customers cannot perceive the value of the service properly even after experiencing it. A customer may experience a good feeling after having observed a painting in an art gallery. When the customer is informed that the painting is Picasso's, the renowned painter's, he will probably get excited. Such value perceptions can be created through external marketing.

"The aim of external marketing is to inform, educate, persuade the target customers to purchase and participate in the service process effectively. As service customers need to perform certain roles in service production, external marketing assumes greater significance."

Often, service outlets operate under certain limitations. The uncertainty over the time taken to handle a customer, demand uncertainties, employee, equipment and infrastructural problems cannot be eliminated totally. Problems of this kind certainly cause inconvenience to the customers and may create negative feelings against the service provider. Through external marketing, the service provider finds an opportunity to inform and convince the customer about possible problems, and it helps increase the level of tolerance. Image building is one of the important goals of external marketing. An organization's image acts as a guard against minor mistakes. One of the major sources of image building is the communication campaign launched by the service provider. Organizational communication must be ethical if high morale and productivity among employees are to be achieved. Communication with other organizations must be ethical if good business relationships are to develop for the benefit of all. Communication with customers and clients must be ethical if businesses are to have satisfied customers and clients that will make long-term profits possible. Communication with the community must be ethical if the organization is to receive the community support and goodwill essential for its survival and to avoid expensive and reputation-damaging legal entanglements.[1]

INTEGRATED MARKETING COMMUNICATIONS

External marketing in services is popularly known as "promotion" in traditional marketing. To continue the traditional identity, promotion was included as one of the components of services marketing mix. Promotion refers to communication campaign of the organization towards external customers to achieve organizational objectives. The five important tools used for marketing communications are

1. Advertising
2. Personal selling
3. Sales promotion
4. Publicity and public relations
5. Direct marketing

A combination of all or a few of them for achieving communication objectives is called communication mix. Figure 17.1 shows the components of marketing communication mix.

- *Advertising*: Advertising is non-personal mass communication by an identified sponsor. Advertising is a cost-effective and powerful means to reach the masses. The cost of per unit (audience) of exposure is the lowest in advertising, when compared to other promotional approaches. It has the capacity to attract the market. Informative, educative and persuasive objectives can be achieved through advertising. Service firms use advertising for the achievement of the above-mentioned objectives.
- *Personal Selling*: If organizations establish communication channels through their sales force with the target market, it is called personal selling. Personal selling is a face-to-face communication. Feedback can be spontaneous and customers can clarify doubts on the spot. However, this approach has a limited application as it is very costly as well as difficult to

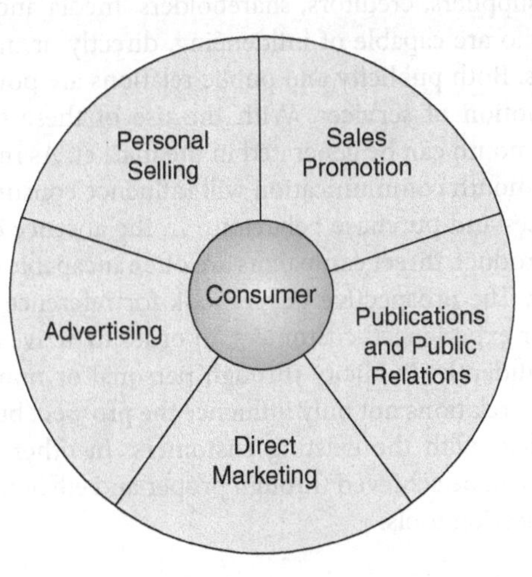

Fig. 17.1
The marketing communication mix

reach the mass market. There are, of course, some exceptions. Life Insurance Corporation of India uses personal selling to reach the market that comprises millions of customers. A large agency network is an extraordinary strength and distinctive competency of the corporation. In spite of the market being flooded with private organizations and MNCs, the sales force of LIC protects its unique position. It may not be possible for any other organization to build such a large sales force and manage it in a short period. Not all service firms can afford to have such a large network of sales personnel. In the case of service firms, sales personnel are not the contact employees involved in service production and delivery. The sales force is used to attract the market to the service outlet and/or to build the image of the organization. However, it is difficult to draw a line that divides the employees as sales personnel and others. All employees in a service organization are marketing employees. Some are full-time marketers and some are part-time marketers. But everyone contributes to sales and promoting image of the company.

- *Sales Promotion:* Sales promotion includes techniques that stimulate demand in a market during a short period and has measured responses. Sales promotion can be implemented through other components of communication mix. Discounts, gifts, coupons, premiums, exhibitions, trade shows and so on are some of the techniques of sales promotion. Service firms use sales promotion techniques, generally, to manage demand to the level of capacity. They are also used to stimulate customer needs beyond the threshold level and thereby generate new demand for the service.
- *Publicity and Public Relations:* Publicity is a communication campaign through a third party (press, opinion leaders and other indirect sources). A business organization's identity and direct payment to the sources are absent in publicity. Public relations is a deliberate attempt by the organization to establish relationships with various people (customers, suppliers, creditors, shareholders, media and social organizations), who are capable of influencing, directly or indirectly, business prospects. Both publicity and public relations are powerful techniques for promotion of services. With the use of these two, a favourable word-of-mouth can be generated in the market. As mentioned already, word-of-mouth communication will influence consumer expectations, preferences and purchase behaviour. In the absence of tangibility of a service product, direct campaigns are often incapable of convincing the customer. The prospective buyers look for reference and advice from experts or experienced customers, in order to arrive at purchase decisions confidently. Publicity through personal or non-personal means and public relations not only influence the prospect but also strengthen the bondage with the existing customers. In other words, customer retention can be achieved through proper and efficient use of these two communication tools.

- *Direct Marketing:* When intermediaries are not involved between producers and consumers, it is called direct marketing. Direct marketing is not a recent concept. It is one of the alternatives for the producer to reach the market. The inclusion of direct marketing as a component of communication mix is a recent phenomenon. The revolutionary changes that took place in the areas of communication system and networking, information technology, transport and technology in recent years promoted the direct marketing concept as one of the powerful communication tools. Direct sales offers through sky shops on television, direct contact of customers through mail, e-commerce and so on are examples. Service providers can use direct marketing for promoting services. By transmitting the service process and other features and options through the electronic media, customers can be motivated and their doubts about the service offer clarified. Direct mail to a prospect initiates need gratification process.

Each of the five components of the communication mix has distinctive capabilities and also limitations of suitability. The major task for service firms is to design a proper mix of these components. The effectiveness of a communication campaign depends upon how efficiently the mix is designed.

> "The elements of a communication campaign include advertising, personal selling, sales promotion, publicity, public relations and direct marketing. The success of the campaign depends on the mix of these elements."

DESIGNING A COMMUNICATION CAMPAIGN

A communication campaign is intended to get a desired response from a target audience. The basic principle that guides any communication campaign is receiver orientation. A proper understanding of the characteristics of the receiver—culture, habits, beliefs, attitudes, abilities, knowledge, experience, exposure, likes, dislikes, associations and so on—should be the foundation for designing a communication campaign. The following are the important decisions the management should take in relation to campaign designing.

Selecting the Target Audience

A clear definition of audience is a prerequisite for the campaign design. The consumers of a service may belong to varied groups. The marketer has to decide which group the company wants to feature in its campaign. The selected group generally should have the capability of leading the other groups in preferring the service. The selection of a target audience provides solutions to many problems relating to communication. The answers to such questions as what to communicate, when to communicate, where to communicate, how to communicate can be obtained accurately with the decision on target audience.

Determining the Objectives of Communication

Once the audience is identified, the objectives of communication should be determined. The objectives are in relation to the response sought from campaign. Although the ultimate objective of the campaign is to generate sales either in the short run or in the long run or both, each of the specific campaigns is directed at achieving specific objectives. Each and every buyer will pass through different stages before arriving at a decision on a purchase. Researchers have identified six stages in the buyer-readiness process. These stages are called the hierarchy of effects. The stages are: awareness, knowledge, liking, preference, conviction and purchase. Buyers need to be stimulated at every stage, either through a single campaign or through a series of campaigns.

Generating the Message

Message generation is vital in designing a communication campaign. Depending on the desired response from the market audience, the message needs to be developed. As per the AIDA model, (attention, interest, desires and action) the message should have the capability of attracting attention, holding interest, arousing desire and making the audience action oriented (purchase of service). There are four important issues to be finalized in formulating the message. They are: message content, structure, format and source.

1. *Message Content:* The message content includes an idea, theme or an appeal which is the unique selling proposition (USP) for the service in the market. Marketers generally use three kinds of appeals. They are rational appeals, emotional appeals and moral appeals. Through rational appeals the marketers try to educate the consumers about the service offer and other environmental factors in the market. The consumers are stimulated to think logically while making a purchase decision. The appeal aims at making the buyer prefer the service offered by the company. Cellular service companies such as BSNL, Tata Indicom, Airtel, Vodafone and so on are campaigning more through rational appeals to build their customer base. Emotion begins when rationality ends. Emotions may be positive or negative. Negative emotional appeals such as fear, guilt or shame motivate people to buy some services. On the other hand, positive emotional appeals such as love, joy, fun, pride, sentiment or celebration motivate the purchase of some services. The moral appeals are directed at social sensitivity. Generally, public and social organizations launch their campaign with moral appeals.
2. *Message Structure:* Message structure relates to the organization of message content in such a way that rightful conclusions are drawn from the message. The effectiveness of message content depends upon how it is structured. Whether to suggest conclusions or leave to the audience to draw conclusions, whether to place one-sided arguments or to present two-sided arguments, whether to put strong arguments in the beginning or the end are the issues that need to be decided.
3. *Message Format:* The format of the message depends upon the medium selected for the campaign. If it is the print media, the decisions relating to headline, space, copy, design, colour and illustration are important. An audio channel like a radio requires the choice of words, voice, modulation, pitch, pauses and so on. For video media, that is, TV, cinema, Internet and so on, the body language, location, visuals, time, music and so on, decide the format.

Mahindra Lifespaces

Mahindra Lifespaces is a company that offers real estate services. The company developed and promoted corporate brand name "Mahindra Life Spaces" in the place of the old company name "Mahindra Gesco Developers Ltd." The new brand name reflects the company's passion and vision of creating spaces for healthy living in both residential and commercial segments. The company logo, created to support the new brand name, is called the "flower of life." It is intended to create perceptual values to customers. The logo encompasses flowers of different colours, with each colour signifying a vital aspect of life. The logo is inspired from a simple and significant insight that flowers form an integral part of one's home. They stand for naturalness, freshness, health, vibrancy, energy and the beauty of life—tenets that inspire Mahindra Lifespaces. The name "Lifespaces" is tucked into the flower of life and is comforted, cosseted and nurtured by it. And when flowers come together they stand for the very essence of life.

Mahindra Lifespaces has taken care of representing all these psychological values in every project it has undertaken. The unique features of the residential projects are openness, greenery, landscaping and various amenities for a healthy lifestyle. It has built a reputation for creating not just buildings but nurturing living, breathing and healthy life spaces. The company's external marketing efforts reached the target audience effectively and as a result the company could get orders from reputed companies and also from the household customers.

4. *Message Source:* Who has to deliver the message is an important decision. Studies have proved that the message source influences the audience. The source selected may be an expert in the field or may be a celebrity who is popular with the target audience.

> *Media options are growing by the day making the job of the marketer critical. Service marketers should decide on media mix for the communication campaign. The print media, audio, electronic media and other media options should be analyzed carefully.*

Selecting the Media

The rapid pace of change in media and the growing complexity of media options make the selection of media channels very complex. Print media, audio channels, electronic channels and tele channels have expanded their scope of operations and business. Each medium has distinctive advantages as well as limitations. Communicators have to ascertain the reach, frequency, credibility and the cost of the preferred medium besides the media habits of the target audience to be able to select wisely. One medium may not fulfil the objectives. A combination of media may be necessary to stimulate audience interest.

Budgeting for Marketing Communications

How much money is required for communication campaign? The answer is critical to marketers. In the absence of accurate evaluation measures and measures to establish cause-and-effect relationships, companies often depend upon traditional approaches in deciding the budget for marketing communication. There are four such methods. The "affordable method" is to use the money the company can afford to spend on communications. The "percentage to sales" method establishes a relationship between sales and expenditure on communications. As the name indicates, the budget for marketing communications is fixed as a percentage to the sales. The "competitive parity method" advocates following the competitor's budget. The "objective-and-task method" calls upon marketers to define specific campaign objectives and list out the tasks to be performed to achieve such objectives. The total estimated cost for the performance of the tasks becomes the budget.

INTEGRATING COMMUNICATIONS MIX ELEMENTS

Communication is the foundation of all human relationships. Only strategically oriented integrated brand communications can help business to reach a sustainable competitive position.[2] It is necessary to integrate the tools of communication such as advertising, personal selling, sales promotion, publicity and public relations and direct marketing, as per requirements. Integrated marketing communications (IMCs) emphasize the benefits of harnessing synergy across multiple media to build brand equity of products and services. The American Association of Advertising Agencies defines IMC as "a concept of marketing communications planning that recognizes the added value of a comprehensive plan that evaluates the strategic roles of a variety of communication disciplines—for example, general advertising, direct response, sales promotion, and public relations—and combines these disciplines to provide clarity, consistency, and maximum communications impact."[3] This definition recognizes the added value aspect of IMC, created by the joint impact of multiple activities in the communication mix; it does not, however, provide a comprehensive articulation of the variety of communication mix elements that comprise IMC.[4] Thus, IMC is a comprehensive plan of integrating all suitable communication tools to campaign company's intentions to the specified target groups of consumers. IMC is a powerful tool in reaching target audiences with persuasive messages.

IMC demands a more coordinated and strategic approach to communication campaign of a company. It is necessary to tie IMC with the overall function, purpose and future direction of the company to achieve the desired results. The marketing strategy needs to address the company's long-term direction, competitive advantage and the scope of the organization's activities.

Marketers may choose to employ any combination of advertising, personal selling, word of mouth, publicity, sales promotion or any other tool that gains attention, awareness and creates an image. One of the great strengths of IMC is its flexibility. A finely crafted IMC effort can influence target audiences that would otherwise be unreachable. IMC's selective use of elements and flexibility allow promotion managers a useful range of applications. Factors influencing IMC include the type of service market, buyer-readiness stage and the service product's life-cycle stage. The communication mix for the industrial market and the consumer market is different. For example, personal selling is of prime importance for the industrial market while advertising leads the mass consumer market. The communication tools and their effectiveness vary at different stages of buyer readiness as well as the service product life cycle. Service companies may use specialist advertisers to have focused campaign designed for their services. The growth of advertising agencies with well-demonstrated expertise in creativity and execution provides greater opportunity to service companies to reach their target audience effectively. The details of select

17.1 Services Marketing Insight | **The New Age Specialist Ad Agencies**

Marketing communication business has undergone several changes in the wake of sustained fragmentation and proliferation of media. The new and emerging media is fast out pacing the traditional media. The evaluation of new media environment in India is paving new ways of experimentation with non-conventional advertising methods. The new-age advertisers are willing to spend on specialist communication offerings.

The growing importance of marketing of services and brand equity promoted new verticals in the brand promotion campaigns. They were digital agencies, brand-promoting companies and design specialists. The Brand Equity Ad Agency Reckoner rated specialist ad agencies operating in India in 2008. The top five ad agencies in different specialist fields are as follows.

Digital specialist agencies	***Design specialist agencies***
1. Webchutney 2. Hungama 3. Contests2win 4. Tribal DDB 5. iContract	1. Ray + Keshavan 2. Elephant Strategy + Design 3. Landor 4. Design Sutra 5. Fitch
Brand promotion agencies	***Agencies with 360° solutions capabilities***
1. Candid Marketing 2. Solutions Integrated Marketing 3. Encompass Events 4. 141 Sercon 5. Kidstuff Promos & Events	1. Ogilvy 2. JWT 3. Mudra 4. Lowe 5. Rediffusion DYR
Agencies with innovation and thought leadership	***Agencies partnering with clients***
1. Ogilvy 2. JWT 3. Lowe 4. Mudra 5. McCann Erickson	1. Ogilvy 2. JWT 3. Mudra 4. Lowe 5. Rediffusion DYR

Source: Brand Equity Ad Agency Reckoner, "A Whole New Act," The Economic Times, *December 17 (2008): 6.*

new-age, specialist advertising agencies are presented in " Services Marketing Insight: The New Age Specialist Ad Agencies".

THE OBJECTIVES OF INTEGRATED MARKETING COMMUNICATIONS

There are basically two important objectives of integrated marketing communications. They are creating right perceptions to customers on the service company and service offers and building brand image.

1. *Creating Right Perceptions:* A communication campaign should create the right perceptions relating to the service. An audience needs support

> "Integrating all communication elements is a critical task. The objectives of the company guide the process of integrated marketing communications. The campaign should be capable of creating right perceptions of the consumers and also building brand image."

to develop perceptions against marketing stimulations. Since the market is overexposed to stimulations, consumers often tend to be selective in their exposure, attention and retention. They are not ready to struggle for assessment of various issues relating to a service in order to develop a perception unless they have a high level of involvement. Communicators should be capable of understanding the perceptual process of the audience and develop a simple methodology to create the desired perceptions in the minds of the customers. They need to select a positioning strategy that is capable of motivating the customers and providing a competitive edge in the market.

2. *Building Brand Image:* Brand image is particularly important to a service because consumers do not know exactly what they are going to experience before the purchase. Therefore, brand image drives customers to make a purchasing decision. Service companies are required to build a brand image and continue to strengthen it with their performance and communicate their performance to the market.

WORD-OF-MOUTH COMMUNICATION

Word-of-mouth communication is considered as one of the most powerful communication channels in services marketing. It has the capability of creating excellent results for the company. If it is not handled properly, the results may be disastrous. "Although word-of-mouth communication can be very influential in any purchase decision, previous research suggests it is particularly important for services."[5] Positive word-of-mouth communication has been recognized as a particularly valuable vehicle for promoting a firm's products and services.[6] Consumers have absolute freedom to communicate each other about a service. Therefore, word-of-mouth communication is not a controllable variable. Organizations can influence the sources, either directly or indirectly, to generate a positive market image. "Empirical research examining the employee-customer interaction has found that encounters that can be characterized as occurring under the broader umbrella of a relationship are likely to produce customer

Colors

Colors is a general entertainment channel that was introduced in 2008. It came with novel programming content which was like a breather to the audience. Noticing the viewer dissatisfaction over several commercial breaks in a half-hour serial, the channel chose to telecast programmes with no more than two or three advertisements. This smart strategy attracted the audience so much that the channel displaced STAR Plus from the top spot—which it occupied for nine years—within a short span of nine months as per TAM data for the 15th week of 2009. The success of Colors can be attributed to the varied programming mix and its content. The channel communicated these core areas effectively to its target market through advertising and publicity in electronic and print media. The successful integration of external and internal marketing (creative programme design, production and transmission) enabled the channel to register a meteoric rise in a highly competitive market.

advocacy behaviours such as positive word-of-mouth communication"[7] It is the general tendency of human beings to indulge in informal communication with others. "Informal communications directed at other consumers about the ownership, usage, or characteristics of particular goods and services and/or their sellers will have powerful impact on consumer perceptions."[8] Marketers should identify the sources of word-of-mouth and develop appropriate strategies. The following are the sources for generating word-of-mouth communication:

- *Contact Employees:* Contact employees of the service generally engage in informal discussion with the customers. They provide information by taking into consideration the anxiety levels of the customer. Customers tend to give greater importance to the informal information provided by contact employees.
- *Other Employees in the Service Outlet:* Customers may contact employees other than contact personnel and share their opinions and information with them. When the waiting time or process time is more, customers are likely to indulge in conversation with other employees.
- *Co-customers:* They are the most important source of communication for customers. Customers share their anxiety with co-customers as both the parties have the same problem and seek a similar solution. Many co-customers also show interest in exchanging information, views and opinions relating to the service that they seek to experience.
- *Experienced Customers:* Prospective buyers generally try to locate experienced customers to get an unbiased assessment of the service.
- *Experts:* Independent consultants in an identified field may also act as informal communicators. Customers seek the advice of the experts in high-involvement services.
- *Opinion Leaders:* Opinion leaders in different fields influence the prospects of a service by spreading their opinions as messages to their followers.
- *General Public Discussions:* When people meet, discussions automatically generate. People during travel time, in clubs, parks, at group events and other places initiate discussions. When a prospective buyer takes part in the group or acts as a spectator, he/she collects information and uses it for assessment before taking a purchase decision.

> **Word-of-mouth communication** *is not controllable but influential. The impact of word of mouth in services is expected to be very strong on business prospects. Marketers should identify the critical sources of word of mouth and influence them.*

Word-of-mouth communication takes place in three ways: (1) when customers contact any of the sources out of anxiety, (2) when any of the source contacts the customer to share its anxiety and (3) an indirect contact between the source and the customer.

THEMES OF EXTERNAL MARKETING CAMPAIGNS

Service companies need to focus on the different themes of communication campaigns in order to achieve organizational objectives. Table 17.1 shows 12 important themes for service organizations.

Table 17.1 External Marketing Campaign Themes

Information	Education	Persuasion
Reinforcement	Training	Efficiency
Leadership	Relationship	Image building
Price Versus Quality	Demand management	Recovery

Information

Information relating to the service package is the focal theme in different situations. When a service company introduces a new or modified service or introduces the service in a new market through a new channel or introduces change in the marketing mix or when the company is new to the service, information becomes the central theme of the communication campaign.

Education

Customers need to be educated properly before they participate in service production and consumption. The educational theme aims at managing service promises and influencing consumer expectations of the service. The management of service promises involves coordinating all promises made by the company and the employees in order to ensure that the execution is consistent and feasible. Service firms should make only realistic promises. It is also necessary to offer service guarantees to strengthen the company's stand on the service promise. In case of any deficiency or failure in service, the company should assure compensation on the loss suffered by the customer. Innovation is a continuous process in services. The changes brought in the service package and process need to be communicated to consumers, otherwise there may be a danger of misunderstanding between the buyer and the seller.

"Customer expectations management" is yet another responsibility of the service company that can be achieved through customer education. It is necessary to study the level of service expectations by the customers and design a communication strategy to influence the customers to have the correct expectations. Some customers develop unrealistic expectations. The company should negotiate these unrealistic expectations and bring them down to realistic propositions without hurting customer feelings. Service employees should have transactional skills to effectively negotiate unrealistic expectations. When a company wants to downsize its activities or shift focus to such services which yield more revenues, it is necessary to reset consumer expectations gracefully without hurting the sales potential. This is called resetting customer expectations. The following four strategies are useful for the purpose:

- *Offering Choice:* Each alternative becomes a separate service package for the customer. The service provider finds a chance to influence customer expectations directly by offering an alternate service package as a choice.
- *Offering Tiered-value Service:* This involves designing need-based service packages to different customer groups. It means offering minimum

services for a low-intensity need segment and high-level immediate service for high-intensity need segment.

- *Communicating Criteria and Levels of Service Expectations:* This involves highlighting the indicators of quality levels to customers. For example, a company may communicate themes such as low price means low quality; the reputation of a firm is critical; the customer base in the market is quality proof and so on to develop consumer expectations.
- *Communicating Realities in the Industry:* This includes providing information to the customers on the competitors' low-level performances, external compulsions like government policy and other social pressures in order to make the consumer have realistic expectations.

Persuasion

Persuasive communication aims at influencing the decision-making process of the consumers. By showing the reasons for preferring a service and service provider, as well as the special benefits and values to consumers, service firms persuade the target market to become the customers of the company. Persuasive communication is used against the defensive or offensive approaches of competition.

Reinforcement

This aims at developing loyalty among the customers. It focuses on the credibility, reliability and continuity of all quality factors and gives an assurance to the target market that they can have similar or better experiences by using the service. Reinforcement reduces cognitive dissonance among consumers. It supports and strengthens the earlier decision of using a service and encourages consumers to continue with the same service.

Training

A typical feature of services is that the consumers are co-producers. The expertise and involvement of the service provider coupled with that of the consumer in service production process results in service quality. Service firms cannot expect all consumers to have the ability and expertise to participate in a service production process. Service firms are responsible for training the customers. There are three phases in the service production process. They are the joining phase, production process phase and detachment phase. The series of activities the consumer has to pass through and the activities they have to perform need to be communicated and proper assistance provided to ensure that consumers are performing their tasks effectively. Designing customer support systems and training customers to access such systems is an important dimension of service campaign.

Efficiency

Service firms proclaim their efficiency in order to motivate the target market to join them. Companies may choose several parameters to exhibit their efficiency. The growth achieved over a period in market expansion and networking, the loyal consumer network, the success percentage in service, the relationship networking with other services and the size and strength of the corporate group in the economy are some of the themes used to communicate efficiency.

Leadership

A leader can attract better prospects. Leadership positioning, either in terms of market share or innovations, creates a solid position for the company in the market. This theme can be undertaken only by leaders either at the corporate level or at the local level.

Relationship

Service companies are taking up special campaigns for building, maintaining and enhancing relationships. The theme focuses not only on customer retention but also on turning each customer into a brand ambassador and an indirect sales person of the company.

Image Building

A company cannot buy its image. It has to build it over a period of time through service excellence. Image-building campaigns are essential for service firms because the image influences customer-perceived quality.

Price Versus Quality

The price vs. quality campaign focuses on attracting different market segments. It also motivates consumers to compare the price-quality offerings of the company with the competitive offerings. The campaign helps customers to choose a service that suits their economic conditions and develop expectations accordingly.

Demand Management

Managing the demand to the level of capacity is one of the major challenges for service companies. A communication campaign is one of the powerful means to manage demand. When the demand is more than the capacity, the campaign is used to shift the demand from peak periods to slack periods. When demand is less than the capacity, the promotional campaign focuses upon demand generation.

Recovery

Service failures and deficiencies are common in service business. Many such failures happen due to uncontrollable factors. But service companies cannot escape responsibility. When such things happen, they have to take recovery measures and communicate to all those who suffered a loss. Right recovery at the right time enhances the image of the organization. The recovery campaigns aim at reducing or eliminating customer anxiety and turn consumer opinion in favour of the company.

> *A communication campaign involves series of activities carrying different themes aiming at nurturing the perceptions of the consumers. Service marketers use different communication themes systematically to promote their services.*

SUCCESSFUL COMMUNICATION CAMPAIGNS

The following are some of the successful communication campaigns of service brands.

- The "Wherever you go our network follows" campaign by Hutch (now Vodafone) is one of the most successful campaigns supported by highly creative advertisements. Cheeka (the pet) became a rage overnight. The pug and the "You and I" slogan helped two changeovers successfully—the brand name and the personification. The campaign "Orange to Pink & Hutch to Vodafone, the Pug Rules" facilitated a very smooth transition. The Vodafone created zoozoos as personification of the brand and timed the campaign strategically using IPL T20 cricket tournament. The 30 creative advertisements really established the new brand in the market touching the hearts of millions across all ages and gender with entertainment fabric.
- The "An Idea can change your life" campaign of Idea Cellular is another successful campaign. It came up with a powerful campaign using celebrity Abhishek Bachchan donning different avatars to target separate consumer sets. The "*what an Idea Sir Ji*" campaign contributed significantly for the growth of business and to strengthen the brand equity.
- The "*Jeetey Raho*" campaign of ICICI Prudential helped to achieve enormous brand recall. The mix of humour as well as seriousness worked well to attract the audience. The sales grew significantly after the campaign.
- The "*Karo Zyada Ka Iradaa*" (Hindi) campaign by Max New York Life is a successful creative campaign. A shift in perception of the consumers is attempted successfully from post-retirement needs to post-retirement life. The basic human emotions are played portraying a similar circle of life. The campaign could have instant connectivity with target audience and contributed for 100 per cent rise in sales in just six months.
- The "*Manoranjan Ka Baap*" campaign by IPL 2009 was an instant success. The T20 cricket was positioned not as just a game but as an entire entertainment package for the whole family. The campaigns attracted a lot of non-cricket audience and led them to have cricketainment.
- The "Incredible !ndia" campaign for promoting tourism in India resulted in increased tourist inflows. The simple and colourful visuals used were appealing and the slogan tugged at the heart.
- The "Surprisingly SBI" campaign focused on attitudinal change in consumers over this good old man of Indian banking. The shedding of the conservative approach of SBI came as a pleasant surprise to the prospects. The campaign positioned the bank as the change leader in public sector banks and a serious competitor of private sector banks.

> *There is no formula for success in external marketing. Consumers expect distinctive values in every offer. The campaigns should be distinctive in communicating value propositions. The successful advertising campaigns stand as guiding elements for effective design of communication campaigns.*

- The "Let Your Heart Fly" campaign of Indian Airlines changed the staid positioning of the state-owned carrier.
- The "Join the Indian Army" campaign launched by the Indian Army convinced many young Indians. The "Do You Have it in You" message was gusty as well as challenging. The campaign moved the minds of the youth and made Indian youth take their decisions to undergo heavy physical training and to jump into the war field when needed. The campaign designed by HTA was successful and resulted in a sharp raise in intake of cadets.
- The "Anything, Anywhere" campaign of Gati, the courier company, repositioned the company as a delivery expert. The storyboard talking of delivering even to a man committing suicide laced with humour has been received by the audience very well. The campaign designed by Enterprise Nexus has changed the boring perception of courier service advertisements.

SUCCESS IN EXTERNAL MARKETING

Service companies need to follow certain guidelines in the development of communication programmes. "Services Marketing Insight: Five Rules of Effective Compaigns" suggests critical areas in designing campaigns. T. D. Peterson and K. S. Porges[9] suggested the following 10 guidelines for communication campaigns, with special reference to services:

1. Be clear on your goal.
   - Goals must be actionable and measurable.
   - Have a descriptive note on goals set.
   - Communicate goals to your employees and make sure they understand them properly.
   - Have only a few major goals.
2. Understand your customer well.
   - Do mystery shopping and observe how the average customer is treated.
   - Employ your confidants to do the same and give you an honest feedback.
   - Use customer letters and phone calls as an important source to understand the customers well.
3. Recognize that there is an emotional side of decision-making. Anatole France once said, "It is human nature to think wisely and act foolishly." Packaging, graphics, casting, music—all can effectively influence the emotional side of a decision.
4. Make sure you're not "talking to yourself" in your ads.
   - Customers should understand the meaning of your ads. Have your ads been reviewed by someone who is not familiar with your services?

17.2 Services Marketing Insight

The Five Rules of Effective Campaigns

It is difficult to spell out what really makes a campaign effective. The campaign design processes are changing fast with digitization and fragmentation changing the landscape through which we communicate. It is not possible to develop a success formula for campaign as it is more a creative art than a science. However, a few general rules minimize the risk of failures and increase the probability of success.

Rule 1: *Find Out What Is Effective:* Agree up front what actually makes the campaign effective. The client agency agreement on effectiveness objectives can save a lot of pain later down the process.

Rule 2: *Build Your Campaign off a Powerful Insight:* Find an insight that resonates in a special way with the customer. It may be related to product, culture or anything that surrounds the brand.

Rule 3: *Find a Powerful Idea:* Ideas are hard to define and breakthrough ideas are the rarest commodity. In the changing media options, the pressure is to create ideas that sit in the ether, floating across all the channels the brand has at its disposal.

Rule 4: *The Right Message through the Right Channel:* Selecting appropriate channels to leverage campaigns is the critical point of marketers particularly when they want to ensure 360 degree marketing communication.

Rule 5: *There Must Be Something to Talk About:* Building an active dialogue with the core customer is an opportunity for the campaigners. Consumers now are interested in interactive communication. The secret is to open up the message to allow people to take part, alter, be creative and actively propagate the campaign.

Source: John Wilkins, "5 Fundamental Rules of Highly Effective Campaigns," 4Ps of Business and Marketing, *IV, no. 8 (April 24th, 2009): 86.*

- After developing your ad, put it aside for a few days. Then review it. Does it still make sense?

5. Time is a sales tool—limit it.
   - Making time-limited offers is one of the best spurs to sales.
   - Use special occasions, such as national holidays and company anniversaries, to limit the time of the offer.
6. Provide for adequate media budget.
   - If two-thirds or three-quarters of your ad budget is not available to place your ad after production costs, rethink your advertising plan.
   - If funds are limited, concentrate your advertising in a niche to achieve a meaningful frequency, rather than spreading it over a large audience.
7. Make sure all your media work together.
   - During any particular period, all your media should communicate the same message for maximum impact.

> *Integrating external marketing activities with internal marketing is essential to ensure the promises made in external marketing. The match between promise and delivery is critical for the success of consumer persuasion and creating positive perceptions on services.*

- The more ways you can manage to communicate your message, the more effective you will be.

8. Use telephone and the Internet to communicate.
9. Experiment with new approaches.
   - No set of guidelines can ever be totally comprehensive. The only limit to ideas for success is your imagination.
   - Every great idea usually has three or four weaker precedents.
10. Break the rules—wherever and whenever required.

MATCHING SERVICE PROMISES WITH DELIVERY

One of the major challenges of the external marketing programme is to match service promises with delivery. The delivery of service should be either more or equal in terms of quality that was promised to the client through external marketing. In case of lower quality in delivery than what was promised, the results would be disastrous. The critical task of the service providers, therefore, is to align these two properly.

MANAGING HORIZONTAL COMMUNICATION

Aligning the activities of external marketing with internal marketing is of pivotal significance in service business. An independent approach for each of these marketing strategies mostly results in either overpromising or under-servicing. Therefore, proper and effective communication channels need to be developed. The channels of communication between advertising and operations and between sales and operations should open. Another approach is to create cross-functional teams for improving horizontal communication. The teams would align their jobs with the requirements of the end consumers. Employees of one function contact the employees in other divisions directly in relation to a customer job. Thus, one employee attends to the whole job of a customer. This kind of design will facilitate employees to understand the total system, its strengths and limitations in realistic propositions.

SUMMARY

- The objective of external marketing is to make every customer ready in all respects to participate in the service process.
- All consumers are overexposed to marketing stimulations. Hence, they are more confused, with respect to services due to the distinctive characteristics of services.
- Service companies should design an effective promotional campaign to inform, educate, persuade, train and encourage buying and experiencing the services offered.
- The critical areas of decision-making are to be handled properly. The themes selected should be appropriate.
- Consumers do develop service expectations. Managing consumer expectations is one of the major purposes of external marketing.
- Services promised during external marketing should be delivered effectively.
- Development of communication mix consisting of elements such as advertising, personal selling,

sales promotion, publicity and public relation and direct marketing is vital.

- The most powerful medium in services is word-of-mouth communication. Service companies should be careful of negative word-of-mouth communication.
- There is a need to integrate external marketing with internal marketing for better results.

KEY TERMS

Advertising *329*	Moral appeals *332*	Rational appeals *332*
Direct marketing *331*	Sales promotion *330*	Message format *332*
Emotional appeals *332*	Message content *332*	Opinion leaders *337*
Personal selling *329*	Message structure *332*	Horizontal communication *344*
AIDA *332*	Publicity *330*	Reinforcement *339*

BRIEF QUESTIONS

1. Why do service companies need external marketing?
2. Explain the components of promotional mix.
3. What is word-of-mouth communication?
4. What is the importance of horizontal communication?
5. Explain the importance of publicity and public relations in services marketing.

ESSAY QUESTIONS

1. What is the role of external marketing in services business?
2. How do you design promotional mix for services? How does it differ from the traditional approach?
3. How do you match service promises with delivery? Discuss the various strategies.
4. Discuss various promotional themes in external marketing.
5. What are the guidelines to be followed for designing a promotional campaign?
6. How can consumer expectations be managed through external marketing?
7. What is word-of-mouth communication? How is it generated? How can it be made useful in external marketing?

ASSIGNMENTS

1. Compare the mass communication campaigns of any two DTH service companies to find out:
   (a) their positioning strategies and their effectiveness
   (b) their promises to customers.
2. Study the external marketing campaigns of two recently released films to identify:
   (a) their campaign objectives
   (b) their communication mix.

REFERENCES

1 Barron Wells and Nelda Spinks, "Ethics Must Be Communicated From the Top Down!," *Career Development International*, 1/7 (1996): 28.

2 Olof Holm, "Integrated Marketing Communication: From Tactics to Strategy," *Corporate Communications: An International Journal*, 11, no. 1 (2006): 24.

3 D. E. Schultz, "Integrated Marketing Communications: Maybe Definition Is in the Point of View," *Marketing News*, 27, no. 2 (1993): 17.

4 Dennis A. Pitta, Margit Weisgal and Peter Lynagh, "Integrating Exhibit Marketing into Integrated Marketing Communications," *Journal of Consumer Marketing*, 23/3 (2006): 156.

5 R. Ettenson and K. Turner, "An Exploratory Investigation of Consumer Decision Making for Selected Professional and Nonprofessional Services," *The Journal of Services Marketing,* 11, no. 2 (1997): 91–104.
6 Dwayne D. Gremler, Kevin P. Gwinner and Stephen W. Brown, "Generating Positive Word-of-mouth Communication Through Customer-Employee Relationships," *International Journal of Service Industry Management,* 12, no. 1 (2001): 44.
7 S. E. Beatty, M. Mayer, J. E. Coleman, K. E. Reynolds and J. Lee, "Customer-sales Associate Retail Relationships," *Journal of Retailing,* 72, (1996): 223–247.
8 R. A. Westbrook (1987), Product/Consumption-based Affective Responses and Postpurchase Processes," *Journal of Marketing Research,* 24, (August, 1987): 258–270.
9 Thad D. Peterson and K. Shelly Porges, "Marketing and Communicating Tools for Services Marketers," *The AMA Hand Book of Marketing for Service Industries.* (New York: American Marketing Association, 1991) pp. 345–365

Interactive Marketing

18

LEARNING OBJECTIVES

After studying this chapter, you will be able to:

- Understand the dimensions of interactive marketing
- Describe the service encounter
- Understand the determinants of employee and customer behaviour at service encounter
- Understand the moments of truth and its management
- Identify the measures to enhance employee and customer participation

Sindhura, Shraddha and Shruti are three boisterous college students who are unhappy with the way they look. Determined to follow in the footsteps of their favourite actors and attain the perfect figure, they consulted a doctor on the best possible ways to lose weight quickly. The wizened old man looked at the three youngsters, asked them about their lifestyle and advised them to reduce their calorie intake and exercise regularly. Fired up with a sense of purpose, all three girls enrolled themselves in a fitness centre. However, within a week of joining the centre, Sindhura decided to quit as she was very unhappy with its services. Shruti, who had been hesitant right from the first day, also voiced her dissatisfaction in no uncertain terms. Shraddha tried unsuccessfully to coax them to change their minds.

Shraddha attempted to understand why her friends' interest in the weight-loss programme waned so rapidly. Sindhura found it discomfiting to perform the exercises in a mixed group in which she felt all her movements were being watched. She found it particularly embarrassing when she could not perfectly execute the trainer's instructions. She did not get along with the trainer either; she found him to be rigid and insensitive. It did not help that she felt that her body weight was only marginally higher than normal and therefore, she did not need to get excessively worried. Shruti, on the other hand, was very lazy and found the new diet-and-exercise regimen quite taxing. The lack of "normal" food left her feeling tired and listless through the day—a feeling that was aggravated by the exercise. Further, she found it rather difficult to refrain from food when her family ate happily without any restrictions. She was looking for an opportunity to escape the routine and seconded Sindhura immediately. Shraddha focused on the aim that they had set for themselves. She chose to ignore their complaints and continue at the centre.

Questions:

1. What are the service interaction issues involved in this problem?
2. How can the fitness centre ensure that Sindhura and Shruti get involved in its services and are satisfied with it?
3. Why does Shradha have a different perception and expectation of the fitness centre?
4. What are the gaps between service consumer perceptions and expectations and service provider perceptions and expectations?

INTRODUCTION

Interactive marketing takes place between contact employees of the service company and service consumers. Through internal marketing, service companies prepare contact employees, physically and mentally, to perform the service. Consumers are also educated and trained to participate in service production and consumption through external marketing. The actual process of service production, delivery and consumption takes place simultaneously during the interactions of contact employees and consumers. The meeting between contact employee and service consumer is called "service encounter." Interactive marketing may be defined as *the managerial process through which a series of interactions between service provider and consumer are organized to facilitate efficient participation in service production and consumption that satisfies the needs and wants of the consumers and creates positive customer-perceived quality.* The employees and consumers have their own ways of perceiving the quality of service performance. In most cases, these two perceptions may not be on similar lines. A customer's perceived quality ultimately is the result of the interactive process. Service process is part of interactive marketing. "Service process is an organized group of related activities that together create a result of value to customers. Internal service processes include simplified standard operations, procedures, and activities that support the front-line business functions that interact with customers."[1] Its significance is reflected by its inclusion as one of the seven components in the services marketing mix.

> "***Interactive marketing*** *may be defined as the managerial process through which a series of interactions between service provider and consumer are organized to facilitate efficient participation in service production and consumption and creates positive customer-perceived quality.*"

CUSTOMER INTERACTION

The basic service package (BSP) involves a series of activities a customer has to pass through. The customer interacts with a variety of variables. Each variable has the capacity to influence the quality perception of the customer. The interacting points from the point of view of a service consumer are:

1. *Physical Setting of the Service Outlet:* Consumers interact with the location, exterior of the service outlet, interior service layout and other elements of the physical environment
2. *Tangibles:* The tools, equipment, furniture and so on
3. *Systems:* The queue system, process system, billing and payment system, recording system, communication system and so on
4. *Co-customers:* The customers who are also seeking service from the service provider
5. *Contact Employees:* The employees at the service counters for interaction with customers
6. *Other Employees on the Line of Visibility:* The support employees who may not interact with customers directly but are visible to the customers

7. *Signage and Other Communication Material:* Signboards, directions, displayed rules and regulations, cautions and other material
8. *Other Facilities:* Drinking water, toilets, ventilation and so on

> *The identification of customers' interaction points/elements is important for interactive marketing. The possible interactions would be with physical settings, tangibles, employees, systems, signage and other facilities at the service outlet.*

QUALITY-GENERATING RESOURCES

The core value provided by the service consumers includes not only the uniqueness of products, but also various factors involved in service processes such as physical facility, styles, images and the quality of service delivery.[2] There are four quality-generating resources in interactive marketing. They are:

1. Customers involved in the process
2. Contact employees
3. Systems and operational processes
4. Physical resources and equipment

Customers are directly involved in the service production system as quality-generating resource. They are active participants and take part in production. "Customer participation can be understood as the extent to which customers provide resources in the form of time and/or effort, information provision, and co-production during service production and delivery process."[3] Contact persons are those employees who directly interact with the customers. Anyone can be a contact person irrespective of his position or job in a service firm. "Service provider and client engage in self-revelation, expend emotional energy, and connect as individuals."[4] Interactions may take place directly or face to face or indirectly over the telephone, fax, mail or the Internet. Contact personnel are the most crucial resource for a service organization. The other resources such as systems, technology and physical resources work to support the contact persons. Systems and operational processes include queuing, billing and payment systems. Systems and operational processes influence the interactive process. When systems and processes are complex and complicated, customers may keep away from the service. It is necessary, therefore, to design service-oriented systems and documents to facilitate an effective interactive process. Physical resources and equipment include all kinds of resources such as computers, documents and other tools that are used in service production system. These not only influence the technical quality of the product but also the functional quality. Contact persons, systems and physical resources form an integral and visible service production system in the minds of customers.

Customer interacts with each one of the above-mentioned factors and registers his/her experiences to form an opinion on the quality. Customers expect simple, speedy, inexpensive yet qualitative processes from the service outlet. It is the interaction through which the core service is getting delivered. Therefore, service organizations should continuously work to improve the service processes through process reengineering to make them simple and effective.

> *Service companies should focus on four quality-generating resources to manage interactive marketing effectively: customers involved in the process, contact personnel, systems and operational processes and physical resources and equipment. Each one has different potential to generate service quality.*

Customer-perceived quality (CPQ) is the ultimate result of the service performance of any service organization. Interactive marketing plays a pivotal role in generating positive CPQ. The customers have equally an important role to perform in the service production and consumption process, as they are the co-producers of service. The generated service quality also depends upon the customers' ability to participate in service process and also their ability to perceive the quality generated.

A SERVICE ENCOUNTER

A service encounter consists of all possible interactive elements between service providers and customers and includes staff, facilities, and other visible substances.[5] It is a fact that no two service encounters are exactly alike. Therefore, the challenges of dealing with new customers and managing customer relationships pose a dilemma for the management of service encounters. "Since the delivery of service occurs during the interaction between contact employee and customers (the service encounter), the attitudes and behaviours of contact employees can influence customers' perceptions of the service."[6] Management of service encounter involves physical, technical, social and psychological issues. A perfect blend of all the elements involved creates desired experiences to both customers and employees. The key elements of a service encounter are employee participation and customer participation.

Employee Participation

Employees should play a proactive role in service encounters. "Employee performance during a service encounter typically involves responding to customer needs, handling special requests, and performing under adverse circumstances."[7] Contact employees should have the clarity of their roles and responsibilities in customer interactions. They should be communicated effectively about the expectations of the management on their performances and be empowered adequately to perform. In case of any ambiguity or conflicting role expectations, the contact employees are likely to exhibit reduced performance and job satisfaction. "Service firms must find ways to effectively manage their customer–contact employees to help ensure that their attitudes and behaviours are conducive to the delivery of quality service."[8] The participation of employees in the service encounter is influenced by the following factors.

- *Work Climate:* Employees' performance in service encounter is also influenced by work climate of the service organization. "Work climate can be conceptualized from a social interactionist perspective as evaluations of environmental attributes that have a social or situational construction component."[9] "Service climate refers to the shared perception of employees concerning the practices, procedures, and kinds of behaviour that get rewarded and supported in a particular setting."[10] The service climate sends the message to the employees about how important the service is in the organization. Employees get this message from the experiences they have during their work time.

- *Empowerment:* Employee empowerment is the powerful influencer of employee performance. Empowerment is necessary because employees need the flexibility to make on-the-spot decisions to completely satisfy customers. "Allowing contact employees to use their discretion in serving customers have many positive influences on their responses and the service encounter."[11] Empowerment influences the attitudinal and behavioural responses of the contact employees positively. They become self-confident in performing tasks and in adapting to changing conditions. Empowerment reduces job stress significantly and makes employees feel better about their jobs.
- *Assignment of Right Job:* The appropriate assignment of job tasks to the well-equipped and motivated persons becomes a factor in competitive advantage. All service tasks may not require specialists. In a service organization, some tasks are strictly the domain of specialized employees, some tasks may be assigned to generic categories of people, it may be better to outsource some tasks from highly skilled firms, some tasks may be performed by intermediary establishments and some tasks are given to customers either in personal contact or via self-service mechanisms. "Assignment of jobs should be based on the ability, suitability and willingness of the employees. When an employee likes the job, the likely output of the employee would be very positive. Organizations must teach employees that they are all service providers, and emphasize their vital role in customer retention."[12] It is necessary to understand the complex behaviours of employees in job assignment. The job and behaviour match really distinguish a highly satisfactory service encounter from a dissatisfactory one.
- *Understanding Customers:* Effective employee participation depends upon the ability of the employee to understand the customers' behavioural dimensions. "Customer-provided cues or characteristics such as speech attributes, mannerisms, dress, and demographic variables such as age and gender that may play a meaningful role in the effectiveness of frontline customer segmentation."[13] Service employees should develop the skill of eliciting information from the customers on various issues like their specific service expectations, participating abilities, pre-purchase perceptions, quality assessment criteria, etc. "The frontline service provider has the opportunity to tailor in real-time not only the services the firm offers, but also the way in which those services are delivered. Customer actions, reactions and other characteristics can have a profound influence on the actions and mannerisms of frontline service personnel."[14] The contact employees should be responsive to the cues from consumers. They should display utmost restraint for negative reactions.
- *Adaptability:* Service employees need to develop inter-personal adaptability to perform well at service encounters. "Interpersonal adaptive behaviour refers to an employee altering various interpersonal communication elements (e.g. tone of voice, vocabulary, gestures) to meet what

they perceive to be the unique needs of individual consumers. Service offering adaptation refers to tailoring or creating a unique bundle of service attributes or benefits based on an individual consumer's needs.[15] Each customer style implies a different employee style. Thus, just like an actor or a comedian learns to read or play off of the audience, so too contact employees must learn this valuable skill in order to better serve customers by meeting their unique expectations."[16] Service companies should search for such employees who are willing to change customer contact styles as situations dictate, who exhibit flexibility in different circumstances and who are not locked into a certain behavioural style.

> "Employees' participation in service encounters needs to be promoted effectively. Service companies should take measures to provide for right kind of work climate, right job to the right person, employees' empowerment, training and motivation for encouraging employees to perform well."

- *Training:* Training is essential for enhancing employee proficiency at service delivery customization. Employees should be trained in how to recognize important cues from customers and in categorization of customers with varying needs and desires. Training not only enriches employee skills but also helps in refreshing and reorienting employees to perform critical tasks.
- *Motivation:* If the employees are truly motivated by a desire to do quality work that meets customer needs, the achievement of that outcome (customer satisfaction) should contribute to their own satisfaction as well.[17] The motivated employees perform all tasks with involvement, exhibit service orientedness, required patience and desire to serve the customer, absorb the mistakes or shortcomings in customer participation and display the feel of enjoyment in work. It allows consumers to perceive employee satisfaction in serving their needs. Such service interactions are perceived by the consumers positively. Employee motivation, thus, is a critical factor in interactive marketing .

Customer Participation

The quality of a service encounter is also influenced by the participative abilities of customers. "Especially in high interaction service encounters, customer participation in service production is critically important in determining service quality and customer satisfaction."[18] The functional quality of customer participation refers to the service customer behaviour, especially interpersonal behaviours, such as friendliness, respect and courtesy, which occur during the service encounter. Service companies should promote functional quality of customer participation by providing necessary inputs for service interactions and environment cues. The level of customer participation is influenced by the types of service encounters, sociability and the presence of co-customers. Customer roles in service delivery are discussed in "Services Marketing Insight: Customer Roles in Service Delivery". Basically three types of service encounters are experienced by customers. They include provider-dominated service encounters; joint user–provider specifications and user-dominated specifications.

In *provider-dominated service encounters*, users have little confidence in their ability to evaluate specifications or little interest in judging specifications. As a result, customers seek relatively little information on service

18.1 Services Marketing Insight — Customer Roles in Service Delivery

Services are jointly produced by service providers and customers. Customers have to play specific roles as per the requirements of a specific service package. The level of customer participation required in a service experience varies across services. In certain services such as entertainment shows, the mere physical presence of the customer is enough. In some cases, such as interior decoration and event management, the involved participation of customer is required for effective service production and delivery. There are yet other services which require the customers to co-create the service along with the service provider. So, depending on the service, customers have predefined roles in service production and delivery. If these roles are not executed properly, the final service outcome may be adversely affected. Bitner and co-workers have identified three roles of customers in service production and delivery.

1. ***The Customer as Productive Resources:*** It recognizes that customers contribute inputs much like employees in the service process. The quality of the service delivery depends to the extent the inputs provided by the customers.
2. ***The Customer as Contributor to Quality, Satisfaction and Value:*** The role the customers play in service delivery may contribute to customer satisfaction and the ultimate quality of the service. The roles played by the customers in services such as healthcare, education, personal fitness and weight loss greatly influence the outcome of the services. The customers should follow the instructions of the service provider and play their roles. Some customers simply enjoy participating in service delivery. This high level of participation of customers in service delivery makes them to feel achievement of satisfaction when things go right. When things go wrong, generally, the consumers blame themselves for their poor performance.
3. ***The Customer as Competitor to the Service Organization:*** In some services, the customers themselves are competent enough to produce the service. In such cases, customers become potential competitors. Housewives are potential competitors for fast food centres. The decision to produce the service on their own or avail the services of a service provider is common enough for customers. Many business organizations face this kind of dilemma in decision making relating to internal production or outsourcing of services. Such competencies of the customers influence the participative role in service delivery.

The three identified roles are not mutually exclusive. Customers may play more than one of the three roles in a given situation.

Source: Mary Jo Bitner, William T. Faranda, Amy R. Hubbert and Valarie A. Zeithaml, "Customer Contributions and Roles in Service Delivery," International Journal of Service Industry Management, *8, no. 3 (1997): 193–205.*

specifications. They do not even look for information to make judgement of specifications that is independent of the judgement of the provider. Legal services, accounting, health care, education services are the examples of provider-dominated service encounters.

Joint user–provider specifications involve joint production of service with almost equal responsibilities. Employees and customers have their own choice specifications. Service organizations monitor the customer's behaviour to make sure that the service is produced efficiently and effectively. In health and fitness clubs, for example, a customer can choose from any of the equipment that is available, but employees usually train customers on how to use the equipment properly.

User-dominated specifications involve using a service where the customer chooses between specifications that are available at his/her discretion. Customers feel that they are able to judge specifications and are interested in doing so. Customers have knowledge of their circumstances, preferences and needs that are important in selecting appropriate specifications. "Customers may not know of all of the specifications available from a specific provider or the outcomes that are likely. Then the customer may seek specifications information. The customer may request a presentation of specifications by the provider, yet the final choice is the customer's prerogative."[19] For example, dining in a restaurant is a common service that is usually customer dominated. Most restaurants have a set menu, and the customer selects from the items listed in the menu. Extreme customer dominance is characteristic of fast food restaurants where customers give their order to service personnel.

Sociality

Sociality is a pattern of verbal and non-verbal communication behaviour with other persons, which includes responsive and immediate behaviours. Sociality has been defined as "performance that encourages a cooperative, social smoothness, void of intense interactions with others."[20] There are four dimensions of sociality: courtesies, pleasantries, sociabilities and privacies. *Courtesies* refer to polite greetings or friendly displays when one person happens to face the other person. *Pleasantries* include small talk on topics related to news, weather, sports or politics. *Sociability* refers to pleasant interactions and disclosures such as sharing gossip and joking. *Privacies* are intimate revelations about oneself to others. The sociable environment encourages the customers to participate in the service process with comfort and confidence. It helps the customers to feel at home and perform naturally.

Gen-Next Lifestyles from Bank of Baroda

Bank of Baroda, the century-old Indian bank, has introduced a product called Gen-Next Lifestyle, a term loan targeted at working executives/professionals with an annual income of INR 250,000 or above. In keeping with the lifestyle of the target market, the bank used its Web site to popularize the product features such as the maximum loan eligibility (product category wise) and the maximum loan the bank can offer, the rate of interest, processing and documentation charges, the repayment process, EMI details, security and other related features. It put up the list of necessary documents and other terms and conditions on its Web site. Any prospective customer visiting the Web site could gather sufficient knowledge and a fair understanding of the terms and conditions of the services offered by the bank. Such communication helps the consumers to conceptualize their service needs and prepare psychologically to pass through various processes without any shortcomings from their side. Their expectations from the bank employees will be realistic and the assessment of service quality will be more rational. Such a preparation on the part of the customer will make it easier for the bank to manage its operations at service encounters effectively.

Presence of Co-customers

The presence of other customers is common in many service encounters. Consumers are required to take the services along with other consumers in case of public transport, shopping, restaurants and bars, beauty care, education, etc. These co-customers may be friends or casual acquaintances or complete strangers. The behaviour of co-customers has an effect on satisfaction/dissatisfaction with the service experience. It may affect consumer purchase intentions also. In some services, such as adventure holidays and academic conferences, the customer-to-customer interactions are planned and made an integral part of the service experience. In some services such as quiz nights and bowling competitions, the service output depends on customer teamwork. "One positive/negative interaction with a fellow customer in a service setting may determine re-patronage decisions. The content and process of customer-to-customer oral interactions can provide insights into the roles that fellow customers adopt in service settings. Some fellow customers can spoil a service experience through inappropriate public behaviour."[21]

> *Customer participation in service encounter is influenced by the roles of customers. In provider-dominated service encounter, customers have a little role to play, whereas in the user-dominated service encounter, they have the major role. The sociable environment and the presence of co-customers also influence it.*

The Participation Problems of Foreign Customers

In cultural encounters, the desired service and adequate service are generally home country based. This means that the service is designed based on customer experiences from the home country. "Foreign customers enter an intercultural encounter with their culturally biased expectations. Consequently, an inter-cultural service provider performance gap occurs when the service performed by a company from one culture is seen as inadequate by a customer from another culture, due to expectations developed by each in their respective home cultures."[22] When foreign customers are not familiar with the service systems of the service provider, they may not be able to perform their role correctly. For example, foreign customers face problems of participation with transport reservation or queuing systems that deviate from those in their home countries.

> *In a cross-cultural interaction, understanding the cultural background of the customers is very important. When it is a mix of domestic and foreign customers, it is often very different to manage service interactions satisfying both the parties.*

MOMENTS OF TRUTH

The concept of the "moments of truth" was promoted by Jan Carlzon[23], the CEO of Scandinavian Airlines. After taking charge in 1981, he adopted a customer-focused approach to turn around the company which was suffering a loss of USD20 million. He identified 50,000 daily moments of truth with the customer. By focusing on improving the moments of truth, he increased the revenues of Scandinavian Airlines to USD 54 million in just 12 months. The concept is simple and easily adaptable. The service company should first identify those moments between employees and customers, customers and service environment, and between customers and systems and other processes that are capable of creating some specific experiences for the customer. The moments thus identified are to be assigned, by categorizing and classifying them into groups, to each employee involved in the

> "*Moments of truth* occurs when a service encounter takes place. The truth is interpreted by the consumers to develop service quality perceptions. Every moment that happens will be having influence at different degrees on consumers directly or indirectly."

interaction process. The employee concerned is responsible for managing the assigned moments. Management of moments of truth effectively is possible only when employees are adequately empowered. It also requires a high level of motivation as well as morale of the employees. This concept makes every employee creative and innovative. The employee becomes conscious of what is happening in the moments assigned to him and becomes accountable for such moments for the company.

Managing Moments of Truth

The moments of truth need to be managed effectively by integrating company policies, procedures, service environment, employees' roles and customer roles.

Figure 18.1 describes that the moments of truth take place when a service encounter occurs.

Determinants of Employee Behaviour at Service Encounter

The determinants of employee behaviour at service encounter include personal needs, self-image, lifestyle, ability to perform, willingness to perform, situational pressures, mood and health.

- *Personal Needs:* Personal needs of the employee influence the interactive behaviour significantly. Employees may have a set of needs they want to satisfy through the performance of the job. An employee may need the job desperately to lead a comfortable life. In such a case, he/she will be careful in performing the job and try not to displease the customer to avoid complaints and negative remarks and try to live up

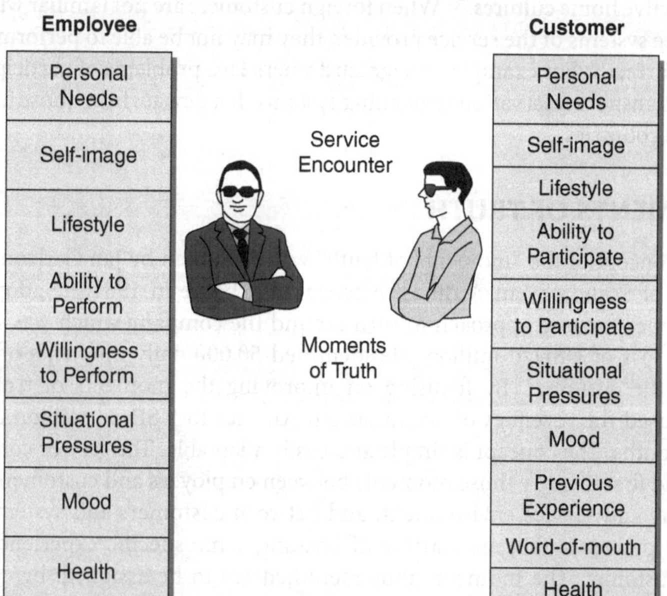

Fig. 18.1
Moments of truth

to employer expectations. The other needs that influence positive behaviour of the employee include recognition needs, achievement needs, promotion needs, work satisfaction needs, learning needs, social needs and relationship needs.

- *Self-image:* Self-image is the image developed by an individual on him/her self. Some employees like to be recognized as a good person, the sociable person, stylish person or positive person or an empathetic person. The perceived status and the expected recognition by the others are part of self-image.
- *Lifestyle:* The way in which an individual leads his/her life is called lifestyle. Every individual develops some uniqueness in leading the life though majority of the life standards are influenced by the group life standards to which he/she belongs to. Lifestyle reflects the opinions, activities and interests of the individual.
- *Ability to Perform:* Employees vary in their ability to perform various tasks at the frontline operations. Knowledge of the job is an important factor influencing the ability of employee in the interactive process. A salesman who does not know the technical features of the product, the competitive brands and their features, the company policies and special packages to the customers, special provisions to different customer groups may not feel comfortable in interactions. If the employee is confident of his/her ability, he/she can participate in interactive process confidently and serve to the needs of the customer.
- *Willingness to Perform:* Willingness to perform is yet another factor that influences the interactive process. The employees may have ability to perform but may not have interest to perform. When the job assigned is not to the interest of the employee who has potential to perform better jobs, but the employee has some dissatisfaction, developed some negative feelings against the customer in the earlier interaction and there are conditions of such nature, they force the employee to participate in the interactive process unwillingly. There may be several other reasons to develop willingness to serve and also to develop unwillingness to serve. The willingness contributes for positive and efficient performance of the employee, and the unwillingness contributes for low or sometimes negative performance.
- *Situational Pressures:* Situational pressures like excessive demand, extended hours of work, observation by superiors, pressures from family side, urgencies and so on do not allow the employee to be cool and perfect in performing the job. Situational pressures may not be a regular phenomenon, but whenever employee undergoes such pressure, his/her interactive behaviour is affected significantly.
- *Mood:* Mood is a psychological state of mind. Individuals may have positive or negative mood in interactions. Mood influences the perception of the employees. The employees with positive mood try to observe positives in the environment and in the interactive persons. Negative mood makes an individual look at the negatives in the environment and

in the interactive persons. There is another position which is called no mood that keeps an individual indifferent and uninterested in handling any job. Such employee may participate in the interaction mechanically because he/she is not supported with positive mood. The mood of the person may be influenced by the ambiance, the positive personalities among co-employees and customers and the interest in the job besides many things.

> *Several factors determine employee participation in a service encounter. The personal needs, self-image, lifestyle, ability to perform, willingness to perform, situational pressures, mood and health of the employees are the vital determinants.*

- *Health:* The condition of health of an employee has a certain impact on interactive behaviour. The healthy person may feel comfortable in facing varied physical and psychological pressures in the interactive process, while an unhealthy person not only will be in inconvenient position to serve the customer, but also may create inconveniences to the customers. Therefore, physical and mental fitness is an important dimension in the interactive process. The employee must be capable of withstanding the work pressures. Sound health is essential for the purpose.

Determinants of Customer Behaviour During a Service Encounter

The determinants of customer behaviour at service encounter include personal needs, self-image, lifestyle, ability to participate, willingness to participate, situational pressures, mood, previous experience, word-of-mouth and health. We examine the contribution of each in this section.

- *Personal Needs:* Consumes seek to satisfy a set of needs from a service provider. The needs may be the services that are identified as requirement for the self and the family, shopping needs such as knowing the choices available, particularly, new services, status needs, social needs, entertainment needs, emergency needs and so on. The group of needs the consumer wants to satisfy is called the *need set.* According to the priority of the needs within the need set, the consumer orients his/her behaviour in the service encounter. For example, if the consumer's buying need is economy, he/she may try to influence the contact person to suggest services in low-price category, discount offer categories, etc.
- *Self-image:* As like the employees, the consumers' interactive behaviour also are influenced by the perception of their self-image. The traditional, the variety seeker, the stylish, the innovator, the dependent, the insufficient, the weak in technical knowledge, the indecisive and the risk taker are some of the self-images the individuals develop. Such self-images may have positive or negative impact at the time of service encounter.
- *Lifestyle:* Consumers of different lifestyles display different behaviour patterns in interacting with others.
- *Ability to Participate:* Consumers often feel deficient in their participative abilities at service encounter. The reasons may be the lack of sufficient, reliable and timely information, lack of adequate knowledge on technical factors, lack of time for shopping, poor communication skills, language barriers and so on. Ability to participate varies from customer

to customer. Customers with ability will display confidence in interactions and take the lead in managing the service encounter.

- *Willingness to Participate:* The willingness to participate also varies from customer to customer, situation to situation and contact person to contact person. The more the consumers are willing to participate, the more will be the customer involvement in the interactive process. When the customers are given a situation wherein he/she is unable to relate the service offer to their needs, the consumer displays unwillingness to participate. For example, in a retail outlet when a consumer is asked to spend his/her time on looking at the products displayed by the salesperson and the consumer finds that the products are of no value to him/her or do not suite his/her lifestyle, there may not be willingness to participate.
- *Situational Pressures:* The pressures like, time pressure, overcrowding of the customers in the service outlet, fatigue or tiresomeness, pressure from children or family members or friends or relatives, etc., create discomfort to the consumer to participate in the service encounter.
- *Mood:* Similar to that of the contact employee, the mood of the consumer influences significantly the interactive behaviour. Consumers with positive mood, indifferent mood or negative mood behave differently.
- *Previous Experience:* The experience that the consumers had at the previous or earlier encounter influences the development of service expectations. Accordingly, the consumer behaves at the service encounter.
- *Word of Mouth:* The information received by the consumers relating to the company from friends, relatives, family members and others who are not related to the company is called word-of-mouth communication. This communication is considered very powerful influence because of the reason that the communication is from the third party. The word-of-mouth communication serves as a credible input to the consumer. Accordingly, the consumer decides the kind of interactive behaviour at the service encounter with the employee of the service organization.
- *Health:* Soundness in health and physical fitness of the consumer play an important role at service encounter. The healthy person seeks more and more interactions as he/she can withstand work pressure and has the ability to convert the interactions as the pleasant experiences. In the case of customers with poor health, the interactions may happen in the opposite direction.

> *"Consumer participation also will be based on the intensity of personal needs, self-image, lifestyle, ability and willingness to participate, situational pressures, mood, previous experience, word of mouth and the health condition of the consumer."*

The employee and the customer with the background of various behavioural determinants face each other at the service encounter and participate in the production and consumption process of the service. In other words, it is the encounter of two different behaviours. Consumer behaviour is not controllable. Employee behaviour can be influenced by promoting service culture and developing interactive skills. A conceptual model of the service encounter is presented in "Services Marketing Insight: Service Cycles".

18.2 Services Marketing Insight

Service Cycles

Service organizations do a lot of work in formulating strategies, policies and operating procedures, although the actual performance of the service takes place at an operative level in a service encounter. The service characteristics indicate the interactive qualities of the service in service encounter. A service provider is encouraged, and performance gets enhanced when there is a continuous response of approval or satisfaction from the service receiver. Contrary to this, an unfavourable or unpleasant response makes the service providers to face disturbance, confusion, tension and a sense of failure. Thus, the production, delivery and consumption of a service in a service encounter are dependent upon service cycles of expectations versus perceptions of a service provider and the service receiver. Svensson developed a conceptual model of services cycles, where the service cycles of interactive service quality consist of four elements:

1. The service provider's expectation
2. The service provider's perception,
3. The service receiver's expectation
4. The service receiver's perception

These elements of the service cycles create four potential gaps of interest to be explored and described:

1. the gap between the service provider's expectation and perception,
2. the gap between the service receiver's expectation and perception,
3. the gap between the service provider's and service receiver's expectations and
4. the gap between the service provider's and service receiver's perceptions.

It is necessary to fill these gaps in order to achieve satisfactory results in interactive service quality. The no-gap situation may be an ideal situation. Preferably, there should be a dissonance indicating that the service receiver's service cycle positively exceeds that of the service provider's in a service encounter.

Source: Goran Svensson, "A Generic Conceptual Framework of Interactive Service Quality," Managing Service Quality, *13, no. 4 (2003): 267–275.*

The interaction between the two under various influencing variables should yield good results for the organization. The customers are not controllable and can only be influenced. As such, only the factors on the employee's side can be regulated. The employee can be made more fit for interaction. Therefore, an employee must be motivated and trained to adapt to the customer's conditions and influence customers to participate well in service encounter. The employee's role in making the moments of truth qualitative is vital. Employees need to be given freedom to participate and design new ways of interactions that delight consumers. Service companies adopt a concept called zero investment improvements (ZIIs) for the purpose. Employees are the best potential to explore ZII in a service.

Let us consider three situations.

1. A consumer enters a service outlet and is unable to identify the right person to contact. The service personnel are basically engaged in their work, and none of them recognizes the customer's presence. The

customer finally contacts a person and enquires about the right person to contact. The service employee guides him properly, and the customer is able to get the work done and leaves the office with a feeling of relief.

2. A consumer enters the service outlet and is unable to identify the right person to contact. One employee of the service outlet greets him with a smile and enquires about the work. The employee guides him to the right person, maintaining all courtesies. The customer contacts the right person and gets the work done. He leaves the office happily.
3. A consumer enters the service outlet and is unable to identify the right person to contact. An employee of the service outlet establishes eye contact immediately, greets him with a smile and offers him a seat. He enquires about the customer's problem, tries to show empathy and reconfirms his understanding of the problem and starts performing the service by contacting the other personnel either over the phone or through the Internet. He contacts other employees quickly and completes the service. The employee thanks the customer for availing the service. The customer leaves the office delighted.

Turning the interactive movements from situation 1 to 3 does not require any extra investment, but the improvement of quality is substantial. The opportunities for improvement in buyer–seller interactions are infinite. Service companies should continuously explore opportunities and strive for improvement of the moments of truth. Phil Weaxler classified the moments of truth into two categories:

1. Magic moments
2. Misery moments

"Moments of truth can be managed by assigning certain identified moments that have a high potential of generating quality to employees and by promoting responsible behaviour in them. The classification of moments into magic and misery moments is one approach."

A moment of magic means that the employee performs a moment of truth with quality service, and the customer feels that he/she has received more than what is expected. The misery moments are quite opposite to the magic moments. The customer feels let down or ill-treated. Excellence in the interactive process occurs only when moments of magic become a way of life for the service organizations. By making every employee familiar with the moments of truth in their jobs, organizations can motivate them to make every moment a magic moment. These may include how to answer a phone, how promptly an action is taken, neatness of the visitors' lounge, appearance of employees, use of signs, company stationary, what employees say to one another, how employees work together and so on. They contribute significantly to customer-perceived quality.

THE SERVICE INTERACTION PROCESS

The service interaction process can be broadly classified into three phases. J. Lehtinen[24] named these phases as the joining phase, the intensive consumption phase and the detachment phase.

The Joining Phase

The joining phase is the first phase of the service consumption process. Some studies identified a pre-joining phase also wherein marketing personnel interact with the customers and persuade or sometimes sell the service. Anyhow, when services are provided at the service outlet, the customer begins with the joining phase. The two important activities in this phase are entry and registration.

At the entry phase, the customers look for parking place. They also interact with the watchman or parking boy and seek assistance. Easy identification of the entry point, the ease of entry and courteous welcome influence the quality perceptions of the consumer. During registration, easy identification of the registration counter, the amount of information to be recorded, the speed of the recording process, the equipment used for recording, the employee and customer roles during recording, the instruments used, the courteous interaction and empathy from the side of contact employee, the understanding of customer problems, the space, furniture and the layout at the registration counter and the direction to the next contact are the issues that influence the consumer.

At the entry level as well as during registration, consumers may need to wait for some time. How the wait line is organized and what facilities are provided for managing the waiting time also matter at this phase. Providing well furnished waiting rooms, latest magazines and entertainment facilities reduce waiting pressure.

The Intensive Consumption Phase

This is a critical phase wherein the service process aims at solving consumer problems. The first step in the process is the perfect diagnosis of the problem. Contact employees will discuss with the consumers and try to define the consumer's problem accurately by getting confirmation from the service consumer. The contact employee proposes the service process and also the cost involved in the service process. The service process will be finalized in consultation with the service consumer and the agreement on BSP results. The service production process starts with defined roles being performed by both parties. If the production process is split into phases, the customers may be directed to move from one phase to another. Precautions are communicated to customers to make participation effective. There are many factors that influence the effectiveness of the process at this stage. Documentation, queue system, time consumed, accuracy, transparency, customer approval, easy flow, equipment used, performance of the equipment, exclusivity (privacy), flexibility and exceptions are some of the factors that influence the quality. Service providers need to identify two important dimensions in managing this phase. These are discussed here.

1. *Customers Contribute to Quality:* The quality of the service depends upon the ability of the consumers to participate and also the ability of the employee to make the customer participate. Customers do seek

clarifications relating to processes and may also suggest improvements in the process. If the customer's queries are clarified properly, they can understand the process well and participate effectively. When their suggestions are implemented, they feel delighted and perceive high quality.

2. *Customers Are Competitors:* One of the choices for the customers in the personal service category is self-service. Due to some pressures and priorities of work, customers want such services to be performed by others, at a cost. However, as they are well aware of the service process and have the capability to perform both sides in the production and consumption process, they become critical evaluators. If the service firm does not perform better than self-service, consumers may not seek the service from the company.

At the end of the intensive consumption phase, the service personnel should try to get confirmation from the customer as to whether the service provided was as per his expectations or not. The collection of feedback from the customers especially for this phase will be of immense help for improving the process.

The Detachment Phase

There are two activities that generally take place during this phase. They are payment and registration for next visit. The payment system that is designed, whether cash, credit, instalment, office billing, credit card and so on, is the factor that influences the customers. The registration system for the next visit, exit facilities and collection of feedback are the other aspects that need to be managed properly.

ITC Welcomgroup

The ITC Welcomgroup invites the customers to interact online for service specifications and other details. It attempts to unfold fears of the customers by way of communicating its privacy policy. As per the policy, the company respects the right to privacy. Any personal information shared such as name, date of birth, address, marital status, telephone number and credit card particulars, shall be entitled to privacy and kept confidential. The policy assures that personal information shall not be used/disclosed by the company, save for the purpose of doing the intended business with the customer, or, if required, to be disclosed under the due process of law. It also assures that in the event of personal information of customers being shared with its subsidiaries, business associated, etc., such sharing of information shall be for the purpose of doing the intended business with the customer. The policy states that the company reserves its rights to collect, analyse and disseminate aggregate site-usage patterns of all its visitors in order to enhance services to its visitors.

The company allots a unique random number called "cookie" to every customer who interacts online to provide personalized experience. The communication of privacy policy to the customers facilitates their free involvement in the service process. When the customers share personal information, it helps the service personnel to understand their needs, wants and expectations clearly and provide services accordingly. The contact personnel can provide highly differentiated and customized services to satisfy the customers.

> *Service interaction process has three phases: The joining phase contributes significantly in shaping first impressions. The intensive consumption phase involves the production, delivery and consumption of core service. The detachment phase helps to ensure the next visit of the customer.*

Integrating the Phases

In the service-interaction process, the phases need to be integrated effectively so that the phase-to-phase delays, communication gaps and flow errors can be either eliminated or minimized. Continuous research is necessary to identify service gaps and also to take measures at the right time to eliminate the gaps.

ENHANCING EMPLOYEE PARTICIPATION

Service companies should initiate appropriate measures to promote effective employee participation in service encounters. Besides the effective internal marketing and issues discussed earlier in this chapter under employee participation, the companies need to train employees particularly on interactive communication skills and transactional analysis. Interactive communication skills refer to both verbal and non-verbal communication skills.

Verbal Communication Skills

Verbal communication skills refer to words used in interactive communication—oral as well as written. The words used by contact employee to welcome, greet, request, suggest, direct, explain, take order, send off, empathize and so on influence the behaviour of service consumers significantly. The excuses, sorry(s), thanks, etc., minimize or eliminate negative perceptions, and many create positive dispositions. Successful service companies with high customer contact standardize words, phrases, and sentences to minimize the risk of failure in verbal communication of their employees. The words are symbols of culture-driven meanings. Therefore, word choice depends upon the cultural background of the customers. Service companies when dealing with cross-cultural customers should take into consideration the positive and negative meanings of different words, contextual meanings, liked and disliked words, word preferences and so on of the people of a culture.

Non-verbal Communication Skills

Non-verbal communication (NVC) is usually understood as the process of communication through sending and receiving wordless messages. Such messages can be communicated through gesture; body language or posture; facial expression and eye contact; object communication such as clothing, hairstyles or even architecture; symbols and info graphics; prosodic features of speech such as intonation and stress and other paralinguistic features of speech such as voice quality, emotion and speaking style. Service employees should be given training on non-verbal communication particularly on the following key elements.

- *Body Language:* Body language is articulation of the body or movement resulting from muscular and skeletal shift. This includes all actions, physical or physiological, automatic reflexes, posture, facial expressions, gestures and other body movements. The body communicates a lot about a person in many ways when interaction is taking place. Body movement can indicate attitudes and feelings while also acting as illustrators and regulators. Body movement includes head movement, eyes, shoulders, lips, eyebrows, neck, legs, arms, fingers, hands and gestures. All these pieces can convey a person is comfortable, unhappy, friendly, anxious or nervous. With so many parts conveying messages, one can see how easily things can get confused and how difficult it is to manipulate non-verbal communication. Body motions such as shrugs, foot tapping, drumming fingers, eye movements (such as winking), facial expressions and gestures communicate meanings to the service consumers.

- *Facial Expressions:* Facial expressions include a smile, frown, raised eyebrow, yawn and sneer—all convey meaningful information. Facial expressions continually change during an interaction and are monitored constantly by the recipient. Facial expressions usually communicate emotions. The expressions tell the attitudes of the communicator. For example, the eyes tend to reveal happiness or sadness and even surprise. The smile, for example, can communicate friendliness and cooperation. The lower face, brows and forehead can reveal anger.
- *Posture:* Posture conveys the degree of formality and the degree of relaxation in interactions. There are some influencing elements in getting the right posture. They are nothing but head position, legs, the angle of the body in relation to others, body relaxation and tension. Posture can influence perceived competence. Closed postures, with features such as folded arms and crossed legs, indicate a closed personality and a lack of confidence. Open posture, with arms spread in a relaxed manner, is a much more confident pose than a closed stance. One should change posture periodically to show confidence because postural stiffness is usually perceived as nervousness. Postural movements should flow with the conversation so that they look natural.
- *Gestures:* Body movements sometimes clearly pass a meaningful message to others. By moving parts of your body, you can express both specific and general messages, some voluntary and some spontaneous. So, gestures are observed actions. Many gestures, for example, a wave of the hand, have a specific and intentional meaning, such as hello or good-bye.
- *Eye Contact:* Eye contact is an event when two people look at each other's eyes at the same time. It is a form of non-verbal communication known as oculesics and has a large influence on social behaviour. Frequency and interpretation of eye contact vary between cultures.
- *Touch:* Touches that can be defined as communication include handshakes, holding hands, kissing (cheek, lips, hand), back slap, shoulder pat, brushing arm, etc. Touch is an extremely important sense for humans. It is vital in conveying physical intimacy.
- *Proxemics:* Proxemics refers to how people use and interpret space. For most of us, someone standing very close makes us feel uncomfortable. We feel that our personal space has been invaded. People seek to extend

their territory in many ways to attain power and intimacy. Customers tend to mark their territory with permanent walls. Personal space is the space one places between self and others.

> "**Non-verbal communication** *plays an important role in a service encounter. Employees should be capable not only of communicating effectively through non-verbal media but also understanding the non-verbal signals of the participant consumers. The impact of non-verbal communication often would be very significant compared to verbal communication in service encounters.*"

- *Appearance and Artefacts:* Personal appearance is a major factor used to judge a person simply because the first impression of a person is based on appearance. People can change their appearance by changing their clothing styles, hairstyles and other accessories or artefacts. Clothing and other artefacts are especially powerful signifiers and convey a great deal of detailed information about someone's job, personality, values and lifestyle. For example, uniforms of one sort or another are a feature in many fields. Some uniforms are obvious like the army, the navy or the air force, the police, hospitals, etc. Personal physical appearance usually provides the first available data about a stranger. To establish credibility, one should wear styles that fit the environment.
- *Paralanguage:* Paralanguage (sometimes called vocalics) is the study of non-verbal cues of the voice. Various acoustic properties of speech such as tone, pitch, accent, etc., can provide non-verbal cues. Paralanguage can be used to modify meaning and convey emotion.
- *Dysfluency:* There are many different kinds of dysfluencies. Dysfluencies heard in the speech of normal speakers include silences, fillers (um, ah), hesitations, whole word and phrase repetitions and revisions.

Transactional Analysis

Transactional analysis[25] (TA) provides a useful framework for focusing attention on how exchanges take place. E. Berne who proposed transactional analysis suggests that there are three basic ways that individuals use to relate to others[26]. These modes of behaviour are called the *parent*, the *adult* and the *child* (see Figure 18.2).

Parent–Adult–Child

The parent model of communication (ego state) is learnt from one's parents. People record the attitudes, values and morals of their parents during their

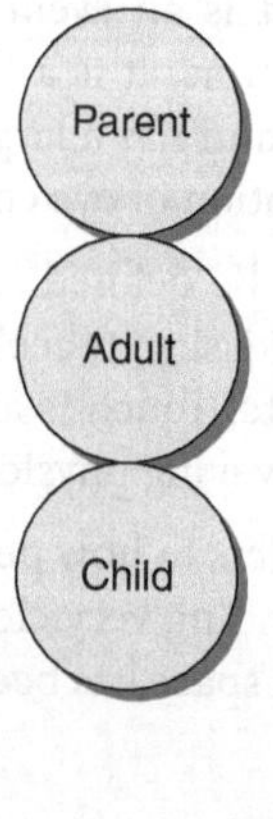

Fig. 18.2
Parent, adult and child ego states

childhood at a time when they are in no position to question or evaluate their parents' ideas. Young children observe their parents' behaviour, how the parents relate to them, etc.; when situations arise which touch on one's parent, the parent ego state is likely to be activated.

Many service providers seem to operate quite often from the perspective of parent when interacting with consumers. If their parent is critical and evaluative, they tend to be critical in listening to the customers and understanding the needs and concerns of the customers. If their parent is warm and supportive, they tend to mother their customers by showing empathy. If the service provider is operating from the perspective of parent, the consumer receives a lot of pressure and generally reacts like the child. They show the behaviour of compliant, dependent, seeking approval, or rebellious, counter dependent or seeking independence.

It is generally easy to recognize parent communication. If the tone of voice is moralistic, the person shakes a finger at the listener, authority is used instead of reasoning and the speech is sprinkled with "shoulds," it is very likely the parent that is speaking.

The *adult* ego state is that part of the individual which is reality oriented and problem centred. The adult attempts to take life's experiences as data and rationally deals with them. The objective of the maturing individual in transactional analysis terms is to emancipate the adult—that is, to free oneself both from the child's feelings of helplessness and dependency ("I'm not OK") and the parent's edicts which cover everything from sex to work. Perhaps, the best indicator of the adult state is the ability to cope responsibility with stress. Adult position is the "I am Ok" position. The person is realistic in his approach and open minded. He seeks information from others to understand the problem thoroughly before arriving at a conclusion. The service provider needs to develop adult state while interacting with the consumers. It is also necessary to adopt an appropriate tactic to manipulate the state of the consumer to be at the adult state. Adult to adult interaction is considered to be the best and more effective which reflects "I am Ok, You are Ok" position.

The *child* ego state contains all the impulses that come "naturally" to a young child. It also contains the memories of childhood experiences and how one responds to them. The child has experienced situations where the individual was helpless and dependent, which may have led him/her to conclude that he or she is "not OK." The child has also experienced being held, loved, consoled and being taken care of. Thus, positive feelings of dependency also reside in the child. The child also contains the playfulness and curiosity that are so obviously a part of the young child's life. Characteristics of the child, which are easily recognized, are rebelliousness, submissiveness, whining, wanting his/her way, impulsiveness, curiosity, playfulness, etc. Thus, the child state symbolizes fearfulness, sentimental, timid, joyous, playful, deceit, etc., having significant impact on interactions with others. Figure 18.3 summarizes the four possible positions in transactional analysis.

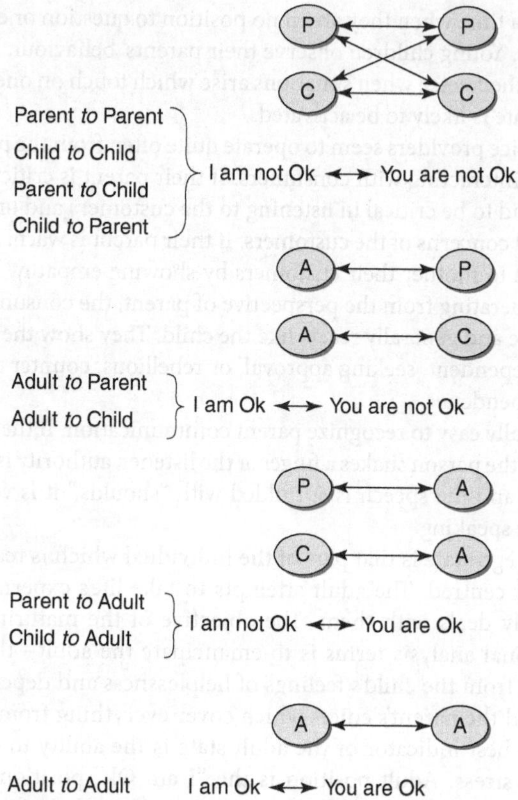

Fig. 18.3
The four possible positions of transaction analysis

> "***Transactional analysis*** *is considered as a very powerful tool for effective interaction with customers. The parent, adult and child ego states in consumers need to be understood and analyzed properly to promote adult to adult interactions.*"

The adult is the only ego state which is interested in and receptive to information. The child is primarily interested in fulfilling wants. The parent assumes the role of the sender in presenting controlling messages. It is the adult which receives, processes and feeds back information in an attempt to understand the other person. Therefore, the employees of the service organization shall be given proper training to master transactional analysis and develop an interactive situation between the service provider and the consumer on an adult to adult basis.

ENHANCING CUSTOMER PARTICIPATION

Enhancing customer participation is the key for effectiveness in interactive marketing. Customers vary in their participative abilities. There are many intervening variables, including the need pressure, customers' goals, time available, situation pressure, mood, impression formed on contact employee, physical environment, other employees, co-customers, importance of the service, value of the service and so on, which influence customers in the participation of service production and consumption. Service companies need to identify the factors influencing customer participation and develop appropriate strategies for encouraging effective participation of customers.

Defining the Processes Where Customers Have to Perform

It is essential to identify clearly the processes where customer participation is vital for service quality. For a medical practitioner, customer participation at the level of diagnosis and following the treatment by consuming medicines, as per the direction of the doctor, are important for service quality. Service companies should communicate effectively what roles the customers need to play and what is the level of expectation from the organization's point of view. The description of customer job cannot be universalized. It varies with the type of service and the organization's desired position within the industry. Some customer jobs may require helping themselves like in self-service restaurants; some jobs require helping others like students in a class helping each other and some customer jobs may be to promote the company by providing word-of-mouth endorsements (for example, introducing a new member to a bank for credit card).

Providing an Appropriate Customer Mix

In services, customers interact quite often with other customers in the process of service production and consumption. The status, culture and behaviour of the other customers influence the level of participation of a customer significantly. Some customers do not want to take the service in the presence of other known customers. Some like to mix with different age groups. Some may have status preferences and some may not have status barriers. The likes and dislikes of customers with respect to the fellow customers vary. The service provider should study the feelings and dispositions of various categories of customers and schedule the services, taking into consideration the compatibility of the customer mix. Compatibility management is critically important for some businesses such as health clubs, hotels, hospitals and so on.

Managing Customer Expectations

Everyone may not be the right customer for a service organization. People may need to possess some qualities, skills and positive attitude for a particular service. The company must be capable of attracting the right customers to make participation more effective. Thus, many educational institutes conduct an entrance test and group interviews to ensure that the right students take the course. Many service organizations offer customer orientation programmes to help customers understand the roles they have to play and the kind of expectations they should have before experiencing the service. Rewarding the best-performing customers increases the involvement of customers and ensures better participation in interactive processes.

In addition to the above, the code of conduct for the customers, training employees to observe customer-to-customer interactions and to be sensitive to potential conflicts help in enhancing participation of customers in the interactive process.

SUMMARY

- Interactive marketing is nothing but managing the process on stage.
- An efficient performance in interactive marketing can save a poorly designed or defective technical product. But an effective technical product with a very poor interactive marketing cannot yield the desired results
- The stages in interactive marketing such as joining phase, intensive consumption phase and detachment phase need to be defined clearly and organized efficiently.
- The foundation for interactive marketing is the integrated efforts of internal marketing and external marketing.
- The moments of truth that take place at the service encounters are to be identified, classified and delegated to service employees for their efficient management.
- Consumers cannot be controlled but can be influenced.
- Service companies should focus on employees and provide them the necessary support for performance.
- Employee empowerment with adequate freedom to perform promotes creativity and innovativeness in employees. They can identify magic and misery moments and can find ways to turn every misery moment into a magic moment.

KEY TERMS

Consumer grievance *348*
Detachment phase *363*
Intensive consumption phase *362*
Joining phase *362*
Magic moments *361*
Misery moments *361*
Moments of truth *354*
Service encounter *350*

BRIEF QUESTIONS

1. What is interactive marketing?
2. What are moments of truth?
3. Explain the concept of a service encounter.
4. How can customer participation be enhanced?

ESSAY QUESTIONS

1. What is the importance of interactive marketing in a service organization?
2. Explain the concept of moments of truth and discuss the important elements in the management of moments of truth.
3. What is a service encounter? How can it be managed?
4. What is the importance of customer participation in interactive marketing? How can customer participation be enhanced?
5. "An integration of internal marketing and external marketing is necessary to perform interactive marketing effectively." Discuss.
6. Analyse interactive processes in the following service encounters.
   (a) A three-star hotel
   (b) A passenger transport corporation
   (c) A healthcare company
7. Examine the moments of truth in a service process.

ASSIGNMENTS

1. Recollect your recent experience with a service organization and prepare a report on
   (a) the experience-generating moments.
   (b) the way those moments are managed by the service company
2. Organized retailing registered substantial growth during the last decade. Shopping malls have come up in almost all urban localities. The malls promise buying experience as well as shopping experience to the consumers in service interactions. You are required to study
   (a) the interactive process in a shopping mall.
   (b) the determinants of employee and consumer participation behaviour.

REFERENCES

1 M. Hammer, *The Agenda: What Every Business Must Do to Dominate the Decade.* (New York, NY: Three Rivers Press, 2001): p. 52.

2 Wen-Bao Lin, "An Empirical of Service Quality Model from the Viewpoint of Management," *Expert Systems with Applications,* 32 (2007): 364.

3 An-Tien Hsieh and Chang-Hua Yen, "The Effect of Customer Participation on Service Providers' Job Stress," *The Service Industries Journal,* 25, no. 7 (October 2005): 894.

4 L. L. Price, E. J. Arnould and P. Tierney, "Going to Extremes: Managing Service Encounters and Assessing Provider Performance," *Journal of Marketing,* 59 (April, 1995): 83–97.

5 M. J. Bitner, B. H. Booms and M. S. Tetreault, "The Service Encounter: Diagnosing Favorable and Unfavorable Incidents," *Journal of Marketing,* 54 (1990): 71–84.

6 D. E. Bowen and B. Schneider, "Boundary-Spanning Role Employees and the Service Encounter: Some Guidelines for Management and Research," in *The Service Encounter: Managing Employee/Customer Interaction in Service Business,* edited by John A. Czepiel, Michael R. Solomon and Carol F. Surprenant (Massachusetts: Maxwell Macmillan; Lexington: D.C. Heath/Lexington Books, 1985) pp. 127–47.

7 M. J. Bitner, et al., "The Service Encounter: "Diagnosing Favorable and Unfavorable Incidents," *Journal of Marketing,* 54 (January, 1990): 71–84.

8 Michael D. Hartline and O. C. Ferrell, "The Management of Customer-Contact Service Employees: An Empirical Investigation," *Journal of Marketing,* 60 (October, 1996): 52.

9 M. J. Burke, C. C. Borucki and A Hurley, "Reconceptualizing Psychological Climate in a Retail Service Environment: A Multiple-Stakeholder Perspective," *Journal of Applied Psychology,* 77, no. 5 (1992): 717–729.

10 B. Schneider, et al., "Linking Service Climate and Customer Perceptions of Service Quality: test of a Causal Model," *Journal of Applied Psychology,* 83, 2 (1998): 150–163.

11 Michael D. Hartline and O. C. Ferrell, "The Management of Customer-Contact Service Employees: An Empirical Investigation," *Journal of Marketing,* 60 (October, 1996): 52.

12 Jennifer Potter-Brotman, "The New Role of Service in Customer Retention," *Managing Service Quality,* 4, no. 4 (1994): 53.

13 Lance A. Bettencourt and Kevin Gwinner, "Customization of the Service Experience: The Role of the Frontline Employee," *International Journal of Service Industry Management,* 7, no. 2 (1996): 7.

14 S. J. Grove, R. P. Fisk and M. J. Bitner, Dramatizing the Service Experience: A Managerial Approach, in *Advances in Services Marketing and Management,* edited by T. A. Swartz, D. E. Bowen and S. W. Brown, Vol.1 (Greenwich, CT: JAI Press, 1992) pp. 91–121.

15 Lance A. Bettencourt and Kevin Gwinner, "Customization of the Service Experience: The Role of the Frontline Employee," *International Journal of Service Industry Management,* 7, no. 2 (1996): 3.

16 A. Thompson, "Customer Contact Personnel: Using Interviewing Techniques to Select for Adaptability in Service Employees," *Journal of Services Marketing,* 3, no. 1 (1989): 57–65.

17 L. A. Crosby, D. B. Grisaffe and T. R. Marra, "The Impact of Quality and Customer Satisfaction on Employee Organisational Commitment," *Marketing and Research Today,* (February, 1994): 19–30.

18 J. E. G. Bateson, "Perceived Control and the Service Encounter", in *The Service Encounter,* edited by J. A. Czepiel, M. R. Solomon and C. F. Surprenant (Lexington, MA: Lexington Books, 1985) pp. 67–82.

19 John E. Swan, Michael R. Bowers and Rajan Grover, "Customer Involvement in the Selection of Service Specifications," *Journal of Services Marketing,* 16, no. 1 (2002): 89.

20 M. E. Pacanowsky and N. O'Donnell-Trujillo, "Organisational Communication as Cultural Performance," *Communication Monographs,* 50 (1983): 126–147.

21 K. D. Hoffman and J. E. G., Bateson, *Essentials of Services Marketing.* (Orlando, FL: The Dryden Press, 1997).

22 Bernd Stauss and Paul Mang, "'Culture Shocks" in Inter-cultural Service Encounters?," *Journal of Services Marketing,* 13, no. 4/5 (1999): 333.

23 http://en.wikipedia.org/wiki/Jan_Carlzon.

24 J. Lehtinen, *Quality Oriented Services Marketing.* (Finland: University of Tampere, 1986).

25 Thomas A. Harris, *I'm Ok You're Ok.* (Great Britain: Jonathan Cape Ltd., 1970).

26 E. Berne, *Games People Play.* (New York, N.Y.: Grove Press, 1964), p. 29.

Service Quality Management

19

LEARNING OBJECTIVES

After studying this chapter, you will be able to:

- Understand the way consumers perceive service quality
- Identify the determinants of service quality
- Describe the managerial process for service quality
- Understand the service quality audit

Star Diagnostic Centre (SDC), established two decades ago, has been functioning on the strength of its relationships with local doctors and hospitals that suggest the centre to their patients. This formula served Star very well till two new diagnostic centres came up which caused many of its old clients to switch loyalties and patronize the new centres despite the doctors and hospitals advising them to visit SDC. Since the time it was established, SDC never focused on the customers—an attitude that became a habit owing to the steadily rising profits. Though many customers clearly expressed their dissatisfaction, SDC did not take any steps to address their grievances. Quite a few customers, though not happy with SDC's services, patronized it either for the sake of convenience or simply for fear of offending their doctor/hospital. SDC took customer loyalty for granted, safe in the knowledge that there was no other service provider in the area to challenge its supremacy. However, the opening of two new centres in the same area changed all that. These centres managed to take away a large share of SDC's business simply because they offered services that were designed with the customer as the focus.

Varun Singh, the proprietor of SDC examined the dropping profits and realized that immediate corrective measures were needed to arrest the rapid customer outflow. To zero in on the problem, Singh interviewed quite a few customers of SDC. He also sent out his employees to visit the new centres and find out on their way of functioning. Based on the information thus gathered, Singh figured that the main problem was the absence of a quality management system at SDC. Singh now plans to design and execute a quality management system in the centre and communicate to all the customers the new system and new promises. He is hopeful that such a measure will bring the customers back to Star Diagnostic Centre.

Questions:

1. How do consumers perceive quality in a diagnostic centre?
2. How can a QMS be designed for the service?
3. Will the old customers who now patronize the new centres believe the new promises and renew their loyalty?

INTRODUCTION

One of the critical tasks of service companies is service quality management. The quality of services is considered to be a critical success factor for contemporary service companies.[1] Quality means the degree of excellence in service performance. Consumers perceive the quality of a service by experiencing the consumption process and comparing the experience with their expectations. Though consumers are co-producers and their participation also affects the quality, service firms cannot blame them for poor quality. Service organizations need to formulate strategies for quality performance. As service quality is antecedent to consumer satisfaction and consumer satisfaction is antecedent to purchase intentions, there is a strong link between quality and customer retention in the services sector.[2] Therefore, how to manage service quality is the pivotal issue for any service company.

Service organizations perceive service quality differently. Quality is related to costs, profitability, customer satisfaction, customer relation, behavioural intention and positive word of mouth. Service organizations ascertain quality by taking either of these variables or a combination of them. However, a common understanding among all is that quality is one of the most influential factors in the consumers' purchase decision process. According to Buzell and Gale, "empirical research clearly shows the positive relationship between service quality and organizational performance. Using a large database of thousands of strategic business units, research shows that the most critical factor affecting a business unit's performance is the quality of its products and services as perceived by the market relative to the perception of its competitors."[3]. A. Parasuraman, V. A Zeithaml and L. L. Berry define service quality as "the degree and direction of discrepancy between consumer's perceptions and expectations in terms of different but relatively important dimensions of the service quality, which can affect their future purchasing behaviour.[4]" This definition clearly indicates that what the consumers assess through their own measurement criteria based on their expectations and perceptions of a service experience is service quality. Service organizations, therefore, have to manage the concept from the customer's point of view. In order to develop services marketing programmes, it is necessary to understand what consumers are really looking for and what and how they evaluate a service.

> *"Service quality management is the most critical task of service companies. Quality may be perceived in many dimensions. It may relate to costs, profitability, customer satisfaction, customer relations or positive word of mouth. Customers assess service quality with their own criteria."*

HOW IS SERVICE QUALITY PERCEIVED?

When service organizations understand how services are evaluated by consumers in terms of quality, it is possible to design strategies to manage these evaluations and influence them in a desired direction. In a service encounter, buyer–seller interactions take place in large numbers. Each interaction obviously has a critical impact on customers' quality perceptions. Thus, a methodology is necessary to understand how customers perceive quality. Grönroos[5] has identified two dimensions of service quality in relation to quality perception by customers: technical quality and functional quality (see Fig. 19.1).

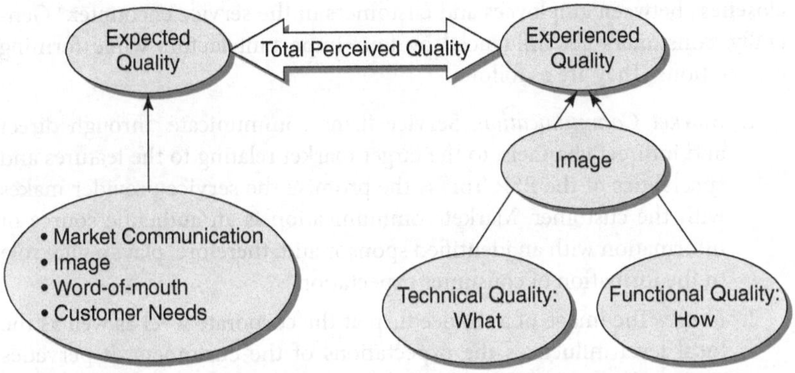

Source: C. Grönroos, "Service Quality: The Six Criteria of Good Service Quality," Review of Business *(New York: St. John's University Press, 1988): 12.* Reproduced with permission.

Fig. 19.1: The total perceived quality

Technical Quality: What is offered to the customer from the organization and what customers receive in their interactions with the service firm is called the technical product. The quality in designing the basic service package (BSP) is reflected in the technical quality of a service. In other words, it speaks of the technical quality of blueprinting and its execution. Technical quality moulds the first impressions of customers.

Functional Quality: Technical quality contributes only to a part of the total quality experienced by the customer. Customers are also influenced by how they receive the service and how they experience the service process in which they also played a part. Research studies indicate that customers are influenced mostly by the way technical quality is transferred to them. The way service processes are handled in a service encounter is called functional quality.

> *"Service quality has two dimensions—technical quality and functional quality. Technical quality refers to the design quality of the service while functional quality refers to performance. Consumers perceive these two dimensions from the perspective of the company image."*

Image

Most consumers evaluate a firm by taking into consideration its resources, history and ways of operating service activities. Therefore, a firm's image at the corporate as well as at the local level is of utmost importance in quality perception. If an organization enjoys a favourable image, customers probably might forgive the occasional minor mistake of the organization. However, if the mistakes are repetitive, there is a danger of spoiling the market image. Customers use a firm's image as a filter or a net while perceiving quality.

Expected Versus Experienced Quality

Every consumer makes an assessment of quality based upon the expectations that they have developed of a service offering. Customers are influenced by the service provider and the quality of the experience. Receiving service is both a personal and psychological experience. There is a psychological and physical closeness between employees and customers in the service encounter.[6] Generally, consumers get influenced by four important factors while forming expectations. They are as follows:

1. *Market Communication:* Service firms communicate, through direct and indirect channels, to the target market relating to the features and specialities of the BSP. This is the promise the service provider makes with the customer. Market communication is an authentic source of information with an identified sponsor and, therefore, plays a vital role in the formation of consumer expectation.
2. *Image:* The image of a service firm at the corporate level as well as the local level influences the expectations of the customers. It pervades various dimensions. An image of proven skills, consistency, innovativeness, care and concern, empathy, ability of handling problems, performance and so on are some of the identities companies develop over a period of time. These identities mould consumer expectations.
3. *Word-of-mouth Communication:* This is an informal communication channel. Word-of-mouth communication is considered to be the most powerful, particularly, in the case of services. As services are intangible and variable, comparison of alternatives and trials is not possible. Consumers often feel less confident about taking a purchase decision, based upon the communication from the service provider. They look for advice and information support from others, whom they consider as having more knowledge and experience in that particular service and will give a frank opinion about the service.
4. *Customer Needs:* Besides the three factors mentioned above, the need intensity of consumers influences the expectations. A relaxed customer may expect quality of a high level compared to a customer who is hard pressed for time. For example, in the case of health care services, at the time of emergency, people expect better and quicker response than in normal conditions.

> *"The total perceived quality results only after the consumers compare expected with experienced quality. When experienced quality supersedes the expected one, the consumers are highly satisfied or delighted. If the result is otherwise, consumers get dissatisfied with the service."*

Total Perceived Quality

The total perceived quality (TPQ) is the outcome of customer's assessment of expected quality and experienced quality. The consumer feels satisfied with the service when experienced quality matches with expected quality. If the expected quality is more than the experienced quality, the consumer is dissatisfied. If the experienced quality is more than the expected quality, the consumer is highly satisfied. The degree of dissatisfaction can be assessed by ascertaining the extent of deviation (negative) between the expected quality and the experienced quality. Similarly, the degree of satisfaction can be ascertained by measuring the deviation (positive) between the two factors. To know the level of satisfaction of the customer, it is necessary for service companies to study and measure expected quality and experienced quality.

DETERMINANTS OF SERVICE QUALITY

What factors really determine the quality of service as perceived by customers? The answer to the question is fundamental for service companies to design their service quality management strategy. The determinants of service quality are not universal but are service specific. However, a general understanding of the identified service quality determinants by various service researchers is useful to policy makers.

Alfrecht and Zemke identified four factors that influence the perceived service quality. They are:

1. *Care and Concern:* How devoted employees and operational systems of a service are in solving the problems of customers.
2. *Spontaneity:* How employees demonstrate willingness and readiness to serve.
3. *Problem Solving:* The expertise and skill of contact employees in performing services.
4. *Recovery:* The special efforts of a service provider in handling a situation when something goes wrong or something unexpected happens

A. Parasuraman, V. A. Zeithaml and L. L. Berry have identified five influencing variables of customer-perceived service quality. The five quality determinant factors are:

- Tangibles
- Reliability
- Responsiveness
- Assurance
- Empathy

Grönroos[7] developed six criteria of good perceived service quality based upon a solid body of empirical and conceptual research. The criteria basically are outcome, process and image related. The six criteria are:

1. *Professionalism and Skills:* Customers should perceive that the employees, operating systems and physical resources of the service provider have the competencies to provide services in a professional way (outcome-related criteria).
2. *Attitude and Behaviour:* Customers should perceive that the employees are positive, friendly and interested in solving their service problems (process-related criteria).
3. *Accessibility and Flexibility:* Customers should perceive that the service provider, its location, operating hours, employees and operational systems are designed and operated in such a way so that it is easy to access the service and the service providers are prepared to adjust to the demands and wishes of the customer in a flexible way (process-related criteria).

> *The identification of service quality determinants is very useful for service quality management. The determinants are not universal but service specific. Further, the influence of each determinant also varies from service to service.*

4. *Reliability and Trustworthiness:* Customers should perceive that the service provider, employees and systems are reliable and keep promises and perform with the best interest of the customers at heart (process-related criteria).
5. *Recovery:* Customers should perceive that whenever something goes wrong or something unpredictable happens, the service provider immediately and actively takes action to control the situation and finds a new, acceptable solution (process-related criteria).
6. *Reputation and Credibility:* Customers should perceive that the operations of the service provider can be trusted and give adequate value for money. The service firm stands for good performance and values that can be shared by customers and the service provider (image-related criteria).

THE PROCESS FOR SERVICE QUALITY MANAGEMENT

Service firms should develop quality-focused managerial processes to ensure continuous quality performance as desired by the customers. In order to achieve

NAAC

The National Assessment and Accreditation Council (NAAC) was established by the University Grants Commission (UGC) of India in 1994 to assess and accredit institutions of higher education in the country. NAAC has evolved a methodology for assessing quality of education services. It has identified seven criteria for assessment and accreditation: Curriculum, teaching—learning and evaluation, research, consultancy and extension, infrastructure and learning resources, student support and progression, governance and leadership, and innovative practices.

Further, it has identified 36 criterion-wise key aspects. Each key aspect of a criterion is further differentiated into a number of assessment indicators which can be used as guidelines/probes by the peer team members to capture the micro-level quality parameters of the institution and arrive at comprehensive grade of the key aspects.

NAAC requires a self-study report (SSR) from each higher-education institution to carry out assessment. After the receipt of SSR, it nominates a peer team comprising well-trained assessors to the respective institution to carry out the assessment. Based on the report of the peer team, the grade is given. NAAC assigns weightages to each of the seven assessment criteria, and, based on the values scored by the institution, it calculates cumulative grade point average (CGPA). NAAC awards A, B, C grade with CGPA. The accreditation given to an institution is valid for 5 years.

NAAC, with a vision to make quality the defining element of higher education in India through a combination of self and external quality evaluation, promotion and sustenance initiatives, is carrying out the assessment and accreditation process. Once accredited, each institution is required to establish an Internal Quality Assurance Cell (IQAC). The prime task of IQAC is to develop a structured mechanism for consistent and catalytic improvement in the performance of institutions. The IQAC is expected to make a significant and meaningful contribution to the institutional quality improvement.

the quality objectives, an integrated and coordinated work of three participant groups is necessary. The groups that influence the service quality are:

- The management of the service organization
- The employees
- The customers

Grönroos[8] has developed a schematic diagram for service quality management framework. (See Fig. 19.2.)

The traditional demand analysis and quality control measurement is the first step in the quality management process. A study of demand patterns of the service at various levels of quality and market responses whenever a change in quality is attempted by the concern need to be studied in detail. Such study

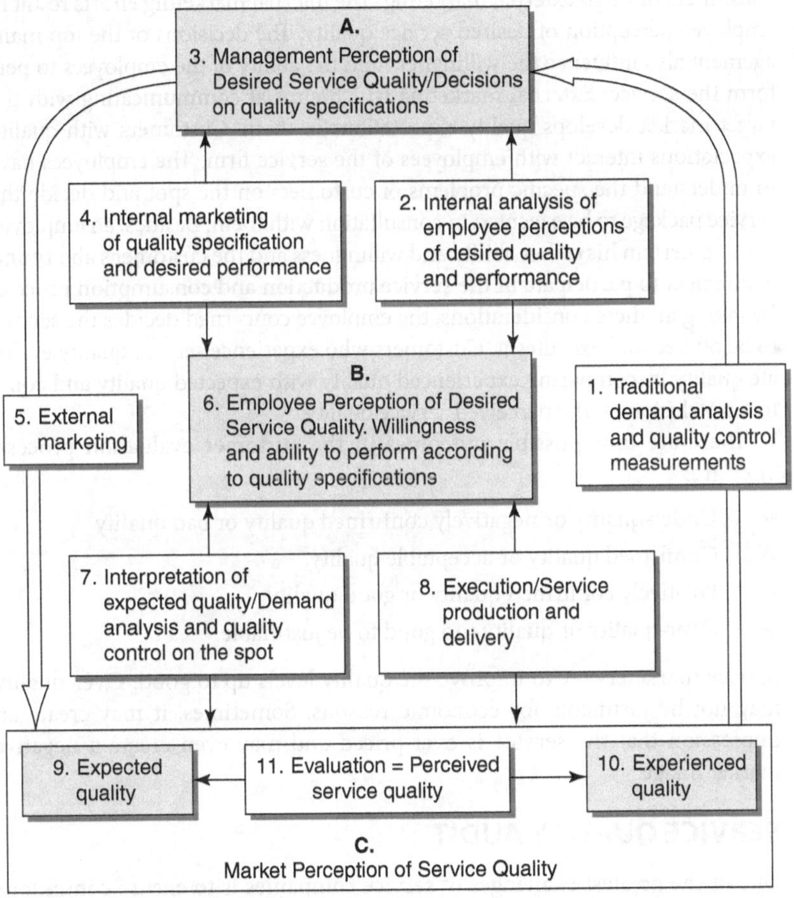

Source: C. Grönroos, Service Management and Marketing; Managing the Moments of Truth in Service Competition, *(Massachusetts: Maxwell Macmillan; Lexington: D.C. Heath/Lexington Books, 1990), p. 55.* Reproduced with permission.

Fig. 19.2: A service quality management framework

develops a basic understanding of desired quality by the customers. The second major source is employees' perception on desired quality and performance. Employees involved in regular interaction with customers in service production and delivery process are in a better position to collect and interpret feedback from the customers. This group, with its knowledge of company's vision, policies, procedures, competencies and limitations and comparative knowledge of competitive offers, is an invaluable resource to the company in developing quality specifications. Management, therefore, has to conduct an internal analysis of employee perceptions of desired quality and performance. The information input from the two processes helps the management to develop their own perceptions relating to desired service quality by the market. After a thorough analysis of various factors, the management can finally arrive at decisions on service quality specifications. The quality specifications thus decided by the management are communicated to employees through internal marketing and consumers through external marketing. The internal marketing efforts result in employee perception of desired service quality. The decisions of the top management also influence the willingness and the ability of the employees to perform the service. External marketing which aims at communicating with the target market develops quality expectations in them. Customers with quality expectations interact with employees of the service firm. The employees have to understand the specific problems of customers on the spot and decide the service package to be executed in consultation with them. Besides, an employee has to ascertain his or her ability and willingness and the customer's ability and willingness to participate in the service production and consumption process. By taking all these considerations, the employee concerned decides the service to be offered and executes it. Customers who experience service quality evaluate quality by comparing experienced quality with expected quality and come to a conclusion on the perceived service quality.

> *"The service quality management framework is useful to understand the inputs, processes, outputs and the roles of management, employees and customers in the process of formulating quality standards, quality performance and quality perceptions."*

There are four possible outcomes in the customer evaluation process. They are:

- Under-quality or negatively confirmed quality or bad quality
- Confirmed quality or acceptable quality
- Positively confirmed quality or good quality
- Over-quality or quality too good to be justifiable

Service marketers try to improve the quality levels up to good. Over-quality may not be justifiable for economic reasons. Sometimes, it may create an impression that the service is over-priced and may even create a negative market image.

SERVICE QUALITY AUDIT

One of the greatest challenges of service companies is to ensure continuous quality services to the customers. The design of effective quality management process alone cannot ensure the achievement of the desired objective. The management should be able to gear the system towards efficient functioning.

A service system operates in a dynamic environment, and, therefore, the system should be capable of adapting itself to the changes. An audit system needs to be designed to locate deficiencies, discrepancies and limitations at various processes. The "GAP" model of service quality which was developed by V. A. Zeithaml, *et al.*[9] serves to the purpose, if executed properly. Figure 19.3 presents the GAP model.

The GAP Model of Service Quality

The GAP model of service is divided into two parts. Part one relates to the internal process in a customer and part two relates to the process involved between service provider and consumer. In the GAP model, five gaps are identified, taking into consideration the possible discrepancies between the elements of the service management process. Each gap arises due to inconsistencies and deficiencies in the quality management process. Let us examine how gaps arise and the possible reasons for each gap to develop in a service organization.

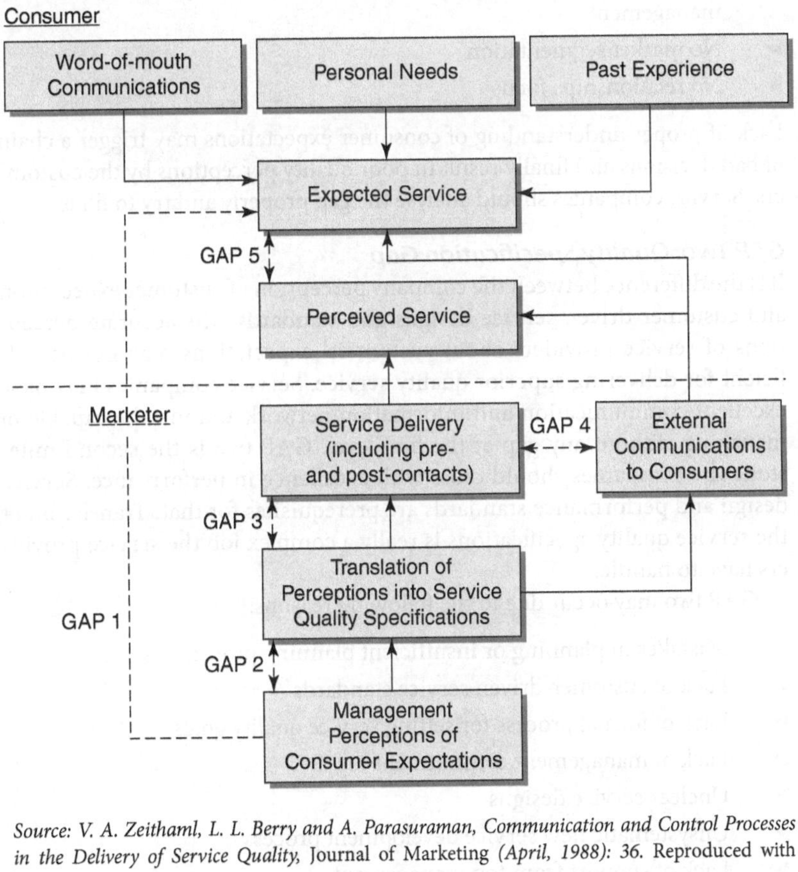

Source: V. A. Zeithaml, L. L. Berry and A. Parasuraman, Communication and Control Processes in the Delivery of Service Quality, Journal of Marketing *(April, 1988): 36.* Reproduced with permission.

Fig. 19.3: Conceptual model of service quality—the GAP analysis model

GAP One: Management Perception Gap

It is the difference between expected service by customers and the management's perceptions of consumer expectations. Service companies often fail to understand properly the expectations of the consumers. Improper understanding or misunderstanding of consumer expectations is one of the root causes for not delivering services that satisfy consumer expectations. The reasons for the gap to arise may be many. The key factors leading to GAP one are as follows:

- Insufficient marketing research
- Inaccurate information from marketing research
- Poorly interpreted information about expectations
- No demand analysis
- Research not focused on service quality
- Lack of interaction between management and the customers
- Insufficient upward and downward internal communication
- Too many organizational layers between contact personnel and top management
- No market segmentation
- No relationships focus

Lack of proper understanding of consumer expectations may trigger a chain of bad decisions and finally result in poor quality perceptions by the customers. Service companies should analyse the gap properly and try to fill it.

GAP Two: Quality Specification Gap

It is the difference between the company perception of customer expectation and customer-driven service designs and standards. The accurate perceptions of service providers about customers' expectations may not be sufficient for delivering superior quality service. Service companies may have excellent communication and information network and may be capable of managing without any gap at the first level. GAP two is the second milestone the companies should cross with excellence in performance. Service design and performance standards are prerequisites for that. Translation of the service quality specifications is really a complex job the service providers have to handle.

GAP two may occur due to the following reasons:

- Mistakes in planning or insufficient planning procedures
- Lack of customer-driven service standards
- Lack of formal process for setting service quality goals
- Lack of management commitment
- Unclear service designs
- Unsystematic new service development process
- Lack of support from top management

GAP Three: Service Delivery Gap

It is the difference between customer-driven service designs and standards and service delivery. Formulation of clear guidelines for performing services may not assure quality service performance. The standards must be supported by adequate and appropriate resources such as people, systems and technology. Employee motivation and satisfaction play an important role in this process. The possible major reasons for GAP three are as follows:

- Complicated and/or rigid process specifications
- Deficiencies in human resource policies such as ineffective recruitment, role ambiguity, role conflict, improper evaluation and compensation system, lack of empowerment, absence of perceived control and team work, poor employee job fit and so on
- Ineffective internal marketing
- Poor management of service operations
- Failure to match demand and capacity
- Inappropriate customer meets
- Lack of proper customer education and training and so on

GAP Four: Market Communication Gap

It is the difference between service delivery and external communications to customers. Service companies make promises through external marketing process to current as well as potential customers. The promises made through communication media potentially raise customer expectations. These expectations serve as standards against which the customer evaluates the experienced quality of service. The discrepancy between actual service and the promised one may occur due to the following reasons:

- Negatively confirmed quality
- Bad reputation
- Lost customers
- Negative corporate or local image
- When a company fails to integrate marketing communication with service operations
- Over-promising in external communication campaign
- Failure to manage customer expectations
- Failure to perform according to specifications

GAP Five: Perceived Service Quality Gap

It is the gap between perceived and expected service. The reasons for this gap are difficult to analyse, but organizations can reasonably expect some negative effects when such a gap arises. GAP five may result in the following: word-of-mouth communication, personal needs, past experiences, service process performance, service promises and service environment.

Service companies need not look for negative results only in this process. This gap can also be positive. If the perceived quality exceeds the expected quality, the customers are satisfied and it benefits the organization.

> *"The five possible gaps identified in the GAP model help the management to develop a workable system to ensure quality performance from the company. Continual gap analysis is necessary for ensuring consistent quality offerings."*

The GAP analysis model guides the management to find out the real reasons for quality problems and to discover appropriate ways to close such gaps. The understanding of the possible gaps will help the management to check various levels and prevent possible errors. A thorough audit of all these possible errors, time and again, makes the service provider confident and such confidence percolates to the frontline employees of the organization; they can then perform well in encounters with customers. This is exemplified in "Services Marketing Insight: Quality Management in Sterilization Services".

19.1 Services Marketing Insight | **Quality Management in Sterilization Services**

Sterilization services are largely provided through a network of public and private sector facilities in India. In most states, camps are a major source of sterilization services. There has been growing concern about the quality of sterilization services being offered. The increase in complications, failures and deaths due to sterilizations has also resulted in increased litigation being faced by the providers, which stood as a barrier in scaling up the sterilization services.

The Research Studies and Standards Division of Ministry of Health and Family Welfare, Government of India prepared a quality assurance manual with the objective of assessing quality and quality needs and to ensure the provision of quality services in sterilization. This manual serves as a guide for assessing service quality and enables programme managers and service providers both in the public sector and in accredited private/NGO facilities to provide quality sterilization services. The elements of quality of care in the specific area of sterilization services are addressed in this manual by using a systems approach—inputs, processes and outcomes.

Inputs include all programme efforts that facilitate the readiness of the facilities to provide services when a client visits the clinic such as qualified providers, physical infrastructure, supplies and equipment, etc. Standards for physical infrastructure for static services have been laid down. The processes include technical and interpersonal dimensions and encompass a range of elements. The outcomes of quality services are assessed in terms of reducing failures, minimizing complications and preventing mortality.

Quality Assurance Management: Monitoring for quality is done at three different levels: at the central level, through proper and well-established reporting systems; at the state and district levels, through quality assurance committees (QACs) and at the service outlet levels, through quality circles.

QACs are formed at the state and district levels to ensure that the standards for female and male sterilization are being followed in respect of preoperative measures, operational facilities and post-operative follow-ups.

Quality circle *(QC)* work includes all the processes involved in the sterilization services being provided at the facility.

Quality Assessment and Improvement: The quality of sterilization services provided is assessed through the already existing documentation tools available at the facilities and instruments/tools specifically designed for this purpose. The areas requiring improvement should be identified using these tools, and this ultimately is beneficial in improving the overall quality of the services delivered.

Source: Research Studies & Standards Division, Quality Assurance Manual for Sterilization Services, Ministry of Health and Family Welfare, Government of India (October 2006).

SERVQUAL

For the purpose of measuring customer satisfaction with respect to different aspects of service quality, a survey instrument was developed by Parasuraman, Zeithaml and Berry[10] in 1988. The instrument is called SERVQUAL. The basic assumption of the measurement was that customers can evaluate a firm's service quality by comparing their perceptions with their expectations. SERVQUAL is applicable to all service industries. The SERVQUAL scale includes five dimensions. They are tangibles, reliability, responsiveness, assurance and empathy. Each dimension can have several items measured on a seven-point scale varying from "strongly agree" to "strongly disagree." Researchers suggested a total of 21 items under the identified five dimensions. The following are the details relating to a study on banks:

> **SERVQUAL** *is popularly used to find out the position of the company in quality performance. The five determining criteria such as tangibles, reliability, responsiveness, assurance and empathy reflect the consumers' view and expectations of service quality.*

Tangibles

Excellent banks will have

- modern equipment,
- visually appealing physical facilities,
- neat, well-dressed employees and
- visually appealing materials associated with the service (such as brochures and statements).

Reliability

Excellent banks will

- carry out what they promise to do,
- show sincere interest in solving problems,
- perform well right from the first time and
- insist on error-free records.

Responsiveness

Employees of excellent banks will

- tell customers exactly when the service will be performed,
- give prompt service to customers ,
- always be willing to help customers and
- have the knowledge to answer customer questions.

Assurance

The employees of excellent banks will

- instil confidence in customers,
- be consistently courteous to customers,
- have the answers to customers' questions and
- ensure safety in transactions with customers.

Empathy

Excellent banks will

- give individual attention to customers,
- have convenient operating hours for all their customers and
- understand the specific needs of their customers.

TOTAL QUALITY SERVICES MARKETING

Service firms should try to achieve total quality in their performance. Total quality marketing aims at achieving quality performance right at the first time. TQM requires cross-functional thinking, planning and doing.[11] The entire organization's orientation should be towards generating quality perceptions to the customers. It is possible for service firms to set targets for 100 per cent performance right from the first time. For some service organizations, 100 per cent quality performance is a must, unlike others. In managing the service process in an airport, the management must insist on 100 per cent performance in all its operations. Any failure anywhere at any point of time may lead to disastrous consequences. "Services Marketing Insight: Five Myths and Truths of Service Quality" focuses on the myths and truths of service quality management.

The concepts of service quality, customer satisfaction and service loyalty are related to each other.[12] Service quality leads to customer satisfaction, and the satisfied customers are likely to purchase the service from the same service company and become loyal customers. Companies' aiming at loyal

Visakhapatnam Port Trust

Visakhapatnam Port Trust is ranked first among major ports in India in terms of annual cargo throughput, for six consecutive years. The port has been complimented by the Government of India as the brightest jewel among all major ports. This recognition is mainly due to quality management efforts of the organization. The port aims at offering cost-effective, reliable and trustworthy services to the customers. The customer-centric philosophy is evident with the set objective of improving organizational effectiveness with a view to reducing the transactional cost to the user. The port achieved quality and productivity in performance through concern for safety and environment, responsive and transparent administration, user-friendly attitude, teamwork and innovation and by creating a learning environment.

Visakhapatnam Port Trust became the only Indian port to have three international certificates for its quality performance. The port achieved:

1. ISO 9001 for Quality Management System
2. ISO 14001 for Environmental Management System
3. OHSAS 18001 for Occupational Health and Safety Management System

The port has defined its quality standards and developed mechanisms for effective execution of the same. As a result, the organization could achieve customer satisfaction and could break the performance records set by the company itself year by year.

19.2 Services Marketing Insight

Five Myths and Truths of Service Quality

Service quality management also develops its myths and truths. The differences identified between goods and services lead to implementation of differentiated approach to many management systems that are proved effective in the manufacturing sector. The following description of myths and truths provides a realistic perspective to understand service quality.

Myth 1: Service quality is difficult to assess because services are intangible. Goods' quality is easy to assess because goods are tangible.

Truth: Service quality is different from goods' quality, but there is no evidence that it is more difficult to assess. Service quality has not been approached systematically enough. It has lived in the shadow of goods' quality management system. The degree of controllability is different for services due to co-production with customers, limited control over certain elements of service delivery process, design of final form of service on the spot and intrafunctional dependency.

Myth 2: Better quality costs more and causes prices to go up. It is more or less a linear relationship between cost and quality.

Truth: "Quality is free", the slogan of Philip Crosby, has become famous for reversing this myth. The truth is that there is no general relationship. Sometimes high quality leads to higher costs; higher costs leads to lower quality; costs may go up and quality may remain the same; costs may go up and quality remains the same and costs may go up and quality may go down. Anything may happen in services in different occasions and in different processes.

Myth 3: Variability of service quality is a major problem because of the customer's role and customer-perceived quality and satisfaction.

Truth: Along with service delivery process, the service design and the ability to manage quality internally with the support of operations management and statistical quality control influence service quality. Service quality must be managed internally and externally.

Myth 4: Market research, training programmes, quality circles, measurement techniques, improved service design, incentive schemes to employees and a host of strategies such as continuous improvements and zero defects will guarantee improved service quality.

Truth: All these are to some extent superficial, if the commitment by management and staff is not genuine and does not come from heart. As services evolve in interaction with customers, empathy, compassion, emotions, involvement, sense of humour, tacit knowledge and intuition—all dimensions of the love factor become essential, in the decisive contributors to service quality.

Myth 5: Improved service quality leads to improved quality perceptions by consumers.

Truth: Not necessarily always. You can improve customer-perceived quality, without changing the service, by putting the expectations on the right level. Raising expectations too much may create dissatisfied customers.

Source: Evert Gummesson, "Truths and Myths in Service Quality," International Journal of Service Industry Management, *2, no. 3 (1991): 7–16.*

customer base must be consistent in service quality performance and direct efforts towards improvements in quality. A. Parasuraman *et al.*[13] stated that service quality is an overall evaluation of an entity's excellence or superiority and that this judgement or evaluation is similar to attitude and related to, but not equivalent to, satisfaction. In order to provide delightful quality experiences to the customers, service firms are required to develop or respect some philosophies relating to service quality. The following are some of the philosophies that promote quality atmosphere in service organizations.

- *Quality Must Be Perceived by Customers:* The employees of the service firm as well as the customers are involved in the service production process. Both perceive the quality in a service encounter. In the service performance process, if an employee is satisfied with the quality and the customer is not satisfied, the service firm cannot claim quality performance. If the perceptions are vice versa, the problem of the service firm is only internal. It can train the employee in such a way that he/she can perceive the quality in customer interactions. The customer-perceived quality is the only end towards which service firms should orient themselves. At the same time it is necessary to orient the employees through appropriate HR methods and make them perceive quality in the service process.
- *Quality Must Be Reflected in Every Company Activity:* A service offer is a bundle of features. Each part of the service product has its own role in contributing to the perceptions of customers. A customer who reserved a hotel accommodation for 5 days may have hundreds of interactions—right from the gatekeeper's welcome salute, to facilitating services performance, supporting services performance and their consistency, co-customers, events and so on. The sum of all these experiences contributes in the development of an overall customer-perceived quality. Excellent performance in some parts, average performance in some and poor performance in some other parts of the BSP cannot contribute to the positive perceptions of the customers. Every activity should reflect quality performance. Therefore, rather than in bits and pieces, organizations should develop a holistic view of the service product to perform quality.
- *Quality Requires Total Employee Commitment:* Employees constitute the core strength for service firms. Quality is a journey, not a destination. Different employees are capable of generating different feelings and experiences in the customers. Satisfied employees exhibit their sense of belonging to the organization and handle varied situations with greater involvement. Employee commitment is an essential prerequisite to those service firms that want to ensure quality services marketing. Internal marketing needs to be operated efficiently to enhance morale and to motivate employees to perform better in service encounters.
- *Quality Can Always Be Improved:* There is no ceiling for quality standards as far as services are concerned. Services are always open to further improvements. Therefore, service firms should not be satisfied with the existing performance standards of quality, even if customers express satisfaction over the service experience. A continuous research on service quality is necessary for the improvement of quality. Service firms should develop quality circles and strategic groups among the

employees, so that they can have a bank of ideas for further improvement. Sometimes, very minor improvements also have the capability to create major quality impressions on the consumers.

- *Quality Does Not Cost More:* Top managements of service firms often hesitate to enhance quality standards with a feeling that it costs them more. They also feel that the opportunity cost of employee time also matters, when they allocate more time of an employee to each customer. However, these perceptions do not hold true in the case of services. The quality of services can be improved without incurring additional costs. Japanese firms developed a concept called ZII, elaborated as zero investment improvements. Employees were encouraged to find out new ways of performing the processes, those that could enhance quality perceptions by consumers, without any further investment. The concept works out very well in quality improvement process. A mention should be made here that it is not possible to improve quality always without additional cost. Yes, certainly, many times quality performance is related to the cost either directly or indirectly. But, the benefits also would be substantial in the short as well as in the long run. Negligence of quality on cost parameters leads to loss of customers or dissatisfaction to customers. Therefore, organizations should orient themselves to the improvement of quality, whenever and wherever there is a possibility.
- *Quality Improvement Sometimes Requires Quantum Leaps:* Service firms should not hesitate to introduce major changes in the organizational set-up when such changes provide more quality to the customers. Computerization in nationalized banks and insurance companies in India was initiated to offer fast and accurate services to the customers. The companies visualized that the service quality to customers will improve significantly with computerization. Though it involved millions of rupees of investment, it resulted in major disturbance in the working for some period, employee resentment to adaptability, fears of retrenchment and other problems, the service companies went ahead of their quality improvement plans. Computerization was taken up, keeping in view the improvement in quality of services to customers. Service firms should prepare for such changes at any point of time in pursuit of quality enhancement.
- *Everyone Contributes to Customer-perceived Quality:* All employees in the organization contribute to customer-perceived quality. Whether an employee is in interaction with the customer or not, whether an employee is within the line of visibility or not, the employee's contribution would be there in quality perceptions. Suppose in a bank, a customer is in the process of depositing money, when some employees, who are not in interaction with the customer, pick up a quarrel on some work-sharing issue. This will definitely have a bad impact on the customer's quality perception, in spite of the fact that he has nothing to do with that incident. Further, suppose a customer is delayed by the frontline employee due to delay in support services. Though the

> *"Service quality must be an organization philosophy. The total quality services marketing aims to achieve quality performance right at the first time and all the time. Companies should believe on certain philosophies and work towards that direction."*

"Quality objective of manufacturing firms is to achieve zero defects while that of service firms is to achieve zero defections. The study of the differences in approach to quality by the two business entities is useful to set quality philosophies differently to that of traditional perceptions of quality."

contact personnel are positive to the customer, beyond a point of waiting, the customer gets frustrated and develops a negative perception of the quality of service.

- *Quality Should Be Monitored by the Employees:* Service employees need to perform with involvement and commitment, if service quality is to be delivered. Unlike in manufacturing organizations, supervision by the managers cannot improve productivity and quality performance in service organizations. In a college, the traditional control mechanism makes a teacher take classes on time and leave on time, but no one can force him/her to teach well or train the students well. Only the teacher himself can ensure this. The presence of a head or principal or vice-chancellor to monitor the teaching may further worsen the situation. Therefore, service firms should have confidence in their employees and provide such mechanisms that provide them a feedback on their performance. Based on the feedback, employees can try to modify their performance and, as a result, improved quality can be achieved.

Zero Defects Versus Zero Defections

A comparative study between manufacturing companies and service companies on total quality management provides an insight into various quality concepts and operational distinctions. Ron Zemke[14] has identified 10 important differences in total quality marketing between service firms and manufacturing firms. Table 19.1 presents the quality performance practices

Table 19.1 Zero Defects vs. Zero Defections

	Zero Defects (Manufacturing Companies)		Zero Defections (Service Companies)
1.	Technical quality	1.	Customer quality
2.	Treating errors as mortal sins	2.	Treating errors as opportunities to excel
3.	Precise standards and performance	3.	Transactions that delight customers
4.	Minimizing the human element	4.	Capitalizing on the human element
5.	Creating standards and protocols for every aspect of transaction	5.	Standards for technical quality. Empowerment and recovery strategies for customer quality
6.	No surprises. Standard operating procedures. Rote and drill	6.	Speed, flexibility and ability to respond, reliability for unique standards
7.	Production quality	7.	Performance quality
8.	Developing satisfactory and mutually beneficial relationships	8.	Building lasting and creative customer relationships
9.	Customer satisfaction	9.	Customer retention
10.	Reworking every policy and procedure to perfection, creating absolutely seamless performance	10.	Experimenting, leap frogging the competition, taking measured risks and learning from them

of manufacturing companies and service companies. A critical study of the work indicates the required shift in quality philosophies of service firms from traditional perceptions of quality.

Zero defects are the target quality standards for manufacturing firms. The products which do not stand to the quality standards are rejected at the points of quality check. However, the total quality management concept that has been widely followed by many manufacturing organizations provides that there should not be any defects in performance, and the goal should be to achieve 100 per cent perfection in the first time itself. In the case of services, customers are sold promises first. If the service firm does not fulfil the promises made to the customers, it is called a defection. Therefore, zero defections should be the goal of service firms. A change in orientation would certainly provide better insights to service firms to ensure total quality services marketing.

SERVICE EXCELLENCE

Service excellence means offering superior quality performance consistently and often beyond the bench-marking performances. It requires well-defined organizational processes, policies, procedures and quality-oriented service culture. Every service company has a model of excellence that it aims for in service offerings. Robert C. Ford, Cherill P. Heaton and Stephen W. Brown[15] have studied the models of the successful firms such as Walt Disney, Marriot International, South West Airlines and Brich Parlton and have developed lessons that can help guide organizations to success. The lessons suggested by the researchers are:

- Base decisions on what the customers want and expect
- Think and act in terms of the entire customer experience
- Continuously improve all parts of the customer experience
- Hire and reward people who can effectively build relationships with customers
- Train employees on how to cope with emotional labour costs
- Create and sustain a strong service culture
- Avoid failing your customers twice
- Empower customers to co-produce their own experience
- Get managers to lead from the front, not the top
- Treat all customers as if they were guests

Achieving excellence in service quality is the inspirational goal of every service organization. The goal becomes attainable only when the management of the company is committed to quality performance all the time. It requires focusing on improving customer experience at the service encounter. Employee empowerment and customer empowerment are the two dimensions that promote positive customer experience. The organization should develop leadership qualities in every employee. The leader in employee makes him/her the future-oriented person and proactive in facing different situations in the service processes. Employees become creative and take calculated risk in experimentation and develop abilities to persuade customers to have new experiences.

RESEARCH ON SERVICE QUALITY

Service firms can obtain information through research on service quality. Research facilitates inflow of required information from internal as well as external sources and provides right information in the right form at the right time to the right manager. With the support of research, the management can take better decisions related to quality. Service companies use several approaches to ensure inflow of information. The following are some of the research approaches through which service firms can have useful information on general or specific issues related to service quality:

- *Regular Customer Surveys:* Customer survey on a regular basis is a useful approach for service firms. It provides customer feedback on various quality parameters and on innovations. In the case of business customers, a census study may be conducive, and, in the case of mass market, a sample survey may be sufficient. With a methodical collection of data and information and the use of analytical and interpretative statistical and mathematical models, useful inferences can be drawn for the benefit of the organization.
- *Use of Consumer Panel:* Consumer panels comprise selected customers, and specific feedback is solicited from them. The panels are also given the freedom to suggest on various issues to the organization for further improvement in service quality.
- *Transactional Analysis:* Service organizations usually encounter grievous customers. The employees involved in the encounter should handle the aggrieved customers with care, concern and empathy. Transactional analysis (TA) is a technical approach that helps to identify the real reasons for dissatisfaction. TA is also used to obtain valuable suggestions from customers. Generally, the grievous customer puts forward the real inner feelings and dissatisfactions that accumulate due to minor deficiencies in service, which might not have been noticed by the service organization. It is certainly an opportunity for service firms to broaden their understanding on customer perception of service quality. However, this approach has a limited application as very few interactions happen through. In the case of employees, this approach is of immense use to understand the reasons for the problems and to take measures to correct them.
- *Perception Surveys:* These surveys aim at knowing the perceptions of the customers on various quality features of the service. Perception surveys are useful for knowing the opinion of customers on technical as well as functional quality of the service.

- *Mystery Shopping:* This approach is being used by many service providers. The top management of the organization personally visits service outlets without revealing its identities, either to customers or to frontline employees, and observe the goings on there. It may interact with customers and also frontline employees to know their experiences and problems and make appropriate changes immediately.
- *Analysis of Complaints:* Consumer complaints are the major source of feedback for service firms. The complaints received should be classified properly and routed to the right personnel at the right time so as to enable them to initiate corrective measures immediately. The complaints should not be viewed only as a source for compensating the deficiencies in service execution. They should be taken as sources for identifying operational defects. Correction should be institutionalized so as to ensure that such defects do not recur in the organization.
- *Employees' Research:* The satisfaction levels of employees should be monitored continuously. Employee research provides required information to the policy makers to develop programmes and policies that make the employees satisfied.
- *Post-Transaction Surveys:* These surveys are intended to collect feedback immediately after the service is performed. It is similar to the guest surveys conducted in hotels.
- *Focus Group Interviews:* Interviewing selected customers as well as employees of the organization to study the qualitative issues in depth is called focus group interview. These interviews provide useful information at low cost and high speed.
- *Similar Industry Studies:* Research studies conducted by service firms on similar businesses also provide some insights over the changing trends in the industry.
- *Intermediary Research:* Some social organizations, research institutes, universities and trade associations also conduct research on service quality. The findings of such research studies are useful for service firms to get market information on service quality.

> *"Service quality research provides information input to service personnel related to quality perceptions of the customers. Different research approaches provide different insights of quality perceptions. It is necessary to select appropriate approach(s) as per the situational requirements."*

SUMMARY

- Quality is a key element in the service business.
- The quality of a service is perceived during buyer–seller interactions.
- Employer–customer interactions at service encounters need to be managed effectively.
- Customer participation in the service production process greatly influences service quality.
- Customers cannot be controlled. They have differing abilities, experiences, attitudes, personalities, lifestyles and self-concepts.
- Customer-perceived quality is the result that should be considered by the service provider.
- Service companies can influence customers to perceive quality through education, training and empathetic interactions.

- Service companies should design the process and take all measures to be 100 per cent correct from their perspective in service offerings.
- They should analyse the market needs and wants properly and design the technical product.
- The functional process should reflect quality dimensions of the organization.
- The determinants of service quality should be identified and appropriate strategies developed.
- The GAP model of service quality is of immense help to service companies to rectify deficiencies in services performance. It helps to conduct a service quality audit and to take appropriate measures at the right time to improve service quality.
- SERVQUAL defines the bench-marking quality parameters for service companies.
- Service companies should promote some philosophies that help in developing corporate vision as well as in motivating employees and gearing the organization as a whole towards quality performance.

KEY TERMS

Expected quality *376*
Experienced quality *376*
Focus group interviews *393*
Functional quality *375*
Image *375*
Mystery shopping *393*
Perception surveys *392*
Service excellence *391*
Service quality audit *380*
SERVQUAL *385*
Technical quality *375*
Total perceived quality *376*
Total quality services marketing *386*
Zero defections *390*
Zero defects *390*
Zero Investment Improvements

BRIEF QUESTIONS

1. What is technical quality?
2. Explain functional quality.
3. How does image influence perceived quality?
4. How do consumers develop total perceived quality?
5. Explain the use of transactional analysis in quality research.
6. What is mystery shopping?
7. Explain two approaches for service quality research.
8. How can service excellence be achieved?

ESSAY QUESTIONS

1. How is service quality perceived by customers?
2. Explain two dimensions of service quality and how they influence quality perceptions?
3. What are the determinants of service quality? How do they influence service business?
4. Explain the managerial process of service quality.
5. How can service quality be audited? Explain the GAP model of service quality.
6. What is total quality services marketing? What are the philosophies that guide service organizations towards total quality marketing?
7. Explain the concept of service excellence. What are the differences in approach of a manufacturing company and a service company in total quality performance?
8. Explain different research approaches for service quality.
9. Select a service company and explain how quality is managed in the concern.

ASSIGNMENTS

1. Management education demands an unconventional approach for developing skills in students. A large number of management institutes have been established in India to produce thousands of management graduates. But as far as employability is concerned, the performance of the majority of the institutions is dismal. You are required to study by interviewing some students and employees to identify:
   (a) The quality determinants of management educational institutions from students' perspective.
   (b) The quality determinant from employees' perspective.
2. The impact of public utility services on day-to-day life is very significant. The services like water supply, electricity, sanitation, maintenance of roads, etc., are critical for all citizens. You are required to:
   (a) Apply SERVQUAL to any two of the services in your locality and rate the quality performance.
   (b) Identify quality gaps and suggest measures for filling the gaps.

REFERENCES

1 A. Karin Venetis and Pervez N. Ghauri, "Service Quality and Customer Retention: Building long-term Relationships," *European Journal of Marketing*, 38, no. 11/12 (2004): 1577.

2 J. J. Jr. Cronion, and S. A. Taylor, "Measuring Service Quality: A Reexamination and Extension," *Journal of Marketing*, 56, no. 3 (1992): 55–68.

3 R. D. Buzzell and B. T. Gale, *The PIMS Principle – Linking Strategy to Performance.* (New York: Free Press, 1987).

4 A. Parasuraman, V. A. Zeithaml and L. L. Berry, "A Conceptual Model of Service Quality and its Implications for Future Research," *Journal of Marketing*, 49 (1985): 41–50.

5 C. Grönroos, *Service Management and Marketing; Managing the Moments of Truth in Service Competition.* (Massachusetts: Maxwell Macmillan; Lexington: D.C. Heath/Lexington Books, 1990), pp. 37–38.

6 Ronald J. Burke, Jim Grahm and Frank Smith, "TQM Implementation – Effects of Reengineering on the Employee Satisfaction – Customer Satisfaction Relationship," *The TQM Magazine*, 17, no. 4 (2005): 358.

7 C. Grönroos, *Service Management and Marketing; Managing the Moments of Truth in Service Competition*. (Massachusetts: Maxwell Macmillan; Lexington: D.C. Heath/Lexington Books, 1990), p. 47.

8 Ibid., pp. 54–57.

9 V. A. Zeithaml, D. D. Gremler, M. Jo Bitner and A. Pandit, *Services Marketing*, 4th ed. (New Delhi: McGraw-Hill, 2008), p. 48.

10 Ibid., p. 158.

11 R. J. Schonberger, "TAM: What's in it for Academics?," *Business Horizons*, (January–February 1995): 67–70.

12 Albert Caruana, "Service Loyalty – The Effects of Service Quality and the Mediating role of Customer Satisfaction," *European Journal of Marketing*, 36, no. 7/8 (2002): 811–828.

13 A. Parasuraman, et al., "SERVQUAL: a Multiple-item Scale for Measuring Customer Perceptions of Service Quality," *Journal of Retailing*, 64 (1988): 12–40.

14 Ron Zemke, "The Emerging Art of Service Management," *Training*, (January 1992): 40.

15 Robert C. Ford, Cherrill P. Heaton and Stephen W. Brown, "Delivering Excellent Service: Lessons from the Best Firms," *California Management Review*, 44, no. 1, (2001): 39–56.

Service Failures and Recovery

20

LEARNING OBJECTIVES

After studying this chapter, you will be able to:

- Understand the reasons for customer grievances
- Understand the customer response to service failures
- Understand the complaining behaviour of customers
- Understand the service recovery strategies

The annual vacation for Mr Singh and his family in 2010 turned out to be a mixed bag thanks to the numerous problems and service lapses they encountered during the trip despite utilizing the services of National Tours and Travels Company, a reputed company based in Delhi. The company offered several tour packages, which included travel, boarding and sightseeing arrangements at every tourist destination. Prior to their departure, Singh received the rules and regulations from the company. The tour started on a promising note. Singh and his family got on very well the other members of the group that comprised 40 people in all. When they all boarded the train at the second destination, which was over three hours late, they found their berths already occupied. It was with great difficulty that the tour guide could manage to find berths for all the members of the group. By the time they reached their destination, their enthusiasm was beginning to flag. Not sufficient rooms were available at the appointed hotel; they had to wait for quite a few hours before a room could be assigned to them since the guides insisted on following the order in which the bookings were made. It was really a horrible experience so much so that they could not enjoy the other services of the hotel. The rest of the tour continued without any major glitches and the Singhs had a good time overall. However, small recurring problems such as interfering and unpunctual co-tourists and uncoordinated support services rendered the experience far from perfect. Though Singh continued to communicate his dissatisfaction to the tour guide, but many a time the guide confessed helplessness. One of the guides went to the extent of suggesting that particular tour was progressing rather smoothly, citing several tours in the past wherein the tourists had faced grave problems. Though Singh felt that some problems were beyond the control of the company, yet he thought that they could have been managed better.

Questions:

1. What are the service failures in this case?
2. What are the expected roles of the service personnel handling the problems?
3. Which recovery strategies could be used in this case to satisfy the consumers?
4. Is it possible for the company to organize tours without any service failures?
5. What are the lapses in service personnel performance and communication?

INTRODUCTION

Providing quality services with zero deficiencies is the desired objective of all service marketers. But problems are common in the service industry mainly due to the unique characteristics of services. "Service failure is commonly defined as a mistake, problem or error that occurs in the delivery of the service."[1] If services are performed, as per the expectations of the customers, right at the first time, the question of deficiency or failure does not arise. Service firms often face problems of poor performance, delayed performance, no performance or part performance. The reasons for such problems include human errors, failure in support services or efficiency variations in contact personnel.

"Service deficiencies and failures affect the interactive process and result in poorly perceived quality by service consumers. When customers suffer from inequalities of the exchange (i.e., service failure), they will demand restitution (i.e., service recovery) or may choose to retaliate (e.g., negative word of mouth, switching behaviour)."[2]

Dissatisfaction due to a service failure and the subsequent service recovery may motivate consumers to indulge in negative word of mouth, that is, telling others about their unsatisfactory experience. Research reports indicate that dissatisfied customers tell between eight and 10 people about bad services they receive, and one in five angry customers tell 20 people.[3] Service failures can lead to negative word of mouth, dissatisfaction and defection, adversely affecting the profitability of the company.

> **Service failures** occur due to distinctive characteristics of services. The more intense the service failure, the more is the customer-perceived loss. The severity of a service failure influences consumer trust and may lead to negative word of mouth, which is dangerous to service companies.

The uncontrollable factors are many in a service encounter. As a consequence, service failures appear to be inevitable. Service companies should learn the ways through which they can nullify the effects of failures. Appropriate recovery strategies are the key to satisfying consumers. Customers react in two ways when they encounter a service failure. They either remain with the service provider or leave (i.e., exit). Some customers may continue to take services from the company with a hope that the failures do not reoccur. Some customers find alternative service providers who can provide better services. The fact, however, remains that service failures do happen, and they influence negatively the satisfaction levels of customers. Service recovery stands as a remedy to the problem. An effective recovery strategy not only is capable of reducing the negative impact on consumers due to the service failure but also is capable of creating and promoting positive perceptions about the company.

REASONS FOR CUSTOMER GRIEVANCES

Many service failures occur when customers interact with service personnel at the service encounter. The behaviour of employees, their ability and willingness to participate in the service process, their intension to solve the problems, and so on may become reasons for customer grievances. Robert

Warlow[4] has identified the following six reasons for the customer grievance due to employee interactions.

1. *Bad Attitude:* Some service employees do not treat the customers properly. They do not acknowledge the presence of customers even when they stand right in front of them. They may engage in chatting over phone; may look at the customer as if the customer is interfering into their daily routine and may not speak politely. Such attitudes of the employees turn the customers against the company. Service marketers should identify such employees and get them away from customers.
2. *Not Willing to Seek a Solution:* Some contact employees acknowledge a customer's problem but just can't be bothered to find a solution. The stock answer is, "I can't help. It's company policy." They do not find anything positive to help the customer. Such interactions make the customer believe that the service company is more in the "can't do" business rather than in the "can do" business.
3. *Not Giving Full-Product Explanations:* The service company may have the capacity to produce services required by the customer qualitatively. If the contact employee does not understand the specific problems of the customer and fails to explain the solution to the problem, the customer is unhappy over the service provider.
4. *Not Willing to Admit a Mistake:* Employees are after all human beings and subject to errors. If the contact employee is unwilling to accept a mistake, it creates a problem. Some employees may try to throw blame on customers for their mistakes. Such behaviour is dangerous for the service company.
5. *Not Keeping Up to Date:* The effective complaint handling process requires communication of up-to-date information to the consumers. The company is taking care of the problem systematically. But the absence of information to the customer on the stage at which the complaint is being processed puts pressure on the customer. A complaint, followed by days of silence, allows doubt and anger to bubble up again. The delay in response becomes another reason for customer grievances.
6. *Broken Promises:* Service companies should not fail in promises, particularly when handling complaints. Customers show high level of dissatisfaction when the promises are broken by the service employees.

> *The behaviour of interacting employees is one of the major areas of consumer grievances. If the attitude and interactions of the employees are not customer friendly, it is likely that consumers become aggrieved.*

CUSTOMER RESPONSE TO SERVICE FAILURES

Customers may respond in a variety of ways when they experience service failures. It is true that every customer develops some kind of dissatisfaction due to the failure of the service either totally or partly. The customers develop a variety of negative emotions such as the feelings of anger, discontent, disappointment, self pity and anxiety. The kind of negative emotions depends on how customers perceive service failures and evaluate the service recovery process.

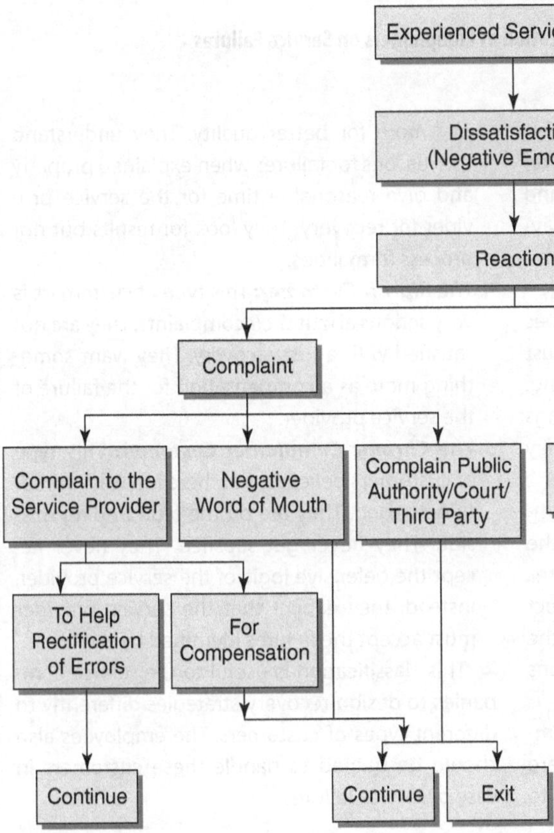

Figure 20.1
Customer response behaviour to service failures

Several factors influence consumers' propensity to complain about a less than satisfactory service experience.[5] All consumers may not settle their grievances in the same manner. For more details, see "Services Marketing Insight: Classification of Complainess on Service Failures". The possible response behaviour of the customers after experiencing the service failure is shown in Fig. 20.1.

The figure indicates that when a customer experiences a service failure there is some kind of dissatisfaction followed by negative emotions. There may be two types of possible actions to display the dissatisfaction or negative emotion. The customers may choose to complain or not to complain. If consumers choose to complain, the following three types of action tendencies can be observed:

1. *Complain to the Service Provider:* Complaints on service failures may be to help the service provider rectify errors in the service process. These customers are rational in their approach. They do not keep quiet when something goes wrong, and look positively for the change in the service provider and expect a sincere response. They provide opportunities to the service provider to rectify gaps and mistakes and improve the service quality to the level of customer expectations. These customers generally do not speak ill of the company in public.

20.1 Services Marketing Insight | **Classification of Complainers on Service Failures**

All customers do not react in the similar way when service failures occur. The reactions are based on beliefs, attitudes, motives and the pressure and importance of needs. Based on the reactive behaviour of the service customers, they can be classified into five types.

1. ***The Meek Customer:*** This type of customers does not complain about any service failures. They just take it easy and consider it a bad happening. These customers look forward for better things to happen. When the failures are consistent they prefer to move on to another service provider.
2. ***The Aggressive Customer:*** This type of customers exhibits opposite behaviour to that of the meek customers. They try to recognize failures quickly and complain immediately. They expect very quick and qualitative response from the service provider. They do not want explanations or excuses but full recovery at the earliest.
3. ***The High-roller Customer:*** This type of customers wants the best services at any cost. They are not aggressive and at the same time ready to pay more for better quality. They understand the reasons for failures when explained properly and give reasonable time for the service provider for recovery. They look for results but not process formalities.
4. ***The Rip-off Customer:*** This type of customers is very serious about their complaints. They are not satisfied with a just recovery. They want something more as a compensation for the failure of the service provider.
5. ***The Chronic Complainer Customer:*** This type of customers believes that there is always something wrong. They are on the fault finding mission. They never get satisfied. They never accept the defensive logic of the service provider. Instead, they expect that the service provider must accept the failures identified by them.

This classification is useful to the service companies to design recovery strategies differently to different types of customers. The employees also should be trained to handle these customers in case of service failures.

Source: Allen F. Wysocki, Karl W. Kepner and Michelle W. Glasser, "Customer complaints and Types of Customers," http://edis.ifas.ufl.edu/pdffiles/HR/HR00500.pdf.

Some customers are not ready to sacrifice their costs due to service failure or deficiency. They react quickly, make a formal complaint and seek compensation. They seriously look for redressal of their grievances and continue to fight with the service provider until they are compensated. They may continue to be loyal to the company or may be in the lookout of some other service providers.

2. *Negative Word of Mouth:* Some consumers actively engage in negative word of mouth as a reaction to the service failure, that is, campaigning the negatives of the company among friends and others. Depending on the outcome of the complaint, the consumers may choose to stay with the company or exit from it.
3. *Complain to a Public Authority/Court/Third Party:* Aggrieved consumers may complain to the respective public authority or court or any other third party to take action against the service company and redress their grievances.

When the choice of the consumers is not to complain, the following three types of action tendencies can be observed:

1. *Take It Easy:* These consumers do not take the service failure seriously and do not try to find faults with the service provider. They generalize the reasons for such failures as their own faults or that of the situation. These people continue their loyalty with the service provider. They will not distort the company's reputation. They react only when the failures are repetitive.
2. *Wait for Failure the Second Time:* These consumers do not want to blame the service provider without adequate reasons. They may express their displeasure over the failure to the contact employees and advise them to ensure that such things do not happen again. When they experience failure for the second time, they move to make a formal complaint.
3. *Vote with the Feet:* These customers are silent but an action-oriented group. They do not believe in complaining to the service provider and settle the grievance. Instead, they simply find a new service provider and break the relationship with the existing service provider. The service provider loses these customers.

> *"Consumer reactions to service failures are not uniform. The behaviour is influenced by several factors. Some may take it easy but some may react seriously. Service companies need to study the reactive behaviours of consumers to develop appropriate recovery strategies."*

COMPLAINT MANAGEMENT

Customer complaint management has become an integral part of business. It is necessary not only from the customer service point of view, but also from the regulatory point of view. In all the countries there are regulatory bodies that have established specific requirements for capturing, investigating, resolving and reporting customer complaints. The best-practiced service organizations consider complaints as opportunities for improvements and achieving excellence in service quality. Companies can obtain priceless knowledge through complaints because complaints contain the direct voice of the customers. Companies should understand the link between complaint resolution and customer loyalty. Studies have established that the efficiency in resolving a complaint leads to stronger customer loyalty.

Complaint management is the formal process of recording and resolving customer complaints. Service organizations develop a system called the customer complaint management system (CCMS).

The Customer Complaint Management System

The objective of the customer complaint management system (CCMS) is to collect, record, classify and resolve customer complaints at the earliest possible time to the satisfaction of the complainers. CCMS provides for systematic processes of complaint handling and recovery. The people engaged in the system are specially trained in complaint management. There are five stages in the customer complaint management process, as shown in Fig. 20.2: complaint registration, classification of customer complaints, analysis and

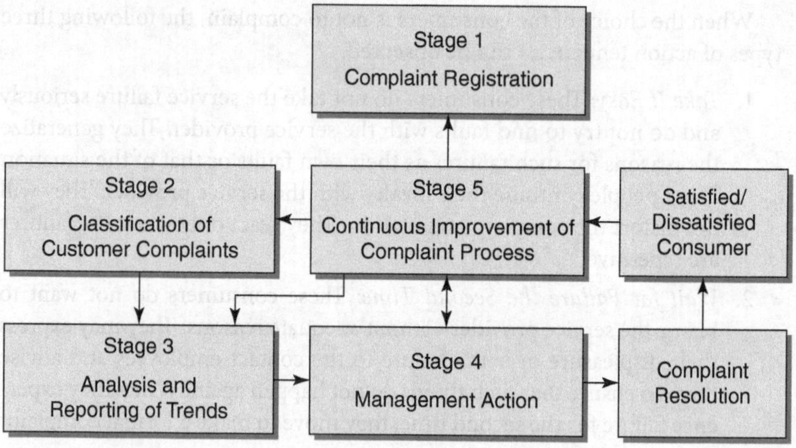

Fig. 20.2
The complaint management process

reporting of trends, management action and continuous improvement of the complaint process.

1. *Complaint Registration:* It is the first stage of the complaint management process. Companies need to develop a process mechanism to facilitate customers to register complaints. Customers should feel convenient to register their grievances with the company. The system designed should eliminate time, energy and other costs of customers. It should encourage the customer to register complaints.
2. *Classification of Customer Complaints:* The complaints registered should be classified based on the nature of the complaint, major or minor, issue wise, department wise, etc. Such classification helps in grouping the complaints to study the reasons and facilitate for speedy resolution.
3. *Analysis and Reporting of Trends:* Classification of complaints should follow analysis and reporting of trends to the management at the corporate and local level. The analysis helps identify themes and workout strategies to prevent such failures. This is done with an eye towards both regulatory matters, and those that help improve customer experiences.
4. *Management Action:* Identification of issues does not help when there is no management action. The actions may be to update customer service standards, improve communications or provide additional training to staff on handling service processes effectively. Changes should be monitored closely to ensure actions, resulting in fewer customer complaints. Research indicates that complaints handled professionally and in a timely manner result in customer loyalty. Therefore, it is essential to satisfy the complainers through the complaint management process. This will not only help retain business, but also reduces the damage that negative "word of mouth" has with existing or potential customers.
5. *Continuous Improvement of the Complaint Process:* Design of the customer complaint management system alone does not serve the purpose. The system should be implemented properly and be improved

continually for yielding effective results. One of the key sources to identify system deficiencies and opportunities for further improvement is customer feedback. The system accessibility, fairness and customer comfort in using the system are the areas that need to be examined, taking different customer segments into consideration.

> *Service companies need to develop the customer complaint management system for effective processing of complaints and responding to them quickly and appropriately to achieve customer satisfaction.*

Customers may stay after they have experienced a problem because they have complained and are satisfied with the service recovery process. This is the ideal situation for service providers who plan for good service recovery.[6] K. Stewart [7] suggests that by the time a customer has decided to exit an organization it is too late to recover him/her. This is often because they are leaving due to the unresponsiveness of the organization, so when the organization does respond when they have decided to leave, this is viewed as ironic. It is necessary, therefore, to formulate certain guidelines for the contact employees for effective management of complaints. The service provider should respond quickly, understand the problem from the point of view of the customer, conversate with customers without arguments and admit frankly the failures in service. The CCMS should focus on regaining customer goodwill. The management should formulate recovery strategies to regain customer confidence.

SERVICE RECOVERY

Service recovery is the process by which an organization attempts to rectify a failure in the service delivery process. Service recovery involves what a service provider does in response to service failures.[8] The service offered by a service organization consists of several features and moments. Service

Tata Indicom Broadband

Tata Communications Internet Service Ltd. is the India's leading provider of International Telecommunications and Internet Services. The company is rapidly growing its retail and corporate services such as high-speed broadband, dial-up internet, net telephony and Wi-Fi through the Internet.

The company offers customers the option to register a complaint at the call centre, if deficiency in the service is noticed. The call centre classifies customer complaints based on existing or new customers; service requests or complaints; billing complaints or technical complaints. The customer then is connected to the complaint management group (CMG) of the company. The CMG executive interacts with the customer to find out complaint details. The executive informs the customer about the status and expected time to resolve. The company provides an organizational mechanism to the customer to get the problem resolved satisfactorily. If the customer is not satisfied with the call centre, he/she may call/e-mail/send letter/fax to the nodal officer of the respective region. As per the standards set by the company:

- The nodal officer calls/writes back to the customer within three days from the receipt of complaint with the unique complaint number and the possible resolution date.
- Complaints such as faults or disruption of the service or disconnection of the service are redressed within three days from the date of registration of the complaint.
- Complaints not pertaining to the above are redressed within seven days from the date of registration of complaint.

> **Service recovery** *is the process by which an organization attempts to rectify a failure in the service delivery process. The ability of a company in resolving consumer problems effectively has a very strong impact on customer satisfaction and loyalty.*

marketers cannot control all aspects of service delivery even through they have taken absolute care in designing the service package. The reason is that service delivery mostly depends on people who deal with customers. It is a known fact in business that it is far less expensive to keep the existing customer than to create a new customer. Service marketers cannot afford to lose good customers who have a potential to become credible campaigners via positive word of mouth, referrals, friends and others. The service marketers reap many benefits from the satisfied customers.

A major factor that affects a customer's perception of a service provider's quality is the number, and extent, of the problems they encounter, and how these problems are handled by the provider.[9] C. Grönroos[10] defined service recovery processes as "those activities in which a company engages to address a customer complaint regarding a perceived service failure." It encompasses all the actions taken to get a disappointed customer back to the state of satisfaction.[11] Research has shown that the ability of a company in resolving customer problems effectively has strong impact on customer satisfaction and loyalty. In other words, the customers who have experienced service failures and are later satisfied based on the service recovery process of the service firm are more loyal than those whose problems are not resolved. Some other studies identified that the consumers who were not satisfied with service recovery were more likely to switch to other companies.

Benefits of Service Recovery

The service recovery paradox addresses the question of whether customers who experience a failure followed by superior recovery might rate their satisfaction as high as or even higher than they would have had no failure occurred.[12] Customers evaluate service recovery in terms of the outcomes they receive and the nature of the interpersonal treatment they receive during the recovery process. Many research studies confirm that satisfactory service recovery contributes to customer retention/loyalty/commitment and other beneficial outcomes. It promotes positive word-of-mouth communication, trust and enhanced perceptions of the firm's competence. It also creates a favourable image in terms of perceived quality and value. "Service firms can go a long way towards turning disgruntled customers into satisfied ones who are likely to maintain the business relationship with the firm through effective service recovery programmes."[13] There are several benefits of a service recovery strategy. The following are the important benefits:

- Service recovery increases customer satisfaction.
- It increases customer loyalty.
- It promotes positive word of mouth.
- It provides information that can be used to improve service quality.
- It helps take preventive actions.
- It reduces the cost of the failure.
- It improves employee satisfaction and promotes healthy internal atmosphere.

- It enhances company's corporate image.
- It provides an opportunity to differentiate the service by providing uniqueness in recovery.
- It promotes good service culture in the organization.
- It reduces employee turnover.
- It enhances employee morale.
- It propagates the value system and ethical behaviour of the organization.

> *Successful companies convert service failures into positive outcomes by resolving them effectively. If companies fail in the recovery process, they may have detrimental outcomes such as customer dissatisfaction and loss of customers.*

Consumer Grievance Recovery Strategies

Service recovery planning ought to be based on research-based knowledge in order to avoid the harmful impact of the service failure.[14] Service recovery should be part of a service firm's quality management strategy. The objective of service recovery should be to maintain the business relationship with the customer. Sincere efforts by the service provider are essential to settle the grievances of the consumers. Negligence on the spot results in another service failure and triggers the consumer grievance further. No service provider can afford to have consumer grievances as that may result in severe customer loss. Therefore, attempts must be made to recover from the damage already done. "Customers evaluate the fairness of a service recovery along the three dimensions of distributive justice, procedural and interactional fairness. Distributive justice refers to the perceived outcome, whereas procedural fairness involves the processes, policies and rules by which recovery effort decisions are made."[15] Service providers must be proactive in finding the possible service failure to eliminate them. Interactional fairness refers to the treatment during the service recovery process which includes apology, courtesy and empathy. Figure 20.3 shows the recovery strategies for services marketing. The variables for measuring customer satisfaction on service recovery are discussed in "Services Marketing Insight: Measuring Satisfaction with Transaction-specific Service Recovery".

> *Designing an appropriate recovery strategy is the critical challenge to the management. It needs to recognize the attitudes and reactive behaviour of customers. The objective should be to maintain the business relationships with the customer. Service companies should ensure the issues such as distributive, procedural and interactional fairness in the recovery are the integral part of the strategy.*

Recovery Strategies

Service recovery strategies involve both what is done (tangible compensation) and how it is done (employee interaction with the customer), and both influence customer perceptions of the service recovery.[16] A major challenge to achieving higher levels of customer retention is the service firm's recovery strategy when customers encounter problems. To turn a dissatisfied customer into a loyal one, choosing the most suitable service recovery option should be considered a critical task for specific incidents.[17] The following strategies are capable of yielding good results in recovery:

- *Acknowledge:* Service failures are observed by the customers. It is not possible to hide or conceal a service failure because customers also are part of the production process. Therefore, it is better to accept the failure immediately after the happening. The service provider should take the blame of the failure. It is improper to share the responsibility with the customer by making him/her partly responsible for the failure. Some

20.2 Services Marketing Insight

Measuring Satisfaction with Transaction—Specific Service Recovery

Service recovery is a multi-dimensional construct. Several factors influence the customer satisfaction on service recovery. Many researchers made attempts to develop an instrument to measure consumer satisfaction on service recovery. One of the useful instruments in this respect was developed by Boshoff in 1999 and named it as RECOVSAT. The instrument was primarily based on the disconfirmation paradigm. The instrument measures satisfaction with the following six dimensions of service recovery:

1. ***Communication:*** It measures clarity of employees' communication, the questions asked to clarify the situation of the consumer, whether employees understood clearly the problem of the consumer and the way employees could communicate reliability and honesty in their endeavours to solve the problem.
2. ***Empowerment:*** It measures the freedom and ability of the first contact employee to solve the problem with out seeking the permission, help and guidance from any other person in the organization.
3. ***Feedback:*** It measures how the customer is communicated with the progress of recovery and whether the problem is acknowledged.
4. ***Atonement:*** It measures whether the service company tendered an apology for the financial loss incurred by the consumer, made sure that the consumer had some money for a comfortable wait and behaved with the customer in a polite manner.
5. ***Explanation:*** It measures the way the service company provided explanation to the customer with the reasons for the service failure, whether such explanation was perceived by the consumers satisfactorily.
6. ***Tangibles:*** It measures the presentability of contact employees, their working style, the speed and the professional handling of processes and the physical environment of the service outlet.

RECOVAST was tested for its usefulness in the banking sector. The results proved its utility in measuring the post-recovery satisfaction of the customer.

Source: Christo Boshoff, "A Reassessment and Refinement of RECOVAST—An Instrument to Measure Satisfaction with Transaction—Specific Service Recovery," Managing Service Quality, *15, no. 5 (2005): 410–425.*

contact employees throw the blame on consumers to save their skin. It really hurts the consumers. Though some consumers accept the responsibility at the situation, they carry the dissatisfaction as they could not get the service rightly. Therefore, acknowledgement from the company side relieves the customer pressure of guilty (if the customer doubts his/her part in the failure) and develops value perception towards the company.

- *Apologize:* Apologizing sincerely to the aggrieved consumer often contributes to reducing the intensity of the grievance. All consumer complaints may not be correct or rational. Some consumers have the habit of finding fault in everything. Some may not be capable of interpreting facts properly and some may not have sufficient information to develop expectations. Business experts suggest that though the consumer may be wrong, the service provider should not feel that he/she has a right to be angry about such complaints. The general rule should be to apologize

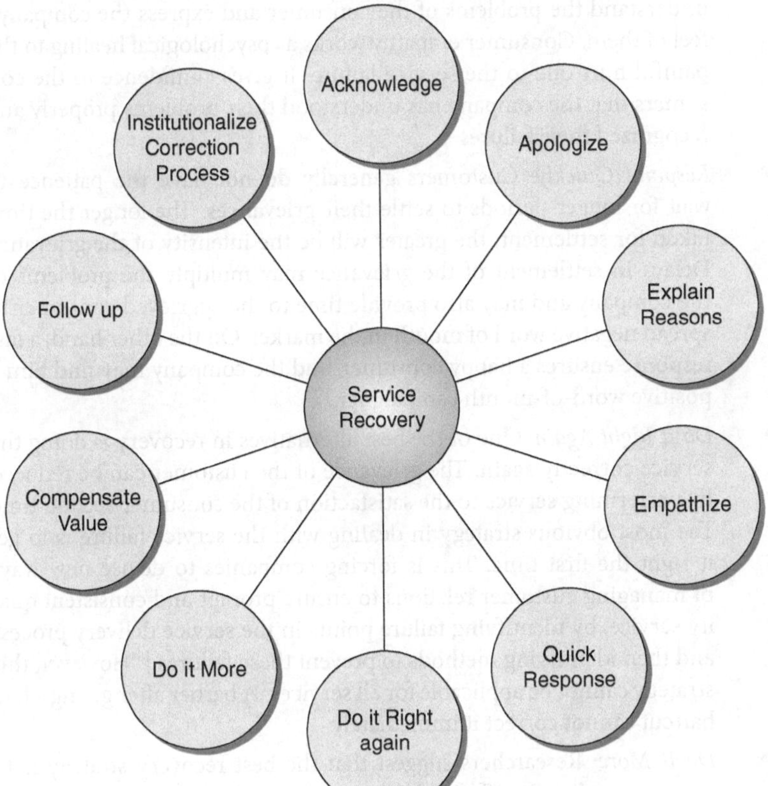

Fig. 20.3
Strategies for recovery

for the inconvenience caused, with a promise to take measures for arresting the recurrence of such failures. R. Johnson and A. Fern,[18] in their study, found that customers have clear expectations of service recovery, but the expectations differ based on the type of the failure. When apology was the appropriate recovery, they found the following:

(i) For less serious failures, a modest apology satisfied, while a follow-up written apology delighted customers
(ii) Serious failures required a managerial apology to satisfy, but no type of apology would delight these customers.

- *Explain Reasons:* Consumers must be apprised of the reasons for the service failure. This explanation makes the consumers understand the problems rationally and respond to the recovery process positively. The understanding of the factors contributed for the failure helps the consumers participate effectively in the recovery process.
- *Empathise:* Service failures hurt the consumers. The effects of service failures on consumers vary based on many factors. The severity is more in some cases, and it is less in some cases. The service provider should

understand the problems of the consumer and express the company's feel of them. Consumer empathy works as psychological healing to the painful hurt due to the service failure. It gives confidence to the consumers that the company has understood their problems properly and recognized their failures.

- *Respond Quickly:* Customers generally do not have the patience to wait for longer periods to settle their grievances. The longer the time taken for settlement, the greater will be the intensity of the grievance. Delays in settlement of the grievance may multiply the problems of the company and may also provide time to the aggrieved consumer to spread negative word of mouth in the market. On the other hand, a fast response ensures a happy consumer, and the company may find him a positive word-of-mouth campaigner.
- *Do It Right Again:* One of the best alternatives in recovery is doing the service correctly again. The grievance of the customer can be reduced by performing service to the satisfaction of the consumer second time. The most obvious strategy in dealing with the service failure is to get it right the first time. This is forcing companies to devise new ways of managing customer relations to ensure prompt and consistent quality service, by identifying failure points in the service delivery process and then identifying methods to prevent these failures.[19] However, this strategy cannot be applicable for all services. A barber after giving a bad haircut cannot correct it immediately.
- *Do It More:* Researchers suggest that the best recovery strategy is to improve quality. By offering better quality to the customer when there is a service failure, the service provider can turn the customers' grievances into delight. Suppose a customer reserves in advance a two-bed accommodation in a hotel. When he reaches the hotel with his family he finds no accommodation. There is every reason for his grievance. If the manager of the hotel tenders an apology immediately and offers a suite for the same price, coupled with a free banquet dinner, the customer is delighted. Offering some free gifts, discounts for future visits, preference in the next visit and so on may influence the customers positively. When the service provider gives a token tangible item to make up for the service failure, customers may feel obliged to change their level of satisfaction. Reciprocity may be a means to explain this phenomenon.[20]

> *"The recovery strategy adopted should have the capability to solve the problem of the customer. Service companies should not take the service failures as the specific outcomes of the employee–customer interactions. They should institutionalize the correction process to prevent reoccurrence of such failures."*

- *Compensate Value:* In some services, there may not be any other way for the service provider except to compensate for the damage done. In healthcare services a service failure may lead to the death of a patient. A service provider may reduce the grievance through the payment of compensation.
- *Follow up:* After the recovery process is completed the service provider should not relax. Follow-up is capable of yielding very good results. An

after-recovery call to ascertain that "are you satisfied now?", a liberal thanks for the cooperation extended by the customer immediately and a follow-up written communication are necessary to have a form of closure and to collect the feedback.

- *Institutionalize the Correction Process:* Service companies should address the grievances of consumers and also focus on correction processes. The corrective measures in the process reduce complaints and improve efficiency. The reasons for failures or deficiencies need to be identified, analysed and appropriate measures have to be initiated for prevention. In the process, the involvement of employees and customers yields good results. The service providers should seek suggestions from customers and employees and incorporate them as per their suitability. Such steps strengthen the bond between the service provider, the employees and the customers. The settlement of a complaint relating to one service outlet should not be the end of the problem. Service companies should study the possibility of the occurrence of such failures in other service outlets and take precautionary measures. Learning from service failures helps in designing BSP or in modifying the existing service packages.

Effective Service Recovery

Service organizations are required to display their commitment in service recovery. They should formulate clear guidelines and effective service recovery procedures. The following practices are important for effective service recovery.

Proactiveness in Service Recovery

The service organization should give priority to the recovery process. The service personnel at the customer contact points should be trained to recognize

Andhra Bank

Andhra Bank, established in 1923, is a public-sector commercial bank. The bank achieved the landmark of INR 1,000 billion business in 2008–2009. The bank achieved the distinction of bringing total branches under the core banking platform and designed a mechanism to settle customer grievances. If a customer experiences service deficiency at any of the branches, the customer can redress the complaint at the branch itself. The bank promises efficient, courteous and fair response to the customer grievances at the branch level. The second tier for grievance settlement, in case of customer dissatisfaction at the branch level, is the zonal office. The next tier is the head office. The branch manger at the branch level and the zonal manager at the zonal level attend customer complaints. At the head office a customer service department is established to handle the customer complaints. The customer can register a complaint by hand writing, on-line or though phone. The bank provided toll-free number for the purpose. In case the consumer is not satisfied at the three organization layers, the general manager and the nodal officer of the customer service attend to the customer. Finally, the customer can approach the banking ombudsman, if the bank fails to satisfy the consumer. Andhra Bank has simplified the redressal process to provide recovery speedily without any additional cost to the consumer.

the signs of dissatisfaction in consumers and enquire the consumers whether they are experiencing any problem. The employees should be directed to look forward to receiving the problems and attending to immediately. It happens many a time that the earlier the problem is recognized, the easier it would be to solve it. It is possible to take a proactive stance to reduce the occurrence of service failures and to equip employees with a set of effective recovery tools to repair the service encounter when failures do occur.[21] The consumers also feel happy over the exhibition of employee concern towards ascertaining the suitability and comfort of the consumers.

Advance Planning for Recovery Procedures

It is necessary to plan in advance the recovery process. The service marketers should expect the possibilities of the occurrence of service failures or deficiencies and develop contingency plans accordingly. It is good to identify the common service problems and develop set solutions in advance, so that the contact employees can follow without any confusion.

Employee Empowerment

Services are produced in buyer–employee interactions. If anything goes wrong, the immediate person to respond is the contact employee. Therefore, the contact employees should be empowered to use their judgment and interactive skills to develop solutions that will satisfy the consumer. Employees need to be given adequate authority to make decisions on the spot. If the employees are to look for the decisions from the superior, the recovery process gets delayed and the consumer gets frustrated. Therefore, employee empowerment is the key for successful resolution of customer grievances.

> *Service companies have two options when the service failure is recognized: proactive or reactive in the recovery process. Proactive recovery refers to the company initiative to rectify the failure without waiting for the customer complaint. Reactive recovery refers to the company action only against the customer complaint.*

Developing Recovery Skills

The interactive behaviour of the employee should be different from that of ordinary transactions. The contact employee has to handle customers who have some amount of dissatisfaction or are frustrated and angry. The employee should be very selective in choosing words in displaying feelings and gestures in interactive communication. He/she should be capable of communicating his/her concerns to the customer problem and assurance that the problem can be handled successfully. For this purpose, employees need to be given appropriate training.

Employee Training

Service employees shall be given training to handle customers with grievances and to make the appropriate recovery decision. In the service recovery training there are at least four areas[22] that need to be specifically addressed. They are: information processing, emotional response, instilling customer confidence, and service recovery versus employee satisfaction.

- *Information Processing:* The employees shall be given training to identify the information sources and the ways to which they can access the system independently and without delay. Information support is essential for quality decision making. The ability of the employee to process information as per the requirements of the problem helps him not to commit further mistakes in the recovery process.

- *Emotional Response:* Consumers' emotional response to service failures is often highly correlated with overall satisfaction judgment of the service encounter.[23] The service employees shall be given special training to handle the emotionally charged customers. If the employees are reactive to the emotional cues of the consumers, the problems get multiplied.
- *Instilling Customer Confidence:* When a service failure transpires, the customer is most likely to be satisfied with the recovery initiative if he/she is convinced that the failure occurred is due to a temporary cause rather than a stable one. Therefore, building customer confidence that the failure is unlikely to happen again is an integral part of the recovery effort. Instilling customer confidence is an advanced service skill and one that must be trained in all recovery programmes.
- *Service Recovery versus Employee Satisfaction:* There is a link between employee satisfaction and the effectiveness of recovery efforts. The service organization should focus on internal marketing to promote motivation and morale among employees. The employees' perception of organizational justice and the extent to which they feel that their values are shared by the company influence their willingness to move the extra mile in a service failure recovery effort. Therefore, the employees shall be involved in the managerial process of the organization, to get them really into the work process.

> *"For service recovery, service contact employees should be trained in information processing, emotional response, instilling customer confidence and employee satisfaction through service recovery. Employee empowerment is critical because the frontline employees have to identify and solve the problems on the spot."*

SUMMARY

- Service failures often occur due to many uncontrollable situations.
- The human factor involved in the service process may cause many service failures.
- Customers recognize service failures immediately as they are part of the production process. Therefore, hiding the failures is not possible.
- All the customers do not react similarly against a service failure.
- The customer reaction depends on the severity of the effect of the failure on the customer.
- Some customers complain against a failure. Some may not take it seriously and some may break relationship with the company.
- It is dangerous for service companies to ignore service failures without initiating the recovery process.
- Customer grievances need to be respected and a mechanism to settle such grievances needs to be developed.
- It is necessary to develop the customer complaint management system and execute it effectively.
- Service companies should encourage customers to complain to gain an advantage of locating deficiencies in the system and to take right measures for rectification.
- A good service recovery provides many benefits to the company.
- An effective recovery strategy strengthens the customer–company relationship bondage.
- Service companies must choose appropriate strategy based on the nature of the failure and the behaviour of the customer at that situation.
- The contact employee needs to be given proper orientation and empowerment to handle the recovery process.

KEY TERMS

Aggrieved customer *400*
Customer Complaint Management System *401*
Service failure *397*
Service recovery *397*

BRIEF QUESTIONS

1. What is a service failure? Why does it occur?
2. What are the reasons for customer grievances due to employee interactions?
3. How do customers react to service failures?
4. What is service recovery?
5. What are the measures to provide effective service recovery?

ESSAY QUESTIONS

1. "In every service failure, customers and employees are equally responsible." Comment.
2. Explain the complaint management process and suggest guidelines for handling complaints.
3. Discuss various service recovery strategies.
4. What kind of training should be given to service employees to make them effective in service recovery?

ASSIGNMENTS

1. Banks, telecom companies, insurance companies, public utility service organizations and so on organize customer meets periodically. You are required to attend any one of the customer meets and find out:
   (a) The customer complaints against the service provider
   (b) The recovery strategies adopted by the organization against the complaints
2. Conduct an exit interview for 30 passengers of a public transport company in your locality with a structured questionnaire to know:
   (a) The service failures identified by them
   (b) Their expectations of recovery and their experiences

REFERENCES

1 M. J. Bitner, B. H. Booms, and M. S. Tetreault, ,The Service Encounter: Diagnosing Favorable and Unfavorable Incidents, *Journal of Marketing*, 54, no. 1 (1990): 71–84.

2 Seungoog Weun, Sharon E. Beatty and Michael A. Jones, "The Impact of Service Failure Severity on Service Recovery Evaluations and Post-recovery Relationships," *Journal of Services Marketing*, 18, no. 2 (2004): 133–146.

3 Mary Ann Hocutt, Michael R. Bowers, and D. Todd Donavan, "The Art of Service Recovery: Fact or Fiction?," *Journal of Services Marketing*, 20, no. 3 (2006): 199–207.

4 Robert Warlow, "Why do you Customers Complain?," www.smallbusiness.biz, dated 18.09.2007.

5 Patrick McCole, "Dealing with Complaints in Services," *International Journal of Contemporary Hospitality Management*, 16, no. 6 (2004): 345–354.

6 R. Zemke, "The Art of Service Recovery: Fixing Broken Customers and Keeping Them on Your Side," in Scheuing, E. and W. Christopher, (Eds.), *The Service Quality Handbook*. (New York: AMACOM Books, 1993), pp. 463–476.

7 K. Stewart, "An Exploration of Customer exit in Retail Banking," *International Journal of Bank Marketing*, 16, no. 1 (1998): 6–14.

8 Seungoog Weun, Sharon E. Beatty and Michael A. Jones, "The Impact of Service Failure Severity on Service Recovery Evaluations and Post-recovery

Relationships," *Journal of Services Marketing,* 18, no. 2 (2004): 133–146.

9 Mark Colgate and Melissa Norris, "Developing a Comprehensive Picture of Service Failure," *International Journal of Service Industry Management,* 12, no. 3 (2001): 215–233.

10 C. Grönroos, "Relationship Marketing Approach to the Marketing Function in Service Contexts: the Marketing and Organizational Behavior Influence," *Journal of Business Research,* 20, no. 1 (1990): 7.

11 C. R. Bell, "Turning Disappointment into Customer Delight," *Editor & Publisher,* 127, no. 32 (1994): 49.

12 M. A. McCollough, L. L. Berry, and M. S. Yadav, "An Empirical Investigation of Customer Satisfaction After Service Failure and Recovery," *Journal of Services Research,* 3, no. 2 (2000): 121–137.

13 Christo Boshoff and Jason Leong, "Empowerment, Attribution and Apologising as Dimensions of Service Recovery: An Experimental Study," *International Journal of Service Industry Management,* 9, no. 1 (1998): 24–47.

14 S. M. Keaveney, "Customer Switching Behavior in Service Industries: An Exploratory Study," *Journal of Marketing,* 59, no. 2 (1995): 71–82.

15 A. K. Smith, R. N. Bolton and J. Wagner, "A Model of Customer Satisfaction with Service Encounters Involving Failure and Recovery," *Journal of Marketing Research,* 36, no. 3 (1999): 356–372.

16 T. Levesque and G. McDougall, "Service Problems and Recovery Strategies: An Experiment," *Canadian Journal of Administrative Sciences,* 17, no. 1 (2000): 20–37.

17 Ting Chi yang, "The Development of an Effective Recovery Programme After Service Failures: A Case Study of Restaurants in Glasgow," *Tourism and Hospitality Planning and Development,* 2, no. 1 (2005): 40.

18 R. Johnson and A. Fern, "Service Recovery Strategies for Single and Double Deviation Scenarios," *The Services Industries Journal,* 19, no. 2 (1999): 69–82.

19 David Cranage, "Plan to Do it Right: and Plan for Recovery," *International Journal of Contemporary Hospitality Management,* 16, no. 4 (2004): 211.

20 Mary Ann Hocutt, Michael R. Bowers and D. Todd Donavan, "The art of Service Recovery: Fact or Fiction?," *Journal of Services Marketing,* 20/3 (2006): 199–207.

21 G. McDougall and T. levesque, "The Effectiveness of Recovery Strategies after Service Failures: An Experiment in the Hospitality Industry," *Journal of hospitality and Leisure Marketing,* 5 (2/3) (1998): 27–49.

22 Vincent P. Magnini and John B. Ford, "Service Failure Recovery in China," *International Journal of Contemporary Hospitality Management,* 16, no. 5 (2004): 276–286.

23 A. K. Smith and R. N. Bolton, "The Effect of Customers' Emotional Responses to Service Failures on Their Recovery Effort Evaluations and Satisfaction Judgments," *Journal of the Academy of Marketing Science,* 30, no.1 (2002): 5–23.

Customer Relationship Management

21

LEARNING OBJECTIVES

After studying this chapter, you will be able to:

- Understand the importance of CRM
- Understand the drivers of successful CRM
- Understand the managerial framework of CRM
- Understand the application of e-CRM

Surya, the newly appoint Chief Manager (Customer Relations) at NextLife Insurance Company was keen on getting to know his team and assessing the utility and functionality of the existent CRM system within the organization. With this goal in mind, he called his entire team together for a meeting. During the meeting, he learnt that the department limited its functions to the extent of responding to customer complaints. Of the customer base of 500,000, it maintained a relationship with only those 50-odd people who complained on any given day. For a complaint, the response time varied from 15 days to 90 days, depending on the nature of the complaint. As per the executives, approximately 10 per cent of the total complaints in a day were unreasonable and, hence, ignored. Surya was not convinced that the company had adopted the right approach to CRM. He felt that the company needed to maintain harmonious relations with all its customers, not just the ones who complain. Also, he did not agree with the way the activities of the department were planned and executed. According to him, there was no excuse for shoddy management of customer relations, particularly in a steadily growing business. He felt it was not justified to put the customer through endless telephonic queues, convoluted IVR systems only to be told that it would take a minimum of 15 days for their complaint to be addressed. Surya is aware that each unanswered complaint causes the unhappy customer to badmouth the organization, switch loyalties and actively dissuade others from employing the services of the organization. Surya intends to overhaul the way the department functions. For starters, he instructs his team to respond to all complaints—reasonable or not. He wants them to have a dialogue with the customers, attend to their grievances with an open mind and respond positively. He wants the department to be proactive in their role and touch the lives of all their customers. He plans to put forward a strong case in favour of the changes he proposes to make to the CMD.

Questions:

1. Do you support the changes proposed by Surya?
2. How can the cost of customer relationship management be defended?
3. Is it necessary to respond to every complaint? Will it not encourage mischievous customers to trouble the company employees?
4. Do you think bad customers should also be allowed to continue under the umbrella of CRM?
5. How would you help Surya in designing a CRM system?

INTRODUCTION

The accelerated pace of change in all facets of business each year has resulted in intense competition, fragmented markets, shorter life cycles and high business risk besides many other problems. The traditional marketing philosophy of customer orientation and providing transactional satisfactions to the customers does not provide convincing margins and support for future development. To face the emerging challenges, companies embraced a customer-centric philosophy wherein every activity in business is defined in terms of value generation to the customer. They realized that the consumer can be used as the value-generating resource. C. K. Prahalad and V. Rama Swamy[1] have rightly pointed out that customers are fundamentally changing the dynamics of the market-place. The market has become a forum in which consumers play an active role in creating and competing for value. The distinguishing feature of this new market-place is that the consumer becomes a new source of competence for the corporation. The competence that customers bring is a function of knowledge and skills they possess, their willingness to learn and experiment and their ability to engage in an active dialogue. Building and strengthening the loyal customer base have become the driving theme of the business. The widely accepted approach to facilitate such theme of the business is customer relationship management (CRM).

CRM directs a shift in the business focus from inside out to outside in. In other words, it is transformation from a producer-driven enterprise to a customer-driven enterprise. The change in the business theme was rightly pointed out by Jill Dyche,[2] stating that the so-called typical customer no longer exists, and companies have been learning this lesson the hard way. Until very recently, business was more concerned about the "what's" than about the "who's." In other words, companies were focused on selling as many products and services as possible, without regard to who was buying them. Most corporations cling to this product-centric philosophy even today, basing their organizational structures and compensation plans on the products they sell, not the customers who buy.

CRM is a comprehensive strategy and process of acquiring, retaining and partnering with selective customers to create superior value for the company and the customer.[3] Relationship customers have far more potential for loyalty as they are often prepared to pay a premium price for a range of reliable goods or services.[4] CRM strategies are only effective if they deliver positive outcomes. It is no longer good enough just to say that you are customer focused, but it matters what you do.[5] Customer relationships are grounded in the ideal of establishing a learning relationship with each customer. "CRM is the development of lasting strategic alliances with customers on a value sharing bases. It implies future orientation and a winning proposition between the sellers and the customers. It helps deliver customer centric relationships."[6] The benefits that business concerns accrue, due to a loyal customer base, should be shared with the customer in order to make CRM effective and future oriented.

> *"Customers have become a new source of competence of service organizations. Building and strengthening a loyal customer base is the most critical function. Customer relationship management facilitates long-term company–customer relations for mutual gain."*

BENEFITS OF CRM

The central theme of CRM is the mutual gain to both the company and the customer through relationships.

Benefits to the Company

Through effective CRM, service companies can:

- Have analytical consumer database
- Identify the most profitable customers
- Have greater understanding of the customers
- Increase market revenues through greater penetration, market expansion and market development, improved channel efficiency and profitable cross-selling and up-selling
- Reduce cost through improved channel efficiency and reduce the expenses due to usage of Internet services
- Design an effective marketing mix
- Design effective participation strategies
- Provide right ambience at the service outlet
- Promote customers' satisfaction, loyalty and responsiveness
- Get ideas from customers for innovation or for improving products or services
- Reduce introductory cost for new offerings
- Promote organizational image
- Provide basic information input for ERP
- Use as the hedge against miner mistakes
- develop loyal customer base

Benefits to Consumers

Consumers also gain some benefits by establishing longer relationship with the service provider. The following are some benefits CRM provides to customers:

- Reliable source of service
- Time saving by not searching for various other service providers
- Minimize information search cost, energy cost and psychological cost
- Confidently get recovery in case the service provided by the seller is deficient
- Effective role play in service production due to familiarity with service organization
- Can get liberal credit terms
- Enhanced social value

THREE DRIVERS OF SUCCESSFUL CRM

Savvy marketers realized the fact that to outperform competitors it is necessary to achieve the full profit potential from each and every customer. Customers should be made the core of the company's organizational culture, across all departments and functions. Each and every employee should perceive exchange with a customer as part of a *customer relationship*, not as a *transaction*. "If the CRM strategy is struggling to influence profitability, after a reasonable period of time, then the organization is clearly failing. Organizations in this position should immediately consider changing direction and adopt alternative strategies. The position for those organizations that have failed may result in a series of circumstances that are hard to recover from. Such companies may find they have a disproportionate number of unprofitable customers that others have jettisoned."[7] The three drivers of successful relationships between marketers and customers are *customer value*, high levels of *customer satisfaction* and building a structure for *customer retention*.

> *The three drivers for the success of CRM are providing customer value, customer satisfaction and customer retention. Customer value is the ratio between the customer's perceived benefits and the resources used to obtain those benefits. Customer satisfaction can be achieved through serving customers as per their expectations. Customer retention is possible through loyalty building strategies.*

Customer Value

Customer value is defined as the *ratio between the customer's perceived benefits (economic, functional and psychological) and the resources (monetary, time, effort, psychological) used to obtain those benefits*. Perceived value is relative and subjective. For example, the perceived value of customers who visit a famous art gallery varies, based on their knowledge, involvement, understanding abilities and other situational factors. Customers who are artists perceive differently to that of art lovers and the both to that of ordinary tourists. Some may perceive exceptionally high value and some may get dissatisfied by comparing costs including opportunity costs against the value they could perceive from the art gallery. Many customers visit McDonald's restaurants to purchase standard, inexpensive meals from franchise owners. The employees are systematically trained by the McDonald's Corporation to deliver the company's four core standards: *quality, service, cleanliness* and *value*. Customers flock to McDonald's outlets repeatedly because the restaurants are uniform, customers know what to expect and feel that they are getting value for the resources they expend.

Customer Satisfaction

Customer satisfaction is the perception of individuals of the performance of the product or service in relation to their expectations. The concept of customer satisfaction is a function of customer expectations. A customer whose experience falls below expectations is dissatisfied, whose experiences match expectations is satisfied and whose expectations are exceeded is satisfied or delighted. Companies should study the levels of customer satisfaction and interpret properly. This information helps the managers understand how satisfied or dissatisfied customers are with both their dealings with the company in general and with the products and services in particular.

Customer satisfaction and customer loyalty generally has a linear relationship. However, research has proved that completely satisfied customers are more loyal to the company or product than just satisfied customers. The information on customer satisfaction serves as a critical barometer of how early the service company is serving its customers. The information is also useful to identify the ways and means to increase customer satisfaction level by level until the majority of the customers are completely satisfied. Therefore, service companies should consider customer satisfaction and loyalty as a priority and take up appropriate strategies for raising customer satisfaction. The vast majority of companies that excel in satisfying customers rank the ability to react when something goes wrong as one of the most important factors in satisfying customers. That ability greatly influences whether customer heap scorn or praise on the company when talking to others. Completely satisfied customers typically believe that the company excels in understanding and addressing their personal preferences, values, needs or problems. To figure out how to satisfy customers in this fashion, a company has to excel at listening to customers and interpreting what they are saying.[8]

Customer Retention

The overall objective of providing value to customers continuously and more effectively than the competition is to have highly satisfied (even delighted) customers; this strategy of customer retention makes it in the best interest of customers to stay with the service company rather than switch to another firm. In almost all business situations, it is more expensive to win new customers than to keep existing ones. Studies have shown that small reductions in customer defections produce significant increases in profits because:

1. Loyal customers buy more services.
2. Loyal customers are less price sensitive and pay less attention to competitors' advertising.
3. Servicing existing customers, who are familiar with the firm's offerings and processes, is cheaper.
4. Loyal customers spread positive word of mouth and refer other customers.

Loyal customers are made, not born; they are made by the process of interaction. When service companies enter into a learning relationship with customers, customers tell what they want. And when customers invest time and effort in this process, very often they do not defect.[9]

Marketers who designate increasing customer retention rates as a strategic corporate goal must also recognize that all customers are not equal. Sophisticated marketers build *selective relationships* with customers, based on where customers rank in terms of profitability, rather than merely strive to retain customers. A customer retention–savvy company closely monitors its customers' consumption volume and patterns, establishes tiers of

SBI Railway Card

IRCTC (Indian Railway Catering and Tourism Corporation) introduced the SBI Railway Card as a collaborative service of two public sector giants—the State Bank of India and the Indian Railways. The SBI Railway Card is the only credit card that gives the customer free train tickets if the customer maintains a regular relationship with the Railways. The package of benefits offered to the customers through this card clearly spells out the relationship benefits. The customers who purchase the SBI Railway Card are eligible for:

- A 10% refund on the AC ticket fare as the Railways points through complimentary membership to Shubh Yatra—the frequent traveller programme of Indian Railways.
- No service charge on tickets booked at www.irctc.co.in using the card.
- 1 SBI Railway point on every INR 125 spent using the card.
- No transaction fee on the purchase of fuel and other lubricants for amounts exceeding INR 400 up to INR 2000, each time, at select IOL and IBP petrol pumps.
- No interest charge for balance transfer for 75 days.
- Complimentary rail accident insurance for INR 1 million.

The introduction of this credit card helps in promoting long-term customer relationships besides promoting business.

customers according to their profitability levels and develops distinct strategies towards each group of customers. For example, some stockbrokers programme their phones to recognize the phone numbers of high-volume traders to ensure that their calls receive priority. Customers who have purchased and registered several of a company's products should receive extensive and expedited customer support. On the other hand, a bank's less profitable customers who make little use of their credit cards or maintain the minimum balance needed to receive free checking should not have penalties waived for bounced checks or late payments. Some service companies also identify customer groups that are unlikely to purchase more if pursued more aggressively; such customers are often discouraged from staying with the company or even fired as customers.

Classifying customers according to profitability levels goes beyond traditional segmentation methods that subdivide consumers on the basis of demographic, socio-cultural or behavioural characteristics. *Customer profitability-focused marketing* tracks costs and revenues of individual customers and then categorizes them into tiers based on consumption behaviours that are specific to the company's offerings. Such a strategy is probably the most effective way to utilize the knowledge of consumer behaviour. T. O. Jones and W. E. Sessor[10] advocated using a customer pyramid to group customers into four tiers:

1. The *platinum tier* includes heavy users who are not price sensitive and are willing to try new offerings.
2. The *gold tier* consists of customers who are heavy users but not as profitable because they are more price sensitive than those in the higher tier, ask for more discounts and are likely to buy from several providers.

> *Customers can be classified based on their contribution to the company's profit. Platinum-tier customers are highly preferred for building relationship. Golden-tier customers are the next best. Iron-tier and lead-tier customers are not worthy of a relationship.*

3. The *iron tier* consists of customers whose spending volume and profitability do not merit special treatment from the company.
4. The *lead tier* includes customers who actually cost the company money because they claim more attention than is merited by their spending, tie up company resources and spread negative word of mouth.

This classification is to develop distinct marketing responses for each group. A corporate philosophy centered on customer value, satisfaction and retention evolves from the marketing concept and also unfolds new dimensions of marketing.

A CRM FRAMEWORK

The managerial framework of CRM includes selection of the list of customers for developing long-term relations, setting the goals of CRM, designing the organizational system and interaction processes and collecting the feedback of customer responses. Figure 21.1 presents various managerial issues involved in the CRM process.

Selection of Customers

Companies need to assess many issues for identifying the customers with whom long-term relationships are expected. The input factors of the selection of the customer are of twofold. They are customer- and organization-related issues. The customer-related inputs are customer classification and analysis,

Figure 21.1
The CRM framework

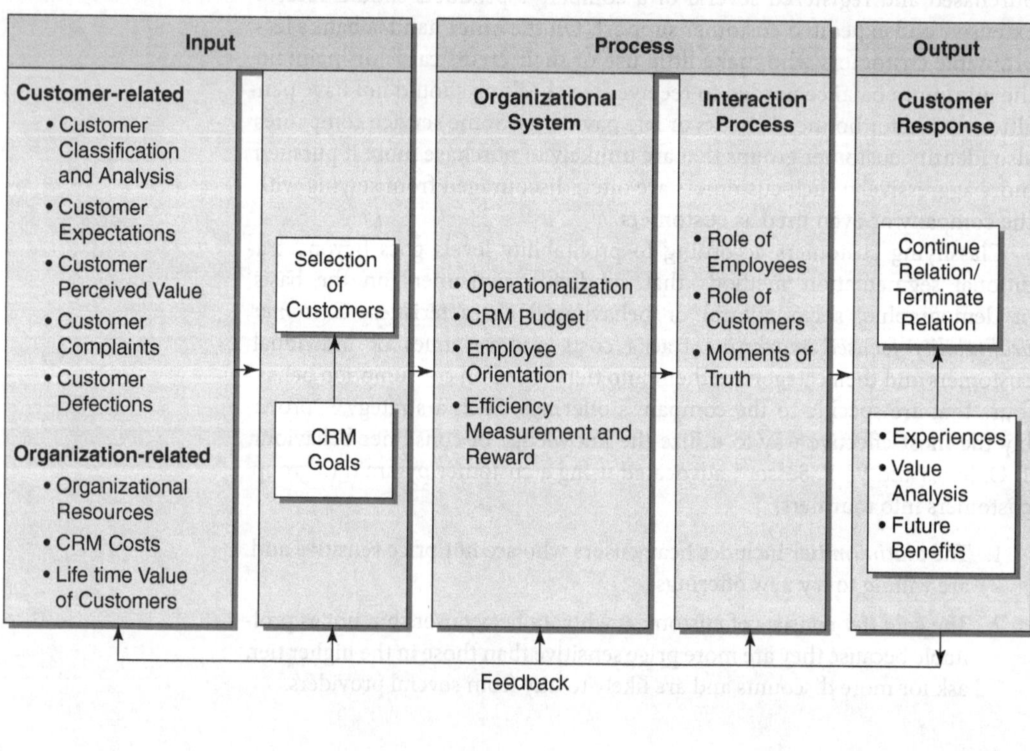

customer expectations, customer perceived value, customer complaints and customer defection analysis. The organization-related issues are organizational resources, CRM costs and life time value of customers.

> "The managerial framework for CRM includes identification of customers for building relationship, goal setting for CRM, designing and execution of the organization system and interactive processes and feedback to know the customer response to the system and to take corrective measures wherever necessary."

Customer-related Inputs

Individual customers vary in their behaviour as each and every customer will have varied behaviour attributes, attitudes, perceptions, motivation and reactive tendencies. Based on the market response, customers broadly can be categorized into the following four[11] types: loyalists, defectors, mercenaries and hostages.

- *Loyalists:* Loyalists are completely satisfied customers. They derive high level of value from the company offerings; therefore, loyalists are the preferred customers to serve. They are the repute buyers and happily invite new offerings of the service company. They recommend strongly and honestly the company products to others.
- *Defectors:* Defectors are customers who shift their loyalty to the competitive companies, due to the reason that they are not happy with the existing company offerings. They are either highly dissatisfied or dissatisfied or taken a neutral stand on the satisfaction measurement scale. Even satisfied customers also defect when they find marginally better offers from competitors.
- *Mercenaries:* Mercenaries are customers who exhibit almost no loyalty to the company. They may be completely satisfied with the company offerings, but still don't like to stick on to any company. Mercenaries are mostly impulse buyers; they like to follow trends in fashion and are lovers of change. It is not possible to establish a long-term relationship for any company with mercenaries.
- *Hostages:* Hostages are the captive customers. The customers continue to purchase the company offerings since they don't have any viable alternative. They continue with the company until they find better alternative to shift their loyalties.

> "Customers can be classified based on their behaviour, attitudes, motivation, reactive tendencies, etc. Companies can divide customers accordingly into four groups: loyalists, defectors, mercenaries and hostages."

The classification of the customers of the company into the above-mentioned four groups facilitates a service company to conduct consumer research with different sets of research objectives. The information thus generated is of immense help in selection of customers, setting CRM goals and development of the CRM strategy.

Customers can be classified into two different ways, based on different levels of value and different needs. The difference between the most profitable customers and the average may be tenfold. "The idea that a company cannot have a profitable relationship with all customers leads to the practice of targeting customers with a differentiated product or service. This practice is already widespread in many financial services, e.g. banking, insurance, credit cards etc."[12] CRM is a useful tool for identifying the right customer groups and deciding the customers to jettison. Customer differentiation helps focus on efforts to gain the advantage with the most valuable customers. It also helps tailor company's behaviour to each customer in order to reflect that customer's value and needs. "The customer base is first segmented by the value they represent to an organization, and then by the needs they may have for specified products/services."[13] The degree and type of differentiation in a company's customer base also help decide an appropriate strategy for a given business situation.[14]

> *Customer expectations are shaped by many factors including company promises, past experience, company image, need pressure, word of mouth and so on. Customer value perception is influenced by socio-cultural, personal and psychological attributes.*

Customer Expectations

Customers do develop expectations while responding to various marketing stimulations. The expectations of the customers depend on various factors which include promises of the company, past experience, company image, word of mouth, need pressure and life style. The level of customer satisfaction mostly depends on customer expectations. When the company offerings exceed the expectations of customers, customers get delighted. When they find the offerings are on par with expectations they derive satisfaction and anything below the expectation creates a feeling of dissatisfaction. The study of expectations of the customers on services of the company and on relationships provides an immensely useful information input.

Customer-perceived Value

Value perception of the customers also varies based on different cultural, social, personal and psychological attributes. The knowledge of the customer value assessment serves as a critical input for the policy makers. The idea that companies succeed by selling value is not new. What is new is how customers define value in many markets. In the past, customers judged the value of a service on the basis of some combination of quality and price. "Today's customers, by contrast, have an expanded concept of value that includes convenience of purchase, after-sale service, dependability and so on."[15]

The value perception of the customers is influenced by several factors. Some customers consider low price is the value. They belong to the price-sensitive group and look for special discounts, distress sales and low-end products and services. Some customers may find value in totality of offerings. These customers do not want to incur search costs and time costs beyond a particular point and ready to pay more for the availability of greater choice and the total set of requirements relating to a particular activity. They prefer service packages for the organization of events, big retail showrooms and malls. These customers represent the creamy layer of the society. Another category of customers follow the rational approach in value assessment of a marketing offer. They take into consideration the customer cost and customer benefit. They continue loyalty of a product as long as it provides more delivered value over competitive products.

Customer Complaints

Customer complaints are the important source to trace out various problems and symptoms of the emerging problems. A customer tends to make a complaint on convincing totally with the problem. The version of the customer may be technically right or wrong. Even if it is wrong the company can identify a communication problem in that. The issues raised by the customers in complaints are useful in formulating a relationship strategy. Complaint classification, analysis and response play a vital role in CRM.

Customer Defections

It is the experience of almost all the companies to find some customers defecting. If the rate of defections is more than new addition of customers, the company may find declining sales volume. When the new additions and defections are equal in number the company may register stagnation in sales. When the company gets more additions than the number of defections, the sales curve may exhibit the progressive movement. Researches have proved beyond doubt that the cost of acquiring the new customer is many times more than the cost of retaining. Identification of defectors, qualifying them and finding the reasons for defection serve as key strategic information for arresting defection of customers. Companies definitely feel happy when they find bad customers in the list of defectors, but they can not afford to lose valuable customers of the company.

Organization-related Inputs

The organization-related input in the CRM process includes the organizational resources, CRM costs and life time value of customers.

Organizational Resources

Internal resources of the company form as core foundation for CRM. Proper analyses of internal competencies and weaknesses are vital. An effective CRM process requires financial resources, human resources, technology, management commitment, internal environment and culture, company's vision where sharing value with the consumers for a long period is an integral part, infrastructure, etc. The assessment of the resources has to be done from the point of view of the customer service. It is necessary to identify the weakness of the prevalent system. The analysis of weaknesses is helpful in setting limitations to the CRM system.

CRM Costs

Companies have to incur cost for customer acquisition and customer retention. They need to pursue different policies and strategies for acquisition of the new customers and for customer retention. In fact, CRM starts with identification of prospects and transforming them in the relationship ladder as the partner of the company. The *relationship ladder* presented in Fig. 21.2 shows the levels of customer relationship management in the hierarchy. Finding prospects and persuading them to become buyers of the company is the first step in the ladder. It requires many efforts to create awareness and interest and to convince them with the superior benefit offerings of the company. In the loyalty ladder, a buyer should be transformed as a customer, a customer as a client, a client as a supporter, a supporter as an advocate and an advocate as a partner. Partnering with customers is considered

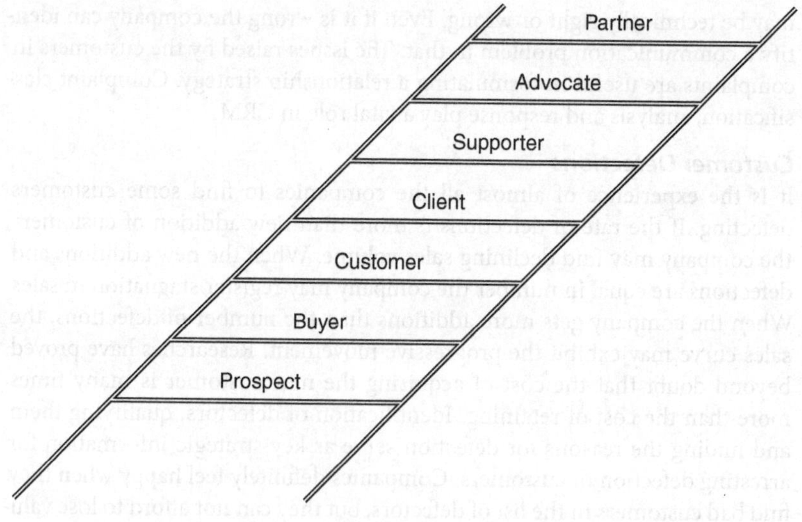

Fig. 21.2 The relationship enhancement ladder

the highest form of relationship. The cost involved in promoting customers through various levels of the relationship ladder is certainly a concern to the companies. The behaviour of all customers is not common in having and continuing relationship with a company. The difficulties and the cost in acquiring and retaining various customers vary.

> *Building, maintaining and enhancing customer relationships is the core principle of the CRM strategy. The relationship enhancement ladder provides the hierarchical direction for the progress of relationships.*

Lifetime Value of Customers

The lifetime value analysis related to customers is an important input for the CRM process. Any wise decision should follow the cost–benefit analysis. The lifetime value of the customers indicates the benefits of CRM—present and future. A comparative analysis of CRM costs and benefits of various categories of customers in various markets is necessary for any company to maximize benefits through CRM.

160by2

160by2 is a free SMS service company supported by advertisements within the SMS. The company was established in 2007 with the innovative business concept of sharing non-monetary value between the seller and the buyer. The exchange was purely on non-monetary terms. The business concept was very well received by the market, and within two years the company became one of the 50 fastest-growing tech companies in India. In the first year, it established a customer base of one million. The company's business philosophy, which reads, "if you take care of your users, your users will take care of you", reflects its commitment to customer relationships. Interestingly, the company did not use advertisements to build its customer base. Word-of-mouth publicity worked very positively for the company. A number of new product introductions such as Templates, WAP site, Widgets, Java Application, Email2Sms, near Instantaneous delivery, Reminders & Alerts, IPL alerts, Contacts & Intelli-text offered to the customers speaks of the company's efforts to add value to the consumers continuously to strengthen the relationship.

SELECTION OF CUSTOMERS

The customer- and organization-related input forms the basis for finalization of customers. The concept of establishing relationships with selective customers is based on the assumption that the larger customer base is costlier to build relationships. Therefore, companies choose the policy of meritocracy. Meritocracy is the selection of the customers on some merits. It demands a shift in the customer care philosophy from providing the highest level of care for every customer to tailored care to each customer needs based on the value of interactions. Meritocracy identifies long-term valuable customers based on historical and future potential value in terms of profits, sales and life style changes. Profitability is one of the serious considerations in the selection of customers for CRM. Customer profitability depends on the factors such as acquisition costs, retention costs, number of face-to-face telephone contacts, sales revenue from the customer, referral value, synergic value and duration of relationship (see "Service Marketing Insight: Customer Classification Based on Acquisition Costs and Retention Costs").

> *The selection of customers for relationships is based on the customer- and organization-related input. There should be a right alignment between the two to find out right customers in right size to serve and to maximize benefits of relationships.*

When the value of customers to the enterprise vary widely, the top customers account for the vast majority of the business; it is called steep skew.

21.1 Services Marketing Insight — **Customer Classification Based on Acquisition Costs and Retention Costs**

The classification of customers—based on acquisition costs and retention costs—made by Jacquelyn S. Thomas, Werner Reinartz and V. Kumar is useful for CRM policy makers. The researchers have classified customers into four groups: casual, low maintenance, high maintenance and loyal. *Casual customers* are easy to acquire and easy to retain. Since acquisition costs and the retention costs are low, the sales staff and relationship management section forget this group to build relations. The second category is *low-maintenance customers*. The cost of acquisition of these customers is high, but the cost of retention is low. These customers are judicious in their approach in the selection of the company; once they establish relationships they prefer to continue loyalty with the company, until the company's CRM personnel commit too many mistakes. The third category is *high-maintenance customers*. The acquisition cost of these customers is low, but their maintenance proves costly to the concerns. These customers are triers and put efforts in evaluating the value of the offering of the existing company with competitive offers. They don't mind cutting off relations, when the company is lagging behind in offering services. The fourth category is *loyal customers*. These customers are difficult both to acquire and to maintain and are highly sensitive of the quality of services. This is the premium group and to tackle them with specialized efforts is necessary. They provide ample opportunities to the company, to maintain and enhance relationships, and require only one thing: the company should treat them as special and offer faultless high-end services.

Source: Jacquelyn S. Thomas, Werner Reinartz and V. Kumar, "Getting the Most out of All Your Customers," Harvard Business Review *(July–August 2004).*

"Relationship marketing is more cost efficient for businesses with a steep skew than with a shallow one. The greater the skew, the more feasible it is to cultivate relationships with the most valuable customers. If the top 2% of the customers generate 50% of profit, the company can protect 50% of the bottom line by fostering learning relationships with just the top few customers. But if the top 20% of the customers make up 50% of the profit, then it will be ten times as costly to achieve the same bottom line benefit."[16]

THE GOALS OF CRM

The goals of CRM should reflect the company's overall strategy towards customers. Each company operates under a set of conditions, opportunities, threats and limitations. Therefore, the goals of CRM cannot be universalized. They are to be company specific. However, the possible goals of CRM are listed here:

- To build, maintain and enhance mutually rewarding relationships with customers
- To promote up-selling and cross-selling to gain maximum wallet share of the customers
- To provide better care and service to customers
- To collect information on customers regularly through consumer research
- To develop and integrate technology and human resources in all customer activities
- To provide highest possible value to the customers better than competitors

THE ORGANIZATIONAL SYSTEM FOR CRM

CRM requires an organizational system that facilitates the achievement of its goals. It requires coordinated and integrated efforts of the total organization. An efficient organization system has the following to achieve high quality in CRM

- Quality assurance processes
- Customer-centric business policies
- State-of-the-art and suitable technology to customer needs
- State-of-the-art and suitable technology to employees needs
- Continuously updated customer database
- Rightly qualified and service-oriented human resources
- Recognition and rewards for employees with customer-centric behaviour
- Mechanism to respond to customer problems and grievances
- Periodic consumer research to understand and anticipate customer behaviour

Operationalization

The organizational system based on the customer-centric philosophy generally follows the four-stage operational process. In the journey of understanding customers the managers of a company will be able to anticipate challenges ahead and plan to utilize organizational resources optimally to face the challenges effectively. Ranjay Gulati and James B. Oldroyd[17] identified the following four stages in their research: communal coordination, serial coordination, symbiotic coordination and integral coordination.

1. *Communal Coordination:* Communal coordination requires creation of a centralized repository of customer information. It requires a two-step process. The first step is to pool all the standardized information from each customer touch point throughout the firm. The second step is to organize the information customer wise, making the customer the fundamental unit and analysis. This process requires establishment of a coordination infrastructure. Instead of contacting one another directly, each organizational unit can contribute information to the common pool and draw information whenever needed. Though the concept of communal coordination is simple, it requires a substantial investment both in time and technology. However, against the huge advantages, the investment requirements may not stand as a limitation.
2. *Serial Coordination:* This stage involves a series of tasks performed by certain functional units in analysing and interpreting the customer data and information to pass to users in the business unit. The objective is to use information in the best way in marketing efforts and also to have the knowledge of local markets. This process is also useful to explore business opportunities and to carry out innovations. It also helps uncover critical gaps in employees' skills.
3. *Symbiotic Coordination:* This stage indicates a shift in the focus from the analysis of past customer interactions to anticipating and even shaping the future. It is to identify customers on their loyalty level and predict their intended relationships with the company in future. For the purpose, companies may create models to predict consumer behaviour or experiment with various interactions to change consumer behaviour and measure the results. Companies may also use feedback from front-line personnel to improve models and business approaches.
4. *Integral Coordination:* This is the stage at which companies use their understanding of the customers to incorporate in day-to-day operations. They see that customer focus pervades in every organizational aspect. In other words, customer focus becomes institutionalized. Getting closer to customers is not only about building an information technology system but it's a learning journey—one that unfolds over four stages, each with its own obstacles, and each requiring people and units to coordinate in even more sophisticated ways. Companies that recognize this invest their customer relationship dollars much more wisely and see their customer-focusing efforts pay off on the bottom line.[18]

> *"Operationalization of CRM should be based on a customer-centric philosophy. There is a need to coordinate organizational resources for the purpose. Communal, serial, symbiotic and integral coordination are the four stages of coordination."*

CRM Budget

CRM is a continuous process that requires formal allocation of resources in the form of budget. Companies cannot dream to achieve good results in CRM without preparing themselves to spend on it. The spending on CRM shall be treated as an investment to build customer equity. The stronger the customer equity, the lesser the risk in current and future endeavours of the business concerns. Companies should select an appropriate method among the available methods such as affordable method, percentage to sales, competition parity and objective and task methods, to provide adequate financial support to the organizational unit to take up CRM activities efficiently.

Employee Orientation

Companies use technology and human resources for the purpose of CRM. Either of the sources alone cannot ensure high level of efficiency in the overall performance of CRM. Employees form a vital resource in rendering qualitative services to the customers. Machines cannot be empathetic towards customers, but employees can. Human touch is precious and solves many physical and psychological problems of human beings. The household customers are human beings and services through employees can make them experience better quality. The role of technology cannot be overemphasized in this respect. Researches in many occasions have proved that technology is not a substitute for human resources in rendering the customer service. In fact, the human resource with the support of the right kind of technology has achieved excellent results.

> *"Employees have to use their physical and mental faculties to deliver quality service and to take active part in relationship management. Employee empowerment is an essential input for the purpose. Employees as internal customers must be supported by qualitative internal services."*

Companies should identify the requirements of CRM and look for people who can deliver the desired experiences to the customers. The recruitment and selection policies should be in tune with the CRM requirements. The employees inducted should be provided with right kind of training, tools and equipment. Employee empowerment is an essential input for CRM. Empowerment means equipping an individual with abilities to perform well. Thus, the employee empowerment means providing right kind of infrastructure, environment, training and authority, to promote the abilities of employees to act with freedom and personal judgment in initiating actions and taking decisions. The employees particularly the frontline employees should be provided with adequate freedom and support environment to design and deliver experiences to the customers.

Another important dimension is to develop organizational culture in which customer focus and customer service are an integral part. The employees are nurtured through policies, practices, design of the work environment, concern towards customer problems, priority of works and other activities to make them believe that the customers are responsible for the present and future existence of the company. It is a known fact that employees deliver satisfactions to the customers only when they are satisfied. Employee satisfaction is an important foundation for customer satisfaction. Companies should identify the needs, wants and expectations of the employees to satisfy them. They should see that the employee satisfaction index (ESI) moves upward always.

Employee motivation and morale are very important for CRM, and the companies should realize the same. An appropriate compensation plan and reward system is necessary to promote employee productivity in customer relations. "A customer relationship commitment will never stand a chance while you pay your staff based on productivity, which gives staff a strong incentive to complete as many calls as possible regardless of their quality. The slogan—'We love you, our customer'—is completely useless when the people on the phone have no power to solve the problems presented to them."[19]

Employees have to use their physical and mental faculties to deliver quality service. They need to play a variety of roles in performing the customer service. The roles of an employee in the service organization include product designer, performer, technician, associate, friend, empathizer, assurer, salesman, marketing intelligence and researcher. Employees' involvement in every part of business activity included in the company's vision is necessary for the companies looking for excellence in employee performance.

Employee Relationship Management (ERM)

> *Employee relationship management (ERM) is critical for CRM. ERM is capable of solving all problems relating to human resources. It ensures much positivity in employee behaviour and promotes health, strength and specialized competencies of the organization.*

Employees are as important as customers. While customer satisfaction is the destiny for companies, employee satisfaction is the means to reach the target. While CRM secure present and future business, ERM makes CRM possible. Companies throughout the world are increasingly realizing the need for relationship with employees. They are promoting the relationships from financial bonds to social and structural bonds. Greater efforts are on the way to achieve high level of employee involvement in all areas. Every employee, irrespective of the rank and file, is a potential knowledge resource. Companies, which exploit the resource optimally, excel in their performance levels. ERM is somewhat easier than CRM. Customers are larger in number than employees and hard to understand, and the management of a company can closely observe and study the employees' behaviour to design relationship policies. ERM is capable of solving all problems relating to human resources. In fact, it is a preventive device for any kind of problems in managing human resources. In addition, it ensures much positivity in employee behaviour and promotes health, strength and specialized competencies of the organization. ERM helps companies communicate, train, and connect employees to their organization base. A study[20] on employee motivation and customer loyalty in retailing business revealed that committed employees build loyal customers. A statistical analysis revealed that employee loyalty explained as much as 40 per cent of customers' loyalty. This meant that a unit shift in employee loyalty could bring about a shift of 0.4 in customer loyalty. Stores which had a higher employee loyalty index (more employees feeling strongly loyal towards the store) showed a significantly higher customer loyalty Index.

Efficiency Measurement and Reward

Companies have to design an efficiency measurement system at the organizational-unit level and at each employee level. The system should have clarity and agreement of those employees of the unit who are subjected to measurement.

"*Companies may use the **customer satisfaction index** (CSI) for the purpose of measuring employees' customer service performance. CSI is developed by surveying the customers about their level of satisfaction and plotting the results over a period of time. CSI can be developed against a department, an activity or an employee.*"

Companies may use the customer satisfaction index (CSI) for this purpose of measuring employees' customer service performance. CSI is developed by surveying the customers about their level of satisfaction and plotting the results over a period of time. CSI can be developed against a department, an activity or an employee. It provides a quick feedback from the customers. The employee or organizational unit concerned need not wait until the completion of the financial year to know the result for drawing inferences on performance. CSI is useful to have feedback almost immediately after the interaction of the customer. The negative change in the index alarm alert signals to check the processes and initiate corrective actions and recovery strategies. Companies may also use traditional quantitative measures, such as number of customer calls attended, increase in sales orders, increase in quantity orders, up-selling statistics, cross-selling statistics, etc., for efficiency measurement of employees.

Measurement alone is not going to help the organization to promote internal atmosphere. Efficiency should be linked with a reward system. The efficiency linked with the reward system promotes productivity and workmanship among employees. It encourages all employees to busily engage in organizational activities. When all the employees engage in work with involvement, they will not have time to damage the internal environment.

THE INTERACTION PROCESS

Employee–customer interaction is the crux of CRM. Employees are basically individuals with a set of needs, wants, egos, sensibilities, abilities and willingness to participate in the customer interactive process. On the other hand, customer participation also is influenced by the pressure of needs and wants, egos, expectations, exposure and knowledge, ability, willingness and other situational factors. The purpose of the interaction between employees and customers is to generate the quality output. It is to note here that the quality judgment is the prerogative of customers. In order to make the interactive process effective it is necessary to identify various interactive points, specific processes at each interactive point, employees responsible for the operations at such interactive points and the infrastructure including ambience, tools, equipment, support services, etc. The roles of employees and customers are to be defined with clarity and communicated to each party before they initiate the interaction process.

Roles of Employees

Identification of the roles of employees begins with listing out the activities that are expected from each employee. As mentioned earlier, employees may need to perform different roles at each interactive point. These interactions are not only confined to customers but also to their coemployees. They may need to take the help of coemployees or to assist them in their work or take or give an advice or work together on a common problem. A proper description of the job, expectations, responsibilities, accountability, etc. and communicating the same effectively are helpful in performing the role of employees.

Roles of Customers

Companies must define the roles of customers in their relationship. The customer benefit programmes devised by the company are to be communicated effectively with all kinds of rules and regulations. To continue the relationship bondage and to become a beneficiary, what a customer has to perform at different situations and periods should be defined properly. Any relationship is a two-way process. No one can continue the relationship without the agreement and continuous participation from the other side. When both the parties are clear in their understanding, know what they have to expect from each other in terms of products, services and benefits, and have belief of achieving prosperity through togetherness, the relationship becomes strong and continuing.

Moments of Truth

During employee–customer interactions at every interactive point several moments take place. Each moment in the interaction is a truth that happened. The truth of the moment is the record of the quality of performance. Companies can explore enormous opportunities when they study critically the moments of truth. Each and every moment may not be having the capability of creating value perceptions to the customers. Customers may be conscious on some moments. Many more moments may not influence the conscious mind but may have influence on subconscious mind. To influence the quality perception of the customers, the primary task of the contact employees is to perform those moments qualitatively if possible beyond the expectations of the customers. The identification of other moments, which are not in the conscious list of the customers, and transforming them as experience-generating moments, is critical in achieving excellence. A careful study with sensible observations is necessary to identify the potential moments. Employees and customers together are responsible for the moments of truth. Both of them should be encouraged individually and together to contribute positively for the improvement of the moments of truth.

THE CUSTOMER RESPONSE

Customer response is the output of the CRM process. CRM provides, as mentioned already, experiences or benefits to the customers. Customer response to the CRM depends on the experience of the customer, value analysis and future benefits. Based on these three variables customer decides whether to continue or terminate the relationship with the company.

> *Customer experience management* (CEM) emphasizes a shift from technology driven relationships to human driven experiences. It believes that people create experiences and concentrates on employee interactions with customers and management of moments of truth.

The Customer Experience

Experiences are built around feelings, emotions, smells, colours, spaces, sounds, human contact, branding, time and many other factors.[21] The great experience is created not only as a result of better product features and services, but also of their ability to make the customer feel. In recent years, competitive pressures are mounting around customer experiences that create ensuring memories and lasting relationships. In fact, a new concept is gaining momentum in the name of customer experience, which is called as customer experience management (CEM). CEM emphasizes a shift from technology-driven relationships to human-driven experiences. It believes that people create experiences. It concentrates on employee interactions with customers and management of moments of truth.

Customers gain experiences with every exposure in their interaction with various facets of the company. They consolidate all such experiences relating to particular activities or experiences relating to a series of activities with the company over a period of time to find out the benefits that they could able to make out.

Value Analysis

Value is a utility-based assessment of a product by an individual. The value analysis of the relationship may include monetary benefit, social value and personal value. The performance of the company in providing satisfaction, service quality and status against competitive offerings is considered by customers for the value analysis.

Future Benefits

Customers show their concern not only on the current benefits but also on expected future benefits. Companies should understand that customers are involved planners and forecasters as well as evaluators of their services. Customers' expectations of future benefits influence future relations with the company. If customers expect more benefits in future, they prefer to continue or strengthen their relationship with the company. If they anticipate future regret, they prefer to discontinue or terminate the relationship.

e-CRM

Implementing CRM is certain to involve the deployment of new technologies. The deployment of such technologies gives an insight into the rate of growth of CRM applications (e-CRM).[22] e-CRM denotes the use of electronics particularly the Internet for CRM. The explosive rise of the World Wide Web (www) in the mid-1990s facilitated the use of the Internet for managing customer relations. Companies realized that the Internet has significant potential for increasing revenue, decreasing costs and retaining customers through improved customer services. "The e-CRM is a combination of business process and technology that seeks to understand a company's customer from a multifaceted perspective. It helps companies to define enterprise-wide business rules that ensure consistent treatment for customers regardless of how they contact the company. CRM-oriented businesses market their products and services through relationships and interactions with multiple markets, most notably the customer market, often taking advantage of IT-based interactivity."[23] CRM frequently uses IT technology to attract and retain customers. "The application of IT technology allows for IT-based interactivity that makes it possible for customers to have access to product and service information much faster than earlier."[24]

Applications of e-CRM

e-CRM system has been recently adopted in the industry as an overall system for managing not only contacts but also accounts, opportunities, activities, marketing, customer support, partner/channel support and many other sales and service processes.[25] e-CRM implies capabilities such as self-service knowledge base, automated e-mail response, personalization of Web contact, on-line product bundling and pricing and so on. "It gives Internet users the ability to interact with the business through their preferred communication channel, and it allows the business to offset expensive customer service agents with technology. So the value is largely on of improved customers satisfaction and reduced cost through improved efficiency."[26] The serious limitations for the use of e-CRM are the electronic infrastructure of the company and net using customer population. During the last one-and-a-half decades the two limitations got marginalized due to the widespread presence and accessibility of Internet facilities."Services Marketing Insight: Markets for e-CRM" discusses the markets.

> *"**e-CRM** refers to the application of electronics to CRM. The advancements in information technology and the emergence of the Internet in a big way as an interactive devise facilitate relationship management through electronic medium."*

BENEFITS OF e-CRM

The world is witnessing the most significant transformation in the business landscape called e-CRM. "Delivering pure Internet applications directly to browsers will empower a global workforce to know, to do, to measure, and to improve their jobs in support of a common, customer-oriented strategy. This is the promise of CRM."[27] e-CRM is useful to companies to optimize value of interactive relationships by way of personalized reach. "The new database technologies enable people to get the knowledge of who the customers are, what they bought and when they bought, and even predictions based on the historical behavior."[28] The available e-CRM technology is capable of delivering significant benefits to service companies when they are driven by well-focused business objectives. With the use of e-CRM, companies can gain the following benefits:

- Data and information can be recorded easily.
- Greater flexibility in classification of data into various subsections and possibility to establish different links for using.
- Fast in processing facilitates and improved response time.

21.2 Services Marketing Insight **Market for e-CRM**

CRM is an information industry term for methodologies, software and usually Internet capabilities that help an enterprise manage customer relationships in an organized way.[29] The CRM market is still immature and seems to include everything from contact management and call centre systems to fully integrated enterprise-wide solutions. Investing in the technologies can be expensive, so companies must have a clear understanding of the requirements and the benefits.[30] The market for e-CRM can be broadly segmented into two parts: market for CRM software and market for CRM services. CRM software is intended to provide the software package for data warehousing and front-end operations. The services segment includes consultation, integration, outsource services and training. The CRM services segment is significantly larger than the CRM software segment. Since CRM services have high potential for growth, a number of companies entering into this business area. The competition is becoming intense day by day. The ever increasing investments by companies all over the world are expanding the market qualitatively and quantitatively. The different CRM solution offerings comprises customer development, sales management and support, market analysis, service centres, virtual marketing, telemarketing, product and brand management, etc.

Seibel Systems is the pioneer in the CRM industry. It is one of the largest CRM vendors in the world. There are many companies such as Oracle, Talisma, SAP and Amdocs competing to capture the market. Indian companies though realized the usefulness of e-CRM their progress in this direction is not impressive. High cost of implementation, inadequate IT infrastructure, less percentage of adaptable customers and product-centric approach of many companies are considered deterrents for the growth of the e-CRM market in the country. However, the financial sector and services sector have taken a lead in implementing e-CRM systems. In the banking sector, ICICI bank and City Bank are the leaders in adopting e-CRM.

- Accesses to relevant information for supporting decision making.
- Cost-effective communication and service.
- Functional all the time.
- Higher revenues through cross-selling and up-selling
- Customer identification and contact at the quickest possible time.
- Reduced complaints from customers.
- Individualized access to the information if necessary by password and pin numbers.
- Improvement in the customer service by facilitating communication in the following ways:
  - Potential problems of the customers can be identified before they occur so that problems can be prevented.
  - It uses Internet cookies to track customer interests and to design customized product offerings.
  - It provides a fast mechanism for after-sales services.
  - Customers are provided with service information and technical assistance on Web sites.

- ▷ User-friendly mechanism is provided for registering and handling customer complaints.
- ▷ Internet promotes collaborative customization.
- ▷ By integrating into other cross-functional systems customers are provided with the information of their interest.
- ▷ Accessibility is provided 24/7.
- ▷ A fast mechanism is provided for managing cognitive dissonance and scheduling follow-up sales calls.

Technically, e-CRM facilitates functioning of an organization in five different ways. First, it provides scalability in the sense that the company can use e-CRM on a large scale and can safely and reliably expand to the greater scales as per the future needs. Second, it provides multiple communication channels by which the company can enhance its interactive abilities with customers by using different devises such as phone and Internet. Third, it facilitates workflow in the organization by automatically routing the work through the system based on a preset programme to different internal customers in the organization. Fourth, it provides data inventory in a centralized storage in the classified form for the use of customer interaction. Last, it takes care of customer privacy when needed by destructing records or data encryption so as to ensure that the records are not stolen or abused.

> *e-CRM provides scalability, multiple communication channels, workflow, data inventory and customer privacy. Companies and customers can exploit the benefits of electronic applications in the CRM process.*

TYPES OF e-CRM

e-CRM systems can be classified into the following three categories: operational CRM, analytical CRM and collaborative CRM.

> *Operational CRM relates to the basic business policies like marketing, sales and service. Analytical CRM is used to analyse raw data and interpret from the point of view of corporate objectives and strategy. Collaborative CRM facilitates customers to perform services on their own through a variety of interactive channels.*

Operational CRM

It relates to basic business policies such as marketing, sales and service. Operational CRM is applied in the following three areas in business: enterprise marketing automation (EMA) that provides information relating to business environment, competitors and trends in the industry. The second area is sales and sales force management. The operational CRM provides sales force automation (SAF) that covers sales and sales force automation functions such as consumer research, performance evaluation of sales personal, etc. The third area is related to consumer service and support (CSS). It covers customer complaints, customer request on information and service, service recovery and so on.

Analytical CRM

Under this system, the raw data generated at various interaction points are used for analysis and interpretation to draw useful inferences. The intelligence gathered is transmitted to different managers and concerned employees to support them in handling situations.

Collaborative CRM

This system is used to facilitate customers to perform services on their own through a variety of communication and interactive channels. While most organizations have the ability to collect information, they don't have a coherent and effective strategy to analyse and process this tremendous amount of data into actionable information. The current wisdom in both the on-line and off-line worlds is that, with storage memory costs continuously falling, "if you don't know what information to keep, keep it all." Such economics have forced businesses into a "data-rich, information-poor scenario." Corporations that have undertaken data warehousing projects have learned the hard way just how complicated and difficult it can be to decide what information to look at, how to analyse it and what to do with the results.[31] Collaborative CRM provides for channeling of the data and information appropriately to the right people at the right time.

CRITERIA FOR THE SELECTION OF e-CRM SOFTWARE

One needs to exercise a lot of caution in choosing a CRM solution. Choosing a wrong CRM solution for a wrong platform can be very expensive, and sometimes it is suicidal. The advice of the consultant, who could add value in its selection process, may be worth considering. Consultants do provide the benefit of experience gained elsewhere and bring in the best practices that are hard to replicate internally. Successful implementation requires understanding and accessing a company's competencies and capabilities to deliver and its commitment to quality of its service.[32] For the selection of software packages for e-CRM the following criteria are used.

- *Functionality:* The features of the system should be capable of solving the business challenges. The system should facilitate the execution of the CRM strategy. It should allow for data synchronization and should support the decision-making process. The package should have relevant architecture suitable to the needs of the company.
- *Flexibility:* Since the business operates in a dynamic environment the software package adapted for CRM should be flexible enough to make changes to the system whenever needed.
- *Integration:* In the process of business growth and development service companies align with other support services or other companies. The package of CRM should be capable of integrating with the database of other firms or services.
- *Scalability:* The system should be useful to accommodate the larger scale of operations and growth of the business to any extent reliably. The system should not experience any down time with the increase of the load on servers.
- *Simple and Usable:* The system should be simple and user friendly.
- *Cost:* The bottom line is that the cost of the CRM package should not be more than the benefits expected from it.

> *"Selection of e-CRM package is an important concern for management. The qualities of a good package include functionality, flexibility, integration, scalability, simplicity and usability."*

SUMMARY

- Customer relationship management is emerging as the core theme of the business in recent years.
- It involves transformation of each and every process of the business from hitherto product-centric philosophy to the customer-centric philosophy.
- Development of adequate loyal and profitable customer base for current and future needs of the company is the objective of customer relationship management.
- Identification of customers for building relationships, designing strategy to build and promote relationships and channelizing the CRM process throughout the organization are the tasks for the management of the company.
- The CRM objective is to establish, maintain and promote relationships with customers. Companies cannot be blind in establishing relationship with every customer. Because CRM involves expenditure, companies should conduct a thorough analysis for the selection of customers.
- The customer- and organizational-related input data help the organization classify customer and finally select them for establishing relationships.
- Companies should carefully design the management framework of CRM reflecting the organizations' desired objectives.
- Each stage in the management process should be supported with suitable technology in the form of hardware and software.
- Selection of the right customers to build relationships and to maintain and enhance relationships is of vital importance.
- Employees are crucial players in the CRM process. Therefore, companies are required to install the employee relationship management system to have a workable and effective CRM.
- The ultimate aim of CRM is to ensure continued relationships with customers through sharing value and delightful experiences.
- e-CRM has become a buzz word in corporate circles.
- Many companies are investing heavily on this to develop customer database and to improve the quality of customer services. Though it is very useful for the effective CRM operations, care should be taken in the selection of right software for the company.

KEY TERMS

Analytical CRM *435*
Communal Co-ordination *427*
CRM costs *423*
Customer experience *432*
Customer loyalty *418*
Customer relationship management *414*
Customer retention *418*
Customer value *417*
Defectors *421*
Efficiency measurement and reward *420*
Employee orientation *428*
Flexibility *436*
Functionality *436*
Hostages *421*
Integral Co-ordinations *437*
Loyalists *421*
Mercenaries *421*
Moments of truth *431*
Operational CRM *435*
Scalability *436*
Value analysis *432*

BRIEF QUESTIONS

1. Explain the concept and importance of CRM.
2. Discuss the following concepts
   (a) Customer value
   (b) Customer satisfaction
   (c) Customer retention
3. Explain different types of customers.
4. How do you analyse the cost of consumer relationship?
5. Explain the types of e-CRM.

ESSAY QUESTIONS

1. What are the differences between traditional marketing and customer retention-focused marketing?
2. Describe customer- and organizational-related input of CRM framework relating to hospitality services.
3. Describe CRM framework by taking a customer service firm as an example.
4. Describe the organizational system of CRM and explain the importance of employee orientation.
5. What is e-CRM? Explain its benefits and applications.
6. What is the criterion for the selection of e-CRM software?

ASSIGNMENTS

1. Select a company, which provides on-line services to the customers, of your choice and study:
   (a) How the company is providing customer value
   (b) How customers are persuaded to become loyal through CRM
2. Mobile teleservices companies are investing heavily to attract the customers of other companies through attractive packages and price offers. Yet customer loyalty is reported to be high in this service segment. You are required to collect the opinion of a few customers of different brands in the category and find out:
   (a) The loyalty switch over behaviour of the consumers
   (b) The role of CRM in building customer loyalty

REFERENCES

1 C. K. Prahalad and V. Rama Swamy, "Co-opting Customer Competence," *Harvard Business Review*, (January–February, 2000): 80.

2 Jill Dyche, *The CRM Handbook: A Business Guide to Customer Relationship Management*. (New Delhi: Pearson Education, 2004), p. 3.

3 A. Parvatiyar and J. N. Sheth, Conceptual Framework of Customer Relationship Management, in Sheth, Parvatiyar and Shainesh (Eds.), *Customer Relationship Management: Emerging Concepts, Tools and Applications*. (New Delhi: McGraw-Hill, 2000), pp. 3–25.

4 F. Newell, *Loyalty.com: Customer Relationship Management in the New Era of Internet Marketing*. (New York, NY: McGraw-Hill, 2000).

5 Christopher Bull, "Strategic Issues in Customer Relationship Management (CRM) Implementation," *Business Process Management Journal*, 9, no. 5 (2003): 595.

6 Yurong Xu et al., "Adopting Customer Relationship Management Technology," *Industrial Management & Data Systems*, 102/8 (2002): 442.

7 Christopher Bull, "Strategic Issues in Customer Relationship Management (CRM) Implementation," *Business Process Management Journal*, 9, no. 5 (2003) 596.

8 Thomas O. Jones and W. Earl Sesser, Jr., "Why Satisfied Customers Defect," *Harvard Business Review*, (November–December 1995).

9 Manoj Kumar, "Driving CRM Practices," *Indian Management*, (November 2002): 10.

10 Thomas O. Jones and W. Earl Sesser, Jr., "Why Satisfied Customers Defect," *Harvard Business Review*, (November–December 1995).

11 Ibid., p. 96.

12 E. Clemons, "Gathering the Nectar, Understanding CRM: Financial Times," *Spring Supplement*, (2000): 24–27.

13 M. P. Jaiswal and Anjali Kaushik, *e-CRM: Business & System Frontiers*. (New Delhi: Asian Books Private Limited, 2002), p. 18.

14 Don Peppers, Martha Rogers and Bob Dorf, "Is Your Company Ready for One-to-One Marketing?," *Harvard Business Review*, (January–February 1999): 153.

15 Michael Treacy and Fred Wiersema, "Customer Intimacy and Other Value Disciplines," *Harvard Business Review*, (January–February 1993): 84.

16 Don Peppers, Martha Rogers and Bob Dorf, "Is Your Company Ready for One-to-One Marketing?," *Harvard Business Review*, (January–February 1999): 157.

17 Ranjay Gulati and James B. Oldroyd, "The Quest for Customer Focus," *Harvard Business Review*, (April 2005).
18 Ibid.
19 Lior Arussy, "The Myth of the Efficient Lover," *Indian Management*, (March 2005): 65.
20 Sanjay Badhe and Sridevi Rao, "Increasing Customer Loyalty Through Employee Focus," *Indian Management*, (March 2004): 49.
21 Alexandra Thusy and Langdon Morris, "From CRM to Experience Management," *Indian Management*, (January 2005): 46.
22 Dotun Adebanjo, "Classifying and Selecting e-CRM Applications: An Analysis-based Proposal," *Management Decision*, 41/6 (2003): 570.
23 L. Ryals and A. Payne, "Customer Relationship Management in Financial Services: Towards Information-Enabled Relationship Marketing," *Journal of Strategic Marketing*, 9 (2001): 3–27.
24 Adam Lindgreen and Michael Antioco, "Customer Relationship Management: The Case of a European bank," *Marketing Intelligence & Planning*, 23, no. 2 (2005): 139.
25 M. P. Jaiswal, Anjali Kaushik, *e-CRM; Business and System Frontiers*. (New Delhi: Asian Books Private Limited, 2002): 12.
26 Paul Greenberg, *CRM at the Speed of Light*, (New Delhi: McGraw-Hill, 2003), p. 54.
27 P. Greenberg, *CRM at the Speed of Light: Capturing and Keeping Customers in Internet Real Time*. (Berkley, CA: Osborne/McGraw-Hill, 2001).
28 Yurong Xu et al., "Adopting Customer Relationship Management Technology," *Industrial Management & Data Systems*, 102/8 (2002): 442.
29 Ibid.
30 Russel S. Winer, A, "Framework for Customer Relationship Management," *California Management Review*, 43, no. 4 (2001): 89–105.
31 V. Venkata Ramana and G. Somayajulu, *Customer Relationship Management—A key to Corporate Success*. (New Delhi: Excel books, 2003): 179.
32 Ibid., p.159.

International Marketing of Services

22

LEARNING OBJECTIVES

After studying this chapter, you will be able to:

- Understand the importance of international marketing
- Understand the international marketing environment
- Understand the market entry strategies
- Understand the trade barriers
- Understand the international marketing programme

Calpana Communications Ltd has been in the business of creative advertising of financial services for the last 15 years in India. During its initial days, it could attract the big brands in India, which enabled it to make a mark for itself in the market. The business has been growing steadily for the last five years—from a single office to branches in all the four metros. The management now plans to expand into the international market. To analyse and comprehend the trends in the international market, the management has appointed a three-member committee chaired by Mr. Pankaj Kapoor. The other two committee members—an academic and a management consultant—have been drawn from outside the company.

To study the trends in advertising services, the company undertook desk research focusing on three important issues—business growth rate, competitiveness, and the number of successfully established international companies in advertising. The committee found that in developed countries there is intense competition in this segment owing to the presence of numerous national and international organizations many of which are well-established multinationals. Though the growth and success rates of foreign companies in these countries are impressive, attempting an entry into such countries may not be ideal for Calpana Communication's maiden venture in a foreign market. Developing countries such as China and South Africa were found to be more suitable for Calpana Communications—both in terms of the business and the cultural environments. The committee, therefore, recommended planning marketing operations in these two countries as a beginning, and, gradually expanding into other markets.

Mr. Kapoor submitted the report to the management with this observation: "The business prospects in these two countries are bright but very few foreign companies are successful in different businesses. In advertising services, the success graph is fluctuative. It is necessary to promote a universal brand name of the company. Marketing strategy is a critical success factor for the company."

Questions:

1. Is it necessary for a successful company in India with a vast potential for growth to enter into the international markets?
2. Do you agree with the observations of the committee? Why or why not?
3. What market entry strategy would you suggest for the company?
4. What are, in your opinion, the key points of success for the company in international marketing?

INTRODUCTION

Services play an important role in world trade. The intense competition due to trade across the borders has promoted innovativeness, quality consciousness and customer orientation in service companies, which helped expand markets and increas trade further. The world imports of services in 2006 stands at USD 2.6 trillion. The United States is the major services-importing country. The share of the USA in the total world services imports was 11.7 per cent in 2006. Germany with an 8.2 per cent share and the UK with a 6.5 per cent share occupy second and third positions in world imports of services, respectively. India occupies the 12th position with a 2.7 per cent share in world service imports in 2006. The major demand for services is from developed countries. According to WTO data, 73 per cent of total service imports are from 30 importers.

The major services with an international business record include transportation, travel, communication, construction, insurance, financial, computer and information, other business services, personal, cultural and recreation services, legal, and accounting services. These services have a global demand. There will be a demand for innovative services in any area provided they are marketed well. The study of international marketing helps understand the critical dimensions of the business.

> *International trade in services is growing fast mainly due to the integration of telecommunications with computer and Internet technologies. The intensified competition due to service trade across the boarders promotes innovativeness, quality consciousness and customer orientation in service companies.*

The last two decades of the twentieth century saw fundamental changes in the international marketing of services in the form of globalization of markets, decline in trade barriers and the emergence of modern communication and information technology. Further, the ability to process and analyse data efficiently and the diffusion of Internet and telecom technologies helped service providers to reach markets outside the country and strengthen their business[1]. However, the characteristics of services stand in the way of general flow of the operational processes compared to international marketing of goods. Intangibility is the key characteristic of a service that creates problems in patenting the services. Therefore, services cannot be protected through patents[2]. Services are perishable and therefore cannot be stored and transported. This creates problems for international expansion. It is more risky for the service firm to go for international expansion as the company, unlike the goods company, does not enjoy the same opportunities for learning from gradual experience. "The international marketer of services has got no choice but to deal directly with the foreign customer[3]." The options available are (1) to offer services at the host country either by establishing own service outlets or by using private and e-channels or (2) to attract the customers from foreign countries to the home-country service outlets or (3) to service in both ways.

> *The challenges of marketing services internationally are many compared to manufactured goods. The service characteristics such as intangibility, inseparability and perishability stand in the way of general flow of processes of international marketing of services. It leaves no choice except to serve the foreign customer directly.*

WHAT IS INTERNATIONAL MARKETING?

International marketing is marketing of goods or services beyond the boundaries of domestic market. If any company sells its services in two or more countries, it is carrying international marketing. "In international marketing, governments, quasi government agencies, and profit seeking and non-profit entities are frequently the buyers[4]." Domestic marketing and international

> **Domestic marketing** *refers to marketing of services in the home country. Service marketers can manage domestic market by facing the challenges of one set of uncontrollables. International services marketer has to face challenges from two or more sets of uncontrollables.*

marketing differ in one major perspective. In domestic marketing, companies have to develop marketing programmes to face the challenges of one set of uncontrollables. In international marketing, companies have to handle two or more sets of uncontrollables in designing marketing programmes.

Many companies, of late, tried to enter into foreign markets to execute their business expansion strategies. There are basically nine facilitating factors for aiming at international marketing:

- Reforms in international trade and tariff agreements resulting lowering trade barriers and tariffs and thus making markets more attractive.
- Developments in logistics and transportation.
- Interdependency in production and operations in many businesses.
- Rapid pace of development in communication and information technology.
- Database availability on various markets of the world.
- Internationalized capital markets.
- Emergence of World Trade Organization to facilitate the trade processes.
- Growing opportunities to exploit the potential of new business ideas.
- Opportunities to utilize capacity fully and to safeguard against demand fluctuations.

COMPANIES' ORIENTATION TO INTERNATIONAL MARKETING

Marketing is a universal discipline, yet needs to be differentiated as per the needs and wants of different groups of people belonging to different regions of the world. Mere extension of one programme designed for a specific market to the other market may not yield similar results. Differentiation is necessary as no two groups or markets are similar in nature any where in the world. International marketing demands adaptation to diverse needs of different groups in different nations. An important task therefore is "to learn to recognize the extent to which marketing plans and programmes can be extended worldwide, as well as the extent to which they must be adopted[5]."

> **Ethnocentricity** *refers to a feeling of superiority of the company products and services over the same in other countries. Due to ethnocentricity, service companies try to capitalize the similarities in the market of the host country.*

The orientation of company's management is an important dimension. This orientation depends upon beliefs of the management of a company toward the markets in the world and their company operations. The orientations of organizations worldwide are broadly classified into three types: ethnocentric, polycentric and geocentric.

Ethnocentricity refers to a feeling of superiority of the company products and services over the same in other countries. Thus, it is a strong orientation of the company toward the home country. The company personnel believe that the services offered in the home country will be accepted as they are in other countries also. The management does not want to change the service package for international markets as it sees more similarities and assumes that its services are superior to that of the similar services available in the foreign market. For example, the American international air transport companies like American Airlines do not change their package of services for Indians when operated in India.

Polycentricity is to differentiate totally the service package as per the needs of the market of the host country. This orientation is totally opposite to that of ethnocentricity. The assumption is that every market is unique with a different set of characteristics. Companies focus on identifying differences between the markets and design the marketing programme in such a way that specifically addresses the differences in markets. The difference between ethnocentric and polycentric philosophies is obvious. Companies with ethnocentric philosophy try to identify the similarities between the home-country market and markets in foreign countries and bank on them to market their services. Companies with polycentric philosophy identify and focus on the differences between domestic market and foreign markets. Localization of services is given priority in the marketing strategy.

> ***Polycentricity*** *refers to total adaptation to the specialities of the foreign market. The service company identifies the differences between home market and host market and develops the service offer differently taking into consideration the unique features of the host market.*

Geocentricity is the widely followed philosophy world over. It is in a way a compromise between ethnocentricity and polycentricity, which directs to two extreme ends. Geocentricity has global orientation rather than to one or two specific foreign markets. Companies identify global similarities and local distinctions and develop programmes to satisfy both the elements. Thus, globalization of similarities and localization of differentials are the key strength of this orientation. *Global plus local becomes "glocal."* The geocentric philosophy promotes glocal orientation. This orientation helps to build global brands and strengthen brand equity globally. McDonald's India is an example for geocentricity.

McDonald's India

McDonald's India is a wholly owned subsidiary of McDonald International. The international giant has a presence in more than 120 countries with about 30,000 restaurants. The company adopted different entry strategies in different markets. The franchisee system is used widely as 70 per cent of the restaurant owners are independent local businessmen and businesswomen. McDonald's entered India by establishing a company and promoting joint ventures—one with Connaught Plaza Restaurants Pvt. Ltd in the northern and the southern parts of the country and the other with Hard Castle Restaurants Pvt. Ltd in the western and southern parts.

The company's philosophy is to maintain a geocentric orientation. It has maintained its global image by maintaining quality, service, cleanliness and value at par with the global standards. The benchmark practices the company pioneered over the years at the international level are followed in all its restaurants. The corporate mission is to provide high-quality products, served quickly and with a smile, in a clean and pleasant environment and all at a fair price. The brand mark and the physical environment of each restaurant reflect its international identity. The local aspects are taken care of by employing local staff, procuring from local suppliers and offering vegetarian and non-vegetarian products with local flavours. To demonstrate its high degree of respect for the local customs and culture, McDonald's India does not offer any beef or pork items.

> *Geocentricity* refers to a balancing approach combining the specialities of the service and local specifications. Service companies try to project and protect certain global features in the service offer and at the same time include some distinctive local features into it. This approach is popularly called as "glocal" approach.

Management orientation is critical to designing and developing marketing programmes for international marketing of services. It is premature to say which of the three is better. It depends upon market conditions (specifically related to the services being marketed) prevalent in the host country. Managements may change their orientation from one philosophy to the other over a period of time based on their experiences.

THE INTERNATIONAL MARKETING ENVIRONMENT

An understanding of the business environment prevalent in various countries is essential to identify business opportunities and to develop strategies for marketing of services internationally. It is particularly important to know and understand the cultural and social, political and legal environments. The following is the brief description of these environments.

> International marketers basically search for cultural universals. They look for similarities in cultural and social systems. When some universal aspects are identified in connection with a service concept the marketers find an opportunity to standardize fully or partially the marketing programme.

- *Cultural and Social Environment:* The influence of culture and society on the behaviour of an individual has been discussed in Chapter 5. International marketers basically search for cultural universals. In other words, they look for similarities in cultural and social systems. When some universal aspects are identified in connection with a service concept the marketers find an opportunity to standardize fully or partially the marketing programme. Basing on the impact of culture on behaviour of people, countries can be classified as high context culture or low context culture[6]. The people of high context culture societies have deep rooted cultural values and traditions. In a high context culture such as South Korea, Taiwan, Japan, China, Arab, Greek, etc, people rely less on verbal communication and infer more from the context of non-verbal actions and environmental settings. In low context culture such as USA, UK, Germany etc. people rely more on verbal communication[7]. Service companies should learn the cross-cultural aspects of various societies as the success of service business is influenced mostly by the quality of interactions. The variations in perceptions due to culture are discussed in Services Marketing Insight: Asian vs. Western Cultures Impact on Travel and Tourism Services.
- *Political Environment:* Political environment refers to governmental institutions and organizations and political parties and their philosophies in the host country. The rulers and people of a country exercise power through the political system that exists. International marketers should necessarily understand the structure of the government and its polity of the host country targeted and analyse critical issues relating to the proposed service business with the country. One of the critical dimensions of the political environment is "political risk." It refers to the risk of changes in government policy. Whenever there is a change in the party in power, the changes in policy are likely to take place. The political parties will have differing philosophies to that of the opposite party, and it is quite obvious that the party in power changes the

22.1 Services Marketing Insight | **Asian Versus Western Cultures: The Impact on Travel and Tourism Services**

The impact of culture on services has become more critical with intense competition in international trade. As culture provides the framework for social interactions, service encounters vary from culture to culture. Service delivery involves customer contact and employee–customer interactions. Cultural factors, therefore, exert great influence on customer-perceived quality. It is especially true in case of high-contact services. It is necessary to adapt service delivery behaviour to the values of differing cultural groups.

The study of Anna S. Mattila on Asian and Western cultures in relation to travel and tourism services provides useful insight. The following are the key findings.

- Business travellers from Asian and Western cultures acted as a homogeneous group, irrespective of their cultural background. The ratings on service encounters were similar. They focused on output but not the style of the service delivery. Output efficiency including speed was more important than the functional quality of interaction.
- Leisure travellers were more heterogeneous in their needs and expectations. Asians gave very low ratings to the service encounter and overall service quality. Asians expected more personal service delivery whereas the Western counterparts expected less personal service delivery.
- Asian leisure travellers expected to be treated as deserving high-quality service irrespective of the type of service encounter. Brief and routine interactions designed to suit Western cultures failed to satisfy Asians as such processes downplay the importance of status difference. Therefore, Asian leisure travellers were less happy with the service than their Western counterparts.
- Asian customers, compared to their Western counterparts, might be less willing to reflect their feelings through their facial expressions.
- Western travellers make more eye contact than Asians and also smile more.
- Purchase motivation is an influencing factor of consumer perception.
- Regardless of the cultural background, the mood of leisure travellers is more positive than business travellers after the service encounter.

The study reveals that Asian and Western leisure travellers differently perceive the quality of the focal service encounter. Business travellers, on the other hand, are similar in their perceptions.

Source: Anna S. Mattila, "The Role of Culture and Purchase Motivations in Service Encounter Evaluations," Journal of Services Marketing, *13, no. 4/5 (1999): 376–389.*

policy to make sure their party philosophies are incorporated. A change in government policy may create opportunities or affect adversely the company's ability to perform. For example, the Industrial Policy 1991 of Indian government created opportunities for many foreign companies to operate their service businesses in India.

- *Legal Environment:* Law is binding on all businesses. International business is governed by international law which includes the law of nations and international commercial law. The key issues connected to legal environment of target countries are establishment of service

> "Political environment influences service business significantly in any country. The political parties, their ideologies and future orientations affect the business either positively or negatively. Political risk is involved in international marketing of services."

outlets and agreements with channel members, jurisdiction of host country courts, tariffs and taxation, patents and trade marks, restrictive business practices, licensing and trade secrets, bribery and corruption, litigation, conflict resolution, and dispute settlement, etc. The laws of the land specify all or many details of all the issues mentioned above. Service companies should design the marketing programmes within the purview of the legal environment. They should also have an understanding of regulatory environment of the host country which consists of governmental and non-governmental agencies that enforce prevailing laws and formulate guidelines for the business in the country.

TRADE BARRIERS

> "International business is governed by international law which includes the law of nations and international commercial law. Every company is obligated to follow the prevalent legal system of the host country."

Market access for services internationally is limited by visible and invisible trade barriers. These barriers continue to exist in spite of consistent efforts by the international trade organizations like World Trade Organization. Service companies face visible as well as non-visible trade barriers. The following are the trade barriers in relation to some specific services.

1. *Financial Services*: There are access problems to operate in the U.S. market under state law for insurance. The fragmentation of the U.S. market into 56 different jurisdictions requiring different licensing, solvency, operating requirements. The regulatory structure also varies among different jurisdictions. Foreign companies have to name a U.S. attorney and lodge a trust fund in a U.S. bank of up to USD 60 million to get approval. In banking services, it is necessary to maintain "asset pledges" in addition to the paid-up capital in their home country.
2. *Legal Services*: The requirements for offering legal services are set by concerned state bar associations in the United States. Though New York, Texas, Washington DC, and California allow foreign lawyers to practice, many states require a minimum of five years' work experience. In Sweden, the use of the Swedish title "advokat" was protected. The non-citizens cannot use this title. Under the conditional revised offers (2005) of the EU, this has been cleverly reworded as "Admission to the Bar necessary only for the Swedish title 'advokat' which is subject to a residency requirement." Though foreign lawyers can freely offer legal services when not appearing under the title "advokat," this protection creates an artificial barrier in the form of Grade A and Grade B lawyers. In Japan also, for legal services, there is the need to be recognized as "Gaikoku-Jimu-Bengoshi" by the Minister of Justice. Legal services have to be supplied by a lawyer qualified as a "Bengoshi" under Japanese law. Japan has refused to remove the most restrictive regulatory hurdle-facing foreign lawyers in the country—the ban on hiring or forming partnerships with Japanese lawyers (Bengoshi) in Japan[8].
3. *Health Care Services*: The national health services system of EC countries like UK denies access to services from outside the country. U.S.

medical insurance companies do not cover medical expenditure incurred abroad. Market access in Germany is restricted to only natural persons in the case of medical, dental and midwives services.

4. *Communication Services*: In the United States, access is denied to non-U.S. firms and foreign-owned firms to invest in radio telecommunications infrastructure and to provide mobile and satellite services due to stringent legislation. The U.S. law enforcement agencies impose strict corporate governance requirements on companies seeking approval to take over a U.S. firm in this business area.
5. *Transport Services*: Restrictions are there in owning air carriers as it is possible to have only up to 49 per cent stake in a U.S. carrier. Many restrictions are imposed in water transport for foreign companies.
6. *IT and TTES*: Some states of the United States passed laws to limit business outsourcing. Restrictions on H1 B visas are the new barrier. The domestic companies are protected and non-U.S. companies are denied access in many fronts.
7. *Audio-Visual Services*: There are restrictions in many countries. In France, there is a rule that 60 per cent of the movies on television must be made in Europe and more than 40 per cent of the programmes must be broadcasted in French. In Arab countries also, many restrictions are there for audio-visual services from outside.

> *Market access to foreign countries is limited by trade barriers. Some barriers are general and some are service specific. Some are direct and some are indirect. Negotiations and trade agreements with respective countries are helpful in breaking the barriers.*

THE WORLD TRADE ORGANIZATION (WTO)

The WTO came into existence in 1995 for liberalizing trade among nations. It has set up a rule-based system of multilateral trading worldwide. WTO agreements are negotiated and signed by many of the world's trading countries. These documents provide legal ground rules in the international trade and help in preventing conflicts.

WTO has inherited trading system of General Agreement on Tariffs and Trade (GATT) which was in existence since 1948. GATT has mainly dealt with trade in goods. The WTO and its agreements expanded its scope to cover trade in services and intellectual property rights. WTO agreements aim to support fair competition in services.

The General Agreement on Trade in Services (GATS) came into existence in 1995 as a treaty of WTO. The GATS agreement covers four modes of cross-border service trade.

1. *Cross-border Supply*: In this mode, the services are delivered within the territory of the member country from the territory of the provider country. For example, an American company providing services to Indians in India without having its physical presence in India.
2. *Consumption Abroad*: In this mode, the services are delivered outside the territory of the member country. In other words, the services are provided in the territory of foreign country to the people of the

> "*The World Trade Organization facilitated the inclusion of services in the international trade agreements. The General Agreement on Trade in Services (GATS) covers four modes of cross-border service trade: cross-border supply, consumption abroad, commercial presence and presence of a natural person.*"

member country. For example, an American company providing services to Indians in America.

3. *Commercial Presence*: In this mode, services are delivered within the territory of the member country by establishing service units in the host country. For example, Indians are served by an American company through its outlets established in India.
4. *Presence of a Natural Person*: In this mode, services are delivered within the territory of the host country through a natural person. A natural person is a human being but not an artificial entity as per law like a company, association, etc. For example, some persons from India may go to foreign countries to serve in different services.

WTO negotiations are taking place in 151 services. The national governments have an option to exclude any specific service from GATS. Many countries are promoting trade in services. The United States supported GATS after it found the potential of this sector to shape interactional trade in future.

22.1 Services Marketing Insight **Measures for Promoting Indian Services Exports**

The services exports from India are growing in volume as well as in number of destinations since the beginning to this decade. The value of services exports was USD 81,330 million in 2006–2007 registering a growth of 32.5 per cent over previous year. Travel, transportation and software services are the major services exported. Business services mainly consisting of architectural, engineering and other technical services, insurance and other financial services have high potential for capturing markets abroad. Service exporters need to be supported by the Government of India on the following lines:

- Supply of relevant market information to the exporters and supporting them to be identified as providers of quality services.
- Export financing with reduced transaction costs.
- Resolving social security benefits issues with target countries by concluding tantalization agreements.
- Simplifying visa process at least for selected countries.
- Inclusion of services trade in regional trade agreements, free trade agreements and comprehensive economic cooperation agreement.
- Focus on exportable services in selected SEZs.
- Working on the removal of trade barriers by way of negotiating with different countries.
- The lines of credit extended by India to many countries through Exim Bank under India's Development Initiative should carry specific lines of focus on promoting service exports particularly construction services, IT-related services and education services.
- The export potential of services such as health care, satellite mapping, project exports, R&D, design and engineering, ship repair services, printing, accounting and auditing, unskilled labour services, etc., should be recognized and promoted.
- Domestic regulations such as licensing requirements and procedures and qualification requirements and procedures need to be liberalized.

Source: Strategy for India's Services Sector: Broad contours, www.finmin, nic.in/workingpaper/1_2007_DEA.pdf.

Singapore, Hongkong, China, Indonesia, India, Malaysia, etc., are also promoting trade in services by incorporating many policy changes in home country. India has high potential for service trade internationally. It has to focus on various issues that stand as barrier of trade. The measures required for the support of international trade in services are discussed in Services Marketing Insight: Measures for Promoting Indian Services Exports.

THE MARKETING PROGRAMME

The marketing programme should begin with the planning for international operations (see Fig. 22.1). It includes the detailed sketch of objectives, orientations and activities of an organization in relation to the international markets. The objectives of the service company should be defined clearly to evolve consistent policy orientation for the domestic and international business. The management of the company needs to spell out the degree of internationalization and the degree of commitment to international marketing. It is related to the proposed composition of domestic and international business, their interdependency, value propositions and the company's interest in operations outside the country. Planning is essential whether the company is planning

> *"The management of a service company needs to spell out the degree of internationalization and the degree of commitment to international marketing. It relates to the proposed composition of domestic and international business, their interdependency, value propositions and the company's interest in operation outside the country."*

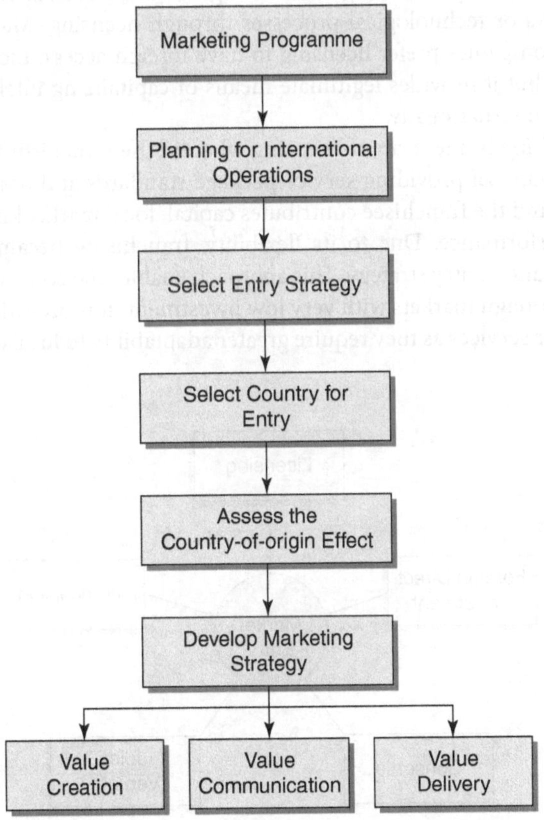

Fig. 22.1 Designing a marketing programme

to enter foreign market for the first time or already is in business with several countries. If it is for the first-time entry in foreign markets or to a new country, market entry strategy needs to be developed along with other market operations. In case of already existing businesses in foreign markets, the marketing programme deals with value creation, value communication and value delivery. International and country-specific business trends need to be analysed from the point of view of company's core competencies to identify business opportunities in various countries. When favourable conditions are identified in a country to operate the business, it is necessary to decide the market entry strategy.

Market-entry Strategies

As mentioned already, GATS agreement covers four modes of international trade in services. Service companies consistent with the defined modes may get into contractual agreements which include licensing, franchising, joint ventures and consortia with a foreign market (see Fig. 22.2). Some companies may establish their own service units or use the Internet to serve the markets (See the caselet on the entry strategy of L&T.).

Licensing is the widely used entry approach as it does not involve heavy investments. Companies can permit foreign firms to use patented products, trade marks or technological processes through licensing. Many small and medium companies prefer licensing to have foreign access. Licensing is less profitable, but it provides legitimate means of capitalizing intellectual property rights internationally.

Franchising is one form of licensing wherein the franchisor fulfils certain responsibilities of providing service package standards and basic interactive processes and the franchisee contributes capital, local market knowledge and service performance. Due to its flexibility, franchising became the fastest growing market entry strategy. This approach enables the company to quickly reach the foreign markets with very low investment. It is proved suitable particularly for services as they require greater adaptability to local environment.

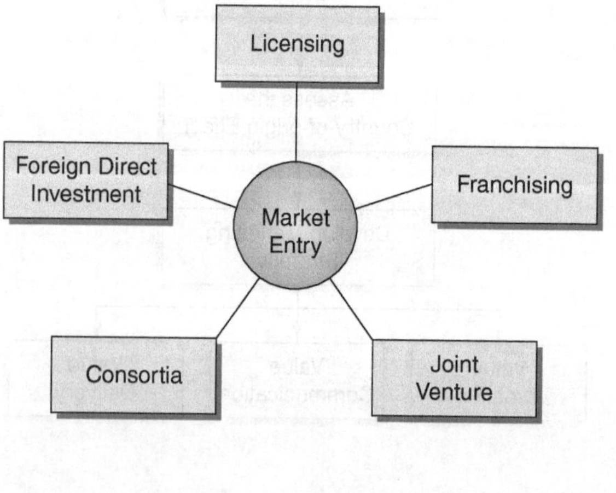

Fig. 22.2
Market entry strategies

Larsen & Toubro

Larsen & Toubro Ltd. (L&T) is India's largest engineering and construction conglomerate. Founded in 1938, it enjoys a formidable presence in India and several other countries around the world. The successful completion of prestigious projects in India firmly established the L&T brand. The company spotted and utilized international business opportunities, particularly on the outstretched arms of the Indian Ocean Rim countries. Currently, L&T has a presence in 20 countries spanning South Asia, South East Asia, the Middle East, Africa and Russia, including several CIS nations.

L&T has used joint ventures, collaborations, public private partnerships and consortia as market entry strategies. In some countries, it has established subsidiary companies to undertake projects directly. Its operations are supplemented by a comprehensive supply chain and distribution network and its benchmark customer services.

The major strength of the company is its human resource. The employees of the company have shown great adaptability to the requirements of foreign markets. The use of company professionals with successful track records in international projects helped it capitalize on and strengthen the image of the company.

The local franchisees' contribution helps to gain customer acceptance quickly and build brand image.

Joint venture is a partnership of two or more companies. It is a separate legal entity. Big companies prefer to have joint ventures as they provide greater access as well as control over operations. That is the reason why many fortune 500 companies are having joint venture in various parts of the world. Joint ventures at foreign countries help to utilize the specialized skills of a local partner, local distribution network, and to overcome certain legal barriers existing in the foreign country.

> *Service companies may get into contractual agreements for market entry by way of licensing, franchising, joint ventures or consortia. They may follow one or more ways to enter into business with foreign markets.*

Consortia are a new form of the joint venture system with two unique characteristics; large number of participants and none of them are active in the land of operation. This mode is used when there is a huge requirement of resources to execute the service. In areas like construction, turn key projects, etc., consortia are used.

Foreign direct investment is another means of entering foreign markets. Many developing countries liberalized their policies to attract foreign companies into their land for operations through this mode during the last two decades; China and India are the front runners in this approach.

Selecting a Country for Entry

Service companies need to develop a comprehensive plan for the entry into foreign markets. The objectives, resources and policies should be defined clearly to carry out international operations sufficiently for a long period to achieve sustainable growth in the international markets. The selection of a market for entry is influenced by the following factors:

1. Business opportunities
2. Company objectives

> "The selection of a country for market entry depends upon many factors including, business opportunities, company objectives, resources, market access, barriers, etc."

3. Resources requirement and availability
4. Market access
5. Political risk
6. Cost and operating conditions
7. Legal barriers
8. Intensity of competition
9. Support services availability
10. Impact of country of origin

Country-of-origin Effect

> "In international scenario, some countries are known for certain specialities which may be capable of influencing positively or negatively the business in host country. Such recognitions are known as **"country-of-origin effects."**"

Market perception of services is greatly influenced by country-of-origin effect. The general image of the home country influences positively or negatively the perceptions of the consumers. Consumers develop vague stereotypes about specific countries and judge them the "best." "German is synonymous with quality engineering, Italian is synonymous with style, and French is synonymous with chic.[9]" Technical education in the United States is perceived qualitative in India. Indian conventional health care system is respected by many foreign markets. The image may be general or service specific. The image is not a permanent one and subject to changes from time to time. Ethnocentrism is part of country-of-origin effect. The marketing proposition is that one has to recognize the influence of country-of-origin perceptions on the marketability of services in foreign markets.

Value Creation

The beginning for value creation is to know value perceptions of the target market in terms of service package, price, interactive processes, quality and physical system of the service company. The value perceptions against each of these variables need not be uniform in all the countries and among different market segments. In fact, it is more likely that the perceptions vary significantly. The value perceptions of Americans, Chinese, Japanese, Koreans, Arabs and Indians vary significantly as they belong to different socio, cultural, economic, political, technological and legal systems.

- *Service Package:* In designing the service product, it is necessary to consider the preferences of the host country, law and regulations and compatibility of the service with the prevalent social system. Service quality is the critical component in this respect. The quality expectations of the consumers and the zone of tolerance should be studied in standardising technical quality and functional performance quality. Managing innovations and diffusion of innovations is another challenge in value creation. Besides the design of a service product and its quality specifications, pricing, contact personnel and physical environment are the critical elements of value creation.

- *Pricing:* It is influenced by cost of production as well as competitive prices in the market. Though the basic approaches for pricing are universally applicable, exchange rate fluctuations, marketing costs, local price competition and tax systems influence the final price and marketing opportunities in international marketing. Multiple levies and duties are one of the serious problems in pricing services in foreign markets. For example, the telecom companies in India have to pay levies at around 26 per cent of adjusted gross revenue as against around 6.5 per cent in Malaysia and around 3.5 per cent in China. The port charges in India are also considerably higher than in many developed countries. The variations in duties and levies will have its impact on final consumer price. Currency issue is yet another factor in international pricing. The service company has choice to set price in terms of its home-country currency, the host country currency or some third-party currency. The decision is influenced by the factors such as buyer preferences, exchange rates, government policy, accessibility of the currency, etc. Exchange rate fluctuations, if higher, impact on profitability of the company. In spite of the dominance of non-price factors in many services, price continues to be the factor in value assessment across all market segments. The importance of price, however, varies among different consumer groups. The higher income group attaches generally less value to the price factor while the lower income group attaches higher value to price. For some services like health care in emergency, price may not be the major influencing factor while the other factors like speed, responsiveness, empathy, etc., are given more value. Price can be effectively used by the service companies as value-generating variable in the international markets. An appropriate pricing strategy with a holistic perspective covering cost, regulation, law, competition, nature of service, service package, consumer group targeted and service positioning help the company to use price as a factor of value perceived by consumers.

> ***Value creation*** *refers to the utility value and perceptual value created in a service offer. It includes primarily the design of service package, pricing, quality specifications, contact personnel and physical environment.*

- *Contact Personnel:* They are the other value-generating resource. Since human interaction is critical for the service processes, the people placed at touch points should be capable of interacting with the people of the host country besides their ability to provide service. Whether to use people from the home country or to employ those of the host country is a critical decision. The home-country people have technical expertise, and they need to be given cross-cultural training to interact with customers of foreign market. If people from the host country are used for customer interaction, they need to be trained on technical aspects and also on cross-cultural issues to improve internal interactions. Foreign customers may get a feel of country of origin when contact employees belong to the home country. It works well when the image of the country is positive. It also helps to differentiate the service as the customers of foreign market may feel the service process original when they interact with the employees of the home country in the service production process. However, there may be some communication and cultural problems when home-country people are used. The selection between the two groups or a combination of them depends upon the value perceptions of the consumers of the host country. Service companies should take support of the database existed or generated database for the purpose for taking a decision on the issue.

- *Physical Environment:* Design and service processes require the companies to take the social and cultural factors of the international markets into consideration. The ambiance, the layout and design, artefacts and signage need to reflect the value perceptions of the people. Physical environment provides innumerable opportunities to value creation. Service companies need to explore opportunities to exploit either the cultural strengths of the home country or the cultural differences of the host country or a combination of them to create value perceptions.

Value creation thus is an integrated approach aiming to generate value that is capable of creating better value perceptions to the customers than the offers from others.

Value Communication

Value communication is the major challenge in international marketing as it involves cross-cultural communication. It is the communication between the people of one culture with the people of another culture(s). Many issues stand in the way to make the communication effective. Language barriers, government regulations, media, consumer behaviour, etc., are the areas needed to be understood well in designing communication campaigns. Words and symbols do not carry the same meanings universally. Their meanings are culture specific. A word or a symbol may convey positive meaning in one cultural group or may spell negative or different meaning in another culture. Therefore, knowledge on cultural diversity is essential for international communication.

> "**Value communication** in international marketing involves intercultural communication. Language barriers, regulations, media, legal system and consumer behaviour of the host market are the major influencers in designing communication campaign."

Communication campaigns are regulated in many countries taking into consideration its negative impact on the society. The use of immeasurable claims, exploitation of sex and misleading advertising campaigns are regulated in the United States, European countries and in many developing countries. In Malaysia, Western-culture images in TV commercials are regulated. In India, China and other high-context culture societies, any commercial campaign that affects the cultural sentiments of the people is regulated.

Media availability, media cost and media reach also vary from country to country. In some countries, too many media options and in some only a few media options are available. In some countries, electronic media is controlled by the governments. "Media prices are susceptible to negotiation in most countries. Agency space discounts are often split with the client to bring down the cost of media. The advertiser may find that the cost of reaching a prospect through advertising depends on the agents bargaining ability.[10]"

Media coverage is a problem to reach certain sections of the society in many developing nations. For example, in Netherlands, there are catholic, socialist, neutral and other specialized broadcasting systems to reach some segments of the society. In Vietnam, there are restrictions on media space coverage. In newspapers and magazines, only 10 per cent of the space can be utilized for advertisements. In case of radio and T.V, 5 per cent of time or 3 minutes per hour is the limitation for commercials.

Communication campaigners should be conversant with all the barriers and opportunities existing in various countries and should be able to differentiate accordingly without affecting the overall international image of the service and the company. Besides the print and electronic media, other channels of communication like direct marketing, sales promotion, publicity and public relations, etc., should be exploited depending upon the suitability to the people of the host country.

Consumer motives, attitudes and learning behaviour vary among different societies. The communication campaign can be effective only when it reflects the trends in these areas. The message development and campaign planning should have the support of database generated through marketing research on these factors periodically. Regular updation of trends and fast adaptation in communication generates more value to the company as well as consumers and helps in establishing competitive advantage.

Value Delivery

Value delivery is the key process of services marketing. The consumers are provided the core value of the service along with augmented value to the consumers through buyer–seller interactions. Service companies may establish their own companies, collaborate with local companies, promote joint ventures or use intermediaries to deliver value to the customers when they have decided to provide services at the host country. Services also can be delivered by being in the home country through attracting the foreigners to the home country or delivering service through electronic channels and other means to the foreigners at host country.

When services are delivered through the outlets established in the home country, the company will have an advantage of having operational control and environment familiarity. They can attract only a limited number of foreign customers for the service as the customer has to incur many costs associated to the consumption of the service (transport, lodging, procedural costs, etc.). Service companies that are highly comfortable in domestic market and are not serious on international reach may adopt this approach. Some service companies may be having high level of cost advantage or resource accessibility in the home country. In such cases also, they prefer to operate at the home country (e.g. software services, ITES, health care, etc). The services like tourism should necessarily attract foreigners to the destinations of the home country.

The majority of the companies deliver value by having their physical presence in the foreign market through the means mentioned above. It is preferable to have own service outlets as it is possible to maintain quality

> "The value generation and value communication will support the value delivery process in achieving the marketing objectives. Service companies should ensure that the basic issues of service quality are addressed effectively in the chosen form of service delivery."

standards, and it is also possible to exercise control over operations. But the problems are also many. Huge investment requirement, political and legal barriers, market knowledge, network development, image building, etc., are the hurdles. Collaborations and joint ventures are the popularly used means for service delivery. These forms will help to get out of many of these problems. Franchisee system and/or agents/brokers are also used by many companies to deliver value. These channels will help to reach the market quickly and with less investment, but the control over value delivery process remains a question mark. The choice of the value delivery system is influenced by many factors, particularly, the business environment of the host country.

The key factor in value delivery process is to generate customer-perceived value positively and better than the competitive offers. The value generation and value communication will support the value delivery process in achieving the objective. The process coordination, internal customer management, customer experience management and the mechanism for service recovery are the critical areas of management in value delivery process. Service companies should ensure that the basic issues of service quality are addressed effectively in the chosen form of service delivery.

The marketing programme of a service company should address the needs, wants and expectations of the consumers of the host country. The resources of value generation, value communication and value delivery should be identified, networked and integrated effectively to create value perceptions better than competitive offers and also to achieve company's present and future business objectives.

SUMMARY

- Services are promoted well in the international markets due to liberalized trade regulations and advancements in technology particularly in telecommunications, computers and the Internet.
- The major services having sound international business record in recent years include transportation, travel, communications, construction, insurance, financial, computer and information, other business services, etc.
- Service characteristics such as intangibility, inseparability and perishability create more marketing challenges than goods marketing in the international arena.
- In domestic marketing, only one set of uncontrollables need to be handled. In international marketing, companies have to handle two or more sets of uncontrollables.
- Service companies need to adopt an appropriate marketing philosophy to reach international markets. Companies may adopt ethnocentric or polycentric or geocentric orientation.
- International marketing environment, particularly the cultural and social environment, political environment and legal environment need to be analysed to identify business opportunities, constraints and threats.
- The trade barriers in various countries need to be analysed.
- GATS came into existence in 1995 as a treaty of WTO. GATS agreement covers four modes of cross-border service trade: cross-border supply, consumption abroad, commercial presence, presence of a natural person.
- Service companies should select appropriate market entry strategy to carry out business operations in foreign markets.
- Service companies may get into contractual agreements which include licensing, franchising, joint

ventures, and consortia. Some companies may establish their own service outlets or use Internet to serve the markets.

- The choice of market entry strategy is influenced by many factors like business opportunities, company objectives, market access, etc.
- The marketing programme should address the needs, wants and expectations of the consumers of the host country. The resources for value generation, value communication and value delivery need to be identified, networked and integrated.
- Value creation should be guided by value perceptions of the people of the host country.
- The service package design, quality specifications, pricing, contact personnel and physical environment are the critical value-generating resources.
- To make value communication effective, language barriers, government regulations, media and consumer behaviour need to be analysed.
- Value delivery is the key process of services marketing. Service companies may establish their own service units, collaborate with local companies, promote joint ventures or use intermediaries to deliver value to the consumers.
- Customer-perceived value is the key factor in value delivery process.

KEY TERMS

Domestic marketing *441*
Ethnocentricity *442*
Polycentricity *443*
Geocentricity *443*
Political risk *444*
Trade barriers *441*
WTO *447*
GATS *447*
Licensing *446*
Franchising *450*
Joint venture *450*
Foreign direct investment *451*
Consortia *450*
Country of origin *452*

BRIEF QUESTIONS

1. What is the difference between domestic marketing and international marketing?
2. Explain GATS.
3. Discuss legal environment and its impact on international marketing.
4. Explain the impact of political environment in international marketing.
5. Explain the problems of service trade internationally.
6. How to select a country for entry into foreign markets?

ESSAY QUESTIONS

1. Why do companies prefer to enter international markets?
2. What are market entry strategies?
3. Explain trade barriers for services.
4. How do you develop a marketing programme for international marketing of services?
5. What is WTO? Explain the place of services in World Trade Agreements.

ASSIGNMENTS

1. Japan is one of the important destinations for Indian services exports. The share of India in Japan's total service imports was only 0.2 per cent while China could achieve 4.3 per cent. All South East Countries have much higher shares than India in service exports to Japan. India could not make serious impact in Japanese market in services, though it has competitive advantage in some commercial services. You are required to study:
   (a) India's service exports to Japan to identify major services exported.
   (b) The reasons for not being successful in Japanese markets.
2. IT and ITES are the services that earned very good image for Indian companies in the international markets. The change in the political and economic environment in the United States causing for concern about the future prospects of the business in the country. You are required to study:
   (a) The key developments during Obama's regime.
   (b) The emerging threats of the business.

REFERENCES

1 Gary Knight, "International Services Marketing: Review of Research 1980-98," *Journal of Services Marketing,* 13, no. 4/5 (1999): 347 and K. Segebath, "Some Aspects of the International Trade in Services: An Empirical Approach", *Service Industries Journal,* 10, no. 2 (1990): 266–83.

2 L. D. Dahringer, "Marketing Services Internationally: Barriers and Management Strategies," *Journal of Services Marketing,* 5, no. 3 (1991): 5–17.

3 B. Nicoulaud, "Problems and Strategies in the International Marketing of Services," *International Marketing of Services*, 23, no. 6 (1998): 58.

4 Sak Onkvisit and John J. Shaw, *International Marketing - Analysis and Strategy,* 3rd ed. (New Delhi: Prentice Hall 1999), p. 7.

5 Warren J. Keegan, *Global Marketing Management,* 7th ed. (Delhi: Pearson Education, 2002), p. 6

6 Edward T. Hall, "How Cultures Collide," *Psychology Today,* (July 1976): 66–97.

7 Courtland L. Bovee, John V. Thill and Barbara E. Schatzman, *Business Communication Today,* 7th ed. (NJ 07458, Prentice Hall, 2003), p. 58.

8 www.finmin.nic.in/WorkingPaper/1_2007_DEA.pdf.

9 Dana Milbank, "Made in America Becomes a Boast in Europe," *The Wall Street Journal,* (January 19th, 1994): B1

10 Michael Flagg, "P&G Picks Starcom, Media Vest to Replace Zenith in China Account," *Asian Wall Street Journal,* (Jan 7, 2000): 5.

Consumer Protection in Services

23

LEARNING OBJECTIVES

After studying this chapter, you will be able to:

- Understand the concept of consumerism
- Understand consumer expectations
- Understand consumer concerns
- Understand the consumer movement in India
- Understand the salient features of the Consumer Protection Act, 1986
- Understand the business response to consumerism

Neelima was throwing a party at her place to celebrate her friend's birthday. She had spent quite some time finalizing the guest list, the menu and other details. She went to a nearby ATM to withdraw money to pay for the various expenses. The transaction failed twice, and she did not receive any cash. To her horror, she found the amount had been deducted twice from her account, leaving it empty. Panic set in as a co-customer informed her that such incidents had become commonplace since the transaction fee on inter-bank ATM usage had been withdrawn. He advised her to lodge a complaint with her bank.

Neelima rushed to her branch and explained her problem to the bank manager who took the matter casually as if it were a regular occurrence. He asked her to put in a written complaint saying that it would take a minimum of seven days for the money to be credited into her account. Despite Neelima's insistence, he maintained that seven days was a reasonable period as the bank had to verify the transaction details from the bank whose ATM was used. Neelima needed the money immediately but the manager was not bothered with her problem. So, she took a personal loan, against her psychological comfort, at a high interest to meet the immediate expenses.

The money was indeed credited into Neelima's account within seven days but she was unhappy with the bank's attitude. During her next visit to bank, the manager explained the technical problems associated with ghost debiting, particularly when other banks' ATMs are involved. She told the manager, "I am not bothered with your technical and process problems. I have incurred monetary and psychological costs in this process. Please tell me how you will compensate me." The manager expressed helplessness.

Questions:

1. Is it justifiable to demand compensation in this case?
2. Do you think the bank manager handled the problem well? If not, state reasons.
3. What is the legal process Neelima can pursue for her grievance redressal?
4. Can she get support under the Consumer Protection Act, 1986?
5. What should Neelima do in this situation?

INTRODUCTION

Consumer protection is an integral part of the broad concept of consumerism. Consumerism means promotion and protection of consumers' interest. A well-protected consumer community is a satisfied community. The ultimate goal of any society is to see every member lead a happy life. Consumerism in this sense drives to an understanding of growth, development and welfare of the society. Many researchers viewed the concept of consumerism as consumer protection against the business community. According to P. Kotler,[1] consumerism is an organized movement of citizens and government agencies to improve the rights and powers of buyers in relation to sellers. The concept of consumerism can be viewed from the perspectives of consumer movement, of business and of society at large. The consumer movement aims at protecting the interest of the consumers by way of seeking redress, restitution and remedy for their dissatisfaction and frustrations caused by the service provider with the help of organized efforts and activities. From the perspective of business, the concept of consumerism advocates self-regulation to the business by not involving in any activity that is against the interest of the consumers. Further, it advocates providing greater value to the customers by using judicially and optimally the natural resources. To achieve the goals of business, the only way that is appreciated has been achieving consumer satisfaction at mutually beneficial propositions. Consumerism, therefore, is the responsibility of the business to safeguard the interests of the consumers and promotes the welfare of the consumers.[2]

> "*__Consumerism__ means promotion and protection of consumers' interests. Consumer protection from all types of exploitations of business is an integral part of consumerism. It advocates self-regulation to the business, consumer movement and provision of greater value to consumers through judicial and optimum use of resources.*"

The case for effective consumer protection is indisputable and therefore, efforts, which are aimed at educating consumers, ensuring their safety and confirming their rights to derive satisfaction from their purchases, are not normally condemned by anyone. Thus, the emergence of consumerism has generally been welcomed, not only by customers, journalists and educators, but even by businessmen who, ostensibly, have most to lose from the activities of an organized consumer movement.[3] Businessmen, wholesalers and retailers need to protect consumers by good ethical practices because if they protect consumers they are also protecting themselves and their nation.[4]

Services marketing focuses on the adverse affects of service failures. Though service failures are most common, the service provider can ill-afford to ignore such failures. For a service failure, the reasons may be many. The failures may be due to the service delivery system failure or due to failures in meeting customers' needs and requests or may occur due to problematic customers. Added to the above failures there is another important reason that significantly contributes to the service failure, that is, the unprompted and unsolicited action of the contact personnel. In case of service failure, it is the responsibility of contact personnel to promptly respond and work for service recovery. The service customer may tolerate even to a greater extent the service failures that occur due to system failure or even the failure in meeting their needs and requests. But if the service failure occurs due to the bad behaviour of the contact personnel or irresponsibility of the service company, it results in customer dissatisfaction and there would be no scope for service recovery paradox in such an event. When there is a service failure, customers respond in a variety of ways. Some customers are passive, some are voicers, some may be irate and some customers are activists. Out of the above categories of complainers, activists are more problematic and they complain on all dimensions. They believe in the positive consequences of complaining. They may even resort to legal action under the provisions of Consumer Protection Act, 1986. In case of court litigation, the service provider, in addition to losing a customer, may also get adverse publicity. The service marketers should know that if business fails to carry out its responsibilities, law intervenes and forces them to carry out such responsibilities. The very fact that 0.191 million cases were filed during 2008, in 657 consumer courts established in India, reveals the impact of Consumer Protection Act on business. Interestingly, majority of these cases are filed against service organizations.

CONSUMER EXPECTATIONS FROM INDUSTRIES AND BUSINESSES

The expectations of the consumers are important to the business community to know, understand and adhere to them in order to see that there is no grievance from the consumers. The following are the five expectations of the consumers that are widely stated throughout the world.

1. Product design and development
2. Product quality and performance including product safety
3. Product representation
4. Optimum use of resources and concern on environment
5. Fairness in transactions

Product Design and Development

The goods and services that are offered to the consumers should necessarily promote the quality of living of the society. The study of consumer needs and wants should form as the basic input for business processes. To demonstrate integrity, the real consumer demand should be satisfied through well-planned product development and design. Business should not create any false needs and desires, through heavy marketing campaigns, those are harmful to the society. It does not mean that business people should not try new ideas. In fact, many positive changes in the society have taken place because of the innovative contributions of great business driving forces like Alexander Graham Bell, George Eastman, Mc Donald, etc., who could impute what the consumers wanted. The justification for any innovation is its value to the consumer. By utilizing the technology and resources optimally, the industry and business should provide enhanced value to the consumers.

Product Quality and Performance

The industry and business should feel responsible for protecting the consumers by ensuring the product quality, its compliance to safety standards and effective performance according to claimed specifications. Service consumers expect the service provider to take care of quality and safety while offering services. The safety standards and quality assurance measures have to be reviewed constantly to see that the latest technology, market changes, consumer requirements and environmental needs are considered. The establishment of International Organization for Standardization (ISO) is the step in the right direction. The ISO sets quality standards and provides right directions to the industry, business as well as government companies. The companies need to have self-regulation in respect of product quality and performance with absolute safety. The excellence in quality assurance enhances not only the corporate image but also increases the competitive edge in the market. It further reinforces the consumer confidence in products or services offered by such companies.

Product Representation

Product representation includes the communication campaign launched by the company to inform and persuade consumers, branding and positioning. In other words, product representation refers to everything other than the product itself, which affects the consumer decision to buy products or services. It is expected by the consumers that the information provided by the businessman is accurate and non-deceptive. It should help the consumers to assess the product for relating it to their needs and wants. They can find a better choice when the product representations are true. Therefore, the product representation influences the consumer confidence on the integrity of the company. The business concerns should identify the information to be communicated and see that such information is well represented in simple, straight and in suitable language. Product representation also should take care of the regulation of the government. Social responsibility of business primarily goes with the company's very operation itself for maintaining proper product quality, proper product pricing and timely distribution and after sales, proper advertising and extending information, proper customer education, etc. The company should also make it a point not to misguide any customer during the course of advertising, information giving and demand creation.[5]

Optimum Use of Resources

Natural resources are valuable and limited. They have to be utilized judiciously so as to preserve them for future generations. The society has no right to deprive the future generation of the natural resources. For providing most of the services, natural resources are utilized. While utilizing such resources, companies should consider the importance to the society and see that every resource is used for the best purpose, economically and without wasting resources. The resources should not be utilized for undesirable services. In other words, the industry and business should not encourage excessive consumption and consumption of such services that are detrimental to the interest of the society.

Fairness in Transactions

Consumers expect that the business should follow fair norms in exchanges. They should not exploit the consumer's weak points like inability to judge the value, inadequate support of information, urgency, requirement of large quantity or small quantity, status consciousness, etc. Consumers expect that the prices of services should be reasonable in the sense that the seller should satisfy with normal profit and should not exploit the favourable market demand because of the poor competitive situations or monopoly conditions. They should be interacted with respect and honour and should not be viewed as the people at the receiving end. Their needs and wants should be understood properly and they should be given an opportunity to express their points of view. They expect that the business concern take responsibility of managing every interaction in a fair and ethical manner.

> *"Consumers expect fairness from business and industry in terms of product design and development, product quality and performance, product representation, optimum use of resources and transactional process. Service firms should try to understand these expectations of the consumers."*

The words of H. Wong[6] are worth mentioning here; "as technology has developed at a tremendous pace in the past century, consumers have been encountering new products, new services, advertising claims flooding the market." Consumer decisions, therefore, take on a greater complexity, especially in a free market open to whatever services industry can provide. It was with this complexity that consumers began to demand protection from sellers by ensuring the quality, safety and performance of their services. This called for some form of market regulation that should not be viewed as completely undermining a free market but rather as setting the rules under which industry and consumers can operate on a fair basis.

CONSUMERS' CONCERNS

The response from the industry and business to the expectations of the consumers in general, however, is not satisfactory. Consumers throughout the world are feeling that they are on the receiving end and are being exploited by the sellers. Due to the outgrowth of the viciousness of the social system, the blind industrialization, profit motive being the primary objective, parallel black economies with lots of funds to produce goods and services at random and the consumer to accept some thing new, something which will help save money, there has been an indomitable and unscrupulously penetrating phenomena of abuse of the consumer.[7] Most businessmen are adapting unfair and unjust marketing practices, such as supply of unsafe products, adulteration, fictitious pricing, defective and deceptive packing and packaging, false and misleading advertisements and sales literature, hoarding, profiteering, black-marketing, price collusion, misuse of brands, planned obsolescence, short measures and weights, face-lifting or cosmetic changes in products and the like. Has the business really had consumer concern and realized the importance of a consumer, there would not have been any scope for malpractices at the market place. There is no substantial change in the attitude of the business with regard to consumer protection. The predominant urge to make a quick buck is diluting the business ethics. Despite the recognition in recent years all over the world that business owes responsibilities to all segments of the society, it is seldom seen the business follows these responsibilities, particularly towards consumers.[8]

Goods and services have multiplied and become more complicated, making it difficult to choose wisely among them. Comforts, conveniences and luxuries unheard of 50 years ago are common now. The right kind of information needed to make intelligent selection among the myriad products is often lacking. We sometimes are not sure what we want to start with, nor do we ordinarily get our advice from sources that are really impartial. We are constantly subject to pressure and persuasions from those whose business depend on the selling of their own particular products at a profit.

The result is that consumer confusion now pervades almost every decision that consumers make—both the life and life-shaping decisions such as choosing a home, doctor, spouse, job, preschool, college or financial plan, as well as the small decisions such as choosing a TV, credit card or evening entertainments. Anyone who has recently tried to select a life insurance policy or differentiate among channel packages offered by DTH companies immediately grasps how many purchasing decisions are based on hunches, sales pitches, brand reputation or sheer fatigue rather than on genuine awareness of value. These poorly informed decisions, made by millions of people every day of the year, profoundly influence the moral, social and economic world around us.

> *"Consumers largely feel that they are on the receiving end. They opine that due to insufficient, improper or misleading information, they are unable to take right purchase decisions. The concerns of the consumers need to be addressed by the industry to prevent a consumer movement."*

The consumers feel they have special interests as consumers, which are frequently neglected, and this neglect makes the ultimate results unworkable. As consumers, they feel they have a vital concern in such questions as the tariff, the regulation of monopoly, the cost of advertising, the fair-trade laws, the conservation of resources, the effect of war on production and prices and many other matters. Nothing is more basic in the make-up of human nature, nothing more central in the concept of the consumer than the urge to get the best standards of living that are possible, within our reach, as individuals and as a nation. This gives the consumer movement a great significance.

THE CONSUMER MOVEMENT IN INDIA

India is the country that has shown concern to the consumer protection right from the Vedic age that spreads between 5,000 and 2,500 B.C. Consumer protection was given due consideration in Dharma Shastras. The ancient code of conduct known as Smritis identifies four broad types of offences against the consumer such as adulteration, high price, falsification of weights and measures and sale of forbidden articles, and punishments are also prescribed against each offence. In Manu's **Dharma Shastra** and the famous Kautilya's "Arthashastra," the problems of consumers were given a great deal of importance. There were historical evidences that the kings of various dynasties used to give severe punishments to the traders and businessmen who were mischievous, deceitful and exploitative in nature.[9] During the British rule of 200 years, several legislations were made to protect the interests of consumers.

The real consumer movement in India finds its beginning only in the 20th century. The two great personalities of India, Swami Vivekananda who gave a call to the business world stating that "Consumer is the King" (with the slogan he wanted the business community realize that if the king is not served properly you will be punished) and Mahatma Gandhi who described the importance of a consumer to a business concern became a source of inspiration to consumer activist. Gandhi said that "A customer is the most important visitor in our premises. He is not dependent on us, we are dependent on him. He is not an interruption in our work, he is the purpose of it. He is not an outsider to our business, he is part of it. We are not doing him a favour by serving him, he is doing us a favour by giving us an opportunity to do so."

Several consumer organizations were promoted during 20th century for the cause of consumer protection. The first known consumer organization of India was Passengers And Traffic Relief Association (PATRA) which was set up in 1915 in Bombay, with a view to ameliorate the hardships and struggles faced by passengers travelling by railways and steamers and also to redress grievances of the Indian trading community. The organization conducted seminars and conferences and had meetings with various government and business organizations. Through judicious persuasion, PATRA achieved good results in its pursuit of consumer protection. At the beginning of 1960s, the consumer movement in India was in the take-off stage, trying to establish a base. In one of the rare instances, where consumers asserted themselves and which has been recorded in the history of consumer resistance, is the Bengalis' refusal to buy fish—their staple diet—when its price really shot up in the late 1960s. Gurbax Singh in his book *Law of Consumer Protection* reports the outrage of the common man in West Bengal when the price of fish, a staple food item, escalated beyond its reach in the late 1960s. Press reports were quiet, and the authorities failed to bring the prices down. The consumers decided to sue with their last weapon, that is, "refusal to buy." A campaign was launched, it spread like wild fire and in just a couple of days, the sellers had to bring down their prices. This is a case in point where the direct action had been employed effectively.[10]

Though a few consumer organizations had come up in early 1960s, it was the Consumer Guidance Society of India (CGSI) that really made an impact on consumer movement. In 1966, nine housewives promoted this organization to fight against the rampant black marketing and food adulteration by dealers and traders. The nine housewives got together "to inform, educate and organize consumers in order to protect their interests. The quality of items of daily use of food stuffs such as milk, oil, tea, etc. were tested by this organization and the test reports created a stir among traders. In its 38 years of existence CGSI created awareness to the public in Mumbai on various consumer issues. The organization fought against the use of metanyl yellow, a dangerous chemical being used extensively in sweetmeats, which was bought mostly by the poor, thus saving them from cancer-producing sweetmeats.[11]

The Karnataka Consumer Service Society (KCSS) which was formed in 1970 by 10 housewives belonging to Bangalore is the other consumer organization that contributed significantly. KCSS organized several seminars and conferences which led to the nomination of its leader Mrs. Mandanna to Karnataka Legislative Council. Being a part of the government, the leadership of the KCSS could influence the government to develop and strengthen the mechanism for the protection of the consumers.

Another consumer organization that could make consumer voice well demonstrated was Visakha Consumer Council (VCC) which was formed in 1973 by a few professors of Andhra University and the noted consumer activist Vasanta Kumar Parigi. The VCC represented the plight of the poor ration card holders and LP gas users. The VCC found that about 0.6 million people in Visakhapatnam were suffering and wasting long hours in queues due to the irresponsible attitude of the concerned authorities. They felt that this was one of the major problems of the masses. They organized a public meeting to voice their grievances. In order to reach the masses, they printed leaflets in Telugu (the local language of Andhra Pradesh) and got them inserted in the local newspapers, inviting the readers to the meeting, which they held on a Sunday morning. They also sent out a press release both before and after the meeting, which was attended by about 500 people. In spite of all the publicity, the collector was not impressed, when the "committee members" met him after the meeting. This small group of about 20 committee members did not lose faith and decided to follow up with a survey of card holders. This was once again released to the press in the conference organized for them. Each newspaper eagerly picked up different aspects and published them. *The Deccan Chronicle* captioned it as "Collapse of Public Distribution System in Vizag" and positioned it right on the front page. This established the VCC as a force to be reckoned with in the consumer movement not merely in Visakhapatnam but throughout Andhra Pradesh.[12] Another significant organization that has been contributing to the cause of consumer protection is Consumer Education and Research Center (CERC) located in Ahmedabad. The centre was started in 1978 to give the consumer movement "The Teeth of Law." The CERC, under the leadership of Manubhai Shah, took the matters relating to consumer protection to courts and fought cases ranging from ordinary day-to-day used products and pubic services to broad issues like misleading advertisements. Over the years, many consumer organizations have come up in the country, and, at present, there are 1,160 voluntary consumer organizations working for consumer protection.[13]

It is generally believed that the consumer movement in India as of today is quite strong when it is compared with other developing countries in Asia, Africa and Latin America. India is a vast country with a very large population of which a sizeable percentage lives below the poverty line. Because of economic inequality, low level of literacy and ignorance, particularly among women, the level of consumer awareness is not too high, and, therefore, the consumers are not able to assert and protect themselves. They easily get exploited by trade and industry and service providers. With the liberalization process which started in 1991, the entire economic scenario is undergoing a complete change from a government-driven economy to a market-driven economy. Protecting the interests of consumers has, therefore, become one of the paramount concerns of the government than ever before. Hence, policies are being designed and legislations were enacted to protect the consumers' interest and grant them the right to choice, safety, information and redressal.[14]

> *Consumer movement in India gained prominence in 20th century due to some active contributions of consumer associations like PATRA, CGSI, VCC, CERC, etc. The movement could not influence the business significantly due to several limitations.*

> *There are more than 30 legislations to protect the interests of consumers in India. The most prominent among them are Consumer Protection Act and Right to Information Act.*

LEGAL AND ADMINISTRATIVE MECHANISMS FOR CONSUMER PROTECTION IN INDIA

In India, there are more than 30 legislations that protect consumer interest. Of these, the two most important pieces of legislation are the Consumer Protection Act (1986) and the Right to Information Act (2005).

The Consumer Protection Act (1986)

Following the United Nations Guidelines for Consumer Protection, the Government of India brought out Consumer Protection Act after having thoroughly discussed with various groups. For the first time, the efforts were made to bring out a comprehensive legislation that takes the justice a step closer to the common man by informalizing the legal process.[15] The act offers protection for the six rights of the consumers, they are:

1. The right to be protected against marketing of goods which are hazardous to life and property
2. The right to be informed about the quality, quantity, potency, purity, standard and price of goods to protect the consumer against unfair trade practices
3. The right to be assured, wherever possible, access to variety of goods at competitive prices
4. The right to be heard and to be assured those consumers' interests will receive the consideration at appropriate forums
5. The right to seek redressal against unfair trade practices or unscrupulous exploitation of consumers
6. The right to consumer education

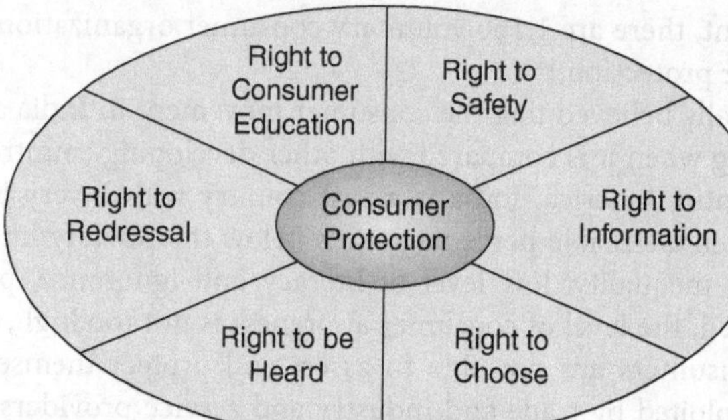

Fig. 23.1
Consumer rights

The consumer rights precisely are shown in Fig. 23.1, and each of the rights is described in detail in the following paragraphs.

> "The Consumer Protection Act provides six rights to consumers: right to safety, right to be informed, right to choose, right to be heard, right to redressal and right to consumer education. It is for the first time Indian consumers got their rights through legislation."

1. *Right to Safety*: The right to safety is intended to protect the consumer against the hazardous goods and services on the health or life and property of consumers. According to the International Organization of Consumer Union, renamed as Consumer International (CI), the right to safety is one "which means the right to be protected against products, production processes and services which are hazardous to health or life." The changing patterns of living and new lifestyles being adopted by the unaffordable middle economic class people provide more opportunities for businessmen to exploit them by offering inferior and unsafe products. Accidents due to faulty electrical appliances, adulterated food, poor sanitary facilities, substandard building materials and so on have become front page news for dailies. Under such circumstances, the right to safety assumes greater significance. This right protects the community at large.
2. *Right to be Informed*: To make an informed purchase decision on goods or services, buyers require adequate information support. If choice is the engine of consumer power, then information is the fuel on which it runs. Individual consumers make judgements about what serves them best without sufficient, accurate and understandable information. The information required is not only on the physical properties or the functions of goods or services but also on the legal implications of the transaction. The relevant information in this respect safeguards the interests of the buyer or consumer. Consumers are generally interested in knowing the price, quantity, quality, size, manufacturer's name, date of manufacturing, expiry date, safety precautions, warranty and other information relating to the product. The right to information ensures the information relating to quality, quantity, potency, purity, standard and price to the consumer. The Government of India has made it mandatory that every packed article sold in the market should contain a detailed label. It is a legal obligation that every manufacturer, retailer and trader gives necessary information

to the consumers in all their transactions. The label should contain the following information:

(i) Description of the articles packed
(ii) Name and address of the manufacturer/packers
(iii) Net weight of contents
(iv) Maximum retail price
(v) Date of packing

3. *Right to Choose*: This right is to provide access to a variety of goods and services at reasonable prices. Thus, consumers have opportunity to select the product that suits their needs and wants. In a market economy, consumer choice is the essential ingredient even for producers to manage their activities efficiently and to realize the consumer's power of choice. The major danger is the strong imbalance of power between producers and consumers. Monopolies are the most common form of imbalance, forcing consumers to accept what is being offered to them. In such cases, it is unlikely that consumers' needs and interests are best served. Even where there is no monopoly, producers may work together in such a way to restrict the choice of consumers. Consumers are distinct in their views, opinions, sense of beauty, sense of satisfaction, sense of reasoning, personality, aspirations and so on. Consumers do not buy products and services, but they buy benefits and satisfactions. Those products or services that can offer maximum benefit and satisfaction to the consumer are preferred. The right to choose ensures opportunity to consumers to evaluate various alternatives available, without submitting themselves to the high pressure and aggressive sales promotions, for exercising their right choice.
4. *Right to be Heard*: The right to be heard is one of the important principles of justice. This right helps individuals make representations on various platforms for consideration against exploitative elements in the society. When consumers identify some defects or problems that may adversely affect their interests as a consumer, this right assures that consumer's interests will receive due consideration at appropriate fora. Appropriate fora may include the business and hence the seller should develop a system to hear the consumers' interests and accordingly modify its marketing plans to suit their requirements. This right encourages the consumers to bring forth their interests before the appropriate fora, be it a government department or a business forum.
5. *Right to Redressal*: The whole concept of consumer protection revolves around the consumer right to redressal against unfair trade practices or restrictive practices or unscrupulous exploitation. It is a well-recognized fact that the markets have become breeding centres for most of the unethical practices devised to cheat the gullible consumer. Markets need discipline so that defrauded consumers are compensated justly. The first and main source of redress for consumers must be the law. The right to redressal has

almost revolutionalized the consumer movement in the country. This right provides opportunity for consumers to demand compensation for the loss they have suffered and the stress they have undergone due to the unfair/restrictive trade practices of the seller. This right is a warning to the sellers not to involve in unfair trade practices and unscrupulous exploitation. Redressal is a natural follow-up which involves in making settlements that is acceptable to consumers as well as sellers. For this purpose, the business houses must establish in-house grievance mechanism to redress the grievance of the aggrieved consumers to their satisfaction or else it may result in confrontation through legal recourse.

6. *Right to Consumer Education*: Consumer education is an important aspect of consumer protection and satisfaction. This right helps a consumer to protect himself against fraudulent, deceitful and misleading information, advertising, labelling or other practices. The consumers must be told what their rights are, under what provisions of law and what remedies are available under the different enactments. Consumer education empowers consumers to make wise purchase decisions and also enables them to protect themselves from the frauds of the market.

The act provides for simple, speedy and inexpensive justice to the consumer grievances. The Act was amended thrice during the last 24 years. The preamble of the Consumer Protection Act states that "It is an act to provide for better protection of the interests of consumers and for that purpose to make provision for the establishment of consumer councils and other authorities for the settlement of consumers' disputes and for matters connected there with."[16]

Salient Features of the Act (as Amended to Date)

1. The act provides for the establishment of three tier quasi-judicial bodies at the national, state and district level known as national commission, state commission and district forum, respectively. The district forum shall have three members including a president who is qualified to be a district judge. The other two members shall be from the society and they must have the ability, integrity and standing in addition to adequate knowledge and experience of 10 years in dealing with problems relating to economics, law, commerce, accountancy, industry, public affairs or administration besides possessing a bachelors degree from a recognized university. One of the three members must be a woman. The district forum is empowered to adjudicate matters having value not exceeding INR 2 million. The state commission must also have three members including the president who should be a judge of High Court. The state commission entertains complaints relating to goods and services where their value exceeds INR 0.2 million, but does not exceed INR 10 million. The national commission is presided by a judge of Supreme Court along with four other members. The complaints valued over INR 10 million and appeals from various state commissions are entertained by the national commission. The functioning of

the National Commission is discussed in "Services Marketing Insight: National Consumer Redressal Commission".

These quasi-judicial bodies observe the principles of natural justice and are empowered to give relief of a specific nature and to award, wherever appropriate, compensation to consumers. These redressal agencies are also empowered to impose penalties for non-compliance of the orders. The Supreme Court of India in a judgement observed that the quasi-judicial bodies/authorities/agencies created by the act known as district forums, state commissions and national commission are not courts, though they have some of the powers of a civil court. They are quasi-judicial tribunals brought into existence to render inexpensive and speedy remedies to the consumers. It is equally clear that these forums/commissions are not supposed to supplant but supplement the existing judicial system. The idea is to provide an additional remedy for providing inexpensive and speedy resolution of disputes arising between

23.1 Services Marketing Insight | **National Consumer Disputes Redressal Commission**

In the hierarchy of three-tier judiciary established, the national commission is the apex body situated in Delhi. It has four types for jurisdictions, namely, territorial jurisdiction, pecuniary jurisdiction (monetary), appellate jurisdiction and administrative jurisdiction. The territorial jurisdiction of the national commission extends to the whole of India, and its monetary jurisdiction is above INR 10 million with no upper limit. It has appellate jurisdiction over the orders issued by various state commissions in the country. With regard to administrative jurisdiction of the national commission, it can exercise administrative control over all consumer courts established in India. It can call for periodical reports from the courts in its administrative jurisdiction. The national commission has the power to suspend proceeding in any matter pending before any lower court and call for the records and issue necessary directions in the matter. It is also empowered to transfer any case pending before any district forum or state commission to any other district forum or state commission. The national commission was constituted by the Government of India in 1988. It is composed of a president and four other members. The president should be a sitting judge or retired judge of the Supreme Court. Other members having honesty and integrity with a degree from any recognized university with 10 years of experience in relevant fields are appointed as members of the national commission. It has a circuit bench and the sittings of the circuit bench are scheduled at places, other than the usual sitting of national commission, that is, at Delhi, as the Central Government notifies from time to time. The national commission prescribes rules and regulations to be followed by the courts below uniformly. Though the national commission is considered as the apex body in consumer justice, however, an appeal can be made to the Supreme Court. Any aggrieved person can prefer an appeal to the Supreme Court within 30 days from the date of the order of the national commission. The national commission has to hear an appeal as expeditiously as possible and should be disposed of within 90 days. The amount of fee payable along with the complaint before the national commission is INR 5,000.

Source: www.ncdrc.nic.in

consumers and suppliers of goods and services. Complaints need not necessarily be filed by the complainant himself. The act empowers any registered consumer organization to file a complaint on behalf of consumers. When a large number of consumers have a similar complaint, one or more consumers can file a complaint on behalf of all. Even the central government and state governments can file complaints on behalf of the consumers. The idea is to help consumers to get justice and fair treatment in the matter of goods purchased and services availed by them in the markets that are dominated by large trading and manufacturing bodies. Indeed, the entire act revolves round the goods and services and is designed to protect consumers' interest.

> *The Consumer Protection Act provides a three-tier quasi-judicial mechanism to provide speedy and inexpensive justice to consumers. Accordingly, the national commission, state commissions and district consumer fora are established.*

The act has created a Central Consumer Protection Council, State Consumer Protection Councils in every state, union territories and district consumer protection councils in each district. These councils deliberate on subjects relating to the promotion and protection of the rights of the consumers and their problems. They pass resolutions recommending appropriate action to correct the situations. The suggestions of the councils are recommendatory.

2. The act provides access to consumer courts to such consumers of goods and services as defined in the Act. As per the Act, consumer is any person who
   (i) buys any goods for a consideration which has been paid or promised or partly paid and partly promised or under any system of deferred payment and includes any user of such goods other than the person who buys such goods for consideration paid or promised or partly paid or partly promised, or under any system of deferred payment when such use is made with the approval of such person, but does not include a person who obtains such goods for resale or for any commercial purpose; or
   (ii) hires or avails of any service for a consideration which has been paid or promised or partly paid and partly promised, or under any system of deferred payment and includes any beneficiary of such services other than the person who hires or avails of the services for consideration paid or promised, or partly paid and partly promised, or under any system of deferred payment, when such services are availed of with the approval of the first mentioned person but does not include a person who avails of such services for any commercial purpose.

According to Section 2 (d) of the Consumer Protection Act, it is not merely the buyer of goods or hirer of services who is called a consumer but any other person who uses such goods or avails of such services with the approval of the original buyer/hirer is also a consumer.

Further, the above definition makes it clear that the Consumer Protection Act primarily brings under its purview all goods and services. But Section 1 (4) says as otherwise expressly provided by the Central Government by notification, this act shall apply to all goods and services. Though the law makers provided an option to the Central Government to exempt certain categories of goods and services from the ambit of this act, no such exemption has been given so far.

> The **Consumer Protection Act** defines a **consumer** as any person who buys goods or hire or avail of any services and any other person who uses such goods or avails of such services with the approval of the original buyer/hirer.

Definition of Service The term "service" has a variety of meanings. It may mean any benefit or any act resulting in promoting interest or happiness. It may be contractual, professional, public, domestic, legal, statutory and so on. The concept of service thus is very wide. How it should be understood and what it means depends on the context in which it has been used. (Supreme Court in *Lucknow Development Authority vs. M.K. Gupta case*[17].)

The definition of service, as given in Consumer Protection Act under Section 2 (o), reads as "Service means service of any description which is made available to potential users and *includes,* but not limited to, the provision of facilities in connection with banking, financing, insurance, transport, processing, supply of electrical or other energy, board or lodging or both, housing construction, entertainment, amusement or the purveying of news or other information, but does not include the rendering of any service free of charge or under a contract of personal service."

Therefore, a service must be made available to potential users who are willing to pay for the service. The service must be rendered for remuneration. Services free of charge do not come under this definition and, hence, are outside the scope of the Consumer Protection Act. Medical services rendered free of charge in a government hospital are not within the purview of the act. The free services rendered by the municipalities in the form of facilities like sanitation, roads, street lights, parks and so on are also outside the purview of this act. In fact, these services are managed by the municipalities or other governmental agencies out of the taxes paid by the citizens. It has been held by the Supreme Court in *Commissioner, Hindu Religious Endowments, Madras vs. Sri Lakshmindra Thirtha Swamiar* case that these taxes do not constitute "consideration" for the services ostensibly rendered gratis by the state to its citizens. Hence, a tax payer does not come under the ambit of the definition of "consumer." Similarly, a claim of pension by an employee from his employer is not covered under the act because he is not hiring his employer's service for consideration.

In the exclusionary clause of the definition for service, the expression, "under contract of personal service" has been used but not defined in the act. It is pertinent here to draw a distinction between a "contract of personal service" and "contract for personal service." The former is the service relationship of a master and servant whereas the latter is the professional or technical services in the performance of which service providers are not subject to detailed direction and control but exercise professional or technical skill and use their own knowledge and discretion. In this case, the person availing of the service does not have control over the service provider and hence may complain about deficiency of service. But in the contract of personal service, an employee can be sent out of service by the master at will, and, therefore, no occasion can arise for the master to complain about the deficiency in the rendering of service by the employee. An employer cannot be regarded as a consumer with respect to the services rendered by his employee in pursuance of a contract of employment.

Whether the relationship between the doctor and the patient is in the nature of contract of personal service had come up for scrutiny in the *Indian Medical Association Vs Vasantha P. Nair*[18] case before the Supreme Court. The Supreme Court held that the relationship between a medical practitioner and a patient carries within it certain degree of mutual confidence and trust, and, therefore, the services rendered by the medical practitioner can be regarded as service of personal nature, but since there is no relationship of master and servant between the doctor and the patient, the contract between medical practitioner and his patient cannot be treated as a contract of personal service and as a contract for personal services and hence not covered by the exclusionary part of the definition of service.

> *As per the Consumer Protection Act, a service must be made available to potential users who are willing to pay for it. Services free of charge do not come under this definition and, hence, are outside the scope of the act.*

If a company is running a bus which is meant to be used by the staff of that company only or is running a canteen exclusively for its staff, it would not constitute rendering "service" for the simple reason that the facilities are not meant to be hired by the potential users.

Definition of Deficiency As per Section 2 (i) (g) of the Consumer Protection Act, deficiency means any fault, imperfection, shortcoming or inadequacy in the quality, nature and manner of performance which is required to be maintained by or under any law for the time being in force or has been undertaken to be performed by a person in pursuance of a contract or otherwise in relation to any service. Deficiency is a breach of an obligation—statutory, contractual or otherwise—to maintain a particular quality, nature and manner of performance of service. Deficiency in service may take many forms such as use of substandard material in construction, other defects and deficiencies in construction, delay in delivering services, delay in settling the claim or belated repudiation of claim by an insurance company and so on. The expression of deficiency is synonymous with negligence. Service companies that do not care for these deficiencies not only lose customers but also need to pay compensation to them.

> ***Service deficiency*** *is a breach of an obligation—statutory, contractual or otherwise—to maintain a particular quality, nature and manner of performance of service.*

Provisions of the Act for Professional Services, Education Services and PSUs

Professional Services

A profession is an occupation requiring either purely intellectual skill or manual skill controlled by intellectual skill. In matters of professional liability, professions differ from other occupations for the reason that professions operate in spheres where success cannot be achieved in every case, and, very often, failure depends on factors beyond human control.

In the sphere of professional services, medical services occupy a predominant place as these services are essential in nature and are required by each

Telephone Services

UNI-Bros got a telephone connection with STD facility installed at Karol Bagh in 1990. The average bill never exceeded INR 1750. Suddenly, the service provider Mahanagar Telephone Nigam Ltd. (MTNL) raised a bill dated 9.3.2001 for an amount of INR 146,260, another bill dated 9.4.2001 for INR 134,635 and the third bill dated 15.5.2001 for an amount of INR 92,365. Though the customer brought these excess bills to the notice of MTNL and requested it to quash the bills, MTNL did not accede. It was only after filing a complaint in Lok Adalat, MTNL offered to waive 30% of the disputed bills. Uni-Bros filed a complaint in the district forum. After a careful consideration, district forum passed the following order:

1. MTNL has to withdraw the excessive three bills and issue three fresh bills at the average of INR 1750 and the telephone be restored if not already restored.
2. MTNL has to pay INR 10,000 towards compensation for causing mental agony.
3. MTNL has to pay INR 2,000 towards cost of litigation.

The appeal by MTNL was dismissed by the state commission, and, hence, MTNL filed a revision petition before the national commission. The national commission observed that though there were clear rules for handling excess billing complaints, there was nothing on record to show that the complaint with regard to higher bills was investigated as procedure laid down in government instructions. There were detailed instructions known as "investigation of an excess billing complaint." Therefore, there was a clear deficiency of service, and, hence MTNL was directed to comply with the order of the district forum.

Source: MTNL Vs. UNI-Bros., CPJ 164 (NC), II (2009).

and every one in society. As such, a duty is cast on the medical practitioner to attend on the patient and exercise reasonable care while treating such a patient. Any medical practitioner who is negligent in his professional career may be held liable for any mishap due to that negligence. But mistaken diagnosis is not an act of negligence unless it is negligence per se. Similarly, paramedical services such as scanning centres, diagnostic centres and medical laboratories also come under the ambit of Consumer Protection Act. A decision pronounced by the Andhra Pradesh State Consumer Disputes Redressal Commission provides more light on this subject. In this case, an 11-month-old boy who was admitted in a hospital with fever and cough was advised blood transfusion. The patient's uncle donated blood which was tested by a blood bank and found to be HIV I and II negative. Although blood was transfused to the child, there was no improvement in the condition of the child. When the child's blood was examined, it was found infected with the HIV virus. The father and mother were tested and found to be HIV negative and hence the possibility of the child contracting the disease from parents was eliminated. It was held that the blood bank had issued the donor card without properly examining the blood of the donor and hence there was deficiency in service. The child was given a compensation of INR 0.1 million .

Educational Services

Imparting education is in the nature of a mission or a noble vocation. A teacher educates children, moulds their character, builds their personality and makes them fit to become responsible citizens. Education is imparted through schools, colleges, institutions and universities. Educational institutions may be private or government owned or a composite activity. The system consists of several components, namely, admission to these institutions, teaching and instructions, conducting examinations, performance appraisal of students, awarding degrees, issuance of certificates and diplomas of achievements and mark sheets and so on. The institution collects fees for examinations and convocations.

Imparting education has never been treated as a trade or business in this country. It has been treated as a religious duty or charitable activity. The vital point as to whether education falls within the purview of the Consumer Protection Act has come up before various state commissions and the national commission. The Maharashtra State Commission, while directing a college to refund the fee of a complainant, observed: "A student is essentially a consumer of services in an educational institution; therefore, when there is no service there is no right with the college to appropriate fees. If it insists on collecting fees without imparting education, it will amount to deficiency." In another case, the Haryana State Commission held that education is generally and prominently a service and, therefore, education would squarely come within the arena of service under the act. The Tamil Nadu State Commission held that education is one of the most valuable services in human society, and this service is not rendered free by the college. Hence, the students are consumers.

The Gujarat State Commission observed that some private educational institutions were making very tall claims and thereby creating big business and recovering by way of fees. It cannot, therefore, be denied that the relationship between the so-called student and such institutes is that of the provider and the recipient of service. The Calcutta High Court expressed that a student is not a consumer. The national commission had decided in earlier cases that a university or the board conducting public examinations, evaluating answer papers, announcing the results thereof and thereafter conducting rechecking of marks of any candidate is not performing any service for hire and there is no arrangement of the hiring of any service involved in such a situation as contemplated by Section 2 (1) (0) of the Consumer Protection Act. A candidate who appears for the examination cannot be regarded as a person who had hired or availed of the service of the university or board for consideration.

Public Sector Undertakings

Public sector undertakings which provide service to potential users are also covered under the ambit of Consumer Protection Act. In a judgement, the National Consumer Disputes Redressal Commission held that it is deficiency in service on the part of railways in not providing water in the compartment. The railway was required to see that water was available in the train. The national commission directed railways to pay INR 10,000 to the complainants, a couple who experienced hardships in procuring drinking water while travelling in the train.

Banking services

Pratima Pal and her husband Gopinath Pal had a savings bank account in Allahabad Bank. On 14.3.2007, the pass book was updated and Pratima Pal issued a cheque in favour of a school. On the said date, INR 178,574 remained in the account. On 19.5.2007, it was noticed by Gopinath Pal, when he went to the bank for updating his pass book, that INR 170,000 was withdrawn from their account fictitiously. It was noticed that on 30.3.2007, INR 50,000 was withdrawn, on 31.3.2007, INR 60,000 was withdrawn and, again on 4.4.2007, an amount of INR 60,000 was withdrawn. The account holders came to know that on 15.3.2007, somebody received a cheque book with 10 leaves in his favour by forging their signatures. The said person did not use any cheque leaf but used the requisition slip and took another cheque book from the bank and, using those cheque leaves from the cheque book obtained subsequently, withdrew the above amounts. As soon as it came to the account holders' notice they informed the bank manager and the manager showed them the encashed cheque in the computer, but the account holders denied the signatures. They wondered how the cheques were issued without proper verification. They further stated that when they went to withdraw INR 1,000 on 12.3.2007, they had to sign thrice on the cheque for verification. According to the customers, all the signatures were forged. The matter was reported to the zonal office, vigilance department and the local police with no redress. Hence, the couple filed the complaint with the district forum. The district forum allowed the complaint and directed Allahabad Bank to pay an amount of INR 170,000 along with interest at 6% p.a. from the date of withdrawal of money till it was credited to the savings bank account. Aggrieved by the order of the district forum, the bank went on an appeal to the West Bengal State Commission and argued that the two cheque books were issued to a third party believing that the transaction was authorized by the account holders and with a view to render effective services it was done. The state commission expressed its surprise on how the bank issued one cheque book on 15.3.2007 against an application and without production of any requisition slip. The state commission carefully compared the signature of the requisition slip with the signature card. Regarding the three cheques, the signatures of those cheques also were not similar to the signature in the signature card. Hence, the signatures of the account holders were forged. Being the custodian of the money of the customer, the bank should have been very cautious in making the payment. The state commission further questioned how the bank issued another cheque book when the cheque leaves of the earlier cheque book were not exhausted. By utilizing the leaves of the second cheque book, the fraud was committed. The bank was not vigilant and hence the judgment of the district forum was upheld.

Source: Allahabad Bank Vs. Pratima Pal, CPJ 42 (West Bengal State Commission), II, 2009.

A complaint can be filled only for deficiency in service, which involves a dispute to the quality, nature and manner of performance of service. The consumer courts do not entertain disputes relating to consideration. But with the recent amendment, the price factor also can be a subject matter of dispute if both parties agree for a particular price and later if one of the parties goes back on the agreement. The disruption of services by illegal strikes also comes under the purview of the act. "Services Marketing Insight: Disruption of Services by Illegal Strikes" discusses the details.

3. The act provides for simple, speedy and inexpensive justice. The procedural formalities to seek redressal are simplified as compared to the existing judicial system. Consumers can make a complaint on a piece

23.2 Services Marketing Insight | **Disruption of Services by Illegal Strikes**

On account of disruption of a large number of flights of Air India, caused due to sudden strike by the Flight Engineers Association, passengers were put to great inconvenience. On a common cause, a voluntary consumer organization filed a case with the national commission. The national commission observed that the persons employed on salary in an organization, which is rendering service for consideration, are equally covered by the provisions of the Consumer Protection Act, along with their management, if they resort to illegal strike.

The national commission gave the following directions in *Consumer Unity and Trust Society, Calcutta vs. C.M.D. Bank of Baroda* case, "Wherever a strike notice is served by the employees or their union on the management of a bank, and a strike appears to be imminent, the concerned bank should insert a publication in the leading newspapers informing the customers about the possibility of a strike in the bank, so that the customers, especially the small account holders, pensioners and so on may not be taken by surprise, but may instead, be enabled to withdraw sufficient amounts to meet their requirements during the period of threatened strike."

of paper, and there is no need of engaging a professional lawyer to represent the consumers in the consumer forum. Until 2002 amendments, there was no court fee for seeking redressal through consumer courts. The 2002 amendments prescribed nominal fee based on the value of the complaint and compensation sought for. The act also imposes a time limit of 90 days for the delivery of judgment. The act provides for establishment of consumer protection councils at central level, state level and also at the district level.

4. The act defines unfair trade practices[19] are the following:

"Unfair trade practice" means a trade practice which, for the purpose of promoting the sale, use or supply of any goods or for the provision of any service, adopts any unfair method or unfair or deceptive practice including any of the flowing practices, namely

(A) the practice of making any statement, whether orally or in writing or by visible representation, which

(i) falsely represents that the goods are of a particular standard, quality, quantity, grade, composition, style or model;

(ii) falsely represents that the services are of a particular standard, quality or grade;

(iii) falsely represents any re-built, second-hand, renovated, reconditioned or old goods as new goods;

(iv) represents that the goods or services have sponsorship, approval, performance, characteristics, accessories, uses or benefits which such goods or services do not have;

(v) represents that the seller or the supplier has a sponsorship or approval or affiliation which such seller or supplier does not have.

(vi) makes a false or misleading representation concerning the need for, or the usefulness of, any goods or services;

(vii) gives to the public any warranty or guarantee of the performance, efficacy or length of life of a product or of any goods that is not based on an adequate or proper test thereof;

provided that where a defence is raised to the effect that such warranty or guarantee is based on adequate or proper test, the burden of proof of such defence shall lie on the person raising such defence;

(viii) makes to the public a representation in a form that purports to be—(a) a warranty or guarantee of a product or of any goods or services or (b) a promise to replace, maintain or repair an article or any part thereof or to repeat or continue a service until it has achieved a specified result;

if such purported warranty or guarantee or promise is materially misleading or if there is no reasonable prospect that such warranty, guarantee or promise will be carried out;

(ix) materially misleads the public concerning the price at which a product or like products or goods or services, have been, or are, ordinarily sold or provided, and, for this purpose, a representation as to price shall be deemed to refer to the price at which the product or goods or services has or have been sold by sellers or provided by suppliers generally in the relevant market unless it is clearly specified to be the price at which the product has been sold or services have been provided by the person by whom or on whose behalf the representation is made;

(x) gives false or misleading facts disparaging the goods, services or trade of another person;

explanation: for the purposes of clause (1), a statement that is

(a) expressed on an article offered or displayed for sale or on its wrapper or container or

(b) expressed on anything attached to, inserted in, or accompanying, an article offered or displayed for sale or on anything on which the article is mounted for display or sale or

(c) contained in or on anything that is sold, sent, delivered, transmitted or in any other manner whatsoever made available to a member of the public;

> *According to the Consumer Protection Act, **"unfair trade practice"** means a trade practice which, for the purpose of promoting the sale, use or supply of any goods or for the provision of any service, adopts any unfair method or unfair or deceptive practice.*

shall be deemed to be a statement made to the public by, and only by, the person who had caused the statement to be so expressed, made or contained;

(B) permits the publication of any advertisement whether in any newspaper or otherwise, for the sale or supply at a bargain price of goods or services that are not intended to be offered for sale or supply at the bargain price or for a period that is and in quantities that are reasonable, having regard to the nature of the market in which the business is carried on, the nature and size of business and the nature of the advertisement;

explanation: For the purpose of clause (2), "bargain price" means (a) a price that is stated in any advertisement to be a bargain price, by reference to an ordinary price or otherwise, or (b) a price that a person who reads, hears or sees the advertisement would reasonably understand to be a bargain price having regard to the prices at which the product advertise or like products are ordinarily sold;

(C) permits

(a) the offering of gifts, prizes or other items with the intention of not providing them as offered or creating the impression that something is being given or offered free of charge when it is fully or partly covered by the amount charged in the transaction as a whole,

(b) the conduct of any contest, lottery, game of chance or skill for the purpose of promoting, directly or indirectly, the sale, use or supply of any product or any business interest;

(D) permits the sale or supply of goods intended to be used, or are of a kind likely to be used, by consumers knowing or having reason to believe that the goods do not comply with the standards prescribed by competent authority relating to performance, composition, contents, design, constructions, finishing or packaging as are necessary to prevent or reduce the risk of injury to the person using the goods;

(E) permits the hoarding or destruction of goods or refuses to sell the goods or to make them available for sale or to provide any service if such hoarding or destruction or refusal raises or tends to raise or is intended to raise the cost of those or other similar goods or service.

The Right to Information Act (2005)

The Right to Information Act[20] is an act to provide for setting out the practical regime of right to information for citizens to secure access to information under the control of public authorities in order to promote transparency and accountability in the working of every public authority, the constitution of a central information commission and state information commissions and for matters connected there with or incidental there to.[21] As per the act on receipt of a request, the information should be provided within 30 days. In case the information sought for concerns the life or liberty of a person, the information should be provided within 48 hours. The act, however, provides exemption for some kind of information that is likely to conflict with other public interests and requires confidentiality. The act provides for accountability of governments and their instrumentalities and also helps to contain corruption.

The Government of India brought out a number of laws to protect the interests of the consumers. The improper implementation of these laws indirectly gave moral strength to the businessmen to continue their unscrupulous activities. The procedural complexities, the time and psychological pressure required to fight against any businessman prevented the ordinary consumers from making a complaint and pursuing the matter.

THE ADMINISTRATIVE MECHANISM

There are several departments working for enforcing control system over the industry and business and thereby protecting the consumer interests. The following are the some of the important functionaries:

- *Department of Drug Administration*: This department is responsible for affective implementation for drug-related laws. The production, distribution and sale of dangerous drugs, cosmetics of substandard quality, narcotic and psychotropic substances and the like are not allowed as per the statutes, and the department takes the responsibility of protecting the people from such hazardous products.
- *Department of Preventive Medicine*: This department is responsible for ensuring the availability of quality food to the consumers. They work for the prevention of food adulteration, contaminated drinking water and the sale of food items in unhygienic conditions.
- *Directorate of Marketing and Inspection*: The directorate focuses on establishing quality standards to the food items. It accords an identity mark labelled as "Agmark" which signifies the standard quality for agricultural products.
- *Department of Consumer Affairs*: This department implements the provisions of Consumer Protection Act. The department establishes Consumer Disputes Redressal Forums and also Consumer Protection Councils. The department also takes care of public distribution system to check the inflationary trends in prices.
- *Bureau of Indian Standards (BIS)*: This bureau is responsible for standardization of products, marking and quality certification of goods. It provides ISI mark to such products that stand to the quality standards prescribed. Standardization is not mandatory but voluntary for the products.
- *Monopolies and Restrictive Trade Practices Commission*: The commission looks after for the control of monopolistic, restrictive and unfair trade practices. The commission receives complaints and takes up prosecution proceedings. As per the Competition Act (2002), the

"The Government of India and the state governments have established administrative mechanism to protect the interests of the consumers. These mechanisms are responsible for implementation of provisions under various acts relating to consumer protection."

commission ceases to exist once the competition commission is established. The proposed competition commission also regulates mergers and amalgamation purporting to cause detriment to the interest of consumers.

- *Department of Legal Metrology*: This department implements the provisions of Standards of Weights and Measurements Act. The department is empowered to take action on traders who contravene the provisions of packaged commodity goods.

BUSINESS RESPONSE TO THE CONSUMER MOVEMENT

The mounting pressure from several consumer organizations, complaints from consumers and the intervention from the Government of India with regulations to protect the interests of consumers forced the business community to respond and develop its own code of conduct. Rama Krishna Bajaj, the then Chairman of the Federation of Indian Chamber of Commerce and Industry (FICCI) (1984) stated that 'the business must formulate a code of conduct for them before the government intervenes and frames a code."[22] A few associations of businessmen have come up during the last four decades to impose self-regulation. They propagated that the consumers do not need any protection when all their rights are met with by the business community. The following are some of the associations of businessmen, which worked for consumers' interests through self-discipline of business.

- *The Council for Fair Business Practices*[23] *(CFBP)*: The council was established in 1966 with 53 members. The council prescribed the following nine fundamental obligations for the member business organizations: (1) to charge only fair and reasonable prices and to ensure that the prices to be charged to the consumers are brought to their (the consumers') notice; (2) to take every possible step to ensure that the agents or dealers appointed by them do not charge prices higher than fixed; (3) in times of scarcity, not to withhold or suppress stocks of goods with a view to hoarding and/or profiteering; (4) not to produce or trade in spurious goods or goods of standards lower than specified; (5) not to adulterate goods supplied; (6) not to publish misleading advertisements; (7) to invoice goods exported or imported at their correct prices; (8) to maintain accuracy in weights and measures of goods offered for sale and (9) not to deal knowingly in smuggled goods. Over the years, the council has tried to propagate the message of self-discipline from every available business platform. Initially, its efforts evoked scepticism; its advocacy was regarded as unrealistic in the prevailing situation. However, the council was gradually able to convince a large section of business of the need to adopt self-discipline in its own enlightened self-interest. The council has thus been able to generate an awareness of the need to adopt norms of self-discipline though its effective enforcement still remains a distant goal.[24]

- *The Advertising Standards Council of India*[25] *(ASCI)*: The Advertising Standards Council of India (ASCI) was established in 1985 and adopted a code for self-regulation in advertising to promote honest advertising and fair competition in market place. The council works for the protection of the legitimate interest of consumers and all concerned with advertising, whether they are advertisers, media, advertising agencies or others who help in the creation or placement of advertising. The code for self-regulation seeks to ensure (1) the truthfulness and honesty of representations and claims made by advertisements and to safeguard against misleading advertisements; (2) the advertisements are not offensive to generally accepted standards of public decency; (3) the advertisements observe fairness in competition so that the consumers need to be informed on the choices in the market place and the canons of generally accepted competitive behaviour in business are both served; (4) safeguard against the indiscriminate use of advertising for the promotion of products which are regarded as hazardous to society or to individuals to a degree or of a type which is unacceptable to society at large. The council established another wing, namely, Consumers Complaints Council consisting of 14 members. To have a fair representation, care has been taken to include eight members of the council neither connected to advertising nor business directly. ASCI has been doing a commendable job though it can exact pressure primarily on ethical grounds. If a complaint is upheld, the ASCI tries its best to ensure that the offending advertisement is either suitably modified or withdrawn.
- *The Associated Chambers of Commerce and Industry of India*[26] *(ASSOCHAM)*: ASSOCHAM is the apex body of industrial representatives and associations and traders. It has set up a Consumer Affairs Committee to take up the work in propagating consumer awareness among its members and also educating consumers through seminars, workshops, discussions and other methods. ASSOCHAM suggests its members to establish the Consumer Affairs Cell (CAC) in their respective organizations. The cell should be headed by a senior executive who reports directly to the chief executive of the company. It also suggested for the organization of consumer meets periodically to know consumer response on the products and services offered and to incorporate changes accordingly. If the aims and suggestions of ASSOCHAM are implemented by its members in right spirit, it would become a great contribution to the consumer movement.
- *The Federation of Indian Chamber of Commerce and Industry*[27] *(FICCI)*: FICCI is the apex body of the Chambers of Commerce and Industry of various parts of the country. It has a very wide network spread even to the remotest parts of the country. FICCI set up norms of business ethics. Its norms, as a measure of self-regulation, required its business community to ensure quality and safety of its products and

adherence to specified standards, accuracy of weights and measures, to avoid hoarding and artificially creating shortages, to avoid knowingly dealing in smuggled or spurious goods, not to publish misleading advertisements and to give good service such as after-sales-services or attendance to consumer complaints or warranty based on adequate data or tests.

- *Association of Indian Engineering Industry (AIEI)*: AIEI is yet another all-India body representing a number of industry and commercial units. It has formulated a consumer code which consists of safety norms, warranties, communications and environmental protection.

"The business also responds through imparting self-regulation to the consumers' concern and consumer movement. A few associations of the businessmen have come up with an internal campaign that the consumers do not need any protection when all their rights are met with by the business community."

In addition to the above, the New Delhi Traders Association (NDTA) and Confederation of Indian Food Trade and Industry (CIFTI) are the prominent bodies propagating self-discipline of the business in various respects.

The response from the business is more subjective rather than objective. The sensibility remained mostly in words, speeches, preaching and promises, but, in practice, business rivalry, competition, profit motives and other selfish considerations took the lead surpassing consumer interests. Marketing philosophers consistently established the fact that successful organization emerges only on the foundation of consumer satisfaction. Consumer retention is not possible through immoral and deceitful practices. It is possible only through fairness and real contribution to the customer value. It is true that some companies may achieve short-term gains by deceiving the people, but such organizations often become short lived. The long-term goals of the organization can be achieved only when consumer is placed as a central focus of the vision of a company.

SUMMARY

- Consumerism is a social movement to protect the interests of the consumer citizens against the exploitative traders and businessmen.
- It is the movement including consumers and government to work out for the welfare of the consumers and also forcing the industry and businessmen to impose self-discipline in serving customers.
- Consumers basically have some expectations from industry and business. They want such products be produced and services be rendered that can satisfy the real demand of the society. Products and services available should be qualitative and perform as per specifications.
- Consumer safety should be the responsibility of business and industry. They should not deceive the people with insufficient and false information.
- The products and services should be presented in the right form to facilitate consumers to select the right product or service.
- Industry and business should make use of the natural resource optimally and should have concern on environment. Besides all, consumers expect fairness in transactions.
- The consumers' concern on the happenings is mounting day by day due to the exploitative tendencies in business.
- In India, more than 30 legislations were enacted for the protection of consumers. The Consumer Protection Act, 1986 is the most comprehensive and benevolent legislation.
- The act provides six consumer rights such as right to safety, right to information, right to choice,

right to be heard, right to redressal and right to consumer education.

- A three tier quasi-judicial mechanism was created to deliver simple, speedy and inexpensive justice to the aggrieved consumers.
- National commission at the central level, state commissions at state level and district consumer forums at the district level were promoted to provide accessibility to justice.
- Consumer councils were formed at the three levels to discuss various problems and suggest measures for strengthening the law and enforcing mechanism.
- The government also developed administrative mechanism at various levels to safeguard the interests of the consumers and to punish traders who indulge in malpractices.
- Several consumer organizations have come up in the country. PATRA, CGSI, VCC, KCSS, CERC and many more consumer organizations are seriously working for the cause of consumers.
- Business organizations also realized their responsibilities and formed into various organizations to develop code of conduct and ethical behaviour in business. In spite of these developments, there are many sellers with unreasonable profit motives trying to exploit the poorly literate, weak and less-informed consumers.
- Marketers believe that the central focus of the business should be consumer value. Companies may gain short-term benefit through unwanted means, but, in the long run, they can be successful only when they adopt fairness and positive value in the business. The success stories of all successful companies proved this beyond doubt.

KEY TERMS

Consumer concern *464*
Consumer movement *460*
Consumer protection *460*
Consumer rights *468*
Consumerism *460*
Product representation *461*
Quasi judicial mechanism *472*
Unfair trade practice *467*

BRIEF QUESTIONS

1. What are consumer rights?
2. According to the Consumer Protection Act, how is the term *consumer* defined?
3. According to the Consumer Protection Act, how are the terms *service* and *service deficiency* defined?
4. What are unfair trade practices?
5. Explain the quasi judicial mechanism provided under Consumer Protection Act?
6. Is consumers' concern justifiable?

ESSAY QUESTIONS

1. What is consumerism? What are the expectations of consumers on industry and business?
2. What are the reasons for growing consumer concern in India?
3. Do you think consumers are being exploited and protection is needed?
4. Describe the growth and development of consumer movement in India.
5. Explain the salient features of Consumer Protection Act, 1986.
6. How is the business community responding to the consumer movement in India?
7. "Consumerism is shame to the business." Discuss.
8. As a consumer of services, what kind of protection do you need? Explain.

ASSIGNMENTS

1. Krishna has been a loyal customer of Vista Bank for a long time. He is not in the habit of verifying his account balances as he reposes utmost faith on his banker. One day surprisingly he found that INR 50,000 from his account was missing. The contact employees failed to give him any

satisfactory answer. No attempts were made by the banker for service recovery. Dissatisfied with the attitude of the employees, Krishna planned to approach district consumer forum for justice and compensation. You are required to:

(a) Suggest a service recovery plan to the banker
(b) Suggest an action plan to the consumer for approaching the consumer forum.

2. Conduct a focus group interview to the customers of private financial services and find out:
   (a) The consumer problems
   (b) The legal protection and administrative mechanism available to protect the interests of the consumer.

REFERENCES

1 Philip Kotler, *Principles of Marketing*. (New Delhi: Prentice Hall, 2002), p. 761.
2 K. Rama Mohana Rao, *Consumer Protection in India*. (Ludhiana: Kalyani Publications, 2005), p. 27.
3 G. Foxall, "Towards a Balanced View of Consumerism," *European Journal of Marketing*, 12, no. 4 (1993): 264–274.
4 Arthur Wate, *Consumer Protection*, 1-10-2005, www.solomonstarnews.com.
5 Aravind I. Kobra, "Consumerism in India – Myth and Reality," Monthly Commentary, New Delhi: The Indian Institute of Public Opinion, XXIX, Nos. 6, 7 (Jan-Feb 1988): 25.
6 Herbert Wong, *Consumer Protection by Industry*, Seminar Proceedings of Consumer Power in the "Free" Market (10-07-1991): 55.
7 Anoop K. Kaushal, *Consumer Protection Law*. (New Delhi: Universal Book Traders, 1993), p. 2.
8 P. V. V. Satyanarayana Murthy, *Consumer Protection in India*. (Visakhapatnam: Andhra University, Unpublished Thesis, 2005), p. 21.
9 K. Rama Mohana Rao, *Consumer Movement in Andhra Pradesh*. (Visakhapatnam: Andhra University, UGC Major Research Project, 2002), p. 21.
10 CERC, *Emergence and Formation of Consumer Groups – A Perspective*. (Ahmedabad: Consumer Education Series, 1992), p. 6.
11 P. V. V. Satyanarayana Murthy, *Consumer Protection in India*. (Visakhapatnam: Andhra University, Unpublished Thesis, 2005), p. 56.
12 K. Rama Mohana Rao, *Consumer Movement in Andhra Pradesh*. (Visakhapatnam: Andhra University, UGC Major Research Project, 2002), pp. 37–38.
13 Satwant Reddy, *Consumer Protection in India – Some Insights*, Key note address presented at National Seminar on Consumer Protection in India – Role of Administrative Mechanism, held at Andhra University, Visakhapatnam, Andhra Pradesh, 8th, 9th October 2004.
14 P. Venkatesan, *Strengthening the Consumer Movement*, http://pub.nic.in/feature/feyr2001/f030820011.html
15 Venkata Rao, *Law of Consumer Protection*. (Hyderabad: Asia Law House, 1998), pp. 7–8.
16 Manoj Jain, *The Consumer Protection Act 1986*. (Indore: India Publishing Company, 1994), p. 2.
17 CPJ 7 (SC), III, 1993.
18 CPJ 1 (SC), III, 1993.
19 Manoj Jain, *The Consumer Protection Act 1986*. (Indore: India Publishing Company, 1994), pp. 7–9.
20 S. Gogia & Company, Hyderabad, 2006.
21 Gazette of India, *The Right to Information Act, 2005*. (New Delhi: 2005).
22 Indian Express, May 17, 1984, reprinted in CFBP Bulletin, 18, no. 5, Sept.–Oct. 1984, p. 6.
23 www.cfbp.org, dated 11-6-2009.
24 Ramakrishna Bajaj, Two Decades of Business Efforts, When a Customer Has a Problem… Who Will Help Out? CFBP 20th Anniversary souvenir (1966–1986).
25 www.ascionline.org, dated 11-6-2009.
26 www.assocham.org, dated 11-6-2009.
27 www.ficci.com, dated 11-6-2009.

Services Marketing in India

24

LEARNING OBJECTIVES

After studying this chapter, you will be able to:

- Understand the marketing of banking services
- Understand the marketing of passenger transport services
- Understand the marketing of tourism services
- Understand the marketing of education services
- Understand the marketing of hospitality services

INTRODUCTION

The service sector has registered a substantial growth during the last two decades in India. Its growth prospects are very high, as per the expectations of industrialists and economists. With the change in government policy, leading to privatization and private participation in service sectors, competition has intensified. The entry of multinational corporations, directly and in collaboration with the private corporate giants of India, has further forced the sector to be market oriented. Under these circumstances, service companies of India have no other option but to adopt the marketing approach to achieve organizational objectives. They also have to recognize the distinctions between marketing approaches followed by manufacturing organizations and service organizations. The application of modern services marketing principles will certainly enhance the internal and external efficiency of service companies and enable them to deliver quality services to the customers.

This chapter examines some important services in India and analyses the services operations from the marketing point of view so that the people concerned can make use of the concepts discussed in the earlier chapters to improve their organizations.

THE MARKETING OF BANKING SERVICES: A CASE STUDY ON THE STATE BANK OF INDIA

Banks are catalytic agents which can create opportunities for the development of national resources and provide employment on a large scale. They perform a very important function in the developmental process by providing facilities for the pooling of savings and making them available to trade and industry, which in turn would work for the expansion of the productive capacity of the people, to satisfy their wants with respect to both goods and services.

The State Bank of India (SBI) is the largest public sector commercial bank in the country. The progress of the bank is intertwined with the history of a newborn independent nation, the growth and development of an emerging economy and the beginning of a new banking system in India. Over the past five decades, the State Bank of India has grown from strength to strength and lived up to its mission of being a premier commercial bank, committed to service and development. It was established in 1955 by the statutory amalgamation of the Imperial Bank and 10 other state-associated banks, namely, the State Bank of Saurashtra, the Bank of Patiala, the Bank of Bikaner, the Bank of Jaipur, the Bank of Rajasthan, the Bank of Indore, the Bank of Mysore, the Hyderabad State Bank, the Bank of Baroda and the Travancore Bank. The setting up of the State Bank was an important step towards the development of a strong commercial banking system in the country.

The State Bank of India is a public sector bank carrying the responsibility of promoting business in the interest and well-being of the society. It has a very wide network of branches spread over various parts of the country. The changing competitive scenario, particularly after the liberalization policies initiated in 1991, forced public sector banks to focus on providing satisfaction to the customers. The State Bank of India over the years had not given adequate focus on this mainly because of the absence of serious competition and the fact that it is the dominant public sector bank. The situation is fast changing due to the rapid change in technology and the entry of private sector and foreign banks. Market orientation has become inevitable to achieve organizational objectives. Considering the above facts, the marketing mix approach is used to analyse the marketing of banking services with particular reference to the State Bank of India.

Product Policies and Strategies

The State Bank of India offers various products to suit the needs of the different clientele. The product mix of the State Bank of India can be broadly categorized into eight product lines: Product line I offers personal banking services, product line II offers agricultural/rural banking services, product line III relates to corporate banking services, product line IV offers NRI services, product line V relates to government business, product line VI relates to various other services offered by the bank, product line VII offers international banking services and product line VIII relates to services offered to small and medium enterprises.

New Product Planning and Development

As competition is strong and dynamic in most markets, it is essential for a service organization to keep developing new products and modifying its current products to meet changing customer needs and competitors' actions. New product development is an essential activity for companies seeking growth. By adopting a new product strategy, firms are better able to sustain competitive pressures on their existing products.

New product design in the State Bank of India takes place at the central level. The central management committee, consisting of nine members, is concerned with the new product design and development. A specific responsibility for product design, development and execution is entrusted with the deputy managing director (corporate development officer). A team of product-designing experts work under him. It is a centralized activity, and the execution takes place all over the country at different branches. The process of making modifications in the existing products and development of new products takes place after a thorough marketing research. The marketing research is undertaken by the research wing of the bank, situated in the central office. The research centre carries work to affect modification in the existing product to increase acceptance, based on customer perceptions, buying behaviour and the likes and dislikes of customers. Customers' suggestions regarding required modifications are given special attention in designing new products or in modifying the existing products.

Product Additions and Deletions

The product mix of a bank cannot be a fixed one. The length and breadth of the product mix needs to be modified so as to make it suitable to meet the changing needs of the society. As product additions are necessary to create new desires and to meet the newly identified needs of the market, product deletions are also necessary to keep the product mix under the span of management and also to minimize loss. The products that are designed keeping in mind specific situations, are not accepted by customers, those that failed to match the needs and wants of customers and so on are required to be dropped out of the product mix. The State bank of India adds products regularly and also drops products by reviewing periodically the performance and prospects.

Pricing Policies and Strategies

In the banking sector, the pricing decision is reflected on the interest rates for loans and advances and on deposits and service charges for various support services performed by banks. The pricing decision of any scheduled bank is in accordance with the RBI guidelines that are in force. The flexibility in pricing is very much limited to the banks. The interest is the payment for the use of funds over a period of time. The rate actually charged depends on such factors as the term of loan/deposit, type of loan/deposit, the creditworthiness of the borrower, the amount of collaterals and the tax treatment of interest for both parties.

Administered Interest Rates

The central fact about bank interest rates in India is that the interest rates are determined by market authorities but not by market forces. Deposit interest rates were regulated for the first time in 1966 through inter-bank agreements. Since 1969, the RBI has taken responsibility for fixing interest rates for banks. The RBI fixes different deposit interest rates and lending interest rates for banks, namely, larger banks, smaller banks, co-operative banks and regional rural banks. The controller of capital issues fixes the ceiling on the coupon rates on industrial debentures and preference shares. The Indian Banks Association fixed the ceiling on call rates from 1973 up to October 1988. The call rates were freed from the ceiling in 1988. The government fixes the interest rates on treasury bills and long-term government securities. The government and RBI regulate the fixation of interest rates on loans to different categories of borrowers and for different purposes. They also fix interest rates on different financial instruments such as commercial bills. Thus, the ruling level and structure of interest rates in India in any given period was an administered one.

Deregulation of Interest Rates

In order to develop and make the banking sector more competitive and market oriented, the Reserve Bank of India initiated a shift from administered pricing to free and flexible pricing system. The Chakravarthy Committee, which was appointed in 1985 to review the working of monetary system, strongly recommended that the administered system should be modified in such a manner that the deficiencies so far referred to were eliminated substantially. The committee recommended that the ceiling on interest rates on bank loans and call loans should be abandoned and that the interest rates on treasury bills, government securities and bank deposits should be appropriately raised so as to yield realistic and reasonable returns to the holders of these claims. The committee also mentioned that the higher interest rates are not really against the goal of social justice, and, in fact, they help small savers who are not in a position to take advantage of fiscal concessions. The recommendation of the committee was approved by the RBI.

Trends during the 1990s and Deregulation

Major financial sector reforms were undertaken in the 1990s with a view to fostering competitive efficiency in the banking sector. One of the major objectives of the banking sector reforms has been to eliminate financial repression, which has been inherent in the administered interest rate structure. The Narasimham Committee, which was appointed in 1991 by the RBI, recommended that the real interest rates should be positive and that concessional interest rates should be done away with. In acceptance of the recommendation, interest rate reforms were undertaken in money, credit and government security markets. In 1992–1993, the structure of interest rates for commercial banks was altered to a more simplified one. As a step towards progressive rationalization of the banks' lending rate structure, the six categories of lending rates were reduced to four in April 1992 and were further reduced to three in April 1993. Effective from October 1994, interest rates on loans above INR 0.2 million were freed and banks were permitted to determine their prime lending rates.

Successive credit policy pronouncements of the RBI during the last decade have brought substantial deregulation and flexibility for banks to evolve their price strategy. The complexities of the interest rates' prescription that rose through the 1970s and the early 1980s were done away with during the 1990s. As recommended by the Chakravarthy Committee, interest rate reforms were undertaken in money, credit and government security markets. The structure of interest rates for commercial banks was altered to a more simplified one. Besides the reduction in the number of slabs, the bank rate was reactivated in April 1997. With the inflation rate under control, the monetary policy was directed towards reducing the minimum lending rate. The gradual introduction of a loan system in place of a cash credit system has facilitated banks in planning their cash flows better. The restrictions on project financing by banks have been increasingly liberalized to enable banks to extend term loans.

SBI's Interest Rate

According to demanding trends in the market and as per the instructions of the RBI, the SBI follows a flexible interest policy. As and when the credit policy of RBI is announced, the SBI changes its interest rates accordingly. In view of decline in the spreads, the bank has been concentrating more on deposit mobilization and disbursements by marketing its activities focussing on safety and liquidity. During 1997–1998 to 2007–2008, SBI changed the interest rates on advances 19 times and the interest rates on deposits 28 times.

The Distribution Network

The SBI follows direct marketing to provide banking services to the target market. The production and distribution outlets of the banking services are the branches and automated teller machines (ATMs) established in various parts of the country. The bank has achieved a phenomenal growth in terms of branch network since its inception. It has the largest network of bank branches in the country. According to the State Bank of India Act, the bank had a statutory obligation to open 400 new branch offices in the rural and semi-urban areas during the first 5 years of its existence. The total number of branches of the bank which was 8,873 in 1997–1998 increased to 9,517 in 2006–2007. The branches in foreign countries increased from 52 to 83 during the same period.

The SBI is a public sector bank and as such it plays a vital role in the development of the economy as a whole. The bank has committed itself to developing a market for banking services in rural areas by cultivating banking habits in the rural population. The underlying principle behind the expansion of branches in the rural areas was the extension of the banking services to the areas that are poorly served and particularly to stimulate banking in rural areas where the commercial banks in the private sector are reluctant to extend their services. The bank is under obligation to mobilize savings from the rural population of the country by opening new branches in rural India. The number of branches established in rural areas was 4,127 in 1997–1998. The management of the SBI had taken a decision to close the non-viable branches. Therefore, the number of rural branches was reduced to 3,825 by the end of 2006–2007.

Information Technology and Customer Service

The bank has adopted and is pursuing effectively its IT policy with the aim of achieving efficiency in operations, meeting customer and market expectations and staying ahead in competition. The introduction of Electronic NOSTRO Account Reconciliation (ELENOR) in December 2000 has helped fast, accurate and fully integrated reporting of forex transactions and has made a major breakthrough in effectively tackling the NOSTRO reconciliation. It has enabled online reporting of forex transactions from 444 forex intensive branches. State Bank Electronic Payment Systems (STEPS) facilitates instantaneous electronic transfer of funds in 1,557 branches. Another product, e-realization, was introduced in October 2001 to facilitate expeditiously reconciliation of outstanding entries in DDP cheques/dividends at 972 branches. These projects were conceived, developed and implemented with in-house expertise, and their success has been widely acclaimed. Apart from the above, 2,000 corporate customers are using remote log-in facilities, which have been implemented in 200 branches. Tele-banking has been implemented at 106 branches, where customers can access their accounts through telephone from anywhere at anytime. With the computerization of all branches, the State Bank of India brought improvement in the customer service, introduced features such as networked ATMs, Internet banking, tele-banking and customer enquiry terminals. Computerization has helped in extension of business hours, faster remittances and speedier collection of instruments.

The SWIFT network has been extended to 447 domestic branches. This has helped faster and automated message transmission. The bank's SWIFT gateway and software at SWIFT Operation Center (SOC) have been upgraded to SWIFT alliance access. The RBI VSAT project, Indian Financial Network (INFINET) backbone, is being used for ELENOR, CMP, STEPS and other messaging, which has resulted in greater efficiency in transaction processing and reporting. The bank has a network covering 164 VSATs in 113 cities extending the coverage to almost the entire country in 2001–2002, and 5,327 VSATs in 612 cities were connected in 2005–2006.

The SBI home page, the bank's Web site, has been redesigned to provide a wide range of information, including profile of all SBI branches. "Online SBI," the bank's Internet banking service, introduced on July 1, 2001, covering retail customers, has been expanded to cover corporate customers also in March 2002. This service covered more than 4,500 branches.

The State Bank Computer Centre implemented various technology-oriented projects to facilitate speedy reconciliation of inter-office transactions and helped the bank in achieving nearly 100 per cent reconciliation. The project e-recon, which is used for transmission of branch clearing and drafts accounts data for reconciliation through the Internet, has been implemented in 2,849 computerized branches.

Corporate communication in the bank has a new look with the video conference facility being available at 24 centres, reducing the need for travel of the executives and, in effect, saving time. The bank is pursuing an aggressive

IT policy as a strategic initiative to meet the growing competition for business and market share, achieve efficiency in internal operations and meet customer expectations. The ATM project, where ATMs are enabled to pay utility bills and college fees, book airline tickets, accept donations, etc., are the new initiatives. Further, bilateral sharing of ATMs was extended to 13 banks, covering 15,700 ATMs, and an MoU has been signed with the Indian Railways for installing ATMs at 682 railway stations.

Core banking solution (CBS) covers 72 million accounts and more than 85 per cent of the bank's business. Financial project for treasury and core banking solution has been implemented at 73 foreign offices in 22 countries, along with Internet banking at all foreign offices. Further, Internet banking has been implemented at 4,498 domestic branches and used by retail banking customers for utility bill payment and booking of rail and air tickets.

The IT policy and IS security policy have been implemented after being benchmarked against best global practices. The bank's central data centre and disaster recovery centres were certified as ISO/IEC 27001:2005 compliant, which is the new international standard for Information Security Management System.

SBI Connect, the wide area networking (WAN) project of the bank, is capable of carrying data, voice and video. All applications requiring connectivity can ride on the SBI Connect backbone in addition to 5,794 branches/offices of SBI and 4,820 branches/offices of associate banks being networked under the SBI Connect Project.

SBI offers customer service and community service banking through the distribution network. It also initiated BPR to promote efficiency in branch operations. These are discussed below.

Customer Service: A number of initiatives were taken up to intensify focus on the customer service. These included conducting of open house or town hall customer meets with participation by circle management; "Operation Samay" at branches to ensure that counters open for business before time and for drawing up of ground rules for the customer service for operating staff. Customers were encouraged to provide frank and honest feedback on services at open house meets.

Community Service Banking: Apart from the normal banking operations, the bank seeks to reinvest part of its profit in various community welfare projects to improve the quality of the life of the poor, neglected, weaker and downtrodden sections of society.

Business Process Reengineering (BPR): The State Bank of India has taken up the BPR project with seven key initiatives with an objective of creating a world class bank. The seven initiatives are core process redesign, CPC design, branch redesign, alternative channel design, sales forces, organizational and performance management implications and change management. The focus of the project is to enhance productivity, efficiency and customer service, to create growth engines and to establish organizational enablers. The bank is focusing on leveraging its IT investment with business process reengineering to bring out the desired change in banking operations.

Further, the bank has taken up the following initiatives to strengthen the distribution network.

- *ATMs:* ATMs have been floated as a means of improving the bank's productivity and extending short-service hours at low cost for routine transactions. ATMs have gained increasing acceptance by both the banking community and the consumers. The SBI makes extensive use of the ATM as a distribution strategy for low-potential/high-personal service cost customers.
- *Model Branch:* As per the guidelines of the RBI, the SBI has identified 220 branches to be developed as model branches. The selection of branches is a proper mix of metropolitan, urban, semi-urban and rural branches from all over the country. The parameters for selecting a branch as a model branch are lay-out, workflow, health and recovery of advances, profitability and productivity, in addition to the quality of the customer service rendered.
- *Personalized Branch Network:* Through the personalized branch network, the SBI provides a range of services under one umbrella. The ambience of these branches is intended to provide comfort and convenience to the customers. Personalized branches are opened for customers who need to complete transactions quickly.
- *Branch Management:* Branch managers are vested with discretionary powers, according to the size of the branch and scale. Sanction of loans is made by the branch manager at his discretion, within the broad policy framework of the bank. Depending on the size of the branch, loans and advances are provided to the customers, based on credit standards. Branch managers do not have the power to take any disciplinary proceedings against the staff. They are held responsible for the safety and security of the premises, accounts, inspection, supervision, coordination of work and performance of the branch. Reporting to the controlling authority is also part of a branch manager's responsibilities.

  There is no fixed formula for deployment of staff. The number of staff is determined according to the volume of business of the branch.
- *Physical Facilities*: Every branch provides seating place, writing pads and signboards to facilitate customers' convenience. Each branch is required to display the timings of the bank, holidays, the branch manager's and AGM's names and the name of the bank and branch.
- *Branch Layout*: There is no specific layout design. Customers should find it convenient to access different areas such as the cash section, accounts section and teller section. The authority concerned in the module is the panel engineer, who visits the branch, and in consultation with the security officer makes suggestions about the layout. From the bank's point of view, the primary motive is to safeguard the "cash chest."

- *Management Information System*: The bank's management information system (MIS) aims at providing timely and accurate information to the management with the help of advanced information technology. With the introduction of MIS for loans and advances (MISLA) in over 7,000 branches, the bank is capable of in-depth analysis of borrowed accounts, which facilitates better credit management. The introduction of the relational database management systems (RDBMS) strengthens the monitoring process. In order to make information available easily to the functionaries at the corporate centre, the "Internet" is available.

External Marketing

The SBI uses advertising and personal selling for communicating marketing offers to consumers. The media used to carry State Bank advertising are the newspapers, radios, televisions, magazines and outdoor and transit advertising. Web sites on the net carry information, which a customer can access on the history of the bank, products and services and different loan schemes offered. Their Web sites include statebankofindia.com and sbi.org.in.

The promotional measures of the SBI are taken at three levels: the central office, the local head office (LHO) and the module (a regional unit). The central office advertises various schemes through newspapers and hoardings at all important customer catchment areas. Certain advertisements, such as introduction of new products, are directly taken up by the central office and are published in all leading newspapers. The central office at Mumbai releases the advertisement budget and allocates funds to various LHOs for the purpose. The LHOs at the state level take up promotion programmes through various schemes. Each LHO mainly concentrates on promotion activity in the capital city in which it is placed. It also gives directions to modules from time to time about the new directives in promotion policies. Module gets advertisement material such as brochures, pamphlets, calendars and other leaflets directly from the LHO and/or the central office. Besides the advertisement amount allocated by the LHOs, a module takes up advertisement in its jurisdiction mainly through the following four categories: hoardings, newspapers, brochures and electronic media. The bank maintains connectivity with its customers through the following measures:

- *Customer Feedback:* At the end of every quarter, a feedback session is conducted by the bank about its product offers and services. Besides this, the bank observes the 15th of every month as the "customer" day. The head of the branch or head of the zone is deputed to redress grievances.
- *Customer Councils:* The bank organizes interactive sessions periodically at different branches, depending on the size of the staff. Branches with a staff strength of 100 and more as well as some specialized branches invite three to six customers who discuss various issues and steps needed to improve customer service with members of the customer service committee.

- *Disposal of Complaints:* The bank has set certain norms to settle the disputes of the customers. All complaints should ordinarily be disposed of within 3 weeks. However, for complaints received through the Director of Public Grievances, Government of India, a fixed time-frame of 6 weeks from the date of receipt of a complaint is set for its disposal. The customer grievance cell at LHOs monitors complaints pending for 3 weeks and above and explains the status to the respective general managers. All complaints pending for over 1 month are put up to the central management committee (CMC) for necessary action. In addition to the above, there is also a customer grievances cell in the Prime Minister's Office (PMO), Ministry of Finance, Government of India and at the RBI. Any grievance registered at the above places is to be redressed within 2 days. Any type of grievance can be registered in the above-mentioned offices, if the customer intends to air any grievance. Any such complaint is answered through a written communication to the customer, besides a copy being sent to the Reserve Bank of India. To ensure efficient customer service, the bank collects feedback on a regular basis through the visits of senior officials from the controlling offices. The system of holding customer meets at regular intervals at branches is another mechanism evolved by the bank to elicit customer reactions about the quality of service rendered.
- *Community Service Banking:* The bank undertakes non-loaning activities or programmes with a high social content, involving voluntary efforts of staff members of branches and other offices throughout the country. Some of the non-banking activities are blood donation camps, medical/health/eye camps for poor persons/children/pensioners, medicine banks, family welfare camps, veterinary camps, literary classes, special programmes such as awards for meritorious students, tree planting and other environmental protection programmes.

Internal Marketing

The staff of the State Bank of India comprises officers, clerks and subordinates. Many efforts are being made to develop the conventional skills and a better attitudinal orientation of the staff. Recruitment to the officers' cadre is done through a national level competitive examination and also through internal promotions of the experienced and talented people. The selection is based on a written test. The selected officers are placed on probation for a period of about 2 years.

Till the 1990s, the SBI used to select people for the clerical cadre through a written test. After 1990, the test was conducted by the Banking Services Commission, until the commission was discontinued. Advertisements for recruitment are now made in all the leading newspapers. After receiving the applications from respondents, the bank conducts a written test followed by an interview. Finally, the selected candidates are placed in respective jobs after an initial induction programme.

There is no selection process for the subordinate staff. Initially, they are taken on a temporary basis, and, based on performance, they are given permanent employment. Subordinates are recruited at the discretion of the bank manager and employed on a temporary basis. Generally, candidates with good manners and polite behaviour are chosen as subordinates.

The central board of the executive committee makes all appointments and promotions for the official cadre in the State Bank of India. There are three channels though which officers are recruited in the bank.

(i) Direct recruitment—probationary officers and rural development officers.

(ii) Promotion as trainee officers.

(iii) Promotion as junior management officials from the clerical cadre.

Employee Training

The SBI makes continuous efforts to enhance knowledge, develop skills and re-orient the attitude of the employees to keep pace with the changing environment. The bank's training network consists of four apex level colleges, namely, State Bank Staff College, Gurgaon; State Bank Staff College, Hyderabad; State Bank Institute of Rural Development and State Bank Institute of Information and Communication Management and over 50 training centres located across the country. In addition to providing training, colleges conduct research on relevant topics. With a view to providing on-site training to employees working in the branches, the bank has a visiting faculty scheme under which faculty from training centres visit branches and conduct training sessions, taking into consideration the local factors also.

The training focus is mainly on adaptation to changes in the work procedures and to update knowledge constantly about the continuous changes in the policies of the government and their impact on the bank's working. For this purpose, training centres were established in various parts of the country. The focus is also on ensuring systems and procedures in the bank, matching with changing business environment, and the continuous review and updating of systems and procedures.

The bank has established adequate support systems to provide necessary information to the employees. For internal communication, the theme of the SBI has been "the customer is the king; he is not at our mercy." The employees are also informed about the developments in the economy, banking trends and the achievements of employees in the business. The media used for internal communication include *The SBI Monthly Review, Gurukula, The SBI Economic Newsletter, Choyanika.*

Employee Benefits

The bank, in order to retain the talented and potential employees, offers financial packages and also provides welfare facilities.

No bank whether in the public sector, private sector, co-operative sector or a foreign bank can really pose a serious challenge to the SBI. The bank has a large and loyal customer base due to its extensive distribution network and its creditability as a public sector bank with a large asset base. However, in the light of the changes in the banking sector with a focus on customer service, new product offerings, persuasive communications, technology-linked services, there is a threat of the SBI losing its supreme position in the market if it does not respond appropriately.

MARKETING OF TRANSPORT SERVICES: A CASE STUDY ON APSRTC

Andhra Pradesh State Road Transport Corporation (APSRTC) is a state-owned passenger transport service organization. It was formed in 1958 by taking over the assets and liabilities of its predecessor, the Road Transport Department. The assets at that time were valued at INR 22.5 million. Within 3 years of the formation of the APSRTC, the nationalized transport services in the state witnessed enormous growth. The APSRTC for the first time in the country started night express services in 1963–1964. The first service was introduced on the Hyderabad–Vijayawada route from May 1, 1963. The corporation had initiated the system of issuing tickets in advance and reservation of seats at a nominal charge of INR 0.25. This facility was extended to all express and deluxe services in 1963–1964 to assure the public of seats without having to wait to buy tickets just prior to departure. Articulated double-decker buses, designed by APSRTC and Hyderabad Allwyn Limited, were introduced in Hyderabad city in April 1963. A departmental training school was opened in Vijayawada during the year for providing training facilities to mechanical and operating staff. As an experimental measure, the system of one-man operation of bus service on long distance, express and deluxe services operating between Hyderabad and Vijayawada was introduced in November 1964. These services were operated without conductors but with experienced and selected drivers to look after the passengers. Special school buses, ladies special buses and limited stop services were introduced in 1966.

The Andhra Pradesh State Government in 1978 had declared its policy of providing bus facilities to all the villages in the state. The APSRTC was entrusted with the responsibility of fulfilling this task. The corporation chalked out a time-bound programme and connected 1,137 villages in the state by the end of June 1978. Further, 484 schemes involving 512 buses on 777 routes were prepared under the Village Link Transport Scheme. These schemes were aimed at providing mechanized transport facility to 3,211 unconnected villages in the state in a scheduled 0.122 million kilometre range.

In pursuance of its policy of nationalization of the entire passenger road transport services in the state, APSRTC implemented various schemes.

This case study has been prepared in association with D. Appala Raju, Professor and Director, Guru Nanak Business School, Hyderabad and Dr. S. G. Rama Rao, Associate Professor, VS Lakshmi Institute of Computer Applications and Management Studies for Women, Kakinada.

APSRTC covered about 83 per cent of the geographical area of the state, representing 75 per cent of the total volume of bus operations. The corporation experienced many ups and downs during the last 2 decades. The customer-oriented approach adopted in recent years drove the corporation through the path of success. By the end of 2008–2009, the APSRTC had 1,14,973 employees, operating 21,324 buses in 7,739 routes covering a route length of 7.762 million km. The corporation carries 14.252 million passengers per day through its 202 operating depots.

The Service Product Mix

Being one of the public utilities, the APSRTC offers its output in the form of road passenger transportation services to various consumers. The service product mix of APSRTC consists of four product lines. They are mofussil services, city services, supplementary services and support services. Mofussil services are those services that are operated in other than city service areas. The services are spread throughout the state and in some interstate routes. Basically, four types of transport services are offered under the category of mofussil services. They are ordinary services, express services, luxury services and hi-tech services.

City services are limited to select urban regions. The services are intended basically to meet the growing needs of the urban population for local transport. There are three types of services offered under the category of city services. They are city ordinary services, metro express services and metroliner services.

Besides passenger transport services in mofussil and city areas, the APSRTC also offers mobility services for certain organizational goods under the head of supplementary services. It has been transporting mail bags for India Post as well as newspapers and magazines. In addition, the APSRTC provides transport facility on special occasions such as festivals and fairs, either regularly or on demand.

The APSRTC also operates services on demand. Buses of the corporation are given on hire to the public for marriages or tours, subject to availability, on receipt of 7 days' advance intimation.

The APSRTC provides a number of value-added support services. Prominent among such services include cloak room facilities for safe keep of passengers' luggage in bus stations and dormitories for resting, space for refreshment stalls/restaurants, required by fruit stalls, fancy stores, medical shops and public telephones, etc. Hygienic toilets, parking facilities, public address systems and information centres are also provided. Closed circuit televisions, drinking water for waiting halls/space for passengers, seating, lighting and maintenance at bus stations along with general security of passengers are provided. In addition, first-aid facilities are made available to the travelling public. The corporation itself takes care of some of the services and some are taken care of by private parties under the supervision of the corporation.

The corporation operates more than 80 per cent of the buses on mofussil routes while less than 20 per cent of the buses are operated on city routes.

The APSRTC-operated passenger transport services on a number of routes are spread over various parts of the state and some selected parts of the neighbouring states.

Pricing

The primary objective of APSRTC is to serve society by providing an adequate, efficient, economical and properly co-ordinated road transport system in the state. The pricing of the corporation services includes both fiscal and welfare objectives, which are often in mutual conflict. Fiscal objectives emphasize a fair return on capital investment, whereas welfare objectives imply maximization of public interest. The APSRTC tries to achieve these two conflicting objectives by adopting strategies such as charging different prices by differentiating the service offer and offering concessions to some sections of society.

The fares charged by the Andhra Pradesh State Road Transport Corporation are generally based on the principle of meeting the costs of operation and earning a fair margin for depreciation and development. Although the corporation has to run on a business principle, it does not have the freedom or power to increase the fares. Whenever the corporation wants to increase the fares, it has to submit the details to the state government and seek permission for increasing the fare. The corporation submits its proposals with all necessary details in support of change in fares to the Ministry of Transport, Government of Andhra Pradesh. The Minister for Transport, if necessary, places the issue either before the state cabinet or the ministerial committee set-up for the purpose. The corporation can incorporate changes in passenger fares only after receiving specific instructions from the Ministry of Transport.

The Distribution Network

A service marketing organization may choose either direct marketing or channels of distribution. Direct marketing involves no intermediaries, and the service producer sells directly to the customers. In the case of channels of distribution, intermediaries are involved between the producer and the consumer. The APSRTC follows direct marketing to facilitate mobility services to the customers. The production and distribution outlets of the corporation are bus stations, bus shelters and bus stops. A bus station is an organized service outlet wherein a service environment is designed to create quality experience for consumers.

The bus stations of the APSRTC are categorized into three classes—major/large, medium and small bus stations. Major/large bus stations are those which are located in the capital city of the state, the district headquarters and other places of importance, where the passenger turnover is very high. The major/large bus stations are managed by the junior scale officers' cadre or by assistant traffic managers assisted by other supporting bus station staff. The medium bus stations are located at divisional revenue headquarters, high traffic junctions and other places of commercial importance. These are managed by senior traffic inspectors (Traffic Inspectors Grade I) or Traffic Inspectors Grade II. The small bus stations are located at the mandal headquarters and other places. The small bus stations are managed by Traffic Inspectors Grade III or traffic controllers. The duties and responsibilities at all the bus stations are almost similar except for certain additional responsibilities including security against thefts, cloak room facility and so on at major bus stations.

The small bus stations will have a minimum of six platforms and a maximum of 11 platforms with a minimum of 1,500 square feet roofed space exclusively for passenger mobility. Besides, the space is provided for commercial establishments, toilets and offices of the bus stations. The medium bus stations will have 12 to 20 platforms with a minimum of 3,000 square feet-roofed space exclusively for use by the passengers apart from additional space to commercial stalls and for administrative purposes. The major/large bus stations have more than 20 platforms and more than 5,000 square feet-roofed space.

The bus stations, apart from providing necessary facilities to the service provider and the service user, are also used to generate non-traffic revenue (commercial revenue) for the corporation. The APSRTC introduced a scheme of appointing authorized agents known as APSRTC-authorized ticket booking agent/agency. Under this scheme, the regional manager of an area may appoint any number of agents based on the need and the competition that exists in that area. The objective of the scheme is to increase the salability of tickets by expanding the reservation/ticketing network. It helps passengers to make advance booking from places close to their dwelling places, instead of having to go all the way to the bus station.

Selling tickets through agencies have been prominently used by private sector bus operators. They have been able to generate business without having formal office structures or bus station facilities. The management of APSRTC realized the threat in this area and introduced the agency authorization system. Although agents were nominated, the business generated through them was not up to expectations. However, private operators were still able to make good business due to flexibility in pricing and commission systems. APSRTC could not transform the agents as sales personnel of APSRTC but could use them only as facilitators.

External Marketing

The need for designing an effective promotional programme has been gaining significance over the years. The function of communication in APSRTC was entrusted to the traffic managers at various levels. The corporation had identified different functions to be taken up under the communication campaign.

Communication at Bus Stations: The corporation provides an enquiry counter in every bus station. This counter is kept open 24 hours in major and medium bus stations and 18 hours in small bus stations.

The enquiry counter is a direct personal interacting unit, wherein the specially trained and designated employees provide information to passengers. Each bus station is equipped with a public address system. The walls and pillars of bus stations are used for the display of information through written media to the customers as well as the employees of the organization.

Communication in Buses: The APSRTC provides the following information in the interior and exterior of the buses through written communication:

- No smoking caution
- Warning against ticketless travel
- Reservation of seats for ladies, physically handicapped persons and public representatives
- Information about the bus timings on a particular route
- Details about emergency exit
- Safety precautions to be observed while travelling

The exterior of the bus is used to communicate the bus stations en route and also to communicate various promotional programmes of the corporation. The corporation also uses print and electronic media for communication. Newspapers, radio and television are regularly provided with information relating to bus routes, timing, reservation details and specific information. Some newspapers and local television channels communicate this information without any charge.

The APSRTC has introduced several promotional schemes for specific target groups. The promotional schemes include advance seat reservation, advance seat reservation by telephone, return journey ticket, Tirumala link ticket, travel-as-you-like tickets, treats, RTC-gift scheme, CAT card, concessions and so on.

The APSRTC uses the print media for releasing advertisements to mobilize public opinion in favour of the corporation and to persuade the target consumers. There is no consistent policy and budget provision for the release of advertisements. But the corporation management uses its discretion to release advertisements whenever necessary.

Apart from all these promotional programmes, the APSRTC conducts the customer/passenger meets regularly at the depot managers' offices. Market surveys are also conducted on various routes to know the feedback and competitive position.

Internal Marketing

Internal marketing is concerned with developing responsiveness, responsibility and unity of purpose among employees. The fundamental aims of internal marketing are to develop internal customer awareness and remove functional barriers to effectiveness. It ensures that all employees understand and experience the various business activities and campaigns and also motivates them to act in a service-oriented manner. The internal exchange must operate effectively between an organization and its employees before facing external markets.

In state road transport undertakings, recruitment and selection are made strictly according to the rules laid down by the respective state governments. The selection of the candidates takes place either through interviews or both written tests and interviews. In APSRTC, there are four classes of employees. Class I (officers' category), class II (supervisors' category), class III (technical employees' category) and class IV (non-technical employees' and workers' category). For Class I and II employments, the recruitment and selection process is centralized at the corporation level. The corporation has decentralized the system of recruitment and selection for Class III and IV employees.

Training helps employees to perform efficiently and deliver service quality. In APSRTC, the newly selected/hired employees are placed in different positions at the beginning. They are provided information about the corporation, its services, areas of operation, scope and standing in the market. The employees are also informed about the corporation's policies towards staff, conditions of employment, promotion policy, facilities and benefits. The objective is to inculcate a sense of confidence in the employee about the organization. After providing this information, the technical category employees are sent to the induction training programme as off-the-job training. The non-technical, administrative and ministerial staff will be assigned to other employees who are performing similar jobs. The new members learn the required skills by observing the work done by the senior employees. At regular intervals, all the employees are sent for refresher training. APSRTC trains one-fifth of its employees every year.

The motto of APSRTC has been "the passenger is the master and the passenger's comfort is above all else." The media used for internal communication include the in-house journal *Prasthanam*, a handbook for drivers and conductors, posters for drivers, a suggestion scheme and interaction between the managing director and other officers with the employees.

The APSRTC offers financial benefits and undertakes various welfare activities. In order to motivate the employees, the corporation supports the employees through several schemes such as house-building advances, car loans, two-wheeler loans, loans for house sites, staff benefit fund, spectacles assistance, funeral expenses, cash awards and educational assistance to children of employees.

MARKETING OF HOSPITAL SERVICES

A hotel is a home away from home where all the facilities and services are available on payment. Over the years, the hotel industry has grown in size. A number of hotels have come up in various parts of the world to facilitate the people who are travelling. The growth and development of the tourism sector

This case study has been prepared in association with Dr. Y. Srinivasulu, Associate Professor, Department of International Business, Pondicherry University.

is reflected in the development of hospitality services. In countries where tourism is progressive, hospitality services are also progressive.

The marketing of hospitality services includes designing the basic service package (product), the physical environment, pricing, internal marketing, promotion and interactive marketing (process). The services (products) offered are mostly market segment specific. The segmentation of the market is largely based on the affordability of the customer. The other criteria used by hotels include the purpose, occasion, individual vs. group, loyalty and so on. Keeping in mind the focussed target segment, a hotel should design a marketing mix strategy. The ultimate goal of the marketing programme is to offer quality services that satisfy the customers and, if possible, delight them. The following are the basic dimensions of the marketing mix of hospitality services.

The Basic Service Package (Product)

The core service offered in a hotel is hospitality. The facilitating services (or goods) are a well-constructed and secure building; rooms with beds and other facilities; toilets, service personnel, reception, parking and so on. The support services (or goods) include restaurants attached to the hotel, shopping malls, entertainment programmes, travel reservation services, local transport, local enquiry and information assistance and services on customer demand.

Hotels develop an appropriate mix of facilitating and supporting services keeping in mind the requirements of the target groups. It is thus necessary to study the expectations of the target market in relation to the elements of the services product and also the quality level of the service. By working out the possibilities of designing such a product and analyzing the demand and cost effectiveness, the management of a hotel arrives at a product decision. A hotel may offer a variety of services in accordance with the requirements of the various market segments. One product may have an independent market and may also act as support service for another service product. For example, a restaurant in a hotel may attract customers, seeking food and/or beverages. Some of the customers may be occupants of the hotel and some may visit the hotel only to use the restaurant. For the customers who come to the hotel only to have a meal, the restaurant is the ultimate product. For those who are staying in the hotel, the restaurant facility is a support service.

Hospitality services are highly competitive. It is not possible to lead the market unless the value delivered to the customer is high. Therefore, efforts ought to be directed to reducing customer cost and increasing the value of the offerings. The potential for the improvement of quality and value, without burdening the customer, has to be explored through continuous research and feedback analysis. A right product mix is the fundamental base for the success of hospitality services.

The Physical Environment

The physical environment of a hotel includes the location, exterior, interior and other physical features. The location of the hotel has strategic significance.

While selecting the location for the hotel, the following issues have to be considered:

- Proximity to travel points
- Availability of quality roads, electricity and communication facilities
- Well-developed surroundings
- Accessibility to other services
- Enough space to provide all desired facilities

The exterior of the hotel creates the first impression on the customers. The design of the exterior should be capable of attracting the attention of the prospective buyers of the service.

The exterior influences the expectations of the quality of services that customers are likely to receive from the hotel. Hoteliers generally take special care while designing the interiors. The architectural values, lighting, air quality, wall hangings, specialized furniture, placing of articles, signage and layout are all parts of the interior of the hotel. The management of the hotel should be flexible and innovative while designing the interiors and introduce modifications to add value perceptions without causing much disturbance to the routine. Customers' perceptions of the ambience determine expectations of the quality of service. The reception and the signage should be customer friendly.

Pricing

Prices are fixed for various services as well as tangibles in hospitality services. Room tariffs are fixed for various categories of accommodation such as single occupancy, double occupancy, air-conditioned rooms, non-air-conditioned rooms, suites, conference/function halls and so on. Prices are also fixed for various food items offered in the restaurants, for special events and for special parties organized inside and outside the hotel.

The decision on pricing is very critical and complex because of the presence of a large number of elements with individual features in the BSP. The problems are not only in arriving at pricing decisions but also in communicating price to customers and influencing them to develop value perceptions of the prices. Besides establishing price–quality relationships, it is necessary to assess the impact of pricing of the competitive offers on the consumer decision-making process. Though services are not closely comparable, consumers definitely keep the pricing of the competitors as reference prices. Cost plus pricing is not very relevant in hospitality services since consumers do not have an idea of the various costs involved in the service offering and the level of efficiency of the management in managing the costs. Consumers are likely to give more weightage to the value they receive. Hence, value pricing is highly appropriate for hospitality services. However, while arriving at a price decision, the prices of similar offers from competition must also be considered. Pricing can also be used to manage the demand fluctuations in this service. During slack seasons, hotels may offer seasonal discounts. Special tariffs may be offered to the customers from business and trade to promote loyalty.

The Distribution Network

Distribution is not a much focussed function in hospitality. Most of the hotels follow zero-level distribution. The hotels directly contact customers without involving an intermediary. The focus is largely on attracting the market to the hotel through communication campaigns. With the emergence of the Internet, the electronic media sells services to customers, anywhere in the world, well in advance.

Some hotels use direct marketing as well as intermediaries for demand creation. The prominent intermediaries are travel agents and tour operators.

Internal and Interactive Marketing

Hospitality service is a highly sensitive market where the attitude, approach and performance of the service personnel contribute to success. The design of the technical and functional products is very important. Hotels attract people from various places with varied cultures, habits, traditions and lifestyles. The customers may experience different problems. All groups of customers have to be offered unique service packages to satisfy their needs and wants. The service personnel should be capable of understanding the needs and wants of the customers and be able to design a product, taking into consideration the available infrastructure and resources. For the purpose, hotels require qualified service personnel, who are dynamic and are committed to work.

The recruitment and selection of the service personnel for a hotel should be as per the requirements of the job. Communication and social skills are assessed in addition to the appearance of the candidates. The employees are given training periodically in technical and interactive skills. Employees are trained in the art of receiving customers, offering various services, organization of operational process, attending to the specific problems of customers and responding and managing the displeasure of the customers, if any. An inclination to service is the key characteristic for hotel employees. Employees are required to control emotions and maintain a pleasant countenance while interacting with customers.

The service job in a hotel is not only physically strenuous but also "stressful." If the employees are not motivated through internal marketing, there is a likelihood of service gaps and failures. Employee satisfaction is the key to success in hospitality services. When employees are motivated, they can deliver excellent services even in the light of some gaps or deficiencies in the technical product. However, if they are de-motivated, in spite of a high-quality technical product, customers may not perceive quality in services.

Recovery from service deficiencies is a major challenge in managing hospitality services. On many occasions, employees are faced with problems, owing to uncontrollable circumstances. Customers may reserve accommodation well in advance. When they arrive, the accommodation may not yet be available. The existing customers may plead for an extension of stay in the hotel for some personal reasons. The employees of the hotel are in a tight situation since they cannot afford to displease either of the parties. They have to explore the possibilities of satisfying both the parties and arrive at a decision on the spot without losing much time. The customers who have arrived find deficiency in service after realizing that the reserved accommodation is not available and may pick up a quarrel with the service personnel. Under such circumstances, the contact service personnel are expected to come out with a recovery strategy by offering a better package, without any additional financial commitment to the customer, and also tendering an apology for the deficiency in service. Such situations need service personnel who are courteous, exhibit empathetic behaviour and use common sense. Human resource policies are to be designed keeping in view the requirement of the job and the challenges associated with it. Employees should be given a clear picture of their roles and responsibilities, and team work has to be promoted.

Interactive marketing is of vital significance in hospitality services. Customers experience many moments of truth during their stay in a hotel. Major as well as minor moments are capable of influencing the quality perceptions of the customers. Interaction with employees generate many moments of significance. An integration of internal and external marketing is necessary for the process to be effective.

External Marketing

In the marketing of hospitality services, customers have to be drawn to the service outlet. External marketing has a major share in the success of this service business. An effective communication campaign for creating awareness and persuading customers to visit and stay in the hotel is necessary in the light of severe competition. Hoteliers use advertising, sales promotion, personal selling, publicity, public relations and direct marketing as the components of the promotion mix. Advertising in print media and electronic media is widely used by large hotels. Sales promotion helps create demand during slack periods. Many hotels announce price discounts and other benefit packages for individuals and families during weekends as room occupancy during weekends is generally low. Some hotels organize special events to attract customers. Sponsoring events, meetings and special programmes are strategies to create publicity. Hotels try to build and maintain relations with business houses so that official visitors make use of their hospitality services.

Direct marketing through the Internet, mailing brochures and interacting with regular customers is used as a powerful promotional tool. Hotels are also tying up with credit card companies to offer special benefits for card holders as a part of the promotional campaign. Many hotels use large-size hoardings placed at vantage points of the town/city to attract tourists. Some hotels distribute cards/pamphlets through sales personnel at various travel points and tourist destinations. Word-of-mouth communication is a powerful influence as consumers are generally highly involved in decision-making as far as hospitality is concerned. Any customer would like to have a comfortable stay with assured safety and security. External marketing efforts should focus on the credibility and reliability of the hotel on such parameters. When they plan a tour, customers verify external marketing campaigns of a hotel with such people who have experience and knowledge in these areas. The guidance and suggestions of their friends, relatives and resource persons have a greater impact on the purchase decision of customers. Marketers, therefore, have to influence the reference groups also to elicit favourable feedback on their services.

MARKETING OF EDUCATIONAL SERVICES

Education is one of the important measures of human resource development in a society. The growth in the education sector results in acceleration of economic growth and prosperity of a nation. Educated people are capable of organizing themselves and the resources of the society. Education promotes innovation and makes society dynamic. Thus, education has been given vital significance in all the societies throughout the world.

After independence, states were responsible for developing education; later the private sector was also encouraged to take part in the process. There are several types of educational services being offered in India. The traditional gurukulas still exist in various parts of the country. Religious education is also being offered through some specialized religious institutions. Formal education is offered at primary, secondary, undergraduate and postgraduate levels by the government, social organizations and the private sector. Specialized skills are imparted through training institutions and research centres established at various places. In addition, adult education programmes are taken up on a large scale by the government to improve the literacy levels in the society. Education is in the concurrent list; therefore, it is the subject for the union and state governments. At the union level, the Ministry of Human Resource Development designs the education programmes and monitors the development in this sector through various funding and promotion agencies like University Grants Commission (UGC), All India Council for Technical Education, Council for Scientific and Industrial Research, Indian Council for Social Science Research, National Assessment and Accreditation Council, National Council for Teacher Education, National Board of Accreditation and so on. The respective state governments plan and monitor the educational mechanism taking the local conditions into consideration.

Marketing of educational services has gained vital importance in recent years in India. The fast-changing economic and business scenario is reflected in the education sector as well. The entry of corporate organizations right from the elementary level to highly advanced specialized education has created a competitive environment in this sector. The business dimension has crept into this service sector and as such marketing has become a key functional dimension. For analysing the marketing of educational services a case of a university was taken. The marketing mix of the university has been analysed in the following sections.

The Product

Every course offered by the university at the undergraduate and postgraduate levels has become a service product of the university. The courses offered can be classified into five categories—linguistics, humanities, sciences, technology, professional courses and others. Universities offer some courses on regular study basis, through distance mode and through private study.

Product Design and Development

Universities follow a systematic product design and development process. For each product or group of products, a board is constituted with experts in that particular discipline. The board is called the Board of Studies with an identity of the discipline that it belongs. The board meets periodically and works out new ideas on new product development. The board also reviews the performance of the existing products and plans on the modifications that are necessary to make the product effective. If the board feels that a particular product has become irrelevant it may recommend dropping the product. The resolutions of each Board of Studies are placed before the Academic Senate (the apex body on academic affairs for a university). The Academic Senate discusses at length the recommendations of the Board of Studies and takes decisions on changes in courses/regulations. The design of each course consists of the following:

- Course objective
- Title of the course
- Course duration
- Eligibility
- Course structure
- Course curriculum
- Student intake
- Organization details of the course
- Evaluation and award of results

The university offers support services that include hostel accommodation, boarding, canteen, library, transport, sports and physical fitness services and so on.

Pricing

The management committee of a university decides the fee structure for various services, after considering the following facts:

- Demand of the course
- Pricing of competitors
- Infrastructure requirement
- Faculty requirement
- Maintenance costs
- Development costs

Universities under the public sector are not profit-oriented organizations. The respective state governments and the funding organizations contribute substantially to the university finances. Hence, the services offered by the public sector universities are highly subsidized. In order to provide quality education even to the economically weaker sections of the society, the services are offered at reasonable prices when compared to private institutions. However, in recent years universities all over the country are facing serious financial crisis. Universities are forced to introduce self-finance courses, payment seats and charge competitive market prices from the students for some professional courses. The fee structure is decided by the management of the university for some courses, and for other courses the state-level bodies such as State Council for Higher Education in consultation with the universities and the colleges offering such courses decide the fees. The fee structure of various courses is modified whenever the institutions feel it necessary, after considering the demand of the course and the cost of executing the course. The payment system may vary from university to university. Some universities collect fees annually, some collect each semester and some at the beginning of the course.

The Distribution Network

Many universities offer educational services not only on the campus but also through affiliated colleges. The area coverage of a state university is decided by the respective state governments. Within that area the university may establish education centres and/or give course-wise recognition to the colleges promoted by the private sector or social and charitable associations. The affiliated colleges are allowed to make admissions based on the prescribed eligibility criteria and admission procedure. The course-wise intake and infrastructure is also decided by the university. The affiliation committees appointed by the university (course wise) visit colleges, periodically, to review the physical facilities, library, laboratories and faculty and submit reports to the university. Based on such reports, the university decides whether to continue or withdraw the affiliation.

Universities take many precautions in selecting a college for granting affiliation. Specific norms are set for the purpose. Colleges that want affiliation strictly adhere to the norms fixed. The land and buildings, caution deposit, appointment of qualitative faculty in required numbers, appointment of the principal or director, library and labs with detailed description stand as norms and the university sends a special committee to see whether the college has the required infrastructure, the ability to run the courses and the prospects of the college in that particular location. The work schedule, the examinations and other evaluation mechanisms are carried out by the university itself. The affiliated colleges (excluding autonomous colleges) have nothing to do with it. The university takes the responsibility of declaring results as well as issuing pass certificates. All the courses carry the brand name of the respective universities.

In case of courses offered through distance mode, the university establishes study centres at various locations. Contact programmes are organized for a brief period every year and course-wise counselling is offered to the students located near the study centre. The study centres may be managed by the university itself or it may permit private institutions to run the study centres. The activities of the centres are limited to facilitating enrolment of the students to various courses, collecting fees and sending it to the university, organizing contact programmes and looking after the arrangements for conducting examinations. The university monitors all the activities of the study centres.

People

Employees form the core strength of any organization offering educational services. The employees of a university can be categorized into three groups: teachers, management and the support personnel. All the three play a vital role in offering educational services and they should have a high level of coordination in performing the tasks. The job description, roles and responsibilities, and reporting and control mechanism are all well defined. Administration is divided into two parts—functional administration and academic administration. The registrar is the functional head of the university whereas the principals of respective colleges function as academic heads. The vice-chancellor of a university coordinates academic and functional activities and provides leadership. The recruitment and selection of employees follow a systematic procedure. Eligible candidates are invited through advertisements in national dailies to appear for an interview. Experts verify the qualities required for the respective position and recommend the panel of candidates selected based on merit. By following the rule of reservation, the university management appoints suitable candidates for respective positions. The teachers of the university are paid salary as per the pay scales suggested by the UGC and approved by the state government. The other groups of employees also follow the same rule, with respect to salary payment. The UGC recommends pay scale revisions and promotion criterion relating to the teachers working in the university to the state governments for every 10 years. The state governments may approve or may make some modifications to the revision proposal before accepting it. The other employees of the university are offered state government scales, which the state government revises periodically.

Teachers with eight years of teaching experience are trained through orientation programmes; refresher programmes are conducted for teachers with more than eight years' experience. Teachers are also encouraged to do research, leading to M.Phil and Ph.D. degrees. The UGC offers fellowships and financial aid to teachers working in universities and affiliated colleges to undertake major or minor research projects. Teachers are encouraged to organize seminars, workshops, conferences, symposia to participate in all such programmes elsewhere in the country or outside; to enhance the knowledge base and to promote inter-institutional understandings.

Teachers are responsible for updating their knowledge in their respective areas and improving their communication skills for better classroom performance. They are role models for students. They should make themselves accessible to students and take the responsibility of nurturing each and every student not only as a superior in knowledge and skill levels but also as a responsible social being. Teachers are the social engineers and their role in shaping the future of the country cannot be overemphasized. The internal marketing concept should be applied to the teachers. The satisfaction of the teachers should be one of the prime goals of any university or educational institution. A periodic assessment of the needs and requirements of teachers has to be done and appropriate measures should be taken to satisfy them. The sensitivities of the profession should be understood by the management. A motivated teacher is capable of developing a very valuable student force that can transform the developmental processes of the society.

Support services are also important. Without the efficient performance of the support personnel, teachers cannot perform efficiently and the system of educational services cannot be run properly. Human resource management policies and strategies are useful in managing the personnel involved in support services.

Promotion

Universities have not given adequate importance to promotion. Over the years the distribution network acted as a principal communicator of various courses offered by the universities. Universities use advertising in print media to communicate about admissions, examinations and results in relation to various courses. Direct mail is prominently used to establish communication with affiliated colleges and to some extent to interact with students. The Internet is also being used by various universities. Distinctions, events, achievements and other relevant information are also communicated through relevant media.

Word-of-mouth communication plays a key role in communications. Candidates seeking admission to universities try to contact persons such as those who are pursuing some course in the university; who were graduates of the university; or who are connected with the university. The opinion of such people influences the potential market of the university significantly.

The image of the university determines its popularity. Universities have to work systematically to develop a positive image. There are several measures that the universities take for promoting a credible image such as:

- Updating and modifying the curriculum periodically and making it flexible for incorporating changes whenever necessary
- Equipping with state-of-the-art technology-based teaching aids
- Recruiting quality personnel and providing an environment for enhancing their knowledge and technical skills
- Promoting result-oriented and socially relevant research

- Introducing new courses in tune with the changing dimensions in the environment
- Following the academic schedule scrupulously
- Participating in programmes related to social development and developing interaction with industry, business and other sections of the society
- Providing placement services
- Building, maintaining and enhancing relations with the old students
- Focussing on a student-oriented, quality education

Interactive Marketing

The students of a university interacts with employees, classrooms, furniture and equipment, library, laboratories, systems, procedures, support services, co-students, senior students, administration and so on. During the period of study, every student experiences millions of moments. All such moments influence the quality perception of the student. In order to improve the quality of the service it is necessary to identify such moments, and see that all such moments are qualitative. The management of moments is a critical exercise for educational institutions. It should be the continuous endeavour of universities and other educational institutions to generate quality experiences for students as they pass through various stages in the process of studying a course.

Educational institutions have social responsibilities. They should not lose track of ethics for short-term benefits. Besides providing knowledge and training to develop technical skills, they should focus on building the character of the student. If educational institutions discharge their responsibilities with honesty, integrity and dynamism, they will definitely contribute to the prosperity of society.

MARKETING OF TOURISM SERVICES

Currently, the tourism sector has become the most powerful growth engine. This "smokeless" industry contributes over 13 per cent of the gross domestic product (GDP). Many countries in the world have recognized the importance of this sector and are trying to strengthen this industry.

Both developed and developing countries are making vigorous efforts to reshape the tourism industry. The main reason behind this attitudinal change in the policy makers is tourism's capacity to generate foreign exchange. This is mainly because almost all countries have realized the need to develop this industry, to keep pace with the changing tastes of potential tourists. Many countries such as Austria, Belgium, Canada, France, Italy, Japan, Singapore, UK, USA, Spain and Switzerland have been successful in contributing handsome dividends to their exchequer, courtesy the tourism industry.

Qualitative improvements in managing this industry became possible when some of the leading global organizations such as World Tourism

Organization, Pacific Area Travel Association, International Union of Official Travel Organization evinced interest in promoting this industry, especially in the developing countries where this industry was in a bad condition. Tourism as an industry operates on a massive scale. It embraces activities ranging from the smallest seaside hotel, to airlines, multinational hotel chains and major international tour operators. The travel agency business coupled with holiday shops represent a significant retail market sector in the UK.

Marketing Approach for Tourism Services

A marketing offer (tour package) may consist of several service providers (owners of tourist destinations); therefore, an integrated and coordinated approach in offering marketing stimulations becomes a complicated process. One distinctive feature is that a majority of the tourist destinations are owned by the governments of the respective countries. Hence, the responsibility of marketing tourism services is with the governments of these countries.

Marketing of tourism involves identifying target markets, anticipating demand for tourism services, developing effective means of providing tourism services, communicating the marketing offers to target consumers and executing service production and delivery to the satisfaction of customers.

Marketing Mix Strategy for Tourism Services

Services marketing mix is a strategic approach to achieve business goals by analysing opportunities and threats in the environment, and interpreting them taking into consideration strengths and weaknesses of internal resources. The services marketing mix consists of several components such as product, physical evidence, price, distribution, people, promotion and process. In order to achieve success, a mix of all these components needs to be developed in such a way that the ultimate mix provides satisfaction to the customers.

The Product

Tourism product is a mix of facilitating services (and/or goods) and supporting services (and/or goods). The product features and managerial aspects are discussed in Chapter 11.

Physical Evidence

The design of the physical environment at tourist destinations is a key factor in influencing the perception of the consumer. Since the product features are varied and often independent, probably with different ownerships, the management of physical environment becomes highly challenging. Everything present at the destination point has the capacity to influence the quality evaluation of the tourist. The issues of concern also vary from destination to destination. If the tourist spot is a natural place, care needs to be taken to preserve the beauty of nature by reducing the effect of the artificial man-made structures and other elements. If there is a traditional monument, a temple, a religious identity or an entertainment and fun environment, an appropriate destination-related strategy has to be worked out to create a tangible feeling of evidence in the minds of the people. The evidence also needs to be developed and communicated with respect to all support services that are associated with the tourism product.

Pricing

The scope of pricing in the marketing of tourism services is very wide. Pricing approaches vary from country to country and also from destination to destination within the country. Sometimes prices are negotiated with the customers and sometimes with the middlemen who design package tours and decide the price for the package. Tourists generally have a wide option to select from, depending on affordability, time schedule and other requirements.

All pricing methods and strategies can be applied to the tourism product. The cost plus pricing, competition-based pricing, demand-based pricing can be decided based on situations and circumstances. Pricing strategies such as fixed price, variable price, charm price, loss leader price, skimming price, penetration price, multistage pricing and seasonal pricing are all suitable for varied situations and to different kinds of customer groups. An appropriate pricing strategy should be developed keeping in mind the long-term objectives, the targeted tourist segment, the loyalty and relationship value of the tourists, their economic status and the impact of price of a tourism product on supporting services and other tourist products.

The Distribution Network

The success of tourism depends mostly on the decision of the channel network and the performance of the channel members. In tourism marketing, both direct and indirect channels are used. The role of direct channels becomes more and more prominent with the development of information technology and –World Wide Web (WWW) network. Consumers throughout the world can interact through the Internet directly for the purchase of tourism products. Traditionally, indirect channels perform valuable services for the development of tourism. The tour operators varying from individuals to big corporations having world wide branch networking are playing the role of intermediaries and facilitating the flow of tourists to various destinations. The intermediaries provide value-added services by designing tour packages, integrating support services, facilitating services and taking all the responsibilities as a seller of a tourism product. In the eyes of the consumer, the channel member is the service provider. The experiences of the tourists at various destinations influence the quality perceptions of the consumers against the services of the distributor. Ironically, the distributor does not have any control over the management of the services offered at various destinations. This critical aspect has to be managed carefully by distributing organizations, by collecting feedback from the tourists and by adopting appropriate recovery strategies.

The tourism departments of various governments have established contact offices at various travel stations (airports, railway stations and bus stations), to facilitate domestic as well as foreign tourists to reach their planned destinations. The contact offices also sell local tourist packages.

Distribution in tourism is mainly an independent business. Typically, these organizations operate on their own without integrating with the philosophies, goals and business approaches of the people/organizations/institutions managing destinations. This gap needs to be managed to strengthen tourism.

People

There are three categories of people involved in tourism. They are employees of the tourism department, tourist guides and distributors/employees of the distributing organizations. The human factor plays a key role in creating value perceptions to the consumers. The people involved in marketing tourism services should possess specialized qualities in communication, knowledge of tourism product offers, support services, foreign languages and cross-cultural facets. These qualities are required because of their interaction with people belonging to different cultures, knowledge levels, lifestyles and personality dimensions. Employees adapt themselves quickly to customers. To develop the qualitative force of service personnel for tourism, the following issues may be considered:

- Recruitment and selection has to be taken up with an objective of taking qualitative personnel, who are capable of creating quality perceptions in the tourists. Service personnel need to be given induction training and periodic training on the basic and required skills for adapting to changing environmental dimensions.
- Tourism is strenuous and challenging since it involves handling of new customers with varied behaviours, abilities and expectations; travel on schedule timings; and many hurdles and disturbances. Therefore, employees need to be kept motivated.
- Employees are to be regularly provided with information relating to development in tourism.
- Support material and services required should also be provided.
- A proper evaluation system and an appropriate reward system have to be designed to identify meritorious performances and to acknowledge them.
- A compensation plan should not only motivate the employees but also help in retaining them.
- The character of service personnel is very important in tourism. Service personnel who are identified with inappropriate behaviour should be removed from the service.

The internal marketing concept should be applied for the management of people in tourism services. Satisfied employees deliver quality services. The needs and expectations of the employees should become the fundamental base for designing all human resource policies. Considering the employees as the first customers and satisfying them is the main theme of internal marketing. When such a theme is followed in tourism, a powerful force of performers gets developed.

Promotions

To attract tourists from various parts of the world, a powerful communications campaign needs to be undertaken. The success of a tourism product mostly depends on the promotional programmes or external marketing efforts. The components of the promotional mix such as advertising, personal selling, sales promotion, publicity and direct marketing are useful for the communication campaign. Word-of-mouth communication is capable of creating a powerful impression in the minds of consumers. By taking into consideration the scope, limitations and applicability of various elements of the promotion, an appropriate mix has to be developed for the external marketing campaign. The design of the message and the selection of media are crucial in this respect. Word-of-mouth communication, which is not controllable, has to be observed and the formal communication campaign should be aligned with it for generating positive results.

External marketing aims at creating awareness and knowledge of tourist destinations. It also aims to persuade and train, if necessary, the target customers to have a qualitative tourist experience. The rapid pace of change in information and communication technology provides powerful arsenal to service organizations. The tourism sector should exploit these strengths to make their promotional campaign effective and demanding.

The Process

Tourists expect that their tour programmes right from the beginning to the end of the programmes should pass freely from stage to stage, without any hurdles. The management of the service process aims at simplifying customer interactions and customer participation in the service process. The systems, policies, procedures, equipment, tools, people and other support services need to be customer friendly. The way the entire service environment responds to the customer needs and requirements reflects the efficiency of the process management.

Tourists get away from their comfortable normal routine. Therefore, their dependency on the service provider for generating a value experience will be very high. They have to manage three stages in the process: pre-tour preparatory process, tour process and return process. The service providers' role in facilitating these three processes is pivotal. These processes are influenced by economic, legal and administrative and infrastructural system of various regions and social, cultural, demographic and psychographic factors of the tourists. It is a Herculean task for tourists to make all the arrangements by themselves. Therefore, they look for someone to relieve them of the burden.

When service firms take on the responsibility of these processes and perform much better than what an individual tourist can do, it adds to the value of the services provided to the customers. The tourist feels relaxed and can concentrate on exploring new values in the tour programme.

KEY TERMS

administered interest rates *489*
authorized agents *501*
customer councils *495*
flexible pricing system *490*
indirect channels *515*
mofussil services *499*
social skills *506*
special events *505*
supplementary services *499*
tourist destinations *507*

BRIEF QUESTIONS

1. Define a mobility service product.
2. How would you design a distribution strategy for a transport company?
3. What is the importance of interactive skills in employees of a transport company?
4. What are the problems in offering quality service to the customers in a hotel?
5. When are recovery strategies useful in hospitality services?
6. How are new products designed in a university?
7. What is the importance of internal marketing in tourism?

ESSAY QUESTIONS

1. Analyse the marketing operations of a transport service company.
2. How do you analyse the marketing operations of hospitality services?
3. Explain the market for educational services and the marketing approach of an educational institution.
4. How do you understand a tourism offer? Explain the marketing strategies of tourism services.
5. How do you apply the marketing concept to a public sector bank? Take a case study and analyse.

Cases

1. Beauty Care by Marico: Kaya Skin Clinics
2. Life Insurance Corporation: Restructuring for Growth
3. McDonald's in India
4. Subway's Marketing Strategy in India
5. Cox and Kings: Service with a Difference

Beauty Care by Marico: Kaya Skin Clinics

CASE 1

Once an unorganized market mostly run by independent dermatologists and beauticians, the Indian skincare treatment market is now attracting some of the leading personal care product manufacturers. Marico Industries, the owner of popular brands such as Parachute, Mediker and Saffola, has entered into the beauty care market through its chain of beauty salons called Kaya Skin Clinic (Kaya) with eight centres spread across India and two centres in Dubai. *Kaya* means "body" or "appearance" in Sanskrit. Kaya points out that a clear and flawless skin is the most attractive aspect of an individual's appearance and its clinics promise to enhance natural skin to make it look healthier, fresher, younger and glow. Kaya offers its customers a wide range of services including laser hair removal, skin polishing and brightening, glycolic and salicylic peels, acne and acne scar reduction, photo-rejuvenation, micro-current facial toning, deep wrinkle removal, and fillers.

Explaining the rationale of a products company entering into the services market, Mr. Rakesh Pandey, CEO, Kaya, says "We are already into haircare and healthcare products; through Kaya we entered skincare." Kaya had by the end of 2004, attracted 10,000 customers and registered INR 10 million of annual turnovers per branch, since its inception in December 2002.

Kaya's goal is to provide long-lasting and result-oriented non-surgical skincare treatment. The company has taken various steps in this direction. Moving against the retail industry trend of a franchisee model, Kaya decided to set up the venture on its own in order to standardize service quality across all its branches. Speaking on this issue, Pandey says, "Since Kaya is a retail medical clinic, it is very important for each branch to be standardized, which is difficult to do with a franchisee model. We want first to perfect our model before we think about it (franchising)."

The company adopts a systematic process in its treatment of clients. At Kaya, utmost care is taken to give the customer an experience that is pleasant and memorable from the time they enter the clinic to the time they leave. Every customer is greeted by skin-practitioners dressed in elegant uniforms designed by Mumbai designer Bhairavi Jaikishen. Then the customer is offered a refreshing welcome Kaya drink (a blend of apple and cinnamon)

---

*This caselet was written by **Satya Srinivas Srikanti,** under the direction of **S. V. Rama Krishna,** ICFAI Center for Management Research. Caselets are intended to be used as a basis for class discussion rather than to illustrate either effective or ineffective handling of a management situation.*

formulated by the noted food consultant, Karen Anand. Once the customer starts feeling at home, the actual treatment begins with a certified dermatologist preparing a detailed "skinscription". The "skinscription" contains in-depth analysis of customer skin and the treatment plan to be followed for the skin. The treatment is based on this prescription, and is required to offer visible results to the customers. For effective results, Kaya offers a wide range of skincare products.

Kaya's treatments range from long-term solutions such as skin peels, skin brightening and polishing, permanent laser hair reduction and pigmentation, and scar reduction therapies to short-term treatments such as face and eye rejuvenation services. The company has adapted a premium pricing policy where prices vary between INR 400 for smaller treatments to INR 150,000 for permanent body hair removal.

The company ensures that the skin practitioners it employs have access to the best equipment, and are well trained to provide effective treatment to the clients. Prior to practising at Kaya, all the dermatologists employed undergo a stringent 45–60 day inhouse training programme. They are certified at the end of the training programme. Under the programme called Continuing Medical Education (CME), the company conducts periodic training programmes (every six months) for its dermatologists to keep them updated about the latest developments in the field. During these programmes, international doctors are invited to conduct workshops on the latest developments and trends in the field of skincare for Kaya medical personnel. Speaking about the importance of training programmes, Mr. Pandey says, "It is necessary to keep up with the trends in this business, so we have ongoing programmes for our staff."

The company is also putting more efforts into research and development, so as to improve its services and offer a larger number of new skin care solutions to its customers. At present the research is focused on acne scar reduction and anti-ageing and skin maintenance. In order to increase its revenues, the company is looking at other revenue-generating opportunities. It is already offering skincare products made in France, which are sold to the customers as standalone products, and are also used by Kaya in its treatments.

Encouraged by the success of its existing branches, the company plans to expand its presence to 50 centres by the year 2006. Its ultimate aim is to become an international skincare retail chain. In the words of Mr. Pandey, "when people think of skin, we want them to think of Kaya."

QUESTIONS FOR DISCUSSION

1. Marico, a product manufacturer, has entered the services segment. What challenges will Marico face while marketing its services?
2. With independent dermatologists and small beauty salons chains dominating the beauty care industry, Kaya clinics will find it difficult to capture the customer mindshare and market share. What tangible elements do Kaya clinics use to differentiate their services from the competition?

ADDITIONAL READINGS AND REFERENCES

1. Bhatnagar, Mohini. "Marico to Set Up Skincare Clinics, Spa Saloons in Indian Metros." *www.domainb.com.* 22 November, 2002.
2. Chatterjee, Purvita. "At Marico, Skin is in." *The Hindu Business Line.* 13 March, 2003.
3. Raghavendra, Nandini. "Beauty and the Business." *The Economic Times.* 06 April, 2003.
4. Chatterjee, Purvita. "Marico Shows its Muscle." *The Hindu Business Line.* 05 August, 2004.
5. "Marico: Its 'Kaya' Improvement Continues." *www.equitymaster.com.* 09 November, 2004.

Life Insurance Corporation: Restructuring for Growth

CASE 2

Till the year 2000, Life Insurance Corporation (LIC) held a monopoly in the life insurance market by virtue of being India's only life insurance company in India. With the opening of the insurance sector to private players, LIC's hold on the market was threatened. Big players such as Tata AIG, ICICI Prudential, Max New York Life, and Bajaj Allianz entered the sector based on the expertise of their foreign partners and the brand equity the Indian company enjoyed with Indian customers. These private players, aided by aggressive marketing and better customer service, started eating into LIC's market share. This prompted LIC to revamp its marketing strategy to take on the competition. In 2000, LIC hired the leading consulting company Booz, Allen & Hamilton to suggest the best modalities to restructure the company and cope with the changing environment in the insurance sector.

Some key recommendations made by the consultants were[1]:

- To undertake product improvements that offer a mix of good returns and bonus
- To launch variable products that appeal to specific customer groups
- To create brand identity that reflects the company's strengths of solidity and Indian-ness
- To make zonal offices autonomous and the corporate office focus on policy making and strategy formulation
- To differentiate service standards to high value agents and customers

On the basis of these recommendations, LIC took various measures. LIC focused on increasing marketing strength through the recruitment of more agents. LIC also doubled its agency network from 550,000 in 2000 to 1.1 million in 2004. The company laid special emphasis on training and development. Agents were given free professional training, mandatory under Insurance

---

*This caselet was written by Satya **Srinivas Srikanti,** under the direction of **S. V. Rama Krishna,** ICFAI Center for Management Research. Caselets are intended to be used as a basis for class discussion rather than to illustrate either effective or ineffective handling of a management situation.*

Regulatory & Development Authority rules. Apart from this, the company also trained its own personnel. For this, LIC tied up with IIM Bangalore for imparting IT skills to its managers and IIM Lucknow to train its staff in marketing. Development officers were sold laptops at concessional rates.

LIC tried to improve its customer service levels through some major customer relationship management (CRM) initiatives. It launched a Wide Area Network (WAN) to interconnect its branches spread across various cities. This offered customers the flexibility to pay the premium or check the policy status at any branch connected to the WAN. At present, 91 cities with 1966 branches have been covered under this network. Another technology initiative LIC undertook was the launch of the Interactive Voice Responsive system (IVRS) that enabled customers to obtain information on their policies through the telephone or fax. This facility is now available in 58 cities. The company also started offering online premium payment services, using which customers can pay their premium online. LIC also concentrated on regaining lost customers. It launched special campaigns to revive lapsed policies to add more customers to its customer base.

LIC also speeded up various service delivery processes. It launched a special drive to clear outstanding claims faster. In the year 2003, LIC set a record by reducing its outstanding claims to just 0.13%. Some divisions even achieved zero per cent outstanding claims. For example, 52 divisions in the South Central Zone achieved zero per cent outstanding claims. Commenting on this, Mr R. N. Bhardwaj, Chairman, LIC said, "It sends a very positive signal to our policy holders that LIC delivers on its promises. Many of them received cheques before the date of maturity."[2]

On the branding front, the company aggressively promoted the LIC brand through successful advertising campaigns like "We know India better" and "*Zindagi ke saath bi, Zindagi ke baad bhi*." Talking about the success of the advertising campaigns and its impact on the brand, Bhardwaj says, "They have played a positive and important role. Our creative slogans that have become catchphrases among the people have been developed by ad agencies. For instance, '*Zindagi ke saath bhi, Zindagi ke baad bhi*' and 'We know India better' helped perpetuate the philosophy of life insurance and its trust among people."

LIC reduced the number of advertising agencies it worked with from 45 to four for better execution of communication strategies. It allocated INR 1 billion towards advertising in the year 2004–05. LIC's present advertising strategy emphasizes strengthening the brand and enhancing its appeal to the younger generation.

Though its market share was eroded by 20% due to the invasion by private insurers, LIC stills holds 80% of market share with 160 million policies in its fold. According to a survey conducted by Taylor Nelson Sofres in March 2004, LIC enjoyed a 75% mind-share among customers. It registered an income of INR 1,000 billion for the financial year 2003. LIC was adjudged number one in the Most Trusted Service Brands survey conducted by *The Economic Times* for 2004.

QUESTIONS FOR DISCUSSION

1. The changing perception about a company among customers is a challenging task for any service provider. To what extent has LIC succeeded on that front?
2. What kind of branding strategy should LIC adopt, given its increasing product mix and the aggressive brand building measures of private insurers?

ADDITIONAL READINGS AND REFERENCES

1. Sen, Sarbajeet K. "Tie-ups for LIC may be Proposed." *The Hindu Business Line.* 10 May, 2000.
2. "Booz, Allen's Advise to LIC." *www.newsnmuse.com.* 30 June, 2000.
3. "LIC Gears Up for Competition—Stress on Good Governance, New Schemes." *The Hindu Business Line.* 05 September, 2000.
4. Narain D. S. "The Business of Better Insurance." *The Hindu Business Line.* 24 October, 2000.
5. ———"Competition in Insurance Sector—Will LIC Still be Market Leader?" *The Hindu Business Line.* 27 November, 2000.
6. "LIC Unveils Steps to be More Customer-Friendly." *The Hindu Business Line.* 04 September, 2001.
7. "LIC's Policy Revival Campaign." *The Hindu Business Line.* 14 October, 2001.
8. Kapoor, Neha & Narayanan, Dinesh. "LIC Call Centre Set to Dial Mumbai." *The Hindu Business Line.* 11 January, 2002.
9. Ram, Anand. "licindia.com: Ensuring Information, Practically." *The Hindu Business Line.* 24 March, 2002.
10. "LIC to Set More Call Centres Across India." *www.domainb.com.* 12 June, 2002.
11. Kurian, Vinson. "LIC Sets Tough Trend for Private Players—To Focus on Expanding Agency Network." *The Hindu Business Line.* 17 October, 2002.
12. Sukumar C.R. "Competition Drives LIC to Fine-Tune Customer Service." *The Hindu Business Line.* 09 March, 2003.
13. "LIC Widens Network for Online Premium." *The Economic Times.* 05 March, 2004.
14. "SBI Life has Third Largest Share of Mindspace." *The Economic Times.* 11 March, 2004.
15. "LIC Pegs Ad Spend at Rs 115 Cr." *The Economic Times.* 03 July, 2004.
16. Pinto, Viveat Susan. "LIC Empanelment Enters Last Round." *www.agencyfaqs.com.* 17 September, 2004.
17. Balakrishnan, Ravi. "Licing the Competition." *The Economic Times.* 15 December, 2004.

ENDNOTES

1. "Booz, Allen's Advise to LIC." *www.newsnmuse.com.* 30, June, 2000.
2. Balakrishnan, Ravi. "Licing the Competition." *The Economic Times.* 15, December, 2004.

McDonald's in India

3 CASE

McDonald's is a leading international fast food restaurant chain with 30,000 restaurants spread across the globe. In India, it launched its operations in 1996 with two stores. In 2003, it had 54 restaurants with a daily inflow of 500,000 customers. It planned to add 15 more outlets by the end of 2004. As per the Informal Eating Out (IEO) survey involving the survey of branded food chains in India, conducted by A. C. Nielsen, McDonald's was found to be the leader in fast food chains. Many factors can be attributed to the success of McDonald's Indian operations.

First, McDonald's has focused on products and changed its menu to suit the tastes of Indian consumers. It launched India-specific items including McVeggie™ burger, McAloo Tikki™ burger and Chicken McGrill™ burger. Considering Indian preferences and sensibilities, the company doesn't offer pork and beef items in India. It offers egg-less sandwich sauces for vegetarian customers; vegetarian items are prepared at a separate counter at the outlets.

On the pricing front, McDonald's has adopted customized pricing for each of the cities depending upon the tax structure, demand, and purchasing power of the population. However, to attract mass-market customers, it launched a new menu called the Happy Price Menu in which select items were priced at INR 20 across all the outlets in the country.

As McDonald's is into the food business, establishing an efficient supply chain infrastructure is of great importance. McDonald's has, therefore, focused on setting up an efficient and effective supply chain. Its supply chain is three tiered, consisting of farms, processing plants, and distribution centres. The company has selected farmers who can meet its quality and supply standards and directly sources the produce from them. They are supported by McDonald's in terms of seed technology and the latest irrigation methods to enable them to obtain higher yields and better produce. The next level of supply chain activities involves the processing of farm produce. For this, the company has tied up with various local suppliers like Vista Processed Foods Pvt. Ltd. a joint venture of OSI Industries Inc., USA, and McDonald's India Pvt. Ltd. that processes chicken and vegetarian food products at its plant situated at Taloja, Maharashtra. Dynamix Diary supplies cheese, butter, ghee, and milk products and Amrit Food

---

*This caselet was written by **Satya Srinivas Srikanti,** under the direction of **S. V. Rama Krishna,** ICFAI Center for Management Research. Caselets are intended to be used as a basis for class discussion rather than to illustrate either effective or ineffective handling of a management situation.*

supplies long life UHT Milk and Milk Products for Frozen Desserts from its fully automated plant situated at Ghaziabad, Uttar Pradesh. The next level of supply chain activity is the distribution of processed food to the outlets. For this, the company has tied up with Radhakrishna Foodland which is into food products distribution. Foodland provides logistics support to McDonald's by providing cold storage facilities and transporting the processed foods to the outlets using temperature-controlled transport vehicles.

To maintain the service standards, the company has made it mandatory for personnel to undergo periodic training programmes. The core principles of McDonald's—quality, service, cleanliness, and value (QSC&V)—guide its training programmes. The company's highly structured training programmes are conducted at four levels: crew development programme, restaurant management programme, mid-management programme, and executive development programme. Entry-level workers are trained under the basic crew development programme. The training is conducted at each restaurant. Crew members are given on-the-job and off-the-job training. The next level of training is the management development programme. This training programme is devised for the employees in the restaurant management team. The programme ranges from the basic level to the advanced level.

McDonald's has also focused on creating a right ambience in its outlets. The company has positioned its outlets as a restaurant that caters to the typical Indian family, and the physical environment reflects that image with the atmosphere being informal and bright. The outlets a spacious for kids to play around and families have the facility to conduct events like birthday parties. In addition, the outlets have been made nonsmoking zones to reflect the sensibilities of Indian families. McDonald's also lays special emphasis on kids. The outlets have low counters for easy accessibility to kids. Besides, vibrant colors and theme-based paintings pleasing to kids have been used.

McDonald's has developed localized ads in line with the advertising strategy of the parent company. Localized ads with the punch line "I'm lovin' it" were created. Humorous ads with the theme "What Your Bahana is" were developed to put the message across to the consumers. The protagonists in the ads cite weird reasons for eating out at McDonald's. In addition, McDonald's also carries out various sales promotion activities to keep up the interest in the brand like offering toys and other accessories, and conducting contests.

QUESTIONS FOR DISCUSSION

1. The services marketing mix consists of three additional elements like people, process, and physical evidence apart from the traditional marketing mix elements such as product, price, promotion, and place. How was McDonald's able to utilize these additional three elements to market its services?
2. The proliferation of western fast-food chains such as McDonald's, Pizza Hut, Subway, and Dominos in the Indian market has only been a recent phenomenon. What are the reasons that have contributed to the increased popularity of western fast-food chains in India?

ADDITIONAL READINGS AND REFERENCES

1. Jagtiani, Anushka. "The Money's in the Eating." *Business India*. 02–15 August, 2004.
2. Shatrujeet, N. "McDonald's: Pumping up the Volumes." *www.agencyfaqs.com*. 22 August, 2000.
3. "McDonald's India Cold Chain." *www.mcdonaldsindia*.com.
4. www.mcdonalds.com.

Subway's Marketing Strategy in India

CASE 4

The Indian fast food industry is pegged at INR 20 billion with an expected annual growth rate of 40%. Several multinationals including McDonald's, Domino's and Pizza Hut have established their presence in India. A new entrant is Subway—leading sandwich chain, which, with 16,900 outlets in Canada and the USA, has surpassed McDonald's branch strength in these two countries. Worldwide, it has a total of 22,361 restaurants, spread across 78 countries. Subway operates in India through a wholly owned subsidiary, Subway Systems India (Subway). Subway increased the numbers of outlets in India to 200 by 2005. Subway sells a wide range of vegetarian and non-vegetarian sandwiches, which consumers can customize. To cater to Indian tastes, it also offers many Indian recipes such as *paneer tikka*, chicken *tikka*, chicken *seekh kebab*, and spicy vegetable. In deference to Indian sentiments and sensibilities, the company does not use beef products in India. The preparation counters for vegetarian food are kept separate. What is special about Subway outlets is that the orders are prepared right in front of the customers, with customers being able to even customize their meal. They can choose the toppings, spices to be added, etc. Speaking about the products that the fast-food chain sells, Chetan Arora, Business Development Manager, Subway Systems India, says, "There is no other fast food chain in India that serves the products we serve. Further, customer interaction is maximum at our stores as the customer can be involved at all stages of the sandwichmaking process, starting from choosing the bread to the meat, the sauces, spices, and so on, which again is unique to us."[1]

Subway has adopted the franchising route to penetrate the market. Each store involves an investment of INR 4.5–6 million. It has an area of 700 sq. ft. to 1,000 sq. ft. with two sections—dine-in and takeaway counters. Justifying the move to use the franchising route, Fred DeLuca, Chairman & Founder of Subway, said, "We have never compromised on quality and services. But you cannot be present in 70 countries to monitor this on a day-to-day basis. So we follow the franchisee route everywhere." The franchisee has to bear the cost of setting up the outlet. These include an initial franchise fee, and purchasing

---

*This caselet was written by **Satya Srinivas Srikanti,** under the direction of **S. V. Rama Krishna,** ICFAI Center for Management Research. Caselets are intended to be used as a basis for class discussion rather than to illustrate either effective or ineffective handling of a management situation.*

or leasing the equipment. The franchisee is also responsible for managing the restaurant and personnel. The franchisee should pay a royalty fee of 8% and 3.5% toward an advertising fund; in lieu, Subway provides assistance in identifying the location for the outlet, in designing the store, in preparing the menu, in setting up operational systems, in conducting training programmes, and in carrying out periodic evaluations.

On the pricing front, the prices range from INR 40–INR 220—depending on the recipe the customer chooses—10–15% higher than its nearest competitor McDonald's. But analysts are not sure about the company's premium pricing strategy. Mr. Arvind Singhal, MD of a retail-management consultancy firm, KSA Technopak, commented, "As such, there is no negative perception about sandwiches in India. However, the premium pricing strategy for the product may have to be altered, keeping the price-conscious Indian consumer in mind."[2]

Subway has a unique arrangement to promote its brand. The advertising expenses are financed from a specially created advertising fund that is operated by the franchisees themselves. The franchisees contribute a certain percentage of the sales proceeds to build the fund. They also promote the brand locally. The development of advertising campaigns is being looked after by Triton advertising agency. The main objectives of the advertising campaigns are to attract customers to the outlet and also to project the image of the outlet as one that offers healthy and fresh food.

QUESTIONS FOR DISCUSSION

1. "We have never compromised on quality and services. But you cannot be present in 70 countries to monitor this on a day to day basis. So we follow the franchisee route everywhere." Do you agree with this statement?
2. Subway has adopted a premium pricing strategy with prices 15% higher than those of its competitors. Do you feel that such a pricing strategy is appropriate for the price-conscious Indian consumer market?

ADDITIONAL READINGS AND REFERENCES

1. Price, Charlene. "Fast Food Chains Penetrate New Markets - Industry Overview." *Food Review.* January-April, 1993.
2. Chakravarty, Chaitali. "You can Go for Global Salad, Subway is Here." *The Economic Times.* 02 November, 2001.
3. Kaushik, Neha. "Subway's Recipe." *The Hindu Business Line.* 12 December, 2002.
4. Awasthi, Raja. "Subway Plans 12 Outlets by March." *The Economic Times.* 15 December, 2002.
5. Bajpai, Rajendra. "India's Fast-Food Nirvana." *Fortune.* 20 February, 2003.
6. Tripathi, Dhirendra. "Global Fast Foods Tickle Desi Palates." *The Economic Times.* 16 December, 2003.
7. "Subway Outlet Opens in Chennai." *Business Standard.* 05 March, 2004.
8. Awasthi, Raja. "The Ever Expanding Subway." *The Economic Times.* 11 April, 2004.

ENDNOTES

1. Neha Kaushik. "Subway's Recipe." *The Hindu Business Line*. 12 December, 2002.
2. Chaitali Chakravarty. "You can Go for Global Salad, Subway is Here." *The Economic Times*. 02 November, 2001.

Cox and Kings: Service with a Difference

5 CASE

Cox and Kings (CKS), one of the prominent tour operators of the world, was established way back in 1758 by Richard Cox when he was appointed regimental agent to the footguards of India. By early 20th century, the company was acting as an agent and banker for the armed forces. In 1922, the company merged with the Henry S. King Bank, subsequent to which the banking business was sold. The travel business grew by leaps and bounds and in the early 21st century, CKS was operating various individual and group tours throughout India as well as abroad. CKS offices abroad were known as Indian tour specialists in their respective markets and had destinations from the Indian subcontinent (amongst other destinations) in their product portfolio. They catered to 50,000 inbound tourists to India in the year 2004. CKS identified various needs of customers in different segments and designed customized packages to suit these needs.

They realized that schools needed to provide a common platform for different children across the country to interact and exchange ideas. Therefore, in association with the Andhra Pradesh Tourism Board, they pioneered "Udaan"—an interschool educational tour—in October 2004. This tour included a four-day and five-night trip to Ramoji Film city in Hyderabad, which offered trips to educational places in the city, interschool competition, workshops, etc. Through this programme, they identified a niche segment to which they could market their services. CKS also saw an opportunity in business visitors who travelled to international trade fairs. They devised a value-based package for these visitors, which included confirmed accommodation for the fair period, Indian meals, and additional services such as factory visits, and buyer-supplier meets. These provided comfort to the Indian traveller in foreign countries. With a growing number of customers seeking tour packages covering religious destinations, CKS ventured to introduce religious packages to select destinations such as Vaishno Devi and Puri. These trips had guides going along for the convenience of the travellers. Their Spiritual Sojourn package offered the Art of Living course to customers seeking spiritual fulfillment. In addition, to cater to the up-market tourist who wanted to be a part of the historic Mahakumbhmela in Allahabad, CKS

*This caselet was written by **Ramya Narasimhan,** under the direction of **S. V. Rama Krishna,** ICFAI Center for Management Research. Caselets are intended to be used as a basis for class discussion rather than to illustrate either effective or ineffective handling of a management situation.*

set up five-star-quality tents which provided hot water baths, massages, and other benefits that were the ultimate word in comfort.

Apart from fulfilling the specific needs of customers, CKS aimed at constantly reinventing itself to provide the best services. In 2002, it tied up with Radius, the world's largest travel company, to offer the best prices on airlines, hotels, and other travel related services, which translated into savings for the customer. This partnership gave CKS access to travel reservations and ticketing to a 24-hour-a-day emergency toll-free travel service combined with a global travel management system that used 72 different currencies. Realizing that Indian travellers, with their specific eating habits, faced a real problem with regard to food while traveling abroad, CKS introduced the Kitchen Caravan on its Europe Tours. The Kitchen Caravan travelled with the Eurail, offering all varieties of Indian food. CKS also had a product development cell which conducted market surveys and obtained customer feedback on a continuous basis. As a result of their findings, it offered a special "two-in-one offer" that combined a domestic and an international holiday at the price of one. This offer was launched in Kolkata in October 2000, to coincide with the annual Puja holidays.

In a bid to offer the customer more access to its services, CKS tied up with MSN India to give information on destinations, air tickets, hotel reservations, foreign exchange, domestic tours, international holidays and tours, and also documentation such as passport assistance, medical insurance, etc. This alliance was obviously successful as CKS managed to get 8–10% of its holiday bookings through the MSN India site. To make its trips affordable, it tied up with ICICI Bank to offer instalment schemes on such travel loans. The premium customer could take their pick from various "one-of-a-kind luxury travel packages" which provided private, group tours as well as group and family safaris, while offering the best of accommodation with personalized service. Apart from these, flexi-holidays were provided where the customers could plan their own dates and schedules so that they could avoid travelling in a group. CKS's unique packages and positioning resulted in revenue generation of around INR 50 million[1] in 2004 from the Indian subsidiary. The figures clearly indicated the effectiveness of the strategies.

QUESTIONS FOR DISCUSSION

1. Cox and Kings (CKS) identified revenue sources by introducing new travel packages. Elaborate on this statement by discussing the niche targeting that CKS adopted for various segments in India.
2. To woo the convenience and comfort savvy customer, Cox and Kings introduced many value added services in its offerings. How have these served to help the Indian traveler in easing his/her travel plans and actual trip?

ADDITIONAL READINGS AND REFERENCES

1. Maakan, Anupama, "Hot Summer Holidays", *Outlook Money*, 10 March, 1999.
2. "Cox & Kings Eyeing a Tie-up with European Company", *www.magindia.com*, 24 October, 2000.

3. Fernz , Charmaine, "Cox & Kings to Offer Enhanced Services Through its Tie-up with Radius", *Express Travel & Tourism*, 16–31 October, 2002.
4. "MSN India Tie-up Helps Boost Cox & Kings' Biz", *www.magindia.com*, 04 August, 2003.
5. Pandya, Kiran. "The Business of Worship Tours Goes Corporate", *www.midday.com*, 31 January, 2004.
6. Ghosh, Shashwati. "Movies, Masti, Magic Lure *Amdavadis* to Europe", *www.cities.expressindia.com*, 21 February, 2004.
7. Byas, Anand. "Cox & Kings ventures into international trade fairs", *The Times of India*, 03 May, 2004.
8. "Cox & Kings announces inter school programme", *www.indiainfoline.com*, 16 September, 2004.
9. Ganguly, Dibeyendu. "Cox & Kings: Down memory lane", *The Economic Times*, 15 October, 2004.
10. Mitra , Prithvijit. "The world is an Oyster", *The Telegraph*, 04 November, 2004.
11. *<http://newsarchives.indiainfo.com/spotlight/y2k/doc23a.html>*
12. *www.msnindia.com*
13. *www.coxandkings.com*

ENDNOTES

1. Dibeyendu Ganguly, "Cox & Kings: Down memory lane", *The Economic Times*, 15 October, 2004.

Index

A

achieved status, 100
advertising, 329
  new age specialist ad agencies, 335
Advertising Standards Council of India (ASCI), 483
affluent consumer, 96
aggrieved customer, 400
All India Council for Teacher Education (AICTE), 84
All India Radio (AIR), 47
Alteon Training, 19
American Marketing Association, 4
analytical CRM, 435
Andhra Bank, 409
Andhra Pradesh State Consumer Disputes Redressal Commission, 475
Andhra Pradesh State Road Transport Corporation, 10–11
  channels of distribution, 500–501
  external marketing in, 501–2
  internal marketing in, 502–3
  pricing of corporation services by, 500
  service product mix of, 499–500
animation industry, 19
Apollo Hospitals, 82
APSRTC, *see* Andhra Pradesh State Road Transport Corporation
ascribed status, 100
aspiration group, 98
ASSOCHAM, 70, 483
Association of Indian Engineering Industry (AIEI), 484
associative groups, 98
attitudes, 103–104
aviation sector in India, 19, 71–72

B

B2C, *see* business-to-consumer e-commerce
Bajaj, Rama Krishna, 482
Balaji Telefilms, 56
Bank of Baroda, 354
basic service package, 220–22, 313, 348
behavioural segmentation, 174–76
behaviour of management and employees, 35
Bharti Airtel Limited, 8, 194
Bharti Enterprises, 17
Big Bazaar, 13
Biyani, Kishore, 13
brand conditioning, 250–51
brand confirmation, 250
brand consistency, 250
brand construction, 250
brand context, 250
brand continuity, 250
brand elements, 243
brand equity, 251–53
brand image, 252
branding, 243. *See also* positioning of a service
  benefits of, 247
  and brand equity, 251–53
  and the brand value chain, 247
  and choice of brand elements, 245–47
"bricks and clicks" retailers, 302
BSNL, 73, 225
BSP, *see* basic service package
bundling services, 211
  pricing of, 287
Bureau of Indian Standards, 481
business systems planning, 302–3
business-to-consumere-commerce, 300
buyer behaviour, 92
buyer–seller interactions, 9–10
160by2, SMS service company, 424

C

call centres, 18
capacity management
  when high demand, 212
  when low demand, 212–13
  strategies for, 211
captive pricing, 288
Carlzon, Jan, 155, 355

Center for Monitoring Indian Economy, 96
Central Consumer Protection Council, 472
channel management strategies, 304–305
closed-ended questions, 140–42
collaborative CRM, 436
Colors (entertainment channel), 336
communal coordination, 427
communication value, 28
competition
  achieving competitive advantage, 194–96
  analysis of, 190–92
  competitive threats, 185–87
  defending market share, 192–93
  from industry perspective, 187–88
  and life insurance market development in India, 189
  from market perspective, 188–89
  monopolistic, 188
  pure, 188
  strategies to overcome, 192–94
Competition Act (2002), 481
competitive positioning, 256
competitive threats, 185
complaints management, 393, 401–403
complimentary pricing, 288
Confederation of Indian Food Trade and Industry (CIFTI), 484
conservativism, 53
consumer behaviour
  factors influencing, 92–104
Consumer Education and Research Center (CERC), 466
Consumer Guidance Society of India (CGSI), 465
consumerism, 460
consumer protection, 460
  administrative mechanism of, 481–82
  movement in India, 464–67
Consumer Protection Act (1986), 461, 467
  definition for unfair trade practices, 478–80
  definition of consumer, 472
  definition of deficiency, 474
  definition of service, 473–74
  protection on account of disruption of services by illegal strikes, 478
  provisions for education services, 475–76
  provisions for professional services, 474–75
  provisions for PSUs, 476–80
  salient features, 470–74
  Section 1 (4), 472–73
  Section 2 (d) of, 472
  Section 2 (i) (g), 474
  six rights of the consumers, 467–70
consumer purchase decision process
  stages of, 109–113
corporate branding, 248–51
corporate social responsibility, 165
Council for Fair Business Practices (CFBP), 482
Cox and Kings, 533–34
credence qualities, 111
culture, defined, 93
customer-centric philosophy, 32
customer complaint management system (CCMS), 401–3
customer delivered value (CDV), 285
customer dissonance, 11
customer expectations, development of, 104. *Also see* service level
customer participation, 11
customer participation, in service encounters
  appropriate customer mix for, 369
  factors influencing, 369
  management of customer expectations, 369–70
customer relationship management (CRM)
  benefits of, 416
  framework of, 420–24
  drivers of, 417–20
  goals of, 426
  organizational system for, 426–27
customers, 35–36, 92
customer value hierarchy, 223
customer-value perception, 25
customization, 11, 179–80
customized service package, 228
custom marketing research firms, 128

D

database marketing, 38
defection, 390–91
delivering value, 28–29
demand management, 26, 208–11
demand patterns, 202–5
demand situations, 200–2
demand variations, 205–8
demographic environment, 48
demographic segmentation, 173
deregulation of business, 36
deregulation of services, 2

detachment phase, 363
differentiated marketing, 170. *See also* market segmentation
direct marketing, 331
Directorate of Marketing and Inspection, 481
disassociate group, 98
distribution of services, 292
  channels for, 296–305
  control strategies in, 304–5
domestic marketing, 441
Doordarshan, 174
downmarket stretch, 235
drop errors, 230
DTDC Courier & Cargo Ltd., 35

E

e-commerce retail market, 301
economies, contribution of services, 3
e-CRM
  applications of, 433
  benefits of, 433–35
  market for, 434
  selection of software, 436
  types of, 435–36
educational services, in India, 83–85
emotional labour, 311
employee participation, in service encounters
  non-verbal communication skills, 364–66
  transactional analysis, 366–68
  verbal communication skills, 364
employment, services sector, 3, 17–19
entertainment and media services, in India, 85–88
entertainment sector, 19
ethnocentricity, 442–43
ethnocentrism, 452
excellence positioning, 256–57
excess demand situation, 204–5
exclusive distribution, 293
expectations of consumer, 24
expected product, 223
expectations of consumers
  fair norms in exchanges, 463
  optimum use of resources, 462–63
  product design and development, 461
  product quality and performance, 462
  product representation, 462
experience qualities, 111
external marketing
  advertising in, 329
  budget for marketing communication in, 333–34
  communication tools for, 329–31
  and delivery of service, 344
  integrated marketing communications, 334–36
  management of horizontal communication in, 344
  message generation in, 332–33
  need for, 328
  objectives of communication, 331–32
  personal selling in, 329–30
  publicity and public relations, 330
  rules of effective campaign in, 343
  sales promotion in, 330
  selection of a target audience for, 331
  selection of media channels for, 333
  successful communication campaigns of service brands, 341–42
  success strategies for, 342–44
  themes in, 337–41
  word-of-mouth communication in, 336–37
extensive distribution, 293

F

facilitating services, 220
falling demand, 202
failure and deficiencies, in service
  complaint management, 401–3
  customer responses to, 398–401
  reasons for customer grievances, 397–98
  service recovery, 403–11
Federation of Indian Chamber of Commerce and Industry, 483
FEMA, 52
Ford, Robert C., 391
forecasting methods, 207
foreign direct investment, 451
foreign investment, 51
foreign technology agreement, 51
formal learning, 93
Fortis Healthcare, 82
franchising, 296–99, 450
full demand situation, 203
full-time marketers, 317

G

GAP model of service quality, 381–84
GDP, relation with services sector, 2, 60–62
General Agreement on Tariffs and Trade (GATT), 447

General Agreement on Trade in Services (GATS), 447
General Insurance Corporation (GIC), 68–69
generalized fixed package, 228
generalized flexible package, 228
geocentricity, 443
geodemographic segmentation, 173
geographic segmentation, 172–73
globalization, 36
go errors, 230
goods marketing, 29–30
goods-producing sector, 14
goods–services relationship, 6–7
Gujarat State Commission, 476

H

health and fitness, 54, 67
healthcare sector, in India, 67, 81–83
health insurance, 83
hidden services sector, 2
high-tech markets, 37
holistic marketing, 33–35
hospitality, 19
horizontal communication, 344
human resources, 19
hybrid category of products, 7

I

ICICI Infotech Services Limited, 311
ICICI Prudential, 255
image of a service, 375–76
implementation, 37
incentives, 210
India Post, 76–77, 151
India, services sector in
- banking sector, 79–81, 487–98
- competitive situation and demand–supply positions, impact of, 66–67
- cultural changes, role of, 65
- developments of markets, 66
- economic liberalization process, impact of, 64, 67
- educational services, 83–85, 508–13
- electricity, development of, 75–76
- employment opportunities, 61–62, 64
- entertainment and media services, 85–88
- export potential, 67–68
- and GDP growth, 60–62
- growth and development of services, 62–68
- healthcare sector, 67, 81–83, 503–8
- insurance business, 68–70
- IT and IT-enabled (BPO) services, 65–66, 74–75
- operational characteristics of, 64
- postal system, 76–77
- retailing, 66, 88
- rural to semi-urban and urban migration, impact of, 67
- social marketing initiatives, 66
- sub-sectors of services, 61, 64
- telecommunications, 72–74
- tourism, 77–79, 513–18
- transport business, 70–72, 499–503
- women, role of, 64–65

Indian Medical Association Vs Vasantha P. Nair, 474
Indian Railways, 10, 71
Indian School of Business (ISB), 278
Indian Telegraph Act, 73
industrial licensing, 51
inseparability of services, 9–10
Insurance Regulatory and Development Authority Act, 2000, 69
insurance sector, 18
intangibility of services, 9
integral coordination, 437
integrated marketing, 33
integrated marketing communications, 334–35
- objectives, 335–36

intensive consumption phase, 362
interactive marketing
- definition of, 348
- quality-generating resources in, 349–50

interactive skills, 317
internal marketing, 34
- challenges in, 316
- concept of, 309
- customer satisfaction and retention in, 310–11
- dimensions of organizing employees, 319–20
- emotional labour, 311
- employee motivation, 321–22
- empowerment strategies, 319
- evaluation of employee performance in, 322–23
- importance of employees in, 310
- objectives of, 311–12
- product in, 313–14
- rewarding system in, 323
- roles of service employees in, 312–13
- staffing for, 314–18

strategies for, 314–18
strategies to retain employees, 323–24
support systems, 320–21
training for, 318–19
international business, of services
business environment, 444–46
international marketing *vs* domestic marketing, 441–42
marketing programme, 449–56
orientation of company's management, 442–44
services exports from India, 448
trade barriers, 446–47
IRDA, 52. *Also see* Insurance Regulatory and Development Authority Act, 2000
irregular demand, 202
IT and IT-enabled (BPO) services, 19
in India, 65–66, 74–75, 214
ITC Welcomgroup, 363

J

joining phase, 362
joint ventures, 451

K

Karnataka Consumer Service Society (KCSS), 466
Karvy Consultants Limited, 160
Kaya Skin Clinic (Kaya), 521–22
Kerala Ayurveda Limited, 94
knowledge process outsourcing, 18–19

L

Larsen & Toubro Ltd. (L&T), 451
latent demand situation, 201
leadership positioning, 256
leading questions, 139
licensing, 450
life-cycle management, of service product, 238–39
Life Insurance Corporation (LIC), 68–70, 524–25
loss-leader pricing, 288

M

macro-environment, 43
demographic environment, 48–49
economic environment, 49–50
natural environment, 50
political and legal environment, 52
social and legal environment, 52–55
technological environment, 50–52
Maharashtra State Commission, 476
Mahindra Lifespaces, 333
manufacturing sector, 3
manpower planning, 315
market challengers, 193
market expansion, 192
market followers, 194
marketing
challenges in, 35–37
core concepts of, 24–29
database, 38
definition, 23
difference between goods and services, 29–30
mix, 38, 162–64
objectives of, 38
philosophies of, 30–35
planning, 37–39
situation analysis, 37
target of, 38
vital tasks of, 39
marketing information system
collecting information, 122–23
definition, 118–19
identifying and assessing information needs, 121–22
information analysis and distribution, 146
sources, 119–21
marketing mix, 33
marketing-oriented philosophy, 32–33
marketing offer, 23–24
marketing programme, international
country-of-origin effect, 452
market-entry strategies, 450–51
selection of a country for entry, 451–52
value communication, 454–55
value creation, 452–54
value delivery, 455–56
marketing research
application and importance, 124–27
online, 136
organizations, 127–28
marketing research, process of
data analysis and interpretation, 145
data collection, 145
defining the problem, 129–31
designing of questionnaire, 138–42
experimentation method, 137–38
marketing research, process of *(Continue)*

interviews, 133–34
mail surveys, 134–35
model development, 130–31
observation method, 135–37
preparing and presenting research report, 145–46
primary data, 132–38
question sequence and questionnaire layout, 142
response format, 139–42
sample selection, 142–45
secondary data, 131–32
situation analysis, 130
market nichers, 194
market-oriented service strategy
external marketing, 161
interactive marketing, 161–62
internal marketing, 160–61
marketing mix, 162–64
problems, 157–59
service-oriented organizational structure, 159–60
service-oriented strategic approach, 158
market segmentation, 26–27
and accessibility, 179
bases for, 172–77
consumer characteristics and, 172–74
criteria for, 178–79
customization, 179–80
and differentiability, 179
differentiated market, 170–72
and measurability, 178
need for, 171
stages in, 181
and substantiality, 178
undifferentiated market, 170
Max Healthcare, 82
maximum service level, 104
McDonald's India, 443, 527–28
mergers and acquisitions, 36
micro-environment, 43
competitors, 46
customer markets, 46
intermediaries, 46
marketing division of an organization, 45
relation with public, 46–47
suppliers, 45
middle class consumers, 99
minimum service level, 104
mission statement, definition of, 152
Mittal, Sunil Bharti, 8
moments of truth, concept of, 355–61
managing, 356–61
monopoly, 187
Monopolies and Restrictive Trade Practices Commission, 481
MRTP Act, 51
MTNL, 73
multi-marketing, 304
mystery shopping, 393

N

National Assessment and Accreditation Council, 84, 378
National Consumer Disputes Redressal Commission, 471
National Council for Teacher Education, 84
National Knowledge Commission, 84
NCAER, 132
needs of consumer, 24
negative demand situation, 200
New Delhi Traders Association, 484
New India Assurance, 318
new service, development of a
business analysis for, 232
categories of new products for, 227–28
commercialization of, 233
concept development and testing for, 230–32
different forms of, 228
evaluation of new ideas for, 230
generation of new ideas for, 229–30
marketing strategy for, 232
market testing, 233
service environment for, 232–33
success factors in, 234
Nielsen India, 128
NIIT, 32
no demand situation, 200–201
non-agricultural labour force, 14
non-government organizations, 18

O

objective language, 262
oligopoly, 187–188
online dotcom companies, 37
online marketing research, 136
open-ended questions, 140
operational CRM, 435

optimum capacity, 203
organizational response, to marketing environment, 56. *See also* macro-environment; micro-environment
ownership, lack of, 11–12

P

Pantaloon Retail (India) Limited, 13
part-time marketers, 312
Passengers and Traffic Relief Association, 465
penetration pricing, 286
performance evaluation, 37
perishability of services, 10–11
personal reference price, 277
personal selling, 329–30
physical evidence
  concept of, 260–61
  elements of, 261–70
  guidelines for developing, 272
  in services marketing, 270–720
pleasantries, 354
polycentricity, 443
positioning, 27–28
positioning of a service, 253. *See also* branding
  frame of reference, 253–54
  strategies, 254–57
potential product, 224
prestige pricing, 287
price bundling, 287
price framing, 287
pricing
  approaches to, 280–85
  attributes influencing decisions on, 277
  and discounts, 286
  objectives of, 279–80
  price discrimination, 286
  price–quality relations, 278–79
  role of non-monetary costs in, 278
  of services, 276–79
  and value perceptions of a service, 282, 285–88
primary group, 98
privacies, 354
privatization, 36
proactive marketing, 32
product augmentation, 224
production philosophy, 31
product philosophy, 31
'Ps,' seven, 33
psychographic segmentation, 173–74
psychological pricing, 286
public sector banks, in India, 79–80
public sector policy, 51
pure service, 7
pure tangible goods, 6

Q

quality-generating resources, 349–50
quality of services
  audit of, 380–84
  determinants of, 377–78
  expected *vs* experienced, 375–76
  functional, 375
  GAP model, 381–84
  perception of, 374–76
  philosophies practiced in service organizations, 388–89
  process for, 378–80
  research on, 392–93
  service excellence, 391–92
  SERVQUAL, 385–86
  in sterilization services, 384
  technical, 375
  in terms of needs, 376
  total quality management, 386–91
quality positioning, 256
questionnaire, 138

R

reactive marketing, 32
reference group, 98
relationship marketing, 33–34
Reliance Communications, 194
Reserve Bank of India, 79
resistance to change, 55
retailing services, in India, 66, 88
Right to Information Act (2005), 467, 480–81

S

sales cycle of a service, 303
sample study, 142
sampling frame, 143
sampling methods, 144–45
sampling unit, 143
Sarva Shiksha Abhiyan, 83
Satellite Imaging for Rail Navigation, 71

SBI Railway Card, 419
Scandinavian Airlines, 355
search qualities, 111
seasonal demand situation, 201–2
secondary group, 98
segmentation of market
segmentation pricing, 287
segmentation system, 178
self-concept, 100
self-servicing, 2
selective distribution, 293
selling philosophy, 31
service application positioning, 256
service attribute analysis, 230
service blueprinting, 231–32
service branding, 243–44
  goods branding *vs,* 244
service consumption process
  detachment phase, 363
  integrating phase, 364
  intensive phase, 362–63
  joining phase, 362
service culture, 319–20
service deliverer, 294
service differentiation, 236–37
service economy, 2
service encounter, 108, 350–55
  appropriate assignment of job tasks, 351
  co-customer management, 355
  and customer satisfaction, 352–54
  and customers' behavioural dimensions, 351
  determinants of customer behaviour at, 358–61
  determinants of employee behaviour at, 356–58
  employee empowerment, 351
  employee motivation, 352
  employees' performance, 350
  foreign customers, 355
  intercultural encounter, 355
  inter-personal adaptability at, 351–52
  quality of a, 352
  training for employee proficiency, 352
service excellence, 391–92
service failure, 397
service flower, 224–27
service interaction process, 361–64
service life cycle, 238
service-line decisions, 234–36
service-line featuring, 235
service-line length, 235
service-line modernization, 235
service-line pruning, 236
service level, 104. *Also see* consumer expectations
  determinants of, 104–108
service perception, of customers
  customer experiences, 108
  evidence of a service, 108
  image of an organization, 108–9
  service encounters, 108
service principal, 294, 304–5
service product
  action on payment, 226–27
  basic service package (BSP), 220–22
  billing, 226
  consultation, 225
  development of new service, 227–34
  exceptions, 226
  hospitality, 226
  information, 225
  life-cycle management, 238–39
  mix, 234–36
  order taking, 225–26
  safekeeping, 226
  and service differentiation, 236–37
  in terms of customer value, 223–24
service recovery
  advance planning for, 410
  benefits, 404–5
  consumer grievance, 405
  development of recovery skills, 410
  employee empowerment for, 410
  measuring satisfaction with transaction, 406
  proactiveness, 409–10
  strategies, 405–11
  training for, 410–11
service (s)
  characteristics, 9–13
  definition, 3–6
  differentiating goods from, 6–8
servicescape
  ambient environment, 264–65
  concept, 261–62
  dimensions, 263–67
  effects on behaviour, 267–69
  impact of colour on, 266
  interpersonal services, 263
  living space and functional support facilities, 265–66
  remote service, 263

self-service environment, 262
signs, symbols and artefacts, 267
socialization of, 268
stimulus-organism-response (SOR) model, 267–68
tangibles used in service, 269–70
types, 262–63
services marketing, 29–30
marketing challenges and strategic options in, 12
need for, 7
services sector, growth of, 13–14
employment opportunities, 17–19
major industries classified under, 18
reasons, 14–17
services with accompanying tangible goods, 7
service tax, 69
service user positioning, 256
SERVQUAL, 385–86
situation analysis, 37
skimming pricing, 287
sociability, 354
sociality, 354
socially responsible marketing, 34–35
social relationships, 53
social skills, 317
specialty-line marketing research firms, 128
Standards of Weights and Measurements Act, 482
State Bank of India, 10, 255, 270
ATMs, 494
branch layout, 494
branch management, 494
core banking solution (CBS), 493
corporate communication, 492–93
customer service and community service banking, 493
distribution outlets of the banking services, 491
Electronic NOSTRO Account Reconciliation, 492
employee benefits, 497–98
employee training, 497
external marketing, 495–96
information technology and customer service, 492–95
interest policy, 489–91
internal marketing, 496–97
management information system (MIS), 495
model branches, 494
new product planning and development, 488–89
personalized branch network, 494
physical facilities, 494
pricing policies and strategies, 489–91
product mix, 489
product policies and strategies, 488
SWIFT network, 492
trends during the 1990s and deregulation, 490–91
Web site, 492
State Consumer Protection Councils, 472
State Cooperative Banks, 79
strategic planning. *See also* strategy evaluation and control; strategy implementation
aim of, 150
based on differentiation, 155
best-cost-provider strategy, 155
differentiation, 154
focused marketing or niche marketing, 155
formulation of a strategy, 153–55
low-cost-provider strategy, 154
mission statement, developing a, 152
steps in, 151–55
SWOT analysis, 152–53
strategy evaluation and control, 166
strategy implementation, 164
Subway Systems India (Subway), 530–31
Sun Direct DTH services, 288
Supporting services, 220
SWOT analysis, 152–53
symbolism, 35
syndicated service research firms, 127

T

Taj Lake Palace, 262
Tamil Nadu State Commission, 476
tangibility spectrum, 8
transformation of intangible services into, 9
tangible goods with accompanying services, 6
target marketing, 27
Tata Communications Internet Service Ltd., 403
Tata Power, 209
TATA Strategic Management Group, 44
team work, 320
technical learning, 93
technical skills, 317
technographic segmentation, 177
technological environment, 54
technological innovations, 36–37
telecommunication sector, India *vs* China, 4

regulated competition in Indian telecom sector, 195
Telecom Regulatory Authority of India (TRAI), 73
teledenstity, in India, 72
Thyrocare Technologies Ltd., 296
Times Group, 87
Tirumala Tirupati Devasthanam, 215
tolerance, 55
total customer cost (TCC), 283
total perceived quality (TPQ), 376
total quality management, 386–91
tourism, in India, 77–79
TRAI, 52
transactional analysis, 366–68, 392
transactions in services, 292–93
two-way market services, 235
two-part pricing, 288

U

undifferentiated marketing, 170
Unit Trust of India (UTI), 81
upmarket services, 235
Urban Cooperative Banks, 79
U.S. labour market, 14
UTI Act, 1963, 81

V

VALS (Values, Attitudes and Lifestyle Systems), 174
value chain analysis, 196
value creation, 28
value perceptions, of a service, 282
value pricing, 287
variability of services, 10
Virgin Mobile, 255
Visakha Consumer Council, 466
Visakhapatnam Port Trust, 386
visual merchandising, 269
Vivekananda, Swami, 465
VLCC, 99

W

waiting-line management
  creating reservation systems, 215
  differentiating customers, 216
  making waiting fun, 216
  operational logic, 213–15
  psychology of people in waiting lines, 216
Wal-Mart, 17
wants of consumer, 24
Wills Lifestyle, 175
Wockhardt, 82
women, status of, 54
word-of-mouth communication, 35, 211, 336–37, 376, 517
World Trade Organization (WTO), 36, 447–49

Y

Yatra Online Pvt. Ltd., 300

Z

zero defections, 390–91
zero defects, 390–91
zone of tolerance, 105. *Also see* service level

Dear Student:

We hope that that this textbook has been a useful resource and learning tool for you. We would appreciate hearing about your experiences with this textbook and its supplements. The feedback you provide will help us to continue develop better textbooks. We thank you for giving us your valuable time, suggestions, and comments.

1. Several features are present in the text to make the material more accessible and interesting. Using other texts as the basis of comparison, please rate the following features on a 5-point scale (1 – least useful and 5 – most useful):

Chapter-opening Cases	1	2	3	4	5
Margin Elements	1	2	3	4	5
Services Marketing Insight Boxes	1	2	3	4	5
Caselets	1	2	3	4	5
Tables/Figures/Charts	1	2	3	4	5

Any other comment:...

....

....

2. The following features are present at the end of each chapter. Please rate each of them on a 5-point scale (1 – least useful and 5 – most useful):

Summary	1	2	3	4	5
Brief Questions	1	2	3	4	5
Essay Questions	1	2	3	4	5
Assignments	1	2	3	4	5

3. Do you find that the book includes recent developments and trends in the area of services marketing?...

....

....

....

4. How would you describe the writing style and readability in these chapters? Is the text easier or more difficult to read and understand than your current text(s)? In what way? ....

....

....

....

5. What is your opinion about the caselets and cases in the book? Do you find them sufficient in number? How can they be improved?...

....

....

....

6. Do you feel that the questions and assignments helped you understand the concepts? Is the number of these sufficient? Please give instances of some specific questions that you feel should be added. …

………

………

………

7. Overall, what did you like most about the book? And what did you like the least? ………………

………

………

………

8. If you have any additional comments or feedback, please share the same with us. ………………

………

………

9. Please tell us about the textbooks that are currently used in your course.

Book No. 1 (Title) ……………………………………………………………………………

Author ……………………………………………………………………………………

Publisher ……………………………………………………………………………………

Book No. 2 (Title) ……………………………………………………………………………

Author ……………………………………………………………………………………

Publisher ……………………………………………………………………………………

10. Where and why did you purchase this book? ……………………………………………………

………

………

Please fill in the form below using CAPITAL LETTERS.

YOUR NAME: ……………………………………………………

AFFILIATION: ……………………………………………………

ADDRESS: ……………………………………………………

E-MAIL: ……………………………………………………

DATE: ……………………………………………………

May we have permission to quote your comments in promotions for *Services Marketing?*

❑ Yes ❑ No

Please send us your feedback, via e-mail or post, to:

PEARSON EDUCATION
A division of Dorling Kindersley (India) Pvt. Ltd.
Head Office: 7th Floor, Knowledge Boulevard, A-8(A), Sector 62, Noida 201309, UP, India

E-mail: hedfeedback@pearsoned.co.in